W9-AHF-428

NEWCOMER'S
HANDBOOK®

FOR MOVING TO AND LIVING IN

Minneapolis-
St. Paul

4th Edition

FIRST BOOKS

503-968-6777
www.firstbooks.com

4th Edition

Newcomer's Handbook® and First Books® are registered trademarks of First Books.

Author: Elizabeth Caperton-Halvorson
Editor: Linda Franklin
Cover and interior design: Erin Johnson Design
Cover and interior layout: Masha Shubin
Interior photos by Sarah Kannenberg
Maps provided by Jim Miller/fennana design

Transit maps courtesy of Metro Transit

ISBN-13: 978-0-9823476-4-5
ISBN-10: 0-9823476-4-2

Printed in the USA on recycled paper.

Published by First Books®, 503-968-6777, www.firstbooks.com.

What readers are saying about Newcomer's Handbooks:

I recently got a copy of your Newcomer's Handbook for Chicago, and wanted to let you know how invaluable it was for my move. I must have consulted it a dozen times a day preparing for my move. It helped me find my way around town, find a place to live, and so many other things. Thanks.

– Mike L.
Chicago, Illinois

Excellent reading (Newcomer's Handbook for San Francisco and the Bay Area) … balanced and trustworthy. One of the very best guides if you are considering moving/relocation. Way above the usual tourist crap.

– Gunnar E.
Stockholm, Sweden

I was very impressed with the latest edition of the Newcomer's Handbook for Los Angeles. It is well organized, concise and up-to-date. I would recommend this book to anyone considering a move to Los Angeles.

– Jannette L.
Attorney Recruiting Administrator for a large Los Angeles law firm

An exceptional book for relocators. However, even non-relocators will find it very enjoyable. It features great coverage of the city of Portland, including the very desirable West Hills and Bridlemile sections, as well as its incorporated suburbs, yet it also covers unincorporated areas…as well as the often-overlooked towns of Wilsonville and Happy Valley, and Vancouver, Washington and its suburbs. Many great ideas for education, dining, house-hunting, shopping, health/fitness, and recreation are included in this book. DON'T PASS THIS BOOK UP UNDER ANY CIRCUMSTANCES!!!!!!!!!!

– "The Footpath Cowboy"
(on amazon.com)

In looking to move to the Boston area, a potential employer in that area gave me a copy of the Newcomer's Handbook for Boston. It's a great book that's very comprehensive, outlining good and bad points about each neighborhood in the Boston area. Very helpful in helping me decide where to move.

– no name given (online submit form)

We were considering moving to Portland, Oregon and recently took a scouting mission there to see whether that was an idea worth pursuing. This book proved invaluable and I would highly recommend it to anyone considering the same thing. Its neighborhood descriptions were spot on and helped us focus our search.

– L. Gillespie
New York, New York (on amazon.com)

TABLE OF CONTENTS

CONTENTS

CONTENTS

T HE MINNEAPOLIS–ST. PAUL METROPOLITAN AREA CONSISTS OF THIR-
teen counties located in both Minnesota and neighboring Wisconsin.
The seven core counties of "The Metro" are Anoka, Carver, Dakota,
Hennepin (includes Minneapolis), Ramsey (includes St. Paul), Scott, and Washington, all within Minnesota. The larger 13-county area extends out to Chisago,
Isanti, Sherburne, and Wright counties, also in Minnesota, and Pierce and St.
Croix counties in Wisconsin. That's an area of 144 by 114 miles. In terms of population, three out of five Minnesota residents live in the Twin Cities area, with
over 70% concentrated in the Western Metro. More than 70% of the region's
jobs and traffic are concentrated on the west side as well, and projections show
that the "western tilt" will continue to grow.

There's no place like the Twin Cities. The trees, the lakes, the snow…the pro
sports, restaurants, music, and theaters! And where else can you teach your kids
to drive on roads plowed on frozen lakes? Really, we've got it all.

But if all you've ever heard about Minnesota is our "invigorating" climate,
the prospect of living here might be daunting. Rest assured, national surveys
consistently pick the Twin Cities as one of the best places in the nation to raise
a family, as well as one of the top 20 for singles. So what's so great about Minnesota? It's the quality of life!

It's 136,900 acres of parks, lakes, trails, ski areas, and golf courses integrated
into our neighborhoods. It's more shopping than you could ever do, two internationally acclaimed orchestras, and nearly as many theater seats as New York
City. It's Fortune 500 companies, a vibrant local music scene, and vital downtowns where people like to live and want to play. It's a small enough population
for breathing room, but big enough numbers to support major league sports
and nightlife—plus, we have relatively safe neighborhoods, decent schools,
and well-maintained houses. Most important, if you decide to move here, you'll
be living in a place where art, culture, sports, and recreation are not only easily

accessible, but also more affordable than in the major cities on the east and west coasts.

But, what about the weather you ask? The sub-zero temperatures? The blizzards? The wind-chill factor? Well, that's what pulls Minnesotans together, giving us something to talk about and an opportunity to brag about our survival skills.

And it doesn't seem to be keeping anyone away. The Twin Cities metropolitan area is the 15th largest in the U.S., according to 2008 updated census information, with three and a half million people (over half the state's population) living in the region. Projections show that we're on track to add another million by the year 2030.

Unfortunately, most of the people moving here head for the suburbs, a pattern of growth that contributes to our biggest problem, urban sprawl. Third-ring suburbs Woodbury, Eagan, and Eden Prairie all doubled their populations during the 1990s, and current growth is occurring even farther out in outlying areas of Chisago, Dakota, Isanti, Scott, Sherburne, and Wright counties, which are expected to double or triple in population in the next 20 years. While urbanization on such a vast scale can have a tendency to blur or erase the unique qualities that give communities their own sense of character, here—at least for now—our communities have managed to remain distinct.

Take Minneapolis and St. Paul, for example. Although they're called the Twin Cities, they are definitely not twins. Sitting on the Mississippi's west bank, Minneapolis (just under 400,000 population) is the power suit—it has demolished layer upon layer of its architectural history in order to create a skyline profile of sleek office towers and glassed-in condos. In contrast, St. Paul (population of almost 300,000), across the river, even though it's the state capital, has a slower, more settled and provincial feel. Having paid attention to architectural preservation, it boasts the low-slung silhouette of some of the Midwest's last remaining Victorian Romanesque blocks. In fact, it's so low-rise that at one time a 14-story ice palace was actually the city's tallest building!

The suburbs, too, have their own look and feel, ranging from post-war practical inner-ring municipalities like Richfield, Roseville, and St. Louis Park to the resort-style villages of Lake Minnetonka and White Bear Lake. Newer suburbs, such as Hudson, Wisconsin, and Blaine, are all about soccer and golf, while upscale Edina is all about shopping; and Excelsior, Wayzata, Mound, Chaska, Elk River, Anoka, Stillwater, and Waconia, though definitely suburbs, are also traditional small towns.

On the economic front, although median household income has fallen during the recession, and unemployment and the number of people living in poverty have increased, the Minneapolis–St. Paul area has still fared slightly better than many U.S. metros. That's thanks largely to the fact that two-thirds of our families have more than one person employed, and to the strength of our locally headquartered corporations such as Target, 3M, Cargill, General

Mills, United Health Group, Travelers, Ecolab, and Medtronic, which have been knocked down, but not out.

The engine that drives Minnesota's economy is our schools. We rank fourth most educated among the 25 largest metropolitan statistical areas—and a whopping 37% of our adults hold Bachelor's degrees. That statistic reflects the fact that an education is easy to obtain here, as the metro is home to the University of Minnesota main campus, a dozen private four-year colleges, six community colleges, nine technical institutes, and several trade schools.

Finally, on the good side of the bad economy, housing has become much more affordable. In fact, the Twin Cities tied with Phoenix as seventh most affordable among the 25 largest metros in 2008, with 72% of homes for sale considered affordable to a median-income family.

The faces of Minnesota are changing as well. Though Minnesotans traditionally consider themselves "Scandinavian," the state is becoming more ethnically and racially diverse, though considerably less so than the national average. In 2007, 14% of Minnesota's population was nonwhite or Latino, according to the American Community Survey, with Hennepin County (35% nonwhite or Latino residents) and Ramsey County (27%) ranked as our most diverse counties. Nowhere is Minnesota's new diversity more apparent than on the streets of Minneapolis and St. Paul. St. Paul (long known for its Irish roots) is now home to the second largest urban Hmong population in the world. The Twin Cities are also host to the largest Somali and Liberian refugee communities in the U.S., as well as one of the largest Native American urban populations. But growth in our nonwhite population hasn't been confined to the inner cities: outer-ring suburbs have actually had the fastest rates of growth in total minority population between 2000 and 2007. Nevertheless, even though we are definitely growing in diversity, the state still has a long way to go before it will mirror the 34% nonwhite and Latino population found in the U.S. as a whole.

HISTORY

A play about Minnesota history opens with the untamed rhythms of a Native American chant in raw counterpoint to the genteel strains of a Victorian waltz—a clear metaphor for the cultural conflict that accompanied the settling of Minnesota and continues today.

The first Europeans arrived in the 1680s in the person of Father Louis Hennepin, a Franciscan adventurer who traveled with a party of Dakota guides up the river to a wide falls, which he named St. Anthony. Where Hennepin was standing is now the center of downtown Minneapolis.

A hundred twenty years later, Minnesota was acquired through the Louisiana Purchase (1803), and Congress sent a military expedition to explore the new territory and find out what treasures the country had gained. Expedition leader Lieutenant Zebulon Pike found two different groups of Native American tribes living here, the Ojibwe and the Dakota. Pike signed an agreement with the Dakotas in 1805 that ceded to the U.S. nine square miles of land at the confluence of the Mississippi and Minnesota Rivers—that's the land Ft. Snelling and the airport are built on today, and includes much of the cities of Minneapolis and St. Paul. Settlement began during the 1820s, and soon fur traders and farmers were comfortably established downriver from the fort. In 1841, an earnest missionary named Lucien Galtier built a log church on the east bank of the Mississippi and named it after St. Paul, the Apostle of Nations. The name stuck for the settlement, which soon became the capital of the new state of Minnesota.

Entrepreneurs also moved upriver to St. Anthony Falls, where they used the hydraulic power of the Mississippi to mill flour and saw lumber, giving Minneapolis its nickname "Mill City." This east bank settlement was originally known as St. Anthony, but Charles Hoag, a teacher, proposed a different name for it, combining *Minne*, the Dakota word for "water," and *polis*, the Greek word for "city," into Minneapolis. Today the cobblestone street of old St. Anthony has been preserved as Saint Anthony Main, a shopping and entertainment district across from downtown on the east bank of the river, in what is known as the Mississippi Mile.

Relations between white settlers and Native Americans in the area were not always harmonious. Despite an agreement by the U.S. to send food and supplies to displaced Indians, during the recession of 1862 federal food rations were not sent, and a group of hungry and desperate Indians raided a homestead and killed the people living there. More violence followed, leading to the Dakota War of 1862. When the fighting ended, 38 Dakotas were executed by hanging, and the Indians were pushed west into what are now called the Dakotas.

It was the Mississippi River that opened Minnesota to the world, and the newborn cities on its banks became boomtowns in the late 19th century as waves of immigrants, particularly Scandinavians, Germans, and Poles, moved to the frontier. In 1867 Minneapolis was incorporated as a city. At first the transportation hub of St. Paul was the larger of the two competing hamlets. During the 1880s, however, Minneapolis began to overtake its neighbor both in population and commerce. Rivalry between the cities was fierce, leading to the Great Census War of 1890. The first census results showed that Minneapolis was population champ, but St. Paul officials charged fraud, and a scandal ensued. A deputy U.S. marshal arrested census workers in downtown Minneapolis and, when results were recounted, investigators found that counters in both cities had inflated numbers with "residents" who lived in cemeteries and office buildings! The recount, however, did confirm that Minneapolis had more residents, and it has remained the larger city ever since.

Although St. Paul has gradually garnered the reputation as the sleepier town, it hasn't always been that way. During the Prohibition years from 1920 to 1933, mobsters running liquor from Canada brought their ill-gotten gains and wild ways to the city. Ma Barker and her sons hid out here, and the infamous John Dillinger was involved in shoot-outs around town. Finally, arrests and indictments in the late 1930s led to the end of St. Paul's "gangster city" era.

With a large rural population, Minnesota was fertile ground for labor and agricultural reform movements. When the state's Farmer-Labor Party merged with the Democratic Party in 1944 (forming the Minnesota DFL), it began producing national leaders with a strong progressive bent. One of the most visible on the national stage was Hubert H. Humphrey, who served first as mayor of Minneapolis, then as Minnesota's U.S. senator. A strong advocate for civil rights, he gave up his congressional seat to serve as vice president under Lyndon B. Johnson, and was the Democratic presidential candidate in 1968, losing to Richard Nixon. Humphrey's protégé, Walter Mondale, succeeded him as U.S. senator, then served as vice president under Jimmy Carter. In 1984, he, too, ran for president. Consistent with Minnesota's progressive tradition, he chose a woman, U.S. Representative Geraldine A. Ferraro, as his running mate, making her the first woman nominated for that position by a major party. Together they campaigned in support of the Equal Rights Amendment and the need to reduce the federal budget deficit, but were defeated by Ronald Reagan and George H.W. Bush.

While the state's political reputation was growing on the national front, the Twin Cities were becoming the industrial, commercial, and cultural center of the vast fertile Upper Midwest region. Unchecked by geography, area growth erupted outward into the surrounding farmlands after World War II, and the rings of suburbs that were created lured population away from both Minneapolis and St. Paul. Extensive redevelopment, begun in the 1960s, continues to this day, bringing people back to the metropolitan core. The early 1970s construction in Minneapolis of the Investors Diversified Services (IDS) building, the area's first skyscraper, signaled the emergence of Minneapolis as a financial center for the upper Midwest. Soon many downtown offices, apartments, stores, and theaters in Minneapolis and St. Paul were connected with indoor, above-ground skyways, making it possible to live and work in the city centers during the bitter months of winter without ever having to step outside.

Also during the 1970s, investors and government officials finally became concerned with building preservation. Numerous revitalization projects were undertaken, including restoring the Landmark Center in St. Paul and renovating the Warehouse District in Minneapolis. These initiatives have kept alive some of the early history of the two boomtowns, and now the presence of these historic buildings is helping to attract affluent professionals, young families, and senior citizens back from the suburbs to live in the cities' central cores.

WHAT TO BRING

- **A car and a coat**—both in good shape to take on winter. The Twin Cities' bus system, MetroTransit (www.metrotransit.org), offers express connections to the suburbs, but getting around totally by bus is difficult and time-consuming. After years of legislative reluctance, light rail transit (www.metrotransit.org/rail) and commuter rail (www.northstartrain.org) have become a reality, connecting the Minneapolis downtown to the airport and Mall of America to the south, and to Fridley, CoonRapids/Riverdale, Anoka, Elk River, and Big Lake in the northwest. But light rail for the rest of the area is still in the planning stage (see the **Transportation** chapter). Finally, while much of the metro is "walkable" for recreational purposes, there are very few places where you can live and walk to a grocery store.

- **A map**—there are places where Twin Cities' streets and highways follow a perfect grid, and places where streets are laid out at crazy angles. This guide will help you get to know the neighborhoods, but for the full picture, you'll need to accompany it with a map. Hudson's Street Atlas (www.hudsonmap.com), which is published locally and sold online and at bookstores, is a comprehensive spiral-bound book that shows every street in St. Paul and Minneapolis and the surrounding communities. Once you get used to using it, you'll never get lost. And iPhone has an app for you, too, the Minneapolis Offline Street Map, which allows you to zoom in and out for the best view (http://openstreetmap.com/). Even better is the iPhone 3GS, which uses GPS and a built-in compass to find your location and get directions.

"MINNESOTA NICE"

Everyone has concerns about moving to a new place and dealing with an entirely new culture, so rest assured the term "Minnesota Nice" is not just an expression—people here really are nice. In contrast to some other parts of the country, Minnesotans feel the need not to offend and to "make the other person feel comfortable." Consequently, they invariably display a positive demeanor when encountering strangers. You can expect them to jump-start your car in the grocery store parking lot, tow your boat when it runs out of gas, lend you their favorite chainsaw, and let you go first at a four-way stop. What they won't do, however, is open up to you in any meaningful way. Try to get personal, and "Minnesota Nice" quickly turns into "Minnesota Ice," making it hard to tell what a Minnesotan is really thinking or feeling about you, and making it very, very hard to make friends when you first move here. In fact, that's the main complaint of nearly everyone who's ever moved here, so don't think it's you. It's merely a cultural (and possibly weather-augmented) lack of willingness to engage at any level beyond the superficial. On the other hand, if you have to hold up the checkout line while you dump the entire contents of your purse out on the counter to find your credit card, it's nice to know that the people behind you, no matter how angry, frustrated, irritated or bent out of shape they may be, will stoically fume in silence and steadfastly refuse to show any displeasure with you!

That said, how do you develop relationships with people who are so reserved? Do the same things you'd do anywhere. Get involved. Volunteer in your child's school or sports. Join a church, club, or civic organization. The League of Women Voters (www.lwvmn.org) talks about important issues at every meeting—and it's a great way to learn about your new state; ditto the library book clubs. Organizations such as Twin Cities Transplants (www.imnotfromhere.com, http://www.meetup.com/Twin-Cities-Transplants) sponsor events for singles and couples that range from happy hours to museum tours and New Year's Eve parties. They also maintain message boards to help people with similar interests find each other and arrange to get together. The local Newcomers and MOMS Clubs (www.newcomersclub.com/mn.html) provide a similar service, sponsoring golf and tennis leagues, bridge, and many social events, though their events are primarily open to women. (See also the **Getting Involved** chapter in this book.)

Finally, if you've moved here in winter, just hang on. In summer your neighbors will come out of their houses—and while they may not be willing to talk about much more than the weather, at least you'll be talking!

LOCAL LINGO

Sisu. Fish house. Hotdish. What are these people talking about? Here's your Minnesota-to-English Translation Guide. For an in-depth understanding of Minnesotan, rent the movie *Fargo* (yes, we do talk like that!) or read Howard Mohr's book, *How to Speak Minnesotan.*

Bars: Cookie squares, such as brownies or lemon bars.

Borrow: Lend, as in, "Will you borrow me your chainsaw?"

Brat (rhymes with trot): Something you eat; officially named bratwurst.

Croppie: How Minnesotans pronounce the name of the panfish the rest of the country calls a "crappie."

Din't: How Minnesotans pronounce the contraction, "didn't."

Duck, duck grey duck: The circle tag game the rest of the world calls "Duck, duck, goose."

Fish house, also ice house: A structure you haul out on the ice so you can be warm and cozy sitting inside a heated shelter while you fish through a hole in the floor. For a sneak peek at what these homes-away-from-home look like, check out *The Fish House Book* by Kathryn Nordstrom, www.dayoopers.com/the.store?page=catalogF.html.

Hotdish: Casserole. The standard formula is some kind of meat plus some kind of soup plus some kind of cooked vegetable. In other parts of the country, if you're invited to a potluck, you typically take enough for eight to ten servings. Minnesotans, however, take enough food for the whole crowd. Not only that, but if asked to bring an appetizer, they will, without fail, arrive with two—and probably some bars for dessert (see above), as well.

Ice dam: A ridge of ice that forms at the edge of a roof and prevents melting snow (water runoff) from draining off the roof. The water that backs up behind the dam eventually gets under the shingles and leaks into the home, causing damage to walls, ceilings, insulation, and other areas. The only permanent fix for ice dams is to properly insulate, seal, and ventilate the attic so that the home's roof remains cold.

Ice-out: Ice is considered to be "out" when it is possible to travel from any shore to any other shore across a lake, even if you have to go around ice to do so. Ice-out is called in different ways. On Lake Minnetonka, for many years it was called when a boat could travel between Wayzata and Excelsior. Older residents remember when someone would put a broken-down car out on the ice in Wayzata Bay or Spring Park Bay and call ice-out when it fell through. Now the Freshwater Institute calls ice-out when a boat is able to navigate in and out of every Lake Minnetonka bay, even if the ice in the middle still looks fairly solid. In the 150 years that ice-out has been recorded on Minnetonka, it has usually gone out the second or third week in April. It has also gone out six times in March and six times in May.

Lutefisk: Fish soaked in lye. This Scandinavian delicacy is usually served at Christmas with melted butter and mashed potatoes. Don't worry—no one will expect you to actually eat this, but they may demonstrate their own superiority to you by going back for seconds. That said, Minnesotans are nothing if not practical, and this stuff stinks, which is why those who choose to indulge normally eat it at a restaurant, church supper, or down at St. Olaf College, where they serve it in the dining hall prior to the St. Olaf Choirs' annual Christmas concerts.

Norski: Norwegian

Not too bad: Very good.

Ole and Lena: Norwegian characters in Minnesotans' favorite Scandinavian jokes. They are often joined by their Swedish friend Sven, as they are in this joke that goes around year after year: Ole died, so Lena went to the local paper to put a notice in the obituaries. Sven, the editor, after offering his condolences, asked Lena what she would like to say about Ole. Lena replied, "You yust put 'Ole died.'" Sven, somewhat perplexed, said, "That's it? Just 'Ole died'? Surely, there must be something more you'd like to say. You were married 55 years. If it's money you're concerned about, don't worry, the first five words are free." So Lena thought about it for a few minutes and finally said, "O.K. You put 'Ole died. Boat for sale.'"

Out East: East Coast

Parking Ramp: A multi-story building where you can park your car (as opposed to a surface lot), called a parking garage or parking structure in some other areas of the country.

Pop: Soda or cola

Rambler: One-level house

Sisu: Finnish word for an almost magical combination of stamina, toughness, and perseverance in the face of adversity. While the term is more commonly seen on bumper stickers than heard in everyday speech, every now and then you can expect to hear somebody say that someone has "sisu." It's most often a reference to a patient fighting a life-threatening illness, or someone who has just suffered a devastating loss—often it's as much as you'll ever hear about someone else's troubles.

Sack: Bag

So...then: The basic construction of a Minnesota sentence, as in: "So, are you through with the chainsaw then?"

SPAM: That iconic canned pork-shoulder-and-ham product with an indefinite shelf life that was invented and is still produced in Austin, Minnesota (www.ci.austin.mn.us) by Hormel Food Corporation (www.spam.com).

Spendy: Pricey; expensive

That's different: Expression of extreme disapproval. In ancient Viking days, those who were different were killed. Consequently, a Scandinavian's foremost wish is to fit in, and anything that is "different" is very bad, indeed.

The Range: Iron Range (www.rangecities.com); Northern Minnesota, around Virginia, Chisholm, Ely, Eveleth, Biwabik, Hibbing, etc., where iron ore and taconite have been mined since the late 1800s. This part of the state was made famous by the 2005 movie *North Country*.

Uff-da: Norwegian expletive that passes for an extreme emotional outburst in Minnesota. It signifies strong disgruntlement on the order of something a carpenter might say when he hammers his finger instead of the nail.

Up North: Northern Minnesota, above Grand Rapids.

Warming house: Temporary, seasonal shelters beside outdoor ice rinks where you put on your skates and go to warm up after skating.

Whatever: This is the ultimate expression of Minnesota's institutional passive-aggressiveness. Do not make the mistake of thinking that the person who has responded to your query by answering "Whatever" has no opinion or preference and is leaving the decision up to you. They are merely keeping you guessing.

Wild rice: Minnesota's State Grain is not actually rice, but a very high protein annual water-grass seed, *Zizania aquatica*. Naturally abundant in the cold rivers and lakes of Minnesota and Canada, wild rice is still harvested in the traditional Indian way, from a canoe using beater sticks to knock the seeds into the bottom of the boat. Wild rice soup, in particular, is a favorite of people who live here.

Ya: Phrase of agreement, as in "Ya sure, you betcha." You'll hear this phrase ten times a day if you go Up North, but around the metro, you're more likely to hear people say, "You bet." The Howard Mohr book, *How to Speak Minnesotan*, says that this phrase is popular because "it is pleasantly agreeable, but doesn't obligate the speaker to a strong position."

Yet: still. You will hear Minnesotans say things like, "Is it raining yet?" (meaning, "Is it still raining?") and it will grate on your nerves, but there is nothing you can do about it.

ADDRESS LOCATOR

There are places where Twin Cities' streets follow a perfect grid, and places where streets are laid out at crazy angles with no relation to east, west, north, or south. The convolutions are due primarily to the Mississippi River winding through both downtowns, oblivious to the needs of city planners. City boundaries, where streets occasionally change names, add additional confusion. Suburban communities often follow Twin Cities' street patterns, but not always. For the full picture, you'll need to accompany this guide with a map. With one in hand, keep the following things in mind:

MINNEAPOLIS

- Street addresses are uniformly divided in hundreds, block by block. Numbers increase moving outward from the Mississippi River on the north side and from Nicollet Avenue on the south side.
- Downtown streets are laid out diagonally to the compass (the pesky Mississippi!) so try not to let compass directions throw you off. Because of their orientation to the river, numbered streets and those running parallel to them are labeled north or south, dividing at Hennepin Avenue.
- South Minneapolis (south of Grant Street) is straightforward and easy to understand. Numbered streets run east-west, with ascending numbers going southward. Avenues for the most part run north-south, and have numbers east of Nicollet Avenue and proper names west of Nicollet, which means, in South Minneapolis, the higher the numbered street, the farther south it is; the higher the numbered avenue, the farther east it is.
- In the University of Minnesota neighborhood, numbered streets generally run east-west, while numbered avenues run north-south. Streets and avenues here are labeled Southeast.
- In Northeast Minneapolis numbered avenues run east-west, with numbers ascending northward. North-south streets are numbered heading east from the river until 6th Street. East of 6th the streets are named chronologically after U.S. presidents, from Washington to Coolidge.

- In North Minneapolis numbered avenues run east-west, with numbers ascending northward. North-south streets have ascending numbers as you go west from the Mississippi, until 7th Street. West of 7th, streets have proper names.

ST. PAUL

Governor Jesse Ventura got into trouble for suggesting that St. Paul was laid out by tipsy Irishmen, but there are many who live here who would agree.

- Along with St. Paul's old-world charm comes a somewhat confusing street system. St. Paul's street numbers don't always follow tidy increments of one hundred for every block; they may change from 100 to 200 in the middle of the block so...get out that atlas.
- West of Downtown, the north-south dividing line is Summit Avenue. Street numbers increase going westward from Downtown.
- Downtown, Wabasha Street is the division between east and west. The Mississippi River is the north-south marker.
- East of Downtown the north-south dividing line is Upper Afton Road. Street numbers increase going eastward from Downtown.

FROM CITY TO CITY

- University and Franklin avenues keep their names going from St. Paul to Minneapolis, but Marshall Avenue in St. Paul becomes Lake Street in Minneapolis, and St. Paul's Ford Parkway becomes 46th Street in Minneapolis. Don't worry too much; there are only a handful of these streets to remember. The river breaks up most of them.
- Some suburbs, especially inner ones, number their streets according to the grid of the Twin Cities. Other older or far-flung suburbs, such as Wayzata, are laid out on their own grids. The simple advice: don't expect address numbers in the 'burbs and cities to match up.

All in all, the Twin Cities are no more difficult to navigate than any other middle-aged American city with local geographical quirks. Take a few trips to different parts of town and it won't be long before you're tooling around like a native.

MINNEAPOLIS AND ST. PAUL, THE CORE CITIES

THE MINNEAPOLIS AND ST. PAUL DOWNTOWN WAREHOUSE BLOCKS, which began morphing into residential districts in the 1980s, have blossomed into tony glass and concrete playgrounds for the childless, with access to both cities' riverfronts and cultural attractions that is unmatched elsewhere in the metro.

Surrounding neighborhoods also shared in the spiffing-up. Northeast's bachelor-on-the-skids scruffiness gave way to a dapper elegance that has turned it into one of the Cities' most sought-after addresses; the North Loop has transformed into a sophisticated haven on the river; and grungy old Elliot Park has taken on the look of a dull brass doorknob that's finally gotten a good polish.

Across the river, St. Paul has struggled with development projects that never came to fruition, as well as a change in needs, with greater demand for rental units and less demand for condos. Nevertheless, the city is focused on making itself "The Most Livable City in America" by 2015. Key to this plan is transit-oriented development along the Central Corridor Light Rail down University Avenue, and redevelopment that will finally give the city a "full-service" downtown.

So where should YOU live?

Here are a few suggestions to get you started in your hunt: Many young single professionals choose to go straight to Uptown or Northeast Minneapolis, or the southwest districts of St. Paul. Young families love South Minneapolis and western St. Paul as much for the niches in the houses' plaster walls as for their easy access to bike paths, children's activities, and shopping; and lofts in St. Paul and Northeast Minneapolis tend to be more affordable than those in Minneapolis Downtown. And Bryn Mawr, in Minneapolis north of I-394, has been voted one of our most livable neighborhoods more than once.

As is true wherever you go in this state, the closer you are to water, the more you'll have to pay. Equally true: Parking is difficult to find in the downtowns and winter exacerbates the situation. You will save yourself a lot of headaches if you limit your search to housing that includes off-street parking.

And of course, there are still sections of both cities that you should check out extra-carefully: North Minneapolis, extending into Robbinsdale and Brooklyn Center, has some great, affordable houses—and a high crime rate; South Minneapolis, south of I-94 and east of Lyndale to the Mississippi River, can be dicey as far down as 46th Street; St. Paul, along University Avenue east of Snelling and north of I-94, as well as the northeastern quadrant of St. Paul, north of I-94 and east of I-35E, has seen a fair amount of drug- and gang-related violence. While these regions do, in fact, include some great older homes and fabulous amenities, there may be safer Twin Cities locales.

When asked where they live, residents in Minneapolis and St. Paul are more likely to give the names of their neighborhoods than their street addresses. This can be confusing, but don't worry, it's actually quite orderly—at least in Minneapolis, which has five geographic areas (Downtown [shown as Central on some maps], South, Southwest, North, and Northeast) divided into 11 communities (Calhoun-Isles, Camden, Central/Downtown, Longfellow, Near North, Nokomis, Northeast, Phillips, Powderhorn, Southwest, and University). The communities are further subdivided into 81 neighborhoods that are usually organized around parks and schools. The Central/Downtown community, for example, includes the following neighborhoods: Downtown East, Downtown West, Elliot Park, Loring Park, North Loop, and Stephens Square/Loring Heights (www.ci.minneapolis.mn.us/about/maps/neighborhoods.pdf).

Thanks to the clear-cut boundaries, in Minneapolis, people tend to be quite specific about their neighborhoods. In St. Paul, on the other hand, even though it is officially subdivided into a much more manageable 17 districts, there are nearly 130 informal "proxy" neighborhoods, many of which coincide with shopping districts, historic designations, or earlier, independent villages that are no longer there. Don't worry, though. If you move to St. Paul, just say you live on Cathedral Hill or in Swede's Hollow, and anybody you're talking to will get the idea.

You can locate Minneapolis neighborhoods and your police precinct by moving your mouse over the Police Precinct and Neighborhoods map posted at www.ci.minneapolis.mn.us/police/about/precincts.asp. Statistical information and pictures can be accessed through clickable links on the city's profiles page, www.ci.minneapolis.mn.us/neighborhoods/index.asp. Neighborhood profiles and news are available at www.nrp.org/R2/Neighborhoods/Orgs/Organizations.html.

In St. Paul, the 17 district Community Councils operate as private nonprofits to engage residents, business owners, and property owners in issues and projects throughout the city. Their web pages can provide you with neighborhood profiles and the latest news. To reach them, click on a link from the city's web site, www.stpaul.gov, under the heading, "I Want To…Find a District Council."

In case you're still confused, browse www.livemsp.org, a web site launched by Minneapolis and St. Paul together to promote home buying, neighborhood information, and current resident resources. A neighborhood map helps, too. Big Stick, www.bigstickinc.com/map_minneapolis.asp, has produced an exquisitely detailed hand-drawn "fire and ice" wall map that shows all the neighborhoods in Minneapolis and St. Paul—and identifies some of the historic areas. Very handy for figuring out WHICH St. Anthony your realtor is talking about! Another resource—Hubbuzz, www.hubbuzz.com/Minneapolis-St.Paul/MetroAreaMap.aspx, has a clickable online map you can use to find out the names of cities and neighborhoods across the metro, as well as to see pictures of cityscapes and properties that are for rent.

> Take a virtual bus ride down Lake Street, one of the main east-west thoroughfares through south Minneapolis, on the Minnesota Historical Society's 21A-Right on Lake Street, www.mnhs.org/exhibits/lakestreet/interactive/master.html.

NEIGHBORHOOD SAFETY

911 is the emergency number throughout the metro area, but for safety information, you will need to contact other sources.

For Minneapolis, you can find out how one neighborhood compares with another by reading neighborhood crime reports online at CODEFOR, www.ci.minneapolis.mn.us/citywork/police/stats/codefor. The Minneapolis Police Department also provides Crime Watch incident information at www.mplscrimewatch.blogspot.com. Looking at these reports, you often see that the largest numbers of violent crimes are reported on the North side of the city. Be sure, though, to note the types of crimes and not just the numbers.

A further resource is the SAFE Crime Prevention team of specialists who work in each precinct. You can contact them by calling 311 or e-mailing them through clickable links on the Minneapolis police department web page, www.ci.minneapolis.mn.us/police/outreach/safe-teams.asp.

To investigate neighborhood safety in St. Paul, check with the St. Paul Police Department, 651-291-1111, www.stpaul.gov/index.aspx?nid=461. Or look online at the department's Crime Analysis page, www.stpaul.gov/index.aspx?nid=674. This has a link to the city's crime maps, where incidents are plotted on density grids, allowing you to compare all parts of the city by crime: assault, auto theft, burglary, robbery, and theft. Rape and murder are not mapped.

Wherever you choose to live, you should also do a ZIP code search of the Department of Corrections Predatory Offender web site (www.doc.state.mn.us/level3/search.asp) to see if any Level 3 sex offenders are living nearby.

A word on safety for renters: Question the landlord closely about tenant screening procedures, what they do about problem tenants, and if they participate in the **Crime Free Multi-housing Program**. If they do, and have completed the required training, they should display a large metal sign that shows they are certified, and the building's literature and advertising should include the program logo.

Finally, once you've narrowed down your choices, give the ZIP codes for the addresses you're interested in to your insurance agent, who can provide you with additional statistical information, including crime rates and how much insurance coverage will cost you if you decide to move into that area.

STORMWATER UTILITY FEE

Into each life a little rain must fall, but in Minneapolis you pay for it according to how much impervious surface you have in your yard. (Impervious areas are hard surfaces, such as roofs, sidewalks, and driveways, which stop rain or melting snow from being absorbed into the ground.) Called a "stormwater utility fee," the city separates this charge out from the rest of your bill so that you can appeal it or apply for up to a 100% credit if you install stormwater management practices, such as rain gardens on your property. Placed in a strategically located shallow depression in the ground, a rain garden will not only act like a sponge and prevent excessive runoff from leaving your property, but will also help to replenish our groundwater supply, all the while taking some of the pressure off the city's already overburdened storm sewer system. For more information, contact the City Utility Billing Office, 311, or check out the city's web site, www.ci.minneapolis.mn.us/stormwater/fee.

MINNEAPOLIS

Water played an important role in the city's development. Known as both the "City of Lakes" and the "Mill City," Minneapolis has 18 lakes, over 11 miles of the Mississippi River, and more than 3,783 acres of parks within its city limits. It's the river that made it the "Mill City." With several flour mills located alongside St. Anthony Falls, in the area we call Historic St. Anthony or St. Anthony Main, Minneapolis was the world's largest flour producer from 1882 to 1930. This era in the region's history is preserved in the Mill City Museum, 704 South Second Street, www.millcitymuseum.org. A National Historic Landmark, this riverfront museum chronicles the ups and downs of the flour milling industry, including the story of Betty Crocker, of cooking fame, who, in 1945, was voted the second most popular woman in America behind Eleanor Roosevelt. Not bad for a gal who never existed! Better yet, she still represents the most successful branding campaign in advertising history.

Fast-forward to 2010, and though the mills are long gone, Minneapolis, in Hennepin County, is still the state's largest city, and one of its fastest growing, having added more than 7,000 new residents between 2000 and 2008. The Metropolitan Council estimates that 390,131 residents sleep in the city every night, and 290,864 work there every day. Add the 100,000 or so who attend the University of Minnesota and other colleges and technical schools within the city's boundaries, and Minneapolis suddenly has a daytime population of approximately half a million. That's 10% of the state's 5 million population!

At first glance, the faces of these Minneapolitans may appear to be overwhelmingly white, but Minneapolis is our most ethnically diverse city, with approximately 17% Black/African Americans, 6% Asians, 11% Hispanics or Latinos, and 1% Native Americans.

New immigrants have repeatedly settled in the same places, making our historic districts far more diverse than the historic districts in many other cities. To learn about the historic districts and hear all the tall tales, sign up for a free Historic Preservation Commission walking tour of Park Avenue, Elliot Park, and more. Tours are given from May through August. Check them out at www.ci.minneapolis.mn.us/hpc/walking-tours.asp or call 612-673-2615. Reservations are not required. Meeting times and locations are posted on the web.

Eleven and a half miles of the Mississippi flow through Minneapolis, and now the city is tying its most Ivy League new developments and recreation amenities to this river. So if you're interested in boating, or merely looking for running room, consider these neighborhoods, all of which have some access to the river: Lind-Bohanon, Webber-Camden, Shingle Creek, Near North, North Loop, Downtown East and West, Cedar Riverside, Seward, and the Greater Longfellow neighborhoods on the west bank; Columbia Park, Marshall Terrace, Bottineau, Sheridan, St. Anthony West and East, Marcy-Holmes, and Prospect Park/East River Road on the east bank. Get the official take on what's been accomplished and what is yet to come by watching the Park and Recreation Board's slide presentation, Minneapolis Riverfront Revitalization Three Decades of Progress, www.ci.minneapolis.mn.us/cped/docs/Riverfront_PowerPoint.pdf.

Live in any of the following neighborhoods and have easy access to the Hiawatha Light Rail: Minnehaha, Ericsson, Standish, Hiawatha, Howe, Corcoran, Longfellow, Seward, East Phillips, Ventura Village, Seward, Cedar-Riverside, North Loop, and Downtown East and West

---

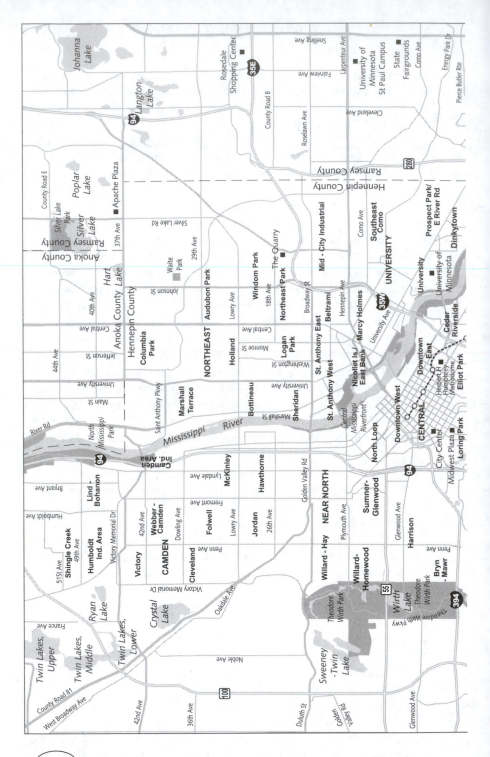

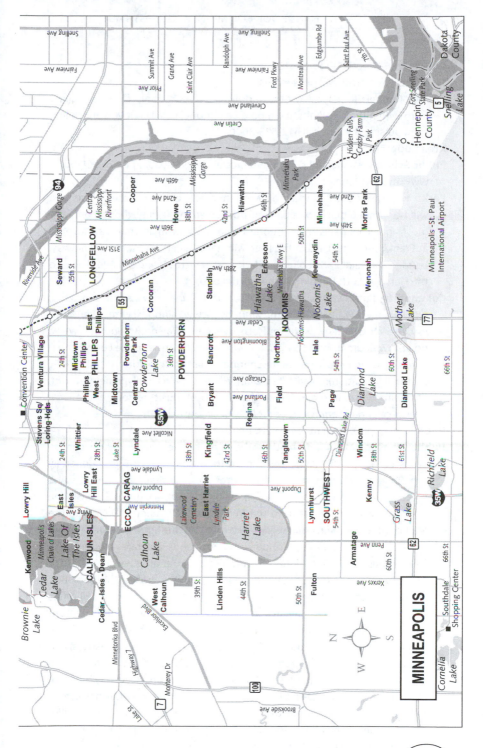

MINNEAPOLIS

City Hall: 350 South 5th St, 55415

Web Site: www.ci.minneapolis.mn.us

Phone Number: To reach any Minneapolis city department, if you are calling from within the city limits, even on a cell phone, call 311. If you are calling from outside the city, call 612-673-3000.

Area Code: 612

Public Schools: Minneapolis, District Office: 612-668-0000, TTY 612-668-0001, www.mpls.k12.mn.us

Parks: www.minneapolisparks.org; no matter where you choose to live, you will be within 6 blocks of a park and/or recreation facility, though only the most significant parks are mentioned below. Off-leash dog parks are located at Franklin Terrace, Lake of the Isles, Minnehaha Park, St. Anthony Parkway, Loring Park, Elliot Park, Columbia Park, and at 3rd St N and 8th Ave N next to the Herschel Lofts Building in the North Loop.

Community Publications: *Minneapolis Star Tribune*, www.startribune.com; *City Pages*, www.citypages.com; *MinnPost*, www.minnpost.com; *Minneapolis Observer Quarterly*, www.mplsobserver.com; *Downtown Journal*, www.downtownjournal.com; *Southside Pride*, www.southsidepride.com; *Minneapolis Civic Garden*, www.wirelessminneapolis.org (provides useful, public sector information); *Twin Cities Daily Planet*, www.tcdailyplanet.net; *Rift*, www.riftmagazine.com, offers samples of local music, reviews and a local events calendar; *Southwest Journal*, www.swjournal.com

Photos: www.phototour.minneapolis.mn.us

Public Transportation: Information about all public transportation can be accessed at 612-373-3333, www.metrotransit.org. *Buses:* Buses generally run along main thoroughfares, but routes and schedules do change, so be sure to check the web site or call. *Trains:* The Hiawatha Light Rail Transit line follows Hiawatha Avenue from the Minneapolis Warehouse District to the Mall of America. Trains run every 5–10 minutes during rush hours and every 10–15 minutes during off-hours and weekends. Rail fares are the same as local bus fares ($2.25 during rush hours, $1.75 at all other times). There are reduced fares for seniors, youth ages 6–12, and people with disabilities. Trains run between 5 a.m. and 1 a.m. The Northstar Commuter Rail offers five morning trips from Big Lake to downtown Minneapolis and five return trips in the afternoon along a 40-mile corridor adjacent to congested highways 10 and 47. There is one reverse commute roundtrip on weekdays, and three weekend roundtrips on Saturdays and Sundays. Fares range from 75 cents station-to-station on weekends to $7 one-way on a weekday between Minneapolis and Big Lake. Children under 5 ride free. HourCar has cars in neighborhoods throughout the city, including Uptown, Bryn Mawr, Elliot Park, Northeast, the Mill District, North Loop, Saint Anthony Park, Stephens Square, Seward, and some LRT stations, www.hourcar.org.

CENTRAL/DOWNTOWN COMMUNITY

Warehouse District and Riverfront; Downtown West; North Loop; Downtown East; Stevens Square–Loring Heights; Elliot Park; Loring Park

Boundaries: North: Plymouth Ave, Mississippi River; **West**: I-94; **South**: Franklin Ave, Hwy 12; **East**: Interstate-35W

> Target, Lund's, the open space of Gold Medal Park, the skyways, shops and cafes, and the Farmer's Market—all these amenities combine to create a real, livable community downtown.

Downtown West centers around Nicollet Mall, an eight-block commercial strip closed to cars, and includes the restored **Warehouse District** that surrounds Target Center. **Downtown East** is the area between Park Avenue and 35W that includes the Guthrie Theater, Hubert H. Humphrey Metrodome, Mill City Museum, and the lovely open space of Gold Medal Park. Both neighborhoods boast a high concentration of office buildings, with Downtown West heavier into entertainment, restaurants and retail stores. Another difference—while the high-rises of Downtown West are filled with rental apartments, many of the old mills and factories of Downtown East have been converted into large, multi-story condos.

But if you're looking for quarters more hospitable to young families, head straight for the **North Loop**, www.northloop.org, which runs along the north edge of the business district from the Mississippi River on the east to I-94 on the west, and Plymouth Avenue on the north to Hennepin Avenue and Glenwood on the south. It's easy to find—just aim toward the Twins' new baseball stadium, Target Field (http://minnesota.twins.mlb.com/min/ballpark/index.jsp).

For years the city turned its back on this area. The warehouse blocks were an entertainment district at night, but by day they were plain old skid row.

Likewise, the **Riverfront** was allowed to become an industrial wasteland, and the river was pretty hard to find, even if you knew it was there. Not any more. Over the past decade trendy condo complexes have emerged in revamped warehouses, and quiet streets of three- and four-bedroom row houses have blossomed on land that used to be home to hobo camps and railyards. Of course, there are rental apartments in this neighborhood, too—some in buildings that are connected to the business district's skyways, though mostly near the ends. (Skyways are enclosed breezeways that connect building to building on the level of the second or third floors.) Controlled access and 24-hour security are standard, as are amenities such as fitness centers and secure parking. Many complexes also set aside space for corporate housing, providing newcomers with an easy way to get to know the area before having to commit.

Recreation amenities here are spectacular, with trails along the Mississippi river and a major park/marina out in the middle on Boom Island. Great bars and restaurants abound, too, including Bar La Grassa, a joint project of the owners of perennial favorites 112 Eatery and La Belle Vie, which is just as good, but less expensive, with a bar that's open until 2 a.m. (800 Washington Ave. N., Minneapolis, 612-333-3837, www.barlagrassa.com) And then there's the stadium. Because of the stadium, the North Loop has become the epicenter of the region's rail transportation system. Another stadium perk—skyways and a pedestrian bridge that will connect the Loop to the existing skyway system at 6th Street. With a high-end Lund's Grocery at 11th and Hennepin (www.lundsandbyerlys.com), and the Nicollet Mall Target (www.target.com), living Downtown has become as easy as living anywhere.

Only a short hop away, **Stevens Square–Loring Heights** is bracketed between the busy streets of Lyndale Avenue, I-35, I-94 and Franklin Avenue, just south of the downtown business district. The original buildings here were constructed roughly between 1890 and 1930. If you're interested in seeing where Minneapolis has come from—and where it is going—just take a walk around these simple-to-sumptuous streets. Loring Heights, west of Nicollet, is a neighborhood of grand houses, developed in one of the upper classes' first moves toward the south and west of the central city. Its layout of curved streets on a ridge is the classic mark of the Victorian romantic suburb. The small apartments of Stevens Square (www.sscoweb.org), on the other hand, were built as a mill town for small families and single tradesmen. Today these apartments are home to many singles, as well as people taking the cure at nearby treatment centers. Though most properties are rental, condo conversions are increasingly popular. One of the neighborhood's landmark buildings is the 12,000-square-foot George W. Van Dusen mansion at 1900 La Salle Avenue South, which was used as a backdrop in the Coen brothers' 2008 movie about the Twin Cities, *A Serious Man*. More interestingly, according to court documents, it was purchased in 2007 with some of the early profits of a massive Ponzi scheme, and then used to impress potential victims and convince them to entrust their

money to the alleged co-conspirators, one of whom is a syndicated talk radio star. A star of a different kind, the Stevens Square Center for the Arts (www.stevensarts.org), 1905 3rd Avenue S, is a nonprofit that rents out studio and gallery space to artists, and hosts Red Hot Art in Stevens Square Park—two days of music, art and fun that are not to be missed!

Nearby **Elliot Park** (http://elliotparkneighborhood.org), surrounding the Hennepin County Medical Center (HCMC) and the Hubert H. Humphrey Metrodome, has suffered from a dicey reputation, but is trending upward with projects such as the mixed-income/mixed-use East Village row house development on 11th Avenue South, and the conversion of some of the historic brownstones and factories into condominium lofts. The South Ninth Street Historic District residential structures located along sections of Ninth and Tenth streets are among the oldest apartment buildings in Minneapolis. One of them has the distinction of being the birthplace of J. Paul Getty, the world's richest man at his death in 1976.

The lovely turn-of-the-20th-century, brick walk-up apartments and large stone houses surrounding Loring Park give the **Loring Park** neighborhood (Lyndale to 12th and Hawthorne Avenue to I-94, www.loringpark.org), an air of grandeur that is further enhanced by the presence of a number of beautiful public buildings—the Basilica of St. Mary, the Woman's Club of Minneapolis, the Cathedral Church of St. Mark, and the Hennepin Avenue United Methodist Church. Connected to the Nicollet Mall by a picturesque pathway known as the Loring Greenway, it is easy to live here and walk to work downtown. Its days as a rental neighborhood, however, may be numbered as more and more of the apartments are converted into expensive condominiums.

Long the center of gay life in the Twin Cities, these hills and hollows are well-supplied with hangouts for gay and straight alike. Visiting film crews and out-of-town celebrities are often spotted in the Café and Bar Lurcat (1624 Harmon Place, Minneapolis, 612-486-5500, www.cafelurcat.com), which

overlooks Loring Park and is arguably the Twin Cities' most cosmopolitan bistro. A slew of interesting coffee shops and cafés line the north side. On the south, the 510 Groveland Building is one of the best addresses in town, and home to what is generally acknowledged as the metro's best restaurant, La Belle Vie (612-874-6440, www.labellevie.us). Numerous independent stages, such as the Red Eye Theater (612-870-0309, www.redeyetheater.org) are all within walking distance, and the Walker Art Center and sculpture garden (612-375-7600, www. walkerart.org) are just across the street over a pedestrian bridge.

ZIP Codes: 55401, 55402, 55403, 55404, 55415, 55487, 55488

Post Offices: Main Office, 100 S 1st St; Loop Station, 110 S 8th St; Commerce Station, 307 4th Ave S

Police Precinct: 1st, 19 North 4th St, 311 or 612-673-5701 (non-emergency); http://www.ci.minneapolis.mn.us/police/about/1st-precinct.asp

Emergency Hospital: Hennepin County Medical Center, 701 Park Ave, 612-873-3000, www.hcmc.org

Library: Central Library, 300 Nicollet Mall, 612-630-6000, www.hclib.org

Community Resources: Guthrie Theater, 818 Second St S, 612-377-2224, www.guthrietheater.org; Hennepin Theatre District, includes the State, Orpheum, Pantages theatres, all located along Hennepin Ave, 612-339-7007, www.hennepintheatretrust.org; Hubert H. Humphrey Metrodome, 900 S 5th St, 612-332-0386, www.msfc.com; Illusion Theater, 528 Hennepin Ave, 612-339-4944, www.illusiontheater.org; Mill City Museum, 704 S Second St, 612-341-7555, www.millcitymuseum.org; Orchestra Hall, 1111 Nicollet Mall, 612-371-5656 or 800-292-4141, www.minnesotaorchestra.org; Target Center, 600 1st Ave N, 612-673-0900, www.targetcenter.com; Target Field, Third Ave between Fifth and Seventh sts, http://minnesota.twins.mlb.com/min/ballpark/index.jsp

Parks: www.minneapolisparks.org; Loring Park; Mississippi Riverfront; Gold Medal Park

Community Publications: *Downtown Journal*, www.downtownjournal.com; *Southside Pride*, www.southsidepride.com

Public Transportation: 612-373-3333, www.MetroTransit.org; you can get around downtown by bus on any major street, and downtown fares are reduced. Minneapolis/St. Paul Inter-city Express buses provide connecting service between downtown Minneapolis, I-94, Snelling Ave, the Capitol Complex, and downtown St. Paul. The LRT travels along S 5th St with 5 stations in downtown Minneapolis: Target Field, Warehouse District/Hennepin Avenue, Nicollet Mall, Government Plaza, and Downtown East/Metrodome.

CALHOUN-ISLES COMMUNITY
Uptown; Bryn Mawr/Cedar-Isles-Dean/West
Calhoun; Kenwood/East Isles/Lowry Hill

Boundaries: North: Bassett Creek; **West**: France Ave; **South**: 38th St; **East**: Lyndale Ave

Visitors and residents alike fall in love with Minneapolis because of the Calhoun-Isles community with its linked "Chain of Lakes" and the myriad activities possible here: shopping, running, rollerblading, biking, swimming, sailing, people-watching, etc. Calhoun is one of the top lakes for windsurfing in the Twin Cities, and the running/biking paths around all these lakes are part of the Grand Rounds Scenic Byway (see **Lakes and Parks**).

This was the first Minneapolis suburb, and it's still one of the most popular places for newcomers (and young people who grew up in the suburbs) to settle. For those who work in downtown Minneapolis, the office is only a short walk, bike ride, or brief bus ride away.

Calhoun-Isles can be divided into three distinct districts: the trendy, populous rental neighborhoods commonly known as Uptown; the meandering streets along the southwest border of the city that make up Bryn Mawr, Cedar Isles-Dean, and West Calhoun; and the city's most expensive neighborhoods, Kenwood, Lowry Hill, and East Isles, which wrap around Lake of the Isles.

Lest you think that all the crime is confined to North Minneapolis, you need to realize that there is a fair amount here as well, particularly burglary and theft from motor vehicles.

ZIP Codes: 55403, 55408, 55416
Post Offices: 110 E 31st St
Police Precinct: 5th, 3101 Nicollet Ave S, 311 (non-emergency), 612-673-5705
Emergency Hospital: Hennepin County Medical Center, 701 Park Ave, 612-873-3000, www.hcmc.org
Library: Walker, 2880 Hennepin Ave, 612-630-6650, www.hclib.org

Community Resources: Purcell-Cutts House, 2328 Lake Pl; Walker Art Center, 1750 Hennepin Ave, 612-375-7600, www.walkerart.org

Parks: www.minneapolisparks.org; Minneapolis Chain of Lakes; Parade Athletic Fields and Ice Garden, 600 Kenwood Pkwy, 612-370-4846; Walker Art Center Sculpture Garden, 1750 Hennepin Ave, www.walkerart.org

Community Publications: *Downtown Journal*, www.downtownjournal.com; *Bryn Mawr Bugle*, www.bmna.org/bugle.html; *Uptown Neighborhood News*, www.carag.org/news/unn.htm

Public Transportation: 612-373-3333, www.MetroTransit.org; bus service is frequent along Lake St, Hennepin Ave, and other major thoroughfares

---

UPTOWN

East Calhoun (ECCO); CARAG; Lowry Hill East (The Wedge)

Uptown (http://ouruptown.com) spreads outward from the Calhoun Square Shopping Mall, which is on the corner of Lake Street and Hennepin Avenue. It has loosely defined boundaries, at least so far as Minneapolitans are concerned, but is generally understood to include **East Calhoun** (ECCO, http://eastcalhountest.ning.com) west of Hennepin, and **CARAG** (www.carag.org) east of Hennepin. Together these neighborhoods extend south from Lake Street to 36th Street, and from the east shore of Lake Calhoun to Lyndale Avenue. There is also a northern section of Uptown, called **Lowry Hill East** or **The Wedge** (www.thewedge.org), a large, roughly triangular shaped rental area that stretches between Hennepin and Lyndale Avenues, north of Lake Street, to the point where the two streets meet near Loring Park. It includes the up-and-coming Lyn-Lake business district and entertainment center, at the corner of Lyndale and Lake streets. Vegan bistros, art-house cinemas, ethnic eateries, and beer-and-burger bars all thrive in this area, along with small theater companies

and trendy shopping. **East Isles** (EIRA), though not officially part of the district, is generally spoken of as Uptown, as well (see the Kenwood/East Isles/Lowry Hill section of this chapter).

As a general rule, housing closest to the lakes is the most expensive. Large homes, many of which have been divided into duplexes, predominate, and stately brick apartment buildings built as far back as the 1890s still survive. Before the building boom of 2000, the last major building period occurred during the 1920s, as part of a plan to convert East Calhoun into an "apartment district." Mediterranean-style structures from this period can be easily identified by their red tile roofs. Low-rise one- and two-bedroom apartment complexes built in the 1960s and '70s are still to be found, but there are also newly constructed condos, particularly near the lakes and along the Midtown Greenway. While these neighborhoods offer rental living quarters and recreation possibilities in abundance, the downside is traffic. The intersection at Hennepin and Lake is said to be one of the busiest in the Twin Cities. In an effort to make commuting by bike easier and safer, area residents asked for—and got the city to build—the Midtown Greenway, a mostly below-grade bike path that parallels Lake Street, running from Chowen Avenue on the west all the way across town to the Mississippi River (www.midtowngreenway.org). Shopping is easy, too, with many unique stores and the cream of TC groceries—Lund's on Lake Street near Hennepin (www.lundsandbyerlys.com), Kowalski's at 24th and Hennepin (www.kowalskis.com), and The Wedge Co-op at 22nd and Lyndale (www.wedge.coop).

BRYN MAWR, CEDAR-ISLES-DEAN, WEST CALHOUN

Close to the parks, but out of the traffic, the hilly wooded neighborhoods on the west edge of the city offer comfortable living in a park-like setting of architecturally varied, well-kept bungalows, ramblers, colonials, and architects' signature houses. High-rise apartment buildings in **Cedar-Isles-Dean** (www.cidna.org) and **West Calhoun**, along Highway 7 and Excelsior Boulevard, boast picture-perfect views of sailing boats beating through the deep green waters of Lake Calhoun.

Back on Cedar Lake, much of the shoreline is occupied by private homes, unusual in this city where most lakes are completely surrounded by public parks. Public access is provided, however, at beaches, boat launches, and fishing piers. Cedar Lake is part of the Grand Rounds Scenic Byway and connects with Theodore Wirth Park and Lake Calhoun/Lake of the Isles via the parkway system, as well as through a channel into Lake of the Isles (in case you're a kayaker). Homes here are beautiful and architect designed, and this hidden neighborhood, though small, is one of the finest in the Twin Cities.

Bryn Mawr (www.bmna.org), located west of downtown, has been picked repeatedly as one of the most livable places in the metropolitan area. Sliced in two by east-west–running I-394, the northern half tends to have slightly smaller houses built closer together on smaller lots. These single-family homes are diverse, yet well kept, and you can find every style here from Tudor to Colonial to Contemporary. Two Minneapolis public schools, Bryn Mawr Elementary/Park View Montessori (http://parkview.mpls.k12.mn.us), and Anwatin Spanish Dual Immersion, are located in the neighborhood. There is a small commercial district on Cedar Lake Road that includes a coffee shop/café, pizza place and market.

KENWOOD, EAST ISLES, LOWRY HILL

While Calhoun/Uptown seems like a summer kind of place, **Kenwood** (www. kenwoodminneapolis.org) and the other neighborhoods that surround Lake of the Isles are at their best in winter when the crowds have gone home. Winter evenings bring groups of sledders screaming down "Suicide Hill," skaters, and

scents of hot chocolate and cinnamon wafting through the frost-bitten air. On nights like these, the most important building on the block becomes the east shore warming house, even though in winter this affluent neighborhood seems twice as impressive as usual, with its large Mediterranean, Colonial, and Arts-and-Crafts homes dressed up in lights and greenery for the holidays. So muffle-up and take the three-mile walk around the lake, and don't miss the Purcell-Cutts house at 2328 Lake Place, which is considered one of the best examples of Prairie School architecture in the country, or the "Mary Tyler Moore house" on the corner of Kenwood and 21st, where Ms. Moore hung her hat after she sailed it in the air in the opening clip of the TV show. While you are walking, keep your eyes open. Some of the "old" houses here are actually new and include elegant twin homes you'd swear were built at the turn of the 20th century. Check out the eight new "old" houses in Kenwood Crest, located next to the historic Kenwood water tower—they even have two- and three-car garages (a rarity for the city!), while fitting comfortably into the ambiance of the 19th-century neighborhood. You'll find that people tend to refer to this whole area as Kenwood, even though Kenwood is mostly on the western side of the lake.

Not all residents live lakeside, of course. Many of the skaters, bikers, and joggers you'll pass live between the lake and Hennepin Avenue, where the hills of **East Isles** sport blocks of architecturally significant houses and a vast number of well-maintained apartments with character. You will find many young professional families here, as well as young professional singles, but the area is in such high demand that to find an apartment, you should look for signs posted in yards or windows, because only rarely do the best apartments make the classifieds.

At the north end of the lake, the steep streets of **Lowry Hill** (www. lowryhillneighborhood.org), from 22nd Street to I-394, west of Hennepin, span the arts and the ages, from turn-of-the-20th-century mill owners' mansions to the Walker Art Center contemporary art museum (www.walkerart.org). Some of the houses here have been pulled down or turned into offices, but many of them still exist as private homes with craftsman details intact, creating a wonderful air of elegance and grace. Despite the heavy traffic, residents of Lowry Hill enjoy their neighborhood, happy to live so conveniently near downtown.

SOUTHWEST COMMUNITY
Armatage/Kenny/Windom; Lynnhurst /Tangletown; Linden Hills/Fulton; East Harriet/Kingfield

Boundaries: North: 38th St; **West**: France Ave, Xerxes Ave; **South**: Crosstown Hwy 62; **East**: I-35W

While young singles head straight for Uptown, hip young families usually prefer the post-Depression bungalows and mini-Tudors of the other southwest communities. Life here, while still close to the city lakes and parkways, is far enough away to make tree-lined streets and well-kept yards feel like small town living. No more than ten minutes' drive from the high-rises of downtown, this is the most heavily residential area of Minneapolis.

Single-family homes and duplexes predominate, with most homes dating to the early 1900s through the 1940s. Homes surrounding Lake Harriet are expensive and some of the most beautiful in Minneapolis. Moderately priced ideal starter homes abound away from the lakes.

Numerous parks add to the tranquility of this community and provide entertainment, too. You can catch a concert at the Lake Harriet bandshell most summer evenings, or stroll through the park's rose garden or bird sanctuary. Lake Harriet also boasts some of the city's favorite swimming beaches. A bike path connects the rose garden to Lyndale Farmstead Park, the original home of Theodore Wirth, the turn-of-the-20th-century "father" of Minneapolis parks. This park, too, has a garden, but it also has ballfields, ice skating rink, nontraditional "imaginative" play space, and a water fountain with a place where dogs can get a drink, too. The Minnehaha Creek Parkway and trail corridor runs through the community to the south. For pictures of Minnehaha Creek and Lake Harriet, look online at Minneapolis Phototour, www.phototour.minneapolis.mn.us.

The southern end of Minneapolis is strongly impacted by airport noise.

ZIP Codes: 55409, 55410, 55419

Post Offices: 110 E 31st St; 110 S. 8th St; 3948 W 49½th St, Edina

Police Precinct: 5th, 3101 Nicollet Ave S, 311 or 612-673-5705 (non-emergency)

Emergency Hospitals: Fairview Southdale Hospital, 6401 France Ave S, 952-924-5000, www.fairview.org; Abbott Northwestern Hospital, 800 E 28th St, 612-863-4000, www.abbottnorthwestern.com

Libraries: Linden Hills, 2900 W 43rd St; Washburn, 5244 Lyndale Ave S; www.hclib.org

Community Resources: Bakken Library and Museum of Electricity in Life, 3537 Zenith Ave S, 612-926-3878, www.thebakken.org

Parks: www.minneapolisparks.org; Minneapolis Chain of Lakes; Lake Harriet Rose Garden; Minnehaha Creek Park

Community Publications: *Downtown Journal*, www.downtownjournal.com; *Southwest Journal*, www.swjournal.com

Public Transportation: 612-373-3333, www.MetroTransit.org; buses run along the main thoroughfares; HourCar, 651-221-4462 ext. 138, www.hourcar.org

ARMATAGE, KENNY, WINDOM

Lined up on the southern border of the city, north of the 62 Crosstown Highway and south of Diamond Lake Road, **Armatage** (www.armatage.org), **Kenny** (www.kennyneighborhood.org), and **Windom** (www.windomcommunity.org) neighborhoods boast well-built two- and three-bedroom starter houses, most of which pre-date the 1940s. Armatage, which runs between 54th Street and

the 62 Crosstown, adjoins Richfield. Homes here are mostly single-family, with some multi-family buildings. Café Maude (54th and Penn, 612-822-5411, http://cafemaude.com) is named for Maude Armatage, daughter of the family which farmed the land that is now this neighborhood. East of Logan Avenue, homes in Kenny tend to be newer, and sometimes larger. According to the Kenny Neighborhood Association, 96% are owner-occupied. Rental homes and apartments can be found in Windom, which runs along I-35W from Diamond Lake Road down to the 62 Crosstown. Here housing runs the gamut, dating from pre-WWII through the 1970s. Retail space in these neighborhoods consists of locally owned stores, located primarily along Penn Avenue and Lyndale. Neighborhood concerns include airport noise and freeway issues.

LYNNHURST, TANGLETOWN

The community milk-cow (you read it right) once grazed in a pasture on 46th Street, and the neighborhood of **Lynnhurst** (www.lynnhurst.org) somehow retains that idyllic sense. Extending from Lyndale west to Penn Avenue, between 46th and 54th streets, this neighborhood boasts very fine period homes as well as parks along Minnehaha Creek and the shores of Lake Harriet. This is one of the most beautiful neighborhoods in the Twin Cities.

Step out of the hustle and bustle of the city in **Tangletown** (www.tangletown.org, formerly called Fuller), where the streets are quiet because most of the passers-through are lost. Nestled between I-35W on the east and Lyndale on the west, from 46th Street down to Diamond Lake Road, this hilly tangle of curved, wooded streets is unusual in the mostly grid-like South Minneapolis layout. Also unique—the neighborhood is capped by the Washburn Water Tower on Prospect Avenue. This majestic water tank is ringed by 16-foot-tall sword-wielding soldiers who have stood sentry since 1932 underneath huge concrete eagles. They're there to protect the city's water supply from typhoid, and apparently they're effective. The water tower was built by Tangletown resident Harry Wild Jones, who also designed Lakewood Cemetery Chapel; check it out on the Minneapolis Phototour web site, www.phototour.minneapolis.mn.us/3005. About a third of the houses here are pre-1920, with most of the rest built prior to 1960. Because development happened over the course of so many years, architectural styles are highly variable, giving these tree-lined streets a real small town feel. Major issues in this vicinity are typical of South Minneapolis—airport noise and the volume and speed of traffic on the straight bits. Shopping is conveniently located in five commercial districts along Penn Avenue, 50th, Bryant, and Lyndale, with many new shops and small restaurants being added every year.

LINDEN HILLS, FULTON

Linden Hills (www.lindenhills.org), on the far southwest edge of the city, was built as a "cottage city" in the 1880s to entice homebuyers away from downtown and out to the waters of Calhoun and Harriet. Only a few cottages remain. Most have been torn down and replaced by bigger houses with two-car garages. The remaining ivy-covered cottages with details like oval windows are consid-

ered desirable remodeling gems. Property values are high, even for houses in deteriorated condition.

Many families choose Linden Hills to be in Southwest High School's attendance district. The sense of community—wine and cheese welcomes and summertime block parties—is another draw. Best of all, it's quiet—a tranquil haven in the middle of the city, with pleasant shopping centered on 43rd and Upton, near which you will find Turtle Bread Company (www.turtlebread.com), and Wild Rumpus books (www.wildrumpusbooks.com). The Linden Hills co-op (www.lindenhills.coop) is near Sunnyside and France.

A neighborhood with a social conscience, it operates a nonprofit, Linden Hills Power & Light, that works to reduce the local carbon footprint and helps people who are having trouble paying their energy bills, www.lhpowerandlight. org.

Fulton (www.fultonneighborhood.org) is a bit less placid. Located between Lake Harriet and 47th streets on the north and 54th street on the south, between France and Penn avenues, it is bisected by the busy artery of 50th Street, with its extended commercial district offering boutique shopping at both 50th and Penn and 50th and France. Housing here consists of 108 square blocks of well-cared-for 1920s- and '30s-built bungalows. Most of them are owner-occupied. This location is one of the most convenient in the city—residents can walk to Lake Harriet, grocery stores, drug stores, the movies, and numerous shops and restaurants, as well as have easy access to Highway 100 and the 62 Crosstown and 35W freeways.

EAST HARRIET, KINGFIELD

Talk about quiet neighborhoods—most of **East Harriet** (www.eastharriet.org) is occupied by Lakewood Cemetery. That's supposed to be a joke; you'll hear it a lot if you move into this neighborhood. You'll also be treated to a list of all your

celebrity "neighbors," including Hubert Horatio Humphrey, Minnesota's senator for many years and vice-president of the United States. Joking aside, this neighborhood does include some of the city's finest open spaces: Lake Harriet and its Rose Garden, and the T. S. Roberts Bird Sanctuary, with its boardwalk through the marsh and an osprey nesting platform. Houses in East Harriet (between 36th Street on the north and 46th on the south, west of Lyndale) tend to be family-sized two-story Tudors, Colonials, and Mediterraneans with charming amenities such as sun-porches. The homes are set back from the streets under leafy, old growth canopies. Many have been divided into duplexes, and there are some apartment buildings, thus splitting this neighborhood about 50-50 between renters and homeowners. For photos of this neighborhood, look online at Minneapolis Phototour, www.phototour.minneapolis.mn.us.

Kingfield (www.kingfield.org), between 36th and 46th, is bordered by I-35W on the east and Lyndale on the west. It takes its name from Martin Luther King Park. Its houses are similar to those closer to Lake Harriet, but a little less expensive. Many have been updated with additional bathrooms and new kitchens. Contemporary housing options include new multifamily residences and live/work condos on Nicollet, as well as apartment buildings. Kingfield, which prides itself on being a forward-looking neighborhood, is the impetus behind developing an off-leash area in MLK Park, as well as the RiverLake Greenway project which, when complete, will create an attractive and safe cross-town route for bicyclists from Lake Harriet to the Mississippi River via 40th and 42nd Streets. For those who embrace the car-free lifestyle, there is an HourCar hub at 38th and Nicollet, conveniently located on the 18 and 23 bus lines (www.hourcar.org).

NOKOMIS COMMUNITY

Hale/Page/Diamond Lake; Standish-Ericsson; Field/Regina/Northrop; Kee-waydin/Minnehaha/Morris Park/Wenonah

Boundaries: North: 42nd St, Hiawatha Golf Course; **West**: I-35W; **South**: Crosstown Hwy 62; **East**: Hiawatha Ave, 47th Ave

"Say, if you'd begin to live, To Oleana you must go/The poorest wretch in Norway, becomes a Duke in a year or so." Those were the words of a song meant to lure Scandinavians to America. Oleana turned out to be a land fraud in Pennsylvania and many of the immigrants wound up here, in Minnesota. The first generation settled on "Snoose Boulevard" (Cedar-Riverside); the second generation built their sturdy post-Depression bungalows in Nokomis, and lived in them for a lifetime.

In the southeast corner of the city, **Nokomis**, which has tree-lined blocks of pleasant yards and tidy houses, is moderately priced, making it attractive to young singles and couples. Luxurious homes line the curved parkways that overlook Lake Nokomis; otherwise, what you'll find here are bungalows, mini-Tudors, and occasional one-story ranch houses. Brick apartment buildings dating to the 1920s can be found along larger streets such as Chicago and Cedar avenues, and small commercial districts dot the area. Housing in this community is largely owner-occupied, by a local population with a range of ages and pocketbooks. This section of the city has an atmosphere much like that of Calhoun/Harriet, but noise from Minneapolis/St. Paul International Airport, to the south, is definitely a factor to consider if you're looking at Nokomis. Keep this in mind and ask pointed questions if you're house hunting in this area.

On the other hand, the ground transportation and recreation amenities are excellent and close at hand. The LRT on the east side of these neighborhoods makes getting downtown, to the airport, or to the Mall of America a quick and easy trip, and the heart of the community, Lake Nokomis, is an expansive body of water with more greenspace around it than any of the other lakes of South Minneapolis. Minneapolis' lake-parkway system winds through this community along Minnehaha Creek and around Lake Nokomis, leading to the public Hiawatha Golf Course and Lake Hiawatha. The Hiawatha Golf Learning Center features a driving range, putting greens, and a variety of sand traps to use for short iron, chipping, and bunker practice. Minnehaha Park, located at the intersection of Hiawatha Avenue and Minnehaha Parkway, is one of Minneapolis' oldest and most popular parks. In keeping with the Scandinavian roots of the community, it is the venue for the Svenskarnas Dag Scandinavian festival held every year near the end of June. The off-leash dog park is at the south end of the park, accessible from the park's 54th and Hiawatha entrance. For a description of Minnehaha Park and Minnehaha Falls, which are on the eastern edge of Nokomis, check **Lakes and Parks**. For information on all these parks look online at www.minneapolisparks.org.

The **Hale**, **Page**, and **Diamond Lake** neighborhoods (www.hpdl.org) are rich with open space. Located between Minnehaha Creek on the north, Highway 62 on the south, Chicago Avenue and I-35W on the west, and Cedar Avenue on the east, they encompass Diamond Lake and a chunk of Lake Nokomis, a long run of Minnehaha Creek Park to the north, and the open fields and wetlands of Solomon Park in the district's southeast corner. Most of the houses here are owner-occupied two-stories, and were built from the 1920s into the 1960s. Homes along Clinton Avenue, between East Diamond Lake Road and Roslyn Place, have large yards that back up to Diamond Lake. Pearl Park, in the geographic center of Page, has a playground, tennis courts, and baseball, football and soccer fields. A highlight of each year is the HPDL Business Association's "Rabbit Hunt." New clues are posted every morning and residents of all ages join in the search. It's a fun way for businesses to say thank you to neighbors for their patronage—and a fun excuse for residents to explore the neighborhood.

Standish and **Ericsson** (www.standish-ericsson.org), north and east of Lake Hiawatha from Cedar Avenue to Hiawatha Avenue, and from 36th Street down to Minnehaha Parkway, are traditional "bungalow communities," with small well-kept stucco bungalows and 1.5-story expansions that boast details like natural woodwork, hardwood floors, and built-in buffets. New housing can be found in the redevelopment zone that abuts Hiawatha Avenue and the LRT line. Two LRT stations (38th Street and 46th Street) service this area. Rich with strong civic groups, active block clubs, and recreational facilities, Standish-Ericsson is home to Hiawatha Park and public golf course, www.minneapolisparks.org, where you can swim, walk, bike and golf in summer and ski groomed cross-country trails in winter. The RiverLake Greenway, when completed, will create an attractive and safe cross-town route for bicyclists along 40th and 42nd streets, and provide connections to several parks and other Southside landmarks like Roosevelt High School and Sibley Field, which has a children's playground, sledding hill, and hockey and skating rinks. If you work in St. Paul, these neighborhoods have easy access to that side of the river over the Ford Parkway Bridge.

In the center of Nokomis, between I-35W and Cedar Avenue, from 42nd down to Minnehaha Parkway, **Field**, **Regina**, and **Northrop** (www.frnng.org) consist primarily of small, two-bedroom pre-1940s stucco and brick houses. The 1970s-era Town Oaks townhomes, in the center of the Regina neighborhood at 43rd Street and 4th Avenue South, was one of the city's first modern townhouse projects. Northrop in particular has some pretty, hilly streets (check out 12th, 13th, and 14th avenues South) and a mix of well-kept, updated housing stock. This area is popular with young couples looking for an affordable alternative to Lake Harriet. Shopping is nearby along Chicago Avenue, with restaurants, banks, and a theater located around the busy hub of Chicago and 48th Street.

Finally, **Keewaydin**, **Minnehaha**, **Morris Park**, and **Wenonah** are spread out from the east shore of Lake Nokomis and Minnehaha Parkway to 54th Street and the 62 Crosstown. Known collectively as **Nokomis East** (www.nokomiseast. org), these neighborhoods abut the airport—and we know what that means—though neighborhoods just north of the airport seem quieter than those farther west. Most of the homes here were built from the 1920s through the 1960s, and include a high proportion of rentals. Prior to 1900, this district was a major American Indian center, and until 1880 there was actually an American Indian village here on the site now occupied by the Nokomis Community Center. The Minnehaha neighborhood includes Longfellow Gardens, a landscaped land bridge over Highway 55/Hiawatha Avenue. Morris Park includes the Minneapolis–St. Paul Air Reserve Station. The area's primary shopping district is at 34th Avenue between 50th and 54th streets. There you will find the library, post office, grocery store, and a variety of other businesses. The success of the Hiawatha LRT (with stations at 50th Street, VA Medical Center, and Ft. Snelling) has brought new condo development to this area.

ZIP Codes: 55404, 55406, 55407, 55409, 55417, 55419, 55423

Post Offices: 5139 34th Ave S; 5500 Nicollet Ave

Police Precinct: 3rd, 3000 Minnehaha Ave, 311 or 612-673-5703 (non-emergency)

Emergency Hospitals: Fairview Southdale Hospital, 6401 France Ave S, 952-924-5000, www.fairview.org; Abbott Northwestern Hospital, 800 E 28th St, 612-863-4000, www.abbottnorthwestern.com; Fairview-University Medical Center, 2450 Riverside Ave, 612-273-3000, www.fairview-university.fairview.org

Libraries: Nokomis, 5100 34th Ave S; Roosevelt, 4026 West 28th Ave S; www.hclib.org

Community Resources: The Rabbithood, www.rabbithood.com: The Hale, Page, Diamond Lake Business Association has dubbed itself the "rabbit-hood" in honor of the seven-foot bronze rabbit that graces the Portland Ave at Minnehaha Pkwy gateway to the neighborhood.

Parks: www.minneapolisparks.org; Hiawatha Park and public golf course; Lake Nokomis Park; Minnehaha Creek; Minnehaha Park and Off-leash Dog Park

Community Publication: *Southside Pride*, www.southsidepride.com

Public Transportation: 612-373-3333, www.MetroTransit.org; buses travel along Chicago Ave, Minnehaha Ave, Bloomington Ave/Ford Pkwy (to St. Paul), 28th Ave S, 34th Ave, 42nd St, and Cedar Ave; the Hiawatha LRT stops at 38th, 46th, and 50th Streets, VA Medical Center, and Fort Snelling

POWDERHORN COMMUNITY

Powderhorn Park; Whittier; Lyndale; Central; Corcoran; Bryant; Bancroft

Boundaries: North: Franklin Ave, Lake St; **West**: Lyndale Ave, I-35W; **South**: 38th St, 42nd St; **East**: Minnehaha Ave

When the snow begins to fall, the rolling hills of Powderhorn Park become a well-used tobogganing area, and skaters take to the outdoor rink. At the heart of Powderhorn's diverse community is this lovely park, a one-square-mile reserve of woods and wildflower-covered hills surrounding a small powder-horn-shaped lake that is home to egrets and great blue herons. It's a welcome expanse amid these urban surroundings, and the ideal setting for Powderhorn's artistically minded neighborhood events, which include May Day, Powderhorn Festival of the Arts, Shakespeare in the Park, July 4th fireworks, and Friday night concerts. Central to all of these events is neighborhood-based In the Heart of the Beast Puppet and Mask Theatre, located in the Avalon, an art deco cinema, 1500 East Lake Street, 612-721-2535, www.hobt.org.

Powderhorn Park neighborhood (www.ppna.org), from Lake Street to 38th between Chicago and Cedar Avenues, which boasts many beauti-fully renovated properties, is working hard to get its residents to put down roots and stay. In that respect, and others, it sits in marked contrast to some of the neighborhoods around it (Central, Corcoran, Bryant), which tend to be economically depressed rental areas with high levels of unemployment, crime, poverty, and substandard housing. What is unusual is that the Powderhorn Park Neighborhood Association is working to promote stability in those less fortunate neighborhoods as well. PPNA has been the impetus behind transforming Lake Street, a project which began with shutting down the local XXX movie house, and continued with the building of a new YWCA at 22nd and Lake (www.ywcampls.org), and the development of the Midtown Exchange offices/condos/global market and Sheraton hotel at Chicago and Lake (www.midtowncommunityworks.org/exchange). The plan is to eventually revamp Lake Street all the way from the Mississippi River to Uptown, accommodating pedestrians as well as vehicles and enhancing the ethnic character of the surrounding neighborhoods. They are working on revitalizing Chicago Avenue, as well. If you're interested in living in this area, contact the Powderhorn Residents Group (www.prginc.org), a nonprofit organization that not only promotes the well-being and success of youth, families and other stakeholders in the greater Powderhorn area, but can also help you find quality, affordable housing here.

Central neighborhood (www.candompls.org), south of Lake Street to 38th, between 2nd Avenue and Chicago, is also home to people who are working hard to return their 1800s and early 1900s houses to their former glory and stabilize their community in the process. This neighborhood's Healy Block, bounded by 2nd and 3rd avenues and 31st and 32nd streets, represents one of the finest surviving collections of Queen Anne architecture in Minneapolis, and is listed on the Historic Register (www.ci.minneapolis.mn.us/hpc/landmarks).

With easy access to downtown via the Midtown Greenway bike trail, good bus coverage, and the Hiawatha Light Rail Transit line down at the end of Lake Street, as well as new condos and many houses that have had a face-lift in recent years, this neighborhood is definitely worth more than a passing thought.

Bancroft (www.bancroftneighborhood.org), from 38th Street down to 42nd, between Chicago and Cedar Avenues, consists mostly of single-family dwellings built before 1940.

Bryant (between 38th and 42nd streets, west of Chicago Avenue to Interstate 35W) is a quiet neighborhood of small apartment buildings and modest single-family homes with detached garages. Some homes boast intact Craftsman details, and some are as tiny as 750 square feet; many have been recently renovated and now feature open floor plans and modern appliances. Access to Minneapolis is easy via 35W and dedicated bike lanes along Park and Portland avenues.

At the far east end of Lake Street, the **Corcoran** neighborhood (www.corcoranneighborhood.org), East Lake Street to East 36th between Hiawatha and Cedar Avenues, is conveniently positioned just west of the LRT line. Home to a diverse and active Hispanic community, this neighborhood hosts the city's annual Cinco de Mayo celebration.

Closer to downtown, **Whittier** (www.whittieralliance.org), from Franklin south to Lake Street, between Garfield and I-35W, is one of the city's oldest neighborhoods. Named for the poet John Greenleaf Whittier, it is sometimes referred to as the "Arts Quarter" because of the presence of the Minneapolis Institute of Arts (www.artsmia.org), Children's Theatre Company (www.childrenstheatre.org), and Minneapolis College of Art and Design (www.mcad.edu)—as well as the bohemian collection of artists and actors who live nearby. This is a largely rental area of mansions sitting next door to Section 8 housing in a patchwork of sometimes posh/sometimes sketchy blocks. With a large percentage of the city's supportive housing and social services concentrated in this neighborhood and nearby Phillips, Stevens Square–Loring Heights, and Central, an ongoing issue is the impact of the group homes on the community's livability and safety. On the other hand, that very abundance of iffy property is what makes this a neighborhood where you can buy something cheap, fix it up, make a profit, and move to a much better place and still stay within the neighborhood. And the neighborhood is rich with "better places." The Washburn–Fair Oaks Mansion District, near the Minneapolis Institute of Arts/Children's Theatre, is listed on the National Historic Register (www.ci.minneapolis.mn.us/hpc/landmarks). More grand houses, some of the oldest in Minneapolis, are found along Blaisdell and Third Avenue, and Stevens Avenue may already have the beautifully restored home you've been looking for. The Gale Mansion here, across the street from Fair Oaks Park, is a local favorite for getting married or holding a reception, 2115 Stevens Avenue South, 612-870-1662, www.galemansion.com.

Running through the middle of the neighborhood, "Eat Street," or Nicollet Avenue, offers an around-the-world tour of restaurants and groceries, as well as loft housing. Four blocks east, Third Avenue South, which runs between Downtown and the MIA/CTC/MCAD complex, has been designated the "Avenue of the Arts," and given streetscaping improvements that include a Frank Lloyd

Wright–inspired freeway bridge. When checking out this area, be sure to visit the Hennepin History Museum, 2303 Third Avenue S, http://hennepinhistory. org. In addition to ongoing exhibits, it offers walking tours around the neighborhood every summer.

Farther south, across Lake Street, the duplexes and apartments in **Lyndale** (www.lyndale.org), Lake Street to 36th and Lyndale Avenue to I-35W, are much like nearby neighborhoods in Uptown, although housing here is generally more affordable and incomes more modest. A quirky collection of restaurants, galleries, and theaters makes the corner of Lyndale and Lake Street, known as Lyn-Lake, a great alternative to the busier parts of town.

ZIP Codes: 55406, 55407, 55409

Post Offices: 3045 Bloomington Ave; 3033 27th Ave S; 110 E 31st St

Police Precincts: West of I-35W: 5th Precinct, 3101 Nicollet Ave S, 612-673-5705 (non-emergency); East of I-35: 3rd Precinct, 3000 Minnehaha Ave, 612-673-5703 or 311 (non-emergency)

Emergency Hospital: Abbott Northwestern Hospital, 800 E 28th St, 612-863-4000, www.abbottnorthwestern.com

Library: Hosmer, 347 E 36th St; www.hclib.org

Community Resources: Children's Theatre Company, 2400 3rd Ave S, 612-874-0400, www.childrenstheatre.org; Minneapolis Institute of Arts, 2400 3rd Ave S, 888 MIA ARTS (642-2787), www.artsmia.org; Minneapolis College of Art and Design, 2501 Stevens Ave, 612-874-3700, www.mcad.edu; Midtown YWCA fieldhouse, childcare, and athletic center, 2121 E Lake St, 612-215-4333, www.ywcampls.org

Parks: www.minneapolisparks.org; Midtown Greenway Bikeway (one block north of Lake St from Chowen Ave to the Mississippi River); Powderhorn Park and Recreation Center; Fair Oaks Park

Community Publication: *Downtown Journal*, www.downtownjournal.com

Public Transportation: 612-373-3333, www.MetroTransit.org; buses travel on all the major thoroughfares and are timed to connect with the LRT at the Lake Street/Midtown and Franklin Avenue Stations

PHILLIPS COMMUNITY

Phillips West; Midtown Phillips; East Phillips; Ventura Village

Boundaries: North: I-94; **West**: I-35W; **South**: Lake St; **East**: Hiawatha Ave

The greater Phillips neighborhood is subdivided into Ventura Village, Phillips West, Midtown Phillips, and East Phillips. Ventura Village, the closest to downtown Minneapolis, occupies the northern part of the community, from I-35/I-94 down to 24th Street, between I-35W and Hiawatha. **Phillips West** runs from 22nd Street down to Lake Street, between I-35W and Chicago Avenue, but because it became a official community only in 2005, most residents still refer to the area as Phillips. East Phillips extends from Bloomington Avenue east to Hiawatha and from 24th Street down to East Lake Street. Midtown Phillips is the bit in the middle, from 24th down to Lake Street, between Chicago and Bloomington Avenues.

The **Phillips** community (www.pnn.org) in south-central Minneapolis has, for years, been the densest, poorest, most diverse community in the city. Plagued by crime and disinvestment despite years of hard work by neighborhood block clubs, corporations, and social agencies, today some parts of this community are rising out of a decades-long slump and becoming leaders in transit-oriented infrastructure development.

You can look at the variety of housing along these streets and see that Phillips has a complex history. Elegant Victorian mansions along Park and Portland avenues are reminders of this neighborhood's past grandeur. So are smaller turn-of-the20th-century houses with Queen Anne turrets and gingerbread trim. Unfortunately, urban decay, due in part to construction of interstate highways 35W and 94, laid waste to much of this area. By the 1990s, neighborhood unemployment was 14% and the streets were blighted with boarded-up drug houses and vacant lots. But then several things happened more or less at the same time. Abbott Northwestern Hospital figured out that the neighborhood murder rate was affecting its bottom line and started hiring locals, as well as helping employees buy houses nearby; in addition, residents started turning the vacant lots into gardens. By 1997, 30 community gardens had sprouted here. Everyone agrees that these gardens played a key role in stabilizing the area. However, as in many cities, the "pacification" of the neighborhood resulted in pressures for redevelopment, and now many of the vacant lots are sprouting townhouses and apartment buildings instead of flowers.

The principal location for new housing here is along the Midtown Greenway bike trail and linear park (one block north of Lake Street from Chowen Avenue

to the Mississippi River), where hundreds of new homes and offices have been built in recent years, particularly in the Midtown Exchange (www.midtowncom munityworks.org/exchange) area of **Midtown Phillips** (http://midtownphil lips.wikispaces.com). Here you will find new multi-unit housing that caters to singles and small families and all sizes of pocketbooks, with units that range from modest apartments and townhomes to million-dollar penthouses. The main floor in this building is home to many small Latino, Kenyan, and Somali businesses and restaurants, gathered together in what is known as the Midtown Global Market (www.midtownglobalmarket.com). This 11-acre "campus," in a landmark early Sears department store, is also home to Allina's corporate offices and a Sheraton Hotel.

A little farther down Lake Street, the Mercado at Bloomington Avenue (www.mercadocentral.net) is bringing a Latin American renaissance to **East Phillips** (http://eastphillips-epic.com), commercially, at least. As if aging housing stock weren't enough of a problem here in one of the city's poorest neighborhoods, high levels of arsenic have been found in many East Phillips yards. The affected properties are near a former pesticide plant at 28th Street and Hiawatha Avenue, where arsenic was used or stored from 1938 to 1963. This is an Environmental Protection Agency Superfund site, with ongoing clean-up of affected properties as they are identified (www.ci.minneapolis. mn.us/inspections/tenantnotification_arsenic.asp). In view of the obstacles, you really have to give the people here credit for persisting in trying to improve their neighborhood. Evidence of their determination is tangible, with the con-struction—finally—of a community center on 17th Avenue that was in the works from 1997 to 2010.

Arsenic has been found in the soil of parts of Corcoran, Longfellow, Midtown Phillips, Powderhorn, Seward, and Ventura Village, and all of East Phillips. Amelioration is under way.

To the north, in **Ventura Village**, most housing is multi-family and rental, with some condos along I-94. Phillips is home to the city's largest population of Native Americans, many of whom live in the Little Earth Housing Complex south of Franklin on Cedar. East Franklin Avenue, which bisects the neighborhood, was once considered the most unsafe street in the city, but has improved signif-icantly in recent years. The diversity of the immigrant groups that have settled here is reflected in the businesses and services offered along this busy commer-cial corridor: a Somali Suuq (Somali Village Market); the American Indian Center (www.maicnet.org); Centro community meeting place for Latino familes (www. centromn.org); a Colombian restaurant; Open Arms (www.openarmsmn.org) which feeds people living with HIV/AIDS, ALS, breast cancer, and MS; a Chine photographer…the list goes on and on.

This part of the city is well-connected to the transit system, with good bus coverage, bike lanes, access to I-35W and I-94, and a Hiawatha LRT station at Franklin Avenue.

To view pictures of this neighborhood, visit www.dawnwangen.com/capstone/default.asp. To take a simulated drive down Lake Street, check out the Minnesota Historical Society's virtual bus ride, 21A-Right on Lake Street, www.mnhs.org/exhibits/lakestreet/interactive/master.html.

ZIP Codes: 55404, 55407
Post Offices: 3045 Bloomington Ave; 110 E 31st St
Police Precinct: 3rd, 3000 Minnehaha Ave, 612-673-5703; Franklin Avenue Safety Center, 1201 E Franklin Ave, 612-871-8090; Midtown Community Safety Center, 2949 Chicago Ave S, 612-825-6138
Emergency Hospital: Abbott Northwestern Hospital, 800 E 28th St, 612-863-4000, www.abbottnorthwestern.com
Libraries: East Lake, 2727 E Lake St; Franklin, 1314 E Franklin Ave, www.hclib.org
Community Resources: American Swedish Institute, 2600 Park Ave, 612-871-4907, www.americanswedishinst.org; Green Institute/Re-Use Center/Phillips Eco-Enterprise Center and Deconstruction Services, 2801 21st Ave S, 612-278-7100, www.greeninstitute.org; Minneapolis American Indian Center, 1530 Franklin Ave E, 612-879-1700, www.maicnet.org
Parks: www.minneapolisparks.org; Midtown Greenway, Peavey Park
Community Publication: *Southside Pride*, www.southsidepride.com
Public Transportation: 612-373-3333, www.MetroTransit.org; buses travel along Franklin Ave, Chicago Ave, Bloomington Ave/Cedar Ave, Lake St, and Park Ave; I-35W express routes board where the highway crosses Lake St; LRT stations are located at Franklin and Lake St

GREATER LONGFELLOW COMMUNITY
Seward; Longfellow/Cooper/Howe/Hiawatha

Boundaries: North: I-94; **West**: Minnehaha Ave; **South/East**: Mississippi River

Greater Longfellow (www.longfellow.org) is the sliver-shaped bungalow community that flanks the gorge of the Mississippi River between I-94 and Minnehaha Falls Park. It is bisected by Lake Street and bordered by Hiawatha Avenue. Ideally located, with a variety of housing, this is another neighborhood in which first-time homebuyers can buy small and (relatively) cheap and move up without having to leave the neighborhood. Another plus—the beautiful drive to work along the river, if you work downtown.

Popular since the 1920s with working-class people, it is well served by public transportation, including the Hiawatha LRT, with stations at Franklin,

Lake Street, 38th, 46th, and 50th Street/Minnehaha Park. St. Paul is just across the river over the East Lake Street/Marshall Avenue and Ford bridges. The building boom associated with the construction of the Hiawatha LRT corridor has brought a number of new condo/apartment/small-scale retail developments to this district, particularly near the 38th Street and 46th Street stations.

Residents here have easy access to nature. Bike trails through the Mississippi River Gorge, Minnehaha Park, and the east-west Midtown Greenway (which crosses both Longfellow and Cooper neighborhoods) combine to make the outdoor amenities in this district every bit as nice as those you will find around the Chain of Lakes in the southwest corner of the city—better, really, because here there is more Nature and less Traffic. Though most of the houses are fairly undistinguished, there are a few homes that have treetop views of city skyscrapers, and ground-level views that are all river and nature.

The Community Council web site, www.longfellow.org features a number of short videos about the community. Of particular interest is the April 2008 "Longfellow Station Meeting" which describes the community's engagement with a developer to make sure community values and priorities were integrated into a transit-oriented development. While you're on the web site, watch the "Mississippi River Gorge" and "Friendly Yard Tour" videos, too—you'll not only get a feel for the housing here, but you'll get to meet some of your prospective new neighbors!

ZIP Codes: 55404, 55406

Post Offices: 3033 27th Ave S; 5139 34th Ave S

Police Precinct: 3rd, 3000 Minnehaha Ave; 311 or 612-673-5703 (non-emergency)

Emergency Hospitals: Abbott Northwestern Hospital, 800 E 28th St, 612-863-4000, www.abbottnorthwestern.com; Fairview-University Medical Center, 2450 Riverside Ave, 612-672-6000, www.fairview.org

Library: East Lake, 2727 E Lake St; Roosevelt Library 4026 28th Ave S; www.hclib.org

Community Resources: Longfellow House, located in Minnehaha Park at 4800 Minnehaha Ave S; 1849 John H. Stevens House (first frame house built west of the Mississippi) is also located in Minnehaha Park

Parks: www.minneapolisparks.org; Mississippi River Parks and Trails; Minnehaha Park and Off-leash Dog Park

Community Publication: *Minneapolis Bridgeland News*, www.bridgelandnews org

Public Transportation: 612-373-3333, www.MetroTransit.org; buses tr Franklin, Minnehaha, 25th, and Lake St and connect with the Hiawath at Franklin, Lake St, 38th, 46th, and 50th

SEWARD

Seward (www.sng.org) has a laidback Colorado commune vibe that is unique in the Twin Cities, although that is changing as increasing numbers of Somali refugee families move into the neighborhood. Stretching between Hiawatha Avenue and the Mississippi River, from I-94 down to 27th Street East, this neighborhood is close to the U and convenient to everywhere. Housing ranges from deteriorated student digs to two blocks of gentrified railroad workers' houses (circa 1880) located on Milwaukee Road and listed on the Historic Register (www.ci.minneapolis.mn.us/hpc/landmarks/Milwaukee_Avenue_District.asp).
In between there are new townhouses and industrial-style lofts, small apartment buildings built in the late 1800s and early 1900s, a slew of early 20th-century 1.5-story bungalows, and even some fairly new family-sized in-fill houses and high-rises. About two-thirds of the properties are rentals. All within walking

distance: vegan cuisine, small shops, the biggest Oriental grocery store in the Midwest (www.unitednoodles.com), a lively bowling alley/local band hot spot (www.memorylanesmpls.com), a co-op (www.seward.coop), two arts centers (the Playwrights' Center, www.pwcenter.org, and Northern Clay, www.northern-claycenter.org), arty cafés, and even a gym. And you can run, walk, ski, or skate along the Mississippi. Who needs more than that?

LONGFELLOW, COOPER, HOWE, HIAWATHA

⸴th of Seward, a patchwork of 1920s to 1960s homes in various stages of
⸴vement characterizes the **Longfellow**, **Cooper**, **Howe**, and **Hiawatha**
⸴orhoods. Houses in the blocks closest to the river have been upgraded

substantially, and more modest homes farther back have also been renovated on a block-by-block basis. At the south end of Hiawatha, Minnehaha Parkway boasts apartment buildings and larger homes with charming decorative details. In Hiawatha, the curvy streets between 46th Ave and Edmund Boulevard, from Dowling down to 42nd Street, are more suburban in feel, with homes that date from the 1960s. Rumor has it that this area is so much newer than the rest of Longfellow because the University of Minnesota owned this parcel until the 1960s. That's also the explanation for the names of the streets—former presidents of the U. For architecturally unique dream-houses or condos, look to the river and shop along Edmund Boulevard.

Much of Longfellow's housing is deemed worthy of rehabilitation, but may fall short of meeting the needs of modern families. Over half the houses in these neighborhoods are bungalows—two-bedroom, one-bath, single-story houses with expansion attics. Two-story, four-square houses built in the 1920s are the second-most prevalent style. So popular is renovation of these existing houses that the Longfellow community commissioned a book, *The Longfellow Planbook: Remodeling Plans for Bungalows and Other Small Urban Homes*, which contains ideas for updating the area's predominant housing types. Plans have been reviewed and approved by the Minneapolis Inspections Division. The book can be purchased from the Longfellow Community Council (www.longfellow.org).

UNIVERSITY COMMUNITY

Cedar-Riverside, Marcy-Holmes, Stadium Village, Dinkytown; Southeast Como; Prospect Park/East River Road; Nicollet Island/East Bank

Boundaries: North: E Hennepin Ave, I-35W; **West**: Nicollet Island, I-35W; **Sout** I-94, East Bank of Mississippi; **East**: city limits

Maroon and gold (the University of Minnesota colors) rule—but so do black, white, yellow, and brown, in these neighborhoods on the banks of the Missis-sippi close to the U, which straddles the river with both East Bank and West Bank campuses. Here Somalis, Russians, Indians, Ethiopians, Kenyans, Asians, Latinos, and Minnesota farm kids of Scandinavian and German descent all crowd the streets, walking as one, talking and laughing in the melting pot of colors and cultures that has been the theme of this neighborhood since its founding.

CEDAR-RIVERSIDE, MARCY-HOLMES, STADIUM VILLAGE, DINKYTOWN

A haven for new immigrants ever since the 1800s, when it was known as "Snoose Boulevard," **Cedar-Riverside** was slated for demolition in the mid-1960s when I-94 was built. It saved itself through a grassroots, counter-culture movement that created the first federally funded, New-Town-In-Town urban redevelopment project in the country. Backers of the project idealisti-cally believed that people of all incomes, ages, races, and cultures could live together in harmony in high-density, high-rise apartments close to shops and cultural activities. While this vision was never fully realized, anyone traveling I-94 between the two cities cannot help noticing the project's distinctive Riv-erside Plaza apartment towers with their multi-colored panels. Locally famous architect Ralph Rapson, who designed the towers, said of this complex: "We had the dream that modern or contemporary design was going to really revo-lutionize and change the way we lived and thought about society….We always had the notion that we could do something that would make the environment better for mankind." A little radical? Maybe. Or maybe just an appropriate edu-cational mission for a neighborhood that is home to two Twin Cities icons of higher education, the U and Augsburg College.

There is less avant-garde housing here as well. Multitudes of student duplexes and apartments are located just off-campus in **Marcy-Holmes** (www.marcy-holmes.org), a neighborhood where new riverfront condos and lofts rub shoulders with the raucous blocks of Dinkytown (www.dinkytownusa.com), which abuts the U campus. Quieter neighborhoods can be found in Prospect Park and Southeast Como. Unfortunately, due to their near-campus location, rents are not a bargain, although house prices are moderate. Dinkytown and Stadium Village (www.stadiumvillage.com), along University/ Washington and Huron Avenues, are the main campus commercial/entertainment districts, with plenty of cheap eateries and many businesses named "Gopher" (for the University of Minnesota mascot). **Stadium Village** has a bank, grocery store, hotel (www.radisson.com/minneapolismn_metrodome), and newer student apartment complexes, as well as the new TCF Bank Stadium http://stadium.gophersports.com. **Dinkytown**, still charming in its way, was the heart of the

Minneapolis folk scene in the 1960s. Bob Dylan (known locally as journalism major Robert Zimmerman from Hibbing, Minnesota) lived over Gray's Drugstore here, in what is thought to be the current Loring Pasta Bar's party room, and performed in the neighborhood's beat coffeehouses. While most places connected with Dylan no longer exist, today's students carry on the tradition as they lounge on the couches at the Varsity Theater (www.varsitytheater.org), listening to Amy Winehouse and Cloud Cult. For full information about where to go and what to do, look online at www.dinkytownminneapolis.com.

Convenient to downtown Minneapolis and St. Paul, this district also enjoys the perks of an academic community—lectures, concerts, the University Film Society; the University's Weisman Art Museum, on the East Bank, is the riverfront's most significant architectural landmark.

There is an LRT station at Cedar-Riverside, though no buses connect with it. The closest bus service is on Cedar Avenue. Wherever you go, think about safety and take your cue from the University of Minnesota, which provides escorts to people who are out on campus at night.

ZIP Codes: 55401, 55413, 55414, 55454, 55455 (University of Minnesota)

Post Offices: 100 S 1st St,; 307 4th Ave S; 2811 University Ave SE; 1311 SE 4th St

Police Precinct: 1st, 19 North 4th St, 311 or 612-673-5701 (non-emergency); 2nd, 1911 Central Ave NE, 311 or 612-673-5702 (non-emergency)

Emergency Hospital: Fairview-University Medical Center, 2450 Riverside Ave, 612-672-6000, www.fairview.org

Libraries: Southeast, 1222 4th St SE, www.hclib.org; University libraries, www.lib.umn.edu

Community Resources: University of Minnesota, www.umn.edu; Cedar Cultural Center, 416 Cedar Ave S, Minneapolis, 612-338-2674, www.thecedar.org; Frederick R. Weisman Art Museum, 333 E River Rd, University of Minnesota, 612-625-9494, www.weisman.umn.edu

Parks: Mississippi National River and Recreation Area, www.nps.gov/miss; Minneapolis Riverfront District: Boom Island, Nicollet Island, Upper St. Anthony Falls Lock and Dam, St. Anthony Falls Heritage Trail, Stone Arch Bridge, First Bridge Park, www.minneapolisparks.org

Community Publications: *Southside Pride*, www.southsidepride.com; *Minnesota Daily*, www.mndaily.com; *Downtown Journal*, www.downtownjournal.com; *Minneapolis Bridgeland News*, www.bridgelandnews.org

Public Transportation: 612-373-3333, www.MetroTransit.org; *Buses:* Numerous routes run from many parts of the Twin Cities to campus, though most of them operate on weekdays only. Campus shuttles are free and run continuously, http://www1.umn.edu/pts/busing/index.html. *Trains:* The Cedar-Riverside LRT station does not have any connecting bus routes, thou buses do run north and south on Cedar Ave. To find them, follow the Cedar Avenue Buses" signs. The proposed Central Corridor Light Ra between Minneapolis and St. Paul will serve this community along University and Washington Avenues.

SOUTHEAST COMO

Often recommended for off-campus housing, Southeast Como, to differentiate it from the Como neighborhood in St. Paul, http://secomo.org, runs from East Hennepin Avenue in the north to the Southeast Industrial Area in the south, between I-35W and the eastern city limits. It is a swath of modest (sometimes dilapidated) early 20th-century bungalows and tall, skinny two-stories mixed with a scattering of newer duplexes and single-family homes. Along Como, 15th and Hennepin avenues, there are post-'60s two-story walk-up apartment buildings and large homes converted into student housing. This neighborhood is home to Joe's Market and Deli at 1828 Como, a market/deli/laundry/pizza complex where you can sit in the little dining area and eat while catching up on weekly chores—and the bulletin board is a great place to find roommates or other necessities. Monday is Lebanese Omelet Day—omelets stuffed with onions, tomatoes, olives, and yogurt are $5 treasures. Other neighborhood amenities including the Como Student Community Cooperative Housing (http://cscc.umn.edu) and University Childcare Center (www.cehd.umn.edu/childcarecenter) make this a desirable neighborhood for students with families. The University is involved in ongoing clean-up of toxic soil near the Como Student Community Cooperative, where an incinerator operated until 1960. The neighborhood has asked the Minnesota Pollution Control Agency to test for contaminants beyond the University's boundaries.

PROSPECT PARK/EAST RIVER ROAD

Across the river from the Seward neighborhood, on the East Bank between the U of M and the city of St. Paul, Prospect Park/East River Road (www.pperr.org) is a place where you can walk out of your modern condo door into a 100-year-old neighborhood. Security is not such a huge concern here, where quiet streets and tree-covered slopes give the neighborhood a tranquil character despite the steady hum of I-94 next door. People who live in "the Park" say they live in a small town with an urban beat, a place where they can walk to work, to recreation, shopping, and community events, and probably recognize everybody along the way. Residents here are 10 minutes by car from each downtown, and centrally located for travel to any place in the Twin Cities. Their strong sense of place probably has as much to do with the area's clear geographic boundaries (the University, river, city limits, and railroad tracks in the north) as its pointy

green witch's hat water tower, which is visible from I-94. Once a year the whole neighborhood climbs to the top and is treated to a panoramic view of the cities all the way to the airport.

The area's civic history dates back to the late 1800s when it was a commuter suburb on the Minneapolis streetcar line. Today, imposing historic residences rub elbows with new condos and public housing on Prospect Park's meandering streets. Though there is a laissez-faire attitude toward landscaping, and the used auto parts business displays "found-art" sculptures, beautiful restoration is appreciated. Many of the homes date from the early 1900s up to the 1930s and feature art glass windows and other elegant details. Popular updates include turning butler's pantries into second bathrooms and putting in modern kitchens. The industrial zone along University has been transformed into mixed-use housing. One of the first of the projects, Emerald Gardens, is located on the exact border of Minneapolis and St. Paul. Anywhere you live in this district you'll be only a short walk or bike ride away from either U campus.

NICOLLET ISLAND/EAST BANK

Another antique refuge with a view of the city skyline is just east of downtown, out in the Mississippi River and also on its East Bank between the Burlington Northern Santa Fe Railroad line on the north and Central Avenue on the south. Forty-seven-acre Nicollet Island (www.nicolletisland.org) is a 19th-century Victorian landmark settlement and park within the St. Anthony Falls Heritage Zone. Most of Nicollet Island's graceful Victorian houses were built between 1880 and 1910, and have been faithfully restored. Today they are joined by new luxury condominiums across the water on Historic Southeast Main Street in a part of the neighborhood that is commonly referred to as **Old/Historic St. Anthony** or **St. Anthony Main** (http://stanthonymain.com/mplsriverfrontdistrict.htm), as this was the location of the original town of St. Anthony, the predecessor to Minneapolis. Confused? It gets worse. People also tend to think of St. Anthony Main as part of "**Nordeast**," which is one of the reasons why Historic St. Anthony is included in the Northeast section below. Don't worry. Just say you live on Nicollet Island or at St. Anthony Main, and everyone will know. Even if you decide not to move to this neighborhood, be sure to take Mobile Entertainment's Segway guided tours of the Mississippi Riverfront, 952-888-9200, www. humanonastick.com (see Transportation). The Nicollet Island Inn (95 Merriam St, 612-331-1800 www.nicolletislandinn.com) is the perfect place to stay while you check out the city. To view some of the best pictures of the island's houses, click on www.umcycling.com/msp2.htm.

NORTHEAST COMMUNITY

Historic St. Anthony/St. Anthony West; Beltrami/Northeast Park; Sheridan/Bottineau/Marshall Terrace; Columbia Park/ Waite Park/Audubon Park/Holland/Logan Park/Windom Park

Boundaries: North: 37th Ave NE; **West**: Mississippi River; **South**: Nicollet Island, Central Ave, I-35W; **East**: city limits

In Minneapolis, the action has definitely moved to this side of the river! Once an industrial area filled with seedy bars that catered to the local workingman and University of Minnesota students, "Nord'east" (www.northeastminneapolis. com) has taken a dramatic upscale turn. Streets filled for over 100 years with Polish, Ukrainian, Scandinavian, German, and Italian laborers who came over to work in the grain and lumber mills are now teeming with empty-nest suburbanites, artists chased out of the Downtown Warehouse District by escalating rents, and young executives equally attracted to the neighborhood's trendy shopping/entertainment scene and to its easy access to offices in downtown Minneapolis, just across the river over the Hennepin Avenue/First Avenue bridge. Although, as someone said on the radio, they're not giving gay walking tours of Northeast—yet—East Hennepin is also starting to develop a large concentration of gay-owned businesses and residents.

Housing in the neighborhoods is changing dramatically as well. Not that swank lofts are replacing all the old warehouses and cottages, but they are replacing a lot of them. The trend is referred to as "Edina-fication" after the Twin Cities' most fashionable suburb. Yet, the industrial and immigrant heritage of this area is still evident along the neighborhoods' stick-straight streets that were named for presidents in order to help immigrants prepare for their citizenship exams. For the most part, buildings here are a few stories, not 50, and brick, rather than glass and steel. And though fancy restaurants and stylish bars are pulling in an upscale clientele, good old red-pleather Nye's Polonaise Room (www.nyespolonaise.com), Mayslack's (www.mayslacksbar.com), and Elsie's Bar and Bowling (www.elsies.com) are still packing them in, too.

While music, churches, bars, and polka lounges have always been an important part of this community, the visual arts have recently come to prominence as well. The area of Northeast Minneapolis bordered by Broadway, Lowry, Central Avenue, and the Mississippi River is designated the Northeast Minneapolis Arts District. It includes the neighborhoods of Bottineau, Sheridan, Holland, and Logan Park, but Historic St. Anthony, St. Anthony West, and Beltrami are home to many artists' studios and galleries as well.

Though the rest of Northeast is not so glam, there is still more to this community than new lofts in old buildings around East Hennepin. Midwest squares built before 1940 and small turn-of-the-20th-century wood houses predominate in the blue-collar blocks of most of the neighbo while the "Parks" (Waite, Audubon, Windom, and Columbia) have newer houses, and are actually quite a lot like the suburbs they adjoin. They even have a South Minneapolis–style amenity, a stretch of parkway that runs along St. Anthony Boulevard from the Mississippi River on the west through Columbia Park, Waite Park, and Audubon Park, to Hillside Cemetery on the east. This parkway is part of the Minneapolis Grand Rounds, and, besides being a great place to run or bike, connects several parks and Columbia and Francis A. Gross golf courses (www.minneapolisparks.org/grandrounds/home.htm).

ZIP Codes: 55413, 55414, 55418, 55421
Post Office: 1600 18th Ave NE
Police Precinct: 2nd, 1911 Central Ave NE, 311 or 612-673-5702 (non-emergency)
Emergency Hospital: Fairview-University Medical Center, 2450 Riverside Ave, 612-672-6000, www.fairview.org
Libraries: www.hclib,org; Northeast, 2200 Central Avenue NE; Pierre Bottineau, 55 Broadway NE
Community Resources: Ard Godfrey House, Central and University Ave SE at Chute Square, www.ardgodfreyhouse.org; Northeast Minneapolis Arts Association, www.nemaa.org; St. Anthony Main, www.saintanthonymain.com/mplsriverfrontdistrict.html
Parks: www.minneapolisparks.org; Boom Island Park; Columbia Park and Golf Course
Community Publication: *Northeaster*, www.nenorthnews.com
Public Transportation: 612-373-3333, www.MetroTransit.org; buses travel along E Hennepin, Johnson St, Stinson Blvd, Central Ave, 2nd St NE, University Ave, Marshall St, and Lowry Ave

HISTORIC ST. ANTHONY/ST. ANTHONY WEST

After you have crossed the river on Hennepin Avenue, Surdyk's Liquor and Cheese Shop (www.surdyks.com), in business since 1934, and Kramarczuk's East European Deli (www.kramarczuk.com), which has done business at 215 East Hennepin since 1954, usher you into the city's old working-class neighborhood of **Historic St. Anthony** (http://stanthonymain.com/mplsriverfrontdistrict.html, www.stawno.org, http://saenaminneapolis.wordpress.com). This is the birthplace of Minneapolis—not to be confused with the nearby suburb of St. Anthony or the St. Anthony Park section of St. Paul. This wedge-shaped neighborhood, bordered by Northeast Central, Broadway, and the Mississippi River, is ome to many historical places of interest including St. Anthony Falls, "discov-d" by Father Louis Hennepin in 1680; the Pillsbury "A" mill, the beginning of City's" flour, lumber, and textile industry; and the Stone Arch Bridge. Other rks—the Russian Orthodox and Ukrainian Orthodox churches, four of

Minneapolis' five historic Polish churches, and the landmark Grain Belt beer sign that looms over Nicollet Island—serve as reminders of St. Anthony's longtime paradoxical reputation for having a church and a bar on every corner.

Successive waves of redevelopment in the 1960s, '70s, and '80s demolished many of the old houses, replacing them with multi-unit housing, including luxury high-rises where residents are treated to spectacular views of the river

and city, as well as the soaring music from National Historic Landmark Our Lady of Lourdes Catholic Church (www.ourladyoflourdes.com), the oldest continuously used church in the city. Housing is split fairly equally between rental and owner-occupied units. If you are looking for a house, Craftsman four-squares, colonials, and bungalows built between 1900 and 1930 can be found in the northern reaches of the neighborhood.

St. Anthony West (www.stawno.org) also experienced several waves of redevelopment, but came through them with some of its Victorians intact. Now designated a Historic Garden District, the demand for its vintage homes far exceeds the supply, resulting in most of St. Anthony West's residents living in some form of multi-housing such as duplexes or townhomes. For those who love the river, this is an ideal place to live. Not only is it a 20-minute walk to offices downtown, it is within biking distance of the university and has Boom Island Park for river access. This 14-acre riverside park features a day-use marina, playground, and picnic area.

BELTRAMI/NORTHEAST PARK

Heading north along Central Avenue, you'll find delis, polka lounges, and supper clubs, as well as rows and rows of small, Midwestern squares and bungalows. Here the Beltrami and Northeast Park neighborhoods, east of Central, are also picking up their pace. Though two-story plain frame houses built during the early 1900s make up the bulk of the homes, more recently constructed housing can be found near the railroad tracks and along East Hennepin. While Northeast is notably lacking in good parks, Beltrami Park, off East Broadway, has a playground, pool, tennis and basketball courts, and soccer and softball fields, and the Northeast Athletic Fields and Jim Lupient Water Park actually take up a huge chunk of Northeast Park. As other warehouse districts have gentrified, some artists are choosing **Beltrami** for its less expensive studio space. It is also conveniently located to the university, Interstate 35W, and to shopping at the Quarry Retail Center, with its grocery store, Target, Home Depot and other national retailers. The rest of the neighborhood of **Northeast Park**, just north of I-94, is made up of quiet, dead-end streets. Really quiet and genuinely dead: the Hillside Cemetery occupies a full third of it. Older homes in the area (c. 1920s and '30s) are being bought by young families looking for starter homes with character, and some of its sturdy ramblers changed ownership for the first time as late as the 1990s.

SHERIDAN/BOTTINEAU/MARSHALL TERRACE

The rental working-class communities of Sheridan, Bottineau (www.bottineauneighborhood.org), and Marshall Terrace may lack the fanciest recreation amenities, but residents can still get their workouts biking the Grand Rounds or dancing the polka at Gasthof Zur Gemutlichkeit at 2300 University, www.gasthofzg.com.

Located within the designated Northeast Minneapolis Arts District, **Bottineau** actually has some houses on the riverfront, and has become very popular with artists. The California Building, at 20th and California, a 90,000-square-foot grain mill built in 1915, now houses 75 artists' studios. Newer construction has added lofts and townhouses to the neighborhood's stock of pre-1940s single-family homes and duplexes. While most of the old houses are best described as utilitarian, there are some rather charming examples of Folk Victorian architecture on Marshall Street.

Other buildings with long histories include Jax Restaurant (1933), and Tony Jaros' River Garden, which is known less for its age than for its lime and vodka "Greenies." Say it like a 'Nordeasterner: "Jare-us's. It's named for former owner and Minneapolis Lakers basketball hero, Tony Jaros.

Rental and industrial property still play a significant role in the neighborhood, but there are increasing numbers of owner-occupied homes. Several commercial areas are within biking distance of Bottineau, including Rosedale and the Quarry shopping centers. Projects to improve bike travel along the river and major streets are included in the city's short-term plans.

The **Sheridan** neighborhood, also part of the Arts District, is a good example of Northeast's unpretentious, working-class style. Plain, often large, and in good condition, these houses are being fixed, not gentrified. A number of small apartment buildings can also be found here. Once considered an iffy place to live, Sheridan is now considered extremely desirable, in part due to its growing art scene, which includes small galleries along its 13th Avenue business corridor, Ballet of the Dolls, and Art-A-Whirl. The Sheridan Neighborhood Organization (SNO) emphasizes community-building by sponsoring events like the SNO Ball and SNO Big Deal. Once the only neighborhood in the city that didn't have a park, the community has acquired a small, undeveloped green area on the bank of the Mississippi River where a foundry formerly stood. Eventually, it will contain a picnic area and a peace garden. If you're interested in this part of the city, be sure to watch Sheridan's online video at www.sheridanneighborhood.org.

Marshall Terrace (www.marshallterrace.org), which sits on the river between St. Anthony Parkway on the north and Lowry Avenue on the south, looks like it would be 100% industrial, until you get into it. Then you see plain turn-of-the-20th-century houses on quiet streets. The houses are affordable, and many have been purchased either by parents of University students, or young professionals. About one-quarter of the houses here are duplexes. For those concerned about living near an industrial zone, current residents say that Northern States Power Co. (NSP) and the other industries that occupy the riverfront are generally good neighbors, and the bulk of their complaints are related to noise. This neighborhood has access to the river bike paths along West River Road, across the Lowry Avenue bridge.

COLUMBIA PARK/WAITE PARK/AUDUBON PARK/ HOLLAND/LOGAN PARK/WINDOM PARK

The Shoreham Yards train, trucking, and bulk-distribution center between University and Central is a source of pollution for this part of the city, as well as the cause of collateral blight (www.ci.minneapolis. mn.us/cped/shoreham_yards.as). Clean-up is under way and redevelopment is planned.

Another well-kept Northeast secret is the upscale **Columbia Park** neighborhood (www.neighborhoodlink.com/Columbia_Park/info), just a chip shot away from Columbia Park and Francis A. Gross golf courses. Columbia Boulevar' which runs north of Columbia Park and Golf Course, looks very much like south Minneapolis parkways, with the same type of housing—stucco and Tudors and two-story colonials. Curvy Architect Avenue, off Columbia P west of Van Buren, is truly picturesque, with houses designed by p

Twin Cities architects over the course of the 1930s, '40s, and '50s. Homes here are elaborate and well kept, with meticulous landscaping and mature trees that contribute to the park-like atmosphere. Most of the industrial part of the neighborhood is west of 5th Street NE, or south of Columbia Park. Most homes here are owner-occupied, but there are some rentals to be found.

Waite Park (www.waiteparkneighborhood.org) and **Audubon Park** (http://audubonneighborhood.org), across Central from Columbia Golf Course, down to Lowry, are known as friendly neighborhoods with well-kept homes ranging from historic bungalows to mid-century ramblers. Houses with 1940s charm and contemporary renovations, located in the vicinity of Johnson Street and St. Anthony Boulevard, are especially popular with young professionals and their families.

South, down Central and across Lowry, the **Holland** neighborhood (www.hnia.org) is often overlooked. Covering 66 blocks, this neighborhood is primarily residential, but is diagonally bisected by a busy rail line and a corridor of light industry. Over 75% of the homes were built in the early 1900s by railroad workers employed at the Shoreham railyards on the northern edge of the neighborhood (see Waite Park above). They consist mostly of modest two-story wood frame or 1.5-story stucco bungalows that lack embellishment. They were sturdy, however, and offer today's buyers an affordable housing option that is difficult to find elsewhere. Though high-rise apartments can be found on Holland's borders, most of the neighborhood's rental units are duplexes or four-plexes. The neighborhood's main commercial/retail areas along Central, Lowry, and University are bustling and evolving, as old Italian and Eastern European shops and restaurants are replaced by Hispanic and Indian-owned restaurants, a food co-op on Central Avenue (http://eastsidefood.coop), pubs, bakeries, dance companies (www.ritzdolls.org) and art galleries. Jackson Square Park features a small YMCA that offers after-school activities for children.

At the center of the Arts District, **Logan Park**, just south of Holland, from 19th Avenue NE down to Broadway, between Washington Street and Central, is a small neighborhood that boasts large houses, including Victorians with dining rooms, built-in buffets, and intact woodwork. Low-rise rental units—duplexes and four-plexes—can also be found here. The heart of the neighborhood is Logan Park, originally a decorative city square in the late 1800s with formal flowerbeds and a Victorian fountain in the center, and now a recreation area. In an attempt to attract more artists, Logan Park set aside neighborhood redevelopment money to support the arts, and now its Northrup King Building complex (www.northrupkingbuilding.com) serves as a creative center for over 90 artists, small businesses, and nonprofits. The NK Building is home to two of Twin Cities' biggest shows: Art-A-Whirl, which takes place in the spring at locations throughout NE Minneapolis; and Art Attack, in the fall.

Windom Park (www.windompark.org) is a long strip of land running Central Avenue, east to New Brighton Boulevard, between 18th Avenue

and Lowry. Central Avenue, the main commercial corridor, is lined with vintage buildings and many ethnic restaurants. Big box retailers (Target, Home Depot, etc.) and a full-service bank with a multi-lingual staff can be found at the Quarry Shopping Center on 18th Avenue. Johnson Street also has a mix of commercial and large residential rental units. The other major thoroughfare, Stinson, on the east side of the neighborhood, is a parkway that is included in the Grand Rounds. Single-family craftsman and Tudor-style homes built in the 1920s and '30s are found along this parkway and to the east, while multifamily buildings are more prevalent in the west. Windom, the park, at the intersection of Johnson Street and Lowry Avenue, features a long, sloping hill that serves as a site for summer concerts and the annual Ice Cream Social, a carnival that attracts families from throughout Northeast.

ZIP Codes: 55413, 55414, 55418, 55421

Post Office: 1600 18th Ave NE

Police Precinct: 2nd, 1911 Central Ave NE, 311 or 612-673-5702 (non-emergency)

Emergency Hospital: Fairview-University Medical Center, 2450 Riverside Ave, 612-672-6000, www.fairview.org

Libraries: Northeast, 2200 Central Avenue NE; Pierre Bottineau, 55 Broadway NE; www.hclib.org

Community Resources: Ard Godfrey House, Central and University Ave SE at Chute Square, www.ardgodfreyhouse.org; Northeast Minneapolis Arts Association, www.nemaa.org; St. Anthony Main, www.saintanthonymain.com/mplsriverfrontdistrict.html

Parks: www.minneapolisparks.org; Boom Island Park; Columbia Park and Golf Course

Community Publication: *Northeaster*, www.nenorthnews.com

Public Transportation: 612-373-3333, www.MetroTransit.org; buses travel along E Hennepin, Johnson St, Stinson Blvd, Central Ave, 2nd St NE, University Ave, Marshall St, and Lowry Ave

NORTH MINNEAPOLIS

Driving through some parts of North Minneapolis now and seeing the deteriorated housing, graffiti, and groups of people hanging out in the streets, it's hard to imagine the bustling multicultural yet peaceful community that thrived here prior to the mid-1960s. Back then West Broadway was one of the largest retailing centers in the metro area, and Plymouth Avenue is said to have looked a lot like Grand Avenue in St. Paul looks now—a street lined with a useful mix of small owner-operated shops.

So what happened? Different things, which happened to converge at a particularly vulnerable time. The construction of I-94 fractured the neighborhoods and the more economically secure residents moved away, choosing—as many other city-dwellers did—to move to the suburbs, where newer, bigger houses were being built on larger lots. Finally, there were the race riots of 1966, when Plymouth Avenue went up in flames. At that point, much of the remaining white population put their homes on the market at fire sale prices and fled, leaving these neighborhoods to the poorest of the poor, most of whom were African American.

Today North Minneapolis exists as a paradox—still largely African American with a high concentration of poverty and crime, but with some of the city's most interesting housing stock and finest public greenspaces. If you like old houses with their interesting woodwork, but can't quite swing the price of a home in south Minneapolis, this might be a place to look.

By 2030, the population of this community and the northwest suburbs along County Road 81 (also known as West Broadway and Bottineau) is expected to increase by 25%. In preparation, the city has come up with a number of projects, including housing development, redevelopment of Lowry Avenue, a bus rapid transit corridor along County Road 81 (www.northwestcorridor.info), and commercial development on the corner of Penn Avenue and Lowry that includes an Aldi's grocery store (www.aldi.com).

WEBBER-CAMDEN COMMUNITY
McKinley/Folwell/Cleveland; Lind-Bohanon; Shingle Creek; Victory

Boundaries: North: 53rd Ave N; **West**: Xerxes Ave N; **South**: Lowry Ave N; **East**: Mississippi River

Webber-Camden (http://comehometocamden.org) is "like a great big flea market," says one resident, "a place where people can find real treasures at affordable prices." About a third of Webber-Camden is taken up by a cemetery. The rest is housing. Although there are some post–World War II apartment buildings, approximately 80% of the houses are single-family two-story wood-frames and Craftsman-style bungalows or 1.5-story stucco Tudors built between 1910 and 1932, some with two-car garages. Many are considered on the small

side for today's families, though just right for first-time home-buying singles or childless couples. The city and organizations such as Habitat for Humanity have worked hard to improve the housing stock here, and many of the most derelict buildings have been torn down and replaced. In the late 1990s, the neighborhood took off, drawing buyers who might traditionally look to buy in Uptown or Highland Park in St. Paul, including young families attracted to Patrick Henry High's International Baccalaureate program, artists, and gays. Webber-Camden's business area is located along 44th Street North and includes a homey coffeehouse, Camden Coffee Company, on the corner of 44th and Humboldt.

In the Shingle Creek and Victory areas, homes are slightly more expensive and incomes slightly higher when compared with the rest of Camden, although all of the neighborhoods are modest in comparison to the rest of Minneapolis.

Shingle Creek (www.scna-mpls.org), west of Humboldt and north of 49th Avenue, is made up of bungalows and ramblers (one-level homes) built primarily in the 1950s after the lowlands were drained. A creek cuts diagonally through the neighborhood and creates a natural greenspace, which connects with a mixed-use trail on the north side of 49th Avenue near the main entrance to the North Mississippi Regional Park and Interpretive Center, www.minneapolisparks.org. The Shingle Creek Common Ground Community Garden includes prairie, wetland, and shade gardens, all maintained by local volunteers.

Victory, west of Penn, between Dowling Avenue and the Humboldt Industrial Area (http://victoryneighborhood.org), contains vintage homes from the 1920s and '30s through the 1960s, as well as some of the city's nicest public greenspaces, among them Victory Memorial Drive, which has been designated a State Historic District.

While most of the housing here is single-family, there are several apartment buildings along Thomas Avenue North, which is also a ma route. Most home sales here, as in the rest of North Minneapolis, ar time buyers. But, in contrast to other nearby neighborhoods, the me of houses in Victory rose more than 30% between the censuses of 1990 and 2000. If you're interested in this area, be sure to check out the pictures of Victory Memorial Drive posted on the Minneapolis Park Board web site, www.minneapolisparks.org/grandrounds.

North of Webber-Camden, **Lind-Bohanon** (www.lindbohanon.org), which stretches from 43rd Avenue to the north city limits, between the Mississippi River and Humboldt Avenue, has a reputation for being a relatively quiet neighborhood with a low resident turnover rate. Some families have lived in their houses here for two or three generations. One of the first public housing projects in the nation—Mississippi Courts—was built in Lind-Bohanon in the 1940s to house soldiers returning from World War II. A recent addition to the community is one of the metro's more successful "New Urban Neighborhoods," the Humboldt Greenway (www.humboldtgreenway.com) community of two-story, single-family homes and townhouses that went on the market in 2005.

North Mississippi Regional Park (www.minneapolisparks.org) snakes along the edge of the neighborhood. It's a great place for hiking, biking, cross-country skiing, and geocaching. Inside the Karl Kroening Interpretive Center, you can take a 1973 Barracuda "for a spin" and discover the impact that I-94 had on the community. Actually, you can look around and see for yourself that it wasn't good.

On the southernmost edge of the community, between Dowling and Lowry, the neighborhoods of **McKinley** (which includes the North River Industrial Area), **Folwell** (www.folwell.org), and **Cleveland** are areas of modest single-family, duplex, and sometimes triplex, houses. The Arts and Crafts/Prairie School Bungalow at 3505 Sheridan Avenue North, known as the Fournier House, has been designated an historic landmark (www.ci.minneapolis.mn.us/hpc/landmarks/map.asp).

The Minneapolis public schools in this area run several innovative programs including the Afro-Centric Middle School Academy and the Elizabeth Hall International Baccalaureate Primary Years magnet school, which includes Chinese language instruction and an all-day kindergarten.

ZIP Codes: 55411, 55412, 55430
Post Office: 2306 Lowry Ave N
Police Precinct: 4th, 1925 Plymouth Ave N, 311 or 612-673-5704 (non-emergency); Broadway Safety Center, 1011 West Broadway, 612-673-2947. The 4th Ward CARE Task force web site, http://4thwardcaretaskforce.org, is designed to inform residents about public safety issues in these neighborhoods.
Emergency Hospital: North Memorial Medical Center, 3300 Oakdale Ave N, Robbinsdale, 763-520-5200, www.northmemorial.com
Library: Webber Park, 4310 Webber Pkwy, www.hclib.org
www.minneapolisparks.org; North Mississippi Regional Park
Community Publications: *North News*, www.nenorthnews.com; *Camden Community News*, www.camdenews.org; *Insight News*, http://insightnews.com

Public Transportation: 612-373-3333, www.MetroTransit.org; buses travel along 26th Ave, Lowry, Thomas, West Broadway, Oakdale, Fremont, Lyndale, and Penn. Bus Route 5, which travels through this community, has a history of having more problems than most. Extra transit officers are sometimes assigned to ride this route, and cameras have been added to buses, but for your own safety, you may not want to ride this or other routes alone.

NEAR NORTH COMMUNITY

Hawthorne; Jordan/Willard-Hay/Willard Homewood; Sumner-Glenwood; Near North; Harrison

Boundaries: North: Lowry Ave; **West**: Xerxes Ave; **South**: Bassett Creek; **East**: I-94, Mississippi River

The Northside of Minneapolis is one of the city's oldest districts, and has been home to many different ethnic populations through the years. Today it is home to the most extensive from-the-ground-up redevelopment the city has ever undertaken.

This project, in the Northside's easternmost neighborhoods of **Sumner-Glenwood** and **Near North**, came about as the result of the settlement of a 1990s lawsuit that required Minneapolis to demolish ghettos of public housing and replace them with mixed-income development. In 2005, the 900-unit mixed-income, mixed-density, culturally diverse redevelopment project that has risen in their place, Heritage Park, was dedicated and people started moving back. Eventually this project will stretch from I-94 on the east to Humboldt Avenue on the west, and from 12th Avenue on the north to Glenwood Avenue on the south. The development includes two new parks, a new boulevard named for Van White, the city's first black councilmember, and connections to the Hennepin County trail system and the downtown business district.

The historic 1915 Sumner Library, on the corner of Olson Highway (55) and Van White Memorial Boulevard, houses the largest black history collection in Minneapolis. Further reminders of Minneapolis' proud past, a strip of Queen Anne "painted ladies," can be found in the 1500 block of Dupont Avenue, just north of Plymouth Road. Dating from 1875 to 1899, at least one of these houses is listed on the National Historic Register. Another area of significance is the 30-square-block Arts-and-Crafts neighborhood of Old Highland (www.oldhighland.org), located from West Broadway down to Plymouth Avenue between Aldrich Avenue and Girard. The "painted ladies" and their Arts-and-Crafts neighbors are some of the biggest houses in North Minneapolis.

Hawthorne (www.hawthornecommunity.org), located north of Broadway to Lowry, and east of Emerson Avenue to the Mississippi River, is a 77-square-block area bisected by I-94. About two-thirds of this neighborhood

consists of rental property. It has history, too: the concrete block houses and row houses, between 3rd and 4th Streets and 26th Avenue North, date from 1885 and are designated historic landmarks (www.ci.minneapolis.mn.us/hpc/landmarks/map.asp). New condos with river views can be found across the street from Orvin "Ole" Olson Park at the end of West River Road, just north of 22nd Avenue.

In **Jordan**, north of Broadway and west of Emerson, where there is a higher rate of home ownership, there is a trend toward rehabilitating houses, rather than tearing them down. The same is true in **Willard-Hay**, south of Broadway, from approximately Penn Avenue to Xerxes. Willard-Hay, which has many dilapidated houses, is the unlikely location of "the poor-man's Kenwood," otherwise known as **Willard-Homewood**, located south of Plymouth Avenue and abutting Theodore Wirth Parkway. This area of large, architecturally interesting Tudor, Spanish, and Arts-and-Crafts style houses was one of the city's first planned developments. Most of the houses were built between 1905 and 1930. Residents fled this neighborhood in the 1960s when north Minneapolis was the scene of racial rioting, and houses here have been selling at fire-sale prices ever since. You can get a lot of house for the money—sun porches, high ceilings, fireplaces, built-in bookcases and buffets, beamed ceilings, hardwood floors, front and back staircases, and libraries. This is, however, a neighborhood for those who have a high tolerance for urban interactions.

The **Harrison** neighborhood, which is south of Highway 55, abuts Theodore Wirth Park on the west, and is adjacent to the more prosperous Bryn Mawr neighborhood on its south border. It is bisected by Glenwood Avenue. Parcels of industrial land occupy the neighborhood east of Cedar Lake Road, while the western part is mainly residential. A "pro-active" community, residents here work hard to make their neighborhood safe and to keep the housing stock from deteriorating. One of the most popular services of the Neighborhood Association is the Tool Lending Library, which allows residents to rent tools from Broadway

Rental to help them do home repairs and remodeling. The Neighborhood Association has also been working for years to promote the redevelopment of Bassett Creek, a small, shallow stream that begins at Medicine Lake in Plymouth and winds through Golden Valley and this neighborhood before draining into the Mississippi River in downtown Minneapolis. It is thought that if Bassett Creek could be cleaned up and uncovered where it's been diverted through tunnels, it would provide the North Side with an amenity on the order of Minnehaha Creek in South Minneapolis. While projects upstream in Plymouth and Golden Valley have focused on improving the creek's water quality, not much has been done to reclaim it at the Minneapolis end, except by volunteers.

ZIP Codes: 55405, 55411
Post Offices: 18 N 12th St; 2306 Lowry Ave N
Police Precinct: 4th, 1925 Plymouth Ave N, 311 or 612-673-5704 (non-emergency); Broadway Safety Center, 1011 West Broadway 612-673-2947
Emergency Hospitals: North Memorial Medical Center, 3300 Oakdale Ave N, Robbinsdale, 763-520-5200, www.northmemorial.com; Hennepin County Medical Center, 701 Park Ave, 612-873-3000, www.hcmc.org
Libraries: North Regional, 1315 Lowry Ave N; Sumner, 611 Van White Memorial Blvd; www.hclib.org
Resources: North Community YMCA, 1711 W Broadway, 612-588-9484, www.ymcatwincities.org
Parks: www.minneapolisparks.org; North Mississippi Park; Theodore Wirth Park and Golf Course and Eloise Butler Wildflower Garden and Bird Sanctuary
Community Publications: *North News*, www.nenorthnews.com; *Insight News*, http://insightnews.com; *My Northside*, www.northminneapolis.com
Public Transportation: 612-373-3333, www.MetroTransit.org; buses travel along Fremont, Emerson, Broadway, Penn, Plymouth Ave, Lyndale Ave, Glenwood, Cedar Lake Rd, and Hwy 55 (Olson Memorial Blvd)

ST. PAUL

St. Paul, the state capital, is often called "The Last City of the East" because early developers laid it out in an East Coast style, with city squares and broad boulevards, and filled it with buildings that featured elaborate ornamentation. Look for examples of the city's superb early architecture in its six designated historic districts: Dayton's Bluff, Historic Hill District, Irvine Park, Lowertown, Summit Avenue West, and University-Raymond Commercial Historic District. Maps of the districts are posted on the city's web site at www.stpaul.gov/index.aspx?NID=1832.

From the horse-drawn golden chariot on the State Capitol's marble dome to Summit Avenue, the longest and best-preserved boulevard of Victorian mansions in the nation, a stately, 19th-century elegance pervades much of this city. Though St. Paul was settled only slightly earlier than Minneapolis, it seems older because so much of the early city survives: blocks of Victorian Romanesque brick buildings, divided boulevards, established neighborhoods—even the trees are old.

Now modern loft conversions have breathed new life into the old buildings. Unfortunately, a commitment by the city to build 5000 new units of housing by the end of 2005 fast-tracked a lot of construction projects, often to their detriment. Still, rather than triggering the demolition of existing buildings, the Big Push did serve to encourage renovation and reclamation of a number of sites. The 1917 Union Depot, for example, which is listed on the National Register of Historic Places, had its upper floors converted into two-level loft condominiums, while its lower floors are being renovated to serve as a transit hub for the new Central Corridor LRT. There have also been several larger, neighborhood-scaled projects developed around the riverfront. One of them, Upper Landing condos and rental apartments, actually sits on a swath of land that was considered flood plain before developers elevated it above the 100-year-flood level.

St. Paul's population (288,055 in 2008) and economy have always trailed Minneapolis, which actually is one of the reasons people like to live here—it feels more like a small town than a big city. The downtown is compact and the streets are more wholly residential than the streets of Minneapolis. At the same time, grocery stores, restaurants, bookstores, and the city's many historical and cultural sites are easily accessible by foot or bus from most neighborhoods. Housing on the east side of the metro also tends to be cheaper than on the west side. Expect rents to be about $100 less per month than in Minneapolis, and houses to cost proportionately less, as well.

A true sense of community is fostered within St. Paul's 17 neighborhoods (here called districts), assisted by district councils that work together with city government, giving neighborhoods a voice in city decisions. District councils are also active in civic beautification, community gardening, home improvement, and recycling, and work closely with the St. Paul Police Department on crime prevention. Call the district councils listed at the end of each neighborhood profile for more information about a specific neighborhood. *Tour Saint Paul Neighborhood Guides* produced by Historic Saint Paul include audio walking tours that highlight historic landmarks in the city's core neighborhoods, www. historicsaintpaul.org. For phototours of several sections of St. Paul, check out http://www.phototour.minneapolis.mn.us/st_paul.

St. Paul's police force is organized into three districts—western, central, and eastern. Each district has several neighborhood substations. For information about crime in a particular neighborhood, look online at the department's reports to district councils, www.stpaul.gov/index.aspx?NID=2399. The police department's monthly crime reports and maps of crime locations (STATMap) are posted on the internet at www.stpaul.gov/index.aspx?nid=674. Annual reports and maps covering several years can be found at www.stpaul.gov/Document-View.aspx?DID=9470. According to the STATMap, St. Paul's "hot spots" for crime tend to be located in the parts of town north of I-94, particularly in the Thomas-Dale, Summit-University, and Dayton's Bluff neighborhoods. But don't read this and automatically mark these neighborhoods off your list; their community councils are working hard to deal with the troublesome blocks—and the police have targeted all these areas for additional patrols. Apparently their efforts have been effective, as Saint Paul Part 1 crimes (homicide, rape, robbery, aggravated assault, burglary, theft, motor vehicle theft, and arson) decreased 26.6% from 2000 to 2008.

Web Site: City of St. Paul, 651-266-8989, www.stpaul.gov/index.aspx

Area Code: 651

Emergency Hospitals: Regions Hospital, 640 Jackson St, 651-254-3456, www. regionshospital.com; HealthEast St. Joseph's Hospital, 69 W Exchange St, 651-232-3348, www.healtheast.org/st-joes.html; United Hospital, 333 N Smith Ave, St. Paul, 651-241-8000, www.unitedhospital.com

Library: St. Paul Public Libraries, www.sppl.org; 13 locations; Central Library, 90 West Fourth Street, 651-266-7000

Police Headquarters: 367 Grove St, 651-291-1111, www.stpaul.gov/index. aspx?nid=461

Public Schools: St. Paul District #625, District Office: 360 Colborne St., 651-767-8100, www.spps.org

Parks: St. Paul Parks and Recreation, 651-266-6400, www.stpaul.gov/index. aspx?nid=243; St. Paul has over 4,000 acres of parkland, an indoor water park, 33 recreation centers, three 18-hole golf courses, 100 miles of paved

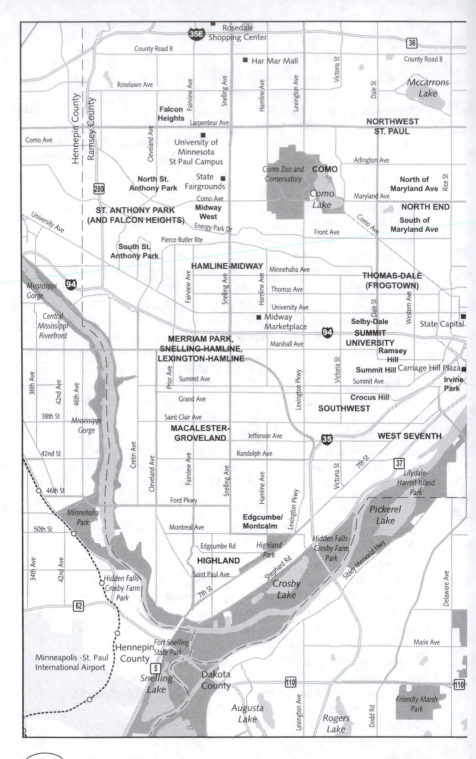

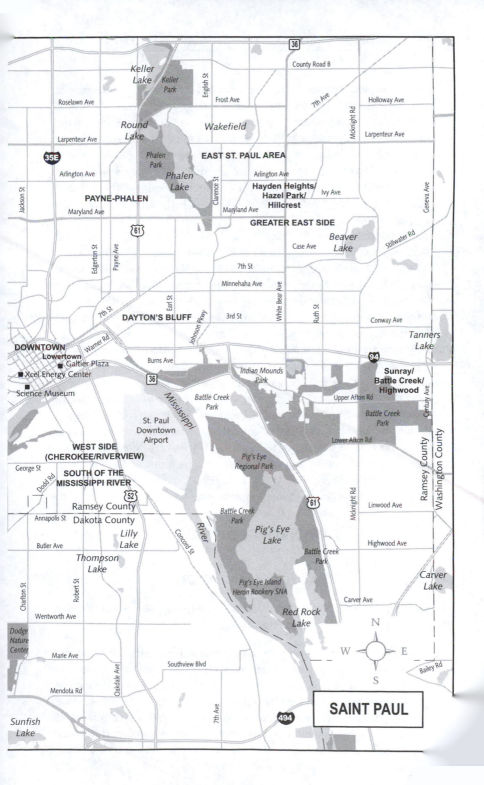

trails, indoor and outdoor pools, a multi-purpose outdoor stadium (home of the St. Paul Saints), a zoo, an indoor garden, a ski and snowboard hill, several ice rinks, and a public beach. Its principal parks are Como and Phalen in the northern part of the city, and Highland and the Mississippi riverfront in the south. Book tee times online at www.golfstpaul.org. Adults who live or work in the city of Saint Paul can use recreation center fitness rooms and indoor walking tracks for a nominal annual fee. Arlington/Arkwright Off-Leash Dog Area, on the corner of Arlington and Arkwright, is the city's only off-leash dog park.

Community Publications: *St. Paul Pioneer Press*, 651-222-1111 or 800-950-9080, www.twincities.com; *St. Paul Villager and Avenues*, 757 Snelling Ave S, 651-699-1462, www.villagercomm.com; *Lillie Suburban Newspapers*, www.lillienews.com, *Sun Newspapers*, www.mnsun.com; *WoNews*, Minnesota Women's Press, 771 Raymond Ave, 651-646-3968, www.womenspress.com

Community Resources: Historic St. Paul, www.historicsaintpaul.org; St. Paul Neighborhood Network, SPNN TV, www.spnn.org

Public Transportation: Information about all public transportation can be accessed at 612-373-3333, www.MetroTransit.org. Buses generally run along main thoroughfares, but routes and schedules do change, so be sure to check the web site or call. The Central Corridor LRT line will connect downtown Minneapolis and downtown St. Paul along University and Washington avenues through the State Capitol complex, Midway area, and University of Minnesota. Service is expected to begin in 2014. Parking information, commuter help, and walking and biking maps can be found at St. Paul Smart Trips, 651-224-8555, www.smart-trips.org. HourCar has several area locations and can be accessed at www.hourcar.org.

DOWNTOWN DISTRICT

DOWNTOWN/LOWERTOWN

Boundaries: North: University Ave; **West**: Marion St, Irvine Ave; **South**: Kellogg Blvd, Mississippi River; **East**: I-94, Lafayette Rd

The beauty of living downtown is that most everything is within walking distance—although, since St. Paul is built on hills, people sometimes opt to take the bus up and then walk down. Bus service is convenient; you can take the bus anywhere within downtown for fifty cents, or use it to get to downtown Minneapolis, the Mall of America, or the Rosedale Shopping Mall. In fact, immediate amenities are so accessible by public transport that many residents don't even a car. However, since downtown shopping is limited, residents who otherwise blissfully car-free recommend joining "HourCar" (www.hourcar.org), a nonprofit pay-as-you-go car sharing service managed by the St. Paul Neighborhood Energy Consortium (www.spnec.org). HourCars are conveniently stashed in Downtown and the Selby-Dale neighborhoods, Macalester College, and near the University of Minnesota. (See the **Transportation** chapter in this book.)

The other beauty of living in **Downtown** is all the new housing. While the neighborhood has long been dotted with high-rise apartment buildings containing both moderate-rent and luxury apartments, recently many of the old corniced and dentiled office buildings have also been converted into condos. Newer units are generally described as "cozy" (as small as 370 square feet) and often equipped with space-saving Murphy beds. Though the units are decked out with the same high-end appliances and trendy finishes, prices tend to be lower than in similar units in Minneapolis. Most of these units are targeted at singles or those who work downtown. The State Capitol building and state offices are here, as are headquarters for a few large companies. Many of these offices and apartments are connected by skyways (enclosed breezeways spanning 40 blocks that connect building to building on the level of the second or third floors). On weekdays these aerial walkways bustle with restaurants and food-courts, coffee shops, markets, and a YMCA. But many shops close in the evenings, and some segments have restricted hours. That said, three hotels, the Central Library, Children's Museum, RiverCentre convention center, and Xcel Energy Center can be reached through the skyways, and the Science Museum is just a short jog across Kellogg Boulevard from the system. Download a map of the skyway system from the City of St. Paul's web site at www.stpaul.gov/DocumentView.aspx?DID=5052.

Despite the weekday buzz in the skyways, Downtown is not a world-class shopping destination, though with more people living in the district, that may change. Downtown does have a small full-service grocery, drug store, fruit market, discount bookstore, and Macy's, and there are plans for a high-end Lund's grocery store. (For more specialized shopping, see the Shopping Districts section of the **Shopping for the Home** chapter.)

Nor does Downtown have many children or places for children to play. Open space, while not as plentiful as elsewhere in the Twin Cities, is available in a handful of small city parks tucked in amid the tall buildings, and in a regional park on Harriet Island. Rice Park is a formal square bordered by the Ordway Center for the Performing Arts, Landmark Center, the Central Library/ James J. Hill Library, and the grand old St. Paul Hotel. More of a plaza than a park, it hosts the ice sculpture contest during the St. Paul Winter Carnival. Kellogg Park is a narrow strip of greenspace that runs between the edge of the river bluff and Kellogg Boulevard, from the Robert Street Bridge to the Wabasha Street Bridge. A popular setting for weddings, it includes sculptures depicting St. Paul's history. Mears Park, another square, features a bandshell and is home to popular summer concerts. Visit in the spring for a stunning display of thousands of tulips. The newest downtown parks are Landmark Plaza located along Market Street, where there is an ice rink in winter, and Wacouta Commons, a neighborhood greenspace in the new North Quadrant development. Harriet Island Regional Park is just a short walk from downtown across the Wabasha Bridge. The region's leading venue for outdoor festivals (such as the Irish Fair) is located here, as are the St. Paul Yacht Club and the Padelford tour boats. Upper Landing Park is located on Shepard Road and Chestnut, on the north side of the Mississippi River, near the Science Museum. This beautiful location is great for company picnics on the lawn, wedding ceremonies near the fountain, family reunions and other gatherings.

What the district does have is nightlife. The Ordway Center for the Performing Arts (www.ordway.org), with its concerts and Broadway musicals, is in the center of downtown on Rice Park, and there's a wellspring of nearby restaurants, pubs, and coffee shops to go to before and after performances. (For more information, see the **Cultural Life** chapter.)

Historic and cultural sites and annual events abound as well, making it easy to entertain out-of-town visitors. People flock to events at the RiverCentre auditorium and convention center (www.rivercentre.org), the Fitzgerald Theater (www.fitzgeraldtheaterpublicradio.org), the Science Museum of Minnesota (www.smm.org), Minnesota Children's Museum (www.mcm.org), and the Minnesota History Center (www.mnhs.org), and to numerous festivals throughout the year. During the summer, on Friday and Saturday evenings, Kellogg Boulevard is closed off between Robert Street and Wabasha for antique car shows, complete with food vendors and live music. The car shows are an intimate tête-à-tête compared to the serious food-fest, the Taste of Minnesota, which is held over the Fourth of July weekend (http://tasteofmn.com). Then restaurants from all over the Twin Cities set up booths on Harriet Island, live bands play throughout the park, and each evening ends in fireworks. There are more fireworks in January during the 120-year-old St. Paul Winter Carnival, a major event that includes an ice castle, sled dog races, parades, and a treasure hunt. The ice castles have always been the highlights of the Winter Carnivals, and throughout the event's history, palaces of all sizes and designs have been constructed. The 1888 ice castle, at 14 stories, was the tallest building in the city at the time; the 1992 ice palace, at 15 stories, was the tallest ice palace on record in the world at the time. (Check out construction of the 1992 ice palace, from cutting the ice to the nightly light shows, on YouTube at www.youtube.com/watch?v=IP7KdIvirFQ&NR=1. Those who enjoy a wee bit of rowdiness will love St. Paul's raucous St. Patrick's Day street party (www.stpatsassoc.org). Rooted in the city's Irish heritage, the festivities kick off at noon with a parade down Fourth Street to Rice Park, and continue into the night with (it seems) nearly everyone in town wearing a "Kiss Me I'm Irish" button and partaking of green beer.

Lowertown, the eastern half of downtown, centers on the beautifully landscaped square of Mears Park. Housing options here include condos and lofts in rehabbed brick warehouses and factories, high-rise apartments, and even a few townhomes. With over 300 sculptors, potters, painters, and performance artists living in the district, Lowertown has one of the largest concentrations of working artists of any city in the Midwest. Each April and October, the members of the Art Collective open their studio doors for the St. Paul Art Crawl. Check www.stpaulartcrawl.org for more information. Site of the lower of St. Paul's two early river landings, commerce has always been key to this area, which boasts, besides the artists' studios, St. Paul's year-round Farmers' Market (http://stpaulfarmersmarket.com) and an international assortment of restaurants and bars.

Web Site: Capitol River District Council (District 17), 101 East 5th Street, Suite 240, 651-221-0488, www.capitolrivercouncil.org

ZIP Codes: 55101, 55102, 55103

Post Offices: Main Office, 180 E Kellogg Blvd; 408 Saint Peter St

Police: Headquarters, 367 Grove St, 651-291-1111; Central District Patrol Team, 401 N Robert St, 651-291-1111 (non-emergency), www.stpaul.gov/index.aspx?nid=461

Emergency Hospitals: Regions Hospital, 640 Jackson St, 651-254-3456, www.regionshospital.com; HealthEast St. Joseph's Hospital, 69 W Exchange St, 651-232-3348, www.healtheast.org/st-joes.html; United Hospital, 333 N Smith Ave, St. Paul, 651-241-8000, www.unitedhospital.com

Library: www.sppl.org; Central, 90 W 4th St

Community Resources: Ordway Center for the Performing Arts, 345 Washington St, Box Office 651-224-4222, www.ordway.org; RiverCentre convention center and Roy Wilkins Auditorium, 175 W Kellogg, 651-265-4800, www.rivercentre.org; Landmark Center, 75 W 5th St, 651-292-3225, www.landmarkcenter.org; Xcel Energy Center, 199 W Kellogg Blvd, 651-726-8240, www.xcelenergycenter.com; Minnesota Children's Museum, 10 W 7th St, 651-225-6000, www.mcm.org; Minnesota History Center and Minnesot Historical Society, 345 W Kellogg Blvd, St. Paul, 651-259-3000, 651-282-6C (TTY) or 800-657-3773 (toll free), www.mnhs.org; Science Museum of nesota, 120 W Kellogg Blvd, 651-221-9444, www.smm.org; Min Women's Consortium, Minnesota Women's Building, 550 Rice St, f

0338, www.mnwomen.org; Minnesota State Capitol, 75 Rev. Dr. Martin Luther King, Jr., Blvd, 651-296-2881, www.mnhs.org/places/sites/msc

Parks: www.stpaul.gov/index.aspx?nid=243; Harriet Island Regional Park; Wells Fargo WinterSkate outdoor ice rink, Landmark Plaza adjacent to Rice Park at the corner of West 5th and Market sts

Public Transportation: 612-373-3333, www.MetroTransit.org; numerous city bus lines run through downtown on Broadway, 5th and 6th, Minnesota, Robert, Cedar, Wabasha, Wall, and St. Peter Streets. Travel between downtown stores, restaurants and businesses on the Downtown Zone fare, which is 50 cents at all times. Pick up a free transit map at the MCTO store in the skyway level of the US Bank Center at 6th and Minnesota sts. HourCars are located at 316 Jackson St, www.hourcar.org. The Central Corridor LRT line will connect downtown Minneapolis and downtown St. Paul. Stations will include the Union Depot, 4th and Cedar, 10th St, and the State Capitol.

SOUTHWEST DISTRICTS

SUMMIT HILL DISTRICT

Crocus Hill; Summit Hill

Boundaries: North: Summit Ave; **West**: Ayd Mill Rd; **East**: Ramsey St; **South/ East**: I-35E; **South**: Summit Hill is separated from W 7th by the bluffs

St. Paul's counterpart to Kenwood in Minneapolis, the neighborhoods of the Southwest district have the ambiance of a library filled with leather-bound books: old, hefty, and rich with historical detail. Variations include the more trendy east end of Summit, and the more academic west end, but all the people who live here have access to the restaurants and shops of Grand Avenue, one of St. Paul's great pleasures. The one surprise is the number of rental units contained within the huge old houses.

The mansions and historic buildings poised high on **Summit Hill** epitomize the grandeur and wealth of boom-era St. Paul. The traditional home of the city's aristocracy (and robber barons), this broad boulevard is lined with superior examples of many styles of turn-of-the-20th-century architecture and ornamentation, including a possible decorative coffin on the roof of Number 456 (on the north side of the street, just west of the University Club). Summit's first mansion, erected in 1862 at 432, also created quite a stir when it was built ecause it incorporated three newfangled features—steam heating, hot and 'd water, and gas lighting.

In the 1880s and 1890s the Crocus Hill and Grand Hill neighborhoods ecame fashionable locations for wealthy families. **Crocus Hill** (south mit) is still one of the Twin Cities' most desirable and eccentric

neighborhoods. If you buy a house in this maze of cobblestone streets, it may come with a ghost, but your garage could be four blocks away. Crocus Hill, the street (Goodrich becomes Crocus Hill just east of Dale Street), is only half a block long, but that's long enough for most deliverymen, because house numbering is not consecutive. One is the first house built on the street, but the second house, built at the opposite end of the street, is Four. In between are Twelve, Two, Eleven, and Sixteen—and Five is around the corner. Only two of the early 1880s houses remain; the rest were built between the early 1900s and 1940s. Crocus Hill, the neighborhood, extends to St. Clair, and, mercifully, the rest of the streets do employ sequential numbering. For real estate advertising purposes, homes anywhere near the St. Paul Cathedral on Summit Avenue are listed as "prestigious Crocus Hill."

All five miles of Summit Avenue, in the Summit Hill/Ramsey Hill area, are protected, either as a national or local Historic District. Out of 440 original homes built along this avenue in the late 1800s, an amazing 373 have survived. Summit Avenue has also survived as St. Paul's power address. The Minnesota governor's official residence is at 1006, although recent governors have chosen not to live there. Railroad baron James J. Hill's 45-room red sandstone mansion, a few blocks away at 240 Summit, was the largest house in the Midwest when it was built in 1891. Across the street is the Renaissance-style Catholic Cathedral of the Archdiocese of Saint Paul and Minneapolis, which looks down on the other domed building in town, the Minnesota State Capitol. The cathedral is host to many concerts, the most popular of which is the annual Christmas performance of Handel's *Messiah*.

F. Scott Fitzgerald was born in the neighborhood, and returned to write *This Side of Paradise* in a shabby-genteel red stone row house on the corner of Summit and Dale. Take a self-guided tour of the St. Paul locations that figured in his life by following the walking tour directions posted at http://home. comcast.net/~caudle2/fscotwlk.htm. Or learn even more about the Gilded Age mansions by joining one of the Minnesota Historical Society's guided walking tours, held every Saturday and Sunday from May through September (651-259-3000, www.mnhs.org). Another tour, the biannual September historic Ramsey Hill House Tour, showcases home interiors and private gardens and serves as a neighborhood fundraiser (651-221-0200, www.ramseyhill.org). Pictures posted on all these web sites will give you a very good idea of what the neighborhood looks like.

Step away from Summit Avenue and you'll find more than a museum that pays homage to the lavish excesses of the late 19th century past. Residential opportunities abound in Summit Hill, and not everyone living here is a millionaire. The neighborhood's last housing boomlet, in the 1920s, included the building of many apartments, particularly along the streetcar lines on major thoroughfares like Grand Avenue. In addition, many single-family houses have been converted into duplexes or rooming houses, making up much of the housing that's available in Summit Hill today. Vacancy rates are low, but if you're lucky, it is possible to find an apartment here that has refinished hardwood floors, tall windows, and a working fireplace. Try the area south of Grand Avenue for more modest housing. People from all walks of life live here, including faculty, staff, and students from nearby colleges.

Proximity to Grand Avenue, one of the Twin Cities' most attractive commercial districts, is another perk to living in Summit Hill. This major commercial artery is loaded with interesting restaurants, specialty stores, taverns and bookstores. The southwest districts' principal summer festival, Grand Old Day, attracts crowds from all over the Twin Cities. Then the street is closed off and its entire length becomes one long party, with live bands, food, beer, games, a parade, and great people watching.

However, the area's popular shopping, coupled with the presence of so many apartments, has created three problems: burglaries, traffic, and parking. So a word to the wise, don't park even for a minute in a space that requires a resident's sticker, and don't leave things in your car. For more information about shopping in this district, see the **Shopping for the Home** chapter.

Web Site: Summit Hill Association (District 16), 860 St. Clair Ave, 651-222-1222, www.summithillassociation.org

ZIP Code: 55105

Post Offices: Main Office, 180 E Kellogg Blvd; 1430 Concordia Ave

Police Non-Emergency: Western District Patrol Team, North: 651-266-5512, General Information, 651-291-1111; www.stpaul.gov/index.aspx?nid=461

Emergency Hospitals: Regions Hospital, 640 Jackson St, 651-254-3456, www.regionshospital.com; HealthEast St. Joseph's Hospital, 69 W Exchange St, 651-232-3348, www.healtheast.org/st-joes.html; United Hospital, 333 N Smith Ave, St. Paul, 651-241-8000, www.unitedhospital.com

Libraries: www.sppl.org; Central, 90 W 4th St; Rondo Outreach Community Library, 461 North Dale St

Community Resources: James J. Hill House and Library, www.mnhs.org/places/sites/jjhh; F. Scott Fitzgerald sites at 481 Laurel, 240 Summit, 260 Summit, University Club at 420 Summit, 475 Summit, 501 Grand Hill, 626 Goodrich; Cathedral of St. Paul, www.cathedralsaintpaul.org

Parks: www.stpaul.gov/index.aspx?nid=243; Linwood Park and Recreation Center, 860 St. Clair, has a dance studio, gym, play area, tennis courts, athletic fields and a 1/2 basketball court.

Public Transportation: 612-373-3333, www.MetroTransit.org; buses travel along Selby, Grand, St. Clair, Dale and Snelling; Summit Hill is fundraising to get an HourCar hub in the neighborhood, www.hourcar.org.

SUMMIT-UNIVERSITY DISTRICT
Selby-Dale, Cathedral Hill/Ramsey Hill (South of Summit)

Boundaries: North: University Ave; **West**: Lexington Pkwy; **South**: Summit Ave; **East**: Irvine Ave, Marion St (also includes buildings on the north side of Irvine St located immediately below Summit Ave, east of Ramsey St)

Like Summit Hill to the south, the streets of Summit-University and Ramsey Hill contain many of the city's oldest, most historic buildings, including stone mansions, charming Victorian wood frames, and elegant 19th-century brick storefronts and row houses. But there is a literal disconnect in this neighborhood, and that, too, has everything to do with history.

"Before there was Interstate 94…there was Rondo," said Mary Sanders in a 1992 book that details the destruction of this district's legendary Rondo neighborhood by the construction of I-94. The book, *In Voices: A Collection of Writings*

and Stories for a Diverse Community, compiled by Mark Clark and available from the Minnesota Historical Society, tells the story of Rondo Avenue, which was the heart of St. Paul's largest black neighborhood. When the freeway went through, the Cedar-Riverside community to the west was able to rally and find a way to remain somewhat intact—Rondo was not. The construction erased it, displacing thousands of African Americans and leaving a legacy of poverty and crime that continues today, especially in the half of this district that is north of I-94.

More like two distinct neighborhoods than one, "Summit-U" straddles the freeway. The north side is heavily commercial and crime-ridden, though currently the subject of much transit-oriented development, including one of the nation's most unusual mixed-use projects, the Rondo Community Outreach Library Apartments and Townhomes at University and Dale. With three floors of apartments above the library, it is home to almost 100 renters and a home base for many small businesses, as well as reading literacy and education programs. It is one of a handful of such projects in the nation in which a library shares a facility with a housing development.

The south of I-94 side of the district, at least once you get a few blocks away from the freeway, is the part we think of as charming and trendy. Stretching out from the St. Paul Cathedral to Lexington, it, too, was a hotbed of porno shops and crime as recently as the early 1990s. At one point, someone even bombed the Selby-Dale police station and blew out all the windows in the neighborhood. Today, those times are past, and the corner of Selby and Dale has become the center of one of St. Paul's most charming residential and entertainment quarters. Houses and brownstone apartments have been restored to the glory of their golden days, and the neighborhood's chic restaurants are always full.

The **Ramsey Hill** neighborhood (www.ramseyhill.org), east of Dale to the Cathedral, between Summit and I-94, is one of the largest, best preserved contiguous Victorian districts in North America and the largest and oldest Registered National Historic District in Minnesota. Every other year the Ramsey Hill Association sponsors a house and garden tour to showcase this neighborhood's beauty and rich history. While most of these properties are single-family homes, in some of them you can find huge apartments with "character" (sometimes even fireplaces) at rents that are lower than in Uptown in Minneapolis. In fact, that's one of the great surprises of this area: there are actually more places to rent than to buy here.

If you're in the market to buy, **Selby-Dale** used to be a great place to find a fixer-upper, especially for those looking for two-story frame houses with front porches and picture windows. That isn't so much the case anymore, though with some homes as small as 700 square feet, this can still be a good neighborhood for first-time homebuyers. In the blocks adjacent to Summit, truly large Italianate, Beaux Arts, and Queen Anne houses can also be found. Thanks to urban renewal, some houses now sit on a lot-and-a-half, with owners having purchased land when next-door derelict houses were torn down. Still, lots are small in proportion to the houses, and it's hard to garden because there's so much shade. Pocket gardens and boulevard gardens are popular, and they have the additional advantage of bringing people out onto the streets where they can keep an eye on what's going on.

Like the other neighborhoods surrounding Summit, shopping on Grand Avenue is within easy walking range, But some of the best local dining is to be found right on **Cathedral Hill**. Sweeney's (www.sweeneyssaloon.com) at Dale and Ashland rocks inside and out all year long thanks to a HUGE stone fireplace; and W.A. Frost, at Selby and Western, www.wafrost.com, not only serves delectable locally sourced organic food, but has repeatedly been selected the Twin Cities' Most Romantic Restaurant. On the supply side, Mississippi Market natural food coop (www.msmarket.coop), at the corner of Selby and Dale, is also a perennial favorite.

The absence of a large open space in the area may be problematic for some. While people walk, run, and bike the city streets—and the Twin Cities Marathon comes right down Summit—there is no place for kids to hit a ball; in fact, the closest open area is along the Mississippi River. However, there are playgrounds every few blocks and many residents work out at the local Y or swim, curl, play squash and croquet at private clubs in the neighborhood (St. Paul Curling Club, vwww.stpaulcurlingclub.org; Commodore Squash & Fitness, http://commodoresquashclub.com; and The University Club, www.university clubofstpaul.com).

Posh though some of this district may be, there is still diversity. Townhouses, plain apartment buildings, and single-family ramblers built from the 1950s to the 1970s sit incongruously among the National Historic Register Victorians. As for the residents, approximately one-third of St. Paul's people of color live in this neighborhood, and minorities make up nearly 50% of its population. For over eighty years, the Hallie Q. Brown/Dr. Martin Luther King Community Center (270 N. Kent Street, www.hallieqbrown.org), has worked to make life here better for everyone and foster cross-cultural understanding. It provides daycare services, after-school and summer programs, and numerous cross-cultural activities. The center is also home to one of the Twin Cities' finest theaters, the Penumbra (Box Office, 651-224-3180, www.penumbratheatre.org), which features plays with African-American themes.

Transportation-wise, this area is so well-connected some families have been able to downsize to one car and others live completely car-free. Not only does bus service crisscross the district, but many of the quiet residential streets are good for walking and biking. An HourCar hybrid is stashed at 632 Selby, www.hourcar.org. And, the Central Corridor light-rail transit (LRT) line, scheduled to begin service in 2014, will connect downtown Minneapolis and St. Paul, with service primarily along University Avenue. For a Smart Trips Kit of neighborhood bus schedules, walking and biking maps, and coupons from neighborhood businesses, look online at www.smart-trips.org/smart_trips_summit_u.php or call 651-224-8555.

Web Sites: Summit-University Planning Council (District 8), 627 Selby Ave, 651-228-1855, http://summit-u.com; Ramsey Hill Association, www.ramseyhill.org

ZIP Codes: 55102, 55103, 55104

Post Office: 1430 Concordia Ave

Police Non-Emergency: Western District Patrol Team, 651-266-5512; General Information, 651-291-1111; www.stpaul.gov/index.aspx?nid=461

Emergency Hospitals: Regions Hospital, 640 Jackson St, 651-254-3456, www.regionshospital.com; HealthEast St. Joseph's Hospital, 69 W Exchange St, 651-232-3348, www.healtheast.org/st-joes.html; United Hospital, 333 N Smith Ave, St. Paul, 651-241-8000, www.unitedhospital.com

Library: www.sppl.org, Rondo Community Outreach Library at University and Dale

Community Resources: Ramsey Hill Historic District, www.ramseyhill.org; Cass Gilbert Society (historical architecture), www.cassgilbertsociety.org; Cathedral of Saint Paul, 239 Selby Ave, 651-228-1766, www.cathedralsaintpaul.org; Hallie Q. Brown/Dr. Martin Luther King Community Center, 270 N. Kent St, 651-224-4601, www.hallieqbrown.org; Mississippi Market (www.msmarket.coop), 622 Selby Ave, 651-310-9499; St. Paul Neighborhood Energy Consortium 624 Selby Ave, 651-221-4462, www.spnec.org; Penumbra Theatre Company, 270 N Kent St, Box Office, 651-224-3180, www.penumbratheatre.org; Commodore Squash Club, 79 Western Avenue N, 651-228-0501, http://commodoresquashclub.com; University Club; Germanic–American Institute, 301 Summit Avenue, 651-222-7027, www.gai-mn.org; Cathedral Hill YWCA, 375 Selby Ave, 651-222-3741, www.ywcaofstpaul.org; William Mitchell College of Law (www.wmitchell.edu)

Parks: www.stpaul.gov/index.aspx?nid=243; Webster Playground at 470 Selby; Dunning Recreation Center, 1221 Marshall Ave, has athletic fields, tennis courts, and a children's play area; Western Park and Sculpture Garden; Oxford Community Center and Jimmy Lee Recreation Center features a water park, basketball, and fitness equipment

Public Transportation: 612-373-3333, www.MetroTransit.org; buses travel along all major thoroughfares. The Central Corridor LRT will go down University Avenue. There is an HourCar location near Mississippi Market on Selby, www.hourcar.org.

MACALESTER-GROVELAND DISTRICT

Boundaries: North: Summit Ave; **West**: Mississippi River; **South**: Randolph Ave; **East**: Ayd Mill Rd

Universities and colleges located in or near the Mac-Groveland neighborhood (Macalester College, the University of St. Thomas and St. Paul Seminary, St. Catherine University, and William Mitchell College of Law) give this district a friendly, college-town feel.

Created in the 1880s when a group of Macalester College trustees bought a farm west of St. Paul and divided it into a campus and lots for houses, Mac-Groveland has become one of St. Paul's epicenters, bustling with academic and commercial energy. Grand Avenue, the main east-west thoroughfare, includes specialty retail shops, restaurants, and scores of places to eat, drink, and argue politics and religion—but there is very little parking.

Once a farm, then a commuter suburb, the history of Mac-Groveland has resulted in an interesting mixture of housing sizes, prices, and designs, with rents and house prices among the highest in St. Paul. Because of high student demand, the best time to look for an apartment is in late spring to early summer when students move out and sublets and leases become available.

More than three-fourths of Mac-Groveland's homes and apartments were built before 1940, so retro styling and mid-century modern architecture abound. Two-, three-, and four-bedroom bungalows and two-stories with garages and amenities such as hardwood floors can be found on most streets, with small apartment buildings, duplexes, and triplexes sprinkled in among the single-family homes. The west end features luxurious Mississippi River–front residences. Other large, gracious older homes line Summit Avenue and the curvy streets skirting Macalester College. High-rise condos and townhomes abut the Edgcumbe Recreation Area. On and near Grand Avenue, small art-deco apartment buildings are interspersed with the cafés and retail businesses that make Grand Avenue St. Paul's most lively commercial district. Because this is such a desirable area, many of the homes and apartment buildings have been extensively renovated, and some of the larger houses have been turned into multi-unit condos.

One hundred-foot-tall bluffs and the Mississippi River gorge lie at the western end of the neighborhood, where miles of river walking or bike riding are accessible via the river parkway.

Professionally staffed, hourly drop-in childcare for infants and preschoolers is available at KidsPark in Desnoyer Park, 651-603-0144, www.kidsparkdropin. org.

Web Site: Macalester-Groveland Community Council (District 14), 320 Griggs St S, 651-695-4000, www.macgrove.org

ZIP Code: 55105

Post Office: 1430 Concordia Ave

Police Non-Emergency: Western District Patrol Team, 651-266-5512; General Information, 651-291-1111; www.stpaul.gov/index.aspx?nid=461

Emergency Hospitals: Regions Hospital, 640 Jackson St, 651-254-3456, www. regionshospital.com; HealthEast St. Joseph's Hospital, 69 W Exchange St, 651-232-3348, www.healtheast.org/st-joes.html; United Hospital, 333 N Smith Ave, St. Paul, 651-241-8000, www.unitedhospital.com

Library: www.sppl.org; Merriam Park, 1831 Marshall Ave

Community Resources: Macalester College, www.macalester.edu; University of St. Thomas, www.stthomas.edu

Parks: Mississippi National River and Recreation Area features walking and biking paths, www.nps.gov/miss/index.htm; www.stpaul.gov/index. aspx?nid=243; Edgcumbe Recreational Area has tennis courts, athletic fields, and a gym

Public Transportation: 612-373-3333, www.MetroTransit.org; buses travel along Grand Ave, Snelling, Smith Ave, and Randolph

UNION PARK (MERRIAM PARK, SNELLING-HAMLINE, LEXINGTON-HAMLINE)

Boundaries: North: I-94, Cleveland Ave, University Ave; **West**: City limits at 33rd Ave, Mississippi River; **South**: Summit Ave; **East**: Lexington Pkwy

---

Merriam Park, Snelling-Hamline, and Lexington-Hamline neighborhoods have been merged into a new district, Union Park, but the name change hasn't caught on, as old residents and realtors still frequently identify these neighborhoods by their original names.
Cartoonist Charles Schultz (Peanuts) grew up in Merriam Park.

Merriam Park's attractiveness derives not only from the aura of urbane wilderness that graces its scenic riverfront and the polish of its well-kept homes, but

also from the interesting people who live here—and the fact that it's extremely convenient, no matter where you work.

Bordered by University Avenue on the north, the magnificent gorge of the Mississippi to the west, and the mansions of Summit Avenue to the south, Merriam Park is a mature community conveniently located midway between downtown Minneapolis and St. Paul. Minneapolis and its Hiawatha LRT are just a short hop away across the Lake Street/Marshall Avenue bridge and the Central Corridor LRT (expected to begin operation in 2014) will provide downtown St. Paul to downtown Minneapolis service along University Avenue.

Although it is in the center of urban activity today, Merriam Park was actually one of the Twin Cities' first suburbs, located—then—a couple of trolley stops outside of St. Paul. Colonel John Merriam, who in the 1880s owned much of the neighborhood's bluff land, envisioned the creation of a rural village built on large estates separated by abundant parkland. He built himself a luxurious house and sold lots to those who would agree to his requirement that homes built on this land cost at least $1,500—a sizable amount at the time.

Traces of Merriam Park's exclusive beginnings are still apparent along the Mississippi where the Town and Country Club (www.tcc-club.com), the state's first country club, and Eastcliff (www1.umn.edu/pres/eastcliff), home to the presidents of the University of Minnesota, lend the neighborhood an air of grandeur.

It seems every size and style of architecture is represented here, from large Queen Anne and Tudor Revivals reflective of Victorian taste to Arts and Crafts bungalows, low-rise Moderne apartment buildings and stunning contemporary row houses. Built to last, these homes and apartment buildings generally exhibit solid construction and craftsmanship, and loving attention to detail. Many of the big old homes have been converted into large duplexes or fourplexes, some with units that have as many as four bedrooms.

Not surprisingly, given the surrounding academic institutions, residents are extremely well educated. Of those 25 or older, over half have four-year college degrees and over 20% hold graduate or professional degrees.

Snelling-Hamline is located to the east of Merriam Park between Snelling and Hamline. The northern blocks of this neighborhood were decimated by the construction of I-94, and are now heavily commercial. Closer to Summit, you will find old brownstone apartments side-by-side with new duplexes and well-maintained older single-family homes that sit on long, narrow lots. The neighborhood pub, O'Gara's, at Snelling and Selby (www.ogaras.com), has a micro-brewery and offers music that ranges from an Irish jam session on Sunday nights to rock. They also offer free shuttle service to all Vikings and Wild home games.

Further east, **Lexington-Hamline** also straddles I-94 between Lexington and Hamline Avenues from University to Summit. North of the freeway is largely commercial, with Rainbow Foods, Cub Foods, Walmart, and Super Target, and a Common Bond Community called Skyline Tower that is home to many immigrants and refugees. Most of the neigborhood's residents live south of the freeway in single-family houses that have often been updated so that they look more appealing on the inside than on the out. The two sides of the neighborhood connect via Lexington and Hamline Avenues and a pedestrian bridge on Griggs Street. Like the neighborhoods farther west, Lex-Ham also has a college, Concordia University (www.csp.edu), a Lutheran liberal arts school that has a strong connection with the Twin Cities Hmong community and has been a significant partner in neighborhood improvement initiatives.

The major streets, Cleveland, Cretin, Selby, Marshall, Snelling, University, and Lexington, are busy and commercial, but add to the general convenience of the district with all the necessary goods and services, plus unique businesses like Choo Choo Bob's Train Store on Marshall (651-646-5252, www.choochoobobs. com). Coffeehouses, bakeries, and specialty shops are found on Marshall and Cleveland. The Midway Shopping Center, at University and Snelling avenues, offers staples at discount stores and supermarkets.

Events at the University of Minnesota and University of St. Thomas and other campuses in the area are only a walk, bike, or bus ride away, and residents of the more southern streets can easily stroll to many of the restaurants, shops, and conveniences of Grand Avenue. (For more about Grand Avenue, see **Shopping for the Home**.) With so many bungalows in the vicinity, the Merriam Park Library, at Marshall and Fairview, maintains a "Bungalow Collection," of books and magazines focused on bungalow homes and the Arts & Crafts movement.

Though not over-endowed with neighborhood parks and playgrounds, life here does offer the open splendor of the Mississippi bluffs. A pleasant hike along the river begins at Merriam Park, goes south to the Ford Parkway Bridge, then across the river and back up to the Marshall Avenue Bridge. Don't miss the color extravaganza in October. During winter, the country club's gates are left open so that neighbors can cross-country ski.

Web Sites: Union Park District Council (District 13), 1570 Concordia Ave, 651-645-6887, www.unionparkdc.org

ZIP Code: 55104

Post Office: 1430 Concordia Ave

Police Non-Emergency: Western District Patrol Team, 651-266-5512; General Information, 651-291-1111; www.stpaul.gov/index.aspx?nid=461

Emergency Hospitals: Regions Hospital, 640 Jackson St, 651-254-3456, www.regionshospital.com; HealthEast St. Joseph's Hospital, 69 W Exchange St, 651-232-3348, www.healtheast.org/st-joes.html; United Hospital, 333 N Smith Ave, St. Paul, 651-241-8000, www.unitedhospital.com; Fairview-University Medical Center, 2450 Riverside Ave, Minneapolis, 612-273-3000, www.fairview-university.fairview.org

Library: www.sppl.org; Merriam Park, 1831 Marshall Ave

Community Resources: Concordia University, www.csp.edu; University of St. Thomas, www.stthomas.edu; Lex-Ham Community Band, www.lexhamarts.org/band/index.html; Town and Country Club, 300 Mississippi River Blvd, 651-646-7121, www.tcc-club.com; Arts US African Diaspora arts programs for children, 221 Marshall Ave, 651-528-6871, www.arts-us.org

Parks: Mississippi National River and Recreation Area, www.nps.gov/miss/index.htm; www.stpaul.gov/index.aspx?nid=243; Dunning Park Recreation Center and Athletic Fields and ARTS US programs for children, Merriam Park Recreation Center has a skate park, basketball court, play area, tennis courts, and athletic fields

Public Transportation: 612-373-3333, www.MetroTransit.org; buses travel along Grand Ave, Snelling, University, St. Clair, Cleveland, Cretin, Randolph, and Marshall/Lake Street; the Central Corridor LRT will travel along University Avenue beginning in 2014; HourCar has a hub at Grand Ave and Macalester, www.hourcar.org

HIGHLAND DISTRICT

Boundaries: North: Randolph Ave; **West/South**: Mississippi River; **East**: I-35W, Homer St from W 7th St to Shepard Rd

Highland Park is a neighborhood where moving up doesn't necessarily mean moving out. From homes with character to ultra-luxe penthouses, there is housing here to fit most tastes and pocketbooks, although demand is such that it has historically been much easier to sell a home here than it is to find one to buy or rent.

Housing consists mostly of single-family homes, with apartments, duplexes, and condos clustered around the University of St. Catherine and West Seventh Street–Shepard Road. Architectural styles are exceptionally diverse. You can find everything from original farmhouses, bungalows and Cape Cods to 1960s split-levels and colonials. A 1950s housing boom brought blocks of small ramblers to the vicinity of the now-abandoned Ford plant. More substantial brick and stucco homes on correspondingly larger lots line Mt. Curve Boulevard and Highland Park Golf Course. The community also boasts a number of unique architect-designed residences including the gracious homes of Mississippi River Boulevard and Edgcumbe Road/Montcalm Place. Many of these have river views.

Highland is also home to two of the Twin Cities' only "Streamlined Moderne" buildings, the 1939 Mann Highland Theater on Cleveland and a stucco–and–glass block house at 1775 Hillcrest Avenue, that was also built in '39. Of less architectural but more historical interest, the elegant house at 1590 South Mississippi River Boulevard served as a prohibition era speakeasy known as the Hollyhocks Club and is said to have been a favorite hangout of gangsters John Dillinger and "Ma" Barker. The neighborhood's signature yellow stone water tower at the intersection of Snelling Avenue and Ford Parkway is listed on the National Register of Historic Places. It is open to residents one weekend every fall so that they can view the autumn colors from above.

Historically the city's primary Jewish neighborhood, this is where you will find kosher Cecil's Deli (651 Cleveland, 651-698-6276 www.cecilsdeli.com) and most of the city's synagogues.

Highland's main commercial area is clustered around the intersection of Cleveland Avenue and Ford Parkway. This shopping destination has it all—big-box and boutique, bookstores, groceries, department stores, bank, an historic movie theater, and some of the metro's favorite restaurants. Other assets in this district include O'Shaughnessy Auditorium at St. Catherine University, which is the St. Paul home of the Minnesota Orchestra and also provides an intimate venue for a wide variety of dance groups and other performances (2004 Randolph Avenue, 651-690-6700 http://oshaughnessy.stkate.edu). Well-regarded private schools Cretin-Derham Hall (www.cretin-derhamhall.org), St. Paul Academy/Summit School (www.spa.edu), and Talmud Torah of St. Paul (www.ttsp.org) are located here as well.

In fact, Highland residents often say that everything they want is right here and within walking distance—and yet no place is more convenient when they need to leave. Handily placed about halfway between the State Capitol and downtown Minneapolis, Highland is only about ten minutes from either the airport or the capitol, and a bus ride across the Ford Bridge connects it with Minneapolis' light rail.

The other major perk of living in this district is its proximity to greenspace and recreation areas. Highland Park (the park) is a hilly expanse with a municipal golf course, outdoor swimming pools, and cross-country ski trails. On the wild side, Hidden Falls and Crosby Farm Regional Park, adjacent to the southern end of Highland, offer walking and biking trails through the woods. The confluence of the Mississippi and Minnesota Rivers, which includes Minnehaha Falls, the Fort Snelling State Park, and the Minnesota River National Wildlife Refuge, is just across the Ford Bridge.

Great as Highland already is, it is also looking at new possibilities. With the closure of the Ford plant mentioned above, St. Paul has gained the largest space for development it has seen in decades, and city planners have an exceptionally "green" vision for these 125 acres that includes transit-oriented development connected to the Hiawatha LRT and the possibility of Jetson-like Personal Rapid Transit cars. Keep track of what the task force is considering at www.stpaul.gov/index.aspx?NID=1318.

Web Sites: Highland Park District Council (District 15), 1978 Ford Pkwy, 651-695-4005, www.highlanddistrictcouncil.org
ZIP Code: 55116
Post Office: 1715 W 7th St
Police Non-Emergency: Western District Patrol Team, 651-266-5512; General Information, 651-291-1111; www.stpaul.gov/index.aspx?nid=461
Emergency Hospitals: Regions Hospital, 640 Jackson St, 651-254-3456, www.regionshospital.com; HealthEast St. Joseph's Hospital, 69 W Exchange St, 651-232-3348, www.healtheast.org/st-joes.html; United Hospital, 333 N Smith Ave, St. Paul, 651-241-8000, www.unitedhospital.com; Fairview-University Medical Center, 2450 Riverside Ave, Minneapolis, 612-273-3000, www.fairview-university.fairview.org
Library: www.sppl.org; Highland Park, 1974 Ford Pkwy
Community Publications: *The Villager*, www.villagercomm.com

Community Resources: Old Highland Park Water Tower, Highland Fest Art Fair, www.highlandfest.com; St. Catherine University and O'Shaughnessy Auditorium, 2004 Randolph Ave, Box Office, 651-690-6700, http://oshaughnessy. stkate.edu

Parks: www.stpaul.gov/index.aspx?nid=243; Highland Park has a Golf Course, Frisbee golf, and a pool; Crosby Farms Regional Park Nature Area, www.nps. gov/miss/planyourvisit/crosfarm.htm

Public Transportation: 612-373-3333, www.MetroTransit.org; buses travel along Snelling Ave, Randolph, Cleveland, Cretin, and Ford Pkwy, connecting with the Hiawatha LRT at the 50th Street Station

WEST SEVENTH/FORT ROAD DISTRICT

Boundaries: North: Bluffs of Summit Hill and I-35E; **West**: I-35E, Homer St; **South**: Mississippi River; **East**: W Kellogg Blvd

Just to the west of downtown is St. Paul's old Uppertown, named for being the location of the "upper" of St. Paul's two boat landings on the Mississippi River. Known also as West Seventh, Fort Road (because the main drag, West Seventh Street/Shepard Road, leads to Fort Snelling), or the West End, this traditional immigrant neighborhood is St. Paul's historic heart and soul. This is where notorious bootlegger "Pig's Eye" Parrant set up his still and founded the city of "Pig's Eye," which we know as St. Paul. It is also the flood-prone docklands where many of St. Paul's earliest residents stepped off riverboats to begin making their homes on the frontier.

Don't get this district confused with "The West Side," which is across the river.

While the houses of West Seventh were not built on as grand a scale as the homes along Summit Avenue, many of them are older and at least as historic. On streets laid out around elegant Irvine Park, you'll find such treasures as Civil War–era Italianate and Greek Revivals, restored red brick row houses, and Victorian Queen Annes. This National Historic District is also the setting for Territorial Governor Alexander Ramsey's stone, two-story Second Empire house at 265 South Exchange Street, which, together with its surrounding English garden, is open for tours and holiday dances. Forepaugh's restaurant, located in one of the district's finest Victorian mansions at 276 South Exchange Street, is considered the grande dame of our local dining scene, 651-224-5606, www. forepaughs.com. In summer, eat on the roof of the portico and enjoy a stunning view of St. Paul.

As St. Paul expanded, earlier residents moved "up the hill" to Summit in the first of many flights away from the docklands, and West Seventh became the destination of workers arriving from Europe in search of jobs on railroads and in grain mills. Irish, German, Italian, and Czech—all the immigrant groups that built St. Paul—passed through here, not unlike Ellis Island. By the late 1800s, there were so many Czechs living in the neighborhood that Czech composer Antonin Dvorak stopped in at the now refurbished Czecho-Slovak Protection Society Hall on South Michigan Street while on his concert tour across America. Poles, too, began moving to the neighborhood in the late 19th century, and their Saint Stanislaus Catholic Church (www.ststans.org) still stands on Western Avenue. Eventually, these immigrants moved on as well and, as is often the case with urban areas, the large old houses became too big to manage for the working classes who were left and were divided up for flophouses and brothels. Many of the buildings, including a house designed by State Capitol architect Cass Gilbert, became so derelict they had to be torn down.

Another part of the history of West Seventh has literally been washed away. As early as the 1850s, Italian families built houses along the levee below 7th Street (the site of today's Shepard Road). Their community, known as Little Italy, with its flocks of chickens and community ovens, was condemned in 1959 after being inundated by a series of floods. Cossetta Eventi restaurant on West Seventh (www.cossettaeventi.com), a block from the Xcel Energy Center, was moved up from the flood plain and has an awning reminding us all that it is "just a piece of the levee." In the meantime, the land along Shepard Road was left to become an industrial mess, with breweries, power plants and a petroleum "tank-farm."

Finally, in the 1970s, when much of West Seventh was in danger of being bulldozed for an industrial park, a group of residents stepped in, rolled up their sleeves and formed the West Seventh/Fort Road Federation (www.fortroadfederation.org). Their efforts resulted in the area's designation as an Historic District. The federation has also undertaken a number of redevelopment projects that have brought a mix of new and rehabilitated single family housing, apartments, condos, lofts, and townhouses onto the market. One of the projects, Upper Landing, off Shepard Road, is a new urban village on the riverfront just steps away from the Science Museum of Minnesota and Xcel

Center (hockey, concerts, etc.). Built by several established local builders, the seven-block complex includes market rate apartments, affordable housing, high-end townhomes, lofts and condominiums, a coffee shop and a 24-hour fitness facility—and excellent access to the river.

With a large stock of modest brick-and-frame homes that have so far stood the test of time, this is also a good place to look for a house to renovate. The West Seventh/Fort Road Federation posts information about city home improvement loan programs on its web site: (http://www.fortroadfederation. org/loan.html). While the bedrock that creates the river channel and underlies this neighborhood sometimes makes renovation of houses and upgrading of utilities difficult, the river itself is an outstanding source for neighborhood rec- reation. Miles of trails along the river offer a bird's eye view of the Mississippi; and Crosby Farm Park, off Shepard Road, is a bluff and floodplain forest com- plete with a boardwalk running through its marsh and a network of hiking and biking trails.

The east end of West Seventh, by Xcel Energy Center in Downtown, is con- sidered the commercial gateway to the neighborhood. Known as Seven Corners, this lively, bustling end of the district is a prime location for antique shops, bars, and excellent restaurants. Try finding a seat at Cosetta Eventi (211 West Seventh, 651-224-8419, www.cossettaeventi.com)! Actually, though the line winds round the building, by the time you get your sausage pizza, you will be able to find a place to sit and will have made a few new friends, too, so don't be deterred. (And don't skip the making friends part—you may need to share a table!) They also do excellent takeout. If your taste runs more to Irish pubs, The Liffey (175 West Sev- enth, www.theliffey.com), kitty-corner from the Xcel Energy Center, is not nearly as chaotic, and is known for its blue-ribbon Guinness and menu of Irish favorites like bangers and mash. It also serves up a wide variety of appetizers you can split before a game. At the beginning of the street, the region's classic diner, Mickey's Dining Car (36 West Seventh, www.mickeysdiningcar.com), serves breakfast and burgers 24 hours a day. You've probably seen Mickey's in the movies (*The Mighty Ducks*, *A Prairie Home Companion*).

Besides all the new housing, the neighborhood has also scored a new Mississippi Market co-op at 1500 West Seventh (www.msmarket.coop). A new Trader Joe's sits just over the line in Highland Park on the corner of Randolph and Lexington (www.traderjoes.com).

Amazingly convenient, West Seventh is well situated for working practi- cally anywhere. West Seventh Street/Fort Road is a high-frequency bus route with buses connecting with the Hiawatha LRT at the Mall of America, 28th Avenue, Bloomington Central Station, and Lindbergh Terminal (airport).

Web Site: West Seventh/Fort Road Federation, 974 W 7th St, 651-298-5599, www.fortroadfederation.org

ZIP Codes: 55102, 55116

Post Offices: 1715 W 7th St, 408 St. Peter Street

Police Non-Emergency: Central District Patrol Team, 651-266-5565; General Information, 651-291-1111; www.stpaul.gov/index.aspx?nid=461

Emergency Hospitals: Regions Hospital, 640 Jackson St, 651-254-3456, www.regionshospital.com; HealthEast St. Joseph's Hospital, 69 W Exchange St, 651-232-3348, www.healtheast.org/st-joes.html; United Hospital, 333 N Smith Ave, St. Paul, 651-241-8000, www.unitedhospital.com; Fairview-University Medical Center, 2450 Riverside Ave, Minneapolis, 612-273-3000, www.fairview-university.fairview.org

Library: www.sppl.org; Central Library, 90 W 4th St; West Seventh Library, 265 Oneida St

Community Publications: *Community Reporter*, http://communityreporter.org

Community Resources: Governor Alexander Ramsey House, 265 Exchange St; West Seventh Community Center, 265 Oneida St, www.west7th.org

Parks: www.stpaul.gov/index.aspx?nid=243; Irvine Park, 281 Walnut St (Ryan Ave & Walnut St) is a popular setting for wedding photographs; North High Bridge Park and Sculpture Garden; Linwood Park and Recreation Center; Palace Recreation Center has athletic fields and a children's play area; Mississippi Riverfront and Crosby Farm Regional Park, www.nps.gov/miss/planyourvisit/crosfarm.htm

Public Transportation: 612-373-3333, www.MetroTransit.org; buses travel along Grand Avenue, W 7th Street, St. Clair, Randolph

NORTHWEST ST. PAUL

(West of I-35E and North of University)

ST. ANTHONY PARK DISTRICT (AND FALCON HEIGHTS)

Boundaries: *St Anthony Park:* North: city limits (Larpenteur); **West**: city limits (Hwy 280); **South**: I-94, B.N. Railroad; **East**: Cleveland Ave, Snelling Ave, St. Paul Campus of the University of Minnesota, and the Minnesota State Fair Grounds; ***Falcon Heights:* North**: Roselawn Ave; **West**: Fulham St; **South**: Hoyt Ave and Como; **East**: Hamline Ave

Tame hills and mature trees provide a park-like setting for a variety of stolid brick apartments and stately older houses in these neighborhoods. Falcon Heights is technically a St. Paul suburb, but hard to differentiate from the rest of this community.

The lovely curved streets of **St. Anthony Park** were laid out in the 1870s by landscape architect Horace Cleveland. His idea was to build a community of large rural estates adapted to the natural contours of the land, thus creating

the meandering streets and oddly shaped parks and greenways that make up this district.

Although "The Park" still offers the original tranquility its designer sought, the city has long since grown up around it, and now the Burlington Northern industrial/commercial rail corridor divides it into northern and southern halves. North St. Anthony Park is an affluent twist of wooded residential streets containing larger Colonials and variations of Midwestern squares, the majority of which were built between 1900 and 1929. Many of the newer buildings are apartments, where university faculty and students make up a good number of the residents. South St. Anthony Park is a more modest area made up mostly of single-family bungalows and Midwestern-square style houses. In 2003, the warehouse district that sits in between these neighborhoods was designated the University-Raymond Historic District. Groups dedicated to creating a better central corridor transit system have recently begun transforming this area from industrial to mixed-use, transit-oriented residential. One of the first of these projects was 212-unit Emerald Gardens (www.egliving.com), which is located on the exact border of Minneapolis and St. Paul.

Small commercial districts containing numerous locally owned businesses are within walking distance of most homes in the St. Anthony Park District. At the west end of Como near Carter Avenue, and often credited with putting St. Anthony on the map, are the Luther Northwestern Theological Seminary (www.luthersem.edu) and the surrounding shopping area that includes Micawbers Bookstore (www.micawbers.com), Muffuletta Café (www.muffuletta.com), Finnish Bistro (www.finnishbistro.com), and The Bibelot Shop (www.bibelotshops.com). The University-Raymond Commercial Historic District is the commercial core of the Saint Paul Midway. Hampden Park co-op on Raymond (651-646-6686, www.hampdenparkcoop.com) is what you imagine when you think "co-op." It sells many bulk products and encourages members to work in the store.

Following the eastern "arm" of the neighborhood, Midway West (Energy Park Drive) is a mixed-use strip of development that went up in the 1980s and includes apartment complexes, office space, and Midway Stadium, home of the St. Paul Saints Northern League baseball team (http://saintsbaseball.com). Although the Saints are a minor league team, their games are the hottest ticket in town, due in part to their wacky promotions, such as free back rubs during games and the famed pig that carries out new balls.

As befits a neighborhood of professional and academic households, a Carnegie library, endowed in 1917 by "the patron saint of libraries," Andrew Carnegie, is the neighborhood centerpiece. St. Anthony also has its own band, and is home to the Music in the Park Sunday Concert Series. The highlight of the year is a 4th of July celebration that starts with a morning run, features a neighborhood bike/trike/lawnmower brigade parade and a patriotic speech contest, and ends with an evening concert and dance.

Several small parks provide children's playgrounds, tennis courts, winter skating rinks, and picnic tables. Access to the trails and parks along the Mississippi River is gained from city streets.

The St. Anthony Park Community Foundation (www.sapfoundation.org) is the city of St. Paul's only neighborhood-based charitable foundation. It provides grants to support activities of the St. Anthony Park community, including energy conservation, the arts, education, health, and housing.

The vast open spaces that take up two-thirds of **Falcon Heights**—the University of Minnesota St. Paul Campus, the Minnesota State Fairgrounds, U of M Golf Course, and Gibbs Farm Museum—create the impression of an almost rural area, and don't leave much room for housing. In fact, most of this 2-square-mile city's streets are east of Snelling, between Hoyt and Roselawn Avenue. Laid out in a standard grid pattern, they are in marked contrast to the west side of the city, where the curvy blocks of the University Grove development take their cue from neighboring St. Anthony Park. Situated on University-owned land, University Grove consists of 103 architect-designed homes built for professors and administrators over a 60-year period from the 1920s into the 1990s. They were described as an "architectural time capsule" of modern America in a 1989 article about the neighborhood in *The New York Times*. While homeownership there is basically limited to University faculty and staff, there are occasional rentals available, usually when professors go on sabbatical. Check the University Grove web page for pictures and information, www1.umn.edu/ugrove.

Conventional suburban-style single-family homes, circa 1920–1970, can also be found here, as well as newer townhomes and condominiums. The city's newest development, Town Square, at Snelling and Larpenteur, combines apartments and townhouses with service-oriented businesses like restaurants and a beauty salon. Located on the fringe of this neighborhood, at 1579 Hamline, Coffee Grounds (www.thecoffeegrounds.net) is the quintessential neighborhood meetup place, with music, coffee, and free WiFi for customers.

As befits the home of a principal campus of the University of Minnesota, Falcon Heights is considered the very best educated city in Minnesota, and one of the best educated in the country (www.city-data.com/top12.html). Nearly three-fourths of its over-25 population holds bachelor's degrees and nearly 40% hold graduate or professional degrees. No surprise here that the most common occupation is post-secondary teacher, followed closely by scientist!

While sleepy most of the time, this neighborhood wakes with a start during the state fair. Then most Falcon Heights streets have parking restrictions to ensure that they remain accessible to emergency vehicles, but the city does provide residents with special parking permits. While the fair can be a nuisance, the increasing willingness of fair visitors to use the bus has made a big difference to traffic in this area over the last few years.

Web Sites: St. Anthony Park Community Council (District 12), 890 Cromwell Ave, 651-649-5992, www.sapcc.org; City of Falcon Heights, 2077 W Larpenteur Ave, 651-792-7600, www.falconheights.org

ZIP Codes: 55104, 55114, 55108, 55113

Post Office: 2286 Como; 2000 County Road B2 W, Roseville

Police Non-Emergency: Western District Patrol Team, 651-266-5512; General Information, 651-291-1111; www.stpaul.gov/index.aspx?nid=461. Falcon Heights contracts police service from the City of St. Anthony, 3301 Silver Lake Rd, Saint Anthony, 612-782-3350.

Emergency Hospitals: Regions Hospital, 640 Jackson St, 651-254-3456, www.regionshospital.com; HealthEast St. Joseph's Hospital, 69 W Exchange St, 651-232-3348, www.healtheast.org/st-joes.html; United Hospital, 333 N Smith Ave, St. Paul, 651-241-8000, www.unitedhospital.com; Fairview-University Medical Center, 2450 Riverside Ave, Minneapolis, 612-273-3000, www.fairview-university.fairview.org

Library: www.sppl.org: St. Anthony Park, 2245 Como Ave

Public Schools: Falcon Heights is part of the Roseville School District, 65-635-1600, www.isd623.org

Community Publications: *Park Bugle*, www.parkbugle.org

Community Resources: Midway Stadium and the Saint Paul Saints baseball team, 1771 Energy Park Dr, Tickets 651-644-6659, http://saintsbaseball.com; Arts Festival, www.stanthonyparkartsfestival.org; St. Anthony Park Community Band, www.stanthonyparkband.org; Gibbs Farm Museum of Pioneer and Dakotah Life, 2097 W Larpenteur Ave, www.rchs.com/gbbsfm2.htm; University of Minnesota St. Paul Campus, www1.umn.edu/twincities/index.php; Minnesota State Fairgrounds, www.mnstatefair.org; University-Raymond Historic Area; Minnesota State Horticultural Society headquarters, www.northerngardener.org

Parks: www.stpaul.gov/index.aspx?nid=243; Langford Park has a playground, tennis courts, and a winter skating rink. Falcon Heights Parks and Recreation, www.ci.falcon-heights.mn.us (click on Parks and Recreation); leashed dogs are allowed in all city parks; Community Park includes tennis courts, athletic fields, playground, and a prairie with a walking trail.

Public Transportation: 612-373-3333, www.MetroTransit.org; buses travel along Snelling Ave, Como Ave, Cleveland, Buford, Gortner, Fairview, University Avenue, Larpenteur, and Raymond. U of M #52 routes run from many parts of the Twin Cities to the St. Paul campus on weekdays; the University Circulator is free and provides service every 15 minutes during the regular University school calendar to bus connections on the St. Paul and Minneapolis campuses. A Park & Ride lot is located at Eustis and Como aves. The Central Corridor Light Rail Line down University Avenue is scheduled to begin service in 2014. There is an HourCar hub at 2265 Como, www.hourcar.org.

HAMLINE-MIDWAY DISTRICT

Boundaries: North: Burlington-Northern Railroad; **West**: Cleveland Ave; **South**: University Ave; **East**: Lexington Pkwy

Just east of St. Anthony Park, midway between the downtowns of Minneapolis and St. Paul, the Hamline-Midway neighborhood is one of the busiest parts of the Twin Cities. In fact, University and Snelling is the busiest intersection in the entire state of Minnesota.

University, which parallels Interstate 94, has always been a major route between the two Twin Cities—first by horse-drawn carriage, then electric streetcar, then by car, now by rail. Central Corridor Light Rail Transit is expected to begin service in 2014, and it's bringing with it a lot of transit-oriented and mixed use development.

Large residences lining the narrow streets that immediately surround Hamline University were built as late as the 1960s, but the farther away you get from the college, the older and more modest the housing becomes.

To learn about the history of individual homes here, including some 1880s Victorians, check out Placeography (www.placeography.org/index.php/Hamline-Midway%2C_Saint_Paul%2C_Minnesota).

Though the neighborhood is not exactly what you'd call charming, it is not without its charms. Neighborhood gardens, for example. With so little open space, several groups have organized to create cooperative gardens in what space there is. At Midway Green Spirit Community Garden, at Taylor and Hamline, people are raising food for themselves and extra to donate to local food shelves. At Horton Park, volunteers maintain a native plant garden that is the setting for many community events. Other volunteers plant and maintain Snelling Avenue planters. The most significant open space, 10-acre Newell Park in the northwest sector of the neighborhood off Pierce Butler Route, boasts a rare rolling landscape and old oak trees.

While shopping runs big-box, Midway Used and Rare Books, at the corner of University and Snelling (www.midwaybook.com), attracts collectors from all over the world for its rare books, vintage comics, and pre-1960 magazines.

Then there's the entertainment. The Turf Club, at 1601 University, (www.turfclub.net/Home.html, 651-647-0486), is one of Twin Cities most rockin' venues, booking both out-of-town and local talent. At the opposite end of the spectrum, Gingko Coffeehouse (721 North Snelling Avenue, www.ginkgocoffee.com) has a family-friendly atmosphere, with local professional and amateur music and weekly art and story hours.

Despite the fact that the Midway area is engaged in a period of significant transition, derelict housing is still a concern, and so is crime.

Web Site: Hamline-Midway Coalition (District 11), 1564 Lafond Ave, 651-646-1986, www.hamlinemidwaycoalition.org

ZIP Code: 55104

Post Office: 1430 Concordia Ave

Police Non-Emergency: Western District Patrol Team, 651-266-5512; General Information, 651-291-1111; www.stpaul.gov/index.aspx?nid=461

Emergency Hospitals: Regions Hospital, 640 Jackson St, 651-254-3456, www.regionshospital.com; HealthEast St. Joseph's Hospital, 69 W Exchange St, 651-232-3348, www.healtheast.org/st-joes.html; United Hospital, 333 N Smith Ave, St. Paul, 651-241-8000, www.unitedhospital.com; Fairview-University Medical Center, 2450 Riverside Ave, Minneapolis, 612-273-3000, www.fairview-university.fairview.org

Library: www.sppl.org; Hamline-Midway Branch Library, 1558 W Minnehaha Ave

Community Resources: Hamline University, www.hamline.edu; Friends School of Minnesota, www.fsmn.org; Hamline Midway Environmental Group, 651-646-1986; Hamline Midway History Corps, www.hamlinemidwayhistory.org

Parks: www.stpaul.gov/index.aspx?nid=243; Newell Park

Public Transportation: 612-373-3333, www.MetroTransit.org; high-frequency buses travel along Snelling Ave, Como Ave, Cleveland, Buford, Gortner, Fairview, University Avenue, Larpenteur, and Raymond; Central Corridor Light Rail down University connects downtown St. Paul to downtown Minneapolis; Amtrak Midway Station, 730 Transfer Rd, www.amtrak.com

THOMAS-DALE (FROGTOWN) DISTRICT

Boundaries: North: B.N. Railroad; **West**: Lexington Pkwy; **South**: University Ave; **East**: I-35E

Because of their high concentrations of foreclosures and vacant properties, Frogtown, the North End, Payne Phalen, and Dayton's Bluff have been named Invest Saint Paul priority areas, and in 2010 the city was awarded Federal Neighborhood Stabilization Program money to help rehabilitate them.

In the 1880s, when Germans first settled here to be near railyard jobs, they called their marshy new home, Froschburg, or Frog City, probably for their croaking companions outside. Today, the marshes, with their frog choruses, are long gone and Frogtown has the lowest ratio of greenspace per resident of any Saint Paul neighborhood.

In place of the marshes are modest worker cottages built by the state's earliest residents, as well as newer two-story Midwestern squares and ramblers. Some of the lots are narrow, apparently the result of subdivisions by enterprising residents, and in some places two houses are built on a single lot, one house behind the other. Over half of the housing is pre-1940, and many of the cottages are over 100 years old. The Ramsey County Historical Society (www.rchs.com) did a survey and found houses dating from the 1860s and

1870s along Sherburne, Charles, and Como avenues east of Rice Street. They also discovered a concentration of 1880s houses along the streets extending westward between Rice and Dale. The historical society says you can recognize these oldest houses by their arched window and door openings, brick window hoods, and frilly open porches.

Thomas-Dale is the city's most diverse neighborhood, with many Hmong, Lao, Oromo, African-American and Latino residents, and a mile-long business district along University Avenue that boasts scores of Asian and African restaurants and markets.

Churches here also have ethnic origins, including a striking monument to the area's early European immigrants, the baroque masterpiece Church of St. Agnes at 548 Lafond Avenue, which is easily recognized by its 200-foot-high green onion bell tower. The Twin Cities Catholic Chorale sings the 10 o'clock Latin High Mass on Sundays. Check the church web site for pictures and more information, www.stagnes.net.

Though the neighborhood is beset by poverty, crime and blight, it does offer modestly priced homes, active and engaged residents, and easy access to the I-94 freeway. The Central Corridor Light Rail Transit line will pass through this neighborhood along University.

Web Sites: Thomas-Dale (District 7), 533 Dale St N, 651-789-7407 (www.d7mix. org)

ZIP Code: 55103

Post Offices: 40 Arlington Ave; 1430 Concordia Ave

Police Non-Emergency: Western District, 651-266-5512; Central District, 651-266-5563; General Information, 651-291-1111; www.stpaul.gov/index. aspx?nid=461

Emergency Hospitals: Regions Hospital, 640 Jackson St, 651-254-3456, www. regionshospital.com; HealthEast St. Joseph's Hospital, 69 W Exchange St, 651-232-3348, www.healtheast.org/st-joes.html; United Hospital, 333 N Smith Ave, St. Paul, 651-241-8000, www.unitedhospital.com

Library: www.sppl.org; Rondo Community Outreach Library at University and Dale

Parks: www.stpaul.gov/index.aspx?nid=243; West Minnehaha Park and Recreation Center has athletic fields and a basketball court; Biff Adams Ice Arena, 743 N Western, www.co.ramsey.mn.us/parks/Ice/communityarenas.htm, 651-558-2200

Community Resources: Church of St. Agnes, 550 W Lafond Ave, on the National Historic Register, www.stagnes.net; Frogtown Gardens, www.frogtowngardens.org; Jackson Street Roundhouse/Minnesota Transportation Museum, www.mtmuseum.org; Hmong Cultural Center, www.hmongcc.org

Public Transportation: 612-373-3333, www.MetroTransit.org; buses travel along Como, Thomas, Rice St, University Ave, Dale St; Central Corridor LRT will travel along University, probably with a station at Dale

COMO DISTRICT

Boundaries: North: Hoyt Ave, Larpenteur Ave, and the City of Roseville; **West**: Snelling Ave and the City of Falcon Heights; **South**: B.N. Railroad, Como Park, W Maryland Ave; **East**: Dale St

When it's minus 25 degrees, and the rest of the folks in the Twin Cities are fantasizing about someplace warm, all Como residents have to do is step next door to the tropical rainforest inside the glimmering glass Victorian Conservatory in Como Park. With a million visitors each year at the zoo alone, Como (www.comozooconservatory.org) is the most-used park in the seven-county metro area. St. Paul's equivalent of Central Park, 450-acre Como Park comprises over 40% of this district. The centerpiece of what is known as St. Paul's "Garden District," the park features the city's main recreation lake, a zoo, amusement park, 18-hole golf course, miles of trails, a Japanese garden, bandshell, and extensive picnic grounds where throngs of picnickers enjoy summer evenings much as they did at the turn of the 20th century when they rode out to the lake in horse-drawn omnibuses.

While this cozy, family-friendly neighborhood surrounds the park and Lake Como, none of the homes are actually lakeside, although many of them enjoy lake and park views. The oldest houses were built on the lake's south and west sides, some of them as summer villas for visitors from the South. Later waves of building in the 1940s, '70s, and '80s added a mix of spacious Craftsman homes with sun porches, Tudors, and moderately priced bungalows, many of whose owners choose to remodel instead of relocating. Two-thirds of the homes in the

district are owner-occupied, but you'll find plenty of rental apartments in the vicinity of Energy Park Drive.

On the western edge of this neighborhood lies the Minnesota State Fairgrounds, which is viewed alternately as an asset and a liability. A perennial controversy at State Fair time has to do with those residents who allow fairgoers to park in their yards. While this brings in extra cash for some, it also clogs traffic and turns the usually tranquil neighborhoods into noisy parking lots for almost two weeks each August.

Shopping is close by at the Midway shopping area, to the south, where there are banks, groceries, discount stores, big-box retail, at Rosedale Shopping Center, as well as at the strip malls along Highway 36 to the north in Roseville. And then there's Java Train Café at 1341 Pascal Street (www.javatraincafe.com). It's a coffee shop…and an ice cream store…and a café that's at the top of the list for kid-friendly dining in the Twin Cities. Great place to stop and visit with the locals when you're out househunting!

On top of all its at-home amenities, it's also easy to get to both downtowns via public transit or car, and five local colleges are only a bike ride away. Not all residents have to be commuters, however. Energy Park Business Center, on the southern end of the neighborhood, is home to Kemps Ice Cream and other national corporations, as well as U.S. Bancorp, which employs over 2000 people.

Web Sites: Como Park Community Council (District 10), 1224 Lexington Pkwy N, 651-644-3889, www.district10comopark.org

ZIP Codes: 55103, 55108, 55117

Post Offices: 2286 Como Ave; 2017 Buford Ave; 40 Arlington Ave E

Police Non-Emergency: Western District Patrol Team, 651-266-5512; General Information, 651-291-1111; www.stpaul.gov/index.aspx?nid=461

Emergency Hospitals: Regions Hospital, 640 Jackson St, 651-254-3456, www.regionshospital.com; HealthEast St. Joseph's Hospital, 69 W Exchange St, 651-232-3348, www.healtheast.org/st-joes.html; United Hospital, 333 N Smith Ave, St. Paul, 651-241-8000, www.unitedhospital.com; Fairview-University Medical Center, 2450 Riverside Ave, Minneapolis, 612-273-3000, www.fairview-university.fairview.org

Library: www.sppl.org: St. Anthony Park, 2245 Como; Hamline-Midway, 1558 W Minnehaha Ave

Community News: *Park Bugle*, www.parkbugle.org; *The Monitor*, www.monitorsaintpaul.com

Community Resources: Twin Cities Model Railroad Museum, 1021 Bandana Boulevard E, 651-647-9628, www.tcmrm.org; Lubavitch Yeshiva of Minnesota; Metro Deaf School, www.metrodeafschool.org

Parks: www.stpaul.gov/index.aspx?nid=243; Como Park, Conservatory, Golf Course, and Zoo; Comotown Amusement Park (www.comotown.com);

Como Aquatic Park (scheduled to open in 2012); North Dale and NW Como Recreation Centers

Public Transportation: 612-373-3333, www.MetroTransit.org; buses travel along Front St/Energy Park Dr, Horton, Larpenteur, Victoria, and Dale

NORTH END DISTRICT

Boundaries: North: Larpenteur Ave; **West:** Dale St, Lexington Pkwy; **South:** B.N. Railroad; **East:** I-35E

Heading north from the State Capitol on Rice Street, you cross the railroad tracks and enter the city's North End District, a mix of residential and commercial/industrial properties with a distinctly small town feel. The streets south of Maryland Avenue (which bisects the district) include an intact working-class enclave of small Victorian wood frames on narrow lots. Weathered but iron-strong, they were built by railyard and millworkers in the 1870s and 1880s.

Adding to the atmosphere of deep time are three large cemeteries. Pre–Civil War Oakland, east of Rice Street, is the Midwest's oldest cemetery, and is the final resting place of many of St. Paul's early statesmen, including founding father Henry Sibley. Their free walking tours are a painless and interesting way to learn about the history of Minnesota (http://oaklandcemeterymn.com). Calvary, west of Como, which dates from 1866, is the Twin Cities' oldest Catholic cemetery and the final resting place of Archbishop John Ireland. Elmhurst Cemetery, off Wheelock Parkway, dates from 1858.

North of Maryland has a more suburban feel, with curving streets, larger lots, and houses built mostly in the 1930s–60s. Housing here includes single- and multi-family dwellings, and large apartment complexes. Picturesque Wheelock Parkway, which begins in Como, winds east-west through the northern part of the neighborhood following the edge of a sheer bluff, connecting lakes Como and Phalen. A great place to run or bike, Wheelock Parkway features newer

split-levels, ramblers, Colonials and a few Tudor style homes. Some come with spectacular views of downtown St. Paul—and even wild turkeys.

Convenient shopping is available on thoroughfares, including Rice Street, and Maplewood Mall is a short drive north on White Bear Avenue. There is also easy access to highways 35E, I-94 and 36, and the U of M campus.

Web Site: District 6 Planning Council, 213 Front Ave, 651-488-4485, www. district6stpaul.org

ZIP Codes: 55103, 55117

Post Office: 40 Arlington Ave E

Police Non-Emergency: Central District, 651-266-5563; General Information, 651-291-1111; www.stpaul.gov/index.aspx?nid=461

Emergency Hospitals: Regions Hospital, 640 Jackson St, 651-254-3456, www. regionshospital.com; HealthEast St. Joseph's Hospital, 69 W Exchange St, 651-232-3348, www.healtheast.org/st-joes.html

Library: www.sppl.org; Rice Street, 1011 Rice St

Community Resources: Jackson Street Roundhouse train museum, off I-35E and Pennsylvania, 651-228-0263, www.mtmuseum.org/jsrh.shtml

Parks: www.stpaul.gov/index.aspx?nid=243; Rice Street Recreation Center has a gym, 1/2 basketball court and athletic fields; Willow Reserve Nature Area; Marydale Park is on Loeb Lake, which has been designated a children's fishing pond and is stocked with crappies and bluegills. Gateway Trail, www. dnr.state.mn.us/state_trails/gateway/index.htmls, is an 18-mile converted rail bed that begins at Cayuga/L'Orient Streets, travels northeast through the cities of Maplewood, North St. Paul, and Oakdale, through Washington County, and ends at Pine Point Regional Park, 4 miles northwest of the city of Stillwater.

Public Transportation: 612-373-3333, www.MetroTransit.org; buses travel Jackson St, Rice St, Dale, Arlington, Maryland, Front St, Larpenteur

EAST ST. PAUL AREA

(East of I-35E and North of I-94)

East St. Paul projects a certain kind of been there, done that ennui, with signs of optimism and complete disillusionment living next door to each other on many blocks. And yet, though it's generally lacking in curb appeal, it is filled with surprises.

Covering nearly a third of the city, this huge area has always been working-class and industrial, but became severely blighted over the last 30 years, as the ~ories that used to be here closed and the workers who lived near them lost jobs. The area began suffering from deteriorating property, increasing ~y, and rising crime. Then, in the late 1990s, in an attempt to turn this district around, the St. Paul Port Authority, University of Minnesota College of Architecture and Landscape Architecture, and a number of nonprofits, as well as corporations such as Wells Fargo and 3M, came together to create the Phalen Corridor. This 10-year, hundreds-of-millions-of-dollars project has won numerous awards, including the EPA's 2005 Phoenix Award, and the "Most Heart Warming Revival of the Metro Area" in 2004 from *Twin Cities Business* magazine. It included the construction of a new street, 2.5-mile-long Phalen Boulevard, which runs from 35-E east to Johnson Parkway, a new YMCA (www.ymcatwincities.org) and connected public school, new single-family homes and townhomes, and the conversion of rundown Phalen Shopping Center into senior housing. It also created Ames Lake, the nation's first wetland reclaimed from a shopping center parking lot.

And it brought new recreation amenities into the area, including linkage of the Bruce Vento, Willard Munger and Gateway bike trails, Vertical Endeavors indoor rock-climbing facility (651-776-1430, www.verticalendeavors.com), and an extreme skate park. Contemporary housing includes several mixed-income projects such as The Brownstones on Swede Hollow Park (www.brownstoneson swedehollowpark.com), just steps from downtown, and Phalen Village near Ames Lake.

Ames Lake, which is now surrounded by suburban front-loaded town-houses and condos, turned out to be a cautionary tale about how good ideas can be subverted by private development, but nearby Lake Phalen is still and always will be available to the public. One of the Twin Cities' treasures, it has a beautiful 18-hole public golf course, St. Paul's only swimming beach, walking/biking/skating paths that are much less crowded than those around the Minneapolis lakes, and a shoreline and surrounding wetlands that have been restored to their natural state. In the summer you can rent sailboats, and in the winter, the park offers cross-country ski lessons. Home to many events during the St. Paul Winter Carnival, it also hosts dragonboat racing in summer.

Long a stepping stone for immigrants, the neighborhood is home now to many Asians, Latinos, and African refugees.

PAYNE-PHALEN DISTRICT

Boundaries: North: Larpenteur Ave; **West**: I-35E; **South**: Grove St, B.N. Railroad; **East**: Johnson Pkwy, McAfee St

While many of the blighting influences that have had a negative effect on property values in the area have been removed, this is still a tough neighborhood, particularly south of Maryland.

If you choose to live here, however, you will not only have easy access to I-35 and I-94, you will also be close to the city's finest recreation amenity, Lake Phalen (see description above). Not only is the park on a par with any park

Minneapolis, but the streets closest to it also boast a variety of attractive, well-built, well-kept, larger homes.

Modest two-story frame houses, bungalows, and Midwestern squares, as well as a smattering of unique turn-of-the-20th-century Victorians, fill out most of the rest of this neighborhood—and some of the houses are quite historic.

There are two historic areas in Payne-Phalen: Railroad Island and Swede Hollow.

Railroad Island (so named because of its surrounding railroad tracks) is located at the southwest tip of the neighborhood, and is the closest East Side neighborhood to downtown. A good place to look for an historic fixer-upper, houses here are typically large, with a tower on one corner. That detail is referenced in the newly constructed Brownstones on Swede Hollow Park (www.brownstonesonswedehollowpark.com), on Payne Avenue, backing up to Swede Hollow Park.

Swede Hollow, a small valley nestled between the Dayton's Bluff and Railroad Island communities, holds a fascinating history and remains a place of beauty here, even though it no longer has residents. Its history began in the 1860s when industry attracted Swedish immigrants to St. Paul. They settled in the little valley and named it Svenska Dalen or Swede Hollow. As the Swedish moved up to fancier digs, other immigrant people moved into the homes: Polish, Italian and then Mexican Americans. But in December 1956, the city Health Department discovered that Swede Hollow had no sewer or city water service and declared the Hollow a health hazard. The city moved out the last remaining residents and burned the buildings, and the area then reverted to the wild. In the 1970s, however, East Side residents and the St. Paul Garden Club joined together to create a nature center in the old ravine. You can get to it from Drewry Street and Beaumont. The unique character of Swede Hollow has provided inspiration to generations of local artists. Many of their original sketches, engravings and paintings are housed at the Minnesota History Center, www. mnhs.org.

Payne-Phalen's primary retail area is Payne Avenue, one of the Twin Cities' most intact turn-of-the-20th-century commercial districts. It offers blocks of neighborhood businesses—delis, antique stores, bars, and old neighborhood fixtures such as Yarusso's Italian Restaurant, a presence in the neighborhood since 1933 (www.yarussos.com). But there's a Latino presence now, too—La Palma Supermercado, a full-service grocery where you can buy several kinds of fresh chili peppers, and a lot more dried. You'll find more shopping on Arcade Street.

Web Site: District 5 Planning Council, 506 Kenny Rd, 651-774-5234 (www. paynephalen.org)

ZIP Codes: 55130, 55106

Post Offices: 1425 Minnehaha Ave; 886 Arcade St

Police Non-Emergency: Eastern District Patrol Team, 651-266-5565; General Information, 651-291-1111; www.stpaul.gov/index.aspx?nid=461

Emergency Hospitals: Regions Hospital, 640 Jackson St, 651-254-3456, www. regionshospital.com; HealthEast St. Joseph's Hospital, 69 W Exchange St, 651-232-3348, www.healtheast.org/st-joes.html

Library: www.sppl.org; Arlington Hills, 1105 Greenbrier St

Community Resources: Minnesota Humanities Commission, 987 E Ivy, http:// minnesotahumanities.org; HOPE Community Academy Hmong School, www.hope-school.org

Parks: www.stpaul.gov/index.aspx?nid=243: Gateway Trail, www.dnr.state. mn.us/state_trails/gateway; Phalen Park and Golf Course; Arlington/Arkwright Off-Leash Dog Area; Bruce Vento Trail along Phalen Boulevard

Public Transportation: 612-373-3333, www.MetroTransit.org; buses travel along Westminster, Arcade, Prosperity, Larpenteur, English, and Maryland. A Park & Ride lot is located at Larpenteur and Arcade St.

DAYTON'S BLUFF DISTRICT

Boundaries: North: Grove St and B.N. Railroad; **West**: Lafayette Rd and State Hwy 3; **South**: Warner Rd; **East**: US Hwy 61, Birmingham St, Hazelwood St, Johnson Pkwy

The charming restored houses that sit high atop Dayton's Bluff, just east of downtown, have a spectacular "front-porch" view of the Mississippi River valle and the St. Paul cityscape below. Developed in the 1850s by land specula Lyman Dayton (hence the name, Dayton's Bluff), this was St. Paul's first up "suburban" neighborhood. Now it is one of St. Paul's five historic distric though many of its Victorian "painted ladies" have been rehabilitat

are some still waiting. Fans of old houses will appreciate the cupolas, dormers, gables, turrets, parapets, and pediments that are common architectural elements in the historic area.

Like Payne-Phalen to the north, this is another neighborhood in transition. In fact, it's always been in transition. While the lower part of the district, "Swede Hollow," was basically a "stepping-stone" where immigrants squatted until they saved enough money to move to better digs, the upper part of the neighborhood—the Bluff—was once called "the most picturesque and beautiful district of the city" (*St. Paul Pioneer Press*, January 1, 1887). In the two decades between 1970 and 1990, however, the Bluff suffered job losses, deteriorated housing, and soaring crime. Then in 1992, the community got organized. An historic district was established, and young professionals started moving in and rehabbing the old houses. The Upper Swede Hollow Neighborhood Association also started buying troublesome properties and turning them around. As a result of the community's efforts, East 7th Street has been largely cleaned up and turned into an ethnic business corridor that is home, now, to the Mexican consulate (797 East 7th Street, 651-771-5494) as well as a new HealthEast clinic.

And though crime is still a problem here, active block clubs and police are working together to clean up the pockets of trouble. The city is also putting Neighborhood Stabilization funds into this district in an attempt to remove problem properties and get new families into currently vacant houses. Unfortunately, Dayton's Bluff not only has the largest stock of Victorian houses in the city, it also has the highest number of vacant houses. So, starting in 2008, the Dayton's Bluff Community Council began conducting spring and fall shopping tours of vacant homes in the neighborhood, many of which are fixer-uppers—though some are move-in ready. Often, financing help is available. And if you don't like Victorians, don't worry. The neighborhood also possesses a great variety in the styles and ages of other housing, including vintage Italianates, bungalows, '60s ramblers, and even new townhomes and row houses.

At the southern end of Dayton's Bluff there is a steep hilltop with a breath-taking view of the Mississippi River Valley and both downtowns. As early as 1000 B.C. the Hopewell Indians chose this area as a burial site, leaving behind a series of oval-shaped burial mounds along the edge of the bluff. The overlook, with the six gravesites that remain, is now Indian Mounds Park, complete with walking paths, picnic areas, and playgrounds. The city's newest park, Bruce Vento Nature Sanctuary, is located along the river below this bluff.

Web Site: Dayton's Bluff Community Council (District 4), 798 E 7th St, 651-772-2075, www.daytonsbluff.org

ZIP Code: 55106

Post Offices: 1425 Minnehaha Ave; 886 Arcade St; 180 Kellogg Blvd

Police Non-Emergency: Eastern District Patrol Team, 651-266-5565; General Information, 651-291-1111; www.stpaul.gov/index.aspx?nid=461

Emergency Hospitals: Regions Hospital, 640 Jackson St, 651-254-3456, www.regionshospital.com; HealthEast St. Joseph's Hospital, 69 W Exchange St, 651-232-3348, www.healtheast.org/st-joes.html; United Hospital, 333 N Smith Ave, St. Paul, 651-241-8000, www.unitedhospital.com

Libraries: www.sppl.org; Arlington Hills, 1105 Greenbrier St; Sun Ray Branch, 2105 Wilson Ave

Community Resources: Mexican Consulate; Metropolitan State University, www.metrostate.edu; Dayton's Bluff Historic District, www.stpaul.gov/DocumentView.aspx?DID=1979; Parkway Little League, 130 3rd St E, 651-774-8113; Mounds Theatre, a venue for community building movies and theater productions, and a home base for local arts and culture organizations, 1029 Hudson Rd, 651-772-2253, www.moundstheatre.org

Parks: www.stpaul.gov/index.aspx?nid=243; Indian Mounds Park, Swede Hollow Park, East Side Heritage Park, Bruce Vento Nature Sanctuary; Margaret Community Recreation Center, 1109 Margaret St; Dayton's Bluff Recreation Center, 790 Conway St, co-located with Dayton's Bluff Achievement Plus Elementary

Community Publications: *Dayton's Bluff District Forum* newspaper is published monthly, March through December, and is downloadable from the internet (www.daytonsbluff.org/news.html) or delivered to residents free of charge

Public Transportation: 612-373-3333, www.MetroTransit.org; buses travel along Arcade, Minnehaha, Payne, E 7th St, 3rd St, Mounds Blvd, Pacific, and Burns

GREATER EAST SIDE

East Phalen; Beaver Lake Heights; Frost Lake; Prosperity Heights; Phalen Village; Parkway-Greenbrier; Lincoln Park; Hayden Heights; Hazel Park; Hillcrest

Boundaries: North: Larpenteur Ave; **West**: Johnson Pkwy, McAfee St; **South**: East Minnehaha Ave; **East**: McKnight Rd

The Greater East Side doesn't look like the rest of St. Paul at all. Instead of old Victorians, it's filled with small- to mid-sized post-1940s Colonials, Cape Cods and ramblers, some of them on curving, suburban-style streets. This predominantly residential area is basically ten small subdivisions. **Hayden Heights**, in the neighborhood's northeastern corner, is organized around Hillcrest Golf Club (www.hillcreststpaul.com), a beautiful, rolling par-72 private club. Some houses face the golf course's meticulously groomed grounds, and many others benefit from the quiet streets that parallel the course. On the west side of the neighborhood, **Frost Lake**, **East Phalen**, and **Phalen Village** border on Lake Phalen and the Bruce Vento Trail. Phalen Village was created by the building of the Phalen Corridor and is home to the new Ames Lake developments of suburban-style townhomes. Back on the eastern edge of the neighborhood, **Lincoln Park** and **Beaver Lake Heights** are built around Beaver Lake, a small, shallow lake with a 10-acre park. **Parkway-Greenbrier** and **Hazel Park** are on the neighborhood's southern edge, while **Hillcrest** is nestled between Frost Lake and Hayden Heights, with **Prosperity Heights** just to the south.

Maplewood, which surrounds this district to the north and east, is the relatively affluent suburban home to 3M Company's international headquarters, and Greater East Side residents enjoy the employment and retail opportunities of living next to this well-off suburb. One perk is Maplewood Mall, a large indoor shopping center on White Bear Avenue. White Bear Avenue is the "Main Street" of this district, with small shops, restaurants and bars, the library, and community center. While there are several small parks, Lake Phalen is close enough to the neighborhood for easy visits. (See **Ramsey County** for more about Maplewood.)

Web Site: Greater East Side Council (District 2), 1961 Sherwood Ave, 651-774-2220 (www.district2council.org)
ZIP Code: 55106
Post Office: 886 Arcade St
Police Non-Emergency: Eastern District Patrol Team, 651-266-5565; General Information, 651-291-1111; www.stpaul.gov/index.aspx?nid=461
Emergency Hospitals: Regions Hospital, 640 Jackson St, 651-254-3456, www.regionshospital.com; St. John's Hospital, 1575 Beam Ave, Maplewood (just west of Maplewood Mall)

Library: www.sppl.org; Hayden Heights, 1456 White Bear Ave Community Resource: Hillcrest Country Club; Academia Cesar Chavez charter school, an
outreach program of the University of St. Thomas, www.cesarchavezschool.
com

Parks: www.stpaul.gov/index.aspx?nid=243; Hazel Park Recreation Center has
a gym, tennis courts, basketball court, play area, and athletic fields; Furness
Parkway, a 16-block "linear park" in Hayden Heights, has a wide, park-like
median and bike trails.

Public Transportation: 612-373-3333, www.MetroTransit.org; buses travel
along Minnehaha, 7th St, 3rd St, Atlantic, Maryland Ave, Larpenteur, Stillwater Ave, White Bear Ave, Nokomis, Rose, Hazel; bus routes converge at the
Sun Ray Transit Center off Ruth St

SUNRAY/BATTLE CREEK/HIGHWOOD

Boundaries: North: Minnehaha Ave; **West**: Hazelwood St, Birmingham St,
Warner Rd; **South**: Mississippi River, city limits; **East**: McKnight Rd

If you're looking for large lots and modern housing stock, SunRay/Battle Creek/
Highwood has it.

Because of the steep, wooded bluffs in the Battle Creek area east of
Highway 61, and immense stretches of marshy land surrounding Pig's Eye Lake
along the Mississippi River, this area remained undeveloped until after World
War II, except for Highwood, where there was an unsuccessful attempt in the
late 1880s to develop a commuter suburb. A handful of architect-designed
Queen Anne and Shingle-style homes dating from this era can be found along
Point Douglas Road and East Howard Avenue.

Most of the rest of the houses, condo and apartment complexes have been
built since the 1970s. Tract housing characterizes the **Eastview/Conway/SunRay**
neighborhood north of I-94, while split-levels, ramblers (ranch houses), and

stylish contemporaries sit on large cul-de-sac lots south of I-94 in the **Battle Creek** and **Highwood Hills** neighborhoods. Both of these southern neighborhoods overlook the river and Pig's Eye Lake, so some homes here have vast lake and river views.

Shopping is close to I-94 on Suburban Avenue, where you will find a Target, Byerly's grocery store and a wide selection of big box retail. Directly across the freeway, SunRay Center, is anchored by a Cub Foods store. Beautiful hiking and biking areas can be found along the rocky ravines of Battle Creek Park and at other greenspaces in the neighborhood. Across State Highway 61 from Battle Creek, Pig's Eye Lake Park, which is home to nesting great blue herons, egrets and cormorants, is a favorite of birdwatchers.

Besides easy access to I-94, this neighborhood also has its own transit hub, located at SunRay Center.

Web Sites: District 1 Community Council, SunRay Shopping Center, 651-578-7600, www.district1council.org

ZIP Code: 55119

Post Office: 1425 E Minnehaha; 1175 N Gershwin, Maplewood

Police Non-Emergency: Eastern District Patrol Team, 651-266-5565; General Information, 651-291-1111; www.stpaul.gov/index.aspx?nid=461

Emergency Hospitals: Regions Hospital, 640 Jackson St, 651-254-3456, www.regionshospital.com; Woodwinds Health Campus, 1925 Woodwinds Dr, Woodbury, 651-232-0228, www.healtheast.org/woodwinds

Library: www.sppl.org; SunRay Branch, 2105 Wilson Ave

Community Resources: Boys Totem Town juvenile residential program, www.co.ramsey.mn.us/cc/boys_totem_town.htm

Parks: www.stpaul.gov/index.aspx?nid=243; Battle Creek Regional Park and Community Center has trails for hiking and skiing, an off-leash dog area, and Waterworks outdoor aquatic center, www.co.ramsey.mn.us/parks/trails; Pig's Eye Island Heron Rookery, www.dnr.state.mn.us/snas/sna01009/index.html

Public Transportation: 612-373-3333, www.MetroTransit.org; buses travel along White Bear Ave, Burns, Ruth, McKnight Rd, Upper Afton Rd, Lower Afton Rd, Londin Rd, and Century (Hwy 120), Hwys 10 and 61; Transit Center at SunRay Shopping Center

SOUTH OF THE MISSISSIPPI RIVER

WEST SIDE (CHEROKEE/RIVERVIEW)

daries: **North/West/East**: Mississippi River; **South**: Annapolis St

Don't confuse the West Side with its neighbor immediately to the south, West St. Paul, which is an independent city.

Cross the arching Smith Avenue High Bridge, and you're in another world—St. Paul's West Side, a world filled with the strains of mariachi bands and the seductive rhythms of salsa music. If you can't tell by the murals and Spanish-language signs along Cesar Chavez Street, you can tell by the lively mix of cantinas and ethnic markets that you are in the oldest Hispanic neighborhood in the Twin Cities. Though Latinos have been settling here in large numbers since the 1920s, this community is also richly diverse. For over one hundred years, Neighborhood House (179 Roble Street E, www.neighb.org), the local settlement house, has opened its arms to waves of immigrants, first from Russia and Lebanon, now from Latin and Central America, Africa, Mexico, Cambodia, and Thailand. At Neighborhood House the newly arrived learn to speak English and are assisted with their transition to American life. The vibrant flux of these new immigrants has turned this drab industrial area into a technicolor melting pot guaranteed to overcome any case of winter blues.

Known for years as "the West Side," the name is confusing to newcomers and oldtimers alike, since the neighborhood, which sits on the west bank of the Mississippi River, is actually south of Downtown. To clear up the confusion, the papers have started listing properties here as being in "**Cherokee/Riverview**," a reference to the neighborhood's Cherokee Heights bluff area that overlooks the river and downtown St. Paul.

The earliest buildings here are farmhouses and workers' cottages dating from the 1880s. The rest of the housing consists of 1920s Midwestern squares and variations on the bungalow, intermingled with modern split-levels, condos, apartments, and townhouses that were built up to the present time. Overlooking it all, the bluffs of Prospect Terrace, once the West Side's Summit Avenue, contain a veritable museum of fine old houses that have fantastic views

across the Mississippi River to downtown. Much to the dismay of many of the current residents, developers have their eyes on the neighborhood's riverfront. One developer proposed a 12-story condo project on the area's West Side Flats floodplain. Another took reservations in advance for units in a 74-acre, 30-story residential, retail, hotel, and entertainment complex, also on the river. Both projects, said the West Side council, flew in the face of the surrounding neighborhood's character and existing streetscape, violated a host of neighborhood and river corridor plans, and chased poor working families out of the district. The residents geared up to fight—and they won! One can only imagine that the developers looked around at the rather handmade texture of this neighborhood and thought it would be a pushover. They must never have shopped here.

The busy commercial streets teem with civic engagement and entrepreneurial spirit. Robert Street, which runs north-south, is a commercial district where you can find everything from cowboy boots to used cars. Cesar Chavez Street is the axis for the Latino strip, recently revitalized and now known as District del Sol (www.districtdelsol.com). Check out the margaritas and the party trays at Boca Chica (11 Cesar Chavez Street, 651-222-8499, www.bocachicarestaurant.com), and the cherry empanadas at El Burrito Mercado (175 Cesar Chavez Street, www.elburritomercado.com). Smith Avenue and Stryker/George are other major commercial arteries, lined with a mixture of longstanding businesses, eclectic shops, and varied housing. On the far eastern side of the neighborhood, on the flats across the river from downtown, Holman Field, a small airplane landing strip used mostly by private aviation and the Minnesota Air National Guard, is only slightly less quiet than this commercial area.

Even if you don't move here, be sure to visit during Cinco de Mayo, when the whole neighborhood turns into one big street carnival. Or go over for one of the productions of Teatro del Pueblo (www.teatrodelpueblo.org). While you're there, stop in at the Riverview Branch Library at 1 George Street. On the National Historic Register, this Carnegie library has a special section for Spanish-speaking patrons.

Go over, as well, to commune with Nature. Set atop a steep sandstone bluff, Cherokee Park offers an awesome panorama of river barges and downtown St. Paul. This is a place for solitude, and an occasional glimpse of the river's wildlife. Bird watchers can spot herons and egrets riding updrafts over the bluff's edge and, once in a great while, a bald eagle soaring overhead. Below the bluffs are the sandstone walls and marshy river flats of Lilydale Park, which contain small caves created by eons of percolation and erosion. At the turn of the 20th century, some of the caves were used by Yoerg's Brewery for cold storage of their product, which was subsequently marketed as "Yoerg's Cave-Aged Picnic Beer." Nearly all of the cave openings are now barred because of cave-ins and other accidents, but the foundations of the brewery, the ruins of an old brick foundry, and the massive cottonwoods standing along the Mississippi flats still make for interesting exploring.

For a preview of this neighborhood, tune in to Radio Rey, 630 AM, and La Nueva Ley, 740 AM (www.radiorey630am.com). Their Spanish programming audibly reflects the diversity of the district.

Download Tour Saint Paul: The West Side, (www.historicsaintpaul.org/files/westside.pdf) produced by Historic Saint Paul, to learn the history of this unique neighborhood.

Web Site: West Side Citizens' Organization (District 3), 127 W Winifred St, 651-293-1708, www.wsco.org

ZIP Code: 55107

Post Office: 292 Eva St

Police Non-Emergency: Central District Patrol Team, 651-266-5563; General Information, 651-291-1111; www.stpaul.gov/index.aspx?nid=461

Emergency Hospitals: Regions Hospital, 640 Jackson St, 651-254-3456, www.regionshospital.com; HealthEast St. Joseph's Hospital, 69 W Exchange St, 651-232-3348, www.healtheast.org/st-joes.html; United Hospital, 333 N Smith Ave, St. Paul, 651-241-8000, www.unitedhospital.com

Library: www.sppl.org; Riverview, 1 E George St

Community Resources: Cinco de Mayo Celebration, www.districtdelsol.com; Neighborhood House, 179 E Robie St (in the Paul and Sheila Wellstone Center for Community Building), 651-789-2500 ,www.neighb.org; Wabasha Street Caves, www.wabashastreetcaves.com

Parks: www.stpaul.gov/index.aspx?nid=243; Harriet Island; Cherokee Park; Lilydale Park has fossil hunting (by permit only)

Community Publications: *Saint Paul Voice* and *La Voz Latina*, 651-457-1177, www.stpaulpublishing.com

Public Transportation: 612-373-3333, www.MetroTransit.org; buses travel along Stryker Ave, Smith Ave, S Robert St, Concord St, Dodd, Humboldt, Plato, Filmore, and Winifred

WEST METRO SUBURBS

HENNEPIN COUNTY

Boundaries: Northeast: Anoka County (Mississippi River); **Northwest**: Wright County (Crow River); **West**: Wright County; **South**: Scott County (Minnesota River); **Southeast**: Carver County, Dakota County; **East**: Ramsey County (Mississippi River); **Area**: 606 square miles; **Population**: 1,140,988; **County Seat**: Minneapolis

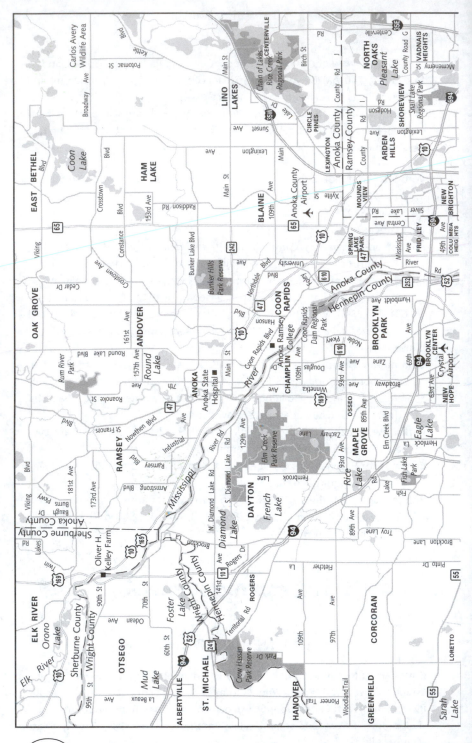

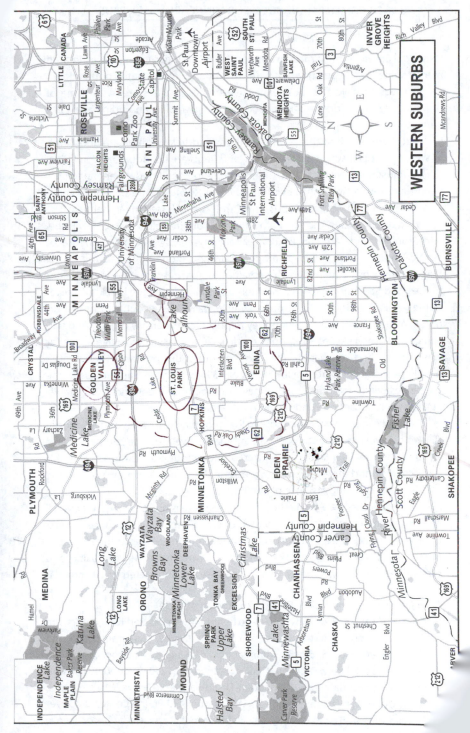

WESTERN SUBURBS

Hennepin County is the largest of Minnesota's 87 counties in budget, estimated market value, and population, with almost a quarter of the state's population.

It tends to have the most expensive homes in the state, with three of the metro's A-list addresses: "Kenwood" (in Minneapolis), and Edina and Lake Minnetonka.

But there's more to this county than posh addresses; there are good jobs, as well. Alliant Techsystems, Nash Finch, and Regis are headquartered in Edina; C. H. Robinson, the Vikings, and Supervalu are in Eden Prairie; General Mills is headquartered in Golden Valley; Best Buy is in Richfield; and Carlson Companies, United Health, Michael Foods, and Cargill are all based in Minnetonka.

And good houses. The northern suburbs (Robbinsdale, Crystal, New Hope, and Brooklyn Park) are chock full of smaller, generally well-maintained economical homes and rentals, as are Richfield and Bloomington in the south. Surprisingly, posh Edina offers good values in apartments, condos, and older homes; and St. Louis Park, a first-ring suburb, is filled with cute blocks of starter homes, as is the City of Minnetonka. Even Wayzata has a couple of neighborhoods of starter homes, although they're priced considerably higher. And you can get on "The Lake" at a reasonable price—if you're willing to live at the far western end and can handle the killer commute. But probably the county's best-kept secret is Golden Valley, north of I-394, which has easy access to the core cities, while featuring mature neighborhoods of older, more affordable, custom-built houses on winding, pretty streets.

Regardless of where you choose to live, shopping will be handy, with Ridgedale in the west in Minnetonka and Southdale —well—in the south, in Edina. Grocery and specialty stores are scattered throughout. But be forewarned: this is car country, and there are very few places in these suburbs where you can live and be within walking distance of anything.

Another car issue—while the county's web site is great for renewals, you'll need to go in person to register your vehicle and get a driver's license the first time. If you must take a road test, most people find the course at the Plymouth Motor Vehicles Service Center (2455 Fernbrook Lane) extremely confusing, and prefer Chaska (418 Pine Street), where road tests are conducted on city streets.

Area Codes: 952 (south of I-394) and 763 (north of I-394)

Hennepin County Web Site: www.co.hennepin.mn.us. Service centers are located throughout the county: Hennepin County Government Center (Downtown), 300 S 6th St, Minneapolis, 612-348-8240; Brookdale, 6125 Shingle Creek Pkwy, Brooklyn Center; Ridgedale, 12601 Ridgedale Dr, Minnetonka; Southdale, 12601 Ridgedale Dr, Edina; Maple Grove Service Center, 9325 Upland Ln N; Eden Prairie Service Center, 479 Prairie Center Dr. Drive-up windows and drop boxes are available at most service centers for license tab renewals.

Police: Hennepin County Sheriff's Office, Minneapolis City Hall, 350 S Fifth St, Minneapolis; Emergency: 911; Administration, 612-348-3744

Library: Hennepin County Library System, www.hclib.org

Emergency Hospitals: Abbott Northwestern Hospital, 800 E 28th St, Minneapolis, 612-863-4000, www.abbottnorthwestern.com; Fairview Southdale Hospital, 6401 France Ave S, Edina, 952-924-5000, www.southdale.fairview.org; Fairview-University Medical Center, 2450 Riverside Ave, Minneapolis, 612-273-3000, www.uofmmedicalcenter.org; Hennepin County Medical Center, 701 Park Ave, Minneapolis, 612-873-3000, www.hcmc.org; Methodist Hospital Park Nicollet Health Services, 6500 Excelsior Blvd, St. Louis Park, 952-993-5000, www.parknicollet.com/Methodist; North Memorial Health Care, 3300 Oakdale Ave N, Robbinsdale, 763-520-5200, www.northmemorial.com; Waconia Ridgeview Medical Center, 500 S Maple St, Waconia, 952-442-2191, 800-967-4620, www.ridgeviewmedical.org (this is the preferred hospital of many who live in the western suburbs); Maple Grove Hospital, 9875 Hospital Drive (just north of I-94 off Maple Grove Parkway), Maple Grove, 763-581-1000, www.maplegrove-hospital.org (the metro's newest hospital, opened in 2010)

Parks: Three Rivers Park District (www.threeriversparks.org) manages nearly 27,000 acres of park reserves, regional parks, trails and special use areas, including three nature centers, four golf courses, two downhill ski and snowboard areas, snow-tubing hill, extensive trails for hiking, biking, horseback riding and cross-country skiing, as well as areas for camping, swimming, fishing/boating, picnicking, and snowshoeing

Community Publications: *Minneapolis StarTribune*, 612-673-4343 www.startribune.com; Sun Newspapers, 612-829-0797, www.mnsun.com

Community Resources: Lake Minnetonka; University of Minnesota Landscape Arboretum, Chaska, www.arboretum.umn.edu; Mall of America, Bloomington, www.mallofamerica.com

Public Transportation: MetroTransit, 612-373-3333, www.metrotransit.org; Buses run from suburban Park & Ride lots and major shopping centers into downtown Minneapolis, but there is little local bus service. I-394 ends in the parking garages behind Target Center in downtown Minneapolis.

SOUTH/SOUTHWESTERN SUBURBS

Bloomington (East and West); Richfield; Edina

BLOOMINGTON

Boundaries: North: I-494; **West**: Town Line Rd; **South**: Minnesota River; Minnesota River; **Area**: 35.5 square miles; **Population**: 85,172

Like yin and yang, the disparate halves of Bloomington fit together to form the state's fourth-largest city. The eastern half, known locally and in the classifieds as East Bloomington, has flat streets laid out in grids, and a large proportion of property that is zoned for business and commercial/industrial uses. When you go shopping at Mall of America, you are in East Bloomington. The western side of the city, which is largely residential, more affluent, and hilly, is known locally as West Bloomington. When you're driving on I-494 and see the ski jump just south of the freeway, you are in West Bloomington.

Bloomington is serviced by two interstate highways, 35 and 494. Large-scale commercial development lines the I-494 corridor. It is the only suburb on the Hiawatha Light Rail Transit line. Its location along major freeways and proximity to the Minneapolis–St. Paul International Airport combine to make it the Twin Cities' principal hospitality center, with numerous hotels, bars, and restaurants lined up along its "494 Strip." Other major industries here include retail, health care, and computer manufacturing—or as they say, in Bloomington, they are a city with "more than 85,000 residents and 100,000 employees."

The two halves of Bloomington are treated separately below.

RICHFIELD AND EAST (HALF OF THE CITY OF) BLOOMINGTON

Boundaries: *Richfield*: **North**: 62 Crosstown; **West**: Xerxes Ave; **South**: I-494; **East**: Minneapolis–St. Paul International Airport; **Area**: 7 square miles; **Population**: 34,440; *East Bloomington* (the eastern half of the City of Bloomington): **North**: I-494; **West**: approximately Penn Ave; **South**: Minnesota River; **East**: Minnesota River

At the end of WW II, returning veterans and their growing families needed homes, so residential development of the area commenced. The result: street after street of modest starter homes.

Those grid-style streets, Cape Cods, and small ramblers are with us still, along with some 1970s split-levels. While the bulk of homes in this area are "maturing," many have been replaced with contemporary housing or "transformed" into more valuable commercial real estate. Look for executive-level homes and condos near Wood Lake in Richfield and along the river bluffs in East Bloomington. That said, most houses still run around 1500 square feet, have detached single-car garages, and sell for less than the rest of the West Metro market. But because of their size and affordability, these houses go quickly (particularly in Richfield), often to young, single professionals.

Surprisingly, for cities that have so many little commercial and retail areas, Richfield nor Bloomington has a real downtown. Bloomington is recthat, however, by building a walkable, mixed-use "downtown" around

its Hiawatha Light Rail Transit Central Station stop. Condos here are pricey, but feature fabulous views across the Minnesota River bottoms and National Wildlife Refuge.

Both Bloomington and Richfield have a number of programs in place to assist homeowners. Each January Richfield holds a very useful "Remodeling Fair" at the Richfield High School. A great reference book, *Cape Cods & Ramblers: A Remodeling Planbook for Post-WWII Houses*, provides ideas for homeowners who want to remodel their homes, and features plans for this area's three most common house designs: a rambler with a detached garage, a rambler with an attached garage, and a 1.5-story Cape Cod. The planbook is available at the city halls for $10 (resident) or $15 (non-resident).

When looking here, keep in mind that these cities abut Minneapolis–St. Paul International Airport and are affected by airplane noise, even at night. Despite this, they are desirable places to live, due in part to their central location along freeways 494 and 35W and excellent bus coverage. About one-third of all housing units here are rentals, and include apartments, double bungalows, and single-family homes.

Both cities have many recreation facilities including Richfield's Wood Lake Nature Center (www.woodlakenaturecenter.org) and the Minnesota Valley National Wildlife Refuge, www.fws.gov/midwest/minnesotavalley, in Bloomington.

Shops and restaurants are on every major thoroughfare, with a Cub Foods at 60th and Nicollet, Rainbow Foods on West 66th, and Lunds and Aldi groceries on Penn.

Richfield is served by Independent School District #280, 612-798-6000, www.richfield.k12.mn.us. It is also home to Academy of the Holy Angels (6600 Nicollet Avenue, 612-798-2600, www.ahastars.org), a Catholic, coeducational high school. Bloomington is served by Independent School District #271, 952-681-6400, www.bloomington.k12.mn.us.

ZIP Codes: 55423, 55431

City of Richfield: 6700 Portland Ave, 55423; 612-861-9700, www.ci.Richfield.mn.us

City of Bloomington: 1800 W Old Shakopee Rd, 55431; 952-563-8700, www.ci.bloomington.mn.us; Interactive Crime Map, http://gis.logis.org/Bloomington/PIMAWeb/PIMAWeb.aspx.

Public Transportation: Buses travel on all the major streets, with many routes connecting at the Mall of America; Hiawatha LRT stations at American Boulevard, Bloomington Central Station, 28th Avenue, and Mall of America

EDINA AND WEST (HALF OF THE CITY OF) BLOOMINGTON

Boundaries: *Edina*: **North**: St. Louis Park and Hopkins; **West**: Washington Ave and Hwy 169; **South**: I-494; **East**: France Ave north of 54th St, Xerxes south of 54th St; **Area**: 16 square miles; **Population**: 54,901; *West Bloomington*: **North**: I-494; **West**: Town Line Rd; **South**: Minnesota River; **East**: Penn Ave

The upscale ambiance of Edina and West Bloomington contrasts markedly with the more working-class atmosphere of easterly neighbors Richfield and East Bloomington.

Although there is no official boundary line, somewhere between Penn Avenue and France Avenue the apartment buildings, hotels, and 1940s tract housing of East Bloomington give way to curved streets, modern housing with multi-car garages, and residents who make a point of telling you that they live in West Bloomington. Custom-built homes grace many of these hilly streets, particularly around Hyland Hills Ski Area and along the Minnesota River Bluffs. In fact, this end of Bloomington is indistinguishable from Edina to the north.

Much is made of Edina and its affluent residents' supposed high-flying lifestyle. But, in many ways, Edina (pronounced Ee-DIE-nah) is more mystique than fact. Though a number of its residents are corporate kings and prominent professionals, at least one fourth of Edina's population is retired and over age 65. And while Edina certainly does have plenty of houses that sell for over a million, it also has a nice selection of plain ramblers dating from the 1950s and '60s, subsidized apartment units, condominiums, and townhouses, as well. Look for less costly real estate near the freeways and major arteries, and in the vicinity of Pamela Park.

More typical of what's considered Edina are the city's multimillion-dollar, brick-and-ivy neighborhoods, among them the 1920s to 1940s houses surrounding the Edina Country Club, which are listed on the National Register of Historic Places. These houses are large in proportion to their lots, a pattern that has served as the template for much of the rest of Edina's development.

The classic styles of these homes offer formal rooms such as first-floor libraries and dining rooms, and many of them boast home theaters and computer-controlled wine cellars, as well. Look for similar amenities in newer homes in the **Braemar** and **Indian Hills** neighborhoods, off Antrim Road, and around **Interlachen Country Club**, where newer homes nestle beneath canopies of mature trees. With very little open land available for development, Edina has had a recent building boomlet as older homes have been torn down and replaced with new construction that is particularly luxurious. Consider that a one-acre lot alone may cost more than a million, and that should give you an idea of what to expect with respect to prices if you're interested in living in one of the swankier sections of the city.

While both Edina and West Bloomington have significant percentages of rental housing, the units tend to be clustered in park-like settings and offer amenities such as tennis courts. One Edina seniors high-rise complex, Edina Park Plaza, off France Avenue and I-494, has the Midwest's largest indoor playground, and an indoor park with real trees. The Residence Inn, which is part of this complex (3400 Edinborough Way, 952-893-9300, 800-410-9649, www.marriott.com/hotels/travel/mspda-residence-inn-minneapolis-edina/), is a great place for a family to stay while you're looking over the city.

One mile north on France Avenue, condos in the new high-end Westin Edina Galleria Hotel and Residences (www.edinagalleriaresidences.com) have beautiful views across the city, as well as amazing convenience—Southdale and the Galleria Shopping Center, which is connected to the Westin via underground tunnel, are just steps away.

Based on its renowned schools and the excellence of its recreation amenities (groomed parks, outdoor aquatic center, ice arena, and public and private golf courses), Edina was chosen a *Family Circle* Best Town for Families in 2009

In the City of Bloomington, 25% of the land is set aside for parks and n areas, mostly located in the western half of the city. The parkland i

Hyland Hills Ski Area, www.threriversparks.org (see **Sports and Recreation**), and the Minnesota Valley National Wildlife Refuge (see **Lakes and Parks**).

Most children in Edina attend Edina District 273 schools (www.edina.k12. mn.us), although some students in the northern part of the city are in the Hopkins District 270 attendance area (www.hopkins.k12.mn.us), and many students attend private schools. West Bloomington is served by Independent School District #271, www.bloomington.k12.mn.us. Two-year Normandale Community College, located at 98th and France Avenue, includes a public Japanese garden that is very popular for outdoor weddings, www.normandale.edu.

While Bloomington and Edina are both known for their shopping, Edina's reputation is more up-market, with a cluster of boutiques, and restaurants centered on Fiftieth and France (www.50thandfrance.com), as well as Southdale and the Galleria malls, farther down France between the 62 Crosstown and I-494. Both these cities are also rich with public transportation. Buses travel along the major roads, and there is a transit hub at Southdale Center.

Finally, for those who do crossword puzzles, Edina is the answer to the clues "Five-letter suburb of Minneapolis" and "Minnesota cake-eaters."

City of Edina: 4801 W 50th St, 55424; 952-927-8861, www.ci.edina.mn.us
City of Bloomington: 1800 W Old Shakopee Rd, 55420; 952-563-8700, www. ci.bloomington.mn.us

WESTERN SUBURBS

Minnetonka; Hopkins; Eden Prairie; Golden Valley; St. Louis Park

MINNETONKA

Boundaries: North: Ridgemont Ave; **West**: Woodland, Deephaven, Shorewood; **South**: 62 Crosstown; **East**: St. Louis Park, Hopkins, and Edina; **Area**: 8 square miles; **Population**: 51,759

The city of Minnetonka barely touches Lake Minnetonka at Gray's Bay, so it isn't the lake that has fueled the city's growth—it's jobs. Major international employers such as Cargill, Carlson Companies, and General Mills, as well as numerous smaller businesses, provide an abundance of white-collar jobs and have placed Minnetonka among the top three cities in the state with respect to job creation. About a quarter of Minnetonka residents work in the city.

Another city with a gilded reputation, Minnetonka features neighborhoods made up of wooded lots with rolling terrain. Many neighborhoods are around wetlands, and land ownership often involves following wetlands which can affect the way you may use your yard.

While the city boasts numerous upper-bracket neighborhoods throughout, for the most affordable housing, check in the neighborhoods that were built circa 1970, off Minnetonka and Excelsior boulevards. Those looking for larger apartments or reasonably priced condominiums will find them around Ridgedale Shopping Center and Cedar Lake Road in the north, or highways 101 and 7 in the southern portion of the city. Settle anywhere in Minnetonka and you won't be far from a playground or park. Among the city's many sport and recreation amenities are city-owned Williston Fitness Center, which offers low-cost memberships to residents, and an extensive network of paved paths. The paths through Purgatory Park, off Excelsior Boulevard east of Highway 101, are particularly good for walking your dog. The city also has a few boat slips on Gray's Bay that are allocated to residents by lottery.

Minnetonka School District #276 (www.minnetonka.k12.mn.us), covers most of the city, but children in the northernmost sections attend Wayzata District #284 (www.wayzata.k12.mn.us/wps). Neighborhoods east of Woodland Road (more or less) are in the Hopkins #270 school district (www.hopkins.k12.mn.us). (For more information, see **Childcare and Education**.) Bus service is organized around commuter service and routes that connect at Ridgedale Shopping Center or the Plymouth Road Transit Center, but basically, you cannot get around out here without a car.

City of Minnetonka: 14600 Minnetonka Blvd 55345; 952-939-8200, www.ci.
   minnetonka.mn.us

HOPKINS

Boundaries: North: St. Louis Park and Minnetonka; **West**: Minnetonka; **South**: Edina and Minnetonka; **East**: St. Louis Park and Edina; **Area**: 4 square miles; **Population**: 17,000

An affordable place to rent or buy a home and a convenient 15-minute commute to Minneapolis, Hopkins is one of the few suburbs that offers a bona fide downtown where you can catch a movie, grab a bite to eat, go to the dentist, or get your car repaired. Other major attractions: the Hopkins Center for the Arts, 1111 Main Street (www.hopkinsmn.com/_hca), which is home to Stages Theatre Company (952-979-1111, www.stagestheatre.org), a wonderful training ground for young actors, as well as an art gallery that showcases local artists and students. Across the street, a former car dealership is the western suburbs' favorite movie theater, www.manntheatresmn.com, with several screens and $3 tickets ($2.50 on Tuesdays). Several restaurants have been added around this core, and the accompanying throngs of customers are bringing a tangible vibrancy and exuberance to Hopkins' streets.

Other amenities are also typical of a real town: sidewalks, a downtown library, grocery store, city hall, post office, and banks and office complexes. A large ballfield, arena, and Main Street School of Performing Arts (www.performing-arts-school.org) are also located in the heart of downtown.

The old-style city has even gone trendy with condos and lofts on Main Street above street-level shops and restaurants. The city also won a Smart Growth Award for turning an abandoned defense plant into a mixed business and residential neighborhood of row houses and townhomes, thus bringing housing and jobs together and turning a blighted industrial property into a community amenity.

While most housing runs to small bungalows, larger homes, including new condos, can be found in the vicinity of Oak Ridge Country Club north of Highway 7, and around Meadowbrook Golf Course, on the east side of town. Another neighborhood of note is **Hobby Acres**, conveniently hidden in the angle created by Highways 7 and 169. Here well-loved 1940s–'50s homes are built on large tree-shaded lots. A place with a real neighborhood feel, its Hobby Acres Association sponsors social events and a book club, a progressive dinner, and an annual garage sale.

In addition to its varied and affordable housing, possibly the best thing going in Hopkins is good schools. The Blake School (www.blakeschool.org) is an outstanding college-preparatory day school, and Hopkins School District #270, which serves the entire city, has a long record of excellence. (See **Childcare and Education**.)

Public transportation is good here as well, with bus routes along all the major corridors. The city will also be a stop on the proposed Southwest Corridor Light Rail Transit high-frequency train line between Minneapolis and Eden Prairie.

Hopkins is the trailhead for the Southwest LRT biking and hiking trails, which continue west past Lake Minnetonka, or south to Chaska. At one time the center of a thriving truck farming community, it still calls itself the Raspberry Capital and hosts a 10-day Raspberry Festival every July. Highlights include a fun run, Little League tournament, fireworks, and human and canine royalty (http://hopkinsbiz.com).

City of Hopkins: 1010 S First St, 55343; 952-935-8474, www.hopkinsmn.com

EDEN PRAIRIE

Boundaries: North: 62 Crosstown; **West**: Chanhassen at Chanhassen Rd and Dell Rd; **South**: Minnesota River; **East**: City of Bloomington, Town Line Rd; **Area**: 36 square miles; **Population**: 60,000

Eden Prairie was the fastest-growing city in Minnesota for ten straight years from 1980 to 1990. Along the way, the farmhouses and barns were bulldozed and the cropland paved, leaving only one farmhouse still standing.

Fortunately for the chai tea and caramel skim latte lovers among us, the city's last 130-year-old farmhouse, on Eden Prairie Road (Highway 4) just south of Highway 5, has been converted into a Dunn Bros. Coffeehouse (www.dunnbros. com). In a city that is without a downtown, it has become the community's gathering place.

The city has made a commitment to "balance" that includes development of life cycle and affordable housing. (Life cycle housing is housing that meets people's needs through all the different stages of life.) Its efforts have resulted in its being rated—several times—by *Money Magazine* as one of the best places in the United States to live and work; named by *Parents Magazine* as a "Best Place to Raise Kids"; and recognized by *U.S. News and World Report* as one of "America's Best Places to Retire." A number of years ago it set goals of having 25% rental housing stock and a total of 43% multiple family housing—both goals that appear

to have been met. Still, one of the city's most interesting developments is one of its first: **The Preserve** (www.preserveassociation.com), built in the 1970s in southeast Eden Prairie off Highway 169 and Anderson Lakes Parkway. With nearly 1700 residential units of all kinds, it was the metro's first successful master-planned community. Residents can walk to an upscale grocery store (Jerry's, www.jerrysfoods.com) and restaurants, and recreation amenities are superb—tennis courts, miles of trails, and a 3/4-acre sand-bottomed pool. Another interesting neighborhood is **Bearpath** (/www.bearpathhoa.com), off Dell Road on the city's western edge, an exclusive, gated golf course development. Less lavish digs can be found near Eden Prairie Center and in the vicinity of Flying Cloud airport. This busy general aviation airport already sees more than 119,000 take-offs and landings each year, and has recently been expanded with a 5,000-foot runway. To meet the ground transportation needs of its residents and the city's workforce, Eden Prairie has joined with Chaska and Chanhassen to develop Southwest MetroTransit (www.swtransit.org, 952-949-2BUS [2287] or www.metrotransit.org), a system that offers express service to downtown Minneapolis and several other popular destinations (see the **Transportation** chapter).

Eden Prairie School District #272 (www3.edenpr.org/public/Home.aspx) serves most of the city, although some areas along the northern edge are in the Minnetonka or Hopkins school districts. The Community Center/Round Lake Park sports complex, on Valley View Road (next to the high school), is the focal point of park and rec activities. It includes skating rinks, a fitness center, athletic fields, and even a beach and fishing pier. Staring Lake Park, near Flying Cloud airport, is a natural area with a nature center and amphitheater, sledding hills, and ski trails. The city also boasts a barrier-free playground at Miller Park.

For those who love theater, the Eden Prairie Players stage several productions every year and are always looking for volunteers, www.edenprairieplayers.org.

City of Eden Prairie: 8080 Mitchell Rd, 55344; 952-949-8300; www.ci.eden-prairie.mn.us

GOLDEN VALLEY

Boundaries: North: Medicine Lake Rd, City of New Hope, City of Crystal, 34th Ave N, 26th Ave, City of Robbinsdale; **West**: Hwy 169, City of Plymouth; **South**: I-394, City of St. Louis Park; **East**: Xerxes, City of Minneapolis; **Area**: 10.2 square miles; **Population**: 20,281

ated roughly along the 45th parallel, exactly halfway between the equator he North Pole, Golden Valley is served by major freeways I-394 and I-694, ected by Highway 55, making it attractive to big corporate employers eneral Mills, as well as those looking for older custom-built homes

with large lots and mature trees. Some of its neighborhoods, such as **North Tyrol Hills**, have such wide expanses of green lawns, they might even be described as pastoral. With very little room for new housing, the emphasis here is on invigorating the existing housing stock (70% of which is single-family homes) through remodeling and infill development (the demolition of existing housing and replacement with new). With a large stock of 1950s and '60s split-entry and split-level houses, the city has developed a remodeling planbook, *Split Visions*, which includes suggestions for ways to update the style. Golden Valley residents can buy the book at City Hall for $10. Also available—*Cape Cods and Ramblers: A Remodeling Planbook for Post WWII Houses*. Multi-family apartments, condos, and townhomes are available, especially near major highways.

Golden Valley is home to the Perpich Center for Arts Education, a public arts-oriented high school, located on Olson Memorial Highway, www.pcae. k12.mn.us; and to Breck (www.breckschool.org), a private Episcopal K–12 college preparatory school. It is also served by two public school districts: Hopkins Independent School District #270 (www.hopkins.k12.mn.us), which operates Meadowbrook Elementary, 5430 Glenwood Avenue; and Robbinsdale Independent School District #281 (www.rdale.k12.mn.us), which has two schools here, an elementary and middle school. Download the school district attendance maps from the city's web site.

Parks include Theodore Wirth Park (www.minneapolisparks.org), with its golf course, wildflower garden, trails, and other recreation amenities too long to list. The 60-mile Luce Line Trail walking and biking trail connects to Minneapolis trails at Wirth Park and runs east–west through Golden Valley. While open on either side of Douglas Drive, it's easy to lose there because there's no sidewalk or pavement, so you have to follow the street to make the connection.

One other feature—Golden Valley is smoke-free. Not only are restaurants smoke-free indoors and out, but the city has banned smoking in public park and on the city-owned Brookview golf course (www.brookviewgolf.com).

City of Golden Valley: 7800 Golden Valley Rd, Golden Valley, 55427; 763-593-8000, www.ci.golden-valley.mn.us

ST. LOUIS PARK

Boundaries: North: Interstate 394; **West**: Hwy 169 and Hopkins; **South**: Edina and Hopkins; **East**: Minneapolis at France Ave; **Area**: 10.8 square miles; **Population**: 44,102

St. Louis Park is home to the movie-making Coen brothers, whose films include *Fargo, O Brother, Where Art Thou?, The Big Lebowski*, and *A Serious Man*, which is loosely based on their own childhoods growing up in what was then the largely Jewish suburb of SLP.

Restaurants, shopping, watering holes where you can grab a drink after work, major medical facilities, top-notch schools—St. Louis Park has something for everyone, including easier access than many Minneapolis residents have to such Minneapolis amenities as the Chain of Lakes.

The array of housing here is probably the most diverse in the Twin Cities, ranging from small and large single-family homes in tree-shaded, often hilly neighborhoods to large apartment complexes and the region's hottest "smart growth" community, **Excelsior & Grand** (www.excelsiorandgrand.com). North of Cedar Lake Road, **Westwood Hills** is a 1960s–'80s development of rolling hills and large homes located between the Minneapolis Golf Club (www.minneapolisgolfclub.com) and 150-acre Westwood Hills Nature Center, a great place to bike or bird watch. Nearby **Aquila** is also filled with parks and open space, including the Hutchinson spur regional bike trail. Across town, in the city's southeast corner, **Minikahda Vista** borders yet another golf course, the Minikahda Club (www.minikahdaclub.org), which is actually in Minneapolis. Houses here were built in the 1920s and '40s, about the same time as neighboring Linden Hills in Minneapolis, which it resembles. Though this is one of St. Louis Park's oldest neighborhoods, it is still one of the most desirable, especially for those looking for houses with character. While this is the perfect place to look for a starter home (only about 25% of St. Louis Park's houses have more than three bedrooms and a bath and a half), many families eventually move out to find more space. In an effort to encourage residents to stay and "supersize" their homes, the city has made a "rehab advisor" available at no cost, and will even pay the cost of a two-hour consultation with an architect. In 2009 the city launched a new assisted home ownership program

that provides employees of St. Louis Park–based businesses with a grant toward the purchase of a home near their workplace.

St. Louis Park is served by nationally recognized St. Louis Park School District #283, www.slpschools.org, as well as by several private schools, including Amos and Celia Heilicher Minneapolis Jewish Day School, www.mjds.net; and Benilde-St. Margaret's Catholic junior high and high school, www.bsm-online.org.

Always innovative, St. Louis Park has a Friends of the Arts group that runs community-wide arts programs. In 2010, it led a yearlong poetry project that included the creation of a community poem called a renga.

Major employers include Methodist Hospital and Park Nicollet Health Center (www.parknicollet.com), one of the country's largest multi-specialty clinics, which are located on Excelsior Boulevard near Highway 100.

Bus transport is easy from the Louisiana Avenue Transit Station to downtown Minneapolis, and there are many routes that run through Knollwood Shopping Center, Methodist Hospital, or along Minnetonka Boulevard and Excelsior Boulevard.

City of St. Louis Park: 5005 Minnetonka Blvd, St. Louis Park, 55416; 952-924-2500, www.stlouispark.org

LAKE MINNETONKA COMMUNITIES

Wayzata; Orono/Long Lake/Medina/Maple Plain/Independence; Deephaven and Woodland; Excelsior/Greenwood/Shorewood; Mound; Plymouth

---

The Lake has always appealed to high society and high-rolling scoundrels. Most recent in the latter category is Wayzata's Tom Petters, who rose from being a stereo salesman at Radio Shack to owner of Sun Country Airlines and Polaroid. In 2009, he and several other Lake residents were convicted of running a $3.65 billion Ponzi scheme based on the sale of nonexistent electronics merchandise. Excelsior played a part in the scheme, as well, with millions of dollars laundered through the Excelsior Car Wash! To learn more about The Lake's long history of rogues and racketeers, take a cruise on one of the tour boats—many of the captains will be glad to point out their current or former residences, and fill you in on all the gritty details. *Queen of Excelsior*, 952-470-VIEW (8439), www.qecruise.com; Al and Alma's, 952-472-3098, www.al-almas.com; Museum of Lake Minnetonka Historic Steamboat Minnehaha, www.steamboatminnehaha.org; Lady of the Lake Cruises, 952-929-1209, www.ladyofthelakecruise.com

Communities Immediately Surrounding the Lake
- Deephaven (see pp.130–133)
- Excelsior (see pp. 130–133)
- Greenwood (see pp. 130–133)
- Long Lake (see pp. 133–134)
- Minnetonka (has a small amount of footage on Gray's Bay) (see pp. 122 – 123)
- Minnetonka Beach (see pp. 130 – 133 and page 197)
- Minnetrista (see pp. 130 – 133)
- Mound (see pp. 130–133)
- Orono (see pp. 130–133)
- Shorewood (see pp. 130–133)
- Spring Park (see page 197)
- Tonka Bay (see page 197)
- Victoria (see page 197)
- Wayzata (see pp. 130–133)
- Woodland (see page 131)

Communities Nearby
- Chanhassen (see pp. 142 – 144)
- Independence (see pp. 133–134)
- Maple Plain (see pp. 133–134)
- Medina (see pp. 133–134)
- Plymouth (see pp. 134 – 135)

Lake Minnetonka (the "Big Water" in the native Dakota language) is located 20 miles west of Minneapolis. The granddaddy of metro-area lake living, "The Lake" from Wayzata (pronounced Y-zeta) in the east to Mound in the west, and lly contains the metro's priciest real estate.

late 1800s were boom years for Lake Minnetonka. Rail lines reached 1867, bringing visitors from all over the country. To accommodate the sightseers, grand hotels were built in **Wayzata**, **Deephaven**, **Excelsior**, **Minnetonka Beach**, **Mound**, and **Tonka Bay**. The summer visitors played tennis, sailed, and participated in amateur theatricals. Excelsior put on pageants at the Excelsior Commons that featured galloping horses and wagons, and included nearly every person and animal that lived in the village. Turn-of-the-20th-century steamboats, among them the *City of Saint Louis*, a 160-foot sidewheeler that is said to have carried 1,000 passengers, ferried visitors on tours of the lake. Excelsior even had a casino overlooking the lake, and Big Island was the site of an amusement park.

Within a quarter of a century, however, most of the resorts had burned down and the summer cottage era had begun.

Today, 100 years later, Lake Minnetonka is still a playground. Cruise boats offer tours of the lake. Day-trippers visit the antique stores, dine at the many restaurants, and swim at the beaches. The lake provides world-class sailing, scuba diving, bass fishing, power-boating, and water skiing. In winter, ice a couple of feet thick is safe for cross-country skiing, ice boating, ice fishing, and snowmobiling.

Connected by a ring of state highways and county roads, the picturesque villages that encircle "The Lake" feature countless multimillion-dollar homes, a shrinking number of cottages and older houses—most of which are destined to be torn down and replaced with "starter castles"—and a growing number of multi-family options such as townhomes, twin homes, and condos. With regular real estate, two-thirds of a property's value is in the buildings; with lake property, two-thirds of the value is in the land—hence builders' willingness to tear down lovely old homes and replace them with McMansions.

Lake homes in the eastern (Lower) Lake Minnetonka communities of **Deephaven**, **Greenwood**, **Excelsior**, **Wayzata**, **Orono**, **Minnetonka Beach**, and **Woodland** boast some of the highest price tags in the metro area. Look in Excelsior, if you'd like to find a house with a garden in a cute, small town. Wayzata also offers in-town living, but mostly in condominiums. Properties at the west end of the lake, around **Mound**, which is less conveniently located and has lower water quality, are more reasonably priced. Homes back from the lake fetch lower prices and don't pay lakeshore taxes, while still offering lake access and, sometimes, water views.

On the south side of Highway 7, near Excelsior, spring-fed Christmas Lake (in **Shorewood** and **Chanhassen**) is another premier Twin Cities address. Clean, cold, and clear, it is small enough that it doesn't have the big boat traffic of the larger lake, making it by far the better place to live if your family likes to swim and water ski, or just putt around. Shorewood, which strings along Highway 7 for about six miles, has all manner of housing, including relatively affordable houses and plenty of new "villas." With big new multi-family complexes springing up all over the lake area, it's easy to find low-maintenance housing and rentals here. Expect to pay the least for apartments and condos near Mound.

Families with school-age children are drawn to this area by more than the desire to live at a good address—Wayzata School District #284 (www.wayzata. k12.mn.us) gets five stars from parents for its academic and sports programs, and for how well it succeeds at integrating new students. Nearby Orono School District #278 (www.orono.k12.mn.us) is small and personal with an excellent music program. Minnetonka School District #276 (www.minnetonka.k12. mn.us) is highly competitive in both academics and sports. (See **Childcare and Education**.)

Shopping is conveniently located in Excelsior, Wayzata, Mound, and Navarre, and at several small malls in Shorewood. Restaurants and bars are plentiful throughout the area.

Area Code: 952

Community Resources: Chanhassen Dinner Theatres, 501 W 78th St, Chanhassen, 952-934-1525, www.chanhassentheatres.com; Gray Freshwater Biological Institute/Freshwater Society, 2500 Shadywood Rd (County Rd 19), Navarre, 952-471-9773, www.freshwater.org; Minnetonka Center for the Arts, 2240 North Shore Dr, Orono, 952-473-7361, www.minnetonkaarts.org; Minnetonka Yacht Club, www.minnetonkayachtclub.org; Museum of Lake Minnetonka and Steamboat Minnehaha, www.steamboatminnehaha.org; Music Association of Minnetonka/ArtsCenter Minnetonka, 952-401-5954, www.musicassociation.org, presents 60 free concerts a year in the western suburbs; Old Log Theater, 5175 Meadville, Excelsior, 952-474-5951, www. oldlog.com; Twin City Polo Club, www.twincitypolo.com; University of Minnesota Landscape Arboretum, 3675 Arboretum Dr, Chaska, 952-443-1400, www.arboretum.umn.edu; Upper Minnetonka Yacht Club, http://umyc. camp8.org; Wayzata Yacht Club, www.wyc.org; Wayzata Community Sailing Center (lessons), www.WayzataSailing.org; Lake Minnetonka Sailing School, www.lmss.us

Parks: Lake Minnetonka Regional Park, 4610 County Rd 44, Minnetrista, Morris T. Baker Regional Park Reserve and Golf Course, and Noerenberg Memorial Gardens, 2840 North Shore Dr, Orono, are operated by the Three Rivers Park District, www.threeriversparks.org. Lake Minnewashta Regional Park, Highway 41 south of Highway 7, includes a swimming beach, boat launch, trails, www.co.carver.mn.us/parks. The Depot, 402 E Lake St, Wayzata, has picnic tables with great water views and is the setting for Wednesday night concerts in summer. Excelsior Commons, Lake St, offers a tennis court, playground, baseball diamond, two beaches, plus a wide green that is popular for Frisbee throwing, kite flying, pick-up soccer games, and summer concerts. Wosfeld Woods Scientific and Natural Area (www.wolsfeldwoods. org), located in Orono and Medina, off County Rd 6, is one of the last remaining examples of the original "Big Woods" that once covered this part of Minnesota.

Local Events: Apple Days, Excelsior (September); Art on the Lake, Excelsior Commons (June); Chilly Open Golf Fundraiser, Wayzata Bay (February); Holiday Open House Tours, Excelsior and Wayzata (November/ December); James J. Hill Days, Wayzata (September)

City of Orono: 2750 Kelley Pkwy, Crystal Bay, 55323; 952-249-4600, www. ci.orono.mn.us

City of Wayzata: 600 Rice St, Wayzata, 55391; 952-404-5300, www.wayzata.org

City of Deephaven: 20225 Cottagewood Rd, Deephaven, 55331; 952-474-4755, www.cityofdeephaven.org

City of Excelsior: 339 3rd S, Excelsior, 55331; 952-474-5233, www.ci.excelsior. mn.us

City of Greenwood: 20225 Cottagewood Rd, Deephaven, 55331; 952-474-6633, www.greenwoodmn.com

City of Shorewood: 5755 Country Club Rd, Shorewood, 55331; 952-960-7900, www.ci.shorewood.mn.us

City of Mound: 5341 Maywood Rd, Mound, 55364; 952-472-0600, www.cityof mound.com

LONG LAKE, MEDINA, MAPLE PLAIN, INDEPENDENCE

Long Lake, just west of Wayzata, is a commercial center on the north shore, offering restaurants, bars, a bank, and other businesses. While it does have a few smaller, older, more affordable houses, and some apartments and new condo complexes, most homes are single-family detached, and very "silver spoon."

Medina is the place to look for homes with real acreage, especially if you want to have a horse. With all the parks and trails here, there's plenty of room to ride. Of course, you'll pay for it. Many of the homes are 10,000 square feet or more, and sell for millions. Though Medina's population is expected to increase

exponentially, a portion of the city will remain "diversified rural," which means a density of no more than one house per ten acres. Other areas, mostly along Highway 55, have been designated "developing," and can (will) have at least three houses per acre.

Maple Plain and the **City of Independence** are located another five miles west on U.S. Highway 12, on the western edge of Hennepin County. Largely rural, they are both loaded with plenty of attractive amenities. The Twin City Polo Club (www.twincitypolo.com) is located here, as is beautiful Lake Independence. Pioneer Creek Golf Course (www.pioneercreek.com) is considered one of the metropolitan area's best golfing bargains, and private Windsong Farm Golf Club (www.wsfarm.com) was ranked by the *Minneapolis Star Tribune* as one of Minnesota's top five courses.

Long Lake and Maple Plain are entirely within the Orono School District #278 (www.orono.k12.mn.us). Children in Medina and Independence attend schools in four districts: Westonka District 277 (www.westonka.k12.mn.us), Orono District 278 (www.orono.k12.mn.us), Delano District 879 (www.delano.k12.mn.us), and Rockford District 883 (www.rockford.k12.mn.us).

City of Long Lake: 450 Virginia Ave, Long Lake, 55356; 952-473-6961, www.ci.long-lake.mn.us

City of Medina: 2052 County Rd 24, Medina, 55356; 763-473-4643, www.ci.medina.mn.us

City of Maple Plain: 1620 Maple Ave, Maple Plain, 55359; 763-479-0515, www.mapleplain.com

City of Independence: 1920 County Rd 90, Independence, 55359; 763-479-0527, http://independence.govoffice.com

PLYMOUTH

Boundaries: North: Maple Grove; **West**: Ferndale Rd/Brockton Ln; **South**: Ridgemont Ave, Luce Line Hiking and Biking Trail; **East**: Hwy 169; **Area**: 36 square miles; **Population**: 70,000

Plymouth, 10 miles northwest of Minneapolis, maintained its rural character well into the 1970s—much longer than most Twin Cities suburbs. Today agriculture is a thing of the past, however, and the city has a diverse economic base that provides the Twin Cities with over 50,000 jobs.

Named a *Money Magazine* Best Place to Live for 2008–09, Plymouth's ed goal is to provide its residents with a strong economic base, preserve tural environment, and foster respect for individuals—and it has taken a of actions to meet this goal. Resources have been committed to pre- en space, and the city now has 70 miles of trails and about 40 parks.

Year-round recreation programs at the Plymouth IceCenter/Life Time Fitness Center (763-509-0909, http://lifetimefitness.mylt.com) have something to offer all ages, from ballroom dance and community garden plots to rock climbing. Other public amenities include a walking-jogging track, pool, and ballroom.

Plymouth has been involved in a planned development process since 1973, and thus has been able to limit its industrial/commercial development to locations along main roads. It has also been able to create a wide range of housing—owner-occupied and rental, single-family detached and multi-family. Though Plymouth is essentially built-out in the south, new development is still taking place in the north/northwest, where you will find higher-end, single-family homes and townhomes. Older neighborhoods, in the southern part of the city near Wayzata, contain a mix of ramblers, 1970s split-levels, and two-story colonials.

I-494, highways 169 and 55, and county roads 6 and 9 run through the city, making it attractive to both corporations and commuters. The city operates its own public transit service and offers express bus service between Plymouth and downtown Minneapolis. Many residents don't need to commute, however, because they work at businesses headquartered in the city. Shopping is scattered throughout the city or located minutes away at Ridgedale (on 394), in Wayzata, or Maple Grove.

Plymouth is served by four school districts: Wayzata #284 (www.wayzata.k12. mn.us/wps), Robbinsdale #281 (http://rdale.org), Osseo #279 (http://district279. org), and Hopkins #270 (www.hopkins.k12.mn.us). (For more information, see **Childcare and Education.**)

City of Plymouth: 3400 Plymouth Blvd, Plymouth, 55446; 763-509-5000, www2.ci.plymouth.mn.us

NORTH/NORTHWEST SUBURBS

Brooklyn Park/Champlin; Maple Grove

BROOKLYN PARK AND CHAMPLIN

Boundaries: *Brooklyn Park*: **North**: 109th Ave N; **West**: Osseo/Maple Grove, Jefferson Hwy, Hwy 169; **South**: Brooklyn Center, Crystal, New Hope; **East**: Mississippi River; **Area**: 26.1 square miles; **Population**: 68,000; *Champlin*: **North**: Mississippi River; **West**: Dayton; **South**: 109th Ave N, Brooklyn Park, Maple Grove; **East**: Mississippi River; **Area**: 8.2 square miles; **Population**: 23,300

Brooklyn Park is located on the banks of the Mississippi River, 12 miles from downtown Minneapolis. The sixth largest city in the state, it is a still-growing second-ring suburb expected to top out at 85,000 by 2030. Though housing here is similar to all the other new housing going up throughout the Twin Cities, single- and multi-family units here are somewhat more moderately priced.

Next-door neighbor **Champlin** is divided roughly down the middle, with older, 1950s and '60s ramblers on the east side of Highway 169, and 1970s split levels and newer homes on the west. Numerous townhouses have sprung up near Highway 169, filling out the middle. Recently constructed executive-level homes can be found along the Mississippi River, off West River Road. Those who would like to build a home might look here, where there are a number of available lots. You'll find information about lots for sale on the city's web site.

Recreation is close at hand for residents of both Brooklyn Park and Champlin. Topping the list are 4900-acre Elm Creek Park Reserve (www.threeriversparks. com), on the western side of Champlin, and nationally recognized Edinburgh USA (www.edinburghusa.com) golf course in Brooklyn Park.

Children in Brooklyn Park attend schools operated by Anoka-Hennepin School District #11 (www.anoka.k12.mn.us), Osseo School District #279 (www.

district279.org), or Robbinsdale School District #281 (http://rdale.org). Children in Champlin attend Anoka-Hennepin Schools (www.anoka.k12.mn.us). Hennepin Technical College (www.hennepintech.edu) and North Hennepin Community College (www.nhcc.mnscu.ed) are both located in Brooklyn Park.

Brooklyn Park is working with Hennepin County and Metro Transit to provide high-speed transit—either Light Rail Transit (LRT) or Bus Rapid Transit (BRT) along the Bottineau Boulevard (County Road 81) corridor into downtown Minneapolis.

City of Brooklyn Park: 5200 85th Ave N, Brooklyn Park, 55443; 763-424-8000, www.brooklynpark.org

City of Champlin: 11955 Champlin Dr, Champlin, 55316; 763-421-8100, http://ci.champlin.mn.us

MAPLE GROVE

Boundaries: North: 109th Ave N; **West**: Hwy 101; **South**: 62nd Ave N; **East**: Hwy 169; **Area**: 36 square miles; **Population**: 64,000

Nearly everything in Maple Grove is new. Since 1999, the city has gone from open land and gravel pits, with half a dozen residential neighborhoods along I-494, to insta-community, with a newly created town center and mile after mile of great room/three-car-garage/granite countertop housing built by all the region's major builders. Townhomes have the same open-plan layouts and trendy finishes, and some of the more expensive units also feature three-car garages. Older (1970s-era) townhouses often have large yards and views across wetlands or other nature areas. The city's much-ballyhooed new downtown has a government center, new library, movie theater, retail shops, townhomes, and the Arbor Lakes "lifestyle" mall. Located just north of interstates 94 and 694, Arbor Lakes has quickly become a popular shopping destination. (See **Shopping for the Home**.)

The community is served by two school districts. Osseo District #279 (www.district279.org) covers most of the Maple Grove area and serves almost 22,000 students, making it one of the largest school districts in Minnesota. Wayzata District #284 (www.wayzata.k12.mn.us) provides service to the southernmost part of the city. Attendance area maps can be downloaded from each school's web site.

Maple Grove Transit: 763-494-6005, provides commuter express service to and from downtown Minneapolis.

City of Maple Grove: 12800 Arbor Lakes Parkway N, Maple Grove, 55311; 494-6000, www.ci.maple-grove.mn.us

OUTER WESTERN SUBURBS

Ten years ago, the properties along Interstate Highway 94 between Maple Grove and St. Cloud weren't suburbs—they were working farms. Today cheap land and easy access to interstates and major highways have turned the west/northwest fringe of the Twin Cities into one of the fastest growing areas in the state—and into a driver's nightmare, as well, putting great pressure on roads whose designs are insufficient for the amount of traffic they are being asked to carry. I-94, which carries the heaviest and fastest traffic, is known for its fatal cross-median crashes and long delays in the vicinity of Highway 101.

HENNEPIN COUNTY

CORCORAN, DAYTON, AND HASSAN TOWNSHIP/ROGERS

The western Hennepin county cities of Corcoran, Dayton, and Hassan Township/Rogers are expected to quadruple in population by 2030. Thanks to the building craze of the 1900s to the mid-2000s, old farmsteads here are already sprouting new townhouses and large single-family homes on suburban-generous lots, some along or near the Crow River. Rogers sports apartments as well. While the current housing woes have reduced development pressure out here, building is expected to resume once the housing market recovers. Trying to preserve the rural character of this area is important to current residents, but to find out what the future really holds, be sure to ask to see a copy of the cities' Comprehensive Plans. (**Hassan** is set to be annexed by the City of **Rogers** in 2012.)

The City of **Corcoran** is split between five different school districts: Buffalo-Hanover-Montrose Schools (www.bhmschools.org), Delano Public Schools

(www.delano.k12.mn.us), Osseo District #279 (www.district279.org), Rockford Area Schools (www.rockford.k12.mn.us), and Wayzata District #284 (www. wayzata.k12.mn.us). Children in Dayton and Rogers attend Elk River Schools, www.elkriver.k12.mn.us. Students in Hassan Township attend Elk River, Buffalo-Hanover-Montrose, or Osseo Area Schools.

While a commute into Minneapolis 20-some miles away on I-94 can be quite trying, **Dayton**, in particular, does have access to the Northstar Commuter Rail at Anoka. Many who live here work at the nuclear power plant close by in Monticello (pronounced mont-i-SELL-o). Park-and-Pool lots are located on either side of I-94 at Highway 101. The closest Park-and-Ride lots that offer bus services to and from the Twin Cities are located in Maple Grove and Plymouth. The Bottineau (County 81) Bus Rapid Transit or (possibly) LRT corridor will extend from downtown Minneapolis to Dayton, Rogers, and Hassan Township.

Recreation is close at hand at Elm Creek Park Reserve and Crow Hassan Regional Park (www.threeriversparks.org), which have lovely, peaceful hiking/biking/horseback riding trails and equally peaceful wildlife to watch. Crow Hassan includes an off-leash dog park and Elm Creek features a designated turf trail for mountain biking.

City of Corcoran: 8200 County Rd 116, Corcoran, 55340; 763-420-2288, www.ci.corcoran.mn.us

City of Dayton: 12260 S Diamond Lake Rd, Dayton, 55327; 763-4274589, www.cityofdaytonmn.com

Hassan Township: 25000 Hassan Pkwy, Rogers, 55374; 763-428-4100, www.townofhassan.com

City of Rogers: 22350 S Diamond Lake Rd, Rogers, 55374; 763-428-2253, www.cityofrogers.org

WRIGHT COUNTY

Boundaries: North: Mississippi River, Sherburne County; **West**: Stearns and Meeker counties; **South**: McLeod County; **East**: Crow River, Hennepin County; **Area**: 716 square miles (31 miles north/south, 36 miles east/west); **Population**: 106,734

Wright County, just west of Hennepin, is another of the fastest growing counties in the country, with thousands of acres of new-style housing to match. Many new developments are clustered around the county's 298 lakes, some of which have very poor water quality because of agricultural runoff. For all its growth, Wright County is still nearly three-fourths agricultural, with farm operations ranging from feedlots to wineries scattered throughout. Most industrial/commercial development is clustered along I-94 and Highways 55 and 12. The

Xcel Energy Nuclear Generating Plant is located along the Mississppi River in Monticello.

Numerous golf courses dot the landscape including Wild Marsh (www.wildmarsh.com) at Buffalo and Riverwood National (www.riverwoodnational.com) near Albertville, where it's also about a different kind of recreation—shopping at the Albertville Premium Outlets' 100 outlet stores.

Web Site: Wright County Government Center, 10 2nd St NW, Buffalo, 55313, 763-682-3900, 800-362-3667, www.co.wright.mn.us

Police: Wright County Sheriff, 1800 Braddock Ave, Buffalo; Emergency, 911; Non-emergency, 763-682-1162

Emergency Hospital: Buffalo Hospital, 303 Catlin St, Buffalo, 763-682-1212, www.buffalohospital.org/ahs/buffalo.nsf; New River Medical Center, 1013 Hart Blvd, Monticello, 763-295-2945, www.newrivermedical.com

Library: Great River Regional Library System, www.griver.org

Parks: 3000 acres of parks, 31.5 miles of trails, 17 miles of ski trails, six fishing piers, a 12-hole disc golf course, seven playgrounds; five swimming beaches; two campgrounds; parks along the North Fork and main branch of the Crow River offer access to one of the region's most scenic and accessible state canoe routes. Ney Nature Center near Maple Lake is an environmental education facility for local schools and the public.

CARVER COUNTY

Chanhassen; Chaska

Boundaries: North: Shorewood; **West**: McLeod and Sibley counties; **South**: Minnesota River; **East**: Eden Prairie; **Area**: 376 square miles; **Population**: 82,000

This is what sprawl looks like. Located just southwest of Minneapolis, this smallest and least populated of the seven metro counties is also one of the fastest growing in the state. The estimated 2006 population of 86,236 is expected to more than double by 2030. To house these new residents, Carver has allowed the farms on the eastern side of the county to be replaced by dense developments of homes and townhomes. As you go west on Highway 5 toward and past Waconia, however, the countryside becomes more rural and you suddenly realize you're counting more horses than townhouses. That's the good news; the bad news is that east-west Highway 5 on which you're driving is a killer—literally, with many fatalities over the years. People who must commute worry about that and the Minnesota Department of Transportation (MnDOT) agrees that the two-lane road was not designed to handle the level of traffic it now receives. That said, money's tight and improving Highway 5 does not appear in any of MnDOT's plans through 2030. Commuters farther south face a bottleneck at the point where Highway 212 goes from four to two lanes.

Web Site: Carver County Government Center, 600 East 4th St, Chaska, 55318, 952-361-1500, www.co.carver.mn.us

Carver County Service Centers: 418 Pine St, Chaska, 952-361-1900; 7808 Kerber Blvd, Chanhassen, 952-361-3900

Police: 606 East 4th St, Emergency: 911; Non-emergency, 952-361-1212

Emergency Hospitals: Ridgeview Medical Center, 500 S Maple St, Waconia, 952-442-2191, www.ridgeviewmedical.org; St. Francis Regional Medical Center, 1455 St. Francis Ave, Shakopee, 952-428-3000, www.stfrancis-shakopee.com

Library: Carver County Library System, www.carverlib.org

Community Resource: The Minnesota Landscape Arboretum, 3675 Arboretum Dr, 952-443-1400, www.arboretum.umn.edu, is part of the Department of Horticultural Science at the University of Minnesota. Its mission is to serve as a resource for horticultural and environmental information, and to develop and evaluate plants and horticultural practices for cold climates.

Parks: Carver County operates three regional Parks: 200-acre Baylor Park and Onan Observatory on Eagle Lake in the western part of the county; 340-acre Lake Minnewashta Park off Hwy 41; and 8-acre Lake Waconia Regional Park on the south shore of the lake. The parks offer swimming beaches, picnic facilities, trails, playgrounds, boat access, and campgrounds, www.co.carver.mn.us/parks.

Public Transportation: SouthwestTransit, 952-949-2BUS, www.swtransit.org, provides commuter and reverse-commuter service between Minneapolis and Eden Prairie, Chanhassen, and Chaska with Park & Ride lots at the intersections of Highways 212/ 41 and Walden Drive/Hundertmark Road in Chaska; and at Southwest Village on the corner of Hwy 212/101 and the Chanhassen Dinner Theater, just north of Hwy 5 in Chanhassen.

CHANHASSEN

Boundaries: North: Shorewood; **West**: Victoria, Chaska; **South**: Minnesota River; **East**: Eden Prairie; **Area**: 24 square miles; **Population**: 20,321

Money Magazine's 2009 Second Best Place to Live in America, Chanhassen grew from a population of 11,000 in 1990 to over 20,000 in 2000, and is expected to reach 38,000 in just a few years. As a consequence of this rapid growth, almost all of the city is new, with over half the homes built since 2000. While single-family detached houses predominate, about a fourth of the city's housing stock is in multi-family units, especially townhomes. Some of the city's prettiest neighborhoods have been built around its lakes, Christmas and Lotus lakes in the north, and Lake Riley in the south, all of which are surrounded by custom-built houses.

Shopping is conveniently located along the city's West 78th Street main drag, which extends in an unbroken line of strip malls from the Chanhassen Dinner Theatre (www.chanhassentheatres.com), at the east end of the street, to Byerly's grocery store and Target at the west. In between you will find a movie theater, hotel (www.countryinns.com/chanhassenmn), banks, medical offices, Cub Foods, the library, and several restaurants. Chanhassen straddles the Hennepin/Carver County border, so children in its northern (Hennepin County) sector attend Minnetonka District 276 schools (www.minnetonka.k12.mn.us). The rest of the city is in the Chaska school district (www.district112.org). Private Chapel Hill Academy (www.chapel-hill.org) is located in the downtown. Many students in this area are home-schooled.

City of Chanhassen: City Hall, 7700 Market Blvd, Chanhassen, 55317; 952-227-1100, www.ci.chanhassen.mn.us/

CHASKA

Boundaries: North: Victoria, Chanhassen; **West**: Laketown and Dahlgren townships; **South**: Minnesota River; **East**: Chanhassen; **Area**: 45 square miles; **Population**: 21,694

The old yellow brick buildings in the historic river city of Chaska sit in marked contrast to the ecru and beige tract-house suburbia that surrounds them. Another contrast: the name "Jonathan" painted on a silo across Highway 41 from a Super Target. Jonathan (www.jonathaninchaska.com) was an early sub-division in Chaska, conceived as an alternative to the sprawling, sterile suburbs that began sprouting in cornfields all over the country in the 1960s. The idea behind it was that people should be able to live, work, and play within a single, ecologically healthy, pedestrian-friendly city. This new urban environment even

had amenities (a concept new for its time) like tot-lots, backyards that melted into parks and greenbelts, and groomed ski trails. The houses, too, were wildly experimental. Some were modular, intended to grow or shrink with a family. Many contained such futuristic gadgets as trash-compactors and a community information system (think early Internet) that allowed residents to be "seen" by doctors at nearby Waconia hospital! The community was so famous in the early 1970s that the *Washington Post* and *Newsweek* covered its construction, and people moved from all over the country to live in it. Then the recession hit and it fizzled. Intended to become a city of 50,000, it topped out at 1500. "Ah, Jonathan, you were such a big, beautiful test-tube baby," wrote *Newsweek*, "but you may never make it to 1990."

Fast-forward to the first decade of the 21st century and Carver County is one of the 100 fastest-growing counties in the nation, with most of its growth taking place in and around its county seat, Chaska, and neighboring Chanhassen and **Victoria**, where large developments of both houses and townhomes now dominate the landscape. Of particular note are new downtown Chaska condos that have Minnesota River views. Farther out, expensive single-family homes are springing up surrounding the Chaska Town Course, a municipal 18-hole golf course near Lake Bavaria (www.chaskamn.com/towncourse/welcome.cfm). Older homes and apartments surround Hazeltine National Golf Club (www. hngc.com), east of Highway 41.

For non-golfers, recreation in *Money Magazine*'s 2009 20th Best Place to Live revolves around the Community Center, www.chaskacommunitycenter. com, which has a walking/running track, pool, gym, skating arena, rehabilitation center, and full-day childcare.

City-owned residential high speed wireless Internet access is available in much of the city of Chaska for about $20 a month. Service is not available in some apartment complexes.

Children here attend Chaska Independent School District #112, www.district112.org. The recent completion of the Highway 212 freeway has cut the 25-mile commute into Minneapolis to about half an hour. Commuters also have the option of taking SouthWest Transit (952-949-2BUS, www.swtransit.org) into town. Express buses operate all day and into the night.

City of Chaska: 1 City Hall Plaza, Chaska, 55318; 952-448-9200, www.ci.chaska.mn.us

NORTH/NORTHWEST METRO SUBURBS

Suburbs Along the Northstar Commuter Rail Corridor

The Northstar Commuter Rail line begins at Target Field (where it connects with buses and the Hiawatha LRT) and heads northwest on the north side of the Mississippi River. It is also well north of I-94. It serves the following cities: Fridley, Coon Rapids/Riverdale, Anoka/Andover/Ramsey, Elk River, and Big Lake. Buses connect at Big Lake and carry passengers on to St. Cloud.

ANOKA COUNTY

Andover; City of Anoka; Blaine; Coon Rapids; Fridley; Lino Lakes; Ramsey

Boundaries: North: Isanti County; **West**: Hennepin and Sherburne counties; **South**: Ramsey and Hennepin counties; **East**: Chisago and Washington counties; **Area**: 424 square miles; **Population**: 327,000

The traditional image of Anoka County is one of blue-collar burgs and right-wing politics: a place where there's very little to do beyond snowmobiling, hunting, and fishing. That's changing—rapidly. Upscale new housing, "smart growth" town centers, and the construction of the Northstar Commuter Rail Line all add up to a county on the brink of a new era. According to the Minnesota State Demographer, the area surrounding the Northstar Commuter Rail Corridor is the single fastest growing region in Minnesota.

Even without the Northstar Commuter Line, this fourth most populous county in Minnesota has exploded! From 1990 to 2000, it grew almost twice as fast as the rest of Minnesota, and is expected to increase its population by another third by 2030. Unfortunately, for a region that desperately needs entry-level housing, most of the development so far has consisted of move-up, single-family homes. That may be remedied soon, as an increasing number of multi-family dwellings are being planned or are already under construction in the cities near the proposed Northstar Commuter Rail Line. Using existing tracks owned by the Burlington Northern Santa Fe (BNSF) Railway, the Northstar Line provides service on a 40-mile route from Minneapolis to Big Lake. There are six stations: Minneapolis, Fridley, Coon Rapids, Anoka, Elk River, and Big Lake. This train has cut the commute between Elk River and Minneapolis from well over an hour to 41 minutes. New town centers along the way are set to add hundreds of thousands of square feet of shopping and thousands of units of transit-oriented housing, including lofts, single- and multiple-family housing, and rentals. Rentals are in short supply, although some can be found in the parts of the county closest to Minneapolis and along major highways and I-35W.

Hard hit by foreclosures, Anoka has used Neighborhood Stabilization Program funds to purchase and rehab tax forfeited and foreclosed homes that are available for sale directly from the county. They are listed on the county's web site. There are a number of vacant lots listed there as well. The county also offers 0%-interest, forgivable rehabilitation loans to purchasers of vacant, foreclosed homes.

While Anoka County lacks good major highway access, it more than makes up for that with abundant natural resources. The gorgeous Rum River flows through the west side of the county, and 16 regional and county parks offer a variety of recreation, including swimming, fishing, horseback riding, hiking, biking, canoeing, boating, golfing and cross-country skiing. They include Bunker Hills Regional Park (Coon Rapids), Carlos Avery Wilderness Area (Columbus Township), Coon Rapids Dam Regional Park, Rice Creek Chain of Lakes Regional Park Reserve (Centerville/Lino Lakes), Sandhill Crane Nature Area (East Bethel), Springbrook Nature Center (Fridley), and Wargo Nature Center (Lino Lakes).

Web Site: www.anokacounty.us

Area Code: 763; 651 in the eastern part of the county

Anoka County Government Center: 2100 3rd Ave, Anoka, 55303; 763-421-4760, 763-323-5289 (TTY)

Driver's and Other Licenses: Anoka License Center, 6111 Hwy 10, Ramsey, 763-576-5777; Blaine License Center, 10995 Club West Pkwy, Blaine, 763-767-3888; Columbia Heights License Center, 3982 Central Ave NE, Columbia Heights, 763-789-7202; Coon Rapids License Center, 455 99th Ave NW, Coon Rapids, 763-785-5999; Ham Lake License Center, 17565 Central Ave NE, Ham Lake, 763-413-9717

Emergency Hospitals: Mercy Hospital, 4050 Coon Rapids Blvd, Coon Rapids, 763-236-6060, www.allinamercy.org/ahs/mercy.nsf; Unity Hospital, 550 Osborne Rd, Fridley, 763-236-5000, www.allinaunity.org/ahs/unity.nsf

Library: Anoka County Library, 707 County Rd 10 NE, Blaine, www.anoka.lib.mn.us

Parks: www.AnokaCountyParks.com; Parks Info Line, 763-767-2820

Transportation: 612-373-3333, www.metrotransit.org; Anoka County "Traveler" bus system, Anoka County Transit Office, 763-422-7075, http://ww2. anokacounty.us/v3_transit/index.aspx; Ramsey Star Express commuter buses to and from Minneapolis, 1-888-528-8880 or www.commutercoach.org

Community Publications: *Anoka County Union, Blaine-Spring Lake Park Life*, and *Coon Rapids Herald*, www.abcnewspapers.com

Community Resources: Lyric Arts Theater, Anoka, 763-422-1838, www.lyricarts. org; Anoka County History Center, Anoka, www.ac-hs.org; Banfill-Locke Center for the Arts, Fridley, 763-574-1850, www.banfill-locke.org; Anoka-Hennepin Technical College, 1355 West Main St, Anoka, 763-576-4700, TTY 711 or TTY 800-627-3529, www.anokatech.edu; National Sports Center, 1700 105th Ave NE, Blaine, www.nscsports.org

ANDOVER

Boundaries: North: 181st Ave NW; **West**: Rum River, City of Anoka; **South**: Coon Rapids; **East**: Ham Lake; **Area**: 34.1 square miles; **Population**: 30,000

You can still find Minnesota's traditional mix of Norwegians, Swedes, and Germans in this little piece of Midwest paradise that residents describe as "not quite in the cities, but not too far out." There, for the price of a 30-minute commute on the Northstar LIne, locals say they get a "not-overpopulated" feeling at the same time that they are still close to shopping at all the big chains—Rainbow Foods, Home Depot, Menard's—which are just off Highway 10 in nearby Coon Rapids. And though most of the houses are quite new, there are still enough old farmhouses, set back from the roads across long front lawns, to give the area a visual connection with its agricultural roots. Development has been steady here since the 1970s, so housing offers a variety of single-family, owner-occupied, family-sized homes whose architecture is typical of each era. Andover is expected to grow to a population of 40,500 by 2030.

Children in a small section in the northern part of the city attend St. Francis District #15 schools (www.stfrancis.k12.mn.us), while Anoka-Hennepin School District #11 (www.anoka.k12.mn.us) serves the rest.

City of Andover: 1685 Crosstown Blvd NW, Andover, 55304; 763-755-5100, www.ci.andover.mn.us

CITY OF ANOKA

Boundaries: North: Ramsey, Andover; **West**: Ramsey; **South**: Mississippi River; **East**: Coon Rapids; **Area**: 6.7 square miles; **Population**: 18,000

Located at the confluence of the Rum and Mississippi rivers, in the southwest corner of the county, Anoka (the county seat) is about 32 minutes from Minneapolis via the Northstar Commuter Rail Line. Since the rail route was proposed, Anoka has been working to develop a residential and commercial Transit Village around the Northstar station site. Apart from the new transit-oriented housing, most homes in Anoka are older, "city-style" properties, with houses built close together on small lots. Garrison Keillor, host of radio's *A Prairie Home Companion*, was born in Anoka and graduated from Anoka High School. His fictional Lake Wobegone is presumed to be based on this town, which also bills itself as the "Halloween Capital of the World."

City of Anoka: 2015 First Ave North, Anoka, 55303; 763-576-2700, www. ci.anoka.mn.us

BLAINE

Boundaries: North: 133rd Ave NE; **West**: University Ave NE; **South**: 85th Ave NE; **East**: Sunset Ave NE; **Area**: 34 square miles; **Population**: 60,000

If you or your children are into sports, you might save yourself hours of driving time by living in Blaine, home of the National Sports Center. The NSC (www. nscsports.org) is a 660-acre campus with 52 soccer fields, the largest ice arena in the world, an outdoor stadium with a 400-meter track, cycling velodrome, and the National Youth Golf Center, an 18-hole golf course built specifically for youth and families. Most of the metro's major tournaments are held here, from soccer and lacrosse to the state high school track and field championships. The facility's biggest annual event, the Schwan's USA CUP soccer tournament (www.usacup. org), is the largest youth sporting event in the Western Hemisphere. For serious adult golfers, the community is home to the Tournament Players' Club (www.

tpctwincities.com), a private 7146-yard, par-72 layout that is the site of the 3M PGA Champions Tour Championships. The upper-bracket housing surrounding the TPC puts Blaine on the map as one of the metro's fancier addresses. In fact, though not all the houses are high-end, most are relatively new—Blaine leads all metro cities except Minneapolis in housing units built since 2000. While you can find a townhome here, most of the houses are single-family.

Some children here attend Centennial School District #12 (www.isd12. org), but most attend Spring Lake Park #16 (www.splkpark.k12.mn.us) and Anoka-Hennepin District #11 (http://anoka.k12.mn.us). Children from the southernmost "tail" of the city attend Mounds View District #621 schools (www. moundsviewschools.org).

Blaine residents can catch the Northstar Commuter Rail at its Coon Rapids station.

City of Blaine: 10801 Town Square Dr NE, Blaine, 55449; 763-784-6700, www. ci.blaine.mn.us

COON RAPIDS

Boundaries: North: Andover; **West**: Anoka, Mississippi River; **South**: Mississippi River, Fridley; **East**: Blaine; **Area**: 23 square miles; **Population**: 62,721

Another stop on the Northstar line, Coon Rapids is a quiet, older suburb located three miles north of I-694 up University Avenue (Highway 47). It is about a 30-minute drive from downtown Minneapolis. Available housing includes single- and multi-family homes, condominiums, townhomes, waterfront homes, riverfront homes, luxury homes, and rentals—with plenty of 1950s ramblers and split-levels, as well as prices that tend to be on the low side for the metro market. The 500-acre Bunker Hills Regional Park (www.anokacountyparks.com) is home to highly rated Bunker Hills Golf Course and water park. Bunker Park Stable offers trail rides, hay and sleigh rides, lessons, and even a walking pony ride for small children. Abundant shopping is centered on Riverdale Mall. The entire city of Coon Rapids is located in the Anoka-Hennepin School District #11 (www.anoka.k12.mn.us). In February, the community turns out for Snowflake Days, a 10-day celebration that includes sporting events, dances, dog sled races, a medallion hunt, and the Miss Coon Rapids Pageant. If you're interested in living in this area, be sure to check out the city's online video tour book.

City of Coon Rapids: 11155 Robinson Dr, Coon Rapids, 55433; 763-755-2880, www.ci.coon-rapids.mn.us

FRIDLEY

Boundaries: North: Coon Rapids, Blaine, Spring Lake Park; **West**: Mississippi River (Brooklyn Park, Brooklyn Center); **South**: Columbia Heights, Minneapolis; **East**: Mounds View, New Brighton; **Area**: 10.89 square miles; **Population**: 25,709

Fridley is known for two things—the World Headquarters of Medtronic, and the 1965 Fridley Tornado. It is located mostly north of I-694 along highways 47 (University Avenue NE) and 65 (Central Avenue NE). While its industries are high-tech, its neighborhoods are modest and affordable. The majority of the city's housing stock was built during the 1960s, after the city was flattened by the tornado, and consists of single-family detached ramblers and split-levels on fairly small cul-de-sac lots. Several small apartment complexes and other multi-unit housing were built about ten years later. Now redevelopment has begun again, especially in the area near the Northstar Commuter Rail Line station at 61st Street and Main.

While a lot of the city has something of a "Rustbelt" appearance, attractive, well-kept homes are to be found along its wetlands and beside the river, and in the Innsbruck neighborhood in the southeastern corner. The city's crowning glory is 127-acre Springbrook Nature Center (www.springbrooknaturecenter.org). The largest park in Fridley, the nature center offers three miles of hiking trails, walkways over wetlands, a Halloween Pumpkin Walk, and summer day camps.

The Fridley School District (www.fridley.k12.mn.us) serves the central area of the city. Children in northwestern neighborhoods attend Anoka-Hennepin School District 11 (www.anoka.k12.mn.us). Children in the northeast attend Spring Lake Park schools (www.splkpark.k12.mn.us). The southern area of the city is served by Columbia Heights School District 13 (www.colheights.k12.mn.us). Banfill-Locke Center for the Arts (www.banfill-locke.org), on East River Road, is the focal point for the city's cultural life, providing classes for adults and children and juried art shows. Shopping is conveniently located along University Avenue or 15 minutes away at Rosedale.

City of Fridley: 6431 University Ave NE, Fridley, 55432; 763-571-3450, www.ci.fridley.mn.us

LINO LAKES

Boundaries: North: Ham Lake; **West**: Blaine; **South**: County Road J; **East**: Centerville; **Area**: 33 square miles; **Population**: 19,123

Located along a chain of 13 lakes in the North Metro, Lino Lakes is committed to the concept of "conservation development," which is intended to provide high-density housing while permanently preserving natural features and open space. Directly up I-35 from St. Paul, it is a popular place to relocate, and has added over 20% to its population since 2000. Ranked #36 among *Money Magazine*'s 2009 Best Places to Live, recreation includes one of the most scenic of all the region's public golf courses, Chomonix (www.chomonixgolf.com), in the Rice Creek Chain of Lakes Regional Park Reserve (www.anokacountyparks.com).

Lino Lakes is served by three school districts: Centennial School District #12, 763-792-6000, www.centennial.k12.mn.us; White Bear Lake Area School District #624, 651-773-6000, www.whitebear.k12.mn.us; and Forest Lake School District #831, 651-982-6000, www.forestlake.k12.mn.us. You can download a map of their attendance areas from the city's web site.

City of Lino Lakes: 600 Town Center Pkwy, Lino Lakes, 55014; 651-982-2400, www.ci.lino-lakes.mn.us

RAMSEY

Boundaries: North: 181st Ave N; **West**, Sherburne County; **South**: Mississippi River; **East**: Rum River; **Area**: 28.8 square miles; **Population**: 23,734

A bedroom community in the far western reaches of Anoka County, Ramsey contains a mixture of newer, large, custom-designed single-family homes on spacious lots, luxurious golf communities, and numerous townhouses. Its population consists mostly of young families, with very few elderly. Like most Twin Cities suburbs, it lacks a real downtown, but the city is working to develop one. Called Ramsey Town Center, it will be a mix of 2,400 homes, parks, and commercial and municipal buildings located along Sunwood Drive. While touted as a model of New Urbanist transit-oriented suburban planning, it has suffered many delays (including no commuter rail station yet), but is expected to

move forward once the economy improves. While this is car country, with many homes featuring three- and four-car garages, residents can hop the Northstar Commuter Rail Line at the Anoka station for a half-hour ride into Minneapolis. Recreation revolves around the city's wetlands and natural areas, including Rum River and Mississippi West regional parks (www.anokacountyparks.com). The Links at Northfork, a true Scottish links–style golf course, is open to the public. Take a virtual tour of the course at www.golfthelinks.com. While there aren't a lot of businesses here, one of them is familiar to discerning coffee lovers around the globe—Paradise Roasters (www.paradiseroasters.com) is one of the top boutique coffee roasters in the world. Children here attend schools operated by Elk River District #728 (www.elkriver.k12.mn.us) or Anoka-Hennepin District 11 (www.anoka.k12.mn.us).

City of Ramsey: 7550 Sunwood Dr, Ramsey, 55303; 763-427-1410, www.ci.ramsey.mn.us

OUTER NORTHWESTERN SUBURBS

SHERBURNE COUNTY

CITY AND TOWNSHIP OF BIG LAKE; ELK RIVER

Boundaries: North: Benton and Mille Lacs counties; **West**: Stearns County; **South**: Mississippi River and Wright County; **East**: Isanti and Anoka counties; **Area**: 431 square miles; **Population**: 88,842

Sherburne County is situated between mid-Minnesota's two principal metropolitan areas, Minneapolis and St. Cloud. Early on, it was hoped that the Northstar Commuter Rail line would extend all the way from Minneapolis to St. Cloud along the I-94 corridor and relieve some of the congestion in this area. The line's actual route (from Minneapolis, through Fridley, Coon Rapids, Anoka, Elk River, and ending at Big Lake) appears not to accomplish that objective. What it has done, however, is increase demand for property out here, and make it much more reasonable to commute into the city for those who live near Elk River or Big Lake. Look here for large acreage or less expensive lakeshore—and lots of new construction. Since 2000, 1100 single-family homes have been built in the City of **Big Lake**, and Elk River added even more. **Elk River**, the county seat, is a genuine small city, with a population of about 24,000 people. In 2010 it asked its residents to perform 1000 random acts of kindness, and the project was a roaring success— librarians paid fines on overdue books, students raised money to keep someone's electricity turned on through the winter,

and someone even hid a $100 bill downtown with a note that said, "Hope this brightens your day!"

Web Site: Sherburne County Government Center, 13880 Hwy 10, Elk River, 55330-4601, 763-241-2700, 800-433-5228, www.co.sherburne.mn.us

Police: Sherburne County Sheriff's Office: Emergency, 911; Non-emergency, 763-241-2500, 800-433-5245

Driver's and Other Licenses: Sherburne County Government Center, 763-422-3401; Department of Motor Vehicles, 600 Railroad Dr, Elk River, 763-441-2110

Emergency Hospital: Fairview Northland Regional Hospital, 911 Northland Dr, Princeton, 763-389-1313, www.northland.fairview.org

Library: Great River Regional Library System, branches in Becker, Big Lake, Elk River, St. Cloud, www.griver.org

Public Schools: Big Lake Independent School District 727 (www.biglake.k12.mn.us); Elk River Area District 728 (www.elkriver.k12.mn.us); Becker I.S.D. 726, www.becker.k12.mn.us; Princeton I.S.D # 477, www.princeton.k12.mn.us

Parks: 30,600-acre Sherburne National Wildlife Refuge (www.fws.gov/midwest/Sherburne) is home to sandhill cranes, trumpeter swans, bald eagles, hawks, a variety of ducks and geese, and other wildlife. The Refuge provides a variety of opportunities for experiencing nature including hiking and cross-country ski trails, fishing, and hunting. Sand Dune State Forest (www.dnr.state.mn.us/state_forests/index.html) includes miles of groomed trails for snowmobiling and horseback riding. Golf courses: semi-private Elk River Country Club, 20015 Elk Lake Rd, Elk River, 763-441-4111, www.elkrivercc.com; Pinewood Municipal Golf Course, 18150 Waco St NW, Elk River, 763-441-3451; Oliver H. Kelley Living History Farm near Elk River on Hwy 10, www.mnhs.org

Community Publications: *West Sherburne Tribune*, 763-263-3602, www.westsherburnetribune.com

Public Transportation: www.metrotransit.org; Northstar Commuter Rail provides daily service from Elk River and Big Lake stations

City of Big Lake: 160 Lake St N, Big Lake, 55309; 763-263-2107, www.biglakemn.org

Township of Big Lake: 21960 County Rd 5, Big Lake, 55309; 763-263-3660, www.biglaketownship.com

City of Elk River: 13065 Orono Pkwy, Elk River, 55330; 763-635-1000, www.ci.elk-river.mn.us

NORTHEAST METRO SUBURBS

RAMSEY COUNTY

Arden Hills; Falcon Heights; Maplewood; Mounds View; New Brighton; North Oaks; North St. Paul; Roseville; Shoreview; Vadnais Heights; White Bear Lake/Dellwood

Boundaries: North: County Rd J; **West**: Silver Lake Rd; **South**: Mississippi River; **East**, Hwy 120; **Area**: 156 square miles; **Population:** 501,428

Ideally situated for easy access to interstate highways 35E, 35W, and 694, these suburbs are only a short commute from the core cities, particularly from downtown St. Paul. Many residents don't have to commute, however, because of all the national companies that have large corporate facilities here: Sysco and Medtronic are in Mounds View; Boston Scientific and Land O'Lakes are in Arden Hills; and international business giant 3M employs 11,000 people at its headquarters in Maplewood.

These suburbs aren't all business though. They are thick with recreation amenities as well. Nine county and five regional parks, extensive bike and cross-country ski trails, golf courses, ice arenas, swimming beaches, and boating facilities combine to give some parts of this region an almost rural flavor. Community centers help to make them function like small towns. North St. Paul and White Bear Lake are small towns, complete with downtown business districts.

What is known as the "Livability Factor" is high here, and residents enjoy a wide range of housing styles and prices, as well as nearby shopping in Roseville and at Maplewood Mall. Roseville alone has one of the largest concentrations of shopping centers in the entire upper Midwest.

Web Site: Ramsey County Government Center West, 50 Kellogg Blvd W, St. Paul, 55102-1664; Government Center East, 160 E Kellogg Blvd, St. Paul, 55101; 651-266-8500, www.co.ramsey.mn.us

Area Code: 651

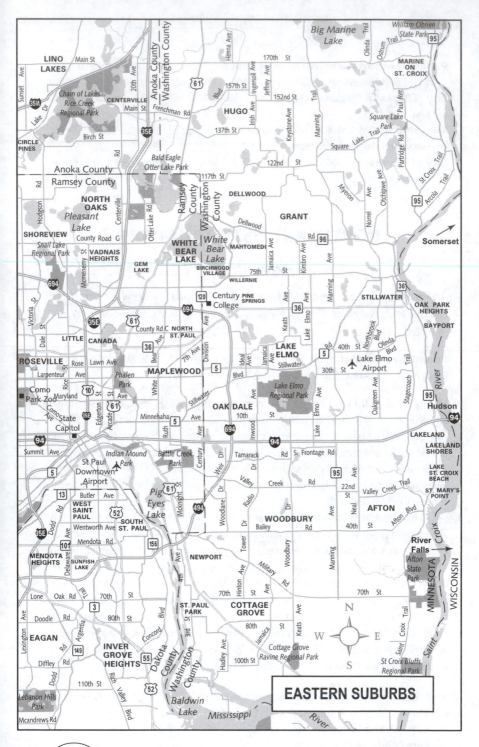

EASTERN SUBURBS

Emergency Hospitals: Regions Hospital, 640 Jackson St, 651-254-3456, www. regionshospital.com; HealthEast St. Joseph's Hospital, 69 W Exchange St, 651-232-3348, www.healtheast.org/st-joes.html; United Hospital, 333 N Smith Ave, St. Paul, 651-241-8000, www.unitedhospital.com; St. John's Hospital, 1575 Beam Ave, Maplewood, 651-232-7000, www.healtheast.org/ st-johns.html; Woodwinds Health Campus, 1925 Woodwinds Dr, Woodbury, 651-232-0228, www.healtheast.org/woodwinds.html
Libraries: Ramsey County Libraries, www.ramsey.lib.mn.us

ARDEN HILLS

Boundaries: North: North Boundary of Twin Cities Army Ammunition Plant; **West**: I-35W; **South**: County Rd D; **East**: Lexington; **Area**: 9 square miles; **Population**: 9900

Eight miles north of downtown St. Paul (see Western Suburbs map), the City of Arden Hills is small and neighborly, with rolling hills, lakes, excellent parks, well-kept houses, and a vibrant commercial and industrial sector. Over half the population 25 and older hold bachelor's degrees, and nearly 20% hold graduate or professional degrees. Housing here is overwhelmingly single-family detached and owner-occupied, with only a small proportion of multi-family and rental units. In the 1970s, Arden Hills was one of the fastest growing cities in the state, and those '70s styles (split-levels, colonials, ramblers) still account for approximately one-third of the city's housing stock. Most are in the moderate to executive price range, and many are situated on scenic wooded lots. The northern third of the city is occupied by the old Twin Cities Army Ammunition Plant. The object of many development schemes over the years, the city's comprehensive plan restricts its use to mixed-use residential/commercial and parkland, including a wildlife area.

City Hall: 1245 West Hwy 96, Arden Hills, 55112; 651-792-7800, www.ci. arden-hills. mn.us

FALCON HEIGHTS

Although technically not part of St. Paul, Falcon Heights is covered, along with St. Anthony Park, under Northwest St. Paul (see page 93).

MAPLEWOOD

Boundaries: North: County Rd D, I-694; **West**: St. Paul, Roseville, Little Canada; **South**: St. Paul at Larpenteur Ave and Newport at Bailey Rd; **East**: North St. Paul

at Ariel St and Oakdale, and Woodbury at Century Ave; **Area**: 19 square miles; **Population**: 36,100

Maplewood wraps around the east and north sides of St. Paul like a puzzle piece. It has been developing constantly since World War II, so housing styles vary greatly. You'll find examples of every era's popular housing types, most of which have been well maintained, often updated. Many are ramblers, dating from the 1950s and '60s, and are smaller than 1500 square feet. Approximately one-third of Maplewood's housing units are townhouses and condominiums. The city's newest, most upscale neighborhoods are located in a six-mile-long, one-mile-wide leg that extends southward alongside Woodbury and Oakdale.

Bracketed by interstates 94, 694, 494, and 35E, and by major state highways 61 and 36, Maplewood is all about shopping and big business. Maplewood Mall is the center of an extensive commercial area; 3M, which has about 11,000 employees at its Maplewood headquarters, is one of Minnesota's largest employers and best-known international corporations.

Maplewood has numerous neighborhood parks and playgrounds as well as the Maplewood Nature Center, Keller Golf Course, Goodrich Golf Course, and Aldrich Arena. The Community Center has a track, racquetball and basketball courts, performing arts theater, and an aquatics center with a 120-foot water slide. The Gateway Trail bike path can be easily accessed from the community center's parking lot. Mountain bikers should head for Winthrop Street Mountain Biking Area in Battle Creek Park, with its 5.5 kilometers of challenging mountain biking trails in hilly, wooded terrain. This is also a thrilling cross-country ski trail in the winter. (See **Sports and Recreation**.) Maps and directions to Maplewood's parks are available online at www.co.ramsey.mn.us/parks.

Children in Maplewood attend North St. Paul/Maplewood/Oakdale (www.isd622.org) or Roseville (www.isd623.org) public schools. Hill-Murray, a private Catholic school for grades 7–12, is known for its sports teams (www.hill-murray.org).

City of Maplewood: 1830 County Rd B East, Maplewood, 55109; 651-249-2000, www.ci.Maplewood.mn.us

MOUNDS VIEW

Boundaries: North: Blaine; **West**: Spring Lake Park; **South**: New Brighton; **East**: Shoreview, Arden Hills; **Area**: 4 square miles; **Population**: 13,000

The city of Mounds View is conveniently located between highways 35W on the east and 65 on the west (see Western Suburbs map). It is home to many businesses, including Medtronic and Sysco. Housing is a mix of post-1960 apartments, duplexes, and townhouses, and single-family detached homes on large wooded lots. The section of the city known as **Knollwood Park** features 1930s-era houses. Children here attend Mounds View Public Schools (www. moundsviewschools.org), a district that has received many accolades over the years. Two of its high schools, Irondale and Mounds View, were ranked among the nation's best by *U.S. News & World Report* in 2009.

City of Mounds View: 2401 Hwy 10 NE, Mounds View, 55112; 763-717-4000, www.ci.mounds-view.mn.us

NEW BRIGHTON

Boundaries: North: Mounds View; **West**: Stinson Blvd; **South**: St. Anthony Village; **East**: I-35W; **Area**: 7 square miles; **Population**: 22,000

Twenty minutes from the downtowns of both Minneapolis and St. Paul, New Brighton is an old town with a lot of new housing options. Originally incorporated in the 1880s, it is primarily residential, offering a range of housing from owner-occupied single-family detached homes on culs-de-sac to rental apartments. The town is split into northern and southern halves by I-694 (see Western Suburbs map)Southe. Most housing dates from the 1970s, but **Wexford Heights**, along Silver Lake Road, just south of the freeway, is comprised of custom homes built in the mid-1990s. **Innsbruck**, located both north and south of I-694, boasts houses that were considered luxury homes when they were built in the 1970s and '80s, and affordable "manor homes" built in the early 1990s.

Recreation amenities include a par-30 executive golf course (with Sunday night family golf!), a network of trails for walking, biking, and blading, and the Eagle's Nest, which was voted Best Indoor Place to Play by readers of *Minnesota Parent Magazine*. Children in New Brighton attend school in the nationally acclaimed Mounds View district (www.moundsviewschools.org). (See **City of**

Mounds View above). The community's principal festival is Stockyard Days, held annually in August to celebrate its heyday as the railhead for the region's cattle industry.

City of New Brighton: 803 Old Hwy 8 NW, New Brighton, 55112; 651-638-2100, www.ci.new-brighton.mn.us

NORTH OAKS

Boundaries: North: County Rd I to County Rd J; **West**: Hodgson Rd; **South**: Hwy 96; **East**: Centerville Rd; **Area**: 7.3 square miles; **Population**: 4689

If you're looking for a quiet wooded setting, you will probably like North Oaks, a private planned community of 6500 acres of open fields and heavily wooded hillsides, private trails, meandering roads, and a community-owned private golf course. Though the average list price here runs well over a million dollars, some older houses have sold for much less. Not a gated community, it is private property, and is run by the North Oaks Home Owners' Association. Though many children here attend private schools, those who wish to attend public school have a choice of Mounds View District #621 (www.moundsviewschools.org) or White Bear Lake Area #624 (www.whitebear.k12.mn.us). Among the city's many community organizations, along with the Children's Hospital Guild and Garden Club, is the North Oaks Singles Network, whose sole purpose is to help singles meet neighbors who are in a similar place in life.

City of North Oaks: 100 Village Center Dr, Suite 230, North Oaks, 55127, 651-792-7750, www.cityofnorth-oaks.com; Home Owners' Association, 100 Village Center Dr, Suite 240, 651-792-7765

NORTH ST. PAUL

Boundaries: North: Radatz St/Beam Ave/Lydia Ave; **West**; Ariel St; **South**: Holloway; **East**: Hwy 120; **Area**: 2.9 square miles; **Population**: 11,885

There may be more to North St. Paul than a snowman, but he's the thing that everybody remembers when they think about this city. Forty-four feet tall and made out of steel and stucco, this landmark grew out of the community's tradition of building a huge snowman every winter. He's been standing at his present location at Highway 36 and Margaret Street (Central Park) since 1990, and has been adopted as the city's official logo. There are actually a lot of interesting things about this city, including its affordable housing, and the fact that

here, in a place where the closest thing most suburbs have to a downtown is a city hall complex, North St. Paul has a real downtown.

A city with environmental sensibilities, North St. Paul distributes its own electricity, offering its customers a chance to "Go Green" by buying power from renewable energy sources, including wind. Housing here is overwhelmingly single-family detached three-bedroom homes. About a third date from the 1950s, with another third from the 1970s. Recent development consists of a few small condo and townhome redevelopments of existing properties. North St. Paul is expected to grow by only 10% by 2030, so for those looking for a fairly stable place that is more small town than suburb, on the north side of metro, this town may be worth a look.

Children here attend North St. Paul–Maplewood–Oakdale schools (www. isd622.org). Residents have access to the **Gateway Trail**, which cuts through North St. Paul on its way from St. Paul to Stillwater.

City of North St. Paul: 2400 Margaret St, North St. Paul, 55109, 651-747-2400, www.ci.north-saint-paul.mn.us

ROSEVILLE

Boundaries: North: County Rd D; **West**: Highcrest Rd; **South**: Roselawn Ave, Hamline, Larpenteur; **East**: Rice St; **Area**: 13.2 square miles; **Population**: 33,000

With two major malls, Roseville is a hub for shopping. Starter homes are also plentiful here, but there is a serious lack of step-up housing. The city is working on that problem by offering home improvement loans and free construction consultations. The parks and recreation amenities are another incentive for families to live here: 34 parks, indoor and outdoor skating facilities (including a speedskating track and what the city claims to be the largest skating party in the state on New Year's Eve), an arboretum, par-3 golf course—the list goes on and on.

City of Roseville: 2660 Civic Center Dr, Roseville, 55113; 651-792-7000, www. ci.roseville.mn.us

SHOREVIEW

Boundaries: North: Hwy 1 (Blaine and Lino Lakes); **South**: County Rd D (Roseville); **East**: Lexington Ave and I-35W (Arden Hills and Mounds View); **West**: Rice St, Hodgson St (North Oaks, Vadnais Heights, and White Bear Township); **Area**: 11.2 square miles; **Population**: 26,500

Three broadcast towers on the north side of I-694 are the tallest structures in Minnesota, and mark the entrance into Shoreview, one of *Family Circle Magazine*'s "10 Best Towns in America to Raise a Family." Located both north and south of I-694, between I-35W and I-35E, Shoreview has 11 lakes, over 1,400 acres of parkland and open space, and a trail system so comprehensive that it has been named a "Bicycle Friendly Community." The city offers a wide variety of housing ranging from affordable neighborhoods of modest ramblers and split levels built in the 1960s–'70s to larger contemporary executive-style single-family homes and luxury townhomes. Snail Lake, one of the larger lakes in the city, has a swimming beach and public boat launch. Shoreview also boasts what may be the best community center in the Twin Cities. A focal point for community life, this facility includes a library, track and fitness center, Tropics Indoor Waterpark, and a fabulous indoor playground.

Most students in Shoreview attend Mounds View schools, www.mounds viewschools.org; but the children in the southernmost part of the city are in the Roseville School District, www.isd623.org.

City of Shoreview: 4600 Victoria St N, Shoreview, 55126; 651-490-4600, www. ci.shoreview.mn.us

VADNAIS HEIGHTS

Boundaries: North: Hwy 96; **East**: Rice St; **West**: Centerville Rd; **South**: County Rd D; **Area**: 8.5 square miles; **Population**: 13,500

Because one-third of Vadnais Heights (pronounced VAD-nays Heights) consists of Department of Natural Resources (DNR)–protected lakes and wetlands, many of its neighborhoods of 1970s–'90s houses back up to open space, giving them a rural, end-of-the-road feel, even though they're only minutes from

I-35E, I-694, and Highway 61. You can find both starter and executive-level homes here, as well as duplexes, townhouses, apartments, and condominiums. The gem of Vadnais Heights' parkland is **Vadnais–Sucker Lake Regional Park**, which boasts 1252 acres of woods and lakes. Home for many years to numerous small truck farms, Vadnais Heights is now home to the Academy for Sciences and Agriculture (www.agacademy.com), a charter high school for grades 9–12. Two public school districts serve this city: White Bear Area Schools (www.white-bear.k12.mn.us) and Mounds View (www.moundsviewschools.org).

City of Vadnais Heights: 800 East County Rd E, Vadnais Heights, 55127; 651-204-6000, www.ci.vadnais-heights.mn.us

WHITE BEAR LAKE, DELLWOOD

Boundaries: North: Hugo; **East**: Washington County (Mahtomedi); **South**: I-694; **West**: Centerville Rd; **Area**: 12 square miles; **Population**: 24,766

White Bear Lake has a racy past. A turn-of-the-20th-century haven for wealthy families from St. Paul, it became a hideout for gangsters in the 1930s, and Zelda and Scott Fitzgerald boozed it up here during Prohibition. In fact, they created such a rumpus, they were asked to leave! Fitzgerald, a St. Paul native, is said to have used it as the setting for his story "Winter Dreams."

Following renovation in the 1990s, the pedestrian-friendly downtown looks more like Fitzgerald's turn-of-the-20th-century summer resort than ever. Ornate lamps and old-fashioned storefronts evoke images of those indolent years and invite visitors to linger and browse in the unique shops. (See **Shopping for the Home**.)

White Bear Lake is to the East Metro what Lake Minnetonka is to the West. Over the past 50 years this one-time summer resort has developed into a bedroom community with a mix of housing, from those that rival Summit Avenue's mansions to others that are modest and cottagey. The lakeshore is where you'll find the most lavish homes, and while the historic lakeside retreats designed by Cass Gilbert and other famous architects have been protected, other less famous houses have been razed and replaced. Back from the shore, there are many tracts of 1950s–'60s split-levels and ramblers, as well as a number of condominium, apartment, and townhome communities. About one-third of the housing here is rental.

White Bear's early reputation as a health and recreation resort persists with relaxation and amusement still revolving around the water. The 2500-acre White Bear Lake is famous for its sailing and fishing. Within ten miles of White Bear there are five public golf courses, including Manitou Ridge (www.manitouridge.com), which features long holes with panoramic views of the

metropolitan area. Swimming beaches and two public launches are located at White Bear Lake County Park. White Bear is also home to the Lakeshore Players (www.lakeshoreplayers.com), the oldest continuously operating community theater in the state.

Many newcomers, attracted by golf and sailing, choose to live close to the Dellwood Golf Club (www.dellwoodhillsgc.org) or the White Bear Yacht Club (www.wbyc.com), both of which are located in neighboring **Dellwood**, which is on the northeastern shore of White Bear Lake in **Washington County** (www.dellwood.us). Dellwood has the distinction of being one of the ten wealthiest cities in America. Among its residents have been members of some of the state's oldest families, as well as our flamboyant former governor Jesse Ventura. Strictly residential, there is no commercial property here except the golf club and apple orchard—not even a city hall! About half its homes are suburban in character and the rest are rural, including a number of farms.

Other lakeshore communities include Mahtomedi (see **East Metro Suburbs/Washington County**), Birchwood (http://birchwood.govoffice.com), and White Bear Township (www.ci.white-bear-township.mn.us), which is notable for its unique annual town meeting form of government, where residents vote on all issues including taxes and expenditures.

Children who live in White Bear attend School District #624 (www.whitebear.k12.mn.us). Mahtomedi Public School District #832 (www.mahtomedi.k12.mn.us) serves students from Dellwood. Post-secondary education is available at Century College (www.century.edu) in White Bear Lake.

Unlike many areas of the Twin Cities, White Bear has abundant transportation. The city is served by several major roads: I-35, I-694, State Highway 61, County Highway 96, and Highway 49. Local buses connect with Metro Transit routes at Maplewood Mall (612-373-3333, www.metrotransit.org).

City of White Bear Lake: 4701 Hwy 61, White Bear Lake, 55110; 651-429-8526, www.whitebearlake.org

City of Dellwood: located at Willernie City Hall, 111 Wildwood Road, Willernie, 55090, 651-429-1356, www.dellwood.us

EAST METRO SUBURBS

WASHINGTON COUNTY

Afton; Cottage Grove; Dellwood (see p. 162), Forest Lake; Hugo; Lake Elmo/ Baytown Township/West Lakeland; Mahtomedi/Grant; Oakdale; Stillwater/ Marine On St. Croix; Woodbury

Boundaries: North: Chisago County; **West**: Ramsey County; **South**: Mississippi River; **East**: St. Croix River; **Area**: 424 square miles; **Population**: 234,348.

The projected growth for Washington County, which currently consists of 27 cities and 6 townships, is staggering: a gain of 66% more households by 2030. Hugo, for example, is expected to grow from a population of 4,000 to 25,000; Woodbury, which is already home to nearly a quarter of the county's residents, is expected to nearly double again, achieving a population of 84,000 by 2030.

For a long time this has been one of the fastest growing counties in Minnesota. Ironically, it developed from farmland to suburb at breakneck speed not only because of its proximity to downtown St. Paul, but also because of its rural, open-to-the-skies landscape, of which nearly three-fourths was still vacant in 1990. That makes most of the housing here quite new, compared to the other close-in suburbs. The county is made up overwhelmingly of single-family, owner-occupied detached houses, though new townhomes are literally popping up everywhere. In fact, most new construction now is multi-family. Older homes are generally set on expansive lots, necessary for private septic systems in a county that had limited access to the metropolitan sewer (MUSA) line until recently. The extension of the sewer line, however, has forced some cities such as Lake Elmo to accept more growth and higher population density than they had previously planned. In spite of all the new houses, these undulating hills, lakes, and forests are still home to hunting, horseback riding, biking, bird watching, and record-book fishing. There are even a few farms left. That said, very few of the county's residents work in agriculture, though many of them work at the small- and mid-sized medical and high-tech companies nearby, or at one of Minnesota's largest employers, 3M, which is headquartered in Maplewood.

One perennial complication of suburban sprawl is education: keep in mind that attendance boundaries are often redrawn as populations change.

With 83 miles of frontage on the St. Croix National Scenic Riverway and the Mississippi River, as well as over 4000 acres of parks, Washington County offers opportunities for diverse experiences: boating; scuba diving in the clear waters of Square Lake; and horseback riding at Lake Elmo Park Reserve, to name just three. In addition to county and regional parks, Washington County also has two state parks, William O'Brien and Afton, as well as a portion of the Gateway State Trail.

Washington County Government Center: 14949 62nd St N, Stillwater, 55082; 651-430-6000, TTY 651-430-6246; www.co.washington.mn.us

Washington County License and Service Centers: open weekdays and Saturdays until noon: Cottage Grove, 13000 Ravine Parkway S, 651-430-4075; Forest Lake License Center, 19955 Forest Road N, 651-275-7200; Stillwater License Center, Valley Ridge Mall, 651-275-7000; Woodbury License Center/ Washington County Service Center, 2150 Radio Dr, Woodbury, 651-275-8600

Washington County Sheriff: 911; Non-emergency, 651-439-9381

Area Code: 651

Fire: each city contracts for its own fire protection, often with volunteer fire departments

Emergency Hospitals: Lakeview Memorial Hospital, 927 West Churchill St, Stillwater, 651-439-5330, www.lakeview.org; Fairview Lakes Regional Medical Center, 5200 Fairview Blvd, Wyoming, 651-982-7000, www.lakes.fairview. org; Woodwinds Health Campus, Woodbury, 651-232-6880, www.healtheast.org/woodwinds.html

Washington County Library System: www.co.washington.mn.us/info_for_ residents/library

Community Resources: Historic Courthouse, 101 West Pine St, Stillwater, is a popular venue for weddings; Washington County Fairgrounds, Lake Elmo, is host to numerous dog and horse shows, lawnmower races, demolition derbies, ATV pulls; equestrian center, www.washingtoncountyfair.org

Community Publications: *St. Paul Pioneer Press*, www.twincities.com

Parks: www.co.washington.mn.us/info_for_residents/parks_division; Big Marine Park Reserve; Cottage Grove Ravine Regional Park; Hardwood Creek Regional Trail; Lake Elmo Park Reserve; Pine Point Regional Park; Point Douglas Regional Park; Square Lake Park

Public Schools: Hastings Independent School District 200, www.hastings.k12. mn.us; North St. Paul, Maplewood, Oakdale Area Public Schools #622, www. isd622.org; White Bear Lake Area Schools #624, www.whitebear.k12.mn.us; Forest Lake Area Schools #831, www.forestlake.k12.mn.us; Intermediate School District Northeast Metro #916, www.nemetro.k12.mn.us; Mahtomedi Public Schools #832, www.mahtomedi.k12.mn.us; South Washington County Schools #833, www.sowashco.k12.mn.us; Stillwater Area Schools #834, www.stillwater.k12.mn.us; Chisago Lakes Area Schools #2144, www. chisagolakes.k12.mn.us; East Metro Integration District# 6067 (Crosswinds Middle School), www.emid6067.net/crosswinds; Intermediate School Dis-

trict #916 (Valley Crossing Community School), www.nemetro.k12.mn.us/
vccs
Public Transportation: 612-373-3333, www.metrotransit.org

AFTON

Boundaries: North: I-94; **West**: Hwy 18 (formerly Hwy 95); **South**: 60th St; **East**:
St. Croix River; **Area**: 26 square miles; **Population**: 2886

If you dream of living in a historic small village, Afton may be the spot for you.
It's the best of all worlds—friendly neighbors, a broad range of housing styles
set in a village-like atmosphere, and only a 30-minute commute to St. Paul. The
charm here is natural: the St. Croix River, the lush floodplain forest, the rolling
fields and country meadows. Like the song, "Flow Gently Sweet Afton," it's
enough to make your heart sing.

Afton's small business district is located along the St. Croix River. There are
no shopping centers, no strip malls, just marinas, restaurants, ice cream parlors,
and other small shops, many housed in buildings left over from the 19th century. New development is being carefully planned to preserve the area's rural
feeling, with requirements for large lots and contiguous open space.

Afton is a major recreation area, with Afton Alps Golf and Ski Area, www.
aftonalps.com, one of the largest ski hills in Minnesota, and Afton State Park,
www.dnr.state.mn.us, located along the St. Croix River flyway—a great place to
hike, camp, and watch hawks, bald eagles, and other birds of prey.

City Hall: 3033 S St. Croix Trail, 55001, 651-436-5090, www.ci.afton.mn.us
Public Schools: South Washington County District #833, www.sowashco.k12.
   mn.us; Stillwater District #834, www.stillwater.k12.mn.us

COTTAGE GROVE

Boundaries: North: Woodbury; **West**: St. Paul Park and Grey Cloud Township;
South: Mississippi River; **East**: Hwy 95 (Manning); **Area**: 34.6 square miles; **Population**: 33,081

Cottage Grove is said to be the birthplace of Minnesota agriculture, and a few
descendants of the original settlers still farm here. Early surviving landmarks
include two "old villages"—Old Langdon School Village, at Jamaica Avenue and
West Point Douglas Road, and Old Cottage Grove, at 70th and Lamar—that date
back to the 1850s.

Cottage Grove was a quiet place until the 1960s, when Orrin Thompson
Homes started the bedroom-community development that brought the

population to nearly 30,000 by 1999. Those original houses sold in the 1960s and '70s for as little as $10,000; now they sell for twenty times that, but given the cost of housing in the Twin Cities, they still qualify as good starter homes. Recent construction, however, tends to be much more pricey. And if you decide to move here, expect to see a lot more building! The expansion of the MUSA (sewer) line is opening vast stretches of Cottage Grove's land to development, and the city's population is expected to nearly double by 2030.

While the fertile soil sustains working farms in Cottage Grove, it is the Mississippi and St. Croix River scenery that is attracting new residents. The river valleys provide space in which to hike, ski, and ride horses. River Oaks Municipal Golf Course (www.riveroaksmunigolf.com) boasts splendid views of the Mississippi River—and isn't a bad golf course. Most commercial development in Cottage Grove is in the downtown portion of the city along Highway 61, where you'll find Rainbow Foods, Cub Foods, and Target. 3M is among the city's largest employers.

City Hall: 7516 80th St S, Cottage Grove, 55016, 651-458-2800, www.cottage-grove.org

Police, Fire, and Emergency Paramedic Ambulance Service: 911; Non-emergency, 651-439-9381

Public Schools: South Washington County District #833, www.sowashco.k12.mn.us

Public Transportation: 612-373-3333, www.metrotransit.org; express buses run to downtown St. Paul. Park & Ride lot is along Hwy. 61 on West Point Douglas Rd between 80th St and Jamaica Ave.

FOREST LAKE

Boundaries: North: 240th St N; **West**: Anoka County; **South**: 180th St N; **East**: New Scandia; **Area**: 36 square miles; **Population**: 17,542

Forest Lake used to be considered "Up North" but now, since it's less than 30 miles from the Twin Cities, it has come to be viewed as a reasonable commute. Located just north of the point at which I-35 splits into 35W (heading for Minneapolis) and 35E (heading for St. Paul), it has easy access to both cities. A fast-growing community (it had a population of 7600 in 2000), it spreads over parts of Washington, Anoka, and Chisago counties. The City of Forest Lake serves as the hub for the area, with shopping malls, major grocery chains, churches, a radio station, and a newspaper, the *Forest Lake Times* (www.forestlaketimes.com).

Another city whose population is expected to double by 2030, it is designated as a "developing community" (higher density housing) in its southwestern corner, where the MUSA (sewer) line has been extended, and "diversified rural" (one house per ten acres) in the east. Homebuyers have a wide variety of choices, including city lots or rural acreage, lake homes, hobby farms, or estates. Prices are generally lower than they would be for properties closer to the Cities.

A quick peek at the city's calendar of events shows that there's always something to do here—Fourth of July parade, ice fishing contest, Chamber of Commerce Golf Tournament, water sports on Forest Lake, and horse racing at Running Aces Harness Park (www.runningacesharness.com), as well as hunting, fishing and cross-country skiing in 23,800-acre Carlos Avery Wildlife Management Area, www.dnr.state.mn.us. Downhill skiing is close by at Wild Mountain at Taylors Falls, 651-465-6315, 800-447-4958, www.wildmountain.com, and at Trollhagen in Dresser, Wisconsin, 651-433-5141 800-826-7166, www.trollhaugen.com.

City Hall: 220 N Lake St, Forest Lake, 55025, 651-464-3550, www.ci.forest-lake.mn.us

Police: 911; Non-emergency: 651-464-5877

Hospital: Fairview Lakes Regional Medical Center, 5200 Fairview Blvd, Wyoming, 651-982-7000, www.lakes.fairview.org

Public Schools: Forest Lake Area District #831, www.forestlake.k12.mn.us

Public Transportation: 612-373-3333, www.metrotransit.org; weekday express service from Forest Lake Transit Center into downtown Minneapolis

HUGO

Boundaries: North: 180th St; **West**: Elmcrest; **South**: 120th St; **East**: Keystone; **Area**: 36 square miles; **Population**: 12,417

While Hugo may or may not be named for French writer Victor Hugo, this rural community located 15 miles north of St. Paul is still one of the fastest-growing cities in Washington County, expected to reach a population of 24,000 by 2030.

Hugo's lakes and fields have historically attracted outdoorsmen, hunters, fishermen, and horse and cattle ranchers. To preserve the country look, the city has adopted policies that encourage cluster housing and field preservation. Post-MUSA (sewer) zoning designates the highest density for the west side of the city and agricultural and rural residential zoning on the east side. Most development has occurred in the southwest corner, near the 35E freeway, with some builders emphasizing master-planned communities that feature multi-family housing, open space, and sports amenities. The majority of the housing is for sale; rentals are scarce. Older housing is largely owner-occupied, single-family detached, built since 1970. By metro standards, Hugo's housing is considered affordable and therefore attractive to young families. There are also executive-level developments, particularly around Bald Eagle Lake. Municipal sewer and water service are only available in the southwest quadrant of the city at this time, with the entire sewer project due to be completed by 2020.

As for shopping, the downtown has the basic necessities, a hardware store, and several restaurants. Major retail stores are located nearby in White Bear Lake and Forest Lake.

City Hall: 14669 Fitzgerald Ave North, Hugo, 55038, www.ci.hugo.mn.us

Public Schools: Forest Lake District #831, www.forestlake.k12.mn.us; Mahtomedi District #832, www.mahtomedi.k12.mn.us; Stillwater District #834, www.stillwater.k12.mn.us; White Bear Lake District #624, www.whitebear. k12.mn.us

Parks: Hardwood Creek Regional Trail extends 9.5 miles from Hugo to Forest Lake along Highway 61.

Community Resources: Hugo Animal Farm, 651-433-4455, www.hugo animalfarm.com, offers a taste of farm and country life through tours and hayrides

Public Transportation: Bus service from Centerville or White Bear Lake, 612-373-3333, www.metrotransit.org

LAKE ELMO

Baytown Township/West Lakeland Township

Boundaries: North: Hwy 36; **West**: Ideal Avenue and Oakdale; **South**: I-94; **East**: Manning; **Area**: 26 square miles; **Population**: 7700

Lake Elmo and its neighbors Baytown and West Lakeland Townships are either an egregious example of urban sprawl or sublime havens that preserve the rural lifestyle, depending on how you look at large houses spaced far apart on acreage. Things are changing, however. **Baytown**, where most of the houses have been built since 1990, has grown from a population of under a thousand in 1990 to 1,587 in 2009, and is expected to reach 3400 by 2030. In **Lake Elmo**, where land-use ordinances tried to preserve the city's rural character by requiring 50% of the land to be set aside as permanent open space, the city has been forced by the advent of sewer service to allow higher density homes and businesses.

Water contamination is an issue in this area, although remediation is taking place. First the history: perfluorochemicals (PFCs) and trichloroethylene (TCE) have been detected in water in Lake Elmo, Baytown, and West Lakeland townships. The largest concentration of TCE appears to be under the Lake Elmo airport, and is spreading eastward toward the St. Croix River. A different kind of contamination, PFCs, has been detected in wells south of Highway 6 in an area centering on Inwood Avenue. That source has been identified—an old

landfill—and clean-up is under way. In the meantime, private wells in several areas have been sealed and municipal water has been extended to some of the neighborhoods in Lake Elmo. In **Baytown/West Lakeland**, older homes that still depend on wells have been fitted with whole-house granular activated carbon (GAC) filter systems, and new developments are required to provide water from a deeper aquifer that has not been contaminated. State law requires homeowners within the Special Well Construction Area (SWCA) who have private wells to notify buyers at the time of sale that the property is within the SWCA. Download information about the Baytown/West Lakeland Townships Special Well Construction Area from the Minnesota Department of Health web site, www.health.state.mn.us/divs/eh/hazardous/sites/washington/baytown/index.html.

Lake Elmo, long a leader in encouraging housing development designed to preserve its rich landscape of prairies, woodlands, open water, and swamps, is home to several "conservation" developments. Its **Fields of St. Croix** (www.engstromco.com/prev_fields) development off Highway 5 was begun in the 1990s, but is still considered one of the most successful cluster housing conservation communities in the country.

Baytown and **West Lakeland**, along the St. Croix River south of Bayport, still enjoy a rural lifestyle and are good places to look for hobby farms that are convenient to the city.

Three school districts serve this area, with an elementary school and junior high school within the Lake Elmo city limits. Lake Elmo's recreation facilities include baseball fields, skating rinks, and playgrounds. Lake Elmo Park Reserve's two-acre chlorinated swimming pond is a family favorite with a sandy bottom and gradual drop-off. The state record tiger muskie was caught in Lake Elmo in 1999. Several parks allow deer hunting.

City Halls: Lake Elmo, 3800 Laverne Ave N, 651-777-5510, www.lakeelmo.org; Baytown Township, 4220 Osgood Ave N, Stillwater, 55082, 651-430-4992, www.

baytowntwpmn.govoffice2.com; West Lakeland Township, 13520 Greenwood Trail, Stillwater, 55082, 651-436-4773, www.westlakeland.govoffice2.com

Public Schools: Stillwater District #834, www.stillwater.k12.mn.us; Mahtomedi District #832, www.mahtomedi.k12.mn.us; Maplewood–North St. Paul–Oakdale District #622, www.isd622.org

Parks: Lake Elmo Park Reserve, www.co.washington.mn.us/info_for_residents/parks_division/parks_and_trails/lake_elmo_park_reserve; Star Trail snow-mobile trail, www.startrail.org;

Community Resources: The Children's Farm School, 651-439-7745, www.childrensfarm.org; Animal Inn dog training facility, 8633 N 34th St, 651-777-2317, www.animalinnboardingkennel.com

Public Transportation: 612-373-3333, www.metrotransit.org; bus service is available along Hwy 5/294 to Stillwater and Oakdale

MAHTOMEDI

Grant

Boundaries: North: Dellwood and Grant; **West**: Hwy 120; area: **South**: I-694 and Pine Springs; **East**: Ideal Ave; **Area**: 2500 acres; **Population**: 8,039

Mahtomedi (pronounced "Ma Toe MEE Die") is a turn-of-the-20th-century resort town on the east shore of White Bear Lake. With its streetcar line and amusement park, it was to St. Paul what Excelsior was to Minneapolis: a summer resort for escapees from the heat of the cities. But the merry-makers had such a good time dancing in the pavilion that they decided to winterize their cottages and stay year 'round. A few of the old buildings are still standing.

Their presence has preserved Mahtomedi's summer resort ambiance despite the rapid growth and development that took place in the 1970s. Because the whole city has municipal sewer and water, it is fully built out,

though it is expected to reach a population of 9200 by 2030, due mostly to in-fill construction of townhomes and condominiums. Some residential developments are centered on small parks.

The **City of Grant** calls itself "A Home in the Country," and it is. Located just east of Mahtomedi and west of Stillwater, a mile from the Highway 36–I-94 interchange, most of its 17,000 acres are agricultural, with a few commercial farms and a lot of hobby farms. The minimum lot size is five acres. With good access to the Gateway Trail—and neighbors who won't complain about animal smells—it is a great place to have a horse.

City Halls: Mahtomedi: 600 Stillwater Rd, 55115, 651-426-3344, www.ci.mahtomedi.mn.us; Grant, 111 Wildwood Rd, Willernie, 55090, 651-426-3383, http://cityofgrant.com

Public Schools: Mahtomedi District #832, www.mahtomedi.k12.mn.us; Stillwater District #834, www.stillwater.k12.mn.us

Parks: Gateway Trail; parks and beaches on White Bear Lake. Parks in Mahtomedi are tobacco free.

Public Transportation: 612-373-3333, www.metrotransit.org; buses travel along 75th St N and Hwy 120 to Century College and SunRay Transit Hub

OAKDALE

Boundaries: North: I-694; **West**: Geneva Ave (also known as Trunk Hwy 120 and Century Ave); **South**: I-94; **East**: Lake Elmo; **Area**: 11.1 square miles; **Population**: 27,066

Ten minutes east of St. Paul, along both I-94 and I-694, this city near 3M's headquarters was among the fastest-growing municipalities in the metropolitan area during the 1990s. Now, with about 8000 owner-occupied properties and 2000 rental units, Oakdale is essentially fully developed, but it still retains something of a small-town feel. Neighborhoods include snug ramblers laid out on suburban-style curbless streets, as well as townhomes and golf developments. Numerous rental units are listed on the city's web site. This is one of the more affordable areas in the Twin Cities.

City Hall: 1584 Hadley Ave N, 55128, 651-739-5086, www.ci.oakdale.mn.us

Police: 911

Public Schools: District #622 Maplewood–North St. Paul–Oakdale, www.isd622.org

Parks: Tanners Lake has a beach and boat launch; Oakdale Nature Preserve includes tennis courts and hiking/biking/cross-country ski trails; Richard

Walton Park is the site of the city's annual Summerfest Concert Series and its farmers' market.

Community Resources: Marcus Oakdale Ultrascreen (3-story screen) Cinema, near the intersection of 36 and 694, 651-779-3795, www.marcustheatres. com

Public Transportation: 612-373-3333, www.metrotransit.org; buses travel along Stillwater Blvd, Hadley, 10th St, 15th Street, and Century

STILLWATER

Marine on St. Croix

Boundaries: North: Hwy 96; **West**: Manning; **East**: St. Croix River; **South**: Hwy 36; **Area**: 7 square miles (the Stillwater *vicinity* encompasses a much larger area); **Population**: 17,764

On the way to **Stillwater** via Highway 36, you'll pass fast-food joints, chain stores, and innumerable cul-de-sac developments. Who would guess that at the end of the four-lane highway lies an entire town that is on the National Register of Historic Places—Victorian "painted ladies," with cupolas, gazebos, leaded glass windows and all.

This old lumber town, which bills itself as the birthplace of Minnesota, celebrates its 19th-century past with antique shops, romantic bed and breakfasts, Lumberjack Days, and paddle-wheeling up and down the St. Croix River. But even though the economic downturn is bringing more of the old houses onto the market, you'll probably still have to get in line. Tourists are always knocking on residents' doors saying, "If you ever want to sell…"

Fortunately, there are a lot of other not-quite-so-old homes on Stillwater's streets, though the number of rental and affordable housing units, both in town and farther out, continues to decline. Newer construction includes everything

from 1970s houses built on pleasant culs-de-sac to brand-new condos in the heart of downtown. The web video for Stillwater Mills condos on Main Street (www.stillwatermills.com) not only promos the building, but also shows footage of the river and scenes downtown. Other newer developments include "New Urbanist" developments such as **Liberty on the Lake**, off Highway 36, which has houses built in styles that reference the older homes of Stillwater; and **The Fields of St. Croix** (www.engstromco.com/prev_fields), between Stillwater and Lake Elmo, which has a distinct New England feel.

Local sporting events and cultural opportunities are well attended by area residents, and the Stillwater high school orchestra has been ranked #1 in the state; and then there is football…

Twelve miles upriver from Stillwater, there is another historic town, **Marine on St. Croix**, founded in 1839, and site of the first commercial sawmill along the St. Croix River. This village is one of the few places in the Midwest where the word "quaint" seems to apply. The 1872 jail has been preserved and turned into a museum. Other historic buildings, the 1870 General Store and 1888 Village Hall, are still in use for their original purposes. In fact, the village hall is the oldest village hall in the state still being used for governmental purposes—and it can be rented for weddings. Yet even Marine is not without more modern development—albeit development that is still in touch with the past. **Jackson Meadow** (www.jacksonmeadow.com), the village's new neighborhood, is a 336-acre conservation development that features 64 simple white frame custom homes clustered near the road like an old-fashioned village. All together, the houses only take up 30% of the land, leaving the remaining 230 acres in woods and open prairie. All the houses have been designed by Duluth architect David Salmela, who received the 2005 American Institute of Architects Honor Award for Regional and Urban Design for his work on the project.

Marine is a great place to go for a Sunday afternoon or weekend. The 1856 Asa Parker House bed and breakfast (www.asaparkerbb.com) is within walking distance of both William O'Brien State Park and the Marine Landing.

City Halls: 216 N Fourth St, Stillwater, 55082, 651-430-8800, www.ci.stillwater. mn.us; Marine on St. Croix City Hall: 121 Judd St, 651-433-3636, http://marine. govoffice.com

Public Schools: Stillwater District #834, www.stillwater.k12.mn.us

Community Publications: *Stillwater Gazette*, www.stillwatergazette.com

Community Resources: Numerous historic buildings and bed-and-breakfasts, www.ilovestillwater.com; Lumberjack Days, www.lumberjackdays.com

Parks: Gateway Trail (virtual tour at www.dnr.state.mn.us/state_trails/gateway/ virtual.html); Lowell Park and Pioneer Park are popular places to take wedding photographs and have reservable parking; William O'Brien State Park, www.dnr.state.mn.us

Public Transportation: MetroTransit, 612-373-3333, www.metrotransit.org: express buses from Stillwater to St. Paul; buses travel along Hwy 5/Stillwater Blvd, Pine St, 4th St, Curve Crest; Park & Ride, St. Croix Valley Rec. Center, 1675 Market Dr (between Orleans and Curve Crest)

WOODBURY

Boundaries: North: I-94; **West**: I-494, I-694; **South**, Cottage Grove; **East**: St. Croix River; **Area**: 36 square miles; **Population**: 60,000

If you've lived in Woodbury for 10 years, you're an old-timer; and if you've lived here since the late 1970s, when the first developer struck out across the farm fields, you can call yourself a founding father, or mother.

Since the 1970s, when the upscale **Evergreen** development was built to lure 3M executives over from Maplewood, Woodbury has been transformed from a sleepy rural township into Minnesota's fastest growing city. Located a mile southeast of St. Paul, Woodbury is expected to grow to a population of 84,000 by 2030. Approximately a fourth of Ramsey County's residents live here already.

Development is ongoing, with projects that are almost exclusively large, multi-phased master-planned communities. It is the city's goal to provide flexible housing options that will enable citizens to live here throughout their lives. Consequently, housing runs the gamut from rental apartments and townhomes to large-lot estates, and includes hard-to-find three- or four-bedroom apartments. Woodbury does not have an established downtown, but it is creating one in the area surrounding City Hall, along Pioneer Road and Valley Creek Road. There they have connected the Southeast Area YMCA at one end and the Washington County library at the other, through an indoor park. Called Cen-

tral Park, it includes "Lookout Ridge," a children's interactive playground, and is home to School District 833's Early Childhood Family Education program.

Bordered by Interstates 94, 494 and 694, Woodbury is strategically located to give residents and businesses alike excellent access to the rest of the metro. Major employers include 3M, The Hartford, Target.com, Assurant, and other high tech and manufacturing companies. The city has also been working to develop Woodbury as a medical destination, establishing a Medical Campus District adjoining Woodwinds Hospital. Combined, these companies have made Woodbury into a place where you can both live and work—unusual in a region where so many experience long commutes.

City Hall: 8301 Valley Creek Rd, 55125, 651-714-3500, www.ci.woodbury.mn.us; License Center: 2150 Radio Dr, 651-275-8600; renew a Minnesota driver's license here or purchase automobile tags, but if you're moving from another state, you must take a written test administered in Stillwater on Wednesdays; call 651-275-7000. The test is also administered at the license substation at 1600 University Ave in St. Paul, 651-642-0808.

Police and Fire: Woodbury Public Safety, 911, Non-emergency, 651-439-9381

Public Schools: South Washington County District #833, www.sowashco.k12.mn.us; Stillwater District #834, www.stillwater.k12.mn.us; North St. Paul/Maplewood/Oakdale District #622, www.isd622.org; Valley Crossing Community School, www.nemetro.k12.mn.us

Community Publications: *The Woodbury Bulletin*, www.woodburybulletin.com; *Woodbury/Maplewood Review*, www.woodburyreviewnews.com

Public Transportation: MetroTransit, 612-373-3333, www.metrotransit.org; weekday express bus service to downtown St. Paul and Minneapolis originates from park-and-ride lots adjacent to Woodbury Lutheran Church (7380 Afton Rd) and in Woodbury Village (express buses to Minneapolis).

WESTERN WISCONSIN

Living in Western Wisconsin appeals to those who want to live in the country but still have access to the Twin Cities. It is considered a reasonable commute for those who work in the East Metro: Somerset is 27 miles from 3M, in Maplewood, and the popular Troy Burne area, south of Hudson, is 18. Hudson, itself, is 20 minutes from downtown St. Paul.

Though Minnesotans make fun of Wisconsin, with its cheeseheads and fiendish native sons like Jeffrey Dahmer, Twin Citians are pulling up stakes and relocating to Pierce, Polk, and St. Croix counties as fast as they can sign with a builder.

There are lots of reasons. For one: Wisconsin is beautiful. With rolling hills and vast stretches of green grass and trees, it's pure eye candy. Then there are the wholesome small towns, straight out of central casting. Finally, there are the prices. At least for now, you can get a three-acre lot in Wisconsin for much less than you'd have to pay for a half-acre lot in Minnesota.

The downside, of course, is the drive.

The commute is all about the bridges over the St. Croix River (the dividing line between the two states). There are two. The 1931 National Historic Register Vertical Lift Bridge between downtown Stillwater and Houlton, Wisconsin, is picturesque, but not sufficient to handle the traffic it gets, with vehicles often backing up all the way through Stillwater and down highways 95 and 36. The I-94 freeway bridge between Woodbury and Hudson was rebuilt in 2004 to add more lanes, and does not have these issues. A new four-lane bridge south of downtown Stillwater has been talked about for decades, and construction is finally slated to begin in 2013—if funding becomes available. In the meantime, when the Stillwater bridge is closed—and that is not a rare occurrence—commuters who use it have to head 7 miles downstream to I-94 or 20 and 30 miles up river to Osceola (connecting WI-35 with MN-95) or Taylor's Falls (Highway 8).

As in any place that is transitioning from agricultural to residential, most people who move here will have to have their own wells, contract for heating oil, and maintain their own septic systems. (For well and septic system information, see the **Getting Settled** chapter.) Because of the need for septic systems, many townships have a 3-acre or more minimum lot size. Look online at the University of Minnesota extension service web site for suggestions on making septic systems blend in: www.extension.umn.edu/distribution/horticulture/dg6986.html and www.extension.umn.edu/info-u/plants/BG442.html.

Heating is another issue. While houses "in town" might have access to natural gas, most homeowners in the country heat with propane. Buy before winter on contract, to lock in the price. While consumption will depend on many factors, such as insulation and whether heat is turned up during the day, expect a three-bedroom house to use at least 1200 gallons each winter.

Childcare is generally offered in the same level of facilities as in Minnesota, but is usually less expensive. For information about schools, see the **Childcare and Education** chapter. Both Hudson and Stillwater offer all the usual activities for children—gymnastics, dance, skating, art, basketball, and hockey, etc.

While Wisconsin may look more backwoods than Minnesota, in some respects it is more forward thinking. For example, people who meet certain age and relationship criteria may apply for a declaration of domestic partnership with the County Clerk in the county in which they reside.

ST. CROIX COUNTY
Hudson; Somerset; River Falls

Boundaries: North: Polk County; **West**: St. Croix River; **South**: Pierce County. **East**: Dunn County; **Area**: 729.45 square miles; **Population**: 80,779

St. Croix County, which includes Somerset, Hudson, and parts of River Falls, is just over the state line (the St. Croix River) on I-94. It is already the fastest growing county in Wisconsin, and one of the 100 fastest growing counties in the nation. Its county seat is Hudson.

St. Croix County Government Center: 1101 Carmichael Rd, Hudson, 54016, 715-386-4600, www.co.saint-croix.wi.us

Police: St. Croix County Sheriff, 1101 Carmichael Rd, Hudson; Emergency, 911; Non-emergency, 715-386-4701

Drivers' Licenses: Hudson Service Center, 2100 O'Neil Road, Hudson; New Richmond Service Center, 156 E 1st St, New Richmond, www.dot.wisconsin.gov/about/locate/dmv/stcroix.htm; schedule an appointment online

Emergency Hospitals: Hudson Hospital, 405 Stageline Rd, Hudson, 715-531-6000, www.hudsonhospital.org; River Falls Area Hospital, 1629 E Division St, River Falls, 715-425-6155, www.allina.com/ahs/riverfalls.nsf

Parks: Willow River State Park, 5 miles east of Hudson, offers beautiful scenery, camping, picnic grounds, nature trails, cross-country ski trails, fishing, and deer and turkey hunting, http://dnr.wi.gov/org/land/parks/specific/willowriver; St. Croix River National Scenic Riverway, www.nps.gov/sacn/index.htm; Apple River, www.appleriver.com, is known for its all-day tubing.

Community Resources: For tourist information for the entire St. Croix River Valley, visit www.saintcroixriver.com. Wisconsin Indianhead Technical College, New Richmond, http://www.witc.edu; Chippewa Valley Technical College, River Falls, www.cvtc.edu/pages/1.asp

Community News Sources: *Hudson Star-Observer*

Public Schools: Hudson School District, www.hudson.k12.wi.us; New Richmond School District, www.newrichmond.k12.wi.us; River Falls School

District, www.rfsd.k12.wi.us; District of Somerset Schools, www.somerset.k12.wi.us

Public Transportation: 612-373-3333, www.MetroTransit.org: the bus system can also be accessed at Guardian Angels Park & Ride at I-94 and Inwood Rd in Woodbury. The Stillwater Park & Ride is off Highway 5 near Orleans Street. Interstate highways 94 and 35, Wisconsin 35, and U.S. Highway 12 provide easy access in all directions.

HUDSON

Fifteen miles from St. Paul, Hudson, with its marina and picturesque Victorian houses, is one of the prettiest towns on the St. Croix River.

Many of the city's 12,000 residents first came to play golf. There are five excellent golf courses nearby: Troy Burne (www.troyburne.com), Clifton Hollows (800-487-8879), Clifton Highlands (www.cliftonhighlands.com), Kilkarney Hills (www.kilkarneyhills.com), and River Falls Golf Club (www.riverfallsgolfclub.com). Greens fees and membership costs are among the lowest in the metro area. The locals' favorite: Clifton Highlands, which also garnered a 4.5 from Golf Digest.

While home to many unique and charming shops in its historic downtown, Hudson has a full complement of big-box retailers on its outskirts, as well. Municipal water/sewer service is available within the city limits of the City of Hudson and the Village of North Hudson.

City of Hudson: 505 3rd St, Hudson, 54016, 715-386-4765, www.ci.hudson.wi.us

SOMERSET

Somerset, founded in 1856, has been known in more recent times for tubing on the Apple River, outdoor summer rock concerts, and camping. One of the fastest growing areas in the fastest growing county in Wisconsin, it is an affluent area being built out by established Twin Cities builders.

Village of Somerset: 110 Spring St; PO Box 356; Somerset, 54025, 715-247-3395, www.vil.somerset.wi.us

RIVER FALLS

Thirty miles east of Minneapolis and St. Paul, this college town is home to the University of Wisconsin–River Falls. Many commute from here to the eastern metro.

Rich with recreational activities, River Falls offers some of the best trout fishing in the Midwest right in the middle of downtown.

City of River Falls: 222 Lewis St, River Falls, 54022, 715-425-0900, www.rfcity. org

PIERCE AND POLK COUNTIES

Though not profiled in this book, Pierce (south of Hudson) and Polk (north of Hudson) counties are both starting to grow with Twin Cities commuters. For information about them, look on their web sites:

POLK COUNTY, WISCONSIN

Government Center
100 Polk County Plaza
Suite 110
Balsam Lake, WI 54810
715-485-9226
www.co.polk.wi.us

PIERCE COUNTY, WISCONSIN

County Courthouse
414 West Main Street
Ellsworth, WI 54011
715-273-3531
www.co.pierce.wi.us

SOUTH METRO SUBURBS

DAKOTA COUNTY

Apple Valley; Burnsville; Eagan; Farmington; Inver Grove Heights; Lakeville; Mendota Heights; Rosemount; South St. Paul/West St. Paul/Sunfish Lake

Boundaries: North: Minnesota River; **East**: Mississippi River; **West**: Scott County; **South**: Goodhue, Rice counties; **Area**: 593 square miles; **Population**: approximately 400,000

Just across the river from Minneapolis and St. Paul, Dakota County feels far away from the hustle and bustle—at least in some places. One-third urban, one-third suburban, and one-third rural—and hoping to stay that way, it offers

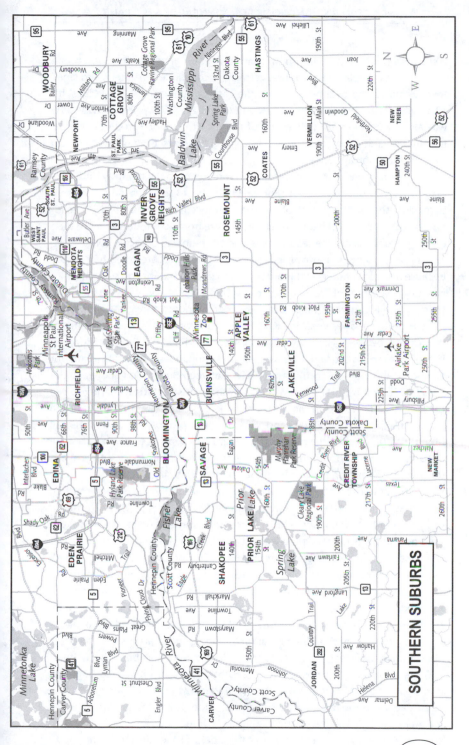

SOUTHERN SUBURBS

residents a wide variety of bedroom communities ranging from intensely urban Burnsville and Apple Valley, to rural Vermillion, collegiate Northfield, and small town Hastings, the county seat. As is the case throughout the Twin Cities, it's all about growth. The county had a population of 275,000 in 1990, and by 2005 was already pushing 380,000. Much of the growth has occurred in Lakeville, Rosemount, and Farmington, which have easy access to the rest of the metro via I-35 and Highway 52.

The word "easy," in this case, means easy to get onto the highways, not necessarily easy to get somewhere. For example, the 13-mile trip on I-35W from Burnsville (the northernmost of Dakota County's cities) to Best Buy's headquarters on I-494 in Richfield can take anywhere from 20 minutes to more than an hour. Problems are the result of insufficient highway capacity, congestion-causing interchanges, and rush-hour carpool lanes that are often half empty because most commuters in this automobile-centered county go solo. The Minnesota Department of Transportation (MnDOT) says that it will be at least 20 years before it can undertake necessary improvements, though it has turned I-35's High Occupancy Vehicle (HOV) lane into a MnPass Express toll lane for solo drivers between Highway 13 in Burnsville and I-494 in Bloomington and between 42nd Street and Highway 65 in Minneapolis. There are plans for extending this lane on northbound I-35W between Burnsville Parkway to the I-35W/I-35E split by 2012. (See MN-PASS in the **Transportation** chapter to see how this system works.) In the meantime, there is commuter bus service from Apple Valley, Burnsville, Eagan, and Rosemount. A proposal for commuter rail from Hastings to Saint Paul is gathering steam and appears to be on track for a 2018 start. The proposed line is known as the Red Rock Corridor, and you can download information about it from the county's web site.

In other transport-related news, a north-south runway has been put into service at Minneapolis–St. Paul International Airport (MSP). While it brought residents of Minneapolis some relief from their overhead noise, the new flight path now impacts Eagan, Apple Valley, Lakeville, Farmington, Burnsville, Inver Grove Heights, Sunfish Lake, and Rosemount in Dakota County, sometimes with as much as 65-decibel (very loud) noise levels. The runway's opening coincided with a lawsuit brought by the cities of Minneapolis, Eagan, Bloomington, and Richfield claiming that the Metropolitan Airports Commission (MAC) had not provided the noise mitigation it promised. As a result of that litigation, MAC was required to provide noise mitigation to homes and apartments in the most heavily impacted areas. In addition, many older planes have been "hushkitted," and many new, quieter planes have been brought into service. For information about the MAC's noise abatement programs as well as maps of the MSP flight paths and the decibel levels recorded under them, look online at www.macnoise.com. Airlake Airport in the more southern part of the county is an additional source of overhead noise for the cities of Lakeville and Farmington.

In recent years Dakota County has attracted the attention of national developers who have built thousands of homes, and purchased thousands more homesites, thus putting pressure on property owners to sell increasingly more ecologically fragile lands. To combat this, the county developed a program that pays landowners for agreeing not to subdivide their properties. It is hoped that, in this way, some Dakota County farmers will be able to keep farming, and that nearly 80,000 acres with cultural, ecological, or historical significance will be preserved. So far, this program has been used to preserve Pilot Knob (see **Mendota Heights** below), the Caponi Art Park in **Eagan**, and Wiklund Wildlife Preserve in **Rosemount**. The county's long-range goal is to create contiguous areas of protected properties. Hence the Caponi project is part of a proposed Eagan Core Greenway that will eventually link Eagan City Hall with Lebanon Hills Park, about three miles away. With a diverse natural landscape that includes lakes, rivers, bluffs, wooded hillsides, and prairies, Dakota County offers particularly high quality recreation opportunities. It also offers jobs. Though hurt by the current downturn in the economy, job growth in Dakota County has been consistently better than either state or national rates, and the county is expected to have 214,150 jobs by 2030, compared with 148,261 in 2000. New construction dominates the market here, especially in Rosemount, Lakeville, and Farmington.

Dakota County Administration Center: 1590 Hwy 55, Hastings, 55033, 651-438-4313, www.co.dakota.mn.us

Service Centers: Western Service Center, 14955 Galaxie Ave, Apple Valley, 952-891-7570; Northern Service Center, 1 Mendota Rd W, West St. Paul, 651-554-6600; Burnsville License Center, 284 E Travelers Trail, Burnsville, 952-891-7850; Lakeville License Center, 20085 Heritage Dr, Lakeville, 952-891-7878. Driver's Licenses written and road tests are given at the South Metro Exam Station, 2070 Cliff Road, Eagan, 651-688-1870; 217 Ramsey St, Hastings.

Police: Dakota County Sheriff Department, Law Enforcement Center, 1580 Hwy 55, Hastings; 911, Non-emergency, 651-438-4700

Emergency Hospitals: Fairview Ridges Hospital, 201 E Nicollet Blvd, Burnsville, 952-892-2000, www.fairview.org; Regina Medical Center, 1175 Nininger Rd, Hastings, 651-480-4100, www.reginamedical.org

Library: Dakota County Library System, www.co.dakota.mn.us/LeisureRecreation/CountyLibraries/default.htm

Community Publications: *Southwest Review News*, www.southwestreviewnews.com

Community Resources: Pilot Knob Preservation Association, www.pilotknobpreservation.org; Historic Village of Mendota and Sibley House Historic Site, www.dakota history.org/county/mendota.asp; UMORE Park Master Gardener Demonstration and Display Garden, Rosemount, www.mggarden.umn.edu;

Caponi Art Park and Learning Center, www.caponiartpark.org; Minnesota Zoo, Apple Valley, www.mnzoo.com; Burnsville Performing Arts Center, www.burnsvillepac.com; Dodge Nature Center, www.dodgenaturecenter.org

Parks: www.co.dakota.mn.us/LeisureRecreation/CountyParks/default.htm; Big Rivers Regional Trail; Lake Byllesby Regional Park; Lebanon Hills Regional Park; Miesville Ravine Park Reserve; Dakota County Mississippi River Regional Trail; Dakota Woods Dog Park, just east of Rosemount, is a 16-acre, fenced, wooded park that's a great place to let your dog run off leash

Public Transportation: MetroTransit: 612-373-3333, www.metrotransit.org; buses travel along Highways 13, 55 and 52, County Rd 42, Johnny Cake Ridge Rd, Yankee Doodle Rd, Pilot Knob Rd, Blackhawk Rd, Cliff Rd, I-35W, I-35E; transit hubs are located in Eagan at Yankee Doodle and Pilot Knob rds, in Burnsville at Highway 13 and Nicollet, and 15450 Cedar Ave in Apple Valley. Park & Ride lots are scattered throughout the area. Minnesota Valley Transit Authority, 952-882-7500, www.mvta.com, provides service on local routes and commuter bus service from Apple Valley, Burnsville, Eagan, Rosemount, and Savage to downtown Minneapolis, downtown Saint Paul, Mall of America, and to the Minneapolis–St. Paul International Airport.

APPLE VALLEY

Boundaries: North: Eagan; **West**: Burnsville; **South**: Lakeville, Rosemount; **East**: Rosemount; **Area**: 18 square miles; **Population**: 48,938

Apple Valley, located 12 miles south of Minneapolis and St. Paul, has quiet streets and affordable housing, including townhomes, starter homes, and mid-range houses, most built by developer Orrin Thompson between 1970 and 1990. According to the city's web site, in 2010, 90% of the homes had a market

value under $250,000, and a third were under $150,000. Look in the "Oaks" neighborhoods for the city's more upscale homes.

The city has a number of sports and recreation facilities, including an outdoor aquatic center, ice arena, and the Minnesota Zoo. Most of the city's children attend schools operated by Rosemount–Apple Valley–Eagan Independent School District 196, www.isd196.k12.mn.us. A small portion of the city, in the northwestern corner, is in the Burnsville-Eagan-Savage district, www.isd191.org.

City of Apple Valley: 7100 W 147th St, Apple Valley, 55124, 952-953-2500, www.ci.apple-valley.mn.us

BURNSVILLE

Boundaries: North: Minnesota River; **West**: Savage; **South**: Lakeville, Scott County; **East**: Eagan, Apple Valley; **Area**: 24.9 square miles; **Population**: 60,220

Those who watched the 2010 Winter Olympics will have heard many references to Burnsville, home of Buck Hill Ski Area and Olympic Gold Medal downhill ski racer Lindsey Vonn. With a vertical drop of only 300 feet, Buck Hill (www.buckhill.com) operates a nationally acclaimed ski racing program, and has put many racers on the U.S. Ski Team. That isn't a bad metaphor for Burnsville, itself, which, while not a glamorous city, still gets the job done with a large stock of entry-level housing, including numerous townhouse and apartment complexes. There are a few luxurious neighborhoods, too, especially west of I-35 in the vicinity of 150th and 155th streets. Though rumors circulate every year that Buck Hill is going to be sold for development, they are not true. In fact, in 2004 the city rezoned the Buck Hill property from single-family residential to Commercial Recreation District, expressly to preserve it. So, if you have children who like to ski, rest assured that the little ski hill that *SKI Magazine* calls the "legendary capital of American ski racing" will be around to send a few more generations of Minnesotans to the Olympics—maybe even a child of your own.

Other recreation facilities include Burnsville Ice Center, a skate park, and soccer dome. The Garage (www.thegarage.net) offers teens a gathering and performance space. The Burnsville Performing Arts Center is home to plays, art exhibits, ballet, and music of all kinds.

Positioned where I-35 splits to become I-35W (heading to Minneapolis) and I-35E (which goes to St. Paul), Burnsville has easy access to both those cities and the airport—on a good day. Throw in a little wet weather or a simple fender-bender, and 35W, in particular, becomes a parking lot. Shopping is conveniently located at Burnsville Mall (www.burnsvillecenter.com) and for miles along County Road 42.

Burnsville is served by three public school districts: Burnsville-Eagan-Savage Independent School District 191 serves approximately 70% of residences in the city, www.isd191.org; Rosemount–Apple Valley–Eagan Independent School District 196 serves approximately 20% of residences in Burnsville, www.district196.org; and Lakeville Area Public Schools Independent School District 194 serves the southernmost residences, www.isd194.k12.mn.us.

City of Burnsville: 100 Civic Center Pkwy, Burnsville, 55337, 952-895-4400, www.ci.burnsville.mn.us

EAGAN

Boundaries: North: Mendota Heights; **West**: Minnesota River, Burnsville; **South**: Apple Valley, Rosemount; **East**: Inver Grove Heights; **Area**: 34.5 square miles; **Population**: 67,448

This former "Onion Capital of the World," just across the river from the Mall of America and MSP airport, has easy access to I-494 and Highway 77 (Cedar Avenue), and ranks high on *Money Magazine*'s list of best places to live. One of the fastest-growing cities in the state, its population of 10,000 in 1970 is expected to top out at 69,000 by 2020. The city is filled with single-family detached homes of every type and price range, as well as a large selection of townhomes and condominiums. It is home to a number of major industries including UPS, Delta Airlines and Blue Cross/Blue Shield of Minnesota—but alas, the farm fields that once grew onions to ship all over the world are long gone.

Eagan contains over 1000 acres of the Minnesota Valley Wildlife Refuge, as well as Cascade Bay, which has been named one of the top ten public water parks in the US. Children here attend schools in three districts: Burnsville-Eagan-Savage District 191, www.isd191.org; Rosemount–Apple Valley–Eagan District 196, www.district196.org; and West Saint Paul/Mendota Height/Eagan District 197, www.isd197.org. Local post-secondary institutions include Argosy University (www.argosy.edu) and Rasmussen Community College (www.rasmussen.edu).

City of Eagan: 3830 Pilot Knob Rd, Eagan, 55122, 651-675-5000, www.ci.eagan.mn.us

FARMINGTON

Boundaries: North: Rosemount; **West**: Lakeville; **South**: Randolph, Hampton; **East**: Vermillion; **Area**: 12.5 square miles; **Population**: 20,000

Farmington is one of those rare things in the metro—a traditional town. One of Dakota County's oldest communities, it was shown on maps even before Minnesota became a state. A number of buildings from those early days survive, including the Oak Street historic preservation area, which is home to a large collection of houses built between the 1870s and the 1930s. New growth suburbs surrounding the town offer a full range of life-cycle options, including high-density, lower-priced townhouses and single-family homes. Children here attend Farmington District 192 Schools, www.farmington.k12.mn.us.

City of Farmington: 430 Third St, Farmington, 55024, 651-280-6800, www. ci.farmington.mn.us

INVER GROVE HEIGHTS

Boundaries: North: South St. Paul, Sunfish Lake; **West**: Eagan; **South**: Rosemount; **East**: Mississippi River; **Area**: 28.6 square miles; **Population**: 32,000, projected 44,000 (2020)

If you're looking for a home with a small amount of acreage that's within 20 minutes of downtown St. Paul, Inver Grove Heights may be the place for you. A wooded community with rolling hills and bluffs that overlook the Mississippi River, it is a place where you can find every sort of housing, from apartments to houseboats and large-lot estates. IGH has been part of every era's building boom, and has a stock of '50s-forward houses to prove it (and even a few that date from the 1890s). While 40% of the housing is valued at $150,000 or less, new construction tends to fall into the high-end range.

Once a community of farms, it still boasts a few agricultural properties, including Triple-S Ranch riding and horse boarding stable (www.triple-sranch. com) and Gerten's Greenhouses (www.gertens.com). The city operates two public marinas, which provide access to the Mississippi River. Children here attend Inver Grove Heights Community Schools District 199, www.invergrove.k12.mn.us or Rosemount–Apple Valley–Eagan District 196, www.district196.org. Post-secondary schools include Inver Hills Community College, www.inverhills.edu.

City of Inver Grove Heights: 8150 Barbara Ave, Inver Grove Heights, 55077, 651-450-2500, www.ci.inver-grove-heights.mn.us

LAKEVILLE

Boundaries: North: Burnsville, Apple Valley; **West**: Scott County; **South**: New Market; **East**: Farmington, Rosemount; **Area**: 38 square miles; **Population**: 50,000

Lakeville is growing like a weed. Strategically located 20 miles south of Minneapolis on I-35, Lakeville bills itself as "The Southern Gateway to the Metro Area." That's because, as you're driving north on I-35, it's the place where farmland suddenly gives way to townhouses. As a designated "developing community" in the metro area regional plan, its population is expected to reach 78,400 by 2020. To accommodate all these new residents, the city has in recent years issued twice as many building permits for townhouses as for single-family homes. Most recently, it has received a lot of publicity for its 2100-unit (eventually) Spirit of Brandjten Farm master-planned community (http://homesofspirit. com), which includes custom-built high-end homes and townhomes. Children here attend schools in three school districts: Farmington School District 192 (www.farmington.k12.mn.us); the Lakeville Area Public Schools (www.isd194. k12.mn.us); and Rosemount–Apple Valley–Eagan District 196 (www.district196. org). You can download the school districts' boundaries from the city's web site.

One local issue of note: Airlake Airport, which is used now as a general aviation "reliever" for Minneapolis–St. Paul International Airport (MSP), is expected at some point to start getting MSP overflow traffic that will include "light" jets. The airport has already been approved for a new crosswind runway and new hangars, although they have not been built yet due to lack of funds.

As for sports—think hockey!

For those who have heard rumors of a "Downtown Lakeville," but have never known where it is, it can be found along Holyoke Avenue in the southern reaches of the city, directly south of the growing commercial district of Heritage Commons. There are some very cute shops there!

City of Lakeville: 20195 Holyoke Ave, Lakeville, 55044, 952-985-4400, www. ci.lakeville.mn.us

MENDOTA HEIGHTS

Boundaries: North: Minnesota River; **East**: Delaware Avenue; **West**: Highway 13; **South**: Eagan; **Area**: 9.4 square miles; **Population**: 11,434

The most beautiful view of the Twin Cities is from Pilot Knob in Mendota Heights. From this bluff at the end of the Mendota Bridge you can see across the confluence of the Mississippi and Minnesota rivers to historic Ft. Snelling and the skyscrapers of Minneapolis beyond. This is the place where the Dakota tribes buried their dead on scaffolds, so they could overlook the river, and where the Dakota signed the Treaty of 1851, which ceded all the land that is now Minnesota to the U.S. government. The name Pilot Knob derives from the promontory's use as a navigation guide by old-time riverboat pilots, and it is featured in one of the most famous paintings of Minnesota, *Distant View of Fort Snelling*, painted in 1846 by Seth Eastman.

Primarily a residential community, with curvy streets built around woods and wetlands, Mendota Heights has an industrial area in its southern quarter that is home to Ecolab and Northland Insurance. Most housing consists of owner-occupied single-family homes dating from the late 1970s to the mid-1980s. The city is short on rental and multi-family housing, but has added a new town center off Dodd Road called The Village at Mendota Heights (www.villagemh.com/the-village.cfm), which includes retail and office space as well as row houses and lofts. Children here attend West Saint Paul/Mendota Heights/Eagan District 197, www.isd197.org. Private schools include Convent of the Visitation School (www.visitation.net) and St. Thomas Academy (www.cadets.com).

City of Mendota Heights: 1101 Victoria Curve, Mendota Heights, 55118, 651-452-1850, www.mendota-heights.com

ROSEMOUNT

Boundaries: North: Inver Grove Heights; **East**: Mississippi River; **West**: Apple Valley; **South**: Vermillion; **Area**: 36 square miles; **Population**: 17,997 (2004); projected 36,700 (2030)

Located approximately 15 miles south of the Minneapolis–St. Paul International airport, the western part of Rosemount is experiencing feverish growth, with residential options that range from upscale custom home communities to affordable townhomes. The city's eastern third is heavily industrial, with an oil refinery and an industrial waste containment facility.

The University of Minnesota owns about 7500 acres of open land just southeast of downtown Rosemount. Known as UMORE Park (University of Minnesota Outreach, Research and Education Park, www.umorepark.umn.edu), it

has been used for many years as an agricultural research station. Now, however, the University plans to turn 5000 acres of it into an education-focused, environmentally friendly, sustainable community that will be home to 20,000 to 30,000 people. The project will begin with sand and gravel mining of the western third of the property, probably in 2011. The mining is meant to provide funding for the project and shape the terrain, leaving behind rolling hills and lakes. The development is expected to take 25 or 30 years, so if you decide to move to this part of the county, expect construction disruption for a long time to come.

Most Rosemount students attend Rosemount–Apple Valley–Eagan District 196 (www.district196.org), which is the second largest district in the state. Those on the east side attend Hastings schools (www.hastings.k12.mn.us), or Inver Grove Heights Community Schools, District 199 (www.invergrove.k12.mn.us).

The city is also served by a number of non-public schools and Dakota County Technical College (www.dctc.mnscu.edu).

City of Rosemount: 2875 145th St W, Rosemount, 55068, 651-423-4411, TTY 651-423-6219, www.ci.rosemount.mn.us

SOUTH SAINT PAUL, WEST SAINT PAUL, SUNFISH LAKE

Boundaries: *SOUTH SAINT PAUL*: **North**: St. Paul; **West**: West Saint Paul; **South**: Inver Grove Heights; **East**: Mississippi River; **Area**: 5.7 square miles; **Population**: 20,167; *WEST SAINT PAUL*: **North**: St. Paul; **West**: Mississippi River, Lilydale, Mendota Heights; **South**: Sunfish Lake; **East**: South Saint Paul; **Area**: 5.01 square miles; **Population**: 19,405; *SUNFISH LAKE*: **North**: Highway 110; **West**: Delaware Ave; **South**: 60th St/Pieper Rd; **East**: S Robert Trail; **Area**: 1.7 square miles; **Population**: 525

Ten minutes from downtown St. Paul, the city of **West Saint Paul** (on the west bank of the Mississippi River) has a wide range of housing that includes a high proportion of rental units, affordable older homes, new condos, townhomes with lake and golf course views, and even a few park-like estates near the Somerset Country Club. Next-door neighbor **South Saint Paul** is best known for its stockyards, which closed in 2008. SSP's homes and condos are among the most affordable in the Twin Cities. It is also home to an active regional airport, South St. Paul Airport (Fleming Field). Owned and managed by the city, it is home to the Southern Minnesota Wing of the Commemorative Air Force (www.cafsmw. org) and the famous *Miss Mitchell* B-25 bomber.

Both West and South Saint Paul are strongly business oriented, boasting nearly as many jobs as they have residents. Major employers include Sportsman's Guide mail-order house, Dakota Premium Foods (meatpacking), Target, Walmart, and Tapemark.

In contrast, neighboring **Sunfish Lake**, one of the wealthiest cities in America, is an island of sylvan serenity. Strictly single-family residential, it has minimum lot sizes of 2.5 acres. Sunfish Lake has no city employees and provides no city services. Look online at the city's web site for information, www. sunfishlake.org.

Recreation amenities in this area include biking/hiking trails along the Mississippi River and 320-acre Dodge Nature Center (www.dodgenaturecenter. org), a place where children can interact with farm animals and explore the natural environment. The Nature Center offers many activities, including preschool and after-school programs and summer camps.

Shopping is conveniently located along South Robert Street in West Saint Paul.

South Saint Paul children attend South St. Paul Public Schools, www.sspps. org, Minnesota's first K–12 International Baccalaureate school district. Students

in West Saint Paul attend West St. Paul–Mendota Heights–Eagan schools, www. isd197.org.

This area is rich with public transportation, with most residents of West Saint Paul living within three blocks of a bus line. Bus routes focus on Downtown St. Paul, but also go to Inver Grove Heights and Mendota Heights.

City of South Saint Paul: 125 3rd Ave N, South Saint Paul, 55075, 651-554-3200, www.southstpaul.org

City of West Saint Paul: 1616 Humboldt Ave, West Saint Paul, 55118, 651-552-4100, www.ci.west-saint-paul.mn.us

SCOTT COUNTY

Credit River Township; Jordan; Prior Lake; Shakopee

Boundaries: North: Minnesota River, Carver County; **West**: Minnesota River, Sibley County; **South**: Le Sueur and Rice counties; **East**: Dakota County; **Area**: 365 square miles; **Population**: 128,937

The extension of sewer service and the building of a flood-proof high bridge over the Minnesota River (Highway 169) have fueled a building boom in Scott County that has made it the fastest growing county in the state. Teeming with young families, its population increased from 57,846 in 1990 to almost 130,000 in 2008, and is expected to hit 220,940 by 2030.

So far, two-thirds of the county's residents live in its three northernmost cities: Shakopee, Savage, and Prior Lake. Another 15% live in posh master-planned communities in Elko–New Market, and in Credit River, in the eastern part of the county, along I-35. The rest of the county has been able to remain somewhat agricultural. That's changing, however, and land is being consumed at a fast pace as the construction of high-amenity developments follows Highway 169 west to Jordan and Belle Plaine, and Highways 21 and 13 south to New Prague. About 70% of the new housing is single-family. Multi-family homes are located primarily in the northernmost cities, although a number of townhomes have been built in golf course developments in Elko. Rentals, too, can be found primarily in the northern cities, where rents are generally slightly lower than in next-door neighbor Burnsville, and significantly lower than in Eden Prairie, which is just across the river over the Highways 101 and 169 bridges.

Bridges are of major importance here, in part because the Minnesota River is prone to spring flooding, and in part because of the way traffic backs up over them during rush hours and busy Renaissance Fair and Valley Fair weekends. Be sure to take them into consideration when contemplating your commute. Four-lane bridges are located on I-35 at Burnsville and Highway 169 at Savage, and two-lane bridges are located on Highway 101 at Shakopee, Highway 41 at Chaska, County Road 45 between Jordan and Carver, and in Belle Plaine. While most commuters here drive solo in their cars, the county does offer commuter transit service five days a week using Minnesota Valley Transit Authority (MVTA) express buses.

The small towns are chock full of locally owned businesses, while big-box retail is available at Savage. Eden Prairie Center is directly across the river and Burnsville Center is minutes away.

Because this is where suburbia and rural Minnesota intersect, those who move here should keep in mind that the proximity of home and farm can create problems ranging from barnyard smells and wild animals/hunters in your yard to teenage keg parties.

This county also tends to have a less settled, more transitory population, a circumstance that has been tied to the county's shrinking high school graduation rate.

Scott County Government Center: 200 Fourth Ave W, Shakopee, 55379, 952-445-7750, 952-445-8170 TTY, www.co.scott.mn.us

Police: Scott County Sheriff's Office: Emergency, 911; Sheriff's Dispatch: 952-445-1411

Driver's Exam Station: 418 Pine St, Chaska, 952-448-3740

Emergency Hospitals: Ridgeview Medical Center, 500 S Maple St, Waconia, 952-442-2191, www.ridgeviewmedical.org; St. Francis Regional Medical Center, 1455 St. Francis Ave, Shakopee, 952-428-3000, www.stfrancis-shakopee.com

Library: Scott County Library System, www.scott.lib.mn.us, has branch libraries in Belle Plaine, Elko, Jordan, New Prague, Prior Lake, Savage, and Shakopee

Attractions: Canterbury Park Racetrack and Card Club, 1100 Canterbury Rd, Shakopee, www.canterburypark.com; Raceway Park (NASCAR), One Checkered Flag Blvd, Shakopee, www.goracewaypark.com; Historic Murphy's Landing, 2187 Highway 101 East, Shakopee, www.threeriversparks.org; Valleyfair Amusement Park, One Valleyfair Dr, Shakopee, 952-445-6500, www.valleyfair.com; Minnesota Renaissance Festival, 3 miles south of Shakopee on Highway 169, www.renaissancefest.com/MRF; Trail of Terror, 3 miles south of Shakopee on Highway 169, www.trailofterrorfest.com; Elko Speedway, 26350 France Avenue, Elko, www.elkospeedway.com; Mystic Lake Casino, 2400 Mystic Lake Boulevard, Prior Lake, www.mysticlake.com

Parks and Recreation: 2400-acre Murphy-Hanrehan Park Reserve, near Savage, off County Road 75, has trails for walkers, bikers, horses, snowmobiles, and cross-country skiers. It is designated an "Important Bird Area" by the National Audubon Society. Cleary Lake Regional Park, near Prior Lake on Scott County Road 27, has a 9-hole golf course, driving range, and facilities for swimming, boating and fishing. Winter activities include cross-country skiing on groomed trails. Both parks are part of the Three Rivers Park System, www.threeriversparks.org. The multi-use Minnesota Valley Trail parallels the Minnesota River from Belle Plain to Chaska, www.dnr.state.mn.us/state_

parks/minnesota_valley/index.html. Golf courses include Stonebrooke Golf Club, 2693 County Rd 79, Shakopee, 952-496-3171, www.stonebrooke. com; The Wilds Golf Club, 3151 Wilds Ridge, Prior Lake, 952-445-3500, www. golfthewilds.com, which was named "Minnesota's #1 Public Course" by *Golf Digest*; and The Ridges at Sand Creek, 21775 Ridges Dr, Jordan, 952-492-2644, www.ridgesatsandcreek.com, which was nominated for "Best New Course" by *Golf Digest* in 2001 and has since garnered accolades as the "Best Value in Golf" in the Twin Cities. The Legends Golf Club, 8670 Credit River Blvd, Prior Lake, with its meandering creek and huge stands of old trees, is one of the most beautiful courses in the Twin Cities, 952-226-1777, www. legendsgc.com.

Public Schools: Jordan District 717, www.jordan.k12.mn.us; Lakeville Area Public Schools, www.isd194.k12.mn.us; Shakopee Public School District 720, www. shakopee.k12.mn.us; Prior Lake–Savage District 719, www.priorlake-savage. k12.mn.us; New Prague Independent School District 721, www.np.k12.mn.us; Burnsville, Eagan, Savage District 191, www.isd191.org

Public Transportation: Minnesota Valley Transit Authority, 952-882-7500, www.mvta.com, provides commuter bus service from Savage. The Savage Park & Ride is located at 141st St and Huntington Ave, one block north of County Rd 42 (behind McDonald's). Dial-A-Ride service takes residents anywhere they want to go within the seven-county metro area, 952-496-8341, www.smartlinktransit.com. Prior Lake's Laker Lines transit service runs express commuter buses each day to downtown Minneapolis, 952-496-8800, www.bluexpressbus.com.

CREDIT RIVER TOWNSHIP

If you're looking for luxurious country living within easy commuting distance of the cities, consider Credit River. Located in the eastern part of the county off I-35W,

this is the fastest growing township in our fastest growing county. Nevertheless, developers here have taken great care to preserve (and market) its rural setting. Among the resort-like planned communities in this area is amenity-rich **Credit River Territory** (www.territoryhomes.com), named "2006 Best New Neighborhood-South" by the Builders Association of the Twin Cities (www.batconline.org). Children here attend Lakeville Area Public Schools, www.isd194.k12.mn.us.

Credit River Township: 18985 Meadow View Ln, Prior Lake, 55372, 952-440-5515, www.creditriver-mn.gov

JORDAN

Located 8 miles south of Shakopee and 25 miles southwest of the major regional intersection of Interstate 494 and Highway 169, Jordan is a flourishing country town with a number of buildings that are listed on the National Register of Historic Places. Housing here ranges from double-wides and townhouses to hobby farms and upper bracket estates. Homes that overlook the Minnesota River have miles of hiking, biking, cross-country skiing, horseback riding, mountain biking, and snowmobiling trails (Minnesota Valley Trail) just outside their doors. While much of the newest construction consists of small homes on 1/2- or 1/4-acre lots, this is still a good place to look for a house on acreage—or acreage to build on. Children here attend Jordan School District #717 schools, www.jordan.k12.mn.us.

City of Jordan: 210 E 1st St, Jordan, 55352, 952-492-2535, www.jordan.govoffice.com

PRIOR LAKE

Prior Lake (the lake) is known for its water skiing, while Prior Lake (the city) is known for being home to Scott County's biggest landowner, the Shakopee-Mdewakanton Sioux Indian tribe, whose reservation is located entirely within the city. This tribe of about 200 members operates the Mystic Lake casino (www.mysticlake.com), which is said to be the second-most profitable Indian casino in the nation. Traffic around Mystic Lake is not inconsequential, as the casino gets over 18,000 visitors every day. To learn more about the tribe, check out their web site at www.shakopeedakota.org.

The city exploded with construction beginning in the 1980s, so you can find contemporary housing here of every type, with many multi-family options, as well as luxurious homes surrounding the lake and The Legends golf course. Recreation, of course, centers on the lake. The Shakopee–Prior Lake Water Ski

Association (www.splwsa.org) is one of the oldest and largest water ski clubs in the country. Buried as Prior Lake is, away from major highways, the commute is no picnic. However the Laker Lines, the city's transit service, does run express commuter buses to downtown Minneapolis each day, www.bluexpressbus.com. Prior Lake/Savage Area School District (www.priorlake-savage.k12.mn.us) serves all of Prior Lake.

City of Prior Lake: 4646 Dakota Street SE, Prior Lake, 55372, 952-447-9800, www.cityofpriorlake.com

SHAKOPEE

Shakopee, population 33,460 in 2009, is expected to grow to more than 50,000 by 2030. The Scott County seat, it is located 23 miles from Minneapolis, at the intersection of Highways 169 and 101. Home to Canterbury Park, Valley Fair Amusement Park, Murphy's Landing, and Raceway Park, it bills itself as "The Definition of Fun." Along with all the nearby "attractions," it is also home to the Shakopee Correctional Facility, the state's only women's prison.

Historic, with a business district full of brick buildings that date from the 1850s, the city boasts so many streets of recently constructed townhouses that it almost has a "new" feel. Most housing falls into the affordable category, with more expensive homes located south of town near Thole and Odowd lakes. Recreation centers around a 920-acre park and open space system which includes a community center, ice arena, skate park, and outdoor aquatic park. The city also operates Enigma Teen Center (www.ci.shakopee.mn.us/enigma.cfm), which gives local young people a place to hang out. Children here attend schools operated by Shakopee School District 720, www.shakopee.k12.mn.us, a district with a large percentage of non-English-speaking students.

City of Shakopee: 129 S Holmes St, Shakopee, 55379, 952-233-9300, www.ci.shakopee.mn.us

OTHER SUBURBAN COMMUNITIES

Today, the Twin Cities are much more than just the metropolitan boundaries of Minneapolis and St. Paul. The post–World War II baby boom, followed by the rapid expansion in the 1960s of the interstate highway system and metropolitan sewer system, led to enormous migration of new families into what had been farms and forests. In fact, over the past 50 years or so the metro area has grown into an amorphous expanse that includes more than 188 distinct suburban communities within the seven-county metro area, alone. If we jump to the 13-county metro area, the suburbs become too numerous to count.

Virtually all of the Twin Cities' growth has been in the suburbs, with seven counties in the 13-county metro statistical area among the 100 fastest growing in the nation: Scott, Sherburne, Wright, St. Croix (Wisconsin), Chisago, Carver, and Isanti.

The appeal of these exurbs is obvious: larger lots, new buildings with floor plans that meet the needs and desires of today's families, and amenities such as private community centers, trails, and pools. For the latest on what sort of homes are being built and where, there is no better source than the Builders' Association of the Twin Cities Parade of Homes, www.paradeofhomes.org.

Below are web addresses for some of the suburban communities not profiled in this book:

WESTERN SUBURBS

- Buffalo, www.ci.buffalo.mn.us
- Greenfield, www.greenfield.govoffice.com
- Minnetonka Beach, www.ci.minnetonka-beach.mn.us
- Minnetrista, www.ci.minnetrista.mn.us
- Monticello, www.ci.monticello.mn.us
- Spring Park, http://springpark.govoffice.com
- Tonka Bay, www.cityoftonkabay.net
- Victoria, www.ci.victoria.mn.us
- Waconia, www.waconia.org

SOUTHWESTERN SUBURBS

- Belle Plaine, www.belleplainemn.com
- New Prague, www.ci.new-prague.mn.us

NORTHERN SUBURBS

- Brooklyn Center, www.ci.brooklyn-center.mn.us
- Cambridge, www.ci.cambridge.mn.us
- Circle Pines, www.ci.circle-pines.mn.us
- Columbia Heights, www.ci.columbia-heights.mn.us
- Crystal, www.ci.crystal.mn.us
- Ham Lake, www.ci.ham-lake.mn.us
- Little Canada, www.ci.little-canada.mn.us
- New Hope, www.ci.new-hope.mn.us
- Robbinsdale, www.ci.robbinsdale.mn.us
- St. Anthony, www.ci.saint-anthony.mn.us

SOUTHERN SUBURBS

- Elko–New Market, www.ci.elko.mn.us
- Hastings, www.ci.hastings.mn.us
- Northfield, www.ci.northfield.mn.us
- Savage, www.cityofsavage.com

The Minneapolis Area Association of Realtors' (www.mplsrealtor.com) annual housing market report is a valuable resource for price trends, and includes maps that will allow you to easily compare median home prices and median square foot prices across the metro.

PRICES HAVE BEEN KNOCKED BACK TO WHERE THEY WERE A DECADE ago and, finally, it's a buyer's market! The building rampage of the last decade has left the Twin Cities with some interesting new digs, a lot of foreclosures, and a huge unsold inventory of recently constructed homes.

With the increase in vacant properties comes an interesting new place to look for a home or lot to build on—city and county web pages. Just click on "Housing" and you will find listings—and sometimes, pictures—of the city's fore-closed homes and vacant lots. Some cities include apartment information, too.

The average cost of an apartment in Minneapolis is about 12% below the national average in 2010, with an average two-bedroom unit going for about $1000. St. Paul apartments are somewhat cheaper, with an average two-bedroom unit going for $800 a month. Ironically, one-bedroom units have actually become more expensive, also averaging around $1000 a month in 2010.

Naturally, there is stiff competition for the most desirable lodgings. That means everyone wants to live in the Southwest Minneapolis and Calhoun/Isles neighborhoods, and in the higher income neighborhoods on the west side of St. Paul. For more affordable apartments look in the Near North, Phil-lips/Whittier, Powderhorn, and Camden areas in Minneapolis and Thomas-Dale, Summit-University, and the North End in St. Paul. You can find the latest rental pricing reports for cities throughout the metro at www.apartmentratings.com.

Real estate crash notwithstanding, the recently constructed lofts and condos in the downtowns, along with the grandiose developments that sprawl along the interstate highways, were unabashedly aimed at affluent buyers, so even their fire-sale prices are high. In addition, first-time buyer incentives have increased demand for starter homes, so that leaves relatively little actually "affordable" new housing to be found.

Consequently, if you are looking for a starter home, you may need to be flexible about your choice of neighborhood—and you may need to get creative about how you're going to pay for it, too. One popular strategy: buy an income-producing duplex in your chosen neighborhood as your first home, then sell it after a few years and use the appreciation on your investment to finance your dream house up the block. To do that, you need to find a neighborhood that has a wide range of housing such as NE or South Minneapolis, or the west side of St. Paul. St. Louis Park (www.stlouispark.org) is another popular get-your-foot-in-the-door town. It has apartments, condos, duplexes (often called double bungalows up here) and a vast number of homes under 1500 square feet. They're ideal for starter homes, but—even better—the city is actively engaged in trying to keep people from having to move away to find family-size housing and has developed a number of programs to help residents enlarge their homes, including help with architects and loans.

Beyond the not-so-well-kept secret of St. Louis Park, the piece of advice most often dished out by locals is this: if you're single, stick with the cities and avoid the 'burbs. Except for St. Louis Park, which counts many young singles among its residents and is closer to the Minneapolis Chain of Lakes than many parts of Minneapolis, the suburbs are almost universally family-oriented. The downtowns of both cities, however, have exploded with tony new lofts that are only suitable for singles or couples. Of course, sophisticated downtown residences can be pretty pricey, which brings us to another urban option—transit-oriented housing.

NEWER HOUSING OPTIONS

TRANSIT-ORIENTED HOUSING

An unfortunate consequence of our existing planning and policy environment is that it is often much cheaper to build on undeveloped farmland in the exurbs than it is to build within existing communities. But the **Hiawatha Light Rail Transit Line** has changed that. Often characterized as "smart growth," transit-oriented housing along the LRT has made it possible for people to drive less at the same time as it has revitalized the neighborhoods along its route. Condos and apartment complexes have joined the old single-family housing stock, and Bloomington has created a whole new downtown around its two LRT stops. North of the cities, the **Northstar Commuter Rail** begins in Minneapolis and travels out 40 miles through Fridley, Coon Rapids, Anoka, and Elk River to Big Lake. Keep your eye on these cities, as they offer a variety of homes and apartments already, and expect to see strong property value appreciation with the advent of their own transit-oriented developments, once the economy improves. Finally, the **Central Corridor LRT** down University and Washington Avenues, which will connect the St. Paul and Minneapolis downtowns, is scheduled to begin service in 2014 and has already spurred redevelopment in the neighborhoods along its route.

ATTACHED OR MULTI-FAMILY HOUSING

For years, most housing in the Twin Cities was either single-family detached or apartments, with relatively few options in between. That is no longer the case. In fact, multi-family units account for the major share of new development, according to the Metropolitan Council (www.metrocouncil.org), our local planning authority. Consequently, twin homes and townhouses now span the region from Shakopee to Princeton, and can even be found within the cities of Minneapolis and St. Paul. Lofts are less widespread, and more concentrated in the two downtowns. Those thinking about buying a loft should be sure to research their preferred buildings to make sure the construction is sound and the building doesn't contain too many unsold units—there have been many such problems caused by financially challenged developers. Those looking for twin homes and townhouses will be able to see a number of new models on the **Builders Association of the Twin Cities Parade of Homes** web site, www.paradeofhomes.org.

HOUSE-HUNTING

ONLINE RESEARCH

The Internet has completely changed how people find their homes. Thanks to the **Regional Multiple Listing Service**'s "broker reciprocity" agreement, you can now sit back home in New Jersey and use the MLS's sophisticated search engine to view all the Greater Metro MLS real estate listings, including property in Wisconsin. Just click on http://msp.themlsonline.com, put in your city choices, price range, and amenities, and in a few minutes you'll have pictures of all the listings that meet your criteria, plus clickable links that allow you to take virtual tours of the properties and links for contacting the listing agents online. You'll also gain a realistic idea of how much the kind of home you're interested in might cost, and be able to identify agents who specialize in the neighborhoods you'd like to look at. Don't worry that you'll be looking at properties that are long gone—the MLS database is updated every 15 minutes. Of course, property that isn't listed with an agent won't be on the MLS web site, so for "For Sale by Owner" listings, check out the *St. Paul Pioneer Press* property search (www.twincities.com/homes), the *Minneapolis Star Tribune* (www.startribune.com), or **Home Avenue**, www.homeavenue.com/fsbo/info/default2.aspx

A different sort of search engine, **www.MNrealty.com**, bills itself as "Your Independent Guide to Minnesota Real Estate On-Line." Not a brokerage, this site lists property for sale and links to information such as schools and sports.

Zillow, www.zillow.com, not only shows home listings but lists median sale prices by neighborhood. **RealtyTrac**, www.realtytrac.com, is a national online real estate listing service that focuses on foreclosed properties, giving detailed information about the foreclosure process and how to buy a home that is in foreclosure.

And of course, there's always **Craigslist**, http://minneapolis.craigslist.org. More and more, people are trying to cut out the middleman by selling their homes through these classifieds.

For those looking for apartments, see the section on **Renting**, below.

OTHER HOMEBUYING RESOURCES

- **Accessible Space, Inc.**, 651-645-7271, 800-466-7722, www.accessiblespace. org, is a nonprofit whose mission is to provide accessible, affordable, assisted/ supportive and independent living opportunities for persons with physical disabilities and brain injuries, as well as seniors.
- **The Home Ownership Center**, 651-659-9336, 1-866-462-6466, www.hocmn. org, is the state's leading independent, nonprofit provider of information and resources aimed at helping Minnesotans begin and maintain home owner- ship. While their services are open to anyone, the Center places an emphasis on supporting low- and moderate-income Minnesotans and those who face barriers to home ownership.
- **Parade of Homes**, www.paradeofhomes.org, is the Builders Association of the Twin Cities' four-times-a-year showcase of new and remodeled construc- tion throughout the metro area.

GETTING TO KNOW THE NEIGHBORHOOD

City web pages are an excellent resource for information, offering profiles of neighborhoods, listings of community events and, sometimes even home tours. You should also call the police precinct that patrols your neighborhood of interest. The numbers are listed at the end of each county or neighborhood profile.

The best advice when house or apartment hunting, however, is to visit pro- spective neighborhoods—have breakfast at a local restaurant and walk around, don't just drive. Find out if services and conveniences you are accustomed to having are available nearby, and pay attention to your comfort level. Check on traffic and noise levels at different times of the day and night. If you are put off by the noise of airplanes taking off and landing (as in South Minneapolis, Rich- field, East Bloomington, Eagan, Mendota Heights, and western St. Paul) or by strangers roller-blading on your street (around the city lakes), factor these into your decision about where to live. There isn't much you can do about crowds of exercise enthusiasts, but for information about airplane noise and possible abatement programs check out the **Metropolitan Airports Commission**'s (**MAC**) web site (www.macnoise.com).

Also consider the commute. According to INRIX, the company that analyzed traffic patterns on highways in the 100 most congested metropolitan areas, the Twin Cities metropolitan area is the 10th most congested area in the nation for its size. In the TC, that means that during peak driving times a random trip on the roads analyzed took 13% more time, on average, than it did when there was no congestion. If you're a fan of audio books, that might not be so bad, but you should still test drive your route at rush hour, morning and night, to be sure of what you're getting into. Lastly, some people are able to commute by bus, but the usefulness of buses depends entirely upon where you live, where you need to go, and at what time. Information about Twin Cities bus routes can be accessed on the Internet at **www.metrotransit.org**. See **Transportation** for more details.

RENTING

Renting for a while is a great way to get to know the town before you commit to a permanent address, and you can easily find an apartment on your own. First check this guide's neighborhood descriptions to learn about the types of housing in different parts of town—then, if possible, use Minnesota's climate to assist your apartment search; many people choose not to move in winter, creating more vacancies in the summer. Begin looking around the first of June, and you might even be lucky enough to find a handsome, turn-of-the-20th-century brick apartment with hardwood floors and tall windows near Uptown or Summit/Grand, two of the most popular neighborhoods for newcomers.

ONLINE AND NEWSPAPER RESOURCES

Numerous online resources such as **www.rent.com** are available. **Hubbuzz**, www.hubbuzz.com/Minneapolis-St.Paul/MetroAreaOverview.aspx, includes good neighborhood descriptions, as well as a clickable map. A national service, **www.sublet.com** has up-to-date listings from all over the metro. Browse it for free, and when you find something of interest, register (for a fee) and they will give you the contact information. Since the same company that owns that site also owns **www.Cityleases.com** and **www.Metroroommates.com**, you'll gain access to those sites at no extra cost. **Craigslist** (http://minneapolis.craigslist.org) also maintains extensive free listings of rental housing, with new postings each day.

Free neighborhood newspapers can be found at businesses and newsstands throughout the Twin Cities. Other papers to watch:

- The **Minneapolis Star Tribune** has the most comprehensive metro-area listings. You can access the classifieds online at www.startribune.com/homes.
- **St. Paul Pioneer Press** is the better resource for St. Paul and the eastern metro area. Access the classifieds at www.twincities.com/rentals.
- **City Pages** is a free alternative weekly, available at businesses metro-wide. The listings are not extensive, but worth checking, especially if you're young and hip. It also lists roommates wanted, www.citypages.com.
- **Minnesota Daily** is the University of Minnesota newspaper, www.mndaily.com.

APARTMENT SEARCH FIRMS

Many landlords contract with rental agents or apartment search firms to find tenants for their units. A search firm can be very convenient if you have a limited amount of time to find a place. Agents will fax you information and arrange appointments for you to view available units. When talking to a rental agent, be specific about your needs; this way you will not waste time considering places that aren't right for you. The following are some of the largest and most well-known apartment search firms. The property owners typically pay their fees, so the service to the tenant is usually free:

- **Apartments.com**, www.apartments.com, has apartments as well as a moving and furniture rental center.
- **Apartment Search**, 800-APARTMENT, www.apartmentsearch.com, offers moving and furniture rental.
- **HousingLink**, 612-522-2500, www.housinglink.org, is a nonprofit service that maintains a directory of affordable housing properties.
- **Park Avenue of Wayzata**, 952-475-1700, www.parkavenueofwayzata.com, lists townhouses and condominiums in the western suburbs.

TEMPORARY HOUSING/SUBLETS/SHARING

If finding a long-term place to live is proving difficult, you may want to consider taking a short-term sublet. Many such sublets are available in May, when students begin to leave town with time remaining on their leases, or during the winter when the "snowbirds" move to warmer climates. But remember, most leases say that a tenant can sublet only if the landlord agrees to it—and that permission should be in writing. (The original tenant remains responsible for unpaid rent and damage done to the apartment by the new tenant.) Check the **Temporary Lodgings** chapter for additional temporary alternatives and see **Online Research** and **Online and Newspaper Resources** above.

CHECKING IT OUT

Your apartment search will be easier if you keep a few things in mind. First, ask yourself how much space you really want to pay for. If you're alone, a studio or efficiency might be most cost-effective. Studios generally are found in downtown Minneapolis and St. Paul and, in 2010, the average monthly rent was about $800. A one-bedroom generally will cost $150–$200 more than a studio, a second bedroom adds anywhere from $150 to $500. Add a third bedroom and your rent will probably increase substantially. The bulk of the larger units can be found in the suburbs.

In Minnesota, an important question to ask is: who will be paying for heat? If it's you and not the landlord, you could be adding a substantial amount to your cost of living during the cold months. You can find out the average cost of heating for an apartment by calling the gas or electric company that provides service to that building (most likely CenterPoint and Xcel—see the **Getting Settled** chapter). Another consideration when choosing a place to live is the availability of parking. Off-street, indoor parking is especially desirable in the winter—your car will start in the morning, you won't have to scrape off ice and snow, and—most important—you won't have to move your car for the city snowplow. City streets are plowed according to several different plans, but no matter the schedule, if your car is parked on a street in the way of the snowplow, it will be towed, and be assured it will be expensive and time-consuming to get your car out of the impound lot. (See **Snow Emergency Parking** in **Getting Settled**.)

Also be sure to check with your city's housing inspection department for a property's past code violations and current citations. Minnesota law requires that landlords disclose any outstanding inspection orders for which a citation has been issued for violations that threaten the health or safety of tenants. However, the law has many loopholes. Better to trust your city's inspections department for current status information. Landlords who rent units built before 1978 also must disclose any known lead-based paint and include a warning in the lease. The National Lead Information Center (800-424-LEAD) can provide information and a copy of the Environmental Protection Agency brochure "Lead Poisoning and Your Children."

Finally, watch for discrimination. In Minnesota, it's illegal to deny housing based on race, religion, age, or any other personal basis. Minneapolis specifically prohibits discrimination based on sexual orientation. However, Fair Housing laws may not apply to owner-occupied complexes of four or fewer units. If you're in Minneapolis and believe you are a victim of discrimination, call the Minneapolis Department of Civil Rights, at 311.

STAKING A CLAIM

When viewing prospective apartments, take along appropriate documentation. That includes job and bank account information, personal references, and the name and telephone number of your previous landlord. Many landlords use tenant screening services and the information they receive is used to approve or deny your tenancy. If a landlord uses the service's information to deny rental, increase your security deposit, or increase your rent, he/she must give you written notice of the adverse action and you have a right to add an explanation of the problem to your file.

LEASES, SECURITY DEPOSITS, AND TAX REFUNDS

The terms of a rental agreement are stated in a lease. Lease agreements should be in writing. Be sure you understand everything in a written lease before you sign it, and get a copy for your files. Remember that a lease is a legally binding agreement and that a tenant does not have the right to break a lease, even for good reasons like moving or buying a home. Following are some clauses you should challenge before signing, or avoid:

- Unannounced entry—Minnesota has a law forbidding a landlord to enter an apartment without permission or reasonable notice (24 hours) except in emergencies.
- Responsibility for repairs without compensation. If you agree to perform any maintenance on your apartment, you can negotiate a rent decrease. Make sure it's in writing.
- Escalation and acceleration clauses—some leases permit an owner to raise the rent during a lease period (escalation). Other lease language may state that upon missing a month's rent, you are immediately liable for the rest of the lease amount, which could be thousands of dollars (acceleration). These kinds of clauses are legal, but you may not want to rent from someone who proposes them. Pay attention and read the fine print.
- Late charges—if your lease does not include information about late charges, then your landlord may not impose them, except for the filing and service fees related to unlawful detainer that are permitted by law.
- As for security deposits, a landlord may require a deposit of any amount in order to pay for damage the tenant might do to the unit. The amount of this deposit may be increased at any time during a month-to-month lease. However, the security deposit must be returned with interest within 21 days after the end of the tenancy, or the landlord must provide a written explanation as to why it is being withheld. If a landlord does not refund the deposit, with interest, the tenant can take the matter to court. Minnesota law also gives tenants the chance to get some of their money back in the form of a partial refund of the property taxes they pay indirectly through their rent. To claim your credit, file a property tax refund form and certificate of rent paid (which your landlord must give you by January 31 of each year) with the Minnesota Department of Revenue, www.taxes.state.mn.us/taxes/prop_refund/refund_information/content/renters_refund.shtml. (See Money Matters.)

LANDLORD PROBLEMS

The Minnesota Attorney General's office offers several free booklets for consumers, including "Landlords and Tenants: Rights and Responsibilities." Download it from the Internet at www.ag.state.mn.us/Consumer/Housing/LandlordTenants.asp.

Other sources of assistance include:

- **First Call for Help** (24 hours), 211, funded by the United Way, is a general information number that can provide housing assistance with respect to lists of available rental housing, advice on landlord issues, loan programs, transitional housing, and referrals to other resources. It's free, confidential, and available 24/7. Cell phone users can call 651-291-0211, 1-800-543-7709.
- **HOME Line**, 3455 Bloomington Ave, Minneapolis, 612-728-5767, 1-866-866-3546 (Greater Minnesota), www.homelinemn.org, provides free legal, organizing, education, and advocacy services so that tenants throughout Minnesota can solve their own rental housing problems. HOME Line serves the entire state of Minnesota except the cities of Minneapolis and St. Paul.

The **Minnesota Legal Services Coalition** (MLSC) provides legal assistance to lower income Minnesotans. Contact MLSC at www.lawhelpMN.org to identify an MLSC location near you.

RENTER'S INSURANCE

Get it. Generally a building owner's insurance covers damage to the building, not your personal possessions. Renter's insurance, however, does provide relatively inexpensive protection against theft, water damage, fire, and, in many cases, personal liability. Insurance companies that sell homeowner's insurance also sell renter's insurance.

BUYING

Minnesota loves homeowners! Yes, property taxes are high, but if you live in the home you buy, the state may offset some of your tax burden by giving you a **homestead property tax refund**. It also allows you to deduct mortgage interest payments from your taxable income, thereby reducing the amount of income taxes you have to pay.

Homes come in many forms, from traditional, **single-family detached houses** to multiple ownership situations: cluster homes, condos, townhouses, patio homes, and co-ops. **Cluster homes** are detached houses built close together with shared outdoor grounds, recreational facilities, and maintenance costs. **Condominiums** are buildings in which you purchase a unit, but all the land and other facilities are jointly owned by the entire condo community. In a **townhouse**, you purchase both the structure and the land under it. A **patio home** is similar to a townhouse; however, in addition to purchasing the unit and the land under it, it will also come with a small yard. **Cooperatives** are buildings in which you own a share in the corporation that owns the building, with a housing unit reserved for each shareholder's use. A **multiple housing complex**, sometimes referred to as **association housing**, is managed by a board of the homeowners, which collects dues and assessments for maintenance and repairs.

Good questions to ask about association housing are:

- What percentage of the units is owner-occupied?
- How much are the association dues and projected assessments?
- What are the rules and regulations?
- Is the development professionally managed?
- Have there been any lawsuits involving the association in the past five years?

When scouting for any home, don't forget the cold climate! Energy costs are high here for both heating and cooling. And, while houses built since the energy crisis of the 1970s may have very tight, energy-efficient construction, they may also have problems with moisture and poor indoor air quality (carbon monoxide, radon). The newest houses solve this problem with balanced mechanical ventilation systems and sealed-combustion appliances that do not draw air from inside the home.

Older houses can be remodeled and/or made more energy-efficient to meet modern families' needs. Three locally produced books have been created to assist those with older homes. *The Longfellow Planbook: Remodeling Plans for Bungalows and Other Small Urban Homes* can be purchased from the Longfellow Community Council (www.longfellow.org, 612-722-4529) for $20, $10 for Longfellow residents. *Cape Cods and Ramblers: A Remodeling Planbook for Post-WW II Houses* will help you time-tune houses from the 1940s, '50s and '60s. It's posted online at www.ci.blaine.mn.us/_Docs/_SafetyServices/_HousingDepartment/ARemodelingPlanbookforPost-WWIIHouses.pdf. Dakota County has produced *Split-Visions: A Planbook of Remodeling Ideas for Split-Level and Split-Entry Houses*. It's online at www.dakotacda.org/pdf/splitvisions.pdf.

A 2004 law requires sellers of residential property to disclose all material facts—of which they're aware—that could significantly or adversely affect an ordinary buyer's use or enjoyment of the property. This not only covers environmental hazards such as lead and mold but also includes information that a prospective buyer would want to know that is not directly associated with the physical condition of the property, such as the expansion of a road that is adjacent to the property, or the expansion of an airport runway that would allow air traffic to fly over the property. Despite this statutory protection, when viewing a prospective home be sure to keep your eyes open. One important thing to look for: roof and structural damage caused by ice dams (see **Local Lingo** in the **Introduction**), which may form if a house is not adequately insulated and ventilated, a common problem in Minnesota. And, since homes often have defects that are not easily visible, it is wise to protect yourself by having a professional roof/mechanical systems inspection prior to purchase. Professional residential inspectors can be found in the Yellow Pages under "Home and Building Inspection," or ask your realtor for a recommendation. The **American Society of Home Inspectors**' web site (www.ashi.com) includes information about what's involved in a home inspection and what to do if your inspection report reveals a problem.

WORKING WITH REALTORS

Even if an agent takes you to see a home, he or she is actually representing the seller, not you. If you want an agent who will act on your behalf, you will need to hire a buyer's broker. This person will not give information about you and what you can afford to the seller and will negotiate the lowest possible price for you. While there are thousands of independent real estate agents of both types working in the Twin Cities area, these are the region's top four real estate brokerage offices by sales. They all have numerous offices throughout the metro:

- **Coldwell Banker Burnet**, www.cbburnet.com
- **Counselor Realty**, www.counselorrealty.com
- **Edina Realty**, www.edinarealty.com
- **Re/Max Results**, www.results.net

PURCHASE AGREEMENTS, CREDIT, AND MORTGAGES

The purchase agreement is a legally binding document between the buyer and seller that states the price and all terms of a sale. It is the most negotiable and variable document produced in the homebuying process. It is also the single most important, since it is the document to which a buyer may attach contingencies. Such contingencies can protect you, the buyer, from being legally bound by the purchase agreement if, for example, you cannot sell the house you live in now, the house you are buying does not pass its mechanical and structural inspection, the seller is not able to give you possession by a certain date, or you cannot qualify for a loan.

Speaking of which, lenders suggest that you prequalify for your loan. To that end, meet with your potential lender to determine the amount of possible financing. Go prepared with documents that pertain to your finances and check your credit report to make sure it is accurate before meeting with a loan officer. You can check your credit report with all three national credit bureaus listed here. You are entitled to one free copy of your report each year, or a new report if you've been denied credit based on your credit report within the last 30 days. For more information about your rights concerning your credit report, check out the Federal Trade Commission's web site at www.ftc.gov. The National Credit Bureaus are:

- **Equifax**, PO Box 105851, Atlanta, GA 30348-5851, 800-685-1111, www.equifax.com
- **TransUnion**, PO Box 1000, Chester, PA 19022, 800-916-8800, www.transunion.com
- **Experian**, PO Box 2104, Allen, TX 75013-9595, 1-888-397-3742, www.experian.com

---

AnnualCreditReport.com is the ONLY authorized source for the free annual credit report that is yours by law.

When qualifying for a mortgage, the rule of thumb is that most people (depending on their existing debt load) can afford a home that is two and one-half times their annual gross income, or monthly payments of about 28% of their gross income. (Known as the 28/36 Rule, the other part of this rule states that no more than 36% of your income should be spent on *all* your monthly debt payments, including mortgage expenses, auto loans, credit cards, and utility payments.)

The **Minnesota Attorney General's Home Buyer's Handbook,** available online at www.ag.state.mn.us, contains information about financing a home, including Veterans Administration (VA) and Federal Housing Administration (FHA) loans, the most popular loans for first-time homebuyers. It also contains a Loan Qualification Worksheet to help you figure out what you can afford.

Banks and mortgage-lending institutions also have web sites that can help you to prequalify for a mortgage. Wells Fargo (www.wellsfargo.com) advertises a "Relocation Mortgage Program," which they say is designed specifically for corporate transferees.

Housing assistance is available for those in need. The **U.S. Department of Housing and Urban Development** (HUD, 920 Second Avenue South, Suite 1300, Minneapolis, 612-370-3000, TTY 612-370-3186, www.hud.gov) can help consumers buy homes, find Section 8 rentals, access HUD properties that are for sale, and figure out how much they can afford to spend on housing. The **Minnesota Housing Finance Agency** (MHFA) (400 Sibley Street, St. Paul, 651-296-7608, or 800-657-3769, TTY 651-297-2361, www.mhfa.state.mn.us) is sometimes able to make loans at below-market interest rates to first-time buyers or those with moderate incomes. For other resources for financial assistance, contact your city hall.

INSURANCE

A common and costly problem in Minnesota is ice dam damage, but your homeowner's insurance policy may not cover it.

Once your loan is approved, your lender will require you to buy homeowner's insurance to protect their investment (your home). A basic homeowner's policy includes liability insurance to protect you if someone is injured on your property, property protection to insure your house and personal belongings against damage or loss, and living expense coverage to pay for you to live elsewhere while repairs are being made. You may also be required to buy mortgage insurance, which pays your lender if you default on your loan, and title insurance, which protects the lender in case the legal title to the property isn't clear. It doesn't protect you, though, so, in addition, you may want to buy an owner's title insurance policy, or get an attorney's opinion on your title. If the seller has purchased title insurance in recent years you may be able to get the same title company to issue you a new policy at a lower cost, so be sure to ask about a re-issue credit. Other consumer tips for buying insurance are available on the **Minnesota Attorney General**'s web site (www.ag.state.mn.us). Advice includes starting to shop as soon as you have signed a purchase agreement, and to purchase a policy with a high deductible in order to lower your cost. A deductible of $1000 to $2500 is often recommended. You may also be able to save money by buying your home and auto coverage from the same company. In addition, subtract the value of the land from the value of the property and only buy insurance to cover the value of your home. After all, your house can burn down, but your land will remain.

Some of the major insurance companies in the area are:
- **Allstate**, www.allstate.com
- **American Family Insurance**, www.amfam.com
- **Farmers Insurance Group**, www.farmersinsurance.com
- **Travelers**, www.travelers.com
- **State Farm**, www.statefarm.com

CLOSING ON YOUR HOME

This is panic time! Most homes close the last week of the month because buyers want to avoid having to pay interest on their monthly loan payment, so underwriters, appraisers, and title companies are always in a mad scramble. Then, once you get to the actual closing you will probably be asked to sign the tallest stack of papers you have ever seen. How to avoid problems? There are a few things you can do. First, schedule your closing at least six weeks from the date your purchase agreement was signed. Then keep in contact with your lender to see if additional information is required. The week you close, ask your closer for a copy of the completed **Settlement Statement** (the HUD-1 form). You have the right to see this form one business day before the closing. It will contain a list of all your closing costs. Compare it to the good faith estimate of closing costs your loan officer gave you when you applied for the loan. The actual closing costs should not differ much from the estimate. If they do, you may be getting scammed. There are some costs, however, such as insurance premiums, the loan origination fee, and mortgage registration, that can only be nailed down after your loan is approved because they are based on the amount of your loan and the final value of the property. Finally, at the closing, be sure you've brought everything necessary: calculator to check addition, your homeowner's insurance binder and receipt showing this has been paid, a photo ID, your addresses for the last 10 years, and a cashier's check to pay the balance of your down payment and unpaid closing costs. For more information on closing, including an explanation of all those papers you'll be asked to sign, download the **Closing Checklist** from the Minnesota Attorney General's web site (www. ag.state.mn.us).

BUILDING

For those who are thinking of building, "location, location, location" is everything. Despite the poor economy, land prices within the Twin Cities have skyrocketed. Property near water sells at a premium, and you also pay higher property taxes to live on it. For those willing to live a 40-minute drive away from the Twin Cities, in communities where the culs-de-sac meet the cornfields, such as Waconia, Chisago City, Northfield, or Hudson, Wisconsin, land prices are more reasonable—though the environmental costs associated with the loss of farmland and long car commutes are high.

Building a new home in the Twin Cities may require the additional expense of drilling a well and putting in a septic system. While there is a lot of water around, many municipalities do not provide it. Be sure to check this out even in established suburbs. (An example: The cities around Lake Minnetonka have sewer service, but they don't all have municipal water.) Well water here, by the way, is likely to be full of iron, requiring the installation of water softeners and high-tech filter systems, all of which add to the cost of a house, as will radon protection (see **Helpful Services**).

MINNESOTA ENERGY CODE REQUIREMENTS

"Build It Tight and Ventilate It Right" is the motto here. Because of our tight air sealing and insulation requirements, a single-family home built after April 2000 must have a mechanical ventilation system. Most builders use either an air exchanger or continuously exhausting fans to meet this energy code requirement. Effective in 2009, passive radon systems are required for all new dwellings. To learn more, call the **Builders Association of Minnesota** (651-646-7959, 1-800-654-7783, www.bamn.org). They can provide general information about building a new home as well as state building code details. Your city clerk or building inspector will also be able to provide building code information, as well as give you a copy of local zoning ordinances. Free information on conservation and renewable energy is available from the **Minnesota Department of Commerce Energy Information** (651-296-5175, 800-657-3710 (Minnesota Only), www.state.mn.us/portal/mn/jsp/home.do?agency=Commerce).

FINDING AN ARCHITECT AND BUILDER

For a listing of local architects, go to the **American Institute of Architects** (www.aia-mn.org). This web site also includes information about working with an architect and questions to ask.

If you're here in the spring or fall, the **Parade/Preview of Homes**, sponsored by the Builders Association of the Twin Cities (www.paradeofhomes.org), is the perfect opportunity to scout locations, check out the latest home designs and construction techniques, and connect with local architects and builders.

Once you collect a few names, be sure to check them out with the **Minnesota Department of Labor and Industry, Residential Builders and Contractors Unit** (443 Lafayette Road North, St. Paul, 651-284-5005, 1-800-342-5354, www.dli.mn.gov/Main.asp). The department's web site contains a directory of licensed contractors, consumer guide to hiring a contractor, complaint information, Contractor Recovery Fund application package, and annual enforcement action listings. The **Contractor Recovery Fund** compensates owners or renters of residential property in Minnesota who have lost money due to a licensed contractor's fraudulent, deceptive or dishonest practices. However, the Recovery Fund will only pay out a total of $75,000 in claims against any one contractor, so you should request that your contractor obtain a performance bond, thus assuring a specific level of protection for your project. For more information, the Minnesota Attorney General's "**The Citizen's Guide to Home Building and Remodeling**" is downloadable off the AG's web site (www.ag.state.mn.us/consumer/housing/citguide/default.asp).

MAXIMIZING POTENTIAL RESALE

In 1970, just 10% of new homes were 2400 square feet; by 2004, 39% of new homes had at least 2400 square feet. In 1970, a bath and a half and two-car attached garage were standard; now multiple bathrooms and three-car garages are a given.

The challenge when buying or building a house is always to find a property that meets your needs while maximizing your potential resale price. So while you think about what you want, keep these construction trends in mind: small is the new "green," but people still like their high-tech kitchens and tall ceilings.

Adaptable homes that will change with you are suddenly coming into vogue, as are walkable urban neighborhoods. "Green" features such as high-efficiency insulation and energy-efficient appliances are often talked about but, in general, prospective buyers are unwilling to pay extra for them. While attached three-stall garages are standard in new construction, buyers do seem willing to pay extra for a fourth stall, so that they will have room to store a snowmobile or a boat. Along with a big garage, mudrooms, fireplaces, a minimum of two bathrooms, and flat driveways (or steep driveways with built-in heating coils to melt the ice) are usually deemed essentials in this market. This being Minnesota, where the mosquito is considered the "state bird," add a screened porch to that list. For the same reason, plus the shortness of the summer season, swimming pools are often, though not always, considered a detriment.

HOME WARRANTIES

Builders usually offer new home warranties, but if your builder does not, you are still protected under state law, and the coverage is basically the same, though it is not "bumper-to-bumper" as we have come to expect with our cars. There is a one-year warranty on workmanship and defective materials that are not in compliance with building standards, but you must notify the builder within six months of discovering the problem or the builder is not liable. There is a two-year warranty on installation of cooling, plumbing, and electrical systems. Major construction defects are covered for 10 years, but your idea of a major construction defect and The Law's may differ widely, as people who have had stucco and mold problems and cracks in their foundations have discovered. Basically, "major structural damage" appears to be limited to the load-bearing walls of the house and to damage that makes a house uninhabitable. For remodeling projects, work is generally covered for a one-year period. Check **Minnesota Statute Chapter 327A** (www.revisor.mn.gov/statutes/?year=2006&id=327A) for the good news/bad news.

Should you discover a defect in your new home, notify your builder immediately by registered letter and also notify your local building inspector. At the very least, the building inspector can give you a copy of your city's building codes and, if you're lucky, a building inspector can be a valuable ally in getting the work done properly. If your contractor ignores you, or if his corrections to the problem are unsatisfactory, you can file a complaint against the contractor with the **Department of Labor and Industry, Enforcement Division** (651-284-5005, 1-800-342-5354, www.dli.mn.gov/main.asp). You might also want to file a report with the **Better Business Bureau** (651-699-1111, http://minnesota.bbb.org). If you think you might need to get a lawyer, contact one early in the process because there is a statute of limitations on home defect lawsuits. Suing is very expensive, but if you win and are still unable to collect from the contractor, you may be eligible to have part of your judgment paid to you from the **Minnesota Contractor Recovery Fund** (see above).

HOME WARRANTY SERVICE PLANS

It is a common misconception that your homeowner's insurance policy will cover breakdowns of your home's mechanical systems. Unfortunately, it won't. Standard homeowners' policies only cover theft and specific disasters. A home warranty service plan, on the other hand, covers repairs or replacement of your property's mechanical systems and all appliances including the heating system, water heater, plumbing, wiring, central air conditioning, and more. It doesn't matter whether your home is one year old or a hundred; it only matters that the covered items were in good working order at the start of the home warranty contract. Home Protection Plans are available through many realtors. According to Bob Vila, formerly on *This Old House,* "Home warranties make great sense when the house and its appliances and systems start to wear, perhaps after 10 years."

MECHANICS' LIENS

Every contractor, subcontractor, or material supplier who has been involved in your construction project is entitled to a mechanic's lien on your property. This means that they may go to court and try to take possession of your property if they are not paid. To avoid this problem, you may pay any subcontractor directly or withhold from your contractor whatever amount is necessary to pay subcontractors until the contractor has provided you with lien waivers signed by the subcontractors. (A lien waiver is a written statement signed by a subcontractor acknowledging receipt of payment and giving up his right to file a lien against your property.) According to the Minnesota Attorney General's **"The Citizen's Guide to Home Building and Remodeling"** (www.ag.state.mn.us/consumer/housing/citguide/default.asp), if you obtain valid lien waivers from the subcontractors, or if you pay the general contractor in full before receiving notice from a subcontractor that he intends to file a lien against your property, you cannot be forced to pay for the services or material a second time, even if the contractor fails to pay the subcontractor. For further information, contact the **Minnesota Attorney General's Office, Consumer Protection** (Hotline 651-296-3353, 800-657-3787, TTY 651-297-7206, TTY 1- 800-366-4812, www.ag.state.mn.us).

BEFORE YOU CAN START YOUR NEW LIFE IN THE TWIN CITIES, YOU AND your worldly goods have to get here. How difficult that will be depends on how much stuff you've accumulated, how much money you're willing or able to spend on the move, and where you're coming from.

But first, a word of caution: watch out for shakedown schemes that begin with a lowball bid off the Internet and end with the mover holding your belongings hostage for a high cash ransom. Despite the fact that federal law says that movers cannot charge more than 10% over any written estimate, it is not unusual for unscrupulous movers to charge you several times their written estimates—and with your possessions in their possession, you may find yourself paying anyway, since companies that operate this way also won't tell you where they're holding your stuff. It's fraud. It's extortion. And sometimes there isn't a lot the police can do to help you. So help yourself first. Check out the **MovingScam** web site (www.movingscam.com) for more information. MovingScam.com is dedicated to providing solid, impartial consumer education and to working for better consumer protections in the moving industry. Its featured articles include "How to Find A Reputable Moving Company," "How to File Moving Complaints," and "Planning an International Move." It also maintains a "superlist" of moving company reviews and a "Blacklist." Its message boards are staffed with experienced volunteers who answer moving-related questions promptly and at no cost to the consumer.

A similar web site, run by the **Federal Motor Carrier Safety Administration (FMCSA)**, is www.protectyourmove.gov. This web site provides one-click checking to make sure that an interstate mover is properly registered and insured, or call 202-366-9805 for licensing and 202-385-2423 for insurance. It also posts news of recent criminal investigations and convictions, and offers links to local Better Business Bureaus, consumer protection agencies, state attorneys general, state moving associations, and the **FMCSA Safety Violation**

and Consumer Household Goods Complaint Hotline (888-DOT-SAFT [888-368-7238], https://nccdb.fmcsa.dot.gov/HomePage.asp). Don't expect much from this hotline, however. It is essentially just a database and you will only hear from the DOT if it looks at your complaint and determines that enforcement action is warranted.

TRUCK RENTALS

The first question you need to answer: Am I going to move myself, or will I have someone else do it for me? If you're used to doing things for yourself, by all means, rent a vehicle and head for the open road. It may well be the best way to get your belongings where you're going. As one web page says, "U-Haul has never held any family's belongings hostage." So look in the Yellow Pages under "Truck Rental," then call around and compare. Below, we list four national truck rental firms and their toll-free numbers and web sites, but for the best information you should call a local office. Note that most truck rental companies now offer "one-way" rentals (don't forget to ask whether they have a drop-off/return location in or near your destination) as well as packing accessories and storage facilities. Of course, these extras are not free and, if you're cost-conscious, you may want to scavenge boxes from liquor stores or purchase them from discounters and arrange for storage yourself. (See **Moving Supplies** and **Storage** sections below.)

Finally, if you're planning on moving during the peak moving months (May through September), call well in advance of when you think you'll need the vehicle—a month at least. And consider timing your move for the middle, rather than the end, of the month, because the prices might be slightly cheaper.

Speaking of price: cheapest is not always best, and some companies in this industry do have a history of unresolved complaints with the **Better Business Bureau**, so be sure to contact your local BBB and request a report (www.bbb.org, or in Minnesota call 651-699-1111, www.minnesota.bbb.org). The following are national truck rental companies with offices in the Twin Cities:

- **Budget**, 1-800-462-8343, www.budgettruck.com
- **Penske**, 1-888-996-5415, www.penske.com
- **Ryder**, 1-800-BY-RYDER, www.ryder.com
- **U-Haul**, 800-468-4285, www.uhaul.com

Not sure that you want to drive the truck yourself? Commercial freight carriers such as **ABF Upack Moving** (1-800-355-1696, www.upack.com) and **PODS** (1-877-770-PODS, www.pods.com) offer an in-between service: they deliver a trailer or container to your home, you pack and load as much of it as you need, and they drive the vehicle or deliver your container to your destination.

MOVERS

Surveys show that most people find movers through the **Yellow Pages**. If that's too random for you, probably the best way to find a mover is through a personal recommendation. If someone recommends a mover to you, though, get names (the salesperson or estimator, the drivers, and the loaders). To paraphrase the NRA, moving companies don't move people, people do. Absent a friend or relative who can point you to a trusted moving company, you can try the Internet; just be careful. For long distance or interstate moves, the **American Moving and Storage Association**'s site (www.moving.org) is useful for identifying member movers both in Minnesota and across the country. Members of **AAA** have a valuable resource at hand in **Consumer Relocation Services**, which will assign the member a personal consultant to handle every detail of the move, free of charge, and which offers discounts of up to 62% on interstate moves as well as replacement valuation coverage of up to $75,000 at no charge. Call 800-839-MOVE or check online at www.consumers relocation.com/aaa-benefits.htm.

But beware! Since 1995, when the federal government eliminated the Interstate Commerce Commission, the interstate moving industry has degenerated into a largely unregulated industry with thousands of unhappy, ripped-off customers annually. In fact, the Council of Better Business Bureaus reports that complaints against moving and storage companies rank near the top of all complaints received by Bureaus every year. And there's more bad news—since states do not have the authority to regulate interstate moving companies, and since the federal government basically won't, you're really pretty much on your own in your dealings with an interstate mover.

Therefore Better Business Bureaus and Attorneys General around the country urge you to take precautions before hiring a mover by doing the following things:

- **Make sure the mover is licensed and insured.** For *intrastate* moves, call the Department of Transportation Office of Freight and Commercial Vehicle Operations (651-215-6300, http://www.dot.state.mn.us/cvo/) to see if a mover is licensed. If yours is an *interstate* move, make sure the carrier has a Department of Transportation MC ("Motor Carrier") or ICC MC number; it should be displayed on all advertising and promotional material as well as on the truck. With the MC number in hand, contact the Department of Transportation's Federal Motor Carrier Safety Administration (800-832-5660 or 202-366-9805 for licensing or 202-385-2423 for insurance), or check online at www.fmcsa.dot.gov or www.protectyourmove.gov, to see if the carrier is licensed.
- If the companies you're interested in appear to be federally licensed, the next step is to **contact the Better Business Bureau** (www.bbb.org) and find out if the Bureau has a record of any complaints against them.
- **Get several written estimates** from companies that have actually sent a sales representative to your home to do a visual inspection of the goods

to be moved. Don't worry about cost here; estimates should always be free. And don't do business with a company that charges for an estimate or wants to give you an estimate over the telephone. Do, however, make sure each company is giving you an estimate for approximately the same poundage of items to be moved, and the same services. Finally, only accept estimates that are written on a document that contains the company's name, address, phone number, and signature of the salesperson. Note that estimates can be either binding or non-binding. A binding estimate guarantees the total cost of the move based upon the quantities and services shown on the estimate. A non-binding estimate is what your mover believes the cost will be, based upon the estimated weight of the shipment and the extra services requested. With a non-binding estimate the final charges will be based upon the actual weight of your shipment and services provided. If you accept a mover's non-binding estimate, you must be prepared to pay 10% more than the estimated charges at delivery (110 Percent Rule).

- **Follow-up with your State Department of Transportation** to find out if the estimate the mover gave you is based on the hourly rate they have filed with the Department of Transportation. Some movers may *quote* below this rate and then, at your destination, attempt to *charge* the higher rate they filed with the state. Also follow up with your mover to find out how the unloading will be handled at the destination end, and ask for references—then check them.

- Be sure you **understand the terms of the moving contract**. Get everything in writing, including the mover's liability to you for breakage or loss. Consider whether to buy additional replacement insurance to cover loss or damage. Check your homeowner's or renter's insurance policy to see what, if any, coverage you may already have for your belongings while they are in transit. If the answer is none, ask your insurer if you can add coverage for your move. You can purchase coverage through your mover. A mover's coverage, however, is normally based on the weight of the items being insured, not on their value. So if you want to cover the actual value of your belongings, you will need to purchase "full value" or "full replacement" insurance. Though it's expensive, it's worth it—and you can lower the cost by increasing your deductible. Better yet, consider packing and moving irreplaceable, fragile or sentimental items, documents, and jewelry yourself. That way you can avoid the headache and heartache of possible loss or breakage of your most valuable possessions.

- **Compile an inventory of all items shipped** and their condition when they left your house, take pictures, and be present for both the loading and unloading of your things. Since checking every item as it comes off the truck is probably impossible when you're moving the contents of an entire house, write "subject to further inspection for concealed loss or damage" on the moving contract to allow for damage you may discover as you unpack.

- **File a written claim** with the mover immediately if any loss or damage occurs—and keep a copy of your claim, as well as all the other paperwork related to your move. If your claim is not resolved within a reasonable time, file complaints with the Better Business Bureau and appropriate authorities, as well. (See **Consumer Complaints—Movers**, below.) To learn more about your rights and responsibilities with respect to interstate moving, check out the United States Department of Transportation (USDOT) publication "Your Rights and Responsibilities When You Move," which is downloadable off the www.protectyourmove.gov web site.

Some general advice, if you've followed the steps above and succeeded in hiring a reputable mover:

Listen to what the movers say; they are professionals and can give you expert advice about packing and preparing. Also, be ready for the truck on *both* ends—don't make them wait. Understand, too, that things can happen on the road that are beyond a carrier's control (weather, accidents, etc.) and your belongings may not get to you at the time, or on the day, promised.

- Treat your movers well, especially the ones loading your stuff on and off the truck. Offer to buy them lunch, and tip them if they do a good job.
- Be prepared to pay the full moving bill upon delivery. Cash or a cashier's check may be required. Some carriers will take VISA and MasterCard but it is a good idea to get it in writing that you will be permitted to pay with a credit card since the delivering driver may not be aware of this and may demand cash.
- Finally, before moving pets, attach tags to their collars with your new address and phone number in case your pets accidentally wander off in the confusion of moving. For more help in this area, you might want to look into *The Pet-Moving Handbook* (First Books, www.firstbooks.com).

INTRASTATE MOVES

When hiring a local mover, follow all the steps above for dealing with interstate movers: check that they are licensed and insured, check with the Better Business Bureau, check estimates, check contracts, and check references. It's a whole lot easier when the company is local! Here are a few Twin Cities–based movers:

- **Fisher Transfer**, 181 James Ave N, Minneapolis (651-774-2250, 612-377-5112, www.fishertransfer.com), is a family-owned company that has been in business in the Twin Cities since 1939. They specialize in moving pianos, but provide full service as well.
- **Good Stuff Moving & Delivery**, St. Paul, 651-488-1902, 866-908-4808, www.goodstuffmoving.com
- **Local Motion** (612-929-6683, 763-476-6683, 651-776-6683, 952-474-6683, www.localmotion.com) is one of the area's largest moving and storage com-

panies. They have portable storage containers that they will bring to you and load.

- **Rose's Daughters** (612-330-3772 or 651-373-1323, www.rosesdaughters. com) provides concierge-type moving services. They'll do everything from planning your local move to cleaning your former home. Their service area includes the seven-county metro area, some out-of-state communities, western Wisconsin, and metropolitan Phoenix, Arizona.

- **Two Men and a Truck**, www.twomen.com, advertises that they will also pick up and deliver appliances and large pieces of furniture. A national franchise, there are several offices in the metro area, including Edina (952-942-4949) and Woodbury (651-645-1279). Click on the Store Locator map on their web site to find an office near you.

MOVING SUPPLIES

Movers' boxes, while not cheap, are usually sturdy and the right size. Sometimes a mover will give a customer free used boxes—it doesn't hurt to ask. But if you need to buy them yourself, UPS stores sell boxes, shipping tape, bubble cushioning, foam peanuts, markers, and labels, as do the office mega-stores.

CONSUMER COMPLAINTS—MOVERS

To file a complaint concerning an **intrastate** Minnesota move, contact the Minnesota Department of Transportation, Office of Freight and Commercial Vehicle Operations (395 John Ireland Boulevard, St. Paul, 651-215-6330, www.dot.state. mn.us/cvo/applications/complaint_tenneson.pdf). If yours was an **interstate** move, your options are limited in terms of government help. The Federal Motor Carrier Safety Administration (www.fmcsa.dot.gov) recommends that you contact the Better Business Bureau in the state where the moving company is licensed as well as that state's consumer protection office to register a complaint. You can also file a complaint with FMCSA in one of two ways: use their complaint Web Site: www.1-888-dot-saft.com, or call their Hotline, toll free: 888-DOT-SAFT (888-368-7238), TTY 800-877-8339, from 10:00 a.m. to 6:00 p.m., Eastern time, Monday–Friday.

If you are uncertain of the appropriate agency to contact, please call 651-215-6330 for assistance.

If satisfaction still eludes you, start a letter-writing campaign. State Attorneys General are responsible for enforcing federal consumer protection laws regarding moving companies, so contact the Attorney General of the state you're moving from as well as the one of the state you're moving to. And because the law offers more protection to the mover than to you, send letters to your congressional representative and newspaper, too, and post your experience on the Internet—the sky's the limit. Of course, if the dispute is worth it, you can hire a lawyer and seek redress the all-American way.

STORAGE

Probably the easiest way to find storage close to your new home is to look online at your new city's web site or at www.move.com, where you can put in your ZIP code and be instantly linked to nearby local businesses, including storage facilities. You can also check the **Yellow Pages** in the phone book or online at www.dexonline.com. Check under "Storage" for complete listings. Given our wild weather swings, units with climate controls are often preferred. Keep in mind that demand for storage surges in the prime moving months (May through September), so try not to wait until the last minute to look for something to rent. Also, if you don't care about convenience, your cheapest storage options may be on the outskirts of the Twin Cities. You just have to figure out how to get your stuff there and back.

A word of warning: unless you no longer want your stored belongings, pay your storage bill and pay it on time. Storage companies may auction the contents of delinquent customers' lockers.

A few area storage companies for you to compare:

- **7th Street Storage**, 2060 W 7th St, St. Paul, 651-698-5777, www.7thstreetstorage.com
- **Acorn Mini Storage**, 612-767-3953, www.acornministorage.com, has storage facilities in North Minneapolis, Northeast Minneapolis, Blaine, Maplewood, Cottage Grove, Inver Grove Heights, Eagan, Chaska, and Shakopee.
- **Great Plains Mini Storage**, 952-657-1019, www.greatplainsministorage.com
- **Minikahda Mini-Storage**, www.minikahda.com, has locations near the University of Minnesota, in the Minneapolis Lakes area, north and western suburbs, and South St. Paul.
- **Minneapolis Self-Storage**, 425 Washington Ave N, Minneapolis, 612-330-9054, www.storageminneapolis.com, has other locations in the South Metro.
- **Public Storage**, 1-800-688-8057, www.publicstorage.com, has locations throughout the Twin Cities.

TAXES

If your move is work-related, and you're not being reimbursed for moving costs by your employer, some or all of your moving expenses may be tax-deductible—so you need to keep your receipts. Though eligibility varies depending, for example, on whether you have a job or are self-employed, generally the cost of moving yourself, your family, and your belongings is tax deductible, even if you don't itemize. The criteria: in order to take the deduction, your move must be employment-related, your new job must be at least 50 miles farther away from your former residence than your old job location, and you must be here for at least 39 weeks during the first 12 months after your arrival.

In general, this is what you can deduct:

- The cost of transportation and hauling from your old residence to your new one.
- The cost of storage-in-transit (limited to 30 consecutive days).
- The cost of shipping your car.
- The cost of moving your household pets.
- The cost of your family's trip to your new residence (this includes lodging, but not meals).

If you take the deduction and then fail to meet the requirements, you will have to pay the IRS back, unless you were laid off through no fault of your own or transferred again by your employer. Consulting a tax expert for guidance about the IRS's rules with respect to moving is probably a good idea. However, if you're a confident soul, get a copy of IRS Form 3903 (www.irs.gov) and do it yourself!

ROAD RESTRICTIONS

A special consideration when you're timing a move or building a house in Minnesota is road restrictions. From March 1 to May 1, when the roads are heaving and thawing, the state, counties, and cities all restrict the weight of the vehicles that may drive here. Many residential streets are closed to heavy trucks. This affects both construction equipment and moving vans. Local contractors are accustomed to working around the road restrictions, but if you're moving from out of state be sure to bring this to your mover's attention. For more information, refer your mover to the **Department of Transportation web site** or from a recording at **651-366-5400**, **1-800-723-6543**, www.mrr.dot.state.mn.us/research/seasonal_load_limits/sllindex.asp; and/or call your (new) city hall.

CHILDREN

Studies show that moving, especially frequent moving, can be hard on children, but there are things you can do to help your children through this stressful time:
- Talk about the move with your kids and, to the extent possible, involve them in the process.
- Make sure your children have their favorite possessions with them on the trip; don't pack "blankey" in the moving van.
- Make sure you have some social life planned on the other end. Your child may feel lonely in your new home and such activities can ease the transition.
- Maintain links to the important people you have left behind.
- If your children are of school age, take the time to involve yourself in their new schools and in their academic life. Don't let them fall through the cracks.

For younger children, there are dozens of good books on the topic. Just a few include *Boomer's Big Day* (ages 4 to 8) by Constance McGeorge; *Max's Moving Adventure: A Coloring Book for Kids on the Move* by Danelle Till, illustrated by Joe Spooner; *Alexander, Who's Not (Do You Hear Me? I Mean It!) Going to Move* by

Judith Viorst; *Goodbye/Hello* by Barbara Hazen; *The Leaving Morning* by Angela Johnson; *Little Monster's Moving Day* by Mercer Mayer; *Who Will Be My Friends?* (Easy I Can Read Series) by Syd Hoff; *I'm Not Moving, Mama* by Nancy White Carlstrom, illustrated by Thor Wickstrom; and *The Berenstain Bears' Moving Day* by Jan and Stan Berenstain.

For older children, try *The Moving Book: A Kid's Survival Guide* by Gabriel Davis; *Amber Brown is Not a Crayon* by Paula Danziger; *The Kid in the Red Jacket* by Barbara Park; *Hold Fast to Dreams* by Andrea Davis Pinkney; *Flip Flop Girl* by Katherine Paterson; and *My Fabulous New Life* by Sheila Greenwald.

For general guidance, read *Smooth Moves* by Ellen Carlisle; *Will This Place Ever Feel Like Home?, New and Updated Edition, Simple Advice for Settling in After You Move* by Leslie Levine; and Clyde and Shari Steiner's *How to Move Handbook*.

ONLINE RESOURCES—RELOCATION

- **American Car Transport**, www.american-car-transport.com.
- **Best Places**, www.bestplaces.net, compares quality-of-life and cost of living data of US cities.
- **The Riley Guide**, www.rileyguide.com; online moving and relocation clearinghouse includes Moving/Relocation Guides, Cost of Living and Demographics, Real Estate Links, and School and Health Care Directories.
- **www.firstbooks.com**; relocation resources and information on moving to Atlanta; Boston; Chicago; Los Angeles; New York; Portland, OR; San Francisco; Seattle; Washington, D.C.; and London, England. Also publisher of the *Newcomer's Handbook for Moving to and Living in the USA; The Moving Book: A Kids' Survival Guide; Max's Moving Adventure: A Coloring Book for Kids on the Move;* and the *Pet-Moving Handbook*.
- **www.moving.org**; members of the American Moving and Storage Association.
- **www.usps.com**, information on how to change your address.

OPENING A BANK ACCOUNT IS ONE OF THE FIRST THINGS YOU WILL need to take care of upon arriving. Many landlords and rental agents will not accept a tenant who does not have a checking account, so it's probably wise to keep your old bank account for at least a short time after moving.

BANK ACCOUNTS AND SERVICES

Both "big" national banks and "little" local banks offer Internet and telephone banking, mortgages, and ATM and debit cards that you can use anywhere in the world. "Little" locally based banks, however, often specialize in personal service. The first three institutions on this list are the "Big Banks" in this region, including homegrown Twin City Federal; the rest are community banks. Many other local banks/savings and loans can be found in the Yellow Pages.

- **Twin Cities Federal (TCF) Savings and Loan**, 612-823-2265, TTY 612-339-3075, www.tcfbank.com, has branches or ATMs in the Minneapolis skyway system, colleges and public buildings, and innumerable gas stations, markets, and grocery stores.
- **US Bank**, 612-US BANKS, 612-872-2657, 800-US BANKS, www.usbank.com, has branch offices and ATMs in a number of grocery stores, Walmarts, and Targets.
- **Wells Fargo**, 800-869-3557, www.wellsfargo.com, has numerous branches and ATMs throughout the metro.
- **Anchor Bank**, 952-808-8083, www.anchorlink.com, is a family-owned, privately held, Minnesota-based national bank holding company with 16 locations in the Twin Cities area. The web site has a clickable map to help you locate their nearest branch to you.
- **Associated Bank**, 1-800-236-8866, International Phone: 1-262-879-0133, www.ibankfnb.com, is one of the largest banks in Wisconsin and has a

growing presence in Minnesota with 10 local branches (input your ZIP code into the Locations search field on their web site).

- **Bremer Financial**, 800-908-BANK, www.bremer.com, is employee-owned and has over 100 locations in Minnesota, Wisconsin, and North Dakota.
- **Cherokee State Bank**, 651-227-7071, www.bankcherokee.com, has branches in St. Paul, North Oaks, and Savage.
- **KleinBank**, 877-553-4648, www.kleinbank.com, has 18 branches located in the North Metro and western suburbs and Madison, Wisconsin.
- **Premier Banks**, 651-777-7700, 800-772-6497, www.premierbanks.com, has 23 branches, and surcharge-free ATMs.
- **The River Bank**, www.theriverbank.com, has branches in Chisago City and Wyoming, Minnesota, and Osceola, St. Croix Falls, North Hudson, and Somerset, Wisconsin.
- **Lake Community Bank**, 1964 W Wayzata Blvd, Long Lake, 952-473-7347, 888-311-3880, www.sblonglake.com.
- **Sunrise Community Banks** are true community banks dedicated to providing custom banking services and investing in the local community. They are:
  ▹ **Franklin National Bank**, 612-874-6000, www.franklinbankmpls.com, has three branches in Minneapolis: 525 Washington Ave N; 2100 Blaisdell Ave S; and 1527 E Lake St.
  ▹ **Park Midway Bank**, 651-523-7800, www.parkmidwaybank.com, has two offices: 2300 Como Ave and 2171 University Ave in St. Paul.
  ▹ **University Bank**, 651-265-5600, www.universitybank.com, 200 University Ave W, St. Paul.
- **Western Bank**, 651-290-8160, www.western-bank.com; centered both physically and philosophically on University Ave in Frogtown in St. Paul, Western Bank has been involved in community development since 1935. It has offices in Edina, Maplewood, Mounds View, Oakdale, and St. Paul.

CHECKING AND SAVINGS ACCOUNTS

Although debit cards are quickly becoming the way to bank and transact business, you might be pleasantly surprised at how readily most Twin Cities merchants still accept personal checks. To open an account, most banks require a minimum deposit (depending on the type of account you want, some have minimums as low as $50), current photo identification, and your Social Security number.

ONLINE BANKING

Every bank offers online banking, making it easy to track your account activity, pay your bills, or even apply for a loan—all from the comfort of your own home. Services vary from bank to bank, and some charge a fee for automatic bill-paying features. See above, under **Bank Accounts and Services,** for area banks' web addresses.

CREDIT UNIONS

Your place of work or neighborhood may offer membership in a credit union—which could be your best banking deal of all. These nonprofit, cooperative financial institutions offer almost all the same products that banks do, usually with fewer fees and higher interest rates. Your employer will be able to tell you if you are eligible for membership in any credit unions through your work. To find other ways of becoming eligible for membership in a credit union, call the Minnesota Credit Union Network (800-477-1034, www.mncun.org) and a representative will help you find credit unions in your area that you are eligible to join. Or use the Credit Union Match Up service (www.findacreditunion.com). For links to all the local credit unions that have web addresses, visit Credit Unions Online (www.creditunionsonline.com). The National Credit Union Administration (www.ncua.gov), the independent federal agency that supervises and insures credit unions, also maintains a searchable database. Here are a few credit unions nearly any Twin Cities resident can join:

- **U.S. Federal Credit Union**, 1400 Riverwood Dr, Burnsville, 952-736-5000 or 800-345-2733, www.usfed.org. This is the oldest credit union in Minnesota. It has branches in the North and South Metro, Minneapolis, and east St. Paul. You are eligible for membership if you live, work, worship, volunteer, or attend school in Anoka, Carver, Dakota, Hennepin, Ramsey, Scott or Washington counties, or in the city of Northfield.
- **SPIRE Federal Credit Union**, 888-34 SPIRE, 651-215-3500, www.spire-banking.com, has nine locations in the Minneapolis/St. Paul metro, and a branch in Princeton, Minnesota. Membership is open to Minnesota and Wisconsin residents who meet certain criteria or who make a $5 tax-deductible contribution to the credit union's foundation.
- **City-County Federal Credit Union**, 6160 Summit Dr, Brooklyn Center, 763-549-6000, www.ccfcu.org, is open to anyone who lives, works, or worships in the seven-county Twin Cities area. It has several locations in Minneapolis, Brooklyn Center, and Minnetonka.
- **St. Paul Federal Credit Union**, 1330 Conway St, St. Paul, 651-772-8744 or 888-439-4239, www.stpaulfcu.org, is open to any person who lives, works, worships or attends school in the Cities of St. Paul or Minneapolis. It has branches in the Minneapolis and St. Paul skyways.

CONSUMER PROTECTION—BANKING

If you have a problem with your bank that you believe to be in violation of a federal law or regulation, first try to resolve the matter by bringing it to the attention of a senior bank officer. If the problem is still not taken care of to your satisfaction, you can file a complaint with the **Board of Governors of the Federal Reserve System, Division of Consumer and Community Affairs,** 888-851-1920, TTY 877-766-8533, www.federalreserveconsumerhelp.gov. Complaints can be filed online.

Complaints about financial institutions that are not supervised by the Federal Reserve System will be forwarded by the Fed to the appropriate agency.

CREDIT CARDS

Department store credit cards are good to use to establish a credit history if you have none. Applications can often be obtained at the checkout counter, and stores frequently offer immediate discounts when you apply for a card. **Macy's** and **Target**, with their metro-wide locations, are particularly good credit cards for this area—they are easy to qualify for, and they're cards you can use often enough to establish a good history. While it's only good at one store, the **Von Maur Department Store** (Eden Prairie Center, 1-800-458-0396, www.vonmaur. com) offers its customers an interest-free credit card with no fees and flexible payments. Search and apply for low-rate, no annual fee, etc., cards on the Internet at **CardWeb** (www.cardweb.com). CardWeb is also a place to look for information on the latest scams.

Call to request a credit card application or apply online:

- **VISA**, 1-800-847-2911, www.usa.visa.com, and MasterCard, 1-800-826-2181, www.mastercard.com, are available from banks.
- Now that local Northwest Airlines has merged with Delta, the **Delta Skymiles American Express** is the card to use to earn miles here, 1-800-223-2670 to apply by phone, 1-800-528-4800 customer service, www.americanexpress. com.
- **Capital One**, 1-800-955-7070 , www.capitalone.com
- **Discover Card**, 800-DISCOVER, (or apply at a Sears store), www.discover card. com

IDENTITY THEFT, CREDIT CARD FRAUD, AND CREDIT REPORTS

Following a steady stream of disclosures of security breaches affecting major banks, credit card companies, and businesses that collect and sell personal data, as well as the vulnerability of the State of Minnesota's own e-business, it seems nearly impossible to do anything to protect yourself from either credit card fraud or identity theft—and yet, if you're a victim, a fraud such as identity theft can nearly ruin your life. Victims spend an average of 600 hours trying to repair their credit; it's a daunting task. For more information, contact the **Identity Theft Resource Center** at 858-693-7935, Victim Assistance Center 888-400-5530, or www.idtheftcenter.org.

That said, there is some good news: by Minnesota law you are not liable for more than $50 improperly charged to your credit card. Industry standards are even tougher and, in practice, consumers are not held responsible for any unauthorized charges on their credit cards. The trick is to check your monthly statements carefully and notify your credit card company immediately when the charges are incorrect. So what else can you do to protect yourself? Security experts recommend several things. Among them—don't carry your Social Security card in your wallet and memorize your PIN numbers and keep printed copies in a secure place. Finally, check your credit rating periodically. You are entitled to one free credit report per year from each of the three major credit reporting companies, so if you request a report every four months from a different credit reporting company, you'll be able to keep tabs on your credit rating—for free. You can also visit **www.annualcreditreport.com** for online access to all three. For more information about your rights concerning your credit report, check out the Federal Trade Commission's web site at www.ftc.gov. The National Credit Bureaus are:

- **Equifax**, PO Box 105851, Atlanta, GA 30348-5851, 800-685-1111, www.equifax.com
- **TransUnion**, PO Box 1000, Chester, PA 19022, 800-916-8800, www.transunion.com
- **Experian**, PO Box 2104, Allen, TX 75013-9595, 1-888-397-3742, www.experian.com

TAXES

Minnesota's 2010 individual income tax rates were 5.35%, 7.05%, and 7.85% depending on whether you're single, married and filing jointly or separately, or head of your household.

Is Minnesota really a high-tax state? It depends on how much you make, how much you spend, and where you live. In fact, income taxes are down. However—since we still have to plow the roads—fees (such as hunting licenses), consumption taxes (sales and excise taxes), and property taxes are up, with much of the burden for paying the costs of government shifted onto homeowners.

According to the 2009 Minnesota Tax Incidence Study, the most recent report available, there is a state and local tax burden on Minnesota households that (in 2006, the most recent year for which figures are available) ranged from 23.8% for the state's poorest residents to 10% for the state's richest, for an average of 11.2%. In 2011, the figures are projected to be much the same with an average tax burden of 11.4% per household. For more information about state income taxes, look online at the Minnesota Department of Revenue Individual Income Tax page, www.taxes.state.mn.us/taxes/individ/index.shtml, or call 651-296-3781, 1-800-652-9094, 711 for Minnesota Relay. For questions regarding other tax types, look online at www.taxes.state.mn.us/taxes/index.shtml.

HISTORY OF TAXATION IN MINNESOTA

Nine years before Minnesota became a state in 1858, the territorial assembly established a property tax levy to support the schools. Property taxes remained the primary source of revenue until the hardships of the Great Depression made property taxes hard to collect. Then the need for dependable government funding, combined with the call for tax relief by property owners, led the legislature to establish the state's individual and corporate income tax systems in 1933. Since that time, Minnesota has relied somewhat more on the income tax, and somewhat less on sales and property taxes, than most other states. That weighting toward the income tax, however, left Minnesota open to the charge of being a high tax state. It also opened the door for the election, in 2002, of a governor and legislature who immediately signed a "No New Taxes" pledge and began shifting the burden of paying for essential services away from the state and income taxes and onto local governments (school districts, cities, and counties) whose only sources of funding are sales and local property taxes.

That's why your property taxes will most likely be higher than your home's previous owner's.

So what can you do about taxes?

Be proactive. Check with your city hall and find out how much of a tax increase you might reasonably expect before you buy. Be sure that you make yourself eligible for all possible tax deductions. If you're moving within Minnesota, be sure that your new main job location is at least 50 miles farther from your former home than your old job was, so that you will be eligible to deduct moving expenses from your federal return. For additional information, refer to the Form 3903 Instructions (PDF) and Publication 521, Moving Expenses, both posted on the **IRS** web site (www.irs.gov), or call 800-829-1040. See **Moving and Storage** for more information.

INCOME TAXES

As a resident here, you will have to pay both federal and state income taxes.

For federal forms, tax help, and information call **1-800-829-1040, 1-800-829-4059 (TDD)**, or look online at www.irs.ustreas.gov. For matters you wish to handle face to face, **Internal Revenue Service Taxpayer Assurance Centers** are located at 1550 American Blvd East - Suite 700, Bloomington, 651-312-8082; 250 Marquette Ave, Minneapolis, 651-312-8082; and 30 East 7th Street, St. Paul, 651-312-8082. Make an appointment in person at the Taxpayer Assurance Center you wish to use. For the **Taxpayer Advocate Service,** call 651-312-7999 in Minneapolis/St. Paul or 1-877-777-4778 elsewhere.

The state income tax is based on federal adjusted income minus exemptions, deductions, and credits. In 2010, the state had three rates that increased with income: 5.35%, 7.05%, and 7.85%. To obtain Minnesota state income tax forms or ask questions call the **Minnesota Department of Revenue** (651-296-3781, 1-800-652-9094, 711 for Minnesota Relay). Forms are available at libraries and post offices during tax season or online at www.taxes.state.mn.us, where you can also file your return online.

Taxpayers who prepare their own taxes may be eligible for free online tax preparation and free electronic filing through a partnership agreement between the Internal Revenue Service and the Free File Alliance, LLC, a private-sector consortium of tax software companies. For a listing of the Alliance members check out the **Free File** web page, www.irs.gov/efile/article/0,,id=118986,00.html.

SALES TAX

The state sales tax (on most goods except food, clothing, and prescription drugs) is 6.875%, with an additional amount collected within certain cities including Minneapolis and St. Paul. Some counties also impose sales taxes. Hennepin, Ramsey, Anoka, Dakota, and Washington counties all collect money for transit development, and Hennepin County levied an additional amount to finance the Minnesota Twins' Target Field. Alcohol is taxed at a rate of 2½% over the regular sales tax, and cigarettes are taxed about $1.50 a pack.

PROPERTY TAXES

First-half Minnesota property taxes are due May 15th. Owners whose taxes are not included in their mortgage payments can pay in person or by mail or credit card. In Anoka, Dakota, Hennepin, Ramsey, and Washington counties, property owners can go online to pay their bills. Second-half taxes are due October 15th. For more information, call your county's assessor:

- **Anoka**: 763-323-5400, www.co.anoka.mn.us/v1_departments/div-property-rec-tax/index.asp
- **Carver**: 952-361-1960, www.co.carver.mn.us/departments/prts/propassess.asp
- **Dakota**: 651-438-4200 or 800-247-1056, www.co.dakota.mn.us/HomeProperty/AssessingProperty/General/default.htm
- **Hennepin**: 612-348-3046, http://hennepin.us
- **Isanti**: 763-689-2752, www.co.isanti.mn.us/depart.htm#assess
- **Ramsey**: 651-266-2000, www.co.ramsey.mn.us/prr/Assessor/index.htm
- **Scott**: 952-445-7750, www.co.scott.mn.us
- **Sherburne**: 763-241-2880 or 800-438-0577, www.co.sherburne.mn.us/assessor/index.php
- **Washington**: 651-430-6175, http://washington.minnesotaassessors.com
- **Wright**: 763-682-7367, www.co.wright.mn.us/department/assessor/

Property taxes (real estate taxes) are different for each city and county and include levies to support school districts, watershed districts, mosquito control, and other services. Several factors determine how much tax is paid, including the market value and type (class) of property, and the amounts levied by each of the taxing authorities. Taxes change each year, but the previous year's taxes for property you are considering buying will always be stated on the property's listing sheet. Minnesota property taxes have increased rapidly in recent years, caused NOT by local governments spending more, but by state policies that have shifted many public costs onto property taxpayers, especially homeowners. Property tax "reform" in 2001 also changed the rates at which different kinds of properties were assessed, protecting some business properties while at the same time removing limits on the rate of tax growth for homes. Now with the decline in property values caused by the housing collapse, cities, counties, and school districts are really feeling the squeeze. And because property owners can't bear any more tax increases, essential services are being cut. Roads are not getting plowed, schools are closing, hospitals are laying off staff. Some cities have even closed their police departments. To find out about property taxes (and changes to services) in the community you are considering, call the city hall or, since school district levies account for the bulk of property taxes, call your local school district (see **Childcare and Education** chapter). For more general information, look online at www.taxes.state.mn.us/taxes/property/index.shtml.

There is also a state general property tax on commercial, industrial and public utility property, and on seasonal residential recreational property, including cabins. Included in your local property tax statement, the state property tax is paid to the county treasurer along with local property taxes, but the money raised from the state general tax does not go to local governments (i.e., counties, cities, school districts, etc.). Instead, it is deposited in the state general fund.

STATE PROPERTY TAX REFUNDS

Minnesota has two partial property tax refund programs for homeowners: the regular refund for those who own and reside in their homes on January 2 (Homestead Credit), and special property tax refund based on your household income and the property taxes paid on our principal place of residence. To apply for either or both of these refunds, use Form M1PR, Minnesota Property Tax Refund. For a fee, you can file your M1PR electronically online at the **Minnesota Department of Revenue**'s web site (www.taxes.state.mn.us). Otherwise, forms and instructions are available at many libraries, or you may download them from the Internet, www.taxes.state.mn.us/taxes/prop_refund/forms.shtml. Minnesota also offers tenants a renter's property tax refund to renters whose income is less than $53,029. Your landlord is required to send you the Certification of Rent Paid (CRP) form no later than January 31. You then have nearly seven months (until August 15th) to fill out your half—the M1PR form—and send both to the state for a refund of the portion of your rent that went to property taxes. Keep an eye on this program, however, because the "No New Taxes" forces keep eyeing cutting this program as a way of raising state revenue without "raising" taxes."

WISCONSIN TAXES

Wisconsin collects income, property, and sales (excise) taxes. Tax information is posted on the **Department of Revenue (DOR)**'s web site (www.dor.state. wi.us). You may also email questions from the web page or call the DOR's headquarters in Madison (608-266-2772). Electronic filing is free.

MONEY ORDERS

Western Union services are available at a number of Twin Cities locations including Rainbow Foods, pharmacies, the Minneapolis Greyhound station, Twin City Federal, and other banks. There are several Western Union/TCF sites in the Minneapolis skyway system. For other **Western Union** locations, use their online worldwide agent locator (www.westernunion.com).

STARTING A BUSINESS IN MINNESOTA

The **Department of Employment and Economic Development (DEED)** publishes an online guide to Starting a Business in Minnesota" that is available free of charge. DEED also offers a wide range of technical assistance tailored to the needs of small and medium-sized businesses in the areas of startup, expansion, or relocation. So does the federal **Small Business Administration** (www.sba. gov) and its corps of business volunteers at **SCORE** (8800 Highway 7, Minneapolis, 952-938-4570; 176 North Snelling Avenue, St. Paul, 651-632-8937; www. scoremn.org). SCORE is an organization of active and retired business people with a wide range of expertise, who volunteer to provide free business counseling—they're well worth a call.

NOW THAT YOU'VE LANDED A PLACE TO LIVE AND OPENED A checking account, you're probably wondering: what will it take to get life back to normal? This chapter covers most of the services you will need: electricity, gas, telephone, water, and garbage and recycling, as well as those essentials of modern life—cable or satellite and Internet. There is also automobile-related information including how to obtain a Minnesota driver's license and register your car, and specifics about getting a library card, voting, and subscribing to the local papers.

UTILITIES

To report gas and electric service problems, call:
- **Electric Outages**: 1-800-895-1999
- **Gas Odor or Gas Leak Emergency**: 800-895-2999

To have utility lines marked before you dig call:
- **Gopher State One Call**: 651-454-0002, 1-800-252-1166; Emergency Only 866-640-3637, or 811

Minnesota's utility industry is comprised of 126 municipal electric utilities, 31 municipal gas utilities, a number of small cooperatives, five large investor-owned gas/electric companies, one garbage/electric company, and practically countless telecommunications providers. Sound complicated? It is and it isn't. In fact, most electricity and gas are provided by **Xcel Energy, Minnesota Valley Electric Coop,** or **Reliant/CenterPoint Energy,** even in Wisconsin; and most communications services are provided by **Qwest or Comcast**. Furthermore, one of the real joys of our computer age is that now you can sign up for all your utilities with just a couple of clicks. You can do this in two ways. Sign up to connect or transfer all your utilities online at a single web site such as **White Fence** (www.whitefence.com) or **Qwest Movers Services** (www.qwest.com/residential/movers/indexA.html). Just put in your address and the web site will automatically locate the providers that serve your area. Then you can compare their packages and prices side-by-side, and order the services that work best for you. Easier still, go to your **new city's home page**, choose **New Resident Information**, and then set up your utilities through the clickable links the city provides.

Note: Before you dig in your new yard call **Gopher State One Call** (651-454-0002, 1-800-252-1166, Emergencys Only 866-640-3637, or 811, www.gopherstateonecall.org). Within a few days they will come out and locate and mark all your buried cables and gas lines. There is no charge for this service. Emergency locate requests are processed 24 hours a day, 7 days a week including weekends and holidays.

COMMUNICATIONS

More often than not these days, communications service comes bundled with phones, high-speed Internet, and cable or satellite TV. So it's convenient, when you're shopping, to buy the whole package. Nearly every company listed below offers bundled packages, no matter how they're categorized.

Qwest is the dominant player in this market. It provides hardwire local and long distance phone service, high-speed Internet, wireless, VoIP, and digital television (DirectTV) throughout most of the Twin Cities area. You can order new residential service and other utilities online at www.qwest.com/homeservice, or call 1-800-244-1111. Most contracts include free installation. If you do not have a previous credit history with Qwest, a service deposit will be required. (Consumer tip: save yourself some money; the phone company's charges for work inside your residence are steep, but dealing with inside wiring yourself is easy, so even if you have to buy a few tools and some materials, you're going to come out way ahead if you do the work yourself. Directions are only a Google search away.)

The other big player here is **Comcast Cable**, 1-800-COMCAST, www.comcast.com.

For easy one-stop shopping for all your digital options, try **DigitalLanding**, 1-800-972-1744, http://direct.digitallanding.com. Just put in your address and all your choices will pop up, including special deals.

Other Twin Cities providers include:

- **Century Link**, 1-800-788-3500, www.centurylink.com
- **Frontier Communications**, 800-921-8101, www.frontieronline.com
- **MediaCom**, 1-888-847-6228, http://mediacomcable.com
- **Verizon**, 1-800-483-4224 (landline phones), www22.verizon.com

CELL PHONES

While the Twin Cities generally have excellent cell phone coverage, there are some black holes where there is no signal for certain carriers, particularly in the western and southwestern suburbs. So to be sure you're not stuck at home with a cell phone that won't work there, you should try to arrange to return the phone if it doesn't work where you need to use it, or try your friends' phones to see how many bars you get from different carriers. Do not depend on the coverage maps.

The following are the metro area's principal cellular providers:

- **AT&T**, 1-800-331-0500 or 611 from your wireless phone, www.att.com, has stores throughout the Twin Cities, including Costco.
- **Sprint**, 866-866-7509, www.sprint.com/local, has numerous stores throughout the Twin Cities. Check its web page or the White Pages for the store nearest you.
- **T-Mobile**, 800-TMOBILE, www.t-mobile.com, sells through dealers at all the major malls, Target, Costco, WalMart, Best Buy, and Radio Shack, and company stores throughout the metro.
- **Verizon**, 800-256-4646, www.verizonwireless.com, is located at all the major malls, Costco, Radio Shack, and numerous other locations throughout the Twin Cities.

AREA CODES

The Twin Cities metropolitan area uses a 10-digit calling system and has four local area codes:

- **612** is assigned to Minneapolis, Richfield, Fort Snelling, and St. Anthony.
- **651** belongs to St. Paul and the East Metro, including Washington County, Eagan, and Dakota County.
- **763** serves suburbs to the north and northwest of Minneapolis and I-394, including Anoka, Sherburne, and Wright counties, and the cities of Becker, Blaine, Brooklyn Center, Buffalo, Cambridge, Circle Pines, Coon Rapids, Delano, Elk River, Fridley, Golden Valley, Isanti, Lexington, Medina, Monticello, Mounds View, Plymouth, Princeton, St Francis, and Waverly.
- **952** includes Apple Valley, Bloomington, Burnsville, Chanhassen, Eden Prairie, Edina, Hopkins, the Lake Minnetonka area, St. Louis Park, Waconia, and other communities south of I-394.
- Outside the metro, northern Minnesota uses area code **218**; western Minnesota is **320**; southern Minnesota is **507**; and Pierce, Polk, and St. Croix counties in Wisconsin, which are considered collar counties of the Twin Cities metro region, use **715**.

WIRELESS

Tiny Chaska was one of the first cities in the world to offer citywide Wi-Fi wireless Internet service to its residents, with big Minneapolis (http://usiwireless.com) following close behind. A few other cities have citywide Wi-Fi in place. But most of the cities that announced projects have either cancelled them or are experiencing technical difficulties. Minnetonka's system ended up costing more and delivering far less than expected; and St. Louis Park, which attempted to have the first solar-powered Wi-Fi in the metro, pulled the plug on that project and is now looking at WiMax. Unlike Wi-Fi, WiMax, which combines Wi-Fi and cell phone technology, is designed for outside use and is expected to provide a stronger signal that will penetrate tree leaves and buildings. Meanwhile, Chaska is unsure whether it will continue investing public funds in its lightly used system. Already in use at some businesses and colleges in the cities, WiMax is also available in the Western Metro exurbs along the I-94 corridor. For Wi-Fi information, check with your city hall. WiMax is available through Implex.net.

A new 4G WiMax wireless option is also on the horizon with Clearwire (www.clearwire.com). *So far* Brooklyn Park, Mahtomedi, Stillwater and White Bear Lake in Minnesota, and Pierce County, Wisconsin, have either approved or are considering giving Clearwire conditional use permits.

For a map of free wireless Internet hotspots around the Twin Cities, look online at www.squidoo.com/wireless_Internet_twin_cities. One thing to remember, **free Wi-Fi hotspots** normally offer open, unsecured connections, so be careful not to access bank accounts or anything very personal, as you could be putting yourself at risk.

VoIP

Most of the companies listed in the "Communications" section above also offer **Voice over Internet Protocol (VoIP),** which allows those who have high-speed Internet to use computers to make calls for free or a flat monthly fee. The biggest players in this market are **Skype** (www.skype.com) and **Vonage**, (1-VONAGE-HELP, www.vonage.com). With Vonage, you can even keep your current phone number and transfer it to a Vonage account. (Consumer tip: don't cancel your old service until your new service is in place; if you let go of your number, you may not get it back!)

VoIP isn't without its problems, however. Chief among them is the fact that VoIP cannot be used to dial 911. For this reason alone, having a conventional landline or cell phone for emergencies is advisable.

PREPAID CELLULAR SERVICES AND LONG DISTANCE CARDS

With only slightly higher rates and no year-long contracts or monthly service charges, prepaid cellular is easily worth the small amount of inconvenience of having to continually replenish minutes. Available at numerous stores in the Twin Cities, phones come with a card representing a certain financial value ranging from $15 to $100. Activate the card and, when the money runs out, replenish it with another payment. This is called "topping up." **T-Mobile Prepaid Mobile To Go** starter kits are available locally at T-Mobile outlets, Target, Radio Shack, Walmart, Best Buy, and Sam's Clubs, or online at www.t-mobile.com. **Verizon's** prepaid phones (www.verizonwireless.com) are available in numerous locations throughout the metro including the downtown skyways, Target, Walgreens, Office Depot, Office Max, Family Dollar Stores, Holiday Stores, many grocery stores, and some colleges. Also online, **Amazon.com** offers pay-as-you-go phones as well as "top-up" cards. Locally, "top-up minutes" can be purchased from many retailers or at U.S. Bank ATMs. Prepaid long distance cards are sold at retailers throughout the area, including those mentioned above, and at gas stations, pharmacies, and grocery stores, as well.

CONSUMER PROTECTION—DO NOT CALL LISTS

Minnesota's Do Not Call law will not stop all your telemarketing calls, but it will stop a lot. Unfortunately for the sanctity of your dinner hour, certain organizations such as nonprofits, telephone surveyors, and political parties are exempt from the law. To put some limits on your phone traffic, however, be sure to sign up for both state and national Do Not Call lists online at www.donotcall.gov or call toll-free, 1-888-382-1222 (TTY 1-866-290-4236), from the number you wish to register. Registration is free. If your number has been on the registry for at least three months, and a telemarketer calls, complain to the FTC online (www.donotcall.gov) or at the numbers above. You'll need to provide the date of the call and the phone number or name of the company that called you, so don't just yell at the caller and hang up. You may also file a complaint if you receive a call that uses a recorded message instead of a live person whether or not your number is in the Registry.

CONSUMER PROTECTION—CRAMMING

"Cramming" used to be what you did before an exam, but the word, when applied to your telephone bill, has a much more sinister meaning now: it's the practice of third parties placing unauthorized charges on your phone bill. So always check your statements thoroughly, and if you do find a problem, remember this: Under the Truth in Billing Act, you cannot lose your phone service for failure to pay a disputed "miscellaneous" charge. That said, be sure to call your carrier's customer service the minute you spot an unauthorized charge in order to ensure your rights. (See **Consumer Protection—Utility Complaints** on page 241.)

DIRECTORY ASSISTANCE

Dial **411** for directory assistance. There is usually a charge for directory assistance, but you can find numbers for free through the Internet via these web sites:

- www.anywho.com
- www.switchboard.com
- www.dexknows.com
- www.twincities.citysearch.com

INTERNET SERVICE PROVIDERS

- **CenturyLink High-Speed DSL**, www.centurylink.com
- **Comcast Cable**, www.comcast.com
- **Hughes Net High-Speed Satellite Internet**, 1-800-428-9570, www.hughesnet.com
- **MediaCom Cable**, http://mediacomcable.com
- **PeoplePC Online Dial-up Service**, www.peoplepc.com
- **Qwest DSL** , www.qwest.com
- **US Internet**, http://usiwireless.com (Minneapolis)
- **Vector Internet Services DSL or Dial-up**, 612-395-9090, www.visi.com; is Minnesota's largest Internet services/hosting firm. Besides e-mail, it offers personal domain hosting and cloud computing.
- **Verizon DSL**, www22.verizon.com

CABLE

Twin Cities cable service is divided geographically.
- **Comcast**, 1-800-COMCAST (1-800-266-2278), www.comcast.net, covers most of the metro and western Wisconsin.
- **MediaCom**, 1-888-847-6228, www.mediacomcc.com, serves parts of the metro including the Lake Minnetonka area; put in your ZIP code to see if they serve your area.

SATELLITE SERVICE

Check out **DishMinnesota** (www.dishminnesota.com) for comprehensive information about this fast-changing business and the latest deals and equipment.
- **DISH Network**, 1-888-825-2557, www.dishnetwork.com
- **Direct TV**, 1-888-777-2454, www.directtv.com; sold locally at Best Buy and Walmart, and by Qwest.
- **Hughes Net High-Speed Satellite Internet**, 1-800-428-9570, www.hughesnet.com

ELECTRICITY AND NATURAL GAS

You can call the companies listed below to see if your new home is in their service area, or save yourself a lot of trouble and ask at your new city hall. Better yet, look online at your city's web page and use its clickable links.

Xcel Energy (1-800-895-4999, **www.xcelenergy.com**) is both an electric and gas utility. Because Xcel's business is regulated by the state, the products and services they are allowed to sell vary in different ZIP codes. To determine what service they provide in your area, go to their web site and type in your ZIP code.

In many areas, residents get their electricity from Xcel, but buy their natural gas from **Reliant/CenterPoint Energy**. You can arrange for both services with one telephone call to 612-372-4727 or 800-245-2377, or online at www.centerpointenergy.com. Service can be connected with only a few days' notice, but it is recommended that you put in your order two weeks in advance. The company's "Budget Plan" is a good way to manage winter payment peaks. The program balances out your payments so you pay more in summer than your actual bills and less in winter. You still only pay for the amount of gas you use.

Some cities operate their own municipal utilities, including South St. Paul, Circle Pines, Anoka, Elk River, Buffalo, Delano, Chaska, Shakopee, and North St. Paul. Of these, Anoka's is by far the largest, serving more than 11,000 customers. These smaller providers are particularly committed to providing energy from renewable sources such as water, wind, and landfill gas. The following are municipal or co-op utilities:

- **Anoka Municipal Utility (Electricity)**, 763-576-2750, www.ci.anoka.mn.us, serves the city of Anoka, and portions of the cities of Ramsey, Coon Rapids, and Champlin.
- **Connexus Energy**, 763-323-2600, 1-800-642-1672, www.connexusenergy. com, provides electricity to the northern Twin Cities in portions of Anoka, Chisago, Hennepin, Isanti, Ramsey, Sherburne, and Washington counties.
- **Dakota County Electric**, 651-463-6212, 1-800-874-3409, www.dakotaelectric. com, serves most of Dakota County including Eagan, Inver Grove Heights, Apple Valley, Lakeville, and Burnsville.
- **Elk River Municipal Utilities**, 763-441-2020, www.ci.elk-river.mn.us
- **Minnesota Valley Electric Cooperative**, 952,492-2313, 800-282-6832, www. mvec.net, serves the southwestern suburbs in Carver, Hennepin, Dakota, and Scott counties. Because it is a not-for-profit organization, MVEC sells electricity to its member-owners at cost.
- **Shakopee Public Utilities**, www.shakopeeutilities.com.
- **Wright-Hennepin Cooperative Electric Association**, 763-477-3000, 1-800-943-2667, www.whe.org, offers electric service in Wright and western Hennepin counties.

HEATING ASSISTANCE/COLD WEATHER RULE

In Minnesota there is a **Cold Weather Rule** that says residential customers who cannot pay their bills in full cannot have their heat cut off between October 15 and April 15—but there are certain procedures that must be followed for you to qualify, including contacting your utility and trying to work out a payment plan. For more information about emergency assistance at the time of disconnection (cold weather shut-off), call your local utility or, look online at www. staywarm.mn.gov.

CONSUMER PROTECTION—UTILITY COMPLAINTS

Try to resolve any billing or other disputes with your phone, gas, or electric company on your own. But if a problem persists, the people to call depend on what you're complaining about. If you have a complaint or inquiry about cellular or mobile phone service, contact the **Attorney General's Office** (651-296-3353, 800-657-3787, www.ag.state.mn.us). For issues related to investor-owned gas and electric utilities, **Dakota Electric Cooperative**, and local and in-state long distance telephone, call the **Minnesota Public Utilities Commission Consumer Affairs Office** (651-296-0406, 800-657-3782, www.puc.state.mn.us). You can also take telephone complaints to the FTC at ftc.gov, or by calling 1-877-FTC-HELP (1-877-382-4357).

SEWER AND WATER

If you are renting an apartment, sewer and water are probably included in your rent. If you are a homeowner or renting a house, call your local city hall to establish service. In Minneapolis, call the **Utility Billing Office** (311 or 612-673-1114, TTY 612-673-2663), or request service online at www.ci.minneapolis.mn.us; a budget plan is available. For water emergencies, call 612-673-5600. St. Paul residents should call 651-266-6350 for billing and general information. Water emergencies are handled at 651-266-6868. St. Paul also supplies water to residents of some its neighboring cities. If the house you are buying has a private well, be sure to have it inspected and tested for bacteria and hardness. A rotten egg smell may indicate that you have iron bacteria growing in your well and plumbing, a common problem, but one that can be hard to solve. In such circumstances, chances are good that the water is safe to drink but you will need a water softener and pre-filter.

Okay. That was the short version of water and sewer. It will work for you if you plan to live in the city or an established suburb. If you're moving to the suburban fringe, however, there's a lot more you need to know.

SEWER

Sewer service is no less complicated than Minnesota's other utilities, and at the same time, equally simple: if your city provides sewer service, sign up for it by calling your city hall. If it doesn't, then you will need to have your own system. Whether your property has—or doesn't have—sewer will be detailed on your Multiple Listing Service (MLS) listing sheet. If you're moving here from a region where everybody has sewer, though, you're probably wondering what's up.

Here's the explanation.

Sewer service is relatively new to Twin Cities suburbs. It started in the early 1970s when the cities surrounding Lake Minnetonka agreed to put in sewer in order to clean up the lake. Since then, the regional sanitary sewer system known as **MUSA (Metropolitan Urban Service Area)** has been expanded twice. Today most of the metro, from Maple Grove to Mahtomedi and Blaine to Lakeville, lies within the MUSA line. But there are still many places that do not, including Inver Grove Heights, Afton, most of Carver and Scott counties, and parts of Hennepin County west of Lake Minnetonka.

So what does that mean to you, a new person in town? If you're looking at houses in a densely developed area, probably nothing, because close-packed development here has had to follow the extension of the MUSA line. But if you're looking at homes or property on the developing edge, get ready to pay an assessment when sewer is extended to your property. Call your city hall and find out what they are projecting for the cost—it will be thousands. (But don't get too excited, the cost will simply be added to your property taxes and paid off over a number of years.) If you will need to have a septic system, don't worry. Taking care of it isn't difficult as long as you follow a few basic guidelines such as keeping trees at least 100 feet away from it, and not overloading it. If you have a big party, rent portable toilets for guests to use. And be careful what you flush. Never flush tampons, cat litter, or large quantities of toilet tissue. Compost kitchen waste, and never pour grease down the drain. For more information, order the **"Septic System Owner's Guide"** from the University of Minnesota (http://shop.extension.umn.edu/PublicationDetail.aspx?ID=941).

WATER

Every spring, when the thawing snow melts into the Mississippi, Minneapolis's tap water smells fishy for a couple of weeks. Never fear, though, the water is safe to drink and it still meets or exceeds all the regulatory requirements on water quality.

Of the 187 municipalities in the Twin Cities seven-county metropolitan area, 123 have municipal water supply systems. St. Paul and Minneapolis both supply their residents with treated water from surface sources such as the Mississippi

River and the St. Paul chain of lakes. Most of the other cities use water supplied from the groundwater system via municipal wells. Some municipalities, such as Shorewood, provide water to some residents, but not to all. Others, including some as close-in as Lake Minnetonka in the west and White Bear Lake in the east, require that people get water from their own private wells. To find out about your water situation, look on your MLS listing sheet and/or contact your city hall.

According to the Metropolitan Council—the agency charged with keeping track of these kinds of things—the average charge for water in the region is $1.92 for 1000 gallons, or 83 cups for 1 penny. The cost of water from a private well, however, depends upon a number of factors, including its depth and whether the water from it will need to be filtered and softened before you can use it (and it probably will). To find out how deep the wells are in your vicinity, put in your address on the Department of Health's online County Well Index (www.health.state.mn.us/divs/eh/cwi). To find a licensed well contractor, check the directory at www.health.state.mn.us/divs/eh/wells.

Keep in mind, though, that even here in the Land of 10,000 Lakes, water is still a threatened resource.

At the time of the writing of this book, finding water isn't difficult. However, it is suspected that the increase in roads and roofs (impervious surfaces) from the building boom we are experiencing may be depleting groundwater supplies. Rain and snowmelt now rush off the paved landscape and into the storm sewers rather than slowly seeping down through the soil and recharging our underground aquifers. That's one reason cities are encouraging rain gardens and limiting the percentage of a property that can be covered by hardscape. Another is the presence in the groundwater of contaminants from run-off that are potential threats to human health. Nitrates from nitrogen fertilizer and herbicides and pesticides have recently been found in residential wells, especially in the eastern metro (not to single them out, since so far that is about the only part of the metro that is testing for them). But don't make the mistake of thinking that those are the only places where's there's a problem. It is reasonable to assume, since we all drink from the same underground aquifers, that the same substances are present in all our well water—and in surface sources, too.

If your city has a municipal system, you can get information about the water's quality from the city's public works department or from the city's annual report. If you have a private well, you'll have to take care of water-testing yourself. The Health Department suggests that well water be tested once a year for bacteria and every other year for nitrates. Wells should also be tested at least once for arsenic. The Health Department maintains a list of certified testing labs at www.health.state.mn.us/divs/eh/wells/#labs. The list includes:

- **Engel Water Testing**, Minnetrista, 952-955-1800, www.engelwater testing. com
- **Flint Hills Resources**, Rosemount, 651-437-0652

- **St. Paul–Ramsey County Department of Public Health**, St. Paul, 651-266-1321
- **Twin City Water Clinic**, Hopkins, 952-935-3556
- **Water Laboratories, Inc.**, Elk River, 763-441-7509

Most private well water needs to be filtered and softened. The principal local water softener companies include:

- **Commers**, www.commers.com
- **Culligan Water Conditioning**, www.culligan.com
- **Eco Water System**, www.ecowater.com
- **Haferman Water Conditioning, Inc.**, 952-894-4040, www.hafermanwater. com

Many of the companies above also supply drinking water, but for home delivery of bottled water, see **Drinking Water** in **Shopping for the Home**.

STORMWATER UTILITY FEE

This fee is discussed early in the Minneapolis section of the **Neighborhoods** chapter (p. 16).

FROZEN PIPES

Even temperatures in the teens can freeze unprotected pipes, but there are steps you can take to keep it from happening to you. Disconnect and drain all outdoor hoses before cold weather hits. Inside, try to keep your pipes warm. On a really cold night, open cabinets under your kitchen and bathroom sinks to get warm air to exposed pipes. If you have just one problem pipe, turn the cold water on there so that it just trickles, and leave it running continuously during extremely cold weather. Wrap water pipes near outside walls with insulation tape. If you leave home for a winter vacation, don't turn the heat off. But if your precautions fail and a pipe does freeze, acting quickly but carefully is key. Place a space heater near the pipe to warm the surrounding air and/or use a blow dryer to warm it at the point of the freeze. Don't use a blowtorch! If water starts leaking from the frozen pipe, it means the pipe has burst, so turn off the water to it and turn it off fast. Once you have the water turned off, you can solder or replace the broken pipe yourself, or call for a plumber. If you don't know a plumber already, companies like **Roto-Rooter** (800-ROTO-911, www.rotorooter.com) usually offer 24-hour plumbing and drain service. After the pipe is repaired, make sure it's properly insulated before next winter.

GARBAGE AND RECYCLING

If you're in an apartment, you can probably skip this section, but if you're renting or buying a house, you'll need to arrange for garbage pick-up, and possibly recycling.

Some cities contract to haul garbage for you. If, however, you have to do it yourself, be sure to check your city's web page for a list of their approved haulers. That said, **Waste Management** (952-890-1100, www.wmtwincities. com) covers nearly the entire metropolitan area, for both hauling and recycling; and **Ace Solid Waste** (763-427-3110, 800-964-4281, www.acesolidwaste. com) covers the North/Northwest Metro including Anoka, Sherburne, and Wright counties, and parts of Chisago, Hennepin, and Washington counties. **Allied Waste**, 651-455-8634, www.alliedwastetwincities.com, covers the North, Southwest, and East Metro.

In **Minneapolis**, the city hauls residential garbage and recyclable materials and provides trash containers for each house. Haulers will also take yard waste as well as up to two extra items (such as discarded furniture) per week. The city also provides vouchers for you to use to dispose of large loads of household debris at the city dump. Minneapolis charges a base fee for garbage of $24 per dwelling plus a rental fee for the disposal cart, tax, and an environmental services fee. Part of this is offset by a monthly recycling credit. For more information look on the city's web page (www.ci.minneapolis.mn.us/solid-waste/ billing.asp), or call 311.

In **St. Paul,** recycling pick-up is provided, but each household must hire a garbage service. (If you are renting, the landlord may already have made arrangements.) Rates vary from company to company and depend on the volume of the trash container you choose. City officials believe this system cuts down on waste, and it does get you to root out recyclables in order to reduce your load. Disposal of large objects must be arranged separately with your hauler. For more information look online at www.stpaul.gov/index.aspx?NID=1947.

For specific information about what can be recycled and when to put it out, call your city hall. **Eureka Recycling**, St. Paul's official recycler, also has an online guide (www.eurekarecycling.org/reu_guide.cfm) that tells you how and where to recycle or safely dispose of anything. Wondering what happens to the materials you recycle? Recycling is a $3 billion business in Minnesota, and Anchor Glass in Shakopee is one of the big dogs in the industry. Each year it recycles 46,000 tons of glass into bottles for Budweiser, La Choy soy sauce, A1 steak sauce, Snapple, and lots of microbrews.

APPLIANCE AND ELECTRONICS RECYCLING

If old computers and appliances are still usable, consider giving them away via **The Twin Cities Free Market web site** (www.twincitiesfreemarket.org). Created by nonprofit **Eureka Recycling** (Saint Paul Recycling Hotline, 651-222-SORT, Ramsey County Solid Waste and Recycling Hotline 651-633-EASY, www. eureka recycling.org), which keeps track of all exchanges, the Internet-based Free Market exchange has kept over 11.4 million pounds of still-useful items out of the landfills to date.

If electronics and appliances are not usable, either ask the retailer you're buying your replacements from to haul the old equipment away, or drop them off at a county recycling center.

- **Hennepin County** has two: 8100 Jefferson Highway, Brooklyn Park, or 1400 West 96th Street, Bloomington. There is no charge for most electronics. Before going, call 612-348-3777 for directions, fees, and to verify that they will accept the item you wish to dispose of, or check online at www.hennepin.us.
- The **Carver County Environmental Center** (116 Peavey Circle, Chaska, 952-361-1835 or 952-361-1800, www.co.carver.mn.us/departments/LWS/env-svc/EnviroCenter.asp) charges $10 for a refrigerator, and recycles many items for free.

Beyond county resources, you might check out:

- **Asset Recovery Corp** in St. Paul (651-602-0789, www.assetrecoverycorp.com) provides "End-of-Life solutions" for computer and electronic equipment.
- **Waste Management Recycling** (www.wm.com) also accepts consumer electronics.
- **Apple** and **Dell** recycle computers.
- **Sony** offers free recycling of Sony-brand consumer electronics at Waste Management eCycle drop-off centers. Find locations online at www.wm.com/WM/takeback/sony/index.asp or call 1-877-439-2795.
- **Sprint, Verizon, Nokia, Best Buy, Batteries Plus, Target,** and **Radio Shack** all recycle cell phones.
- You might also consider the **Call to Protect**'s Donate A Phone campaign, which collects wireless phones to benefit victims of domestic violence. Look online for Minnesota drop-off sites, www.wirelessfoundation.org/CallToProtect/index.cfm.
- For a complete list of household recyclers and recycling events, go to www.pca.state.mn.us/oea/plugin/recyclers-household.cfm#recyclers.
- **Rethink Recycling** (www.rethinkrecycling.com) is another guide for waste and recycling here—just input what you want to dispose of, and the web page will give you clickable links to collection sites in your county.

RECYCLING CLEAN-UP, PAINT-UP, FIX-UP PRODUCTS

Whenever possible, leftover latex paint should be allowed to dry out and may then be disposed of along with the regular trash. Unopened full gallons or larger containers of paint are a welcome—and tax-deductible—donation to the **Reuse Center** (2801 21st Avenue South, Minneapolis, 612-724-2608; 1727 East Hwy 36, Maplewood, 651-379-1280; www.thereusecenter.com).

Oil-based paint, paint thinner, paint remover, primers, stains and varnishes, wood preservatives, furniture stripper, glue with solvents, adhesives, roofing tar, driveway sealers, and concrete cleaners should be disposed of at a Hazardous Waste Disposal site such as the **Carver County Environmental Center** (see above), or the **Dakota County Recycling Zone**, located off Highway 149 between Yankee Doodle Road and Highway 55 in Eagan (www.co.dakota.mn.us/EnvironmentRoads/RecyclingZone/default.htm, 651-905-4520). Consider donating unopened containers to the Reuse Center.

Construction debris can be disposed of at the **Dem-Con landfill**, south of Shakopee (952-445-5755, www.dem-con.com). They will also accept mattresses, box springs, and furniture.

Still usable building materials and tools may be donated, for a tax deduction, to the following organizations: the Reuse Center (see above); or the **Habitat for Humanity ReStore retail outlet** (510 County Road D West, New Brighton, 612-588-3820, www.tchabitat.org). **Furnish Office and Home,** sponsored for Project for Pride in Living (850 15th Avenue NE, Minneapolis, 612-789-3322, www.furnishofficeandhome.org), is always looking for new and used office equipment, artwork, home furnishings, and computers in good condition to sell in its nonprofit store.

COMPOSTING SITES

Take your grass, leaves, and small brush to the following locations, and go there to buy your mulch, compost, soil, and other landscaping materials, too.

- **Ramsey County**: Midway Yard Waste Site, north side of Pierce-Butler Route at Pryor; Summit Hill, Pleasant Ave just south of St. Claire; Eastside St. Paul, corner of Frank and Sims; Battle Creek/Highwood, Winthrop just south of London Lane
- **Hennepin County**: SKB Environmental, 630 Malcolm Ave, Minneapolis, 952-946-6999, www.mulchstoremn.com; Maple Grove Yard Waste, west of County Rd 121 on 101st Ave N, 763-420-4886
- **Washington County**: Composting Concepts, 4600 Cottage Grove Dr, Woodbury, 651-436-1213 www.ci.woodbury.mn.us/environ/compost.html

AUTOMOBILES, DRIVER'S LICENSES, AND STATE IDs

DRIVER'S LICENSES AND STATE IDs

You have 60 days from the date you move to Minnesota to obtain a Minnesota driver's license. The minimum age to receive a driver's license is 16. If you have a valid out-of-state license, only a written test and eye exam are required. Take your current driver's license and another form of ID such as a passport or birth certificate with you to the licensing station (a county service center). If you changed your name when you got married, take your marriage certificate as well. If your current license is no longer valid, or you are not a licensed driver yet, you will be required to pass a behind-the-wheel driving test.

Information regarding vehicle and driver licenses and state ID cards may be obtained from the **Minnesota Driver and Vehicle Services** (445 Minnesota Street, Suite 168, St. Paul, MN 55101, 651-296-6911, TTY 651-282-6555, www. dps.state.mn.us/dvs). The Minnesota Driver's License Manual is posted online at www.dps.state.mn.us/dvs/DLTraining/DLManual/DLManual.htm. Examining stations are located throughout the metro area; call to schedule a driving test.

- **Anoka County**, www.co.anoka.mn.us; State Exam Station, 530 W Main St, Anoka, 763-422-3401; North Metro Exam Station, Highway 35W & County Rd I, Arden Hills, 651-639-4057
- **Carver County**, www.co.carver.mn.us; Chaska Exam Station, 418 Pine St, Chaska, 952-448-3740
- **Dakota County**, www.co.dakota.mn.us; South Metro Driver's Exam Station, 2070 Cliff Road, Eagan, 651-688-1870; 217 Ramsey St, Hastings, 651-437-4884
- **Hennepin County**, www.co.hennepin.mn.us; 2455 Fernbrook Ln, Plymouth, 952-476-3042
- **Ramsey County**, www.co.ramsey.mn.us, 445 Minnesota St, St. Paul, 651-639-4057
- **Scott County**, www.co.scott.mn.us, Customer Service Center, Government Services Building, located at 200 W Fourth Ave, Shakopee, 952-496-8150
- **Sherburne County**, www.co.sherburne.mn.us, Department of Motor Vehicles, 600 Railroad Dr, Elk River, 763-422-3401 to schedule a road test appointment
- **Washington County**, www.co.washington.mn.us, Stillwater License Center, Valley Ridge, 1520 W Frontage Rd, Stillwater, 651-284-1000
- **Wright County**, www.co.wright.mn.us, 15 1st Ave S, Buffalo, 763-682-3963

WISCONSIN DRIVER'S LICENSES

Driver's License and Vehicle Registration information is available online at www.dot.wisconsin.gov/drivers/drivers/apply/nonreside, as are addresses for Division of Motor Vehicles Service Centers. The phone number for all service centers is 800-924-3570. The **Hudson Department of Motor Vehicles**, 2100 O'Neil Road (near Carmichael Road), offers driver's licenses and IDs only.

AUTOMOBILE REGISTRATION

You have 60 days from the time you move here to register your car with the state of Minnesota. After two months you can be hit with a fine, so it pays to get this done as quickly as possible. You can register your vehicle at one of your county's service/licensing centers or at an **Automobile Association of America (AAA)** office (952-927-2600, www.aaa.com) if you are a member. Take your car's certificate of title, proof of insurance, and your personal identification. Motor vehicle licenses must be renewed each year. The registration tax depends on the value of your car; it will be no less than $35 a year, and could be as much as several hundred dollars (ouch!). To determine your registration tax, contact the Minnesota Department of Public Safety's central office, 651-296-6911, www.dps.state.mn.us/dvs. Once you're registered, you should receive an annual renewal notice several weeks before your registration expires. You may renew license tabs online at the Department of Public Safety web site, www.mvrenewal.state.mn.us.

Wisconsin vehicle registration information is posted online at www.dot.wisconsin.gov/drivers/vehicles/veh-forms.html. Those living in Hudson can register their vehicles at the St. Croix County Government Center, 1101 Carmichael Road, Hudson; register in the Clerk's office, 715-386-4609.

AUTOMOBILE SAFETY

In Minnesota, approximately one-third of all traffic deaths involve alcohol. Consequently, the state has strengthened its intoxication laws and judges have toughened their sentencing. On August 1, 2005, Minnesota became the last state in the union to lower the legal limit for alcohol concentration in a driver's blood to 0.08%. We now have "zero tolerance" for underage drinking and driving, as well. A first conviction for DWI (Driving While Impaired) is punishable by a fine and possible jail time of a year, or both; a second offense can result in the forfeiture of your car. A fourth drunken-driving arrest in 10 years is a felony carrying mandatory prison time and a very stiff fine. For more information, visit the **Department of Public Safety**'s web site (www.dps.state.mn.us) and click on Office of Traffic Safety.

Another law to promote public safety is **mandatory seat belt use** by all drivers and passengers regardless of where they are sitting. Children under age 8 and shorter than 4 feet 9 inches must be fastened in a child safety seat or booster. Under this law, children cannot use a seat belt alone until they are age 8 or 4 feet 9 inches tall — whichever comes first. Child safety seats must meet federal safety standards. That means the car safety seat must bear a stamp of approval from the Federal Department of Transportation. For help finding the best seat for your child and car, check out www.carseatsmadesimple.org, a web site sponsored by **the Minnesota Safety Council, AAA Clubs of Minnesota,** and the **Minnesota Department of Public Safety, Office of Traffic Safety.**

CONSUMER PROTECTION—AUTOMOBILES

If you are looking for a new car, Minnesota has a lemon law that covers new vehicles that have been purchased or leased in the state. The law defines a "lemon" as a vehicle that continues to have a serious defect which substantially impairs its use, value, or safety, after a reasonable number of attempts to repair it. A car that you have been unable to use, due to warranty repairs, for 30 or more cumulative business days may also be covered by this law. In any case, if you report the defect within the warranty time period, the manufacturer must repair, refund, or replace the defective vehicle. If, after four or more attempts, the manufacturer is unable to repair the defect, you may go to court or go through a manufacturer's arbitration program to seek a full refund of the car's purchase price.

For those interested in purchasing a used car, Minnesota has a used car warranty law requiring used car dealers (not private sellers) to provide basic warranty coverage for cars that cost more than $3000. The terms of this warranty vary according to the age and mileage of the car. A car that does not meet the warranty guidelines will be marked "as is" on the window sticker, meaning that the seller has no obligation to fix any problems that arise.

For a guide to Minnesota's Lemon Law, Used Car Warranty Law, and Truth in Repairs Law, look online at the **Minnesota Attorney General**'s web site (www.ag.state.mn.us), or call 651-296-3353 or 800-657-3787, TTY 651-297-7206 and 800-366-4812.

AUTOMOBILE INSURANCE

Minnesota law requires owners of motor vehicles to maintain personal injury and liability protection, as well as underinsured coverage and uninsured coverage. Violation of the law can result in fines or imprisonment and revocation of driving privileges. Another law requires that proof of insurance be in the vehicle at all times and shown to a peace officer upon demand. Some of the major insurance companies in Minnesota include **AAA** (952-927-2600, www.aaa.com); **Allstate** (www.allstate.com); **American Family** (www.amfam.com); **Farmers Insurance Group** (www.farmers.com); and **State Farm** (www.state-farm.com). Check the Insurance listings in the Yellow Pages or look online to locate agents near you. The Minnesota Department of Commerce regulates the insurance industry. If you need to ask a question or make a complaint, contact them at www.state.mn.us/portal/mn/jsp/home.do?agency=Commerce, 651-296-2488 or 800-657-3602.

PARKING

Parking in Minneapolis is tight, and you might have to look for a while to find parking at the price you want to pay. The city operates 17 parking ramps and 7 lots conveniently located in the warehouse, entertainment, and business districts. I-394 (which comes into downtown Minneapolis from the western suburbs) goes directly into three parking ramps in the Warehouse District. Find a ramp and see rates on the **Minneapolis Public Works Department**'s web site www.ci.minneapolis.mn.us/parking. If you're determined to commute into downtown every day by car, consider purchasing a monthly ramp pass. The costs at this writing ranged from $80.00 at the Mill Quarter Municipal Ramp on the downtown fringe to $270 a month at centrally located 10th and Lasalle. A number of office buildings offer parking underneath, including the IDS building, Hennepin County Government Center, and Marquette Plaza.

Minneapolis also has 6800 parking meters. For those who find a parking space on the street, take the meter seriously. An expired meter will get you a ticket and may get your car towed. Confusion often arises because meters in different parts of town have different time restrictions and rates. Meters accept only quarters and U.S. dollar coins, or parking cards that work in meters the same as money. Cards are sold from parking card dispenser machines located in parking ramps and at City Hall. The Parking Card Dispenser Machine accepts $5 bills and higher. It does not accept $1 or $2 bills. When you buy a new card, be sure to insert the card back into the machine to add value. Download a map of parking meter locations at www.ci.minneapolis.mn.us/parking/meters.asp

The same parking cards work in St. Paul, where much of the parking is on-street and metered. For information about ramps in St. Paul, there is a clickable map posted at www.smart-trips.org/parkingmap.php. Click on any facility and see its monthly and hourly rates. Convenient ramps are attached to RiverCentre, the St. Paul Hotel, Science Museum, and the Minnesota History Center. Parking is harder to find around the state capitol. Meter debit cards can be purchased at the City Hall Annex, 25 West Fourth Street; from a vending machine located between the RiverCentre Ramp and the Xcel Energy Center; and at the Public Works office at 899 Dale Avenue North.

For information on parking at the University of Minnesota, including rates and maps, look online at www1.umn.edu/pts/parking/index.html or call 612-626-7275.

RESIDENTIAL PARKING PERMITS

In Minneapolis, St. Paul, and most of the surrounding suburbs, there are designated **Critical Parking Areas**. Residents in these areas are given, or can buy, stickers that permit them to ignore the parking restrictions on their streets. In Minneapolis, stickers cost $25 a year and can be obtained at City Hall. Download a map of Minneapolis' Critical Parking Areas at www.ci.minneapolis.mn.us/parking/critical/index.asp. Some cities, such as Deephaven, give one free parking permit to each household and charge for second and third permits. Apply for permits at your own city hall.

SNOW EMERGENCY PARKING

Those moving here from more southerly climes should pay particular attention to yet another peculiar aspect of life in the North: the "snow emergency." This is when Minneapolis, St. Paul, and many of the suburbs restrict on-street parking in order to accomplish necessary plowing. Snow emergency rules require that you move your car from one side of the street to the other in some municipalities, or stay off certain streets entirely in others. Residents are expected to pay attention to the weather and take steps to know when Snow Emergencies have been declared. There are several ways to do this, including checking the local media. *Every* station broadcasts the snow emergency news and runs it on their weather blogs and iPhone apps. You will not miss it! You can also sign up for email alerts with virtually every TV station and city, or follow the snow news for Minneapolis at http://twitter.com/minneapolissnow or on Facebook. Many other cities are looking at the social media as a way to get their news and alerts out.

In Minneapolis, residents may call the **24-hour Snow hotlines**: English, 612-348-Snow (7669); TTY 612-673-2116. Minneapolis residents may also subscribe to the city's own **Email Snow Alert** service (www.ci.minneapolis.mn.us/snow). The city also sends email alerts to mobile devices such as cell phones and PDAs, and also has an automated voice messaging alert service, the **Snow Emergency Phone Alert,** which calls all listed numbers in the city automatically. For those who have caller ID, the phone number displayed is 612-348-7669, which is the **Minneapolis Snow Emergency Hotline** number, and the "caller" will appear as "MPLS SNOW EMERG." The system will leave a recorded message on your answering machine if you're not home. Add or remove a listed phone number, or add an unlisted phone number (cell phone, direct work line, unlisted land line) to the system at www.ci.minneapolis.mn.us/snow/phone-alert.asp. The city cannot guarantee that you will receive a telephone call alerting you of a Snow Emergency, so it's important that people keep an ear to the news or call **612-348-SNOW** whenever snow falls and you think a Snow Emergency might be declared. Minneapolis helps to make parking less of a concern by opening some of its ramps for free or reduced-price overnight and first day of the emergency parking. The city uses the word "snOasis" to describe these garages, which have, in the past, included ramps in downtown and at the university. Check the city's web site (www.ci.minneapolis.mn.us/snow/SnOasis-home.asp) for the current year's ramp locations.

In St. Paul, watch for "Night Plow Route" signs. These are the sides of streets that will be plowed between 9 p.m. and 6 a.m. the first night after a snowfall. "Day Plow Routes" begin the next morning, but there are NO SIGNS on them. Day Plow Routes are mostly east-west residential streets **PLUS** one side of north-south residential streets—the side **WITHOUT** the plowing signs. There are some exceptions to these rules but they are all well marked. St. Paul snow emergency information can be obtained by calling **651-266-PLOW** or visiting the city's web site (www.stpaul.gov/depts/publicworks/ senews.html). Sign up for email notification of snow emergencies on the city's web site or follow them on Twitter.

Don't worry that you might somehow miss the relevant information—it's all over the airwaves. But do take it seriously. Parking restrictions are strictly enforced and cars are tagged and towed quickly and unceremoniously. One last piece of advice: don't go off on vacation and leave your car parked on a street—any street. Standing in a three-hour line at the impound lot is not a fun way to end a vacation. See **Surviving the Weather** for more winter-related tips.

TOWED VEHICLES

Hope you never need these numbers! The **Minneapolis Impound Lot** is at **51 North Colfax Avenue**. For directions and information call 612-673-5777, or go to www.ci.minneapolis.mn.us/impound-lot. Have your license plate number ready, or be able to provide your vehicle's VIN number. You will also need proof of insurance in your name; current registration, title, or lease agreement; and a picture ID. The impound lot is open 8 a.m. to 10 p.m., Monday–Saturday, and from 9 a.m. to 5 p.m. on Sundays. It's also open 24 hours a day on Days 1 and 2 of Snow Emergencies. The regular towing fee is $138. The heavy-duty towing fee is $175 plus Winch Time @$45 per half hour. Storage costs $18 per day, and is assessed at midnight. The impound lot will accept a check, cash, money orders, traveler's checks, cashier checks, or a credit card.

St. Paul has two impound lots: **830 Barge Channel Road** for cars towed south of I-94 (651-266-5642); and **1129 Cathlin Street,** a few blocks west of Snelling and across the street from the State Fairgrounds, for cars towed north of I-94 (651-603-6895). It will cost $186.00 in cash, checks, or VISA or MasterCard to get your vehicle out of the impound lot if you pick it up before midnight the day it is towed. A $15 storage fee is added to that amount for each additional day the vehicle is left there. And, of course, you must also pay for your parking ticket. If you have questions about a towed vehicle, call 651-603-6895. For maps to the impound lots and other information, go to www.stpaul.gov/index.aspx?NID=2094.

VOTER REGISTRATION

- -

Minnesota is one of the best states in the nation for voter turnout.

- -

Minnesota has a colorful political tradition that went neon in 1998, when we elected former professional wrestler and Brooklyn Park mayor Jesse "The Body" Ventura to be our governor. Perhaps you caught him in his purple boa singing "Werewolves of Minnesota" at his inaugural party? Unfortunately, he had a somewhat controversial tenure as governor and wound up in an adversarial relationship with both the state legislature and local news people. Nevertheless, if you're riding the Hiawatha LRT to work everyday, it's Jesse you should thank.

More recently, you have probably heard about our 2008 U.S. Senate election. Republican Norm Coleman was originally reported the winner by 206 votes. However, the tight margin triggered an automatic recount. Because Minnesota uses Opti-scan voting machines, which preserve the actual paper ballots which voters mark, we were able to do an accurate recount, at the end of which

Democrat Al Franken led by 225 votes. Then Coleman sued. A trial that went to the state Supreme Court and a further recount that included absentee ballots that had been improperly rejected on election night increased Franken's vote totals and, eight months after Election Day, he was finally declared the winner and now serves as one of our senators.

The interesting thing about all this is what we learned. First, we learned the value of having paper ballots to recount. Then we learned that there had not been any fraud in our election. We also learned that absentee voting can be an iffy thing because getting your vote counted depends upon tired poll workers trying to match signatures on ballot applications with signatures on actual absentee ballots—and doing it late at night at the end of Election Day. Finally, we learned that you shouldn't let your girlfriend fill out your ballot application or try to fill it out yourself using your computer mouse. (True stories from trial testimony!)

We also learned how to fix our absentee ballot problems, and that is being worked on now. In 2010 the legislature passed a law that provides for validating absentee ballots based on matching identification numbers instead of matching signatures. The new law also requires that absentee ballots be processed by county and city officials with special training in absentee-ballot processing, and that election officials must either send replacement ballots to voters whose ballots are rejected or notify the voters that they need to cast new ballots. Minnesotans will still have the option to replace their absentee ballots if they change their minds after voting; however, absentee voters will no longer be able to cast a ballot at their polling place to override their absentee ballot. So lucky you will not have to worry about whether your vote was counted, as long as you get it in to the proper authorities in a timely manner.

So let's get you registered.

To register to vote, you must be a United States citizen, 18 years old or older, and neither legally incompetent nor a convicted felon deprived of rights. You must have lived in Minnesota for at least 20 days immediately preceding Election Day. It is easiest to register when you apply for your driver's license. Otherwise, you can also register in person at your city hall, county or government center, or by mail using a **Minnesota Voter Registration Form.** Download it from the **Secretary of State**'s web site (www.sos.state.mn.us) or pick one up at any library or city hall. Mail it to the Secretary of State at the address shown on the form or take it to your city clerk. After the Secretary of State processes your registration, you will be sent a postcard confirming your eligibility and telling you where to vote. It will also tell you in which congressional, legislative, school, or other special districts you live. Keep this card and take it with you when you go to vote the first time. If you have your card, you'll be ahead of the game if you are challenged.

ELECTION DAY REGISTRATION

If you don't have time to register in advance, you can still register at your polling place on Election Day. First call your city hall and find out where you're supposed to vote, or look it up online at http://pollfinder.sos.state.mn.us, or on the **League of Women Voters** web site (www.lwvmn.org). Then go to your polling place, taking with you a Minnesota driver's license or other photo identification card that shows your new address in the precinct. You may also wish to ask a neighbor who can vouch for your residency to accompany you. If your Minnesota license shows a former address, you must take a recent utility bill with you to prove your current address. (The utility bill must have your name and current address, and be due within 30 days of the election. Utility bills may be for electric service, gas, water, solid waste, sewer, cell or landline telephone, Internet service, or satellite or cable TV.) College students may use a student fee statement, student picture ID card, registration card showing their address in the precinct, or a rent statement dated within 30 days of Election Day that itemizes utilities. If your first Election Day turns out to be a primary, don't worry, we do not register a party affiliation here, and primaries are open to all registered voters.

ABSENTEE VOTING

changed?

Minnesota law discourages absentee voting and allows it only if you're going to be out of your precinct on Election Day. Because absentee voting is considered a privilege, you have to jump through some hoops to do it—and you'd better do it right. Best chance to get your vote counted: get an absentee ballot application from your municipal clerk, then vote in the clerk's office. Hopefully, the clerk will tell you if you've done anything wrong. You may also request an absentee ballot be sent to you and mail your ballot back. Be sure to do so in plenty of time to arrive before the deadline. Otherwise, your ballot will not be counted.

Finally, if you're sick or injured, or for some reason unable to go into your polling place on Election Day, you have the right to ask the election judges to come out to you at your car. To find out what else you are entitled to, read this Voters' Bill of Rights.

MINNESOTA VOTER'S BILL OF RIGHTS

1.   For all persons residing in this state who meet federal voting eligibility requirements:
2.   You have the right to be absent from work for the purpose of voting during the morning of Election Day.
3.   If you are in line at your polling place any time between 7:00 a.m. and 8:00 p.m., you have the right to vote.

4. If you can provide the required proof of residence, you have the right to register to vote and to vote on Election Day.
5. If you are unable to sign your name, you have the right to orally confirm your identity with an election judge and to direct another person to sign your name for you.
6. You have the right to request special assistance when voting.
7. If you need assistance, you may be accompanied into the voting booth by a person of your choice, except by an agent of your employer or union or a candidate.
8. You have the right to bring your minor children into the polling place and into the voting booth with you.
9. If you have been convicted of a felony but your civil rights have been restored, you have the right to vote.
10. You have the right to vote without anyone in the polling place trying to influence your vote.
11. If you make a mistake or spoil your ballot before it is submitted, you have the right to receive a replacement ballot and vote.
12. You have the right to file a written complaint at your polling place if you are dissatisfied with the way an election is being run.
13. You have the right to take a sample ballot into the voting booth with you.
14. You have the right to take a copy of this Voter's Bill of Rights into the voting booth with you.

POLITICAL PARTIES

You won't be here long before you'll notice references in the news to the "DFL" and the "IR," which are the Democratic Farmer-Labor and Independent Republican parties. These aren't upstart third parties; they're the state's Democrats and Republicans. (Actually, the Republicans dropped the "Independent" from their name in 1995, but people still talk about the IRs, so you may as well know what they're talking about.) The DFL was formed in the 1940s, when Minnesota's Democrats, led by Hubert Humphrey, merged with the populist Farmer-Labor Party. At about the same time, Minnesota's Republicans added "Independent" to their name in the hope of attracting more independent voters. Truly independent parties here have included the Green Party, the Reform Party, and the Independence Party. In 1998, Jesse Ventura ran as a candidate for the Reform Party and, as he said, "shocked the world" when he unexpectedly beat the major party candidates. As a result of those elections in the 1990s, the Independence Party (then the Reform Party) fulfilled Minnesota's statutory requirements and became a major party. In the last few elections the Constitution and Green Parties have also won—and lost— major party status. As of the writing of this book, the third party movement in Minnesota seems to have collapsed for the time being, though the Green Party does have a few current office holders.

Some statistics: As of 2010, the Republicans have held the governorship for 17 of the last 21 years. At the time of the writing of this book, the governor is a Republican, but Democrats are in the majority in the Minnesota House of Representatives and Minnesota Senate. Both our U.S. Senators are Democrats, but our Congressional delegation is divided with five Democrats and three Republicans. For more information about Minnesota's principal political parties, contact them at the addresses below. For TDD service to contact the parties, call (metro) 651-297-5353, or (Greater Minnesota) 800-657-3529.

- **Democratic Farmer-Labor State Office**, 651-293-1200, www.dfl.org
- **Green Party**, 651-288-2820, www.mngreens.org
- **Independence Party**, 651-487-9700, www.independenceminnesota.org
- **Republican State Office**, 651-222-0022, www.mngop.com

For nonpartisan information about Minnesota's candidates and issues, visit the League of Women Voters web site (www.lwvmn.org). The League also has videos on YouTube explaining Voter Registration and Primary and General Elections.

CAUCUS SYSTEM

As de Tocqueville observed a couple hundred years ago, the principle that distinguishes the United States from all other societies is the belief that good government leadership, the kind that represents and serves people best, starts at the grassroots (local) level. In Minnesota we serve that principle through our caucus system.

A caucus is a meeting of local members of a political party to nominate candidates and plan policy. Held in every voting precinct in the state in even numbered years on Caucus Night (the first Tuesday in February), by all the major parties, caucuses give voters a voice in the political process at the absolute grassroots level. They are an opportunity for you and your neighbors to discuss issues that are important to you and to influence the selection of your party's candidates and political platform. At the caucus you can introduce resolutions and offer to serve as a delegate to the next level of your party's meetings—district, state, and national conventions. Everyone who is a qualified voter (or will be by the next election) may participate in one party's precinct caucus in any one year. (Older children are encouraged to attend, though not participate in the voting.) Each party determines its own specific procedures. For example, in the DFL party, there must be equal numbers of men and women on every committee, at every level. So how do you decide which party's caucus to attend? Well, which party's policies and candidates do you generally support? It's that easy.

Something to think about: In recent years some have put forward the idea that Minnesota should not hold caucuses, but just have primaries instead. That, however, is missing the point that caucuses are the one and only place that we Regular Janes and Joes can stand up and say, "I think our party ought to advocate for THIS policy," and actually see that opinion move up to become part of a party's official platform.

For detailed information about participating in caucuses, see the **League of Women Voters of Minnesota** web site (www.lwvmn.org), or watch the League's "Road to Election Day - Part 1, Precinct Caucuses and Party Conventions" on YouTube (www.youtube.com/watch?v=bbYcO-vAY6M).

POLITICAL CONTRIBUTION REFUND PROGRAM

Minnesota voters who contribute gifts of money to candidates for state office or to state political parties have in the past been eligible to apply for a refund of all or a portion of the contributions they have made during the calendar year, up to a limit of $50 an individual and $100 for a married couple. However, the current governor has "unallotted" funding for this program for the 2010–11 biennium. The legality of the governor's elimination of this program is before the courts at the time of the writing of this book. If the program is reinstated, this is how it works: The political committee you contributed to will automatically send you a refund form along with a receipt. All you have to do is fill it out and send it in. Each individual may apply for only one refund per year. The underlying goal of the program is to make it unnecessary for candidates to accept large contributions from individual donors or lobbying groups by providing candidates with enough small contributions to adequately finance their campaigns—and to give small donors a voice in our elections process.

LIBRARY CARDS

Hennepin County (includes Minneapolis), St. Paul, and surrounding counties all have separate library systems, but they are connected: once you get a card in one library system, you can use it to get a card in another one, search for a book and have it delivered from one system to the other, and even check out a book from one system and return it to the other. The library systems are online, so you can scan for titles, place requests, and check your borrowing records from home. To get a card, you'll need to visit a library in person with identification and, if you don't yet have a Minnesota driver's license, a piece of mail with your new address on it. Check the **Neighborhoods** chapter of this book for the library nearest you.

- **Anoka County Library System**, branches in Anoka, Circle Pines, Coon Rapids, Blaine, Fridley, Ham Lake, and St. Francis, www.anoka.lib.mn.us
- **Carver County Library System**, branches in Chaska, Chanhassen, Norwood-Young America, Waconia, and Watertown, www.carverlib.org
- **Dakota County Library System**, branches in Apple Valley, Burnsville, Eagan, Hastings, Inver Grove Heights, Lakeville, Rosemount, and West St. Paul, www.co.dakota.mn.us/LeisureRecreation/CountyLibraries/default.htm

- **Hennepin County Libraries**, 41 branches throughout Minneapolis and Hennepin County, with large libraries on Nicollet Mall in Minneapolis and near Ridgedale and Southdale malls, www.hclib.org
- **Ramsey County Library**, branches in Arden Hills, Maplewood, Mounds View, North St. Paul, Roseville, Shoreview, and White Bear Lake, www.ramsey.lib.mn.us
- **Scott County Library System**, branches in Belle Plaine, Elko–New Market, Jordan, New Prague, Prior Lake, Savage, and Shakopee, www.scott.lib.mn.us
- **St. Paul Public Library**, central library at 90 W 4th St, and 13 branches throughout the city, www.sppl.org
- **Washington County Library**, branches in Bayport, Cottage Grove, Forest Lake, Lake Elmo, Lakeland, Mahtomedi, Newport, Oakdale, Stillwater, and Woodbury, www.co.washington.mn.us/info_for_residents/library

PASSPORTS

Getting a passport can take weeks, so be sure to give yourself plenty of time. If your need is urgent, you can pay a fee and receive expedited service. If you need super-fast service, look on the Internet for a passport expediter. If you're applying for a passport for the first time, take with you two identical, full-face photographs of yourself, proof of U.S. citizenship (an original or certified birth certificate, an expired passport or a naturalization certificate), and a valid form of photo identification such as a driver's license. The **Minneapolis Passport Agency**, located in the United States Federal Office Building at 212 3rd Avenue South, serves customers who are traveling, or submitting their passports for foreign visas, within 14 days of their trips. To apply at the Agency, you must schedule an appointment by calling 1-877-487-2778. If you are not traveling, or needing to submit your passport for foreign visas within 14 days, you must apply at a **Passport Application Acceptance Facility**. To find the facility nearest you, do a ZIP code, state, or city search at the Passport Acceptance Facility Search Page (http://iafdb.travel.state.gov). There are many here, including city and county service centers and post offices.

Simple renewals can be handled by mail. Download application forms and get complete information from the **U.S. Department of State Bureau of Consular Affairs National Passport Office Information Service**, http://travel.state.gov/passport/passport_1738.html. Schedule an appointment or speak with a representative at 1-877-487-2778, TDD/TTY: 1-888-874-7793. General travel information and advisories are available at http://travel.state.gov/travel/travel_1744.html.

Minnesotans often travel to **Canada**—Voyageurs National Park is half in Minnesota and half in Canada, and Winnipeg is a popular long-weekend destination. When crossing the border, U.S. citizens must show a U.S. passport, U.S. passport card, or Nexus card (see below). A single parent traveling with children, or grandparents or other guardians traveling with children, should carry notarized proof of custody or an affidavit of consent from the non-accompanying parent(s) or legal guardian authorizing travel. (This is in addition to proof of the child's citizenship.)

Hunters may take ordinary rifles and shotguns into Canada, but fully automatic and assault-type weapons are prohibited. A complete list of prohibited firearms can be found at the **Canada Border Services Agency** web site (www.cbsa.gc.ca). In addition, anyone with a criminal record (including a Driving While Impaired charge) is considered inadmissible for at least five to ten years; contact the Canadian Embassy or nearest consulate for rehabilitation requirements. Both the U.S. and Canadian governments urge frequent travelers to join the Nexus program for low-risk, pre-approved travelers, www.cbsa.gc.ca/prog/nexus/menu-eng.html. Nexus members receive a special travel card that allows expedited border crossings in both directions. For complete information about traveling to Canada, check the **U.S. Consular Services** web page (www.amcits.com/travel.asp).

PRINT, ONLINE, AND BROADCAST MEDIA

TELEVISION

For old-fashioned broadcast (free) TV, the Twin Cities offer the national networks, plus a few independents. Of course, if you've ordered cable or satellite, the channels may differ from those given here. These are the major local affiliates:

- Channel 2 KTCA TPT, Twin Cities Public Television PBS, www.tpt.org
- Channel 4 WCCO-TV CBS, www.wcco.com
- Channel 5 KSTP-TV ABC, www.kstp.com
- Channel 9 KMSP-TV FOX, www.myfoxtwincities.com
- Channel 11 KARE11-TV NBC, www.kare11.com
- Channel 17 KTCI TPT, Twin Cities Public Television PBS, www.tpt.org
- Channel 23 KMWB CW Twin Cities CW, www.thecwtc.com
- Channel 29 WFTC-TV Fox, www.my29tv.com
- Channel 41 KPXM-TV ION, www.iontelevision.com
- Channel 45 KSTC TV Independent, http://kstc45.com

RADIO

Here's a brief guide to what's available on the radio airwaves in the Twin Cities. Be aware that radio programming can be subject to (rapid) change, so you may want to check web sites before settling on your favorites:

ADULT CONTEMPORARY
- KQRS 92 FM, www.92kqrs.com

- KSTP 94.5 FM KS95, plays Hot Adult Contemporary music, www.ks95.com.
- KTCZ 97.1 FM CITIES 97 puts out extremely popular music "sampler" CDs every year, www.cities97.com.

ALTERNATIVE ROCK

- KUOM, Radio K, Real College Radio from the University of Minnesota, 770 AM, 106.5 FM, 100.7, and online, is possibly the oldest station in the state, and plays an eclectic mix of music that includes many local artists, http://radiok. cce.umn.edu.
- KCMP 89.3 The Current, is a non-commercial, member-supported Minnesota Public Radio station that plays new, legendary, indie and alternative music and features lots of local artists, www.thecurrent.org.
- KVSC 88.1 FM, St. Cloud State University, plays college-format rock, www. kvsc.org
- KXXR 93.7 FM (93X) plays hard rock and sponsors the 93X Fest (formerly EdgeFest) every summer in Somerset, Wisconsin, www.93x.com.

CHILDREN'S PROGRAMMING

- KDIZ 1440 AM Radio Disney, http://radio.disney.go.com/music/yourstation/ minneapolis/index.html

CHRISTIAN/RELIGIOUS

- KTIS 900 AM, 98.5 FM, http://ktis.nwc.edu
- WLOL 1330 AM, www.relevantradio.com

CLASSICAL MUSIC

- KSJN 99.5 FM Minnesota Public Radio, http://minnesota.publicradio.org
- Country
- KEEY 102.1 FM—K-102, 2005 Country Music Association Station of the Year, www.k102.com

EASY LISTENING

- WLTE 102.9 FM, http://wlte.radio.com

ETHNIC

- KFAI 90.3 AM, 106.7 FM, "Fresh Air" is a volunteer-based community radio station that exists to broadcast information, arts and entertainment programming for an audience of diverse racial, social and economic backgrounds, www.kfai.org.
- KMOJ 89.9 FM, "The People's Station," broadcasts an adult urban format. The station provide broadcast communications training for People of Color living in the Twin Cities, and serve as an information and communications vehicle

for the African-American community as a whole. Its call letters were inspired by the Swahili word for Unity, Umoja, www.kmojfm.com.

- WREY 630 AM, Radio Rey is a Spanish-language station, www.radiorey630am.com.

JAZZ

- KBEM 88.5 FM also partners with the Minnesota Department of Transportation to provide traffic reports, http://jazz88.mpls.k12.mn.us.

NEWS, TALK, WEATHER

- WCCO 830 AM has been one of the area's top-rated stations since the 1920s, and is probably the area's most trusted station for weather reports and school closings, www.wccoradio.com.
- KSTP 1500 AM broadcasts nationally syndicated and local programs and sports, www.am1500.com.
- KTNF 950 AM is member-supported and broadcasts politically progressive talk shows, www.am950ktnf.com.
- KTLK 100.3 FM, carries Rush Limbaugh and Glenn Beck, www.ktlkfm.com

OLDIES

- KQQL 107.9 FM, KOOL 108, www.kool108.com
- WGVX LOVE 105 105.1, 105.3, 105.7 FM, www.love105.fm
- WDGY 740 AM, www.wdgyradio.com.

POP, TOP 40S

- KDWB 101.3 FM, www.kdwb.com
- KZJK 104.1 FM Jack, http://1041jackfm.radio.com

PUBLIC RADIO

- KNOW 91.1 FM, Minnesota Public Radio, broadcasts news including the BBC World Service, http://minnesota.publicradio.org

SPORTS/TALK

- KFAN 1130 AM, www.kfan.com

WEB RADIO AND VIDEO MUSIC AND NEWS

- Misplaced Music is a nonprofit devoted to broadcasting local music on the web, www.misplacedmusic.org.
- WCCO/The Wire allows users to watch and contribute to stories as they develop over time, http://wcco.com/thewire.
- TheUptake, www.theuptake.org is a news site run by some pros and a lot of citizen journalists. It provides live coverage of the legislature as well as other events of interest throughout the state—and sometimes Washington. Recent

coverage included a young biker's trip across Minnesota to bring attention to climate change, as well as live coverage of the Federal Communication Commission's debate on Net Neutrality. Volunteers are the backbone of the organization, and donors keep it going. Follow TheUptake on Twitter at http://twitter.com/theuptake.

NEWSPAPERS & MAGAZINES

Whether your interest is in politics, entertainment, restaurants, or parenting, there is a local (and probably free) newspaper or magazine for you. The *Star Tribune* (612-673-4343, 1-800-775-4344, www.startribune.com) and *St. Paul Pioneer Press* (651-222-1111, 1-800-950-9080, www.twincities.com) are the two major news dailies. For an edgier read, try *City Pages* (612-375-1015, www.citypages.com), a free alternative weekly available online and at businesses metro-wide. *City Pages* covers the local arts/entertainment and news scene, offering its own take on everything from politics to the personals. The *Minnesota Daily* (www.mndaily.com) is the student-produced newspaper of the University of Minnesota. The *Sun* suburban newspapers (www.mnsun.com), and a number of other neighborhood and special-interest, feature-driven weeklies, are always available next to grocery store entrances. Latest editions usually hit the newsstands on Wednesdays. *Southwest Journal* (www.swjournal.com) and *Downtown Journal* (www.downtownjournal.com), cover civic issues, arts and culture for neighborhoods in Southwest Minneapolis and the urban core. The *Utne Reader* and *Utne.com* (612-338-5040, 800-736-8863, www.utne.com) reprint articles from over 1500 media sources, touching on everything from the "environment to the economy, politics to pop culture."

MinnPost, www.minnpost.com, is only available online. It provides news and analysis Monday through Friday, based on reporting by professional journalists, most of whom have decades of experience in the Twin Cities media. Basically, everybody we liked to read in the print news who got fired seems to have moved over to MinnPost. The site features video and audio as well as written stories. Follow it on Twitter at http://twitter.com/MinnPost. You don't have to contribute to read it, but donations are tax deductible.

Two local glossies, *Mpls/StPaul Magazine* (www.mspmag.com) and *Minnesota Monthly* (www.minnesotamonthly.com), are great guides to life in the Twin Cities. They include reviews of area restaurants, trends, recreation, environmental issues, music, the arts, people profiles, shopping, getaways, and children's activities.

The Twin Cities offer a multitude of parenting magazines and newspapers. Probably the most popular is *Minnesota Parent* (www.mnparent.com), which describes itself as an "eclectic journal of family living" and contains essays as well as useful parenting information.

Two publications specializing in news for "minorities" are *Insight News* (612-588-1313, http://insightnews.com), a free newspaper serving Minnesota's growing African-American community, and *Minnesota Women's Press* (www.womenspress.com), also free, which has a mission to tell women's stories in ways that create community and encourage change. The Women's Press also hosts a number of events, including Friday night "Salons" with important women writers. Sign up for its newsletter and get clued in about what's going on here with respect to women's interests and issues. Both of these papers can be found at co-ops and coffee shops.

For those interested in the moves and shakes of local finance and commerce, *MinnesotaBusiness Magazine* (www.minnesotabusiness.com) will keep you informed about the whos and the whats, as will *Minneapolis/St. Paul Business Journal* (http://twincities.bizjournals.com/twincities). A subscription to *Politics in Minnesota* (www.politicsinminnesota.com) will keep you on top of Minnesota politics. And for local consumer information you can't beat *Twin Cities Consumer Checkbook*, a magazine that rates local service providers. Pick up an issue at your local bookstore, download articles, or subscribe (800-213-7283, www.checkbook.org). Finally, if you're looking for local LGBT information, check out bi-weekly *Lavender Magazine,* www.lavendermagazine.com (see the **Helpful Services** chapter for more LGBT information and publications).

K NOWING WHERE TO GO FOR A SPECIFIC SERVICE IS PARTICULARLY important when you first move. The following information, which includes particulars about renting furniture, hiring a house cleaner, pest control, shipping services, and consumer protection, might make your life a little easier. Also included in this chapter is a section on services for the disabled, one to assist new residents from abroad, and information about gay and lesbian life in the Twin Cities.

RENTAL SERVICES

If you don't own everything you need to set up housekeeping, have no fear—someone has it and they're ready to rent.

FURNITURE, APPLIANCES, COMPUTERS, AND TELEVISIONS

Most rental stores now rent everything—including electronics and appliances. When you go shopping, take a list of what you need and a floor plan drawing; staff at the showroom will be able to help you figure out what will fit.

- **Carefree Rentals**, 122 E Lake St, Minneapolis, 612-284-1711, www.carefree rental-mn.com
- **Cort Furniture Rental**, 1-888-360-CORT, www.cort.com
- **Quality Furniture Rental**, 2900 Rice St, St. Paul, 651-487-2191; 2845 Anthony Ln S, Minneapolis, 612-782-9585; 1-800-547-5852, www.qualityfurniturerental.com

COMPUTER AND AUDIOVISUAL RENTAL
- **Audiovisual and Video Resources**, 801 American Blvd, Bloomington, 952-814-9898, 8800-238-2887, www.avvr.com
- **Carefree Rentals**, 122 E Lake St, Minneapolis, 612-284-1711, www.carefree rental-mn.com

- **Computer Rental Systems**, 411 W 60th St, Minneapolis, 612-798-1958, www.crsrental.com
- **FedEx Kinko's Copy Centers** have PCs and Macs available for in-store use; numerous locations, www.fedex.com/us/office.
- **First Choice Computer Rental**, 7600 W 27th St, St. Louis Park, 952-975-9926, www.fccrents.com

DOMESTIC SERVICES

HOUSE AND SPECIALTY CLEANING

In addition to taking care of routine chores on a regular basis, most cleaning services also offer a one-time cleaning service, including a once-over after moving day (or after your house-warming party). This list is just to get you started, and recommendation should not be implied. Before you employ any cleaner or cleaning service, be sure to check references, and hire only those services that are insured. Check the Yellow Pages for additional services or ask your friends or co-workers for recommendations. Most of the companies listed below have searchable web sites, so you can put in your new address and find the affiliate who services your area.

- **1-800-GOT-JUNK removal service**, will remove nearly anything from old furniture and appliances to garden debris and estate leftovers, 1-800-GOT-JUNK, www.1800gotjunk.com/TwinCities.
- **Coit Services** has been in business for over fifty years. They clean carpet, upholstery, draperies, air ducts, tile, and grout, and can handle fire and flood restorations, as well. Call 1-800-FOR-COIT, www.coit.com. Appointments can be scheduled online.
- **Distinctive Cleaning** does general cleaning as well as window washing and professional cleaning, 1321 E 66th St, Richfield, 952-922-2457, www.distinctivecleaning.com.
- **EcoMama Clean**, is a licensed, insured, and bonded green cleaning service for homes and offices that uses Mrs. Meyers eco-friendly products, 612-280-3470, .http://www.ecomamaclean.com/
- **Green Cleaning Cooperative** is a unionized collective of about 40 owner-members who have experience in commercial and residential cleaning. Members use less toxic cleaning products, such as those produced by Seventh Generation. The Cooperative was organized with the help of the Latino Economic Development Center, a Minneapolis nonprofit that fosters development of Latino-run businesses, 612-454-5377.
- **Jack Pixley Sweeps**, fireplace cleaning and repair, 763-422-0481, 952-922-4034, 651-646-3872, www.jackpixleysweeps.com
- **Junk Squad** specializes in estate, moving, and garage clean-ups, 952-828-9999, www.junksquad.com.

- **Maid Brigade of Minneapolis/St. Paul**, 952-830-4600, 651-686-0900, www. mnmaidbrigade.com
- **Merry Maids**, 1515 Main St, Hopkins, 952- 471-2541, www.merrymaids.com
- **Molly Maid**, 1-800-MOLLY-MAID, www.mollymaid.com
- **Sedgwick Heating and Air Conditioning**, furnace and air duct cleaning, 952-881-9000, www.sedgwickheating.com
- **Stanley Steemer**, carpet, tile and air duct cleaning, 1-800-STEEMER, www. stanleysteemer.com
- **Two Bettys Green Cleaning Service**, 612-720-8768, http://twobettys.biz/ about

PEST CONTROL

Apart from mosquitoes, Minnesota pests tend to run to squirrels and bats that move into your attic, and raccoons and wood ducks that fall down your chimney. With that in mind, your first line of defense should be to make sure that all your chimneys and air vents are properly screened. Carpenter ants can also be a problem, so trim shrubbery back away from your foundation. Because mosquitoes present a serious health hazard, many people treat their yards with granules to keep the beasts away. Fogging your yard before an evening you want to be outside is a temporary solution. And a repellent that actually works is Off PowerPad lamps, which last about four hours. Should you develop a problem that requires a professional solution, here are some local services:

- **Curbside Landscaping,** 952-403-9012 www.curbsidelandscape.com, uses a flower extract to naturally kill and repel mosquitoes.
- **Diversified Spraying Services**, 952-934-7064
- **Metropolitan Mosquito Control,** 651-645-9149, www.mmcd.org, controls mosquitoes and monitors tick populations throughout the metro. If you see a low-flying helicopter swooping across your swamp, or people in Hazmat suits spraying in your yard, they'll most likely be from MMC. Look on their web site for mosquito, gnat, black fly, and tick information. Call them to report high mosquito annoyance, and they may come out and spray.
- **Midsota Mosquito Control**, 320-240-6908, http://midsotamosquito.com
- **Mosquito Squad**, 763-434-2483 www.mosquitosquad.com
- **Orkin**, 1-877-250-1652, 1-866-949-6043, www.orkin.com
- **Plunkett's Pest Control**, 877-571-7100, www.plunketts.net
- **Terminix Pest Control**, 6988 Oxford St, St. Louis Park, 952-926-4297, 1-866-224-4661, www.terminix.com
- **Wildlife Management Services**, 612-852-8657 612-926-9988

MAIL SERVICE

Look for your nearest post office by using the interactive map on the U.S. Postal Service's web site, www.usps.com, or call 800-ASK-USPS (800-275-8777).

Minneapolis' main post office is located downtown at 100 South First Street. Hours of operation are: Monday–Friday, 7 a.m.–8 p.m., Saturday, 9 a.m.–1 p.m. St. Paul's main post office at 180 East Kellogg Boulevard is open Monday–Friday, 8:30 a.m.–5:30 p.m., Saturday, 9 a.m.–12 p.m. For mail that needs to go out immediately, the post office at the MSP airport is open around the clock (5001 Northwest Drive, St. Paul). If you don't need personal service, use the online interactive map to look for the Automated Postal Center nearest you; most of them are open 24/7.

JUNK MAIL

To curtail the onslaught of mail newcomers always receive after relocating, register with the Direct Marketing Association to stop receiving mail from individual companies within each of four categories—Credit Offers, Catalogs, Magazine Offers, and Other Mail Offers—or from an entire category at once. To stop mail from being sent to a deceased individual, you'll need to register for the **Deceased Do Not Contact List** on the same web site, www.dmachoice.org. Because the three major credit bureaus sell lists of individuals who meet certain credit criteria, you can remove your name from the generated lists by calling their "Opt Out" hotline, 1-888-5-OPT-OUT (1-888-567-8688) or click "Opt Out" online at: www.optoutprescreen.com.

MAIL RECEIVING AND FORWARDING SERVICES

- **Greendog Packing & Shipping**, 5413 Nicollet Ave, Minneapolis, 612-827-0700
- The **UPS Stores** rent mailboxes and provide 24-hour access and call-in Mail-Check; numerous locations throughout the Twin Cities, www.theupsstore.com

SHIPPING SERVICES

Most shipping services offer freight service for large items as well as package and same day delivery.
- **DHL Worldwide Express**, 800-CALL-DHL, www.dhl-usa.com
- **Federal Express** has drop-boxes outside most post offices, as well as authorized shipping centers at OfficeMax and Kinko's/FedEx Office Print and Ship Centers throughout the metro; 800-GoFedex, www.fedex.com
- **YRC** (formerly Yellow and Roadway), 12400 Dupont Ave S, Burnsville, 1-800-610-6500, www.yrc.com
- **United Parcel Service (UPS)**, 800-PICK-UPS (742-5877), www.ups.com
- **U.S. Postal Service**, 800-ASK-USPS, TDD/TTY 1-877-TTY-2HLP (877-889-2457), www.usps.com

CONSUMER PROTECTION—RIP-OFF RECOURSE

The best defense against fraud and consumer victimization is to avoid it. So read all contracts down to the smallest print, save all receipts and canceled checks, get the names of sales and service people with whom you deal, date every paper you sign, and check with the Attorney General's office or the Better Business Bureau for complaints.

- **Minnesota Attorney General's Office Consumer Division**, 651-296-3353, 800-657-3787, TTY 651-297-7206, TTY 800-366-4812, www.ag.state.mn.us
- **Better Business Bureau of Minnesota**, 2706 Gannon Rd, St. Paul, 651-699-1111, 800-646-6222 http://minnesota.bbb.org
- **Minnesota Department of Human Rights** is the state agency charged with protecting people from discrimination. Write them at 190 E 5th St, St. Paul, MN 55101, or call 651-296-5663, 800-657-3704, TTY 651-296-1283, www.humanrights.state.mn.us.

IDENTITY FRAUD

Identity fraud is on the increase and since it can take years for the victims of such fraud to clear their names, the best defense is to avoid becoming a victim in the first place. That said, it's hard to do when the State of Minnesota sells your driver's license data to anybody willing to plunk down $1000 for the list and $450 for monthly updates—even though virtually nobody checks the box giving the state permission to do so. There are some aspects of data privacy over which you do have control, however. Don't have your Social Security number printed on your checks. Shred undesired pre-approved credit offers. Don't carry credit cards, social security cards, birth certificates or passports, except when you need them. Cancel all unused credit card accounts. Always take credit card and ATM receipts away with you and never toss them in a public trash container. Keep a list of all your credit cards, including information on customer service and fraud department telephone numbers. And never give out credit card or social security information over the phone unless you initiated the call.

If you have been a victim of identity fraud, call the three major credit reporting bureaus immediately.

- **Equifax**, 1-800-685-1111, to place a fraud alert on your credit report call 1-888-766-0008, www.Equifax.com
- **TransUnion**, 800-888-4231, to report fraud 800-680-7289 www.transunion.com
- **Experian (TRW)**, 888-397-3742, www.experian.com

You can file your request online at **www.annualcreditreport.com** and view your reports immediately.

Also contact the **Identity Theft Resource Center** at 858-693-7935, **Victim Assistance Center** at 888-400-5530, or **www.idtheftcenter.org**. It has lists and timelines for the things you need to do to keep your life from spinning out of control.

While you're at it, call the Minnesota Attorney General's office (see address and phone number above). Every year they successfully help many people recover their losses—and someday they may even be able to get the state to stop selling our data!

SAFETY ISSUES

HANDGUNS

Probably the first thing you noticed upon arriving in Minnesota was the conspicuous "Guns Prohibited On These Premises" signs posted on the doors of many buildings, including grocery stores and libraries, and you're probably wondering what's going on. If it's any consolation, so are most of the rest of us! The fact is that the signs are there because they are the only way to ban guns from public premises under the Minnesota Personal Protection Act (conceal-and-carry law). This law threw out Minnesota's previous statutory provisions with respect to granting handgun permits, and replaced them with an expedited application process at the same time that it prohibited the barring of firearms from public facilities such as city halls, parks, recreation centers, and municipal liquor stores.

RADON

> Over half the homes in St. Croix and Pierce counties in Wisconsin have high concentrations of radon; fewer than 20% in Anoka County do. Most metro counties are in the 30% range.

Most people understand that outdoor air pollution can harm their health but may be unaware that indoor air pollution from radon can be every bit as dangerous. In fact, the Surgeon General has warned that radon is the second leading cause of lung cancer in the United States, next to smoking. For non-smokers, radon is the number one cause of lung cancer. So what is radon? It's a colorless, odorless, tasteless radioactive gas produced by the breakdown of minerals such as uranium and radium in the soil. Because of our geology and the way our homes are built to be airtight and negative pressured, radon can be a serious problem here. Indeed, the Minnesota Department of Health estimates that one in three homes in Minnesota has a high enough radon level to pose a risk to the occupants' health. One important factor is that many homes in Minnesota have basements that are used as living spaces, and that radon levels are often highest in the level of a building in closest contact with the soil. So what do you do about it? First, test for it. There are short-term and long-term radon test kits.

The short-term test kit takes four to seven days to complete, offering a snapshot of radon levels during those days; the long-term test kit takes 91 days to a year to complete, producing a time-averaged picture of radon levels. Test kits cost between $5 and $25, and the price includes laboratory analysis. Buy them at hardware and home supply stores, or purchase a discounted kit through **WCCO Television** (www.radon.com/sub/mn/). Donate $10 and get a free kit from the **American Lung Association** (ALA), 651-227-8014, www.alamn.org.

If your levels are high, you can reduce exposure by using mitigation techniques. According to the ALA, most homes can be fixed for between $800 and $2500 (simple caulking and painting are NOT a fix). If you're building a new home, you can reduce the amount of radon coming in by using radon-resistant construction techniques. The ALA Health House builder guidelines include radon-reduction strategies. For more information on these builder guidelines, call the **Health House program** (877-521-1491, or look online at www.alamn. org). For complete information, look online at the **Minnesota Department of Health** web site (www.health.state.mn.us/divs/eh/indoorair/radon/index. html), which includes a list of certified and trained radon mitigation contractors. To find out about radon levels in your county, look online at http://mn-radon. info.

Wisconsin residents can access general radon information, get a map of radon test results by ZIP code, and learn about radon-resistant construction at the **Wisconsin Radon Program** web site (http://dhs.wi.gov/DPH_BEH/Radon-Prot/index.htm), or by calling 888-569-7236 (888-LOW-RADON).

Nationally, the U.S. **Environmental Protection Agency** (EPA) also maintains a radon web site that includes scientific findings and the latest news (www.epa.gov/radon/index.html/, 800-SOS-RADON [800-767-7236]).

SMOKING BANS

Minnesota bans smoking in bars, restaurants, stores, private clubs such as VFWs and American Legion halls, bowling alleys, country club lounges, lobbies of hotels and motels, public transportation, taxis, home offices where employees work or customers visit, home day cares when children are present, and smaller commercial vehicles carrying more than one person. Some places, such as Bloomington and Golden Valley, go further and restrict outdoor smoking, also.

KEEPING THE BUGS AWAY

Mosquitoes are so common in Minnesota that they're facetiously referred to as our state bird. In fact we are home to roughly 50 species of them. We are also home to 13 species of ticks, including deer ticks. The bites of most of these insects are usually only a minor annoyance. On rare occasions, though, they can cause serious illness and even death. Mosquitoes can carry encephalitis and West Nile virus, and deer ticks can transmit Lyme disease. The **Centers for**

Disease Control (CDC) strongly recommends that people who live in Minnesota use a repellent to lower the danger of insect-borne diseases. DEET, which is the active ingredient found in Deep Woods Off, Skintastic, Ultrathon, and many other repellents, is highly effective against both mosquitoes and ticks, and is a popular choice. For those who dislike DEET's strong odor or the damage it can do to some synthetic fabrics, plant-based picaridin, found in Cutter Advanced, has tested effective against mosquitoes and biting flies. Permethrin is widely available in products like Fite Bite and bug-repellent clothing. It repels mosquitoes about as effectively as 7% DEET (two hours' protection), and is quite effective on ticks. Because it's a neurotoxin, it is not recommended for children under three. Many DEET products contain much higher concentrations than 7%, and therefore last longer. Ultrathon, a 3M product, contains an additive that inhibits absorption, so that it lasts eight to twelve hours, making it the repellent of choice for many serious gardeners or those who go camping in the Boundary Waters.

Many people here spray their yards or have mosquito-killing chemicals spread in their grass. (See **Pest Control** on page 267.) For short-term comfort, try Off PowerPad lamps, which last about 4 hours.

And while you're protecting yourself, don't forget to protect your pets. Mosquitoes spread heartworms in dogs, so dogs here need to be tested for heartworm every spring and given a heartworm preventative. Dogs can also catch Lyme disease. There are vaccines to prevent Lyme disease in dogs, as well as topical insecticides such as fipronil (Frontline) that are applied to the skin between the dog's shoulder blades once a month. Horses in Minnesota need to be vaccinated against mosquito-borne diseases, too, including West Nile virus and Eastern (EEE) and Western (WEE) encephalitis. Potomac fever, which may be transmitted by ticks from horses to people, has also occurred here. It is currently recommended that horses be vaccinated in April or May and then again in the latter part of the summer, i.e., August. This schedule is a change from earlier recommendations, and is timed to offer the greatest protection during the time of the year when infection is most likely to occur.

SERVICES FOR PEOPLE WITH DISABILITIES

The slogan for a disabled advocacy program on community radio station KFAI is "Disabled and Proud—Not an Oxymoron!" This slogan could also describe the supportive environment for the disabled in the Twin Cities. Here the physically challenged will find visibility (a reporter for one of the local TV stations works from a wheelchair), organization, communication, schools that meet special needs, and reliable mobility. Of course, the reviews are mixed, and the past several years of state budget deficits have resulted in changes to eligibility and service delivery for many programs used by people with disabilities. MinnesotaCare and home and community waiver programs to keep people out of institutional care have been favorite targets of budget cutting proposals, as have services to the mentally ill.

On the other hand, in accordance with the 1990 Americans with Disabilities Act, public buildings are handicapped-accessible, and every parking lot has handicapped spaces. Non-disabled people who park in them face fines of up to $200, and police are generally tough on enforcement. Most city sidewalks have curb cuts, and in the downtowns, with ramp parking and skyways, it is possible to go for miles without stepping outside, although parking spaces for oversized vans are still hard to come by. On the cultural front, theaters and concert halls set aside special sections for people in wheelchairs, and many facilities offer hearing augmentation devices or signed performances.

By state law, Minnesota schools are required to offer special needs students a full range of services. Contact the **Department of Education** (651-582-8200, http://education.state.mn.us/mde/index.html) for more information. The **library systems** offer services for the hearing and vision impaired, such as books-on-tape and high-magnification lenses. Call 952-847-8850 for At Home Services of Hennepin County libraries, www.hclib.org; Ramsey County, 651-486-2200, www.ramsey.lib.mn.us; St. Paul Public Library has assistive technology available at its Central, Highland Park, and Rondo Community Outreach branches, 651-632-5089, www.sppl.org; and Washington County, 651-731-1320, www.co.washington.mn.us.

There is an active community of animal lovers who train assistance dogs in several programs including: **Helping Paws of Minnesota** (952-988-9359, www.helpingpaws.org); and **Can Do Canines** (formerly Hearing and Service Dogs of Minnesota), 763-331-3000, www.hsdm.org, http://can-do-canines.org/).

The area also offers a multitude of sports and outdoor recreation opportunities for the physically challenged, including interscholastic adapted athletics (see **Adapted Athletics** in **Childcare and Education**).

On the downside, although all MetroTransit buses are equipped with wheelchair lifts, winter weather can make it hard to get to them. Winter plowing, unshoveled walks, and the process of freezing and thawing may make it impossible to get around for days or weeks at a time. And, though the downtown has an extensive skyway system, most downtown parking ramps will not accommodate large vans.

For the latest disability information, be sure to read *Access Press* (www.accesspress.org), a monthly newspaper available free at over 235 metro locations, as well as on audiotape and online. To subscribe, call 651-644-2133 or sign up online.

The United Way's First Call for Help (211) is a comprehensive information source for any social service need.

TAX REDUCTIONS DUE TO DISABILITY

Homeowners who are disabled may be eligible for a reduced homestead property tax based on the source and amount of their income. Apply through the Minnesota Department of Revenue, http://www.taxes.state.mn.us/taxes/property/index.shtml.

FREE FISHING LICENSES

Disabled veterans and others with disabilities may qualify for free fishing licenses. Contact the Minnesota Department of Natural Resources License Center in St. Paul. http://www.dnr.state.mn.us/index.html, Consumer Information Line: 651-296-6157, 1-888-646-6367, TTY: 651-296-5484 or 1-800-657-3929.

GETTING AROUND

DISABLED CERTIFICATES AND CAR LICENSE PLATES

To apply for a Minnesota disability certificate or disabled car license plates call the **MN Department of Public Safety** at 651-297-3377, www.dps.state.mn.us/dvs/Disability/disability%20frame.htm, or contact the **Minnesota State Council on Disability** at 651-296-6785 or 1-800-945-8913 V/TTY. You may apply after a physician or chiropractor certifies that you meet the state requirements for a disabled person. If your disability is permanent and you are the owner/primary driver of a vehicle, you may apply for disabled plates at the time of vehicle registration.

Find information about Wisconsin disabled parking licenses and disability parking identification cards at the **Wisconsin Department of Transportation** web site, www.dot.wisconsin.gov/drivers/vehicles/disabled/displate.htm, or go in person to a DMV office. The office in Hudson (St. Croix County Government Center, 1101 Carmichael Road, 715-386-4609) is handicapped-accessible (many are not).

TRANSPORTATION

Buses are lift-equipped, and all MetroTransit drivers are trained to assist people in wheelchairs and to recognize "bus identifier cards" used by the vision- or hearing-impaired to display the bus route number they are waiting for. Call **MetroTransit Customer Relations,** 612-373-3333, www.metrotransit.org) for information about these cards. **Metro Mobility** is our door-through-door transport service. Certification takes a few weeks, but once certified, participants receive rides for any purpose. Reservations should be made in advance. A shared-ride system, it works especially well to get people to and from work or doctor's and therapist's appointments. To apply, you must complete an Americans with Disabilities Act (ADA) application obtainable from **Metro Mobility Customer Services** (651-602-1111, TTY

651-221-9886 between 7:30 a.m. and 4:30 p.m., Monday–Friday), or download an application form online at www.metrocouncil.org/transportation/MetroMobility/Forms/forms.htm. The Metro Mobility peak fare is $4 per one-way trip; the off-peak fare is $3. ADA-certified customers also are entitled to use regular route transit for $.75. Look online at www.metrotransit.org/newrider/howride/howaccessible.asp for detailed information about using buses, trains, and Metro Mobility.

Care Cab offers wheelchair, ambulatory, and stretcher service for doctor appointments, dialysis, routine transfers, and even errands, 1-800-535-7190, 1-320-251-6261, www.caretransportation.com. Other transportation resources include **HealthEast Transportation**, St. Paul, which provides emergency and scheduled transport, 651-232-1700, 651-232-1717, 800-887-6221, www.healtheast.org/transportation.html; **Helpful Hands Transportation,** Minneapolis, 763-546-0094; **Family Alliance Transportation**, 763-464-4804, 763-483-2053; and **Discover Ride**, 612-823-6000.

MOBILITY AND SPECIAL CARE EQUIPMENT

If you need to rent or purchase a scooter or motorized wheelchair, specially outfitted van, or other medical devices and supplies, here are some places to start looking:

- **Ability Solutions Showroom**, 1528 Cliff Road E, Burnsville, 952-808-3646, www.abilitysolutions.net
- **IMED Mobility**, 1915 W County Rd C, Roseville, 651-635-0655, 800-570-0236, www.imedmobility.com
- **Jackson Medical Equipment**, 982 Thomas Ave, 651-645-6221, www.jacksonmobility.com
- **Mobility for Independence,** 1622 W 31st St, Minneapolis, 612-825-1845, www.mobilityforindependence.org, gives grants toward the purchase of mobility equipment.
- **R.C. Sales and Manufacturing**, 14726 Wake St NE, Ham Lake, 763-786-6504, is a specialized builder of wheelchair-accessible vans.
- **RollX Vans**, 2200 Hwy 13, Savage, 952-890-7851, 800-956-6668, www.rollxvans.com, sells new and previously owned handicapped-accessible vans and mini-vans, power openers, ramps and lifts, transfer seats, and driving controls, and provides "At Home" service.
- **Waldoch Crafts and Customs**, 13821 Lake Dr, Forest Lake, 651-464-3215, 800-328-9259, www.waldoch.com

GOVERNMENT AND OTHER SERVICES

DEAF AND HARD OF HEARING

Minnesota's Deaf and Hard of Hearing Services operates eight regional offices. The Metro office is located at 85 East Seventh Place, Suite 105, St. Paul (mailing address: Department of Human Services, 444 Lafayette Road, St. Paul,

MN 55155-3814), telephone 651-431-5940, VP 651-964-1514, TTY 888-206-6513, www.dhs.state.mn.us.

BLIND AND VISUALLY IMPAIRED

In addition to offering a special homestead tax credit, Minnesota provides many adaptive services to the blind and visually impaired. To find out about either, make your first call to the **Minnesota Department of Employment and Economic Development, Services for the Blind** (651-642-0500, TTY 651-642-0506, or toll free Voice/TDD 800-652-9000, www.positivelyminnesota.com). The main Services for the Blind office is located at 2200 University Avenue, Suite 240, St. Paul. This office offers job and independent living classes, including group classes for the blind elderly. Its communications center provides Radio Talking Books and voice-edition newspapers. It also has a store that sells adaptive aids at cost. Transportation is provided to group classes. Additional resources to consider:

- **BLIND Inc.** (Blindness Learning In New Dimensions) is a nonprofit training facility where people learn to live independently, use Braille, cook, clean, and sew. It also teaches industrial arts and job readiness skills, 100 E 22nd St, Minneapolis, 612-872-0100, www.blindinc.org.
- **Minnesota Braille and Talking Book Library** (http://education.state.mn.us/MDE/Learning_Support/MN_Braille_Talking_Book_Library/index.html) provides direct library service to eligible Minnesotans who are legally blind or visually impaired, or have physical disabilities that prevent them from using standard printed materials, To access the service, you must first complete the online application available at the NLS BARD Website, www.loc.gov/nls. Then they'll send you a library code and password.
- **Vision Loss Resources Inc.** (formerly Minnesota Society for the Blind) provides services, plus fun and games, for all ages. Their West Metro facility houses a rehab and community center, 1936 Lyndale Ave S, Minneapolis, Voice/TTY 612-871-2222. Their East Metro facility is located at 216 S Wabasha, St. Paul, Voice/TTY 651-224-7662; www.visionlossresources.com.

HEALTH CARE

Minnesota is in terrible financial trouble and many of the state's efforts to get its budget under control have targeted health and human services programs. Many basic health care programs for our most vulnerable residents have been reduced or terminated, and the cost of providing services has been shifted onto hospitals and other providers.

In the meantime, we do, for the time being, still have MinnesotaCare, a publicly subsidized insurance for Minnesota residents who do not have access to affordable health care coverage. We also have UCare, www.ucare.org, an independent, nonprofit health plan for residents of Minnesota and Wisconsin.

UCare has three special needs plans including *UCare Connect* for adults ages 18 to 64 who have a certified disability or developmental disability. For information, call UCare at 612-676-3554 or 1-800-707-1711 (toll free). If you are hearing impaired, call 612-676-6810 or 1-800-688-2534 (toll free).

In Hennepin County, Cornerstone Solutions (HMO) connects residents with disabilities to social supports and health care coverage. Call 1-866-601-8962 (Toll free), 8 a.m. to 8 p.m., seven days a week; TTY 1-800-627-3529 or 711.

HOUSING

There is a critical shortage of affordable housing in the Twin Cities, so it may take a long time to locate an acceptable apartment. Start your search early.

Minnesota law requires that a disabled person and his/her family must be given priority with respect to handicapped-equipped rental housing. This means that if a family without a disabled member is living in handicapped-equipped housing, they can be asked to move to another unit in the same rental complex to make way for a family that does include a disabled person.

- For help finding barrier-free housing or housing assistance programs for the disabled, contact the **National Handicap Housing Institute** (651-639-9799, www.nhhiaccessiblehousing.com/barrierfree.html), which builds and rents apartments to the disabled.

- **Accessible Space, Inc.** (ASI) provides accessible, affordable, assisted/supportive and independent living opportunities for persons with physical disabilities, brain injuries, and seniors, 651-645-7271, 1-800-627-3529 (Voice/TTY), www.accessiblespace.org.

- **CommonBond Communities** is a nonprofit developer and manager of affordable rental homes in Minnesota, Wisconsin, and Iowa. They have built a variety of accessible housing throughout the metro. Search online for housing that meets your needs, and apply for it online, too; 651-291-1750, www.commonbond.org,

- If you own a home and are no longer able to live in it because of disability, there may be **Fix-Up Fund Accessibility Loans** available to help you make necessary changes, www.mnhousing.gov.

For information about accessible hotels and motels in the Twin Cities area check the **Temporary Lodgings** chapter in this book.

INDEPENDENT LIVING

The **Metropolitan Center for Independent Living** (www.mcil-mn.org) is one of eight such centers in Minnesota. Its Disability Linkage Line (1-866-333-2466, www.minnesotahelp.org) offers up-to-date information including disability benefits programs, home modifications, assistive technology, personal assistance services, accessible housing, employment, social activities, and disability rights. This organization is an amazing resource. It lists job openings, provides peer mentoring, accessible conference space, a computer lab for consumer use, advocacy, subsidized personal assistance, and classes for people with disabilities to acquire the skills they need for independent living. Their **Ramp Project** assists those needing ramps. Their **Transition Program** assists students and young adults with disabilities to make a successful transition from high school to post-secondary education, employment, and adult independent living, 651-646-8342, www.mcil-mn.org.

ADDITIONAL RESOURCES

Following is a variety of resources, both governmental and nonprofit, that may be of use to those with special needs:

- **ADA Minnesota** (651-603-2015, TTY 651-603-2001, 888-630-9793, www.adaminnesota.org) is the Minnesota resource for information about the Americans with Disabilities Act.
- **Advocating Change Together** (ACT), 651-641-0297, 800-641-0059, www.selfadvocacy.org
- The **ARC of Minnesota** provides advocacy, referrals for services, and educational materials, 651-523-0823, 800-582-5256, www.arcmn.org.
- **City Housing and Redevelopment Authorities** (HRA) operate public housing and take applications for Section 8 subsidized housing. For information, call the St. Paul Public Housing Agency (651-298-4444, Hearing Impaired 711, www.stpaulpha.org) or Minneapolis Public Housing Authority, Main Number 612-342-1400, Section 8 612-342-1480, TTY 612) 342-1480, www.mphaonline.org. Applications for subsidized units are actually processed by building managers. It's a good idea to have your name added to the waiting list at all of the buildings in which you'd like to live.
- **Closing the Gap**, www.closingthegap.com, provides the information and training necessary to locate, compare, and implement assistive technology.
- **Courage Center**, 3915 Golden Valley Rd, Golden Valley, is Minnesota's most famous rehabilitation center, with locations in GoldenValley, Stillwater, Burnsville, and Forest Lake. For service and program information, call 763-520-0312, 888-846-8253, www.couragecenter.org.
- **Disability Linkage Line**, 866-333-2466, www.minnesotahelp.info (see above).
- **"Disabled and Proud"** airs on Tuesday nights at 7:00 p.m. on KFAI, 90.3 FM in Minneapolis and 106.7 FM in St. Paul.
- **Lutheran Social Services**, 651-642-5990, 1-800-582-5260, www.lssmn.org; services include transitional housing and permanent supportive housing.
- **Minnesota Disability Law Center**, 430 1st Ave N, Suite 300, Minneapolis, 612-332-1441, TDD 612-332-4668, www.mndlc.org, provides free civil legal assistance to individuals with disabilities.

- **Minnesota State Council on Disability**, Voice/TTY, 651-361-7800, 800-945-8913, 711, www.state.mn.us/portal/mn/jsp/home.do?agency=MSCOD; whatever your disability, this is the agency to contact when you are looking for any kind of assistance.
- **National Handicap Housing Institute** (NHHI) 651-639-9799, www.nhhiaccessiblehousing.com/barrierfree.html, rents apartments to the handicapped and disabled.
- **PACER Center** is a parent training and information resource for families of children and youth with all disabilities from birth through 21 years old; 8161 Normandale Blvd, Bloomington, 952-838-9000, www.pacer.org.

INTERNATIONAL NEWCOMERS

A variety of helpful information can be found online at the **US Citizen and Immigration Services** Web Site: http://uscis.gov. For answers to specific questions and to schedule appointments contact the USCIS national customer service center, 1-800-375-5283, TDD 1-800-767-1833. Once you know what you need to do, you'll undoubtedly have to fill out paperwork. Order the proper forms online or call 800-870-3676.

Below are the addresses of local USCIS district and satellite offices:

- USCIS Application Support Center, 1360 University Ave W, Room 103, St. Paul, 55104
- St. Paul Field Office (serving Minnesota, North Dakota, South Dakota, and parts of Wisconsin): 2901 Metro Dr, Ste 100, Bloomington, MN 55425
- Asylum Office: 401 S La Salle St, 8th Floor, Chicago, IL 60605, 312-353-9607
- Nebraska Service Center: processes most forms filed in this area.

PUBLICATIONS

International newcomers experiencing culture shock can get a quick overview of American culture, etiquette, expectations, and quirks in the *Newcomer's Handbook for Moving to and Living in the USA* by Mike Livingston, published by First Books (www.firstbooks.com).

LOCAL CONSULATES

We have two permanent consulates in Minnesota and many honorary consuls:

Canadian Consulate General

701 4th Ave S
Minneapolis, MN 55415-1600
612-333-4641
www.canadainternational.gc.ca/minneapolis

Consul of Mexico
797 E 7th St
St. Paul, MN 55106
651-771-5494
www.sre.gob.mx/saintpaul

Honorary Consul of Austria
1814 Hillcrest Ave, Suite 300
St. Paul, MN 55116
651-222-2052
www.austria.org

Honorary Consul of Belgium
238 S Mississippi Blvd
St. Paul, MN 55105-1111
651-699-2528

Honorary Consul of Bolivia
18036 65th Ave N
Maple Grove, MN 55311
763-424-0265
www.bolivia-usa.org

Honorary Consul of Costa Rica
6 W 5th St, Suite 201
Saint Paul, MN 55102
651-293-1816

Honorary Consul of Czech Republic
SOKOL Hall/C.S.P.S. Hall
383 Michigan St.
St. Paul, MN 55102
651-221-0016
www.mzv.cz/washington

Honorary Consulate of Denmark
1417 E River Pkwy
Minneapolis, MN 55414
612-338-7283
www.ambwashington.um.dk/en/menu/TheEmbassy/

Honorary Consul of Finland
2429 Girard Ave S
Minneapolis, MN 55405-2537
612-374-2718
www.finland.org

Honorary Consulate of France
150 S 5th St, Suite 2300
Minneapolis, MN 55402-4223
612-338-6868
www.info-france-usa.org

Honorary Consul of Germany
Heino Beckmann, Ph.D.
University of St. Thomas
SCH 103
1000 LaSalle Ave
Minneapolis, MN 55403-2005
651-962-4080

Honorary Consul of Great Britain
800 Nicollet Mall, Suite 2600
Minneapolis, MN 55402-2041
612-338-2525
www.britainusa.com

Honorary Consul of Guatemala
2105 1st Ave S
Minneapolis, MN 55404-2505
612-870-3459

Honorary Consul of Honduras
20 Cygnet Place
Long Lake, MN 55356-9650
952-473-5376
www.hondurasemb.org

Consulate General of Iceland
6428 Nordic Circle
Edina, MN 55439-1140
952-942-5745
www.iceland.org/us

Honorary Consul General of Japan
16 Woodland Rd
Minneapolis, MN 55424-1631
952-926-1907
www.us.emb-japan.go.jp/english/html/index.html

Honorary Consul of Luxembourg
5012 Nob Hill Dr

Edina, MN 55439
952-927-1196
www.luxembourg-usa.org

Honorary Consul of Malta
332 Minnesota St, Suite W 3090
St. Paul, MN 55101-1332
651-224-1844

Honorary Consul of the Kingdom of the Netherlands
100 S 5th St
Minneapolis, MN 55402
612-373-8831

Honorary Consul of Norway
901 Marquette Ave
Minneapolis, MN 55402-2929
612-332-3338
www.norway.org/Minneapolis

Honorary Consul of Romania
1250 Moore Lake Dr E, Suite 242
Fridley, MN 55432-5135
763-574-9472
www.roembus.org

Honorary Consul of Spain
766 Linwood Ave
Saint Paul, MN 55105
651-227-4439
www.maec.es

Honorary Consul of Sweden
American Swedish Insitute
2600 Park Ave
Minneapolis, MN 55407
612-332-6897
www.swedenabroad.com

Honorary Consul of Tanzania
5429 Lyndale Ave S
Minneapolis, MN 55419
612-821-2704

MOVING PETS TO THE USA

- *The Pet-Moving Handbook* (First Books) covers domestic and international moves, via car, airplane, ferry, etc. Primary focus is on cats and dogs.
- **Cosmopolitan Canine Carriers**, 801 Wigwam Ln, Stratford, CT, 1-203-655-7295, 1-800-243-9105, www.caninecarriers.com, has been shipping dogs and cats all over the world for about 40 years. They provide door-to-door global pet relocation, and can tell you all about vaccinations and quarantine times.

GAY AND LESBIAN LIFE

With the second-largest per capita Lesbian/Gay/Bisexual/Transgender (LGBT) population in the U.S., Minnesota—and Minneapolis, in particular—has long been a leader in extending gay rights to its citizens. Openly gay people serve on city councils and, years ago, one of St. Paul's council members went through well-accepted gender reassignment. Many of the largest companies in our private sector also support the LGBT community by extending domestic partner benefits to their employees, and, since 1991, same-sex couples have been able to register as domestic partners at Minneapolis City Hall.

For years we lived complacent in the thought that our state had some of the strongest civil rights protection laws in the country for gays, lesbians, bisexuals, and transgender people. However, Minnesota politics have recently taken a hard right turn, and those protections are under attack.

Nevertheless, we still have a well-established LGBT community, and it has created a service center, clearinghouse, and information line that is the envy of non-gays, called **OutFront Minnesota** (www.outfront.org). The Info Line (612-822-0127 or 800-800-0350) provides hours of recorded information about gay life in Minnesota. For visitors to the Twin Cities, OutFront can make hotel reservations and supply an itinerary for a three-day visit.

ENTERTAINMENT

The Metro doesn't have one gay neighborhood or "strip," but we do have some traditionally "gay" bars that have been around for a long time, as well as new places opening up in Northeast Minneapolis along East Hennepin. We are also home to the **Twin Cities Gay Men's Chorus**, which performs six times a year at the Ted Mann Concert Hall at the University of Minnesota. For tickets call 612-624-2345, or purchase them online (www.tcgmc.org).

- **19 Bar**, 19 W 15th St (east of Loring Park), 612-871-5553, is the oldest gay bar in the Twin Cities.
- **Gay 90s Theatre Café and Bar**, 408 Hennepin Ave, Minneapolis, 612-333-7755, has been voted the Twin Cities' best gay bar many, many times, although its drag shows and three dance floors probably attract at least as many straight college students and bachelorette parties as gays.

- **Jetset**, 115 N 1st St, Minneapolis, 612-339-3933, www.jetsetbar.com
- **Minneapolis Eagle, Bolt, and Bolt Underground**, 501, 513, and 515 Washington Ave S, Minneapolis, www.minneapoliseagle.com, hosts the Booby Trap girls' night every 3rd Saturday in the Underground.
- **Town House**, 1415 University, St. Paul, 651-646-7087, www.townhouse bar. com

HOUSING

If you're looking for like-minded LGBT neighbors, you can cast a wide net. Gays are integrated into neighborhoods throughout the Twin Cities. Some places to start your search in Minneapolis: Lowry Hill, Uptown, Stevens Square, Powderhorn, Longfellow, East Isles, anywhere in South Minneapolis, Bryn Mawr, Tangletown, Downtown, or in the North Loop. Gays are also leading the way to gentrify Northeast and the Camden area of North Minneapolis. However, Loring Park, traditional center of gay activity in the Twin Cities, is becoming less of a rental community than it used to be, as many of the apartments are being converted into condominiums. In St. Paul, consider Como, anywhere on the west side, or the new lofts downtown. In the suburbs there are well-established LGBT communities in Edina, St. Louis Park, and Golden Valley.

CHURCHES

- **All God's Children Metropolitan Community Church**, 3100 Park Avenue S, Minneapolis, 612-824-2673, www.agcmcc.org
- **Dignity Twin Cities** meets at Prospect Park United Methodist Church (22 Orlin Ave SE) on the 2nd and 4th Sundays of the month, www.dignitytwincities. org.
- **Spirit of the Lakes United Church of Christ**, 4001 38th Ave S, Minneapolis, 612-729-7556, www.spiritucc.org
- **St. Joan of Arc**, 4537 3rd Ave. S, Minneapolis, 612-823-8205, www.stjoan.com
- **St. Paul-Reformation Lutheran Church**, 100 North Oxford Street, St. Paul, 651-224-3371, www.stpaulref.org

OTHER LGBT RESOURCES

- **District 202** offers a variety of programs and services to LGBTQQI (lesbian, gay, bisexual, transgender, queer, questioning, and intersex) youth ages 13–21 throughout the metro. Check the calendar posted on the web site for upcoming events, 651-340-6167, www.dist202.org.
- **KFAI-FM Community Radio**, 90.3 FM and 106.7 FM, www.kfai.org, broadcasts several LGBT-themed shows including "Fresh Fruit" and "This Way Out" (www.thiswayout.org).

- **Lavender Magazine** covers culture, arts, news, and the local bar scene. It is free at bookstores, coffee shops, restaurants and bars, or available online, 612-436-4660, www.lavendermagazine.com.
- **Minnesota AIDS Project**, 1400 Park Ave, Minneapolis, 612-341-2060, www. mnaidsproject.org
- **Northern Lights Women's Softball League**, www.nlwsl.org
- **Out for Equity, St. Paul Public Schools**, 651-523-6322, http://outforequity. spps.org, provides support to students, staff, and families, including special events.
- **Out 4 Good, Minneapolis Public Schools**, 612-668-5482, http://sss.mpls. k12.mn.us/Out4Good.html
- **PFLAG (Parents & Friends of Lesbians & Gays)** sponsors monthly programs and discussions; call 612-825-1660, or check online for a chapter near you, http://community.pflag.org.
- **Quatrefoil Library**, 1619 Dayton Ave, St. Paul, 651-641-0969, www.qlibrary. org
- **Rainbow Families and Family Equality Council**, 1821 W University Ave #109, St. Paul, 651-644-4848, www.familyequality.org

MOVING TO A NEW PLACE MEANS RUNNING LOTS OF ERRANDS—from buying new curtains to replacing mops and brooms that didn't make it into the moving truck. The Twin Cities present you with many shopping choices, from major national department stores to flea markets. If you're looking for something trendy, start in Uptown; if sophisticated is your style, try 50th and France; and if it's toilet bowl brushes, school supplies, or a good price on a small appliance, beat feet to Target. If your passion is fashion, there are choices from Ragstock's vintage jeans to designer boutiques—and there is no sales tax on clothing!

HYPERLOCAL, COMMUNITY-ENHANCING SOCIAL COMMERCE

"Hyperlocal" in computer speak translates as "shopping Mom-and-Pop stores down the street"—or buying from your neighbors. Three guys from St. Anthony Park in St. Paul have set up a web site to help you do this. **Buythechange** (www.buythechange.com) is based on the Craigslist model, but with a few twists. You not only find goods and services being sold by neighbors and local businesses, but 1/3 of all membership fees are contributed to nonprofits. Check the webpage to see if your neighborhood participates—lots do, including Mac-Groveland in St. Paul and Powderhorn in Minneapolis. **Localtweeps** (http://localtweeps.com/about/), from the same developers, is an opt-in ZIP code level means of connecting local like-minded individuals—whether their interests are social or commercial. Members may use it to promote specific events and tweet-ups throughout a targeted ZIP code. Happy hour at the local, anyone?

SHOPPING MALLS AND DISTRICTS

MALLS

Partly because of our climate and partly because of the massive urban sprawl and resultant car culture, indoor malls dominate retail shopping here, with

Southdale Mall in Edina said to be the first indoor retail center built in the United States (1955). There are dozens more now and the list below will help guide you. In the meantime, if you can't get out, try shopping the Made in Minnesota Gift Guide, www.mn2020.org/giftguide.

Planes full of shoppers fly in from all over the world to spend their yen at the multimillion-square-foot **Mall of America** (Highways 77 & I-494 in Bloomington, 952-883-8800, www.mallofamerica.com). This is the largest fully enclosed shopping and entertainment complex in the United States, as well as one of the nation's most visited tourist attractions. Easily accessible from downtown Minneapolis or the airport via the Hiawatha LRT and many bus lines, the mall's anchor stores are **Bloomingdale's**, **Macy's**, **Nordstrom**, and **Sears**, but you can find over 500 other stores there, including Nike, Apple, Lego, and H&M, plus a wedding chapel. The Twin Cities retail scene is also home to the latest trend in buzz-word shopping, the "Lifestyle Mall," which features upscale retailers in Disney-esque storefront-on-Main-Street settings. We have two, so far: the **Shoppes at Arbor Lakes**, I-94 and 694 in Maple Grove (www.shoppesatarborlakes.com), and **Woodbury Lakes** at I-94 and Radio Drive (www.woodburylakes.com). Stores at these malls are very much the same as those you find at 50th and France—**Hot Mama**, **Anthropologie**, **Ann Taylor**, **Banana Republic**—plus **Coldwater Creek**, **Gap** and **Baby Gap,** as well as some independents you won't find elsewhere.

Given our weather, enclosed malls are still the standard, and most of the ones below offer a mix of practical and pricey shopping. The four "Dales" and Burnsville Center were our mega-malls before the Mall of America came to town, and they are still hubs for a vast array of surrounding shopping. They are generally where you'll find Macy's, JC Penney, and Sears.

- **Brookdale Center**, off Brooklyn Blvd in Brooklyn Center, www.brookdale-shoppingcenter.com
- **Burnsville Center**, County Rd 42, Burnsville, www.burnsvillecenter.com
- **Eden Prairie Center**, I-494 and Hwy 212, Eden Prairie, www.edenprairie-center.com, is anchored by Sears, Target, a mutiplex movie theater, Kohl's, and the only Twin Cities branch of Iowa-based Von Maur. Though you can practically see the mall from the freeway, getting to it is a real test of navigational skills, even for locals. Follow signs for Hwy 212 or Prairie Center Dr, and you won't stray too far off course.
- **Galleria**, 69th St and France Ave, Edina, www.galleriaedina.com, includes upscale shopping at Gabbert's Furniture and Design Studio, Tiffany, Williams-Sonoma, and locals Sonnie's women's fashions and Three Rooms (where Shakopee's own *Project Runway* contestant, Christopher Straub, sometimes sells his accessories), as well as several restaurants and a Rocco Altobelli Salon and DaySpa.
- **Maplewood Mall**, I-694 & White Bear Ave, St. Paul, www.simon.com
- **Ridgedale**, I-394 and Ridgedale Dr, Minnetonka, www.ridgedalecenter.com

- **Rosedale**, Hwy 36 and Fairview Ave, Roseville, 651-633-0872, www.myrosedale. com.
- **Shops at West End**, at I-394 and Highway 100 in St. Louis Park, has some stores you won't find at every other mall in town—Love Culture, Republic of Couture, and Lululemon yoga wear, www.theshopsatwestend.com.
- **Southdale**, 6601 France Ave S, Edina, www.simon.com, includes numerous restaurants and a huge theater complex.

SHOPPING DISTRICTS

- **Uptown (Lake St and Hennepin Ave)**, www.uptownminneapolis.com, is as urban and edgy as Minnesota gets. Besides the numerous cafés, bars, and art galleries, close to a hundred trendy clothing, housewares, furniture, and home decorating stores are located here. Hennepin and Lake is the center of the district. A few blocks east, the Lyn-Lake intersection is packed with global restaurants, niche shops like the Smitten Kitten sex toys (www.smitten kittenonline.com), and performing arts venues such as the Jungle Theater (www.jungletheater.com) and Intermedia Arts multi-disciplinary, multicultural arts community (www.intermediaarts.org). (See **Cultural Life** for more information.) Check out the massive Uptown Art Fair in August.
- **Grand Avenue, St. Paul**, www.grandave.com, is a treasure trove of interesting bars and restaurants and unique specialty retail shops. During **Grand Old Day** in June, the whole street becomes one long block party with bands and beer and games for the children.
- **Minneapolis Midtown Exchange/Midtown Global Market** (www.midtownglobalmarket.org), at the east end of Lake St (intersection of Chicago and Lake), is the place to look for small ethnic shops, markets, and restaurants.
- **Warehouse District, Minneapolis**, dubbed "The Design District," the old warehouses clustered around Washington Ave have been rehabbed and turned into chic lofts, galleries, design studios, and restaurants. There is an LRT station on Hennepin and at Target Field, and many Warehouse District establishments will even provide an LRT ticket for you if you stop in for a drink or meal before a Target Center or Target Field game; www.mplswarehouse.com.
- **Northeast Minneapolis/Historic St. Anthony** is across the river from downtown via the Hennepin Ave and 3rd Ave bridges. "Nordeast," one of the oldest parts of Minneapolis, has recently blossomed with a lot of trendy new lofts—and a mix of trendy new/old and ethnic shops to serve them; www.northeastminneapolis.com.
- **Nicollet Mall**, Minneapolis, www.downtownminneapolis.com; the city's famous downtown pedestrian mall is home to sophisticated housewares, home furnishings, and department stores such as Macy's, Neiman-Marcus, Saks, Target, and Williams-Sonoma. Getting around from store to store in winter is made easier by the second-story skyway system. There is an

on-the-mall farmers' market in summer, and the Holidazzle Parade enlivens shopping between Thanksgiving and Christmas. Shop for bargains at Saks Off 5th and Neiman Marcus Last Call. Target has everything, including groceries.

- **Linden Hills**, 43rd St and Upton Ave S, Minneapolis, www.linden-hills.com, just west of Lake Harriet, is home to several first-rate, locally owned shops, including two especially good stores for children: Wild Rumpus children's bookstore (2720 43rd St, 612-920-5005, www.wildrumpusbooks.com) and Creative Kidstuff (4313 Upton, www.creativekidstuff.com).
- **50th and France Avenue**, Edina, www.50thandfrance.com, has a hundred classy boutiques, trendy accessories, an indie movie theater, bakeries, restaurants, and a Lund's grocery. In June, this crossroads and its surrounding streets are transformed into an exotic bazaar by the **Edina Art Fair**.
- **Midway**, centered on University Ave at Snelling, midway between Minneapolis and St. Paul, provides the necessities: grocery stores, banks, Big Box and discount department stores, second-hand furniture, and clothing retailers. Farther down University Ave, past Lexington, the neighborhood known as **Frogtown** is home to countless Asian markets.
- **South Robert Street**, West St. Paul, transcends nationality with ethnic groceries and national department and discount stores such as Menard's, Walmart, and Target.
- **Stillwater** (see **Quick Getaways** chapter)
- **Wayzata on Lake Minnetonka**, about 20 minutes west of Minneapolis out I-394; the sign on the Wayzata Home Center at 1250 Wayzata Blvd says it all: "London, Paris, Wayzata." Antique shops here have something for everyone; other stores tend to be upscale. When exploring Wayzata in warm weather months, park your car and walk or use the trolley; www.wayzatachamber.com.
- **West Seventh, St. Paul**; those who think that shopping in St. Paul is tatty and dull haven't been to West 7th, a major commercial artery which heads west/southwest out of downtown through the city's few remaining intact Victorian Romanesque commercial blocks, and is home to many antique shops and interesting taverns and restaurants.
- **White Bear Lake** features one-of-a kind shops clustered in a friendly downtown that has cobblestone streets and a turn-of-the-20th-century resort quality. Make this a day trip, especially if you like to knit, sew, or quilt. The local summer festival, Manitou Days—held in late June—includes a Lake Shore Art Fair, "Then and Now" walking tour, sailboat regatta, 5K run, water ski show, and beach dancing; www.explorewhitebear.org.

OUTLET MALLS

- **Albertville Premium Outlets**, www.premiumoutlets.com, right off I-94 in Albertville, between Minneapolis and St. Cloud, features 100 outlet stores, including Adidas, Ann Taylor Factory Store, Banana Republic, BCBG Max Azria, Calvin Klein, Coach, Gymboree, Kenneth Cole, Nike, Polo Ralph Lauren, and Tommy Hilfiger. On a vacation trip to the Mall of America and want to take in Albertville as well? Book a limo or shuttle: All Day and Night Limousine Service offers special packages from the Bloomington airport area, www.all-daylimo.com, 763-561-0407.

- **Medford Outlet Center**, 45 miles south of the metro on I-35 at exit 48, has Oshkosh, Liz Claiborne, and Columbia Sportswear—but nothing high fashion.
- **North Branch Outlets**, I-35 North, Exit 147, North Branch, www.northbranch outlets.com, is home to Gap, Old Navy, Bass, Carter's, Liz Claiborne, and a Zales Outlet. Check its web site before you go, and download the coupons.

DEPARTMENT STORES

If you'd have trouble living without Bloomingdale's or some other top-of-the-line department store, you can breathe easier—most of the national one-stop shopping giants are here. But before you settle down and become a regular customer at one of the more familiar stores, pay a visit to **Von Maur** at Eden Prairie Center (952-829-0200, www.vonmaur.com). This family-owned, Iowa-based department store carries the same brands of clothing and gifts as the other high-end department stores, but they'll give you free hemming, an interest-free credit card with no fees and flexible payments, and their shoe salesroom is legendary. Von Maur doesn't have "sales," as such, but moves this season's merchandise to sale racks every week as newer merchandise comes in. For an easy way to find weekly specials at all the local stores, check online at www.shoplocal.com.

- **Bloomingdale's**, Mall of America, Bloomington, www.Bloomingdales.com
- **Herberger's**, www.herbergers.com; Rosedale; Midway Marketplace (1400 University), St. Paul; Southtown Mall, Bloomington; Northtown Mall, Blaine; 2001 Washington Ave, Stillwater.
- **JC Penney**, www.jcpenney.com, has stores in "The Dales" and in Maplewood, Woodbury, Burnsville, and Eden Prairie.
- **Kmart**, www.kmart.com, has stores in New Hope, Lake Street in Minneapolis, Burnsville, Blaine, Anoka, West St. Paul, and East Maryland Ave in St. Paul.
- **Kohl's**, www.kohls.com; 10 metro locations, Kohl's runs sales almost continuously on everything from clothing to coffee makers.
- **Macy's**, www1.macys.com, anchors "the Dales" and also has stores in downtown Minneapolis and St. Paul and the Mall of America.
- **Neiman-Marcus**, 505 Nicollet Mall, Minneapolis, www.neimanmarcus.com
- **Nordstrom**, Mall of America (Bloomington) and Arbor Lakes (Maple Grove), www.nordstrom.com; this chain has built its reputation on excellent service and great shoes for both men and women. Check out the clearance items at Nordstrom Rack on the third floor MOA, as well as its "Half-Yearly" sale in June.

- **Sears, Roebuck & Co**., www.sears.com, which started as a catalogue business in Minnesota, has several stores throughout the metro including an appliance outlet at 2700 Winter St NE, Minneapolis.

DISCOUNT STORES

Costco (www.Costco.com) and Sam's Club (www.samsclub.com) are membership discounters.

- **Costco** is a little more polished, and generally preferred, but has only five stores here, most on the western side of town: 5801 16th St W, St. Louis Park; 11330 Fountains Dr N, Maple Grove; 1431 Beam Ave, Maplewood; 12011 Technology Dr, Eden Prairie; and 12547 Riverdale Blvd, Coon Rapids.
- **Sam's Club** has many more locations, and they're conveniently scattered throughout the metro area. Though it is not generally advertised, both Sam's Club and Costco sell liquor to non-members; and while both chains offer the standard mix of food, electronics, and pharmacies, etc., some locations also have gas stations.
- Sam's Club's parent company, **Walmart** (www.walmart.com), is also represented in the Twin Cities with 20 stores.

Dwarfing these chains, however, is our homegrown trendsetter, **Target** (www.Target.com). There may not be a Target on every street corner, but with 70-some stores in the state, it certainly seems like it. Known for its huge selections of cheap chic wares, it is a one-stop shopping mecca for everything from groceries and prescription drugs to designer housewares, clothing, toys, and electronics. Target's flagship store is in downtown Minneapolis at 900 Nicollet Mall. If you spend a certain amount, they will validate your parking at the nearby LaSalle ramp. And while you're there, sign up to be notified about the Target Direct warehouse sale. This is the e-commerce division of Target, and when it unloads its inventory, it is one of the best sales around.

Other local discount stores include:

- **Big Lots**, www.biglots.com, sells name brand closeouts (including frozen food, wine and beer, and furniture) for up to 70% off retail; 5930 Earle Brown, Brooklyn Center, 763-503-9833; 8950 Highway 7, St. Louis Park, 952-933-3831.
- **DSW Shoe Warehouse**, www.dswshoe.com, Knollwood Mall, St. Louis Park; Mall of America, Bloomington; Riverdale Plaza, Coon Rapids; Rosedale Center, Roseville; Fountains at Arbor Lakes, Maple Grove; Woodbury Lakes, Woodbury.
- **H&M (Hennes & Mauritz)**, www.hm.com, Mall of America, Southdale Center, and Woodbury Lakes Mall sells designer knockoff fashions at bargain basement prices.
- **Nordic Ware Factory Outlet Store**, Hwys 7 and 100, St. Louis Park, www. nordicware.com, manufactures bundt pans and other cooking equipment. If

you ever find you need a krumkake iron, this is the place to go, but check the web site first for open dates and times.

- **Sportsman's Guide**, 411 Farwell Ave in South St. Paul, 1-800-882-2962, www. sportsmansguide.com, is both a liquidation showroom and mail-order house. It sells name brand shoes, hunting gear, and outdoor apparel.
- **Tuesday Morning**, www.tuesdaymorning.com, sells seasonal merchandise at 50–80% off. It always has good deals on towels and bedding. Check their web site or the Yellow Pages for locations nearest you.

HOUSEHOLD SHOPPING

APPLIANCES, COMPUTERS, AND ELECTRONICS

The Twin Cities are well-supplied with all the larger appliance and electronics vendors, such as **Sears** (www.sears.com), **Radio Shack** (www.radioshack.com), and homegrown **Best Buy** (www.bestbuy.com). If you can't find the equipment or service you require there, try one of the following vendors:

- **Apple Stores**, www.apple.com, Mall of America, Bloomington; Southdale, Edina; Ridgedale, Minnetonka; Rosedale, Roseville.
- **ApplianceSmart**, www.appliancesmart.com, is a factory-authorized liquidation outlet for Whirlpool, Maytag, Jenn-Air, Kitchen Aid, GE, and Frigidaire; Como Ave and Hwy 280, St. Paul; 7350 Excelsior Blvd., St. Louis Park; and several other metro locations.
- **Hi-Fi Sound Electronics**, 825 Glenwood Ave, Minneapolis, 612-339-6351, www.hifi-sound.com; besides the seriously high-tech new stuff, this store sells refurbished electronics and repairs old equipment as well.
- **Excelsior Appliance Sales and Service**, 237 Water St, Excelsior, 952-474-7200, is just one example of a locally owned non-chain store that will give you good prices and great service.
- **FirstTech**, 2640 Hennepin Ave S, Minneapolis, 612-374-8000 (main), 612-374-8050 (service), www.firsttech.com; sells and services Macintosh Apple computer products.
- **Micro Center**, "The Ultimate Computer Store," 3710 Hwy 100 S, St. Louis Park, 952-285-4040, www.microcenter.com
- **Warners' Stellian**, www.warnersstellian.com, has been in business for 50 years. The odd name "Stellian" comes from the combination of the founders' names, Steve and Lillian. The stores' kitchen displays feature working appliances that customers are urged to try before they buy: 1711 N Snelling Ave, St. Paul, 651-645-3481, and several other locations. Its semi-annual Appliance Extreme Warehouse sale (550 Atwater Circle, St. Paul, 651-222-0011) features over-stocks and scratch-and-dents priced below cost. Brands include Bosch, Miele, Viking, Sub-Zero, and Jenn-Air.

BEDS, BEDDING & BATH

MATTRESSES

A good selection of mattresses can be found at most major department stores or at specialty retailers such as **Mattress Giant** (www.mattressgiant.com), but for those who'd rather buy from the source, the places listed below are local manufacturers. For consumer bed-buying tips, check out www.consumersearch.com.

- **ComfoRest Adjustable Beds**, 5019 University Ave NE, Columbia Heights, 763-572-8361, http://comforest.com.
- **Original Mattress Factory**, www.originalmattress.com: Minnesota Factory and Store, 1261 E Hwy 36, Maplewood, 651-482-9338, and several other locations.
- **Restwell Mattress Company**, 8229 Hwy 7, St. Louis Park, 952-908-3348; Southtown Center, Bloomington; 17436 Kenwood Trail, Lakeville; www.restwellmattress.com
- **Sleep Number Bed by Select Comfort**, 888-411-2188, www.selectcomfort.com; Rosedale, Ridgedale and many other locations.
- **Slumberland Furniture**, www.slumberland.com, has numerous stores throughout the metro. It carries major brands plus their own private label.

LINENS

Department stores, **Bed Bath & Beyond** (www.bedbathandbeyond.com), and **Ikea** (www.ikea.com) can handle all your bath and bedding needs, from the beds themselves to shams and comforters, but if you don't want to spend a bundle, check out **Tuesday Morning** (www.tuesdaymorning.com), which always has some designer linens on sale at closeout prices. And if price isn't an issue, try **F & B Specialty Linen**, 1085 Grand Avenue, St. Paul, 651-602-0844, 800-268-2993, www.fblinen.com, which specializes in fine linens.

FURNITURE AND HOUSEWARES

Gabbert's Furniture and Design Studio (3501 Galleria, Edina, www.gabberts.com) is the gold standard here for furniture and decorative accessories. Shop their Odds and Ends room for high-style bargains; they restock designer floor samples twice a week. **International Market Square** (275 Market St, Minneapolis, www.imsdesigncenter.com) is the local to-the-trade designers' showroom. Go there with a designer or catch the twice-a-year sample sales in April and September. For everyday housewares, **Target** (www.target.com) is always a good choice, as is **Tuesday Morning** (www.tuesdaymorning.com), which sells everything at 50%–80% off. Other local favorites:

- **Becker Furniture**, 13150 First St, Becker (Hwy 10 at Becker between the Twin Cities and St. Cloud), 800-261-4188, www.beckerfurnitureworld.com, is the largest furniture and home furnishings showroom in the Twin Cities. They also sell electronics, cabinetry, flooring, paint, and tile.

- **Cooks of Crocus Hill**, www.cooksofcrocushill.com; 877 Grand Ave, St. Paul, 651-228-1333; 3925 W 50th St, Edina, 952-285-1903; loved by avid cooks—both for its classes and its top-of-the-line cooking equipment. They also sell crop-shares, lamb, eggs, and other top-quality locally produced meats, eggs, fruits and vegetables.
- **Dave's**, 1218 West 96th Street, Bloomington, 952-484-0834, has some of the best deals around. Check the web site for open hours: www.davesfurnitureworld.com.
- **Designer Marketplace**, 160 Glenwood Ave N, Minneapolis, 612-381-8508, www.designermarketplacemn.com, is an outlet for the designers at International Market Square. Every item is marked down at least 50% from retail showroom prices.
- **DESQ/DeZign A Space**, www.desqus.com: 5300 West 35th Street, St. Louis Park, 952-830-1010; sells modular office and home office furniture including wall beds that make even the most cramped space look roomy.
- **Great Finds Designer Home Furnishings Sample Sale**, International Market Square, 275 Market St, Minneapolis, is an annual October event where designers sell one-of-a-kind furnishings, accessories, and rugs at 50–80% off. www.imsdesigncenter.com, www.facebook.com/Greatfinds.
- **IKEA**, 8000 Ikea Way (adjacent to the Mall of America), Bloomington, www.ikea.com
- **Macy's**, 800-BUY MACY, www.macys.com: 700 On the Mall, Minneapolis, 612-375-2200; Southdale, Edina, 952-896-2160; Rosedale, 651-639-2040; offers furniture, mattresses, accessories, and carpeting.
- The **Midwest Home Show**, held in November, attracts around 200 designers, who sell their showroom samples at a high-end flea market every year. Purchase tickets at Cub Foods stores. The Minnesota chapter of the National Kitchen and Bath Association (www.mnstatenkba.org) also participates in this sale. Minneapolis Convention Center, 1301 Second Ave S, Minneapolis, www.midwesthomeshow.com.
- **Odds & Ends Furniture Gallery** is open Thursday–Sunday. It sells close-outs, discontinued pieces, showroom samples, and slightly imperfect furniture at very significant savings; 3740 Louisiana Ave, St. Louis Park, 952-924-1061, www.oddsandendsfurniture.com.
- **Room and Board**, www.roomandboard.com; 7010 France Ave S, Edina, 952-927-8835, sells contemporary and children's furniture. The outlet store, 4680 Olson Memorial Hwy, Golden Valley, is open Saturdays and Sundays only.
- **Rosenthal Furniture**, 22 N 5th St, Minneapolis, 612-332-4363, www.rosenthalfurniture.com, is a warehouse-type showroom full of contemporary furnitures. Its March sales event features huge markdowns.

- **Slumberland Outlet**, www.slumberland.com, sells special purchases, close-outs, and scratch-and-dents. Six metro locations, including 4140 Excelsior Blvd., St. Louis Park.
- **Swank Retro**, 1910 W University Ave, St. Paul, 651-646-5777, www.swankretro. com, dips into the 1950s, '60s, and '70s for its stock of furniture, electronics, kitschy housewares, and textiles. Open Friday–Sunday.
- **USA Baby and Childspace Galleries**, 515 W 77th St (northeast corner of 494 and Lyndale), Richfield, 612-798-0055, www.cpostores.com/usababymn/ index.htm.
- **Williams-Sonoma**, www.williams-sonoma.com; Mall of America, Bloomington; Galleria, Edina; The Shoppes at Arbor Lakes, Maple Grove; Rosedale, Roseville

LAMPS AND LIGHTING

- **Citilights**, 1619 Hennepin Ave, Minneapolis, 612-333-3168, www.citilights. com
- **Creative Lighting**, 1728 Concordia Ave (I-94 at Snelling Ave), St. Paul, 651-647-0111, www.creativelights.com, has the Twin Cities' best selection of lighting fixtures, and runs a great Bargain Room sale every fall.
- **Muska Lighting Center**, 700 Grand Ave, St. Paul, 651-227-8881, www.muska lighting.com

FLOORCOVERINGS

- **American Rug Laundry**, 4222 E Lake St, Minneapolis, 612-721-3331, www. americanruglaundry.com, is the local favorite for rug cleaning.
- **Carpet One Floor and Home**, 907 Hopkins Center and numerous other locations throughout the metro, 952-479-4518, offers nearly next-day installation.
- **Cyrus Carpets**, Galleria, Edina, 952-922-6000, www.cyrusrugs.com, deals in fine artisan rugs.
- **Gabberts**, 3501 Galleria, Edina, 952-927-0725, www.gabberts.com, carries medium to expensive carpeting and Oriental rugs.
- **Kate-Lo Tile and Stone** (www.katelotile.com) sells new and recycled tile, granite mini-slabs, metal accents, in-floor heating systems, stone and porcelain, pottery and glass vessel sinks, and travertine-look furniture: Outlet Center, 701 Berkshire Ln N, Plymouth, 763-545-5455; 3201 W County Rd 42, Burnsville, 952-890-4324; 1358 Helmo Ave N, Oakdale, 651-730-1975
- **Seestedt's Floors To Go**, 282 E 6th St, St. Paul, 651-224-5474, http://saint paul.floorstogo.com

HARDWARE, PAINT, AND WALLPAPER

Hirshfield's (www.hirshfields.com), with numerous stores dispersed throughout the metro, has been the TC's go-to paint and wallpaper store for over a hundred years. Now, of course, even the Big Box retailers such as **Menard's** (www.menards.com) and **Home Depot** (www.homedepot.com) carry paint and match colors as well, but for best quality, you may still want to try a paint and wallpaper specialty store. The same is true for hardware. In addition to many **Ace Hardware** (www.acehardware.com) and **True Value** (www.truevalue.com) stores, the metro has a number of other neighborhood hardware stores that are staffed with seasoned associates capable of giving you all the help you need. Below are some local favorites:

- **Beisswenger's Do It Best Hardware**, 1823 Old Hwy 8, New Brighton, 651-633-1271, www.beisswengers.com, has a small engine repair shop.
- **Frattalone's**, 650 Grand Ave, Saint Paul, 651-292-9800, www.frattallones.com, and many other locations.
- **Guse Hardware**, 4602 Bryant Ave S, Minneapolis, 612-824-7655
- **Mills Fleet Farm**, 8400 Lakeland Ave N, Brooklyn Park; 10250 Lexington Avenue NE, Blaine; 17070 Kenrick Ave, Lakeville; 5635 Hadley Ave N, Oakdale; www.fleetfarm.com (check the White Pages for other locations), is a locally owned small chain that sells hardware, paint, and building materials in addition to housewares, toys, and auto parts. Most stores have auto service centers, car washes, and sell gas.
- **Rockler Woodworking and Hardware Stores**, 800-279-4441, www.rockler.com: 2020 W County Rd 42, Burnsville; 1935 Beam Ave, Maplewood; 12995 Ridgedale Dr, Minnetonka; 3025 Lyndale Ave S, Minneapolis; the Minneapolis store offers classes, some on a walk-in basis.
- **Seven Corners Ace Hardware**, 216 W 7th St, St. Paul, 651-224-4859, www.7corners.com, also repairs power tools.

These two stores are best known for their decorative hardware:
- **The Brass Handle**, 3605 Galleria Mall, Edina, 952-927-7777, www.brass-handle.com
- **Nob Hill Decorative Hardware**, 7630 Wayzata Blvd, Minneapolis, 763-225-8794, www.nobhillhardware.com, is a showroom that special orders from a number of manufacturers.

GARDEN CENTERS AND NURSERIES

One of the biggest problems for any gardener is choosing the right plants for his/her hardiness zone. The Twin Cities metro is in hardiness zone 4a, which means that our average minimum temperature is in the minus 25–30 degrees Fahrenheit range. Unfortunately, summer temps often climb into the 90s (and occasionally over 100), creating a climate that is inhospitable to many popular garden plants. Good advice: start cultivating a fondness for hostas, peonies, shrub roses, and daylilies—four plants that thrive here. Get your gardening questions answered online at the U of M Extension Service, www.extension. umn.edu/gardeninfo or by the **Minnesota State Horticultural Society** (651-643-3601, 800-676-6747, www.norrtherngardener.org). (For more gardening information, see **Gardening** in the **Sports and Recreation** chapter.)

- **Ambergate Gardens**, 8730 County Rd 43, Chaska, 952-443-2248, www.ambergategardens.com, specializes in vigorous, cold-hardy perennials. The Ideas and Advice section of their web site provides all the information you need to grow reliable perennials in this climate.
- **Bachman's**, 612-861-7311, 1-866-222-4626 (phone orders), www.bachmans.com, with locations throughout the Twin Cities, is the longtime go-to garden center for the entire area.
- **Gerten's** is popular with serious gardeners because of their exceptionally well-grown plants; 5500 Blaine Ave, Inver Grove Heights, 651-450-1501.
- **Holasek's**, 8610 Galpin Blvd, Chanhassen, 952-474-6669, http://Holasekgreen houses.com, grows the plants that are sold by many local retail garden stores, but home gardeners can shop their greenhouses, too. Many local groups sell plants grown here for Spring and Christmas fundraisers. They also operate "Great Gardens by Grandma" in the Southwest Metro.
- **Linder's Greenhouse & Garden**, 270 W Larpenteur, St. Paul, 651-488-1927, www.linders.com, is another all-inclusive garden center.
- **Otten Bros. Nursery and Landscaping**, 2350 W Wayzata Blvd, Long Lake, 952-473-5425, www.ottenbros.com
- **Plants and Things USA**, US Hwy 10 & Sunfish Lake Blvd, Anoka, 763-427-4103, www.plantsandthingsusa.com, specializes in lightweight boulders, waterfalls, lawn furniture, etc....and they deliver!
- **Prairie Restorations**, Princeton, Minnesota, 800-837-5986, www.prairi-eresto.com, specializes in installing and maintaining natural landscapes.
- **Sam Kedem Nursery/Town & Country Roses**, 12414 191st St E, Hastings, 651-437-7516, www.kedemroses.com, is famous for roses, vines, and shrubs suitable for our climate.
- **Savory's Gardens**, 5300 Whiting Ave, Edina, 952-941-8755, www.savorys gardens.com; founded by a former president of the Hosta Society, this nursery offers its own hosta introductions in addition to other shade-tolerant plants.
- **University of Minnesota Landscape Arboretum**, 3675 Arboretum Dr, Chaska, 952-443-1400, www.arboretum.umn.edu, is the local expert on winter-hardy plants. Become a member and enjoy unlimited access to "The Arb's" 1000 acres of public gardens and classes that will teach you everything you need to know to be a successful gardener here.

SECOND-HAND SHOPPING

For those of you whose idea of a good deal is something free, check out the **Twin Cities Free Market** (www.twincitiesfreemarket.org), a listing service that allows local residents to get or give away still-useable goods. You'll find appliances, sports equipment, computers, and furniture among the many offerings here, but no live animals, firearms, or cars. Created by St. Paul–based Eureka Recycling, which keeps track of all exchanges, Twin Cities Free Market has kept over 11 million pounds of still-useful items out of the landfills to date—and that's none too trashy!

ARCHITECTURAL SALVAGE AND RESTORATION

- **Art and Architecture**, 3338 University Ave SE, Minneapolis, 612-904-1776, www.artandarch.com
- **Building Materials Outlet, Midwest, Inc.,** 2795 Hwy 55 E, Eagan, 651-454-8840, www.cannonrecovery.com, sells liquidation merchandise, overruns, and extra inventory; most items are at least half off retail.
- **John's Antiques**, 261 7th St W, St. Paul, 651-222-6131, is a good place to look for vintage light fixtures.
- **Lumber Liquidators** advertises that it has the lowest prices on hardwood flooring and will meet competitors' prices; 8901 Hastings St NE, Blaine, 763-784-3440; 2973 Water Tower Place, Chanhassen, 952-314-4975; www.lumberliquidators.com.
- **The Reuse Center**, 2801 21st Ave S (enter and park on 29th St), Minneapolis, 612-724-2608, www.thereusecenter.com, markets high-quality salvaged and green building products and provides living wage jobs for residents of Phillips and surrounding neighborhoods. Because they are called in to dismantle and salvage reusable building materials from many older homes in the area, your chances are good for finding a match for your own old doors here—plus they'll even show you how to hang them in one of their many do-it-yourself classes.
- **Surface Renew**, www.surfacerenew.net, resurfaces bathtubs, wall tile, and kitchen counters; Southwest suburbs, 952-946-1460; North suburbs, 763-253-2300; Minneapolis, 612-869-7242; St. Paul, 651-251-2100.

ANTIQUE SHOPS AND FLEA MARKETS

The Twin Cities' multitude of antique and junk shops tend to be clustered together in places such as West 7th Street in St. Paul, or the cities of Excelsior, Hopkins, Wayzata, Stillwater, and Buffalo. In Minneapolis, venerable dealers are found in the warehouse district along 1st and 3rd Avenues North. The **Decorative Arts Council of the Minneapolis Institute of Arts** also brings in some of the nation's premier dealers for their **Antiques Show and Sale** every October

(612-870-3039, www.artsmia.org). The weekend includes a preview party and lectures and is used as a fundraiser for the Institute. There are also many interesting shops and flea markets to be found off the beaten path. So hitch up the U-haul, and happy hunting!

- **Antiques Riverwalk**, 210 3rd Ave N, Minneapolis, 612-339-9352, www.antiquesriverwalk.net, is home to nearly twenty dealers.
- **Elko Traders Market Antique Show and Flea Market**, www.tradersmarket.us, off I-35 at Elko/New Market exit: Memorial Day, 4th of July, and Labor Day weekends.
- **Medina Flea Market**, in the Medina Ballroom parking lot on Hwy 55 west of Minneapolis, Sunday mornings from 6 a.m. to noon.
- **Osowski's Flea Market**, 1479 127th St NE, Monticello, www.osowskisfleamarket.com, claims to be the state's biggest flea market. It's open Saturdays and Sundays year-round.

GARAGE SALES, THRIFTS, AND VINTAGE SHOPS

If your idea of the perfect Saturday afternoon is spending a few hours poking through tempting tubs of other people's flotsam, then rejoice—you have moved to the right place. The Twin Cities are garage sale heaven, with a season that runs every weekend from April to September. Some swank sales draw thousands of customers year after year, especially the the **Wayzata Community Church Sale** in August (www.wayzatacommunitychurch.org); and the **American Cancer Society World's Largest Garage Sale** in the fall (800-227-2345, www.cancer.org). To find out about these and all the other garage sales in between, look in the papers on Wednesdays and use the ads as a guide to map out your route. Estate sales are also held on weekends, and are often the better place to look for nice furnishings; Edina and Lake Minnetonka are considered the ultimate hunting grounds. Also posh: the **Goodwill** boutiques where they stockpile all the good stuff. Called **Second Debut** (www.goodwilleasterseals.org), they're at 4300 West 36½ Street in St. Louis Park and 1825 University Avenue in St. Paul.

Finally, for those who are looking for a funky outfit, or gently used designer clothing, the vintage and consignment stores included in this list have been vetted by some serious local shoppers, and while it is in no way comprehensive, they say it should get you off to a good start:

- **Andrea's Vintage Bridal**, 723 W 26th St, Minneapolis, 612-716-8006, www.andreasvintagebridal.com
- **ARC Value Village Thrift Stores**, www.arcsvaluevillage.org: 6330 Brooklyn Blvd, Brooklyn Center, 763-503-3534; 6528 Penn Ave S, Richfield, 612-861-9550; 2751 Winnetka Ave N, New Hope, 763-544-0006; 1650 White Bear Ave N, St. Paul, 651-788-8300
- **Blacklist Vintage**, 2 E 27th St, Minneapolis, 612-872-8552, www.blacklistvintage.com, is a retro boutique specializing in 1950s through 1980s clothing and home décor.

- **CostumeRentals**, www.costumerentals.org, a combined project of the Guthrie Theater and The Children's Theatre Company, has an inventory of about 30,000 costumes available for use year-round. 855 E Hennepin Ave, NE, Minneapolis, 612-375-8722.
- **Everyday People**, www.everydaypeopleclothing.com, 2912 Hennepin Ave, Minneapolis, 612-824-3112; 323 14th Ave SE, Minneapolis, 612-623-9095, 1599 Selby Ave, St. Paul, 651-644-4410, has a huge selection of vintage and brand-name consignment clothing.
- **Furnish**, 850 15th Ave NE (in the historic Northrup King Bldg), Minneapolis, 612-789-3322, www.furnishofficeandhome.org, is operated by Project for Pride in Living, a nonprofit whose mission is to help low- and moderate-income people become self-sufficient. They accept donations of high-quality used office equipment and home furnishing from local companies and homeowners, and sell them for 70%–80% off retail.
- **Gage and Gage inventory clearance sale**, 660 Industrial Circle, Shakopee, 952-233-2081, www.gagewarehousesale.com/aboutoursale.html, is the place to shop for 40-90% off retail prices on giftwrap and other paper products. Sales are usually held in April and November.
- **Go Vintage**, 1560 Selby Ave, St. Paul, 651-646-4455, www.govintageshop.com, is the place to shop for everyday fashions as well as really special designer pieces.
- **Hope Chest for Breast Cancer Retail Store** is rich with ritzy items; 3850 Shoreline Dr, Navarre/Orono, 952-471-8700; 571 Snelling Ave N, St. Paul, 651-642-2850; www.hopechest.us.
- **My Sister's Closet**, 2741 Hennepin Ave S, Minneapolis, and 1136 Grand Ave, St. Paul, 651-222-2819, www.mysistersclosetmn.com; twice a year it drops the prices 50% on everything in stock, including vintage and designer consignment items.
- **Nu Look Consignment**, 4956 Penn Ave S, Minneapolis, 612-925-0806, www.nulookconsignment.com, stocks women's, men's, and children's clothing, including designer maternity fashions.
- **Once Upon A Child**, numerous locations throughout the metro, www.onceuponachild.com.
- **Opitz Outlet**, www.opitzoutlet.com, 4320 Excelsior Blvd, St. Louis Park, 952-922-2435, carries designer fashions for women, men, and children.
- **Plato's Closet**, www.platoscloset.com, is strictly for teens; several locations throughout the Twin Cities.
- **Plums Plus Size**, 301 37th Ave NE, Columbia Heights, 763-788-7588, www.plumsplussize.com
- **Rags from Riches**, www.shopragsfromriches.com, 848 E Lake St, Wayzata, 952-473-1435, sells couture women's clothing.
- **Ragstock Clothing**, www.ragstock.com: many locations; is tops with teens and college kids.

- **Saint Paul Retro Loop** is a consortium of five of the best mid-century shops in Minnesota specializing in '50s–'80s housewares, accessories, fashion & design for mod lifestyle. Clustered near each other in Mac-Groveland, they are **Lula** (1587 Selby Ave, 651-644-4110), **Succotash** (781 Raymond Ave), **Up Six** (157 Snelling Ave N, 651-917-0470), **Classic Retro @ Pete's** (2145 University Ave W, 651-224-5235), and **Swank** (1910 University Ave W, 651-646-5777). Look online for a map and more info about each store, www.stpaulretroloop. com.
- **Salvation Army**, www.thesalarmy.com: 900 4th St N, Minneapolis, 612-332-5855, and other locations.
- **SR Harris Fabric Outlet**, www.srharrisfabric.com, 8865 Zealand Ave N, Brooklyn Park, 763-424-3500.
- **Tatters Clothing**, 2928 Lyndale Ave S, Minneapolis, 612-823-5285, http://tattersvintageclothing.com, has men's and women's vintage clothing, as well as new versions of vintage stuff.
- **Turn Style consignment shops**, www.turnstyleconsign.com, sell clothing for the whole family, and some home furnishings; several locations in the Twin Cities including Highland Village Shopping Center, St. Paul, 651-690-3438; Plymouth, Lakeville, Roseville, Linden Hills, and Hudson, WI. Look online for the store nearest you.

FOOD

GROCERIES

`Locally based **Cub Foods** (www.cub.com) and **Rainbow** (www.roundys.com) are warehouse food stores. Their aisles are lined with formidable towers of boxes, cans, and produce, but they also include some ethnic foods and feature highly regarded bakeries and delis. Both are 24-hour enterprises, enabling you to go on late-night shopping sprees. Many of the stores in these chains also offer in-store banking, Western Union money orders, DVD rental, Ticketmaster outlets, full-service pharmacies, and express clinics (see **Health Care** chapter for pharmacies and clinic information). A few Cubs even sell gas and liquor. With nearly 70 Cubs and over 30 Rainbows spread throughout the metro, there is bound to be at least one near you, no matter where you choose to live.

National warehouse stores **Costco** (www.Costco.com) and **Sam's Club** (www.samsclub.com) also have a presence in this market, though you will need to become a member if you want to shop there for anything other than liquor (see **Discount Stores** above).

Up-and-comer **Aldi** (2100 E Lake St, Minneapolis, and 20 other locations, www.aldifoods.com), is another low-cost chain. This group of smaller grocery stores carries a limited assortment of private label products and holds down overhead by charging for shopping bags, requiring a deposit for carts, and not accepting credit cards (they do accept debit cards). Aldi does not publish its phone numbers, so to find an Aldi store near you, check the store locator on their web page. Also expanding in the Twin Cities is **Trader Joe's**, which offers an array of high-quality foods, plus beer and wine, at reasonable prices (4500 Excelsior Boulevard, St. Louis Park; 11220 Wayzata Boulevard, Minnetonka; 12105 Elm Creek Boulevard North, Maple Grove; 484 Lexington Parkway South, St. Paul; 8960 Hudson Road, Woodbury; www.traderjoes.com).

And don't forget **Target**, Minnesota's homegrown retail chain, which has numerous stores throughout the metropolitan area. (See **Discount Stores** above.) Though they have relatively small grocery departments, they, too, boast highly regarded bakeries and delis, and many who shop there praise them for the quality of their produce. The downtown Target is located at 900 Nicollet Mall, and if you spend a certain amount, they will validate parking for you at a nearby ramp. (Check online at www.target.com for other locations.)

For fancier shopping, **Lunds** and **Byerly's** (www.lundsandbyerlys.com), and **Kowalski's** (www.kowalskis.com) are all gourmet supermarket chains that charge premium prices but offer first-rate service, specialty products, restaurants, catering, cooking schools, pharmacies, and wine shops. There isn't much difference between them, though Kowalski's tends to be preferred for some of the local products they carry. Each of these enterprises has stores throughout the metro area. **Jerry's Foods** is also in this category but limits its local stores to Edina and Eden Prairie (9625 Anderson Lakes Parkway, Eden Prairie; 5101 Vernon Avenue South, Edina; www.jerrysfoods.com).

Somewhere in the middle, between the cut-rate and gourmet chains, are the last few remaining neighborhood supermarkets: **Festival Foods** (http://celebrate. festivalfoods.net/), **Rick's Markets** in Navarre and Plymouth, **Coborn's** (www. coborns.com), and **Fresh Seasons** in Minnetonka and Victoria (www.freshseasons. com). **SuperValu**, which owns CUB, is the major food distributor in this area, so no matter where you shop, you're likely to be buying SuperValu's food.

Want to buy your weekly groceries and help others at the same time? Participate in promotions that benefit **Second Harvest Heartland**, the Upper Midwest's largest hunger-relief organization. Second Harvest volunteers pack 35-pound boxes of nutritionally balanced food every month and distribute them at no cost to approximately 10,000 income-eligible pregnant and postpartum women, children up to the age of six, and seniors age 60 and older. You can help by "rounding up" your bill at Cub—the extra will be given to Second Harvest. A number of other businesses—grocery stores, restaurants, garages—participate in other promotions. Volunteers are always welcome, www.2harvest.org.

FOOD CO-OPS AND NATURAL FOODS

Besides offering unsprayed produce and the gamut of "free" foods (wheat-free, free-range, etc.), co-ops sell many foods in bulk, allowing you to buy the exact one tablespoon of celery seed that you need to make your favorite rib rub. Most stores also feature take-out delis offering good-for-you gourmet fare. Co-ops sell shares and distribute dividends to members, and some allow you to volunteer at the store for a discount on groceries. Look online at www.themix. coop for directions to the co-op nearest you. Following are well-known grocery co-ops in the metro area:

- **Eastside Food Co-op**, 2551 Central Ave NE, 612-788-0950, www.eastside food.coop
- **Hampden Park Co-op**, 928 Raymond Ave, St. Paul, 651-646-6686, www. hampdenparkcoop.com
- **Lakewinds Natural Foods**, www.lakewinds.com; Hwy 101 and Minnetonka Blvd, Minnetonka, 952-473-0292; 1917 2nd Ave S, Anoka, 763-427-4340; Chanhassen, 435 Pond Promenade, off Great Plains Blvd, 952-697-3366
- **Linden Hills Co-op**, 2813 W 43rd St, Minneapolis, 612-922-1159, www. lindenhills.coop
- **Mississippi Market**, www.msmarket.coop; 1810 Randolph St, St. Paul, 651-690-0507; 622 Selby Ave, St. Paul, 651-310-9499
- **River Market**, 221 N Main St, Stillwater, 651-439-0366, www.rivermarket. coop
- **Seward Co-op Grocery and Deli**, 2823 E Franklin Ave, Minneapolis, 612-338-2465, www.seward.coop
- **Valley Natural Foods**, 13750 County Rd 11, Burnsville, 952-892-1212, www. valleynaturalfoods.coop
- **Wedge Community Co-op**, 2105 Lyndale Ave S, Minneapolis, 612-871-3993, www.wedge.coop

In a class of their own are Tao Natural Food, Whole Foods, and Traditional Foods of Minnesota. **Tao Foods** (2200 Hennepin Avenue in Minneapolis, 612-377-4630, www.taonaturalfoods.com) is a small shop that combines food and medicine, offering homeopathic remedies, herbal tonics, and a juice bar. **Whole Foods** (3060 Excelsior Boulevard, Minneapolis, and 30 South Fairview Ave, St. Paul, www.wholefoodsmarket.com) is a national chain offering organic and health foods as well as gourmet treats and a bakery. This is not a place to shop for bargains. **Traditional Foods** (302 West 61st Street, Minneapolis, 612-861-0097, www.traditionalfoodsmn.com) is a membership buying club and "real food warehouse" that offers locally produced farm-fresh foods. A lifetime membership costs $75.

MAKE-AND-TAKE MEAL ASSEMBLY

An option that might be more of a bargain than you'd expect is **Make-and-Take meal assembly**, where the store does the prep and all you do is the assembly. Some offer ready-made meals to pick up.

- **Let's Dish**, www.letsdish.net; Apple Valley, Blaine, Eden Prairie, Edina, Maple Grove, St. Paul/Highland, Woodbury
- **Sociale**, 7625 Egan Drive, Savage, 952-447-2300, www.socialegourmet.com, offers meal pick-up at its Savage kitchen and will deliver to Prior Lake, Savage, and Lakeville for a small fee.

FARMERS' MARKETS AND HOME-GROWN PRODUCTS

Corn, raspberries, apples, Christmas trees…nothing beats buying them directly from the growers, and it's easy to do. Seasonal garden produce, flowers, and farm-raised meat are sold at scores of farmers' markets, vegetable stands, orchards, farms throughout the metro area. CSAs (crop shares) are available from most co-ops, or make the connection for yourself. Go to **Minnesota Grown** (www.minnesotagrown.com) for a list of markets, farms, and CSAs closest to your ZIP code.

- **Minneapolis Farmers' Market**, www.mplsfarmersmarket.com: one block south of Hwy 55 on Lyndale Ave N, open daily, 6 a.m.–2 p.m., April 24 to December 24; Nicollet Mall, Thursdays, 6 a.m.–6 p.m., May to November. Winter markets include locally produced fresh meat and eggs.
- **St. Paul's Farmers' Market** has locations in St. Paul and its suburbs. Look online at www.stpaulfarmersmarket.com for locations and hours. The largest market is at Fifth and Wall St, St. Paul, and is open year-round, and includes fresh meat.
- **Midtown Farmers' Market**, Lake Street and 22nd Ave (between the Lake Street/Midtown station of the Hiawatha Light Rail Line and the Midtown YWCA), Minneapolis, www.midtownfarmersmarket.org, is held on Saturday mornings from May to October, and Tuesday afternoons/evenings from July to October. Food stamps and VISA/MasterCard may be used to purchase tokens to use like cash throughout the market.
- **Fresh and Natural Foods** in Plymouth, Shoreview and Hudson, WI, sells locally produced farm-raised meat, www.freshandnaturalfoods.com.
- **Clancey's Meats & Fish**, 4307 Upton Ave S, Minneapolis, 612-926-0222, www.clanceysmeats.com.
- **Grass Roots Gourmet**, 920 E Lake St, Minneapolis, 612-871-6947 (Midtown Global Market), specializes in small-batch products made within a 100-mile radius, www.midtownglobalmarket.org.

COMMUNITY GARDENS

Many neighborhoods have community gardens, particularly in Minneapolis. These are available for free or for a nominal rental fee to people who want to grow vegetables and flowers. Check with your own city for possibilities or contact the **Minnesota State Horticultural Society** (651-643-3601, 800-676-6747, www.northerngardener.org).

HOME DELIVERY

- **Meyer Brothers Dairy/Cass Clay Creamery**, 105 E Lake St, Wayzata, is the last of the original home delivery dairies in the Twin Cities. Started in 1936 by the Meyer Brothers (Bob milked the cows, Cliff bottled, Herb drove the Lake Minnetonka route, and Ted took the Minneapolis route), the company is still going strong—but now offers eggs, juice, meat and deli meats, bakery products, and fruits and vegetables, too. Order online at www.meyerbrosdairy.com, or call customer service at 952-473-7343.
- **Milkman Delivers/Kemps Home Delivery**, 612-627-8709 , www.milkman delivers.com, is a network of independently owned delivery routes that serves most of the metro area. They offer hormone-free dairy products, meat, bread, desserts, juice, and even household cleaning products.
- **Schwan's** has been delivering ice cream and other frozen products to Minnesota homes for over 50 years, Call 888-SCHWANS or order online, www.schwans.com. Their meal kits can be prepared in under 30 minutes, and feature individually wrapped portions.
- **CobornsDelivers**, 763-971-4900, www.cobornsdelivers.com, delivers food and wine throughout the Twin Cities—and to your cabin Up North, as well!

ETHNIC MARKETS

The foods available in the Twin Cities' ethnic markets and restaurants reflect the growing diversity of our state. In Minneapolis, take a walk down "Eat Street," the 17-block stretch of restaurants along Nicollet Avenue north of Lake Street, and you will smell and hear the world. In the same spirit, the Mercado (1515 East Lake Street, www.mercadocentral.net) and Cesar Chavez Street in West St. Paul are centers for the Hispanic community. University Avenue east of Lexington and Rice Street in St. Paul serve that purpose for members of several Asian communities. Other ethnic markets are scattered throughout the Twin Cities. Even though many of the local supermarkets and co-ops offer a selection of foods for ethnic cooking, try some of these below for a more authentic experience—and, remember, in no way is this a complete list:

AFRICAN
- **Afrik Grocery and Halal Meat**, 607 Cedar Ave, Minneapolis
- **Makola African Market**, 31 University Ave, West St. Paul, 651-644-5344

GREEK, MIDDLE EASTERN
- **Abu Nader**, 2095 Como Ave, St. Anthony Park, 651-647-5391
- **Bill's Imported Foods**, 721 W Lake St, Minneapolis, 612-827-2892, www.billsimportedfoods.com

- **Holy Land Bakery & Deli**, 2513 Central Ave NE and 920 E Lake St, Minneapolis, 612-781-2627, www.holylandbrand.com, is possibly our most comprehensive international specialty shop.

INDIAN
- **Patel Grocery and Video**, 1835 Central Ave NE, Minneapolis, 612-789-8800

ITALIAN
- **Broder 's Cucina Italiana**, 2308 W 50th St (50th and Penn), Minneapolis, 612-925-3113, www.broders.com; delivers.
- **Buon Giorno Italia**, 981 Sibley Memorial Hwy, Lilydale, 651-905-1080, www.bgimarket.com
- **Cossetta Eventi**, 211 W 7th St, St. Paul, 651-222-3476, www.cossettaeventi.com; catering.
- **Delmonico's Italian Foods**, 1112 NE Summer St, Minneapolis, 612-331-5466, has been operating in "Nordeast" since most of the people who lived in the neighborhood were Italian immigrants.

LATINO/MEXICAN
- **El Burrito Mercado and Cafeteria**, 175 Cesar Chavez St, St. Paul, 651-227-2192; www.elburritomercado.com
- **Joseph's Mexican & Lebanese Market**, 736 Oakdale Ave, St. Paul, 651-228-9022
- **Cosecha Imports**, 1515 E Lake St (at the corner of Lake and Bloomington), Minneapolis, 612-728-5457, www.midtownglobalmarket.org
- **Marissa's Bakery**, 2750 Nicollet Ave S, 612-871-4519, Minneapolis

ASIAN
- **Dragon Star**, 633 Minnehaha Ave. W, St. Paul, 651-488-2567
- **Phil Oriental Foods**, 789 University Ave W, St. Paul, 651-292-1325
- **Shuang Hur Grocery**, 2710 Nicollet Ave. S, Minneapolis, 612-872-8606
- **United Noodles**, 2015 E 24th St, Minneapolis, 612-721-6677, www.unitednoodles.com, is the largest oriental grocery in the Midwest.

SCANDINAVIAN/RUSSIAN/EASTERN EUROPEAN
- **Ingebretsen's Food and Gifts**, 1601 E Lake St, Minneapolis, 612-612-729-9333, 800-279-9333, www.ingebretsens.com
- **Kramarczuk Sausage Co.**, 215 Hennepin Ave E, Minneapolis, 612-379-3018, www.kramarczuk.com
- **Olsen Fish**, 2115 N 2nd St, Minneapolis, 612-287-0838, www.olsenfish.com, has been processing lutefisk and pickled herring on the north side of Minneapolis since 1910. For those who've never heard of this delicacy, lutefisk is gelatinous lye-soaked cod which Scandinavians eat with copious amounts

of melted butter, especially at Christmas. To order, call their Lutefisk Hotline, 800-882-0212.

- **Taste of Scandinavia**, www.tasteofscandinavia.com, 845 Village Center Dr, North Oaks, 651-482-8285; 2900 Rice St, Little Canada, 651-482-8876; 401 W 98th St, Bloomington, 952-358-7490; both a traditional bakery and a café that serves breakfast, lunch, and dinner.

SPICES

The co-ops sell bulk seasonings, but **Penzeys** carries spices you can't find anywhere else; 674 Grand Ave, St. Paul, 651-224-8448; 3028 Hennepin Avenue, Minneapolis, 612-824-9777; 7626 160th Street West, Lakeville, 952-953-1788; 800-741-7787.

GLUTEN-FREE

Many stores carry gluten-free products. Gluten-free/dairy-free is a little harder to find, but the co-ops have a large selection, as do the Fresh Seasons stores.

- **Madwoman Foods**, 4747 Nicollet Ave S, Minneapolis, 512-825-6680, sells only gluten-free (and many dairy-free, egg-free, corn-free, and vegan) breads, cakes, and pies, as well as cereals, pastas, and packaged meals. Shop online at their web site, www.madwomanfoods.com.

DRINKING WATER

Minneapolis and St. Paul supply municipal water to their residents and some suburbs from surface sources, principally the Mississippi River. Others drink groundwater from municipal or private wells. Increasingly, people here have become concerned about the quality and taste of their water. As a result, sales of bottled drinking water (which may or may not, depending on the supplier, be any better than your own water) have soared. Grocery stores sell bottled water, and there are a number of drinking water delivery services that rent coolers as well. Those who wish to collect their own spring water can do so from a natural spring located at the Richard T. Anderson Conservation Area in the southwest corner of Eden Prairie (18700 Flying Cloud Drive). The following companies provide home delivery:

- **Culligan**, 7165 Boone Ave N, Brooklyn Park, 763-535-4545, www.culligan bottledwater.com
- **Glenwood Inglewood Co.**, 225 Thomas Ave N, Minneapolis, www.glen woodinglewoodwater.com
- **Premium Waters**, 2125 Broadway NE, Minneapolis, 612-379-4141 www. premiumwaters.com

EATING OUT

The Twin Cities has restaurants for every taste, many clustered in the Minneapolis warehouse district and around Uptown. Nicollet from Lake Street North is even called "Eat Street" because of its blocks of ethnic eateries. More rainbows of restaurants line Selby, University, Como, West 7th, and Grand avenues in St. Paul. Look for restaurant listings, plus reviews, online at www.twincities.citysearch.com.

One quick tip: If you're looking for a place to celebrate a special occasion, **La Belle Vie** (510 Groveland, Minneapolis, 612-874-6440, www.labellevie.us) is generally regarded as the best restaurant in the state.

For the best Ju(i)cy Lucy (a Minneapolis-invented cheeseburger where the cheese is inside the meat patty), head to "Food Wars" winner Matt's Bar (3500 Cedar Ave S, http://mattsbar.com), or the 5-8 Club (5800 Cedar, www.5-8club. com).

OTHER SHOPPING

AUTOMOBILES

A list of metro area new car and truck franchise dealerships (with clickable links) can be found on the **Greater Metropolitan Automobile Dealers Association of Minnesota, Inc**. web site (www.gmada.com/). But don't limit your choices to dealerships that are close to home—you may well get a better deal and enhanced customer service from a dealer located on the metro fringe. For more information about shopping for a car, Minnesota laws, and consumer protection, see the **Getting Settled** chapter of this book.

- **AAA**, ww1.aaa.com; besides offering emergency road service and license tab renewal, AAA can help you find a car, negotiate the deal, arrange the financing, and perform the diagnostics and service for the vehicle during the time you own it.
- **Andrews Saab and Subaru**, www.saabpros.com; in Princeton, about an hour northwest of Minneapolis, 763-389-3805, 800-882-7220; Minneapolis/St. Paul Metro Line: 763-633-Saab (763-633-7222); sends trucks to the Cities on a regular schedule to pick up vehicles that need repair or maintenance—and leaves you with a loaner to drive for the day.
- **HourCar car sharing**, www.hourcar.org, is managed by the nonprofit Neighborhood Energy Consortium (NEC) and has car hubs on bus lines in neighborhoods throughout Minneapolis and Saint Paul. Members include individuals, families, and businesses. HourCar offers pay-as-you-go and flat rate plans.
- **U-Pull R Parts Salvage Yard**, www.upullrparts.com: 2875 160th St W, Rosemount, 651-322-1800; 20418 Hwy 65 NE, E Bethel, 763-434-5229, is a self-service auto salvage yard.

- **Victoria AutoHaus**, 1900 W 80th St (Hwy 5), Victoria, 952-443-3000, www. victoriaautohaus.com, handles new, used, imported, and domestic cars, vans, and trucks. They will find the car you're looking for and deliver it.

ART

Artists who live and work in Northeast Minneapolis and Lowertown in St. Paul periodically open their studios for public sales. Keep an eye on the paper for time and details, or check out **Art-A-Whirl** on the Northeast Minneapolis Arts Association's web site (www.nemaa.org) and **St. Paul Art Crawl** at www.stpaulartcrawl.org. The spring **St. Croix Valley Pottery Tour and Sale** is a similar event, except that it's spread out over a 75-mile route northeast of the Twin Cities, along Highway 95, from Stillwater to Cambridge. Check their web site for a map and details (www.minnesotapotters.com). There are also numerous galleries, especially in Uptown, NE, and the Minneapolis warehouse district. And don't forget the art schools. **The Minneapolis College of Art and Design** (612-874-3654, www.mcad.edu) holds a students' art sale early every December, and the **Minnetonka Center for the Arts** (2240 North Shore Drive, Orono, 952-473-7361, www.minnetonkaarts.org) has frequent shows and sales.

ART SUPPLIES AND COSTUMES

- **Artstarts' ArtScraps Creative Materials Reuse Store**, 1459 St. Clair Ave, St. Paul, 651-698-2787, www.artstart.org/reusestore.html, stocks surplus goods and manufacturing scraps, and sells them at starving artist prices.
- **Dick Blick Art Materials**, 2389 Fairview Ave, Roseville; 3867 Gallagher Dr, Edina, www.dickblick.com
- **MCAD Art Cellar**, 2401 Stevens Ave, Minneapolis, 612-874-3775, http://mcadartcellar.blogspot.com; open summer weekdays, regular hours during the school year, selected City Pages'"Best Art Supply" store in 2010.
- **Mosaic on a Stick**, 595 N Snelling, St. Paul, 651-645-6600, www.mosaic onastick.com, is where the serious crafters shop and take classes.
- **Theatrical Costume Company**, 1226 Linden Ave, Minneapolis, 612-339-4144, www.theatricalcostumeco.com, carries thousands of theatrical, costume, and party items.
- **Wet Paint**, 1684 Grand Ave, St. Paul, 651-698-6431, www.wetpaintart.com, was selected City Pages'"Best Art Supply" store several years running.

CHILDREN'S TOYS AND CLOTHING

Superstore children's retailers such as **Toys "R" Us/Babies "R" Us** can be found in the major mall shopping areas throughout the Twin Cities. You won't have trouble seeing them from the freeways, but you can always use their web page store locators to find them (www.toysrus.com, www.babiesrus.com).

Gymboree (www.gymboree.com), a local favorite in new moms' gift registries, also has a number of stores throughout the metro. Finally, **Target**, of course, carries toys and children's clothing and equipment, along with everything else. We are also well-outfitted with many independent children's specialty retailers:

- **Baby Grand**, 1137 Grand Ave, St. Paul, 651-224-4414; 1010 Mainstreet, Hopkins, 952-912-1010; www.babyongrand.com
- **Cribz**, 3545 Galleria, Edina, 952-922-0109
- **Creative Kidstuff**, 1665 West End Blvd and 4313 Upton Ave S, Minneapolis; 1074 Grand Ave, St. Paul; 11647 Fountains Dr, Maple Grove; 7150 Valley Creek Plaza, Woodbury
- **The Glasses Menagerie**, 3142 Hennepin Ave (Uptown), Minneapolis, 612-822-7021, www.Kidseyes.com
- **Lakeshore Learning**, 5699 W 16th St, St. Louis Park; 1721 Beam Ave, Maplewood; www.lakeshorelearning.com; educational toys, arts and crafts supplies.
- **Little Feet Children's Shoes**, 11632 Fountains Dr, Maple Grove, 763-315-0895; Ridge Square North (by Ridgedale), Minnetonka, 952-546-3188; www.littlefeetkids.com
- **Peapods Natural Toys & Baby Care**, 251 Snelling Ave S, St. Paul, 651-695-5559, www.peapods.com
- **Toy World**, Colonial Square, Wayzata, 952-249-1707
- **Von Maur** (see **Department Stores** on page 290.)

MINNESOTA FASHION

- **Voltage** is a runway and rock show held each spring as the highlight of Spring Mnfashion week. This is where local designers debut their warm-weather collections. **Mnfashion** (http://mnfashion.org) is a local nonprofit dedicated to providing resources and professional development to local designers in hopes of creating a thriving fashion industry here.
- **Christopher Straub**, Shakopee's own *Project Runway* contestant, sometimes sells his designs at **Three Rooms** in the Galleria, Edina, http://christopherstraub.myshopify.com.

MUSIC, CDs, AND RECORDS

Local independent record stores sell a variety of music—especially local artists'—which you can't find at the chain stores. Here are just a few:

- **Cheapo**, www.cheapodiscs.com, 1300 W Lake St, Minneapolis, 612-827-8238; 80 N Snelling Ave, 651-644-8981; 170 89th Ave NE, Blaine, 763-574-2308
- **Eclipse Records**, 1922 University Ave, St. Paul, 651-645-7724, is part record store, part concert venue, and part video arcade. It hosts early evening all-ages punk and indie rock shows at least three nights a week, with extra shows when willing touring bands come through town. Check it out online at www.myspace.com/eclipserecords651.

- **Electric Fetus**, 2000 4th Ave S, Minneapolis, 612-870-9300, www.electricfetus. com
- **Tree House Records**, 2557 Lyndale Ave S, Minneapolis, 612-872-7400, http:// treehouserecords.blogspot.com/
- **Urban Lights Music**, 1449 University Ave W, St. Paul, 651-647-9650

MINNESOTA WINES

- **Carlos Creek Winery**, 6693 County Rd 34 NW, Alexandria, 320-846-5443, www.carloscreekwinery.com, makes fruity wines, like Hot Dish Red, and offers dogsled rides to winter visitors. The wine is perfect for serving with casseroles (or hotdishes, as they say here) and leftovers, and the winery is available for rental for weddings and other events.
- **WineHaven Winery and Vineyard**, 9757 292nd St, Chisago City, 651-257-1017, www.winehaven.com; its Slippery Slope Ice Wine, made from grapes that are allowed to freeze on the vines before being picked, was awarded "Best Specialty Wine" in the 2009 International Cold Climate Wine Competition.

WINTERWEAR

In the introduction, we warned you about the winter months and the need for warm clothes. No kidding, even with global warming, winters here are no joke. If you arrived without the right winter gear, the following are a few places where you can get the coats and boots you'll need to stay warm and happy from Thanksgiving to Easter. Don't forget the department stores.

- **Burlington Coat Factory**, www.burlingtoncoatfactory.com; several locations including 3700 S Hwy 100, St. Louis Park, 952-929-6850
- **Hoigaard's**, Miracle Mile Shopping Center, 5425 Excelsior Blvd, St. Louis Park, 952-929-1351, www.hoigaards.com
- **L.L. Bean Catalogue**, 800-441-5713, www.llbean.com; L.L. Bean not only guarantees its merchandise, it also rates it. Buy a 50-below coat and you'll be dancing comfortably on the ice on New Year's Eve.

HARD-TO-FIND GOODS AND SERVICES

- **Angie's List** (www.angieslist.com) advertises itself as a list of plumbers, auto mechanics, painters, etc., recommended by "neighbors," but you still need to check references. There is a fee to join.

FURNITURE RESTORATION AND CONSERVATION

- **American Society of Appraisers**, www.appraisers.org
- **Anthony's Furniture Restoration**, 4553 Bryant Ave S, Minneapolis, 612-824-1717, offers French polishing and cleaning for your fine antiques, as well as refinishing and repair.

- **Minnesota Historical Society**, 651-259-3000, www.mnhs.org, offers workshops on "Preserving Your Treasures."
- **Randy Bohn and Associates**, Hastings, 651-437-1785, specializes in European and early American antique finishes and repair.
- **Upper Midwest Conservation Association**, Minneapolis Institute of Arts, 2400 Third Ave S, Minneapolis, 612-870-3120, www.preserveart.org

SHOE REPAIR

- **Bob's Shoe Repair**, Wayzata Bay Center, Wayzata, 952-473-8248, stays open until 8 p.m.
- **George's Shoe & Skate Repair**, 672½ Grand Ave, St. Paul, 651-227-8258, www.hockeyrepair.com

SHOES FOR HARD-TO-FIT FEET

- **Schuler Shoes**, www.schulershoes.com, Har Mar Mall, Roseville, 651-631-8344, and other locations.
- **Nordstrom**, Mall of America, http://shop.nordstrom.com

HAIR SALONS AND SPAS

> Here is a hairdresser's tip for finding a salon: Look on the web sites of the products you like to use for salons that use those same products.

- **Aveda Institute**, 400 Central Ave SE, Minneapolis, 612-331-1400, www.avedainstitutemn.com/guest_information.html
- **Ficocello's Salons** are in the East Metro, and include a training school at 496 Snelling Ave S, St. Paul, 651-698-7272, www.ficocellos.com.
- **Juut Salonspas** are located in Downtown Minneapolis, Uptown, Edina, Wayzata, Grand Avenue in St. Paul, Wayzata, Woodbury, and Roseville, www.juut.com.
- Edina-based **Regis** hair care company started out nearly 90 years ago as a single salon; today it is worldwide. Salons are located in popular shopping malls across the metro, www.regissalons.com.

Care Cabs for Kids will pick up your child when you cannot, 24-hour Dispatch 1-800-535-7190, 1-320-251-6261, www.caretransportation. com.

DAYCARE

Probably the best way to find a good daycare provider is by referral from someone you know and trust. You'll want to look for daycare centers that are accredited by the **National Academy of Early Childhood Programs** (www. naeyc.org) or the **Minnesota Association for the Education of Young Children** (651-646-8689, www.mnaeyc.org). In addition, various agencies and centers may be helpful:

- **Minnesota Child Care Resource and Referral Network**, www.mnchildcare. org, is a statewide information service, 651-665-0150, 888-291-9811. Call with your ZIP code and they will transfer you to the agency that provides childcare referrals in your area, or use their user-friendly online map. Their listings include nanny services.

- For University of Minnesota–affiliated families, the **University of Minnesota Child Care Center** operates year-round in a state-of-the-art facility on the East Bank, 612-625-2273, www.cehd.umn.edu/childcarecenter.

- In St. Paul, the **University of St. Thomas Child Development Center** at Grand and Finn (651-962-5040, www.stthomas.edu/childdevelopment) accepts infants as young as six weeks. The waiting time is long—one to two years—but you can put your child on the waiting list before he or she is born.

- Another option: **YWCA** (www.ywcampls.org) and **YMCA** (www.ymcatwin cities.org/day-care-child-care) childcare centers. The Y is the largest nonprofit provider of childcare in the United States. They offer before and after school care, school release care, half-day programs for preschoolers, and full-day care for age 6 weeks to kindergarten. A full-time kindergarten program is offered at the **YWCA's Downtown** location, 1130 Nicollet Mall, Minneapolis, 612-215-4189. Check out other locations (which are spread throughout the Twin Cities and even include Hudson, Wisconsin); **YMCA Midway/St. Paul**, 651-646-4557; **YMCA of Minneapolis**, 612-371-8740.

When searching for the best place for your child, be sure to visit prospective providers—and make an appointment. Security-conscious providers should not allow you on their premises unless you have an appointment and can be accompanied by a staff member at all times. In general, look for safety, cleanliness and caring attitudes on the part of the providers. Check that the kitchen, toys, and furniture are clean and safe. Ask for the telephone numbers of other parents who use the service and talk to them. It's a good idea to request a daily schedule—look for both active and quiet time, and age-appropriate activities. In this part of the country, four to five months of the year are spent indoors, so you should ask about active play in the winter.

Keep in mind that being licensed does not necessarily guarantee quality. If you think a licensed provider might be acceptable, be sure to call your county's childcare licensing bureau. They will be glad to tell you if there are any complaints against the provider in their files. The numbers to call are **Hennepin County** (Minneapolis), 612-348-3883, www.co.hennepin.mn.us; **Ramsey County** (St. Paul), 651-266-3779, www.co.ramsey.mn.us; **Washington County**, 651-430-6600, www.co.washington.mn.us. For further information, contact the **Minnesota Department of Human Services**, 651-431-2000, TTY/TDD 800-627-3529, http://www.dhs.state.mn.us.

For drop-in childcare while you go shopping or to a movie, **Clubkid** (www.clubkidfun.com) is a popular choice. It accepts children age 16 months to 10 years at two locations: Edina Centennial Lakes Plaza, 952-831-1055; and Minnetonka Ridge Square North, 952-545-1979. In 2010, rates were $8.50 per hour for a toddler, 16–30 months.

ONLINE RESOURCES

Search for childcare at www.mnchildcare.org. In addition, Minnesota has an online childcare rating tool called **Parent Aware**, www.parentawareratings.org. Use the program's star ratings to help you find the quality of care you're looking for.

NANNIES

In the Twin Cities you can expect to pay at least $600 per week for a live-in nanny, more for a nanny with more experience, and more if housekeeping is expected. **Ramsey County Resources for Childcaring** (651-641-6601, www.resourcesforchildcare.org) provides referrals to nanny agencies. Or look online at **www.nannylocators.com/minnesota.htm**, a web site that connects nannies with families. Local nanny referral services include the following:

- **Nannies from the Heartland**, 5490 Balsam Ln N, Minneapolis, 763-550-0219, www.nanniesheartland.com
- **Nanny Professionals**, 2456 Arkwright St, St. Paul, 651-221-0587, www. nannyprofessionals.com

Minnesota State Southeast Technical College in Red Wing (651-385-6300, 1-877-853-TECH, www.southeastmn.edu) offers an Associate in Applied Science Professional Nanny/Family Child Care degree-granting program. They do not run a placement agency, but contact the school and any interested graduates will call you back. These graduates are much in demand.

Be sure to check all references given to you by applicants. Do-it-yourselfers may visit the **Bureau of Criminal Apprehension**, 1430 Maryland Avenue East, St. Paul, 651-793-2400, www.bca.state.mn.us. A printed copy of a public search costs $4. You may also search online at the **Minnesota Public Criminal History Search**, https://cch.state.mn.us/. This web site contains public data on criminal convictions. Be aware that convictions for driving while intoxicated may not always be reported to the state. To obtain a FULL (public and private) criminal history, you will need notarized informed consent of the subject of your investigation. Instructions are posted on the BCA web site.

If you prefer a professional background check, **Verified Credentials** (952-985-7200, 800-473-4934, www.verifiedcredentials.com) is a Lakeville, Minnesota, firm that specializes in pre-employment screening.

If you are contracting directly with your nanny for his or her services (rather than through an agency), there are certain taxes that will have to be paid, such as social security, Medicare, federal and state unemployment and income taxes. These obligations apply to both full- and part-time in-home workers. You will also need to carry workers' compensation, which you may be able to purchase through either your homeowner's or automobile insurance provider. For assistance call the **Minnesota Department of Labor and Industry**, 651-284-5005, 1-800-DIAL-DLI, www.dli.mn.gov. For more information about nanny-taxes, download *Hiring a Nanny in Minnesota, Your Tax Responsibilities as an Employer* at www.redleafinstitute.org/pdfs/nannymn.pdf. Also check the **HomeWork Solutions** web site, www.4nannytaxes.com. This web site features a free online payroll tax calculator.

AU PAIRS

Au pairs are young adults between the ages of 18 and 26 who provide a year of in-home childcare and light housekeeping in exchange for airfare, room and board, and a small stipend. The program offers a valuable cultural exchange between the host family and the (usually European) au pair, as well as a flexible childcare schedule for parents. The downside is that the program only lasts one year (at most, two), and that an au pair doesn't have the life or work experience of a career nanny. **European Au Pair**, 952-476-4236, 800-333-3804 Ext.2, www.euraupair.com, located in Wayzata, is a U.S. not-for-profit, public benefit organization founded to improve understanding among people of different countries through cultural exchange. It is also one of the oldest au pair organizations in the United States. The weekly stipend to your nanny is fairly small, but there are other fees, typically in the $6,000–$8,500 range. These include application fees, annual program fee (covers liability, life, and medical insurance, training, and an international roundtrip airline ticket), and the cost of a domestic airline ticket.

SCHOOLS

Families moving to Minnesota with school-age children have four choices for their children's education: public schools; private schools; charter schools; and homeschooling.

Public schools, operated by elected school boards and paid for with a combination of state funding and property taxes, must accept any and all students who live within their geographic boundaries. Unlike some other states, Minnesota's districts do not necessarily correspond to city or county lines. Thus Hennepin County (in which Minneapolis is located) has 16 autonomous public school districts, as well as some that offer special shared services. Overall, the state has 417 public school districts, which served 822,412 students in grades K–12 in 2008 (the most recent year for which figures are available). With a long-standing reputation for providing quality education, the public schools offer a variety of programs including magnet schools, language immersion, English as a Second Language, special education, and birth to age 21 services for the disabled. (For more information, see **Public Schools** below.)

Private schools are operated by parent boards and paid for through tuition and fundraising. They are free to set their own standards for admission and decide what sort of program they wish to provide. The Twin Cities' private schools include several nationally acclaimed institutions such as Breck, Blake, and St. Paul Academy. (See **Private Schools** below.)

Charter schools—regarded by proponents as a way for parents to become more involved in their children's education, and by detractors as an interim measure for destroying the public schools—are something of a hybrid. They are paid for with public money, but organized and run by a board of directors composed of teachers, parents, and community members. They are exempt from many regulations relating to public schools, and are free to organize curricula around the needs of the students they intend to serve. Minnesota's 150 charter schools served over 33,000 students in 2008–2009, and include institutions as diverse as the four **Sobriety Highs** (www.sobrietyhigh.org), **High School for Recording Arts** in St. Paul (http://minnesota.hsra.org), and **Minnesota Agricultural and Food Science Academy** in Vadnais Heights (www.agacademy.com).

The **University of Minnesota's Center for School Change** used a multi-million-dollar grant from the Bill and Melinda Gates Foundation to help found several charter schools including the **St. Paul Conservatory for Performing Arts** (www.spcpa.org) and the **Great River School** (www.greatriverschool.org), a St. Paul high school based on the Montessori philosophy.

Curriculum control, teacher choice, and greater opportunity for parental involvement are touted as positive aspects of charter schools; the cons include difficulties with transportation, financial accounting issues, and charges that charter schools take the best students (and a lot of money) away from struggling school districts. For more information, contact the **Minnesota Association of Charter Schools**, 651-789-3090 651-644-0432, www.mncharterschools.org. Consumer tip: Since several charter schools have been forced to close during the school year, primarily because of financial mismanagement, if you are interested in this concept, you might want to look for schools that are overseen by school districts or colleges. They seem to have the best track records, both academically and financially.

Homeschooling is defined as the education of children under the supervision of their parents. Parents wishing to homeschool their children must meet minimum standards, including a bachelor's degree or a passing score on the state's Pre-Professional Skills Test. For further information, contact the **Minnesota Homeschoolers' Alliance**, 612-288-9662, 1-888-346-7622, www.homeschoolers.org. MHA holds Information Stations throughout the year for new homeschooling families and those considering homeschooling. For times and places, look on their web site.

PUBLIC SCHOOLS

Minnesota's public schools face many challenges including rapid growth in districts on the urban fringe, declining enrollments in the inner cities and older suburbs, and the increasing diversity of the student population.

At the same time, years of cuts in state funding have left cash-strapped public schools hustling homeowners for new property tax levies and asking parents to fundraise for program essentials such as books, buses, and heat. And because each student comes with at least some state funding, school districts are advertising to recruit students away from other districts, as well.

It hasn't always been this way.

Prior to 1971, schools in Minnesota were financed solely through property taxes. As a result, there were huge disparities between property-tax–rich and property-tax–poor districts. By 1970, property taxes had risen so high in some places that those on fixed incomes were selling their homes because they couldn't pay the taxes. And even that high level of taxation couldn't make up for the growing inequality between rich and poor communities. Finally, in 1971, the Democratic governor and Republican legislature got together and revised the tax structure, shifting the burden of paying for education away from the localities and onto the state, i.e., away from property taxes and onto income taxes. In that way, they sought to ensure that everyone would receive adequate public services at similar property tax rates throughout the state. This collection of laws became known as the **Minnesota Miracle**. It provided a stable source of funding for more than 30 years until 2002, when a "taxcutting" governor and legislature renounced the Miracle and shifted the burden of paying for schools back toward local residential property taxpayers.

So that's where we stand now. Property taxes are rising—sometimes by astronomical amounts. But since homeowners can only bear so much, school districts have had to put everything on the chopping block. Districts have closed buildings, cut bus transportation, laid off teachers, shortened the length of the school day, cut the number of days kids go to school, and reduced the number of credits required for graduation.

That's the bad news. The good news is that Minnesota's 417 public school districts have fought to save the programs that set them apart, and still offer a wide range of options: year-round programs; magnet schools, Early Childhood Family Education; college credit for high school students; language immersion; adapted athletics; half-day and full-day kindergartens; and extended-day child-care. One notable program is the **Northwest Suburban Integration School District #6078** (www.nws.k12.mn.us), which operates a number of multicultural arts, science, and International Baccalaureate magnet schools in the Northwest Metro area. And, so far, the budget cutting hasn't done away with our public, residential arts high school, the **Perpich Center for Arts Education** in Golden Valley (www.mcae.k12.mn.us). Likewise, the **Fine Arts Interdisciplinary Resource School** (wmep.k12.mn.us/fair) in Crystal and downtown Minneapolis is going strong. Several year-round schools are going strong as well, including **St. Paul's Four Seasons A Plus School** (http://fourseasons.spps.org), **Valley Crossing K–6 Community School** in Woodbury (www.nemetro.k12.mn.us/vccs); **Harambee Community Cultures/Environmental School** in Maplewood (www.emid6067.net/harambee/); and **Crosswinds East Metro Arts and Science Middle School** in Woodbury (www.emid6067.net/Crosswinds).

We also have **Open Enrollment**, so that if the schools in your district don't meet your needs, your children may still be able to attend public school outside the district in which you live. To learn more about the districts you're considering, you may want to try **SchoolMatch**, a firm that maintains a database on public and private schools, including student-teacher ratios, test scores, and per-pupil spending. Order their School Report Card online at www.schoolmatch.com. Please keep in mind, however, that no amount of number crunching can tell you as much about whether a school is right for your child as your own gut feeling when you walk through the door.

That said, if you are determined to try to quantify your school-selection process, there are a few figures that teachers believe really do help to tell a school's story. The turnover rate, the percentage of students who move in or out of the district in any given year, can have a huge effect on a school. Too few new kids and the schools might become cliquish; too many and there may be problems with teachers having to spend most of their time getting new students up to speed. Other figures worth looking at include size of student body, what percentage of students participate in extracurricular activities, and how many of a school's graduates go on to graduate from college or technical school. But, please, don't get too hung up on test scores—they may mean nothing more than that teachers in that school are doing a good job of teaching to the tests. Or, as is often pointed out by administrators, one class of students, such as special education, can make what is deemed to be insufficient progress and cause a whole school to fail.

MAKING YOUR PRESENCE KNOWN IN THE DISTRICT

Even if your oldest child is not yet in school, call your school district's administration office to assure your child's inclusion in the district's database, and to ensure that you will be notified about early childhood screening and kindergarten registration. It will also connect you with the district's **Early Childhood Family Education** (ECFE) services. All school districts provide ECFE programs for infants, preschoolers, and families. These include parent education and support as well as child learning experiences. School districts also provide free **Early Childhood Health Screening** for children ages three and four. This includes a check for vision, hearing, developmental and growth status, and an immunization review.

VISITING A SCHOOL

Most of the literature tells you to compare costs per pupil, graduation rates, and test scores. While these objective measures may support your choice, there really is only one way to choose a school: visit.

When visiting a school, your gut reaction will probably tell you everything you need to know. Ask yourself these questions: Am I comfortable here? Are elementary-age students moving around naturally, but staying on task? What are the halls like in junior high and high schools when classes change? Are students engaged in discussions or projects? Is student work displayed? Ask elementary teachers about reading and math groups and if children move up as they build skills. Find out if there are any special programs offered to assist new students with the transition into a new school. Ask if parents are encouraged to volunteer in the classroom. Finally, look at the facility and equipment. Are the computer labs up-to-date with enough computers? Are instructional materials plentiful and new? Do you see opportunities for your child to do things he/she likes to do—art, music, science, etc.? If all passes muster, then the next step is registering.

SCHOOL REGISTRATION

Register in person at the school your child will attend, and call first to make sure the staff member you need to see will be available. If you are registering a kindergarten student, you will be asked to bring proof of birthday—children need to be five by September 1st in order to enter kindergarten. You don't need to bring anything to register students who are in first grade or higher, but you will be asked to sign a form allowing the district to request records from your child's previous school. Take medical records with you, if possible, because you will have to provide proof of vaccinations at the beginning of the school year.

IMMUNIZATIONS

Minnesota's School Immunization Law requires documentation of students' immunizations before entering school. Requirements vary by grade.

All **kindergartners** must have written proof, either from their doctor or from their parents' records, of the following immunizations: five DTaP/Td/Tdap (diphtheria, pertussis, tetanus); four polio; two MMR (mumps, measles, rubella); two varicella (chickenpox) or history of having the disease; and three Hepatitis B.

All **seventh graders** are required to show proof of a second MMR (measles, mumps, and rubella), Hepatitis B series immunizations, varicella (chickenpox) or history of having the disease, and TD (tetanus booster).

Beginning September 1, 2010, Minnesota schools can no longer accept a parent/guardian's signature as proof that a child has had chickenpox and is therefore exempt from the varicella vaccine requirement. Instead, a health care provider must sign a form stating that the child does not need varicella shot(s) based upon medical verification that the child is indeed immune.

PARENT COMMUNICATION

"Parent portals" are a popular wrinkle in the dialogue between schools and parents. With names like "Schoolview" and "ParentConnect," these computer software programs allow parents to track their children's school attendance, class schedules, assignments, and grades by logging onto a web page or receiving email alerts.

GRADUATION REQUIREMENTS

In order to graduate from high school, Minnesota students are required to complete 21.5 course credits and pass the state's **Graduation-Required Assessments for Diploma** (GRAD) tests. These tests measure student performance on essential skills in writing, reading, and mathematics. Students who do not pass the tests are given opportunities to retake them until they do pass. Most schools offer remediation in the form of test-preparation courses. While first-time tests require both multiple-choice and constructed-response answers, retests require only multiple-choice answers.

STATEWIDE TESTING

Given in April, the **Minnesota Comprehensive Assessments** (MCAs) are part of the **No Child Left Behind** accountability system. Reading and mathematics tests are given in grades 3–8, 10, and 11. Science tests are given in grades 5 and 8 and once in high school, depending on when students complete classes in life sciences.

A snapshot measurement of student achievement, they chart the progress of schools and districts (NOT students) over time in a measurement called **Adequate Yearly Progress** (AYP). Each year schools must increase the number of students who achieve state standards, or make Adequate Yearly Progress (AYP). The goal is that, by 2014, all students in all schools will be able to pass all the tests.

But will they? The **Minnesota State Office of Educational Accountability** ran a computer simulation to see, and came to the disturbing conclusion that "even if there are large, sustained improvements in student achievement (as measured by these tests)," by 2014, every school will be labeled a failing school. That said, new federal initiatives are heading in different directions, and it seems likely that NCLB, itself, may soon be left behind.

Those wishing to learn more about education issues in the state should check out the **League of Women Voters** web site (www.lwvmn.org) for non-partisan information, or **Education Minnesota** (www.educationminnesota.org), for the teachers' view.

QUESTIONS TO ASK ABOUT TESTING AT YOUR CHILD'S SCHOOL

- How has this testing changed the nature of teaching and learning at your school?
- Is this one of the at-risk schools?
- Do your school's test results fairly describe the education that's taking place here?
- How much time is spent practicing test-taking skills and memorizing lists?
- What is being sacrificed to make time for test-prep activities?
- How does your school make use of test results?
- What do you do about students or subgroups of students who consistently score below grade level?

WRITTEN CURRICULUM STANDARDS

The state's written standards are posted online at the Department of Education's web site, http://education.state.mn.us.

ADVANCED PLACEMENT (AP) VS. INTERNATIONAL BACCALAUREATE (IB)

Parents in some school districts have lobbied against the International Baccalaureate program, a demanding curriculum taught at many levels in schools across the metro. The principal charge appears to be the IB curriculum's international focus. Conversely, they characterize Advanced Placement (AP) courses as "homegrown American." Students who have taken both AP and IB courses say they have found nothing "un-American" in the IB curriculum, but that the two programs do constitute very different approaches to advanced work: AP courses move swiftly through a large body of material so that students will be able to do well on the long AP tests; and the IB program moves slowly, exploring topics in depth, with emphasis placed on students conducting their own inquiry, as in science classes, where students conduct their own experiments. The IB program also allows internationally mobile students to transfer from one IB Diploma Program school to another—a real boon to the families of Minnesota's numerous international businesses. For more information, visit the International Baccalaureate Organization's web site, www.ibo.org. For AP information, check with your local school district.

ADAPTED ATHLETICS

In 1992, the Minnesota State High School League became the first association in the nation to sanction interscholastic sports for kids with disabilities. With one division for cognitively impaired athletes (CI) and another for the physically impaired (PI), kids with disabilities have, since that time, been able to earn varsity letters and participate in state tournaments, just like their able-bodied counterparts. Adapted athletics are unlike other sports in that they are usually coed, not organized along school district lines, and players using walkers, wheelchairs, and prosthetic limbs all share the same field or floor. So far, there are four adapted sports—soccer, floor hockey, bowling, and softball. For information contact the Minnesota Adapted Athletics Association (MAAA), http://www.mnadaptedathletics.org. Rules, teams, and schedules can also be found on the Minnesota State High School League web site, www.mshsl.org.

METRO AREA PUBLIC SCHOOLS

This guidebook has usually included fairly detailed information about individual school districts. However, state investment in schools has declined significantly since 2003, and now it's sink or barely stay afloat for many districts. This has meant teacher layoffs, program cutbacks, redrawing of attendance boundaries, and building closures. Some districts have resorted to four-day weeks or cutting the length/number of periods in the school day. In times like these, it is difficult—and probably meaningless—to attempt to provide you with school district descriptions. Our best suggestion is that you decide roughly where you might want to live, then contact nearby school districts and see what you think. Contact information is listed below:

ANOKA-HENNEPIN #11
11299 Hanson Blvd NW

Coon Rapids, MN 55433
763-506-1000
www.anoka.k12.mn.us/
Cities Served: Anoka, Champlin, Dayton, Ramsey, parts of Brooklyn Park, Coon Rapids, and Andover

BLOOMINGTON #271
1350 West 106th St
Bloomington, MN 55431
952-681-6400
www.bloomington.k12.mn.us
Cities Served: Bloomington

BROOKLYN CENTER #286
6500 Humboldt Ave N
Brooklyn Center, MN 55430
763-561-2120 www.brookcntr.k12.mn.us
Cities Served: Brooklyn Center

BUFFALO, HANOVER, MONTROSE #877
214 NE First Ave
Buffalo, MN 55313
763-682-8700
www.bhmschools.org
Cities Served: Buffalo, Hanover, Montrose, and the surrounding townships

BURNSVILLE, EAGAN, SAVAGE #191
100 River Ridge Ct
Burnsville, MN 55337
952-707-2000
www.isd191.org
Cities Served: Portions of Burnsville, Eagan, Savage, Apple Valley and Shakopee

CHASKA/EASTERN CARVER COUNTY #112
11 Peavey Rd
Chaska, MN 55318
952-556-6100
www.district112.org
Cities Served: Carver, Chanhassen, Chaska, and Victoria

CENTENNIAL #12
4707 North Rd
Circle Pines, MN 55014

763-792-6000
www.isd12.org
Cities Served: Blaine, Centerville, Circle Pines, Lexington and Lino Lakes

CHISAGO LAKES #2144
13750 Lake Blvd
Lindstorm, MN 55045
651-213-2000
www.chisagolakes.k12.mn.us
Cities Served: Chisago City, Lindstrom, Taylors Falls

COLUMBIA HEIGHTS #13
1400 49th Ave NE
Columbia Heights, MN 55421
763-528-4500
www.colheights.k12.mn.us
Cities Served: Columbia Heights, Hilltop, parts of Fridley

DELANO #879
700 Elm Ave
Delano, MN 55328
763-972-3365
www.delano.k12.mn.us
Cities Served: Delano, Corcoran, Independence, Loretto, Maple Plain, Medina, Minnetrista, Montrose, Watertown, and parts of Franklin, Rockford, and Woodland townships

EDEN PRAIRIE #272
8100 School Road
Eden Prairie, MN 55344-2292
952-975-7000
www3.edenpr.org
Cities Served: Most of Eden Prairie (some areas along the northern edge of the community are in the Minnetonka and Hopkins school districts)

EDINA #273
5701 Normandale Rd
Edina, MN 55424
952-848-3900
www.edina.k12.mn.us
Cities Served: Edina

ELK RIVER AREA SCHOOL DISTRICT (ERASD) #728
815 Highway 10
Elk River, MN 55330
763-241-3400
www.elkriver.k12.mn.us
Cities Served: Albertville, Dayton, Elk River, Otsego, Ramsey, Rogers, St. Michael, Zimmerman, townships of Big Lake, Baldwin, Burns, Hassan, Livonia, Nowthen, Orrock, and Stanford

FARMINGTON #192
421 Walnut St
Farmington, MN 55024
651-463-5000
www.farmington.k12.mn.us
Cities Served: Farmington

FOREST LAKE #831
6100 N210 St
Forest Lake, MN 55025
651-982-8100
www.forestlake.k12.mn.us
Cities Served: Forest Lake, Marine on St. Croix, Wyoming, Columbus, Linwood, Lino Lakes, New Scandia, East Bethel, Ham Lake, Hugo, Stacy

FRIDLEY #14
6000 W. Moore Lake Dr
Fridley, MN 55432
763-502-5000
www.fridley.k12.mn.us
Cities served: Fridley

HASTINGS #200
1000 W 11th St
Hastings, MN 55033
651-437-6111
www.hastings.k12.mn.us/
Cities Served: Hampton, Hastings, Miesville, New Trier, and Vermillion, and portions of Denmark, Douglas, Hampton, Marshan, Nininger, Ravenna, and Vermillion townships

HOPKINS #270
1001 Highway 7
Hopkins, MN 55305

952-988-4000
www.hopkins.k12.mn.us
Cities Served: Hopkins, Minnetonka, Golden Valley, Eden Prairie, Edina, Plymouth, St. Louis Park

INVER GROVE #199
2990 80th St E
Inver Grove Heights, MN 55076
651-306-7101
www.invergrove.k12.mn.us
Cities Served: Inver Grove Heights

JORDAN #717
500 Sunset Dr
Jordan, MN 55352
952-492-6200
www.jordan.k12.mn.us
Cities Served: Jordan

LAKEVILLE #194
8670 210th St W
Lakeville, MN 55044
952-232-2000
www.isd194.k12.mn.us
Cities Served: Lakeville, a portion of the City of Burnsville, the City of Elko, and Credit River, Eureka, and New Market townships

MAHTOMEDI INDEPENDENT SCHOOL DISTRICT #832
1520 Mahtomedi Ave
Mahtomedi, MN 55115
651-407-2000
www.mahtomedi.k12.mn.us
Cities Served: Dellwood, Mahtomedi, Pine Springs, Willernie, Grant, Hugo, Lake Elmo, Oakdale, and White Bear Lake

MINNEAPOLIS PUBLIC SCHOOLS
807 NE Broadway
Minneapolis, MN 55413
612-668-0000
www.mpls.k12.mn.us
City Served: Minneapolis

MINNETONKA #276
5621 County Rd 101
Minnetonka, MN 55345
952-401-5000
www.minnetonka.k12.mn.us
Cities Served: Minnetonka, Chanhassen, Deephaven, Eden Prairie, Excelsior, Greenwood, Shorewood, Tonka Bay, Victoria, and Woodland

MONTICELLO #882
302 Washington St
Monticello, MN 55362
763-272-2000
www.monticello.k12.mn.us
City Served: Monticello

MOUND WESTONKA PUBLIC SCHOOL DISTRICT
(see Westonka Public School District #277, below)

MOUNDS VIEW #621
350 Highway 96 West
Shoreview, MN 55126
651-621-6000
www.moundsviewschools.org
Cities Served: Arden Hills, Mounds View, New Brighton, North Oaks, Roseville, Shoreview, Vadnais Heights and portions of Spring Lake Park and White Bear Township

NORTH ST. PAUL—MAPLEWOOD—OAKDALE #622
2520 East 12th Ave
North St. Paul, MN 55109
651-748-7622
www.isd622.org
Cities Served: Lake Elmo, Landfall, Maplewood, North St. Paul, Oakdale, Pine Springs, Woodbury

ORONO INDEPENDENT SCHOOL DISTRICT #278
685 Old Crystal Bay Rd N
Orono, MN 55356
952-449-8300
www.orono.k12.mn.us
Cities Served: Independence, Long Lake, Maple Plain, Medina, Minnetonka Beach, Orono

OSSEO AREA SCHOOLS DISTRICT #279
11200 93rd Ave N
Maple Grove, MN 55369
763-391-7000
www.district279.org
Cities Served: Brooklyn Park, Maple Grove, Plymouth, Brooklyn Center, Osseo, Corcoran, Hassan, and Dayton

PERPICH CENTER FOR ARTS EDUCATION
6125 Olson Memorial Hwy
Golden Valley, MN 55422
763-591-4700
www.mcae.k12.mn.us
Cities Served: Statewide

PRIOR LAKE–SAVAGE #719
5300 Westwood Dr SE
Prior Lake, MN 55372
952-226-0000
www.priorlake-savage.k12.mn.us
Cities Served: Prior Lake, Savage,
Credit River Township, Spring Lake Township, Sand Creek Township, Cedar Lake Township

RICHFIELD #280
7001 Harriet Ave S
Richfield, MN 55423
612-798-6000
www.richfield.k12.mn.us
Cities served: Richfield, part of Edina

ROBBINSDALE AREA SCHOOLS #281
4148 Winnetka Ave N
New Hope, MN 55427
763-504-8000
http://rdale.org
Cities Served: Brooklyn Center, Brooklyn Park, Crystal, Golden Valley, New Hope, Plymouth, and Robbinsdale

ROSEMOUNT–APPLE VALLEY–EAGAN #196
3455 153rd St W
Rosemount, MN 55068
651-423-7700

www.district196.org
Cities Served: Rosemount, Apple Valley, Eagan, Burnsville, Coates, Inver Grove Heights, and Lakeville, and rural Empire and Vermillion townships

ROSEVILLE INDEPENDENT SCHOOL DISTRICT #623
1251 West County Rd B2
Roseville, MN 55113
651-635-1600
www.isd623.org
Cities Served: Roseville, Falcon Heights, Little Canada, Lauderdale, Shoreview, Maplewood, and Arden Hills

SHAKOPEE SCHOOL DISTRICT #720
505 South Holmes St
Shakopee, MN 55379
952-496-5000
www.shakopee.k12.mn.us
Cities Served: Shakopee, Savage, Prior Lake and Jackson, Louisville, and Sand Creek

SOUTH ST. PAUL SPECIAL SCHOOL DISTRICT #6
104 5th Ave S
South St. Paul, MN 55075
651-457-9400
www.sspps.org
City Served: South St. Paul

SPRING LAKE PARK #16
1415 81st Avenue NE
Spring Lake, MN 55432
763-786-5570
www.splkpark.k12.mn.us
Cities Served: Spring Lake Park, parts of Fridley, parts of Blaine

ST. ANTHONY–NEW BRIGHTON #282
3303 33rd Ave NE
St. Anthony Village, MN 55418
612-706-1020
www.stanthony.k12.mn.us
Cities Served: New Brighton, St. Anthony Village

ST. LOUIS PARK #283
6425 West 33rd St

St. Louis Park, MN 54426
952-928-6000
http://rschooltoday.com/se3bin/clientschool.cgi?schoolname=school468
City Served: St. Louis Park

ST. PAUL #625
360 Colborne Ave
St. Paul, MN 55102
651-767-8100
www.spps.org
Cities Served: St. Paul

SOUTH WASHINGTON COUNTY SCHOOLS #833
7362 East Point Douglas Rd S
Cottage Grove, MN 55016
651-458-6300
www.sowashco.k12.mn.us
Cities Served: Cottage Grove, St. Paul Park, Newport, Woodbury, Afton, and
Denmark

STILLWATER AREA SCHOOL DISTRICT #834
1875 South Greeley St
Stillwater, MN 55082
651-351-8340
www.stillwater.k12.mn.us/
Cities Served: Afton, Bayport, Baytown Township, Grant, a portion of Hugo, Lake
Elmo, Lakeland, Lakeland Shores, Lake St. Croix Beach, Marine on St. Croix, May
Township, Oak Park Heights, St. Mary's Point, Stillwater, Stillwater Township,
West Lakeland Township, Withrow, and a portion of Woodbury

WACONIA PUBLIC SCHOOLS #110
512 Industrial Blvd
Waconia, MN 55387
952-442-0600
www.waconia.k12.mn.us
Cities Served: Waconia, St. Bonifacius, New Germany

WAYZATA #284
210 County Rd 101 N
Wayzata, MN 55391
763-745-5000
www.wayzata.k12.mn.us/wps

Cities Served: Corcoran, Maple Grove, Medicine Lake, Medina, Minnetonka, Orono, Plymouth, and Wayzata

WEST ST. PAUL, MENDOTA HEIGHTS, EAGAN #197
1897 Delaware Ave
Mendota Heights, MN 55118
651-403-7010
www.isd197.org
Cities Served: West St. Paul, Mendota Heights, Eagan, Inver Grove Heights, Lilydale, Mendota, Sunfish Lake

WESTONKA PUBLIC SCHOOL DISTRICT #277
5901 Sunnyfield Rd E
Minnetrista, MN 55364
952-491-8000
www.westonka.k12.mn.us
Cities Served: Mound, Minnetrista, Spring Park, Shorewood, Lyndale, Navarre, Independence, Orono

WHITE BEAR LAKE AREA SCHOOLS #624
4855 Bloom Ave
White Bear Lake, MN 55110
651-407-7500
www.whitebear.k12.mn.us
Cities Served: Birchwood, Gem Lake, Hugo, Lino lakes, Little Canada, Mapalewood, North Oaks, Vadnais Heights, White Bear Lake, White Bear Township

WRIGHT COUNTY SCHOOLS
District 876: Annandale, Clearwater, South Haven, Silver Creek; www.annandale.k12.mn.us
District 877: Buffalo-Hanover-Montrose; www.bhmschools.org
District 466: Cokato, Dassel; www.dc.k12.mn.us
District 879: Delano; www.delano.k12.mn.us
District 2687: Howard Lake, Waverly, Winsted; www.hlww.k12.mn.us
District 885: St. Michael, Albertville; www.stma.k12.mn.us
District 881: Maple Lake; www.maplelake.k12.mn.us
District 882: Monticello; www.monticello.k12.mn.us
District 728: Elk River Area Schools; www.elkriver.k12.mn.us District 883: Rockford; www.rockford.k12.mn.us

INTERDISTRICT SCHOOLS
Intermediate District #287, www.district287.org, is a consortium district, serving about 10,000 special needs students in more than 100 districts

throughout the state. Most of its services are directed toward a crescent of west suburban districts stretching from Bloomington in the south to Brooklyn Center in the north. While it serves special education students and 500 to 600 alternative learning students, who can't function in a regular school environment, it also offers foreign languages and programs for gifted and talented students.

Northwest Suburban Integration School District #6078, www.nws.k12.mn.us, was created in 2001 in response to Minnesota's Desegregation Rule. The NWSISD includes the districts of Anoka-Hennepin, Brooklyn Center, Buffalo, Elk River, Fridley, Osseo and Rockford, and helps them to work together to create a voluntary desegregation plan.

West Metro Education Program, District #6069 (612-752-7201, www.wmep.k12.mn.us), is a joint powers school district consortium of western metro districts: Brooklyn Center, Columbia Heights, Eden Prairie, Edina, Hopkins, Minneapolis, Richfield, Robbinsdale, St. Anthony/New Brighton, St. Louis Park, and Wayzata. It operates two schools, **Fine Arts Interdisciplinary Resource (FAIR) School** Downtown at 10 South 10th St, Minneapolis (612-752-7100); and **Fair School Crystal**, 3915 Adair Ave N, Crystal (763-971-4500). The district's mission is to eliminate the racial achievement gap.

WESTERN WISCONSIN SCHOOLS

Like Minnesota, Wisconsin has a set of state academic standards for public education; however, the state standards are voluntary. Read them on the Wisconsin Department of Public Instruction's web site at www.dpi.state.wi.us/standards.

SCHOOL DISTRICT OF HUDSON
644 Brakke Dr
Hudson, WI 54016
715-386-4900
www.hudson.k12.wi.us

SCHOOL DISTRICT OF RIVER FALLS
852 E Division St
River Falls, WI 54022
715-425-1800
www.rfsd.k12.wi.us

SCHOOL DISTRICT OF SOMERSET
645 Sunrise Dr
Somerset, WI 54025
715-247-3313
www.somerset.k12.wi.us

PRIVATE SCHOOLS

The metropolitan area is home to many excellent private and parochial schools, most of them located in Hennepin and Ramsey counties. Here are just a few of the best known. For information about all of them, including Montessori schools, check out Private School Review, www.privateschoolreview.com.

BLAKE
110 Blake Rd
Hopkins
952-988-3420
www.blakeschool.org

BENILDE–ST. MARGARET'S (BSM)
2501 Hwy 100 S
St. Louis Park
952-927-4176
www.bsm-online.org

BRECK
123 Ottawa Ave N
Golden Valley
763-381-8100
www.breckschool.org

INTERNATIONAL SCHOOL OF MINNESOTA (ISM)
6385 Beach Rd
Eden Prairie
952-918-1800
www.ism-sabis.net

MINNEAPOLIS JEWISH DAY SCHOOL
4330 Cedar Lake Rd S
St. Louis Park
952-381-3500
www.mjds.net

ST. PAUL ACADEMY AND SUMMIT SCHOOL
1150 Goodrich Ave (Grades K–5), 651-696-1560
1712 Randolph Ave (Grades 6–12), 651-698-2451
St. Paul
www.spa.edu

THE TWIN CITIES METROPOLITAN AREA IS HOME TO OVER A DOZEN colleges and universities, and an equal number of technical schools. Oldest among them is **Hamline**, founded in 1854. The land grant **University of Minnesota** followed soon after. Five of the colleges, Hamline, Macalester, Augsburg, University of St. Thomas, and The College of St. Catherine, have joined together to form the **Associated Colleges of the Twin Cities** (ACTC) (www.associatedcolleges-tc.org). Students at these schools may sign up for courses at any of the ACTC campuses, and parents whose children are enrolled in some of these schools may audit courses there for free.

REDUCED OUT-OF-STATE TUITION OPTIONS

Minnesota has agreements with several neighboring states to provide lower tuition for Minnesota residents who attend public colleges and universities in those states. Called **tuition reciprocity**, the agreements cover **Wisconsin, North Dakota**, and **South Dakota**. The state also has an agreement with the Canadian province of **Manitoba**, and a limited agreement with **Iowa Lakes Community College** in Iowa. Students wishing to apply for tuition reciprocity can get started online at the **Minnesota Office of Higher Education**'s webpage, www.getreadyforcollege.org. State students wishing to attend colleges in Indiana, Kansas, Michigan, Missouri, Nebraska, North Dakota, and Wisconsin may also be eligible for tuition reductions through the **Midwestern Higher Education Compact Student Exchange Program** (612-626-8288 www.mhec. org/MidwestStudentExchangeProgram).

Those interested in attending a public Minnesota college should visit **the Minnesota State Colleges and Universities**' (MnSCU) web page (www. mnscu.edu). It has links to campus profiles, a searchable program index, and transfer and financial information; you can also call them at 651-296-8012, 888-667-2848, or TTY 651-282-2660. The **Minnesota Private Colleges**' homepage (www.mnprivatecolleges.org) has links to 17 private, four-year liberal arts colleges as well as financial and admissions information. (Newsflash! Our own **Minneapolis College of Art and Design, Hamline, Carleton**, and **Macalester** are consistently ranked among the nation's best colleges!)

For those who can't get away to take classes, **Minnesota Online** (www.mnonline.org) makes it possible for you to access over 1500 online courses from the state's 25 two-year public colleges and seven public universities.

Finally, many people have graduated from high school and immediately started to work, finding it impossible to attend any of the state's four-year degree-granting colleges or universities. For them, the two-year community college system is starting to offer some four-year degree programs. Near the metro, **Anoka-Ramsey Community College** (www.an.cc.mn.us) offers four-year degree programs in education, nursing, business administration, and psychology and counseling. Check the **Minnesota State Colleges and Universities System** web site (www.mnscu.edu) for information about this and other community college programs.

TWIN CITIES UNIVERSITIES AND COLLEGES

- **Augsburg College**, 2211 Riverside Ave, Minneapolis 55454, 612-330-1001 (Admissions), 800-788-5678, www.augsburg.edu; known for its ability to work with special needs students, it also offers non-traditional adult education programs, where adult students can earn a college degree or develop a job-related skill. Enrollment: about 3,000.
- **Bethel University**, 3900 Bethel Dr, Arden Hills 55112; 651-638-6400, 800-255-8706, www.bethel.edu; a four-year, liberal arts Christian college located about 15 minutes from downtown St. Paul and Minneapolis. Enrollment: about 3000.
- **Concordia University-St. Paul**, 275 N Syndicate St, St. Paul, 55104; 651-641-8230, 800-333-4705, www.csp.edu; a private, Lutheran, liberal arts college. Enrollment: about 1700.
- **Dunwoody College of Technology**, 818 Dunwoody Blvd, Minneapolis 55403-1192; 612-374-5800, 800-292-4625, www.dunwoody.edu; one of the top technical schools in the US in automotive, electronics, and tool and die manufacturing.
- **Hamline University**, 1536 Hewitt Ave, St. Paul 55104; 651-523-2207, 800-753-9753, www.hamline.edu; a nationally recognized coeducational Methodist liberal arts college with a School of Law and several graduate programs. Enrollment: undergraduate, 2000; graduate, 1300.
- **Hennepin Technical College**, 952-995-1300, 9000 Brooklyn Blvd, Brooklyn Park 55445; 13100 College View Dr, Eden Prairie 55347; www.hennepintech.edu; educating people for careers that do not require a baccalaureate degree for entry, such as computer science and nursing. Enrollment: over 8,300.

- **Macalester College**, 1600 Grand Ave, St. Paul 55105; 651-696-6357, 800-231-7974, www.macalester.edu; has a reputation for producing dedicated social activists. Enrollment: about 2000.
- **Metropolitan State University**, 730 Hennepin Ave, Minneapolis; 700 7th St E, St. Paul; www.metrostate.edu; offers vocationally oriented bachelor's degrees. Enrollment: about 10,000. Register through their online catalogue.
- **Minneapolis College of Art and Design**, 2501 Stevens Ave S, Minneapolis 55404, 612-874-3760, 800-874-6223, www.mcad.edu; located adjacent to the Minneapolis Institute of Art, this four-year private liberal arts college is one of the top art schools in the country. Enrollment: approximately 750.
- **Minneapolis Community and Technical College** (MCTC), 1501 Hennepin Ave, Minneapolis 55403; 612-659-6200, 800-247-0911, TTY 612-659-6731, www.minneapolis.edu; a non-residential two-year community college located near downtown by Loring Park. Its motto is, "If you don't chase your dreams, who will?" This is the most ethnically diverse campus in the state, with a large English as a Second Language (ESL) program and state-of-the-art technical equipment. Enrollment: 10,500.
- **Normandale Community College**, 9700 France Ave S, Bloomington 55431, 952-487-8201, 866-880-8740, TTY 952-487-7032, www.normandale.edu; offers 2-year associate degrees; its engineering and health sciences departments, in particular, are highly regarded by graduates who started there and continued to higher degrees in other institutions. Enrollment: over 13,000.
- **St. Catherine University**, 2004 Randolph Ave, St. Paul, 55105; 651-690-8850, 800-656-KATE, www.stkate.edu; this Catholic liberal arts college for women admits men to its master's programs and its two-year campus in Minneapolis. Enrollment: about 3600.
- **University of Minnesota**, Washington Ave at E River Rd, Minneapolis; Como Ave at Cleveland Ave, St. Paul, 612-625-5000, www1.umn.edu/twincities/; "the U" Twin Cities campus has a student body of over 65,000, making it the second-largest campus in the nation behind Arizona State. One of the top universities in the country, it is highly regarded as a major research institution, particularly with respect to agriculture, business, medicine, and public service. The heart-lung machine, cardiac pacemaker, flight recorder (black box) for aircraft, and retractable seat belt for cars were all invented by University researchers. It is also the world's leading kidney transplant center. It has four additional campuses—Crookston, Duluth, Morris, and Rochester.
- **University of St. Thomas**, 2115 Summit Ave, St. Paul 55105; 651-962-6150, 800-328-6819, www.stthomas.edu; the largest private school in Minnesota, this coeducational Catholic university has satellite campuses in Anoka, Chaska, Mall of America, Woodbury, Owatonna, Rochester, Downtown Minneapolis. Enrollment: approximately 11,000.
- **William Mitchell College of Law**, 875 Summit Ave, St. Paul 55105; 651-227-9171, 888-962-5529, www.wmitchell.edu; founded in 1900, this 1100-student

private law school set among the mansions of Summit Ave boasts two Chief Justices among its alumni. Entering classes of about 375.

NEARBY COLLEGES

- **Carleton College**, 100 S College St, Northfield, 55057; 507-222-4190, 800-995-2275, www.carleton.edu; regarded as one of the country's best small liberal arts colleges. Enrollment: 1936.
- **College of Saint Benedict** and **St. John's University**, P.O. Box 7155, Collegeville 56321, 320-363-5308, 800-544-1489, www.csbsju.edu; "St. Ben's" is a Catholic four-year liberal arts college for women. It shares a common undergraduate curriculum, identical degree requirements, and a single academic calendar with neighboring St. John's University, a Catholic school for men. Enrollment: 4000.
- **Gustavus Adolphus College**, 800 W College Ave, St. Peter 56082; 507-933-7676, 800-GUSTAVU(S), www.gustavus.edu; this private, residential liberal arts college of Swedish heritage is located in a small town about an hour and a half from the Twin Cities. Enrollment: about 2500.
- **St. Olaf College**, 1520 St. Olaf Ave, Northfield 55057; 507-786-3025, 800-800-3025, www.stolaf.edu; a four-year, coeducational, residential, Lutheran liberal arts college with a beautiful campus and nationally recognized music and mathematics programs. The St. Olaf College Christmas Festival is the hottest holiday ticket in Minnesota. Check it out online at www.stolaf.edu/christmasfest. Enrollment: about 3000.

Other notable institutions:

- **Century College**, 3300 Century Ave N, White Bear Lake, 651-773-1700, www.century.edu
- **College of St. Scholastica**, Duluth, 800-249-6412, www.css.edu
- **College of Visual Arts**, St. Paul, 651-757-4000, www.cva.edu
- **Concordia College**, Moorhead, 800-699-9897, www.concordiacollege.edu
- **Minnesota State University–Mankato**, 507-389-1822, www.mnsu.edu
- **Minnesota State University–Moorhead**, 800-593-7246, www.go.mnstate.edu
- **Southwest Minnesota State University**, Marshall, 800-642-0684, www.smsu.edu
- **St. Cloud State University**, St. Cloud, 877-654-7278, www.stcloudstate.edu
- **St. Mary's University of Minnesota**, Winona, 800-635-5987, www.smumn.edu
- **Winona State University**, Winona, 800-342-5978, www.winona.edu

AREA COMMUNITY COLLEGES

- **Anoka Technical College**, Anoka, 763-576-4850, www.anokatech.edu

- **Anoka-Ramsey Community College**, Coon Rapids, Cambridge, 763-422-1100, www.anokaramsey.edu; offers two- and four-year degree programs and some graduate-level classes.
- **Dakota County Technical College**, Rosemount, 651-423-8000, www.dctc.edu, offers the nation's only wood-finishing technology program.
- **Inver Hills Community College**, Inver Grove Heights, 651-450-8500, www.inverhills.edu
- **North Hennepin Community College**, Brooklyn Park, 763-424-0702, www.nhcc.edu
- **St. Paul College**, St. Paul 651-846-1600, www.saintpaul.edu

A S RECENTLY AS 2003, MINNESOTA WAS THE STATE WITH THE HIGHEST percentage of residents with some kind of health care coverage— nearly 90%. Following the recession—and a number of state budget cuts that hit public health programs particularly hard—that is no longer the case. On paper, though, we still look pretty good. We *are* home to the world-famous **Mayo Clinic**, and we do have the longest life expectancy in the contiguous U.S. According to a 2009 Harvard study, our life expectancy is 81.8 years for females and 76.2 years for males, substantially more than the rest of the country, except for Hawaii. That's thanks to our good genes, a low prevalence of smokers, and excellent access to primary care doctors who are experts at delivering preventive care.

After all, Health Care is our biggest industry.

That doesn't mean that acquiring good, affordable health coverage is any less of a challenge here than it is in other parts of the country. Hopefully, health care reform will change that, but in the meantime, some local providers have come up with their own versions of lower-cost health care reform. These end-runs around the insurance companies range from neighborhood clinics such as **Central Clinic**, in northeast Minneapolis, which charges according to a sliding-scale fee, to **Dr. Sam**, an artist/physician who sells low-cost monthly memberships to his practice. Another benefit of seeing this particular doctor—if you need to wait, you can spend your time browsing the exhibits in the doctor's Conduit art gallery next door, http://conduitgallerympls.com (Dr. Sam Willis, 1300 Quincy Street NE, Suite 100, Minneapolis, 612-353-4034, http://doctorsam.us).

HEALTH CARE PLANS

PRIVATE HEALTH INSURANCE PROVIDERS

Insurance providers such as **Medica** (www.medica.com), **Blue Cross and Blue Shield** (www.bluecrossmn.com), and **HealthPartners** (www.healthpartners.

com) offer scores of insurance plans with innumerable variations with respect to premiums, deductibles and benefits. The choices are all very confusing, and if you have to purchase your own insurance, you might want to work with a broker who can cut through the jargon and find the best plan for you. But if you work for a company that offers health coverage, your employer will undoubtedly present you with a limited list of options, usually organized around networks of clinics and hospitals. But how do you know which network to choose?

You can compare hospitals, physicians, medical groups, and health plans at **www.minnesotahealthinfo.org**, a web site created by the state to help consumers understand options, costs, and quality. Click on "Adverse Health Events in Minnesota," for annual hospital-level statistics on how many patients died in each facility because of wrong care, how many foreign bodies were left in patients after surgery, and so forth. You can also do a quality check on hospitals and clinics by name or ZIP code through the **Joint Commission on Accreditation of Healthcare Organizations** web site (www.jcaho.org).

Finding objective information about physicians is infinitely harder, but **Health Grades** (www.healthgrades.com) does rate hospitals, nursing homes, and doctors. You can research a doctor by name and find out his or her board certifications, education, training, and disciplinary actions, but not malpractice suits.

Of course, where choosing a physician is concerned, there is no substitute for word of mouth. Lacking that, however, the **Neighborhood Health Care Network** (651-489-CARE, 866-489-4899 toll-free outside the metro area, or www.nhcn.org) provides medical and dental referrals. Or buy the **Mpls/StPaul Magazine**'s annual special issue that lists the top docs in the Twin Cities (www.mspmag.com). Their information is usually pretty good. The trouble is that the physicians you find most interesting may not be part of your own provider network—which brings us to information about insurers and provider networks.

But first two words of warning:

If you're young and healthy, have no known health conditions, no family—and don't expect to start one any time soon—the most cost-effective provider might be just fine for you. However, if you have—or plan to start—a family, you may want to think twice before cutting yourself off from high-quality specialty providers such as the Children's Hospitals, with their neonatal intensive care and child-friendly surgical departments.

Beware of "health discount plans." The average annual premium for family coverage in Minnesota hit an unaffordable $14,498 in 2009, so numerous companies have begun offering low-cost health discount plans to those priced out of the market. However, health discount plans are not insurance policies and do not provide insurance protection or coverage; all they really do is purport to offer discounts from the retail price charged by certain doctors and clinics. They do not cover claims or pay doctors, and are not licensed or regulated by the State of Minnesota.

To check out an insurance company you're unsure of, contact the **Minnesota Department of Commerce**, 651-296-2135, www.commerce.state.mn.us.

SERVICE PLANS

The following provide services to the majority of Minnesota residents:

- **Allina Hospitals and Clinics**, 2925 Chicago Ave, Minneapolis, 612-262-5000, www.allina.com, has 12 clinics in the Northwest Metro and owns Abbott Northwestern, Mercy, Unity, and United hospitals, Phillips Eye Institute, and Sister Kenny Rehabilitation Institute.

> Allina's Sister Kenny Rehabilitation Institute has a Performing Artists Clinic for treating injuries related to music practice and performance.

- **Blue Cross and Blue Shield of Minnesota**, 3535 Blue Cross Rd, Eagan, 651-662-8000, 1-800-382-2000, TDD 1-888-878-0137, www.bluecrossmn.com; offers numerous insurance plans including short-term (30-, 60-, 90-day) coverage.
- **Cigna**, www.cigna.com
- **Fairview Health Services**, www.fairview.org, has 8 hospitals and numerous clinics throughout the metro area.
- **HealthPartners**, www.healthpartners.com, operates a network of 25 medical and dental clinics, and accepts most major insurance plans. It owns Regions Hospital and a large specialty center in St. Paul, and has affiliations with Abbott Northwestern, North Memorial, St. John's, Fairview Ridges, Fairview-University, Children's, Mercy, and several hospitals in Wisconsin.
- **Mayo Clinic**, Rochester, 507-284-2511, www.mayo.edu, offers a full range of health services through a network of community-based providers, primarily in southern Minnesota; check out your health concerns on their web page.
- **Medica Health Plans**, www.medica.com; 96% of Minnesota's health care providers participate in this network.
- **Metropolitan Health Plan**, 612-348-3000, www.mhp4life.org, is Hennepin County's licensed HMO. It provides care through Hennepin County Medical Center and a number of community clinics.
- **Patient Choice**, www.patientchoicehealthcare.com, offers what it terms "value-based purchasing programs," to self-funded employers in Minnesota and the Dakotas.
- **UCare Minnesota**, www.ucare.org, administers Medical Assistance and MinnesotaCare, and offers plans for seniors, and adults who have physical disabilities.
- **UnitedHealth**, www.unitedhealthgroup.com

COMPLAINTS

If you have a health care concern or complaint, contact the **Minnesota Attorney General's Office Consumer Division** (1400 Bremer Tower, 445 Minnesota Street, St. Paul, MN 55101, 651-296-3353, TTY 651-297-7206, www. ag.state.mn.us).

PUBLIC HEALTH CARE ASSISTANCE PROGRAMS

In addition to private health insurance, government plans cover some people. The plans are described in detail at **www.dhs.state.mn.us**. Here is a brief overview:

- **Medical Assistance** pays for medical care for low-income senior citizens, children and families, and people with disabilities. For information, contact your county Health and Human Services department.
- **Medicare** is the federal government's health insurance program for people 65 and older and qualified disabled individuals of any age, www.medicare. gov.
- **MinnesotaCare** (MNCare) is a minimal subsidized insurance program for Minnesotans who do not have access to other health care insurance, www. dhs.state.mn.us.
- **Minnesota RxConnect Online** helps people find affordable drugs, 1-800-333-2433, www.mnaging.org.

AREA HOSPITALS AND SPECIALTY CLINICS

The **Minnesota Board on Aging**'s web site (www.mnaging.org) includes a downloadable copy of a Minnesota-legal "Health Care Directive." Having one in hand is a good idea for anyone who's heading for the hospital.

Below is a list of TC-area hospitals and specialty clinics, all in Minnesota unless otherwise noted:

- **Abbott Northwestern Hospital** (Allina), 800 E 28th St, Minneapolis 55407, 612-863-4000, www.abbottnorthwestern.com
- **Bethesda Rehabilitation Hospital** (Health East), 559 Capitol Blvd, St. Paul 55103, 651-232-2000, www.healtheast.org/bethesda.html
- **Buffalo Hospital** (Allina), 303 Catlin St, Buffalo 55313, 763-682-1212, www. buffalohospital.org
- **Cambridge Medical Center** (Allina), 701 S Dellwood St, Cambridge 55008, 763-689-7700, www.cambridgemedicalcenter.com
- **Children's Hospitals and Clinics of Minnesota**, 2525 Chicago Ave S, Minneapolis 55404, 612-813-6100, www.childrenshc.org
- **Children's Hospitals and Clinics of Minnesota—St. Paul**, 345 N Smith Ave, St. Paul 55102, 651-220-6000, www.childrenshc.org

- **Fairview Northland Regional Hospital and Clinic**, 911 Northland Dr, Prince ton 55371, 763-389-1313, www.fairview.org
- **Fairview Ridges Hospital**, 201 E Nicollet Blvd, Burnsville 55337, 952-892-2000, www.fairview.org
- **Fairview Southdale Hospital**, 6401 France Ave S, Edina 55435, 952-924-5000, www.fairview.org
- **Fairview-University Medical Center**, 2450 Riverside Ave, Minneapolis 55455, 612-273-3000, www.fairview.org
- **Gillette Children's Specialty Healthcare**, 200 E University Ave, St. Paul 55101, 651-291-2848, www.gillettechildrens.org
- **Hennepin County Medical Center**, 701 Park Ave, Minneapolis 55415, 612-873-3000, www.hcmc.org, is our Level 1 Trauma Center.
- **Hudson Hospital**, 405 Stageline Rd, Hudson, WI 54016, 715-531-6000, www.hudsonhospital.org
- **Lakeview Memorial Hospital**, 927 W Churchill St, Stillwater 55082, 651-439-5330, www.lakeview.org
- **Maple Grove Hospital**, 9875 Hospital Dr, Maple Grove, 763-581-1000, www.maplegrovehospital.org. Owned jointly by North Memorial and the Fairview system, the hospital just opened in 2010. If you are a patient in the Allina or Park Nicollet systems, you may not be able to use this hospital.
- **Mayo Clinic**, 200 First St. SW, Rochester 55905, 507-538-3270, www.mayoclinic.org/rochester
- **Mercy & Unity Hospitals** (Allina), 4050 Coon Rapids Blvd, Coon Rapids 55433, 763-236-6000, www.allinamercy.org
- **Methodist Hospital Park Nicollet Health Services**, 6500 Excelsior Blvd, St. Louis Park 55426, 952-993-5000, www.parknicollet.com/methodist
- **New River Medical Center**, 1013 Hart Blvd, Monticello 55362, 763-295-2945, www.newrivermedical.com
- **North Memorial Health Care**, 3300 Oakdale Ave N, Robbinsdale 55422, 763-520-5200, www.northmemorial.com
- **Phillips Eye Institute** (Allina), 2215 Park Ave S, Minneapolis 55404, 612-775-8800, www.allina.com/ahs/pei.nsf
- **Regina Medical Center**, 1175 Nininger Rd, Hastings 55033, 651-480-4100, www.reginamedical.org
- **Regions Hospital** (Health Partners), 640 Jackson St, St. Paul 55101, 651-254-3456, www.RegionsHospital.com
- **Ridgeview Medical Center**, 500 S Maple St, Waconia 55387, 952-442-2191, www.ridgeviewmedical.org, is the preferred hospital for many who live in the West Metro.
- **River Falls Area Hospital** (Allina), 1629 E Division St, River Falls, WI 54022, 715-425-6155, www.riverfallsareahospital.com
- **St. Francis Regional Medical Center** (Allina), 1455 St. Francis Ave, Shakopee 55379, 952-428-3000, www.Stfrancis-shakopee.com

- **St. John's Hospital** (HealthEast), 1575 Beam Ave, Maplewood 55109, 651-232-7000, www.healtheast.org/st-johns.html
- **St. Joseph's Hospital** (HealthEast), 45 W Exchange St, St. Paul 55102, 651-232-3000, www.healtheast.org/st-joes.html
- **Sister Kenny Rehabilitation** (Allina), 800 E 28th St, Minneapolis 55407, 612-863-4200, www.allina.com/ahs/ski.nsf
- **TRIA Orthopaedic Center**, 8100 Northland Dr, Edina 55431, 952-831-TRIA (8742), www.tria.com, allows walk-in appointments to its Acute Injury Clinic,
- **United Hospital** (Allina), 333 N Smith Ave, St. Paul 55102, 651-241-8000, www.unitedhospital.com
- **Unity Hospital**, 550 Osborne Rd, Fridley 55432, 763-236-5000, www.allinaunity.org
- **VA Medical Center–Minneapolis**, One Veterans Dr, Minneapolis 55417, 612-725-2000, www.minneapolis.va.gov/
- **Woodwinds Health Campus** (HealthEast), 1925 Woodwinds Dr, Woodbury 55125, 651-232-0228, www.healtheast.org/woodwinds.html

MAKING HEALTH CARE AFFORDABLE

FREE AND LOW-COST CLINICS

Many community clinics use sliding fee scales based on income.

CEDAR RIVERSIDE PEOPLE'S CENTER MEDICAL CLINIC
425 20th Avenue S, Minneapolis
www.peoples-center.org
612-332-4973

DR. SAM
1300 Quincy Street NE, Minneapolis
www.doctorsam.us
612-353-4034

FAMILY TREE CLINIC
1619 Dayton Ave., Suite 205, St. Paul
www.familytreeclinic.org
651-645-0478, TTY 651-379-5127

FREMONT COMMUNITY CLINICS
www.fremonthealth.org
Fremont Clinic: 3300 Fremont Ave N, Minneapolis, 612-588-9411
Central Avenue Clinic: 2610 Central Ave NE, Minneapolis, 612-781-6816
Sheridan Women & Children's Clinic: 342 13th Ave NE, Minneapolis, 612-362-4111

HENNEPIN COUNTY MEDICAL CENTER (HCMC)
Owned by Hennepin County, the state's premier Level 1 Trauma Center consists of a downtown Minneapolis medical center and several satellite clinics, including one in Brooklyn Center and another at The Hub shopping center in Richfield. The cost of treatment is discounted for those who apply and qualify.
701 Park Avenue, Minneapolis
www.hcmc.org
612-873-3000

MIDWEST HEALTH CENTER FOR WOMEN
Has provided reproductive and sexual health care services to women for over 35 years
33 Fifth Street S, 4th floor, Minneapolis
www.midwesthealthcenter.org
612-332-2311, 800-998-6075

NEIGHBORHOOD INVOLVEMENT PROGRAM (N.I.P.) COMMUNITY CLINIC
2431 Hennepin Ave S, Minneapolis
www.neighborhoodinvolve.org
612-374-3125

NEIGHBORHOOD INVOLVEMENT PROGRAM (N.I.P.) RAPE AND SEXUAL ABUSE CENTER
2431 Hennepin Ave S, Minneapolis
612-374-9077, 24-hour Helpline 612-825-4357, TTY 612-377-4163

NORTHPOINT HEALTH AND WELLNESS CENTER
Offers medical, dental, and mental health services
1313 Penn Ave N, Minneapolis
www.northpointhealth.org
612-543-2522

OPEN CITIES HEALTH CENTER
Operates two fully integrated medical, dental and mental health care clinics
409 N Dunlap St, St. Paul, 651-290-9200
135 Manitoba Ave, St. Paul, 651-489-8021
www.ochealthcenter.com

PHILLIPS NEIGHBORHOOD CLINIC
Free walk-in clinic operated by University of Minnesota health professions students who are supervised by licensed professionals
Oliver Presbyterian Church, 2647 Bloomington Ave S, Minneapolis
www.student.med.umn.edu/pnc
612-724-1690

PILLSBURY HOUSE INTEGRATED HEALTH CLINIC
3501 Chicago Ave S, Minneapolis
www.puc-mn.org
612-824-0708

PLANNED PARENTHOOD OF MINNESOTA
Operates Express Care Clinics in Apple Valley, Eden Prairie, and Woodbury, and full-service clinics in Brooklyn Park, Burnsville, Minneapolis-Uptown, and St. Paul-Rice Street. Well known for their reproductive health services for women, they also provide a wide range of health services for men. These include infertility and cancer screenings, vasectomy, and routine physical exams. Both state and national web sites provide for a state or ZIP code search for clinics near you.
www.plannedparenthood.org, www.ppmns.org
1-800-230-PLAN

RED DOOR
Provides confidential treatment for sexually transmitted diseases
525 Portland Ave S, Minneapolis
612-543-5555
www.reddoorclinic.org

ROBBINSDALE CLINIC, P.A.
A primary care medical clinic that also offers first-trimester abortion services. Note: check the address as people often confuse this clinic with the Robbinsdale Women's Center, which is located directly across the street.
3819 W Broadway, Robbinsdale
763-533-2534
www.robbinsdaleclinic.com

ROOM 111 STD CLINIC
555 Cedar St, Room 111, St. Paul
651-266-1352
www.co.ramsey.mn.us/ph/yas/about_room_111.htm

SOUTHSIDE COMMUNITY HEALTH SERVICES
4730 Chicago Ave S, Minneapolis
612-822-3186
www.southsidechs.org

ST. MARY'S HEALTH CLINICS
Provide free primary health care to the uninsured with 14 clinic sessions each week, at donated facilities throughout the metro area. Clinics are staffed by vol-

unteer doctors and nurses, as well as interpreters. Call to see if you are eligible and schedule an appointment.
www.stmaryshealthclinics.org
651-690-7029

TAMS (TEEN AGE MEDICAL SERVICE)
An adolescent outpatient program of Children's Hospitals and Clinics
2425 Chicago Ave S, Minneapolis
612-813-6125
www.childrensmn.org

WEST SIDE HEALTH CENTER
153 Concord St, St. Paul
651-222-1816
www.westsidechs.org

WEST SUBURBAN TEEN CLINIC
478 Second St, Excelsior
952-474-3251
www.teenhealth411.org

"MINUTECLINICS"

If you don't have time to sit in a doctor's waiting room, try the **MinuteClinic** at your local CVS Pharmacy. Staffed by certified nurse practitioners and physician's assistants, MinuteClinics provide quick, walk-in care for simple ailments such as strep throat, female bladder infections, or sinus infections. They also give flu shots. The charges for most services range from $30 to $110, www.minuteclinic.com.

LOW-COST DENTAL

The **University of Minnesota School of Dentistry's Dental Clinics** provide general and special dental care in Moos Health Sciences Tower, 515 Delaware Street SE, Minneapolis, on the East Bank Campus. They accept state health plans and most insurance, 612-625-2495, www.dentistry.umn.edu.

PRESCRIPTION ALERT

From time to time it is reported that pharmacists have refused to fill prescriptions for emergency contraception and other birth control pills and devices. Minnesota law does not directly address the issue of a pharmacist's obligation to fill prescriptions, so in the interest of saving yourself a lot of trouble, be sure to ask the pharmacist if he/she will fill your prescription before you hand it over. If the pharmacist says no, most drug stores have policies that require that he/

she transfer the prescription to another nearby pharmacy or pharmacist, so that your prescription can be filled the same day. Be aware that this procedure has not always been followed, however, so it's better to find out up front.

PHARMACIES

Most large clinics have pharmacies. So do most **Cub** (www.cubpharmacy.com), **Target** (http://target.com/pharmacy), **Rainbow**, and **Byerly's** (www.byerlys. com) stores. Finding a pharmacy that's open at night, however, can be a challenge, but these have 24-hour pharmacies, and sometimes drive-up windows or home delivery. Use their web page store locators to find a location near you.

- **Walgreens stores**, 1-800-WALGREENS, www.walgreens.com, offer drive-through service and are open 24 hours at many locations.
- **CVS/pharmacy**, www.cvs.com, has in-store MinuteClinics, and will deliver prescriptions to your door. The store locator also shows local phone numbers for the pharmacies.

HEALTH LAW—PROTECTING PRIVATE INFORMATION

Minnesota has a number of state laws that restrict the use and dissemination of personal health information by health care providers. The general rule is that a provider cannot share your health information with a third party unless you have given written consent or there is a law that authorizes the provider to share your information. If you believe your right to privacy has been violated, contact the **Minnesota Attorney General's Office** (651-296-3353, www. ag.state.mn.us) for assistance with your complaint.

APPS

Medica, a health insurance company headquartered in Minneapolis, has recently added a mobile app to its online comparative cost information webpage (www.MainStreetMedica.com). Both the mobile app and web site are available to all consumers, not just Medica members. Comparison prices are based on the health plan's Medica Choice contract rates. Download the mobile app at www.Medica.com.

MINNESOTA'S CLIMATE MAY BE COLD, BUT LOCAL CULTURE IS ON fire—and it isn't all polka bands and *A Prairie Home Companion,* either. It's Tony Award–winning theater companies—the Guthrie and Children's Theater—and other arts and entertainments as diverse as the calligraphed St. John's Bible and the always-quirky **Fringe Festival** (www.fringefestival.org), 11 days of live stage performances in a variety of neighborhood venues throughout the cities. Then there's Walker Art Center, internationally famous for its contemporary exhibits, and its venerable traditional counterpart, the Minneapolis Institute of Art. The Minnesota Orchestra and St. Paul Chamber Orchestra are held in high regard by classical music aficionados around the world; and the Grammy Award–winning Sounds of Blackness got its start at Macalester College in St. Paul. Popular music acts from Bob Dylan to Soul Asylum to Prince, Atmosphere, Har Mar Superstar, and Marcy Playground (named for the Marcy Open School in Minneapolis) originated in the thriving club scene here. Did we mention the hundreds of small galleries, ballet troupes, and avant-garde theater stages? By some measures, the arts activity is hotter here than it is in New York—and a ticket is much cheaper. And while Minnesotans don't sing along or dance in the aisles, they nearly always show their appreciation for performers with a standing ovation.

A word about TC celebrities. People move to the Twin Cities expecting Prince to play gigs at Paisley Park every Friday night and thinking they'll run into Josh Hartnett during their weekly shopping trip to Cub. Sadly, that just doesn't happen. BUT, The Purple One does occasionally invite fans out to his Paisley Park studio in Chanhassen for surprise late night shows that benefit his favorite charity, Love 4 One Another, which helps those in need throughout the Twin Cities. So keep your eyes on the local newspapers or join Prince's fan club to get tweets of his news—Our Hometown Hero doesn't give much advance notice. Paisley Park is located at 7801 Audubon Road, Chanhassen.

355

KEEPING CURRENT

Of course there's print, especially **City Pages and Rift Magazine** (www.riftmag azine.com), but…

- **3-Minute Egg** (or, as they say on their web site, "The Twin Cities arts seen") is a daily blog that puts the local arts scene on video. It covers a wide spectrum of disciplines—dance and theater, film and visual art, performance art, rock, jazz and hip-hop, comedy, literature, slam poetry, and even the classics.
- Another web site, **Twin Cities Metromix**, will keep you up-to-date and tell you where to eat near the venue you're going to, http://twincities.metromix. com.
- Touring bands that don't play the arenas usually book into the State, Orpheum, or Pantages Theaters. Together those make up the Hennepin Theatre trust, **www.HennepinTheatreTrust.org.** Sign up for the Trust's weekly e-mails and you'll be among the first to hear about upcoming shows.
- Finally, check **RadioK 770AM** (http://radiok.cce.umn.edu) and **89.3FM The Current** (http://minnesota.publicradio.org/radio/services/the_current/) for upcoming alternative, indie, and local music gigs.

> **VitaMn** (www.vita.mn) covers the entire metro with a clickable events calendar of movies, music, art, performances, bars/clubs, and restaurants. Its "Best" lists are The Best, and the site is so comprehensive, it even includes council meetings in the 'burbs.

TICKETS

Ticket prices are lower than New York's, but you can still drop a bundle on a good seat. If you take training as an usher you can often enjoy performances for free. Many venues have their own box offices, and most organizations sell tickets online. Rush tickets usually go on sale few minutes before a performance starts. Many places also use **Ticketmaster** (www.ticketmaster.com), which has a user-friendly web site as well as retail centers located at Macy's and Herberger's department stores. For community-level events such as Designers' Showhouses and the Fringe Festival, check out **www.ticketworks.com** (612-343-3390). Other venues, such as the Open Eye Figure Theatre, only deal with **Brown Paper Tickets**, a Fair Trade ticketing company. A portion of BPT's service fee goes back to the community, **24/7 Ticket Hotline**: 1-800-838-3006, www. brownpapertickets.com. For those who don't like to commit to non-refundable seats, **Theater All Year** ticket vouchers (6 for $99) offer a flexible and affordable way to enjoy a variety of Twin Cities theater offerings throughout the season, www.theaterallyear.com.

MUSIC—SYMPHONIC, CHORAL, OPERA, CHAMBER

The level of artistry in the Twin Cities is extraordinary. For classical music, start with the **Minnesota Orchestra** and **St. Paul Chamber Orchestra,** or take your pick from the following:

- **American Composers' Forum**, 332 Minnesota St, St. Paul, www.composers-forum.org, presents concerts that showcase emerging composers.
- **Minnesota Boychoir**, www.boychoir.org; this concert choir, made up of boys ages 7–18 from all over the Twin Cities, often performs at local churches—when not away on tour.
- **Minnesota Chorale**, www.mnchorale.org; this 150-voice professional chorus performs regularly with the Minnesota Orchestra and the St. Paul Chamber Orchestra.
- **Minnesota Opera**, 620 N 1st St, Minneapolis, www.mnopera.org; this professional opera company has achieved an international reputation for originating opera productions. The company offers four productions each season at the Ordway Music Theater, as well as occasional smaller productions in its rehearsal hall.
- **Minnesota Orchestra**, Orchestra Hall, 1111 Nicollet Mall, Minneapolis, 612-371-5656, 800-292-4141, www.minnesotaorchestra.org; courtesy parking is available in front of Orchestra Hall while you are visiting the Box Office. For those who aren't sure about "highbrow" music, be sure to catch Sommerfest, a four-week festival of food, dancing, and some free concerts presented every summer from July into August.
- **Minnesota Youth Symphonies**, www.mnyouthsymphonies.org, provides preprofessional orchestral training for young people, elementary through college. Three major concerts are presented each season at Orchestra Hall, Minneapolis, and O'Shaughnessy Auditorium, St. Paul.
- **The Saint Paul Chamber Orchestra**, Hamm Building, Ste 500, 408 St. Peter St, St. Paul, 651-291-1144, www.thespco.org, performs at the Ordway, its own performance center, and several churches.
- **The Schubert Club**, 302 Landmark Center, 75 W Fifth St, St. Paul, www.schubert.org, presents eight concerts annually, operates a Museum of Musical Instruments, provides after-school music lessons, presents master classes, commissions new musical works by American composers, and produces recordings and books.
- **VocalEssence** is an arts outreach program of the Plymouth Congregational Church in Minneapolis. This innovative series hosts world-famous orchestral and choral performers and assists emerging composers. Call 612-371-5642 for tickets or buy online, www.vocalessence.org.

COMMUNITY MUSIC

There are over a hundred community bands in the state, and innumerable community choral societies, orchestras, and musical theaters, ranging from ensembles of professionals to volunteer organizations whose purpose is simply to give people who love music a chance to participate. So if you're interested in performing, this list of organizations will give you a place to get started. If you're only interested in listening, these groups are a treat—and many of their concerts are free! For a comprehensive listing (and photos) of community bands and calendar of their concerts, visit the **Community Band Resource Center**, http://mcbrc.us.

- **Apollo Male Chorus**, Eisenhower Community Center, Hwy 7, Hopkins, 952-933-6322, www.apollomalechorus.com; this is ranked one of the top 10 male choruses in the world.
- **Greater Twin Cities Youth Symphonies**, 528 Hennepin Ave, Minneapolis, 612-870-7611, www.gtcys.org
- **Medalist Concert Band**, www.medalistband.com; this 70-member adult concert band has been described by the National Band Association as "one of the foremost community bands in the nation." It presents over 20 concerts each year throughout the area at venues including the Lake Harriet Bandshell.
- **Metropolitan Boys Choir**, www.mbchoir.com
- **Minneapolis Pops Orchestra**, www.mplspops.org; these professional musicians play together only in July in city parks, in a concert tradition that started over 60 years ago.
- **Music Association of Minnetonka**, 18285 Hwy 7, Minnetonka, 952-401-5954, http://musicassociation.org, has several orchestras and choirs.
- **Twin Cities Gay Men's Chorus**, 528 Hennepin Ave, Ste 701, Minneapolis, 612-339-SONG, www.tcgmc.org

MUSIC—CONTEMPORARY

Listen to **MN Soundtrack** on Friday nights, and in a little over an hour and change, you'll be an expert on the incredibly vibrant and diverse music scene that is Minnesota. MN Soundtrack airs from 7:30 to 9 p.m. on KFAI 90.3 in Minneapolis and 106.7 St. Paul.

The Twin Cities have a long, rich history of great popular music. From Bob Dylan, who started out playing the coffeehouses of Cedar-Riverside to Atmosphere rockin' the house at First Avenue, bands such as the Jayhawks, Replacements, and Soul Asylum, rappers Brother Ali and P.O.S., and country-blues star Little Jonny Lang, have made—and continue to make—the Twin Cities a place to catch great gigs and perhaps experience history in the making.

Twin Cities Radio (www.twincitiesradio.net) broadcasts local and world Indie music and video of live shows 24/7.

Little known fact: The disco-era hit "Funkytown" was written by Minneapolis ad man Steven Greenberg and sung by Cynthia Johnson, a secretary at the Maplewood Police Department. It topped the charts for four weeks back in May 1980, and went platinum again in 2005 on the *Shrek 2* soundtrack. You can see Funkytown's original gold record at The Minneapolis Hard Rock Café, 600 Hennepin Avenue, which also displays Prince memorabilia.

The following venues are best known for the category under which they're listed, although many of them book acts of every genre. Unfortunately, most local music is relegated to the downtown areas of Minneapolis and St. Paul.

BLUES

- **Famous Dave's Blues and BBQ**, 3001 Hennepin (Uptown), Minneapolis, www.famousdaves.com
- **Minnesota Music Café**, just off the corner of 7th St E and Payne, on the edge of downtown St. Paul near Metropolitan State University, www.minnesotamusiccafe.com; this is where Little Blues Brother Jim Belushi, Mick Jagger, Jonny Lang, and Keb' Mo' go to jam when they're in town.

COUNTRY, BLUEGRASS, FOLK

- **Dulono's**, 607 W Lake St, Minneapolis; this family-style pizza joint is home to jam sessions on the first and third Wednesdays of every month, and live bluegrass with no cover charge on weekends.
- **Homestead Pickin' Parlor** is bluegrass central, THE place to go for jam sessions, recordings, instruments, and sheet music, 6625 Penn Ave S, Richfield, 612-861-3308, www.homesteadpickinparlor.com.
- **Lee's Liquor Lounge**, 101 Glenwood Ave, Minneapolis, www.leesliquorlounge.com; country, rockabilly, swing, hardcore cowboy—lots of local bands and some nationals, all playing music you can dance to.
- **Minnesota Bluegrass & Old-Time Music Association**, www.minnesotabluegrass.org, sponsors four annual bluegrass festivals, plus numerous concerts, jam sessions, and workshops.

LITTLE BIT OF EVERYTHING

- **Cedar Cultural Centre** presents acoustic jazz, blues, folk, indie rock and world music, 416 Cedar Ave S, Minneapolis, 612-338-2674, www.thecedar.org. Learn about artists and shows, watch videos of past performances, listen to podcasts, and buy tickets to hot shows with The Cedar Cultural Center iPhone app.

- **Ginkgo Coffeehouse**, 721 N Snelling Ave, St. Paul, tickets at 651-645-2647, www.ginkgocoffee.com

IRISH

- **Kieran's**, 600 Hennepin Ave, Minneapolis, www.kierans.com
- **The Liffey Irish Pub**, 175 W Seventh St, St. Paul, www.theliffey.com
- **The Local**, 931 Nicollet Mall, Minneapolis, www.the-local.com
- **O'Gara's Irish Pub and Restaurant/O'Gara's Garage**, 164 N Snelling Ave, St. Paul, www.ogaras.com

JAZZ

- **Artists' Quarter**, 408 St Peter St, 651-292-1359, St. Paul, www.artistsquarter.com
- **Dakota Jazz Club and Restaurant**, 1010 Nicollet Ave S, Minneapolis, 612-332-1010, www.dakotacooks.com
- **Dixie's**, 695 Grand Ave, St. Paul, 651-222-7345, www.dixiesongrand.com
- **Fine Line Music Café**, 318 First Ave N, Minneapolis, 612-338-8100, www.finelinemusic.com

POLKA, LOUNGE MUSIC

- **Nye's Polonaise Room**, 112 Hennepin Ave E, Minneapolis, www.nyespolonaise.com; the only place you're likely to hear "The World's Most Dangerous Polka Band."

ROCK/HIP HOP/R&B

- **First Avenue and 7th St Entry**, 701 1st Ave N, Minneapolis, Info Line 612-332-1775, www.first-avenue.com
- **501 Club**, 501 Washington Ave S, Minneapolis, www.501.mn
- **Triple Rock Social Club**, 629 Cedar Ave, Minneapolis, www.triplerocksocialclub.com
- **Turf Club**, 1601 University Ave, St. Paul, www.turfclub.net

SPORTS BARS

- **Alary's**, 139 7th St E, St. Paul, www.alarys.com, runs a shuttle over to the Excel Center. Check it out before you go on their Bartender Cam.
- **Mac's Industrial**, 312 Central Ave SE (University and Central, where Southeast turns into Northeast), Minneapolis, 612-379-3379, www.macsindustrial.com

ALL-AGES CLUBS AND SHOWS

- **Eclipse Records**, 1922 University Ave, St. Paul, 651-645-7724, has Thursday, Friday, and Saturday night shows every week—and sometimes more when touring bands stop by to pay a visit.
- **First Avenue** (see above under Rock)
- **The Garage**, 75 Civic Center Pkwy, Burnsville, 952-895-4664, www.thegarage. net

NIGHTCLUBS AND DISCOS

- **Bryant-Lake Bowl**, 810 W Lake St, Minneapolis, Ticketline 612-825-8949, www.bryantlakebowl.com
- **Gay 90s**, 408 Hennepin Ave, Minneapolis, www.gay90s.com
- **Kitty Cat Klub**, 315 14th Ave SE (Dinkytow), Minneapolis, www.kittycatklub. net
- **Loring Pasta Bar**, 315 14th Ave SE, Minneapolis, www.loringcafe.com
- **Varsity Theater and Café des Artistes**, 1308 Fourth St SE (Dinkytown), Minneapolis, 612-604-0222, www.varsitytheater.org

CONCERT HALLS, ARENAS

- **Benson Great Hall**, Bethel College, 3900 Bethel Dr, Arden Hills, 651-631-3768, www.bethel.edu
- **Fitzgerald Theater**, 10 E Exchange St, St. Paul, Box Office 651-290-1221, http://fitzgeraldtheater.publicradio.org; home base for Garrison Keillor's long-running nationally broadcast *A Prairie Home Companion*.
- **Guthrie Theater**, 818 Second St S, Minneapolis, Box Office 612-377-2224, www.guthrietheater.org
- **Landmark Center**, 75 W 5th St, St. Paul (on Rice Park), Events Hotline 651-292-3235, www.landmarkcenter.org
- **Northrop Auditorium**, 84 Church St SE, Minneapolis, Tickets 612-624-2345, www.northrop.umn.edu
- **Orchestra Hall**, 1111 Nicollet Mall, Minneapolis, Tickets 612-371-5656, 800-292-4141, www.minnesotaorchestra.org
- **Ordway Music Theater**, 345 Washington St, St. Paul, 651-224-4222, www.ordway.org
- **O'Shaughnessy Auditorium**, 2004 Randolph Ave, St. Catherine University, St. Paul, Tickets 651-690-6700, http://oshaughnessy.stkate.edu
- **RiverCentre/Roy Wilkins Auditorium/XCEL Energy Center**, 199 W Kellogg Blvd, St. Paul, www.xcelenergycenter.com
- **Target Center**, 600 1st Ave N, Minneapolis, Events Line 612-673-0900, www.targetcenter.com; the 5th and 7th St ramps are connected to the center by skyways; the facility is one block from the Warehouse District LRT Station.

MUSIC LESSONS

- **Homestead Pickin' Parlor**, 6625 Penn Ave S, Richfield, 612-861-3308, www. homesteadpickinparlor.com
- **MacPhail Center for the Arts**, 501 South 2nd St, Minneapolis; 14750 Cedar Ave S, AppleValley; Birch Lake Elementary, White Bear Lake; 612-321-0100, www.macphail.org
- **West Bank School of Music**, 1813 S 6th St, Minneapolis, 612-333-6651, www. westbankmusic.org

DANCE

PERFORMANCE GROUPS

Some of the following groups are cross-listed below as organizations that also offer dance lessons:

- **Ballet of the Dolls**, 345 13th Ave NE (Ritz Theater), Minneapolis, Tickets 612-436-1129, www.ritzdolls.com
- **Ethnic Dance Theater**, 3507 Clinton Ave South, Minneapolis, Tickets 612-436-1129 and online at www.ritzdolls.com/tickets, www.ethnicdancetheatre.com
- **James Sewell Ballet** (www.jsballet.org) is known for its technically challenging, yet accessible dances.
- **Minnesota Dance Theatre & The Dance Institute**, 528 Hennepin Ave, Minneapolis, 612-338-0627, www.mndance.org
- **Zenon Dance Company**, 528 Hennepin Ave, Minneapolis, 612-338-1101, www.zenondance.org

LESSONS

Belly dancing, square dancing, salsa, hip-hop, Irish ceili dancing, or swing—dancing is so much fun, you forget it's exercise! Most school districts include dance in their **Community Education** (also called **Early Childhood and Family Education**) classes, as do many community recreation centers and YW/YMCAs. For information on classes in the St. Paul area, call 651-266-6400 (press 4) or look online at www.stpaul.gov/parks. In Minneapolis, find schedules for all 49 park and rec centers at www.minneapolissparks.org or call 612-230-6400.

- **Attitude Dance** teaches group and private classes in swing, waltz, tango, etc., at several locations, 651-245-6670, www.attitudedancing.com.
- **Ballet Minnesota/Classical Ballet Academy**, 249 E 4th St, St. Paul; 7650 Currell Blvd, Woodbury; 651-290-0513, www.balletminnesota.org
- **Conway Recreation Center** in St. Paul (651-501-6343) offers free Irish ceili dancing.

- **Foster's Champion Ballroom**, 550 Market Street, Chanhassen; 1637 Hennepin Ave, Minneapolis; 3742 23rd Avenue South, Minneapolis; 952-934-2160, www.championballroomdance.com
- The **Martin Luther King Center** in St. Paul (651-290-8695) is the place to go for Chicago-Style Steppin'.
- **Minnesota Dance Theater** offers classical and contemporary training for children as young as 3½, 528 Hennepin Ave, Minneapolis, 612-338-0627, www.mndance.org.
- The **Minneapolis YWCAs** (www.ywca-minneapolis.org) and **Oxford Community Center/Jimmy Lee Rec Center** in St. Paul (651-642-0650) offer Zumba dance classes set to calypso and island music.
- **Tapestry Folk Dance Center**, 3748 Minnehaha Ave S, Minneapolis, 612-722-2914, www.tapestryfolkdance.org
- **Zenon Dance Company**, 528 Hennepin Ave, Minneapolis, 612-338-1101, www.zenondance.org

THEATERS

The Twin Cities have something for everyone—from Broadway musicals to avant-garde experiments, plus all the new shows that preview here before opening on Broadway.

- **Chanhassen Dinner Theatres**, 501 W 78th St, Chanhassen, Box Office 952-934-1525, www.chanhassentheatres.com
- **Children's Theatre Company**, 2400 3rd Ave S, Minneapolis, Tickets 612-874-0400, www.childrenstheatre.org. Costume rental, 855 East Hennepin Ave, 612-375-8722, www.costumerentals.org
- **Great American History Theatre**, 30 E 10th St, St. Paul, 651-292-4323, www.historytheatre.com
- **Guthrie Theater**, 818 Second St S, Minneapolis, Box Office 612-377-2224, 877-44STAGE, TTY 612-377-6626, www.guthrietheater.org
- **Jungle Theater**, 2951 Lyndale Ave S, Minneapolis, Box Office 612-822-7063, www.jungletheater.com, presents both contemporary and classic plays and numerous community outreach/education programs for all ages. This is a great place to volunteer!
- **Minnesota Fringe Festival** is an 11-day performing arts extravaganza held in August at venues in Minneapolis and St. Paul. The lineup of productions is unjuried, and participants are selected by lottery. Some productions are good, some bad, but they're always edgy. There are lots of ways to be involved: volunteer, give an artist your spare bed, become a sponsor—or mount your own production, www.fringefestival.org.
- **Old Log Theater**, 5175 Meadville St, Excelsior, 952-474-5951, www.oldlog.com, is the oldest continuously operating dinner theater. It stages comedies and British farces.

- **Open Eye Figure Theatre** is known for its evenings of stimulating, inexpensive music and theatre, as well as their irreverent seasonal favorite, The Holiday Pageant, a family-friendly spectacle which tells the Nativity story from the Devil's point of view. 506 E 24th St, Minneapolis, 612-874-6338, www.openeyetheatre.org
- **Ordway Music Theater**, 345 Washington St, St. Paul, Box Office 651-224-4222, www.ordway.org
- **Orpheum, Pantages, and State Theatres**, 910, 710, and 805 Hennepin Ave, Minneapolis, 612-339-7007, www.hennepintheatretrust.org
- **Penumbra Theatre Company** is Minnesota's only African-American professional theater company, 270 Kent St, St. Paul (Selby-Dale), Box Office 651-224-3180, www.penumbratheatre.org.
- The **Playwrights' Center** nurtures writers and presents new plays by the Center's Core Writers. Its Ruth Easton Series is FREE, but seating is limited. Call ahead to RSVP, 612-332-7481, Extension 10. Center playwrights have won Pulitzers, the Tony, numerous Obies, and a New York Dramatists Critics Circle Best New Play Award. See their work here before it goes to Broadway, 2301 E Franklin Avenue, Minneapolis, www.pwcenter.org.

MOVIE THEATERS

> **Switchblade Comb** reports daily on the local movie scene. The brainchild of three guys who worked together at the Uptown Theater, it's THE place to find out about upcoming films and events that don't get much attention anywhere else, www.switchbladecomb.com.

If it's first run, major studio blockbusters you enjoy, the Twin Cities can offer you a mega-multiplex in downtown Minneapolis or practically any major mall. But if your taste runs to classics, documentaries, or little gems given limited release, ah…then you have really moved to the right place.

- The **Uptown and Lagoon** (www.landmarktheatres.com), and **Parkway** (http://theparkwaytheater.com) theaters all show independent releases.
- The **University of Minnesota Film Society** (www.mnfilmarts.org) shows a combination of international movies and genre-based retrospectives and documentaries at the Bell Auditorium.
- The **Walker Art Center** and **Minneapolis Institute of Art** host film screenings in conjunction with other events.
- **Science Museum of Minnesota** and **Minnesota Zoo** each have theaters designed to make you feel like you're part of the action.
- To see local filmmakers' original work, take in the **Minneapolis Underground Film Festival** (MUFF) hosted by the Minneapolis College of Art and Design

(MCAD). Films are followed by audience Q & A, and there's an informal lounge where audience members can interact with filmmakers from around the world. Audiences vote on awards following the screenings, www.minneapolisunder groundfilmfestival.com

For all local movie listings, check the newspapers (especially on Fridays when there are reviews) or look online at www.startribune.com/entertainment/movies, or http://twincities.citysearch.com.

COMEDY

- **Acme Comedy Company**, 708 N First St, Minneapolis, 612-338-6393; purchase tickets online.
- **Brave New Workshop Comedy Theater and School of Improvisation** is the nation's oldest ongoing satiric theatre, 2605 Hennepin Ave S, Minneapolis, 612-332-6620, www.bravenewworkshop.com.
- **Bryant-Lake Bowl**, 810 W Lake St, Minneapolis, Ticketline 612-825-8949, www.bryantlakebowl.com
- **Plymouth Playhouse** is home to the long-running musical, *How to Talk Minnesotan*, 2705 Annapolis Ln (I-494 and Hwy 55), Plymouth, Box Office 763-553-1600, www.plymouthplayhouse.com.

ART

"Gallery crawls" and open studio events are popular in both Minneapolis and St. Paul warehouse districts.

- Don't miss **Art-A-Whirl**, the six-square-mile, free-floating studio party/art sale presented by the Northeast Minneapolis Arts Association, www.nemaa. org. It's fun and easy to bike from location to location.
- **The Northrup King Building** at 1500 Jackson St. NE is home to over a hundred artists. Its studios are open to the public the first Thursday of every month, www.northrupkingbuilding.com.
- In St. Paul, **Lowertown** galleries are open the first Friday of every month, with official "crawls" in April and October, www.stpaulartcrawl.org.
- The November Minneapolis College of Art and Design (MCAD) **Student Art Sale** is one of the best places in the area to find hip, unique, moderately priced gifts or fine art for your own home, www.mcad.edu. All pieces are creations of MCAD students and recent graduates. Prices top out at $1000 and all proceeds benefit the artists.

Finally, we have an easy way to become a collector—you know how popular it is to buy crop shares? Here you can also buy **Art Shares**. Buy a share and get a box of original art each month all season long—plus a party where you'll pick it up, www.mnartists.org or www.springboardforthearts.org.

MUSEUMS

- **Minneapolis Institute of Arts**, 2400 S 3rd Ave, Minneapolis, www.artsmia. org
- **The Museum of Russian Art**, 5500 Stevens Ave S, Minneapolis, www.tmora. org, is the only institution in the United States dedicated to Russian art.
- **Walker Art Center**, 1750 Hennepin Ave, Minneapolis, www.walkerart.org
- **Frederick R. Weisman Art Museum**, 333 E River Rd, U of Minnesota, Minneapolis, www.weisman.umn.edu, features American art from the first decades of the twentieth century.

HISTORY AND CULTURAL MUSEUMS

- **American Swedish Institute**, 2600 Park Ave, Minneapolis, www.american swedishinst.org
- **Bell Museum of Natural History**, U of Minnesota, Minneapolis, 10 Church St SE, Minneapolis (the corner of 17th and University), 612-624-9050 , www.bell museum.org. Fun for kids—a slumber party at the Bell: bring your sleeping bags, explore the museum by flashlight, and fall asleep to a spooky animal bedtime story.
- **Historic Fort Snelling State Park**, Hwy 5 at Hwy 55, Minneapolis, www. mnhs.org/places/sites/hfs/tour/tour.html; costumed guides present demonstrations, give tours, and talk to you like it's still 1827. Take a tour of the fort, then hike the beautiful trails.
- **Mill City Museum**, 704 S Second St, Minneapolis, www.millcitymuseum. org; built within the ruins of the Washburn A Mill, this riverfront museum chronicles the flour milling industry that dominated world flour production for roughly a half-century, thus fueling the growth of Minneapolis, which is known around the world as the "Mill City." The museum's "Ruin Courtyard" is often used for summer concerts.
- **Minnesota History Center and Minnesota Historical Society**, 345 W Kellogg Blvd, St. Paul, 651-259-3000, 800-657-3773, www.mnhs.org
- **Science Museum of Minnesota and Omnitheater**, 120 W Kellogg, St. Paul, www.smm.org; the Science Museum is a multi-level extravaganza of hands-on exhibits and creative demonstrations, with a 3D multimedia laser-theater and 180-degree screen Omnitheater that shows science-related films.

BREWERY TOURS

- **August Schell Brewing Company**, New Ulm, www.schellsbrewery.com, is the second oldest family owned and managed brewery in the United States. It's open for tours Friday through Sunday afternoons, and on several special occasions, including Oktoberfest. New Ulm is an easy two-hour drive west of Minneapolis.

- **Great Waters Brewing Company**, creators of many award-winning hand-crafted beers, offers one of the most entertaining outings in the TC, assuming you're a beer drinker—the **Ultimate B.E.E.R. (Beer Enthusiasts Educational Retreat) Tour**. It starts at 8 a.m., with breakfast at GW and ends about 12 hours later with dinner. In between, you'll be bused to brewing facilities within reach of the metro and treated to private tours and all the beer you can drink. Great Waters' patio on St. Paul's pedestrian mall becomes the Ice Patio during St. Paul's Winter Carnival. Great place to go before a game or show downtown, 426 St. Peter St N in the historic Hamm Building, St. Paul, www.greatwatersbc.com.
- **Summit Brewing Company** brewery offers tours Tuesdays, Thursdays, and Saturdays. 910 Montreal Circle, St. Paul, 651-265-7800, www.summitbrewing. com

LITERARY LIFE

BOOKSTORES

The Twin Cities are home to many excellent new and used bookstores. They include chains such as **Barnes & Noble** (www.barnesandnoble.com) and **Borders** (www.borders.com), which have many locations. But, as befits the #2 Most Literate place in the country, we are rich with independent booksellers, as well. They survive by virtue of their customer service and erudition and tend to be tucked away in neighborhoods where they are harder to find—and these are but a few of them listed below:

- **Amazon Bookstore Cooperative/True Colors Bookstore**, 4755 Chicago Ave S, Minneapolis, 612-821-9630, www.amazonfembks.com, is the oldest independent feminist bookstore in North America.
- **Big Brain Comics**, 1027 Washington Ave S, Minneapolis, 612-338-4390, www.bigbraincomics.com
- **Birchbark Books**, 2115 W 21st St, Minneapolis, 612-374-4023, www.birchbarkbooks.com, is owned by author Louise Erdrich.
- **Book House**, 429 14th Ave SE, Minneapolis, 612-331-1430, www.bookhouseindinkytown.com
- **Common Good Books**, 165 Western Ave, St. Paul, 651-225-8989, is owned by Garrison Keillor of *Prairie Home Companion* fame.
- **Excelsior Bay Books**, 36 Water St, Excelsior, 952-401-0932, is a real neighborhood bookstore known for its children's books and taste in fiction. No webpage, but they post in-store events on Facebook.
- **Half Price Books Records and Magazines**, www.halfpricebooks.com/minnesota.html, has several locations around the Twin Cities.
- **The Loft Literary Center and Open Book Literary Arts Center**, 1011 Washington Ave, 612-215-2575, www.loft.org, is where emerging writers hone

their craft and readers can listen to outstanding writers discussing their literary influences.

- **Magers & Quinn Booksellers**, 3038 Hennepin Ave S, Minneapolis, 612-822-4611, www.magersandquinn.com; for the friendly atmosphere, scholarly staff, and a sense that there are treasures to be found among the rare and collectible volumes here, this new and used bookstore is a perennial favorite.
- **Micawber's Books**, 2238 Carter Ave, St. Paul, 651-646-5506, www.micawbers.com, is tucked away in the St. Anthony neighborhood near Muffuletta Restaurant.
- **Open Book**, 1011 Washington Ave S, Minneapolis, www.openbookmn.org, is home to the Minnesota Center for Book Arts, The Loft Literary Center (above), and local publisher Milkweed Editions.
- **The Red Balloon**, 891 Grand Ave, St. Paul, 651-224-8320, www.redballoon bookshop.com, is a fantastic children's bookstore that stages many fun family events throughout the year.
- **Uncle Edgar's Mystery Bookstore and Uncle Hugo's Science Fiction Bookstore**, 2864 Chicago Ave, Minneapolis, 612-824-9984, 612-824-6347, www.unclehugo.com
- **Wild Rumpus**, 2720 W 43rd St, Minneapolis, 612-920-5005, www.wildrumpus books.com, in Linden Hills, has a kid-sized door and lots of pet animals. The ambiance alone is certain to turn children into bookworms.

LIBRARIES

Local library systems are all part of MELSA, the **Metropolitan Library Service Agency**, an alliance of metropolitan libraries (www.melsa.org). With MELSA, as its motto says, "Your library card is good at over 100 locations!"

The **Hennepin County Library System** (www.hclib.org) serves Minneapolis and suburban Hennepin County residents through 41 libraries and extensive outreach services. It has developed special collections to serve the area's many immigrant populations, as well as an extraordinary African-American history and culture collection housed at the **Sumner Library** (611 Van White Memorial Boulevard) in North Minneapolis. Many of the libraries are designated "Homework Helper" locations. All branches offer free wireless Internet. The Ridgedale Library also has a bookstore where discarded and donated books are sold. These main libraries, which boast larger collections and bigger computer labs, are open longer hours and on weekends:

- **Brookdale Library**, 6125 Shingle Creek Pkwy, Brooklyn Center
- **Eden Prairie Library**, 565 Prairie Center Dr, Eden Prairie
- **Maple Grove Library**, 8351 Elm Creek Blvd, Maple Grove
- **Ridgedale Library**, 12601 Ridgedale Dr, Minnetonka
- **Southdale Library**, 7001 York Ave S, Edina

- The **St. Paul Public Library** (www.sppl.org) includes a Central Library (90 W Fourth St, St. Paul, 651-266-7000) and branches in most St. Paul neighborhoods. Call 651-642-0379 for Bookmobile Service.

Other county libraries are as follows:
- **Anoka County Library System**, www.anoka.lib.mn.us
- **Carver County Library System**, www.carverlib.org, operates two libraries convenient for Hennepin County residents: Chanhassen Library, 7711 Kerber Blvd, Chanhassen, and Chaska Library, 3 City Hall Plaza, Chaska. When the reserved list is long for a book in the Hennepin County system, you can usually get it here, with a much shorter wait.
- **Dakota County Library**, www.co.dakota.mn.us/LeisureRecreation/County Libraries/default.htm
- **Great River Regional Library**, www.griver.org, serves Wright, Todd, Stearns, Sherburne, Morrison, and Benton counties with 32 branches.
- **Ramsey County Library System**, www.ramsey.lib.mn.us
- The **Scott County Library System**, 13090 Alabama Ave S, Savage, www.scott.lib.mn.us, is another place to locate materials that are on long reserve lists elsewhere.
- **Washington County Library**, www.co.washington.mn.us/info_for_residents/library/

CULTURE FOR KIDS

- **Children's Theatre Company** presents plays for children as young as four, 2400 3rd Ave S, Minneapolis, Tickets 612-874-0400, www.childrenstheatre. org.
- The **Flint Hills International Children's Festival** is sponsored by the Ordway Center for the Performing Arts and Flint Hills Resources. This celebration of arts from around the world includes performances, food, and take-home projects; 345 Washington St, St. Paul, 651-224-4222, www.ordway.org/festival.
- **James Sewell Ballet** presents 50-minute Saturday morning First Chance Dance events at O'Shaughnessy Auditorium that are geared for very young children. Audience members are encouraged to come and go as they please, and children under three attend free! Tickets 651-690-6700, www.jsballet.org.
- **MacPhail Center for the Arts**, 501 S 2nd St, Minneapolis; 14750 Cedar Ave S, AppleValley; Birch Lake Elementary, White Bear Lake; 612-321-0100, www. macphail.org
- **Minnetonka Center for the Arts**, 2240 N Shore Dr, Wayzata, 952-473-7361, www.minnetonkaarts.org, offers numerous classes for kids (and adults), and a really fun summer arts camp. Some classes are held at Ridgedale Mall in Minnetonka.

- **Minnesota Children's Museum**, 10 W 7th St, Downtown St. Paul, 651-225-6000, www.MCM.org; buttons, gizmos, interactive make-believe, a theater, and hands-on exhibits that change frequently make every trip an adventure. Admission is free on the third Sunday of every month.
- **Minnesota Orchestra** presents **Young People's Concerts** to school groups and special family concerts for the general public. Young Listener packages are priced as low as $12 per concert. 1111 Nicollet Mall, Minneapolis, Tickets 612-371-5656, 800-292-4141, www.minnesotaorchestra.org.
- **Nickelodeon Universe** is a seven-acre indoor theme park inside the Mall of America, www.nickelodeonuniverse.com
- **Stages Theatre Company and Acting Conservatory** (ages 7–17), 1111 Main St, Hopkins, Box Office 952-979-1111, www.stagestheatre.org, is a professional theater environment that offers terrific classes and always-entertaining productions. Plus it's easy to get to and park.
- **Stepping Stone Theatre for Youth Development** offers numerous classes and performing arts camps for children as young as 3½. The first Sunday of each show is Free Family Fun Day. The first Saturday of each show is $5 a seat for people who live nearby, 55 Victoria Street N, St. Paul, Box Office 651-225-9265, www.steppingstonetheatre.org.

Bob Hope once said, "If you watch a game, it's fun. If you play it, it's recreation. If you work at it, it's golf." You'll have plenty of chances for all three here, and many other sports besides. To the hale and hearty, this climate is not an impediment but an opportunity. Ice boating, anyone?

The four major sports venues are: **Hubert H. Humphrey Metrodome** (900 South 5th Street, Minneapolis, www.msfc.com), **Target Center** (First Avenue North between 6th and 7th Streets, Minneapolis, www.targetcenter.com), **Target Field** (1 Twins Way, Minneapolis, minnesota.twins.mlb.com), and **Xcel Energy Center** (on the corner of Kellogg Boulevard and West Seventh Street in downtown St. Paul, www.xcelenergycenter.com). The Metrodome, Target Field, and Target Center are all on the **Hiawatha LRT** line. Target Field can also be reached via **North Star Commuter Rail,** which literally lets you off at the door. For those traveling to events by car, there are parking ramps that connect directly to Target Center through the skyway system; park here for Target Field as well. Here's a tip: To avoid congestion, park at the City Center ramp on 7th Street—it's just two blocks away from the 6th Street skyway to Target Field. Parking for the Xcel Center is located in the **River Center Ramp**, which has an entrance off of Kellogg, across the street from the arena. In addition, many local bars offer free rides to patrons on game nights, as do MetroTransit buses (See **Transportation** for more information.)

PROFESSIONAL SPORTS

Sports fans in Minnesota teeter between ecstasy and frustration, with successes that are few and far between. They remember with pride the performances of hometown heroes like **Kirby Puckett**, who helped the Twins win the World

Series in 1987 and 1991. The same goes for Hopkins High School's ESPY winner, **Blake Hoffarber**, who scored the winning point in the 2005 Minnesota Class 4A state basketball title game from flat on his back, with the clock about to run out.

But fame is fleeting, and years of lackluster seasons and pro athletes' brushes with the law were enough to make Vikings fans take down their purple mailboxes, and Twins fans exchange their "Homer Hankies" for pigs' snouts and head over to St. Paul for **Saints** games and cheaper beer. Now things have picked up again. In 2010, Brett Favre led the Vikings *almost* to the Superbowl, and the Twins got a new outdoor stadium complete with food favorites from a lot of local restaurants. Now even those of us who can't tell an R.B.I. from a BBQed r.i.b. have something to look forward to on game day.

BASEBALL

The American League's **Minnesota Twins** play 80 or so games a year at Target Field in Minneapolis. For tickets, call 612-33TWINS (338-9467). For game stats, schedules, player information, and daily ticket specials visit the Twins' web site at http://minnesota.twins.mlb.com. Across town, the **St. Paul Saints**, a professional minor league team, plays dozens of home games at tiny Midway Stadium. Off-diamond sideshows include grandstand massages, fat-suit races, a pig mascot that carries out the ball, lots of giveaways, and affordable tickets, food and drink. Call 651-644-6659 for ticket information or buy tickets online at www.saintsbaseball.com.

BASKETBALL

The **WNBA's Minnesota Lynx** and **NBA's Minnesota Timberwolves** play at **Target Center** in Minneapolis. Tickets are available at the Target Center Box Office or www.ticketmaster.com. For team updates and statistics visit www.wnba.com/lynx and www.nba.com/ timberwolves.

FOOTBALL

Perennial contenders in the National Football League, the **Minnesota Vikings** play eight regular season home games at the **Humphrey Metrodome** each year, as well as several pre-season games. The NFL schedule comes out in May. In July, when single-game tickets go on sale, die-hards camp out in front of the Vikings ticket office at the Metrodome to be first in line. For those who don't know already, the Minnesota version of the Hatfields and McCoys is the Vikings' rivalry with Green Bay, whose fans wear "cheeseheads." In comparison, the Minnesota fans' Viking horns and milkmaid braids don't look half bad. For season tickets, call 612-33-VIKES (338-4537). For team information check www.vikings.com.

HOCKEY

The **Minnesota Wild** drop their pucks on the ice at state-of-the-art Xcel Energy Center in downtown St. Paul. Check www.wild.com for details or call 651-222-WILD. Minnesota is also home to the **U.S. Hockey Hall of Fame**, about three hours north of the Twin Cities in Eveleth, 800-443-7825, www.ushockeyhall.com.

HORSE RACING

- **Canterbury Park Racetrack and Card Club**, Shakopee, thoroughbred and quarterhorse races throughout the summer months, www.canterburypark.com
- **Running Aces Harness Park and Card Room**, Columbus (near Forest Lake), www.runningacesharness.com

LACROSSE

The National Lacrosse League **Minnesota Swarm** (www.mnswarm.com) play indoors at the Xcel Energy Center. Their 16-game regular season schedule begins in December and runs through April. Buy tickets online or call 651-602-6000.

ROLLER DERBY

Minnesota Rollergirls, Roy Wilkins Auditorium, 612-296-4743, www.mnrollergirls.com/. Tickets are sold online at www.ticketmaster.com and at Pizza Luce, O'Gara's, Electric Fetus, and a few other local outlets.

SOCCER

NSC **Minnesota Stars** play April through September at the National Sports Center in Blaine. Purchase tickets online, www.nscminnesota.org.

COLLEGE SPORTS

The biggest college draw is, of course, the **University of Minnesota**, which plays in the Big Ten Conference, www.gophersports.com. "**Golden Gopher**" basketball and hockey each have a particularly large following. In football, the U's biggest rival is **Iowa**, which they play for a bronze pig known as "**Floyd of Rosedale.**" Their other big rivalry is with nationally ranked **University of Michigan**, over **The Little Brown Jug**. Finally, in 2005, after 16 consecutive years of losing, the Gophers brought that venerable trophy home to Minnesota as fans of both teams sat there and watched the game in disbelief. To learn about this historic moment and get the latest (unofficial) word on all Gopher sports, read The GopherHole, online at www.gopherhole.com. For schedules and tickets to any U of M event, contact the Minnesota Athletics Ticket Office at Mariucci Arena, 4 Oak Street SE, Minneapolis; 612-624-8080 or 1-800 UGOPHER. Home games are held at the TCF Stadium located on campus.

PARTICIPANT SPORTS AND RECREATION

Minnesota is all about sports. From babies to grannies, everybody participates in something. People moving into the area who want to play team sports should call their local Community Services or the **Cities Sports Connection**, 612-929-9009, www.cscsports.com. Sign up on their web site for social outings as well as adult recreation. Sports include broomball, volleyball, kickball, basketball, football, softball, bowling and soccer. Games are played at locations throughout the Twin Cities, all year 'round.

AUTOMOBILE RACING

- **Brainerd International Raceway and Resort**, www.brainerdracewayand resort.com. For tickets call 1-866-444-4455.
- **Elko Speedway**, 26350 France Ave, Elko, 952-461-7223, elkospeedway.com
- **Minnesota Street Rod Association** meets monthly to talk cars and sponsors a "Back to the '50s" car show at the Minnesota State Fairgrounds, www.msra. com.
- **Raceway Park**, 1 Checkered Flag Boulevard, Shakopee, 952-445-2257, gorace waypark.com

BICYCLING

According to *Bicycling Magazine* (May 2010), Minneapolis is the #1 Bike City in the country.

From the **National Sports Center's Velodrome** bike track in Blaine (www.nsc-sports.com/velo) to the interconnected web of trails that stretches from the western suburbs to Stillwater in the east, the Twin Cities are blessed with an abundance of places to bike. Recreational biking has exploded, and bike commuting has also taken off. It's not unusual to see bikers wheeling to and from work dressed in suits, with important papers stowed in backpacks—even in winter! Minneapolis and St. Paul both promote bike commuting by offering low-cost bike lockers at numerous locations and by providing guaranteed rides home in bad weather. (See **Transportation** for more information.)

Throughout the rest of the metro, increasing numbers of off-street bike routes have either been built or are under construction. Download bike info from any city's web site. An excellent way to find the best routes is by using **Cyclopath**, http://cyclopath.org. This "geowiki" provides an editable regional map where other Twin Cities cyclists enter tags about special problems and fix map problems such as missing trails.

The Twin Cities have been named one of *Bike Magazine*'s 15 best cities in North America for mountain biking. Try these popular and scenic trails, many of which are also used for walking and skating, and cross-country skiing in winter:

- **Afton Alps Mountain Bike Area**, Hastings, www.aftonalps.com.
- **Gateway Trail** begins just south of Wheelock Pkwy and east of I-35E in St. Paul, and extends 18 miles to Pine Point Park in Stillwater, www.dnr.state.mn.us.
- **Luce Line Trail** from Plymouth west to Cosmos, www.luceline.com/.
- **"Minneapolis Grand Rounds,"** 50-mile National Scenic Byway loops around the Minneapolis Chain of Lakes, www.minneapolisparks.org/grandrounds.
- **Mississippi Gorge** trails on both sides of the Mississippi River between the Franklin Avenue Bridge and Ford Parkway Bridge create an 8-mile loop, www.nps.gov/miss.
- **Southwest Regional LRT Trail** from Hopkins west to Victoria or southwest to Chanhassen; or from Hopkins east to Minneapolis, to connect with the Midtown Greenway, www.fbiw.org/Trail/trailguide.htm.
- **Theodore Wirth Park** has an off-road cycling trail north of Highway 55, between Twin Lakes and Wirth Parkway, www.minneapolisparks.org.

For out-of-town biking, the trails below are just a sampling. Most of them are also open for horseback riding, cross-country skiing, and snowmobiling. **The Bicycle Vacation Guide, Minnesota and Wisconsin**, www.littletransport.com, is a good guide to help you plan a trip.

- **Cannon Valley Trail** from Cannon Falls to Red Wing, www.cannonvalleytrail.com.
- **Gandy Dancer** is a 98-mile trail from St. Croix Falls to Superior in northwestern Wisconsin, www.nps.gov/sacn.
- **Heartland State Trail** is a 49-mile multiple-use route between Park Rapids and Cass Lake about 200 miles north of Minneapolis, dnr.state.mn.us/state_trails/heartland.
- **Lutsen Mountain Bike Park**; on the North Shore, www.lutsen.com.
- **Root River Trail** from Fountain to Houston in the far southeastern corner of Minnesota is a 42-mile paved multiple-use trail that offers outstanding views of the Red River Valley, www.rootrivertrail.org.

BICYCLING RESOURCES

- **Angry Catfish Bicycle and Coffee Bar** has a very nice bike-repair station and amazing Intelligentsia coffee that pairs up well with the high-quality, unique-to-the-Twin Cities bikes/clothing/equipment they stock, 4208 28th Ave S, Minneapolis, 612.722.1538, www.angrycatfishbicycle.com.

- **Capricorn Bicycles** hand-makes workhorse steel bike frames and racks, both custom and stock, Minneapolis, www.capricornbicycles.com.
- **Explore Minnesota**, www.exploreminnesota.com, offers excellent information on trails and mountain-biking locations all over the state, as well as lodging and trail pass requirements.
- **Freewheel Midtown Bike Center**, 2834 10th Ave S, 612-238-4447, http://freewheelbike.com) is a joint effort of Allina Health Systems and the City of Minneapolis to provide the Midtown Greenway and larger Twin Cities community with a full-service bike transportation station complete with bike storage, rentals, café, public restrooms and showers, repair classes, and a shop where you can do your own maintenance. They also have a full-service repair shop, bicycle and accessory sales.
- **Hennepin County Bikeways & Trails**, www.threeriversparks.org.
- **Minnesota Bike Trails & Rides**, http://mntrails.com, is the Minnesota Department of Natural Resources' online trails magazine.
- **Rehbeins Arena**, Lino Lakes, offers year-round BMX racing, www.rehbeinsbmx.com.
- **Two Wheel View** coordinates environmental stewardship with local, regional, and international bike trips, www.twowheelview.org/.

LOCAL BICYCLING CLUBS

- **Minneapolis Off-Road Cycling Advocates** (MOCA) designed, built, and maintains the Wirth Park trail, www.mocatrails.org.
- **Minnesota Off-Road Cyclists** (MORC) has a "complete and authoritative" guide on its web site, www.morcmtb.org.
- **Minnesota Rovers Outdoors Club** emphasizes quiet sports such as hiking, canoeing, climbing, bicycling, and skiing. Trip costs (day/weekend/extended) are shared and coordinated by members. Hotline: 612-782-7139, www.MNRovers.org.
- **Ski Hawks Sport and Social Club**: This more social club sponsors bike, ski, and snowboarding trips, rollerblading, and happy hours, www.mnskihawks.org.
- **Twin Cities Bicycling Club**: TCBC is the largest recreational bicycling club in the Minneapolis–St. Paul area, www.biketcbc.org
- The **Wheelmen** is a national organization whose mission is to promote the restoration and riding of pre-1918 cycles. Early Wheelmen pushed the Twin Cities to pave their streets and create the Chain of Lakes system that we all enjoy today. You won't have any trouble recognizing the members—they ride funny-looking cycles and wear funny-looking clothes and are usually surrounded by curious onlookers. Check the national web site, www.thewheelmen.org, for current local contact information.

BIKE POLO

Bike polo is just starting to catch on in the TC, so they have frequent "New Player Days" and special sessions for beginners. Look online at Minneapolis Bike Polo for all the local news and schedules, www.mplsbikepolo.com.

BILLIARDS AND POOL

- **Fat Boy Billiards**, 1920 Central Ave NE, Minneapolis, 612-789-9750.
- **Shooters Billiards Club and Café** is the see-and-be-seen pool hall of the-Twin Cities. It's open from 10 a.m. to 4 a.m, 1934 Hwy 13 E, Burnsville, www.shootersbilliardclub.com.

BIRDING

Located along the **Mississippi River flyway**, the Twin Cities are home to eight unique birding habitats, and it is possible to see nearly 300 species of birds here without ever venturing far from home. To find out where to go and when, get a copy of **The Twin Cities Birding Map**. It is available at bookstores, bird-seed outlets, and interpretive centers throughout the metro. For those who'd rather explore the world of birds in comfort with a cold drink in their hands, the **Mississippi National River & Recreation Area** (www.nps.gov/miss) sponsors occasional cruises down the Mississippi on **"The Birding Boat."** Cruises depart from Harriet Island, St. Paul. For tickets, contact the **Padelford Packet Boat Company**, 651-227-1100, www.riverrides.com. Guided van tours through the **Minnesota Valley National Wildlife Refuge** will also net glimpses of bald eagles, great blue herons, and wild turkeys close enough for even the near-sighted to see. Tours are run by volunteers and available on a reservation-only basis, www.friendsofmnvalley.org, 952-881-9055. Online sign up for email updates about bird and butterfly migrations at **Journey North**, www.learner.org/jnorth, an educational web site for school children, teachers, scientists, and nature lovers. The **Minnesota Ornithologists' Union** web site posts recently sighted bird photos as well as a ton of local birding information, www.moumn.org.

BOATING

Minnesota isn't called the **Land of Ten Thousand Lakes** for nothing. There are hundreds of lakes within the metro area alone, and most of them are host to boats of some kind. **Lake Minnetonka**, the **St. Croix River**, and the **Mighty Mississippi** are the most popular big boat waters and have numerous public launch sites. In the East Metro, **White Bear Lake** is home to world-class sailors. In the South Metro, **Prior Lake** is loved by water-skiers for its calm waters.

(Water-skiing was actually born at **Lake City**, Minnesota, on the Mississippi River, www.lakecity.org.)

If you've got a craft already, you'll need a **license**. A boat license is good for three years, and the cost depends on the type of boat. **Register your watercraft** in person at any Deputy Registrar of Motor Vehicles office (where you license your car). Look on the **DNR** web site (www.dnr.state.mn.us) for a license center near you. The DNR web site includes the **Minnesota Boating Guide**, a downloadable booklet that summarizes Minnesota's boating laws and regulations.

If you're looking for a loaner, you can rent small canoes and paddleboats at most city lakes. Call one of the following for bigger boat rental. Most of the popular lakes Up North offer plenty of rentals for those on vacation.

- **Excel Boat Club**, Excelsior, is a membership boat club that rents a variety of powerboats, 952-401-3880, www.excelboatclub.com.
- **Rockvam Boat Rental**, Spring Park, rents fishing boats and pontoons by the day, 952-471-9515,www.rockvamboatyards.com.

If you're looking for a boat to buy, you won't have to travel far. Minnesota seems to have as many boat dealers as it has car lots, and they sell everything from fishing boats to luxury yachts. If it's a fine vintage boat you're looking for, though, try **Mahogany Bay** in Mound, which sells, services, restores, and stores classic boats, 952-495-0007, www.mahoganybay.net.

Contact the local Power Squadrons for courses in how to operate a boat safely:

- **Minnetonka Power Squadron**, 612-253-2628, minnetonkaps.org
- **St. Paul Sail and Power Squadron**, Mound, 952-472-9300, stpaulsquadron. org

---

H20 Towing & Taxi/Towboat U.S. provides salvage, emergency pump-out, towing, and jump-starts on Lake Minnetonka, 612-282-8616. Towing costs over $100 an hour, so become a member of **BOATUS.com** (800-395-2628) and save yourself a bundle.

CANOEING, KAYAKING, ROWING

- **Above the Falls Sports**, www.abovethefallssports.com, sells and rents kayaks, canoes, and rowboats, instructs, and offers group touring on the Mississippi River above St. Anthony Falls. Its location in the North Loop neighborhood of Downtown Minneapolis means that river access is within walking/rolling distance of the shop, 120 N 3rd Ave, Minneapolis, 612-825-8983.

SAILING AND SAILBOAT RENTAL

Minnesota waters are known to boaters across the country. **Lake Minnetonka** and **White Bear Lake** in the Twin Cities suburbs and **Lakes Calhoun** and **Harriet** in the shadows of Minneapolis' skyscrapers are home to nationally competitive yacht clubs and experienced sailing schools. **Lake Superior** is one of the finest sailing grounds in the world. Rent small sailboats at Phalen-Keller Regional Park in St. Paul, www.friendsoftheparks.org. To learn to sail or race contact:

- **Calhoun Yacht Club** and **Lake Calhoun Sailing School**, 612-822-8238, www.lakecalhoun.org
- **Lake Harriet Yacht Club** maintains a fleet of boats on Lake Harriet for the use of its members, 612-920-9420, www.lhycsailing.com.
- **Lake Minnetonka Sailing School**, 952-404-1645, www.lmss.us
- **Minneapolis Parks and Recreation Board**, www.minneapolisparks.org, offers beginner-level evening lessons for adults at Lake Harriet.
- **Minnetonka Yacht Club**, Deephaven, 952-474-4457, www.minnetonka yachtclub.org
- *Northern Breezes* is the free local sailing news magazine, www.sailingbreezes. com.
- **Sailboats, Inc.** offers instruction and charters on Lake Pepin and Lake Superior, 800-826-7010, www.sailing-instruction.com.
- **St. Paul's Come Sail Away** sailing program on Lake Phalen teaches basic and intermediate sailing to people age 14 through adult, Phalen Lakeside Activities Center, 651-266-6406, www.stpaul.gov/parks.
- **Twin Cities Sailing Club** offers a great opportunity for experienced and novice sailors to sail regularly and inexpensively at Lake Harriet. Membership provides access to the club's fleet of small boats and the chance to crew with the experienced sailors of the Lake Harriet Yacht Club, http://www.tcsailing. com/scum/.
- **Upper Minnetonka Yacht Club**, 4165 Shoreline Dr, Spring Park, www.umyc. org
- **Wayzata Yacht Club and Sailing School**, 1100 E County Rd 16, Wayzata, 952-470-1468, www.wyc.org
- **White Bear Yacht Club and Sailing School**, Clubhouse 651-429-8395, www. wbycsail.org

SAILBOAT DOCKAGE AND STORAGE

Once you have a boat, finding a place to keep it can be difficult and expensive, though many cities offer good deals on dockage to their residents. Check with your city hall about waiting lists and fees. Most facilities require that boat owners remove their boats for the winter, but **French Regional Park** on Medicine Lake in Plymouth rents slips for sailboats under 22 feet in length, and offers winter storage, too. Slips and storage spaces are available on a lottery basis, 763-694-7750, www.threeriversparkdistrict.

ICE BOATING AND WINDSURFING

Ice boating and windsurfing are not as organized as sailing, but there are some races and there are plenty of guys out there experimenting with their "sleds," particularly on **Lake Minnetonka**, **Lake Calhoun,** and **Lake Waconia**. Those interested should contact one of the yacht clubs listed above, or just show up where you see a group of ice boaters gathered, often on Wayzata Bay of Lake Minnetonka. For windsurfing, these places can outfit you with equipment and arrange for lessons:

- **The House Boardshop**, located at the junction of 35E and I-694 at 300 S Owasso Blvd, St. Paul, 800-409-7669, www.the-house.com
- **Scuba Center Windsurfing**, 5015 Penn Ave S, Minneapolis, 612-925-4818, www.scubacenter.com

BOWLING

Over and over again Twin Citians have picked bowling alleys as the best places to go on a first date. Several local bowling alleys offer other entertainment as well.

- **Bryant Lake Bowl**, 810 W Lake St, Minneapolis, www.bryantlakebowl.com, also offers a wine and espresso bar and performance space.
- **Elsie's Bowling Center**, 729 NE Marshall St, 612-378-9701, www.elsies.com
- **Park Tavern Bowling and Entertainment Center**, 3401 Louisiana Ave S, St. Louis Park, www.parktavern.net
- **Ran-ham Bowling Center**, 490½ S. Hamline Ave. St. Paul, 651-698-0252

BRIDGE

- The **Twin Cities Bridge Center** offers lessons and sponsors duplicate tournaments, 6020 Nicollet Ave, Minneapolis, 612-861-4487, www.district14.org/Minnesota/Minneapolis.

CASINOS

Indian gaming is one of Minnesota's biggest industries, and most casinos remain open all night. You have to be 18 to gamble, though most establishments have some kind of facility for children, such as an arcade. For more information on casinos in Minnesota check **casinosminnesota.com**.

- **Little Six**, Prior Lake, 952-445-6000, www.littlesixcasino.com
- **Mystic Lake Casino**, Prior Lake, 800-262-7799, www.mysticlake.com
- **Treasure Island Casino**, Hwy 61 and 316, Red Wing, 800-222-7077, www.treasureislandcasino.com

CHESS

- **Castle Chess Club**, 1121 Jackson Street NE, Minneapolis, www.chesscastle.com, holds "rated chess" events. Look on their web site for information about other local clubs and where they play.

- **Chess Club of Minnesota** (www.mnchess.com) plays at locations in the western suburbs. It offers free and fee-based chess, mini-camps, and tournaments for all ages from kindergarten up.
- **Minnesota State Chess Association** (http://minnesotachess.org) sponsors tournaments, including the state championships and other events.
- **School Chess Association**, www.schoolchess.org, promotes chess for students K–12.

CURLING

Part housecleaning, part shuffleboard, the game of sailing a rock across a sheet of ice is probably the least known winter sport in the U.S.—unless you live in St. Paul, home of the 1200-member St. Paul Curling Club, the largest curling club in the USA. They play a world-class game here. Minnesota's own Allison Pottinger competed in the 2010 Olympics and many other members have won numerous U.S. national and world medals.

- **St. Paul Curling Club**, 470 Selby Ave, St. Paul, 651-224-7408, www.stpaul curlingclub.org.

DANCE

Twin Cities dance clubs offer lessons, host dances, participate in competitions, and perform at festivals and fairs. For **square dance lessons**, visit www.square danceminnesota.com. For regular **ballroom dancing**, check the Yellow Pages under "Dance Instruction." Local dance resources include:

- **Arthur Murray**, 5041 France Ave, Edina, 612-920-1900, www.arthurmur-raympls.com.
- **Four Seasons Dance Studio** is a dancers' co-op that offers instruction in a number of partner dances and a four-hour crash course for wedding couples, 1637 Hennepin Ave S, Minneapolis, 612-342-0902, www.4seasonsdance.com.
- **Tapestry Folkdance Center** offers beginner instruction in International Folk Dancing, Contra, and Swing, and features live music on weekends, 3748 Minnehaha Ave, Minneapolis, 612-722-2914, www.tapestryfolkdance.org.

DISABLED ATHLETES

In 1992, the **Minnesota State High School League** became the first association in the nation to sanction interscholastic sports for kids with disabilities (see **Adapted Athletics** in the **Childcare and Education** chapter). **Courage Center** (www.couragecenter.org) offers numerous sports opportunities for all ages. Here are some other things to try:

- If it's camping or canoeing you like to do, **Wilderness Inquiry** creates outdoor adventures for people of all ages, abilities, and backgrounds (612-676-9400, 800-728-0719, www.wildernessinquiry.org).

- For those who love horses, Minnesota has **We Can Ride** (www.wecanride. org), which offers therapeutic horseback riding and cart driving for children and adults at several locations, 952-934-0057, www.wecanride.org; and Hoofbeats and Heartbeats Equestrian Learning Center, 12301 95th St NE, Elk River, 763-441-2274, www.hoofbeatsheartbeats.org.
- The **Power Hockey** league allows anyone in a power wheelchair to participate. If you want to sign up, call the US Electric Wheelchair Hockey Association, 763-535-4736, www.usewha.org.
- **Special Olympics MN** offers year-round training and competitions, 100 Washington Ave S, Minneapolis, 612-333-0999, 800-783-7732, www.special olympicsminnesota.org.
- **U.S. Blind Tandem Cycling Connection**, http://bicyclingblind.org, provides an online resource for blind and sighted cyclists to team up for a bike ride. By creating a profile, riders can search for either a sighted pilot or a blind/visually impaired stoker in their local area.

DISC (FRISBEE) GOLF

Disc golf is played at a growing number of metro-area parks. The **Minnesota Frisbee Association** (MFA) maintains an up-to-date clickable course map on its web site, http://mnfrisbee.ning.com.

DOG-RELATED RECREATION

For additional information, see the **Pets** chapter.

DOG SLEDDING

Many resorts and dogsled outfitters offer opportunities to mush across the frozen tundra behind a line of powerful huskies. For a complete list, look online at www.exploreminnesota.com. Here are a just few:

- **Boundary Country Lodge to Lodge Adventures**, Grand Marais, 218-388-4487, 800-322-8327, www.boundarycountry.com.
- **Cragun's Resort**, 11000 Craguns Dr, Brainerd, 800-272-4867, www.craguns. com
- **Outward Bound Wilderness**, Ely, 866-467-7651, 720-497-2340, www.out wardboundwilderness.org
- **Points Unknown**, Watertown, 612-327-6965, www.points-unknown.com, maintains a kennel of traditional sled dogs and offers training and adventure dog-sledding trips, where you learn how to mush a small team of sled dogs, navigation, and other wilderness skills.
- **Wilderness Inquiry**, Minneapolis, 612-676-9400, 800-728-0719, www.wil dernessinquiry.org; can take you on safari in Africa, too!
- **Wintergreen Dogsled Lodge**, Ely, 218-365-6022, 877-753-3386, www.dog sledding.com

SLED DOG RACES

Check out **www.sleddogcentral.com** for race dates and locations. Here are a couple, not too far away, where you can watch the Big Dogs run:

- **John Beargrease Sled Dog Marathon**, Duluth, www.beargrease.com
- **Pine River Sled Run**, Merrill, Wisconsin, www.witrailblazers.org

HERDING

Shepherd's Harvest Sheep and Wool Festival, www.shepherdsharvestfestival.org, not only has lots of stock dogs and textiles on display, but activities for children, such as weaving, music and llama walking. There's even a sheepherding class, Washington County Fairgrounds, Lake Elmo, on Mother's Day Weekend.

- **Training Camp Inc.,** herding classes and clinics, 15040 Old Marine Trail N, Scandia, 612-922-1114, www.trainingcampinc.com

GAME FAIR

Minnesota Game Fair, www.gamefair.com, is held at **Armstrong Ranch Kennels**, between Anoka and Elk River, www.armstrongkennels.com. This late August weekend event is a family affair where there are activities for the whole family, including your dog.

SKIJORING

A dog, a harness, and some skis are all you need for skijoring—a sport that combines cross-country skiing with dog power for an exhilarating sprint across the snow. The Midwest Skijorers Club offers lessons and demo days where you can hook up to a trained dog and see what it's like, www.skijor.org. Several Three Rivers Parks have skijoring trails (www.threeriversparks.org), as does Lake Byllesby Regional Park in Dakota County (www.dakotacounty.us).

FISHING AND HUNTING

Becoming an Outdoors Woman is a program of half-day clinics and weekend workshops that teach outdoor skills, including hunting and fishing, to women age 18 and older, www.dnr.state.mn.us/education/bow/index.html.

You are now in hunting and fishing country! Everything stops for the season openers, spring and fall. Really! Including homebuilding—so don't expect your painters to show up on the fishing opener. Though many people routinely go "Up North" for their recreation, you really don't have to leave your neighborhood to fish here because the **Department of Natural Resources** (DNR) stocks metro lakes, as well as the waters Up North.

Don't forget **ice fishing**. Most who fish in summer enjoy "hardwater fishing" in winter, too—sometimes in two-story houses outfitted with amenities such as stoves, big screen TVs, underwater cameras, and enough beds to sleep a crowd. In fact, whole communities of ice houses (or fish houses), complete with plowed roads and street signs, spring up every winter on otherwise desolate frozen lakes. Fish houses can be homemade, purchased, or rented. Rent a heated 2-holer (that's fishing holes) on Lake Minnetonka or Lake Waconia from **Minnetonka Fish House Rental** (952-221-4386 http://minnetonkafishhouse.com) for about $100/day. To rent an ice house on famed **Lake Mille Lacs**, look online at www.millelacs.com.

The latest craze: **darkhouse angling**. That's when you spearfish through a hole in the ice that is enclosed in a darkened space. For information and help getting started, contact the **Minnesota Darkhouse and Angling Association**, www.mndarkhouse.org.

Remember that all forms of fishing and hunting require a **license**. You can purchase hunting and fishing licenses and apply for hunting lotteries online, by phone, or in person. **Online**, buy your licenses through the DNR's web page, www.dnr.state.mn.us/licenses. Purchase licenses **by phone** at 1-888-665-4236 (1-MN-LICENSE). Finally, you can buy your licenses **in person** from a state licensing agent. Agents include bait shops, marinas, sporting goods stores, hardware stores, gas stations, and county license centers. Search the DNR web site by county to find a licensing agent near you.

Though noted metro-area lakes are often surrounded by homes, they are still crowded with walleye, bass, northern pike, muskies, and crappies (up here people say "croppies"). Hang your hook in **Lake Minnetonka, Lake Elmo, Lake Waconia,** or **Forest Lake** and you might come home with a record-breaker. Or cast your jig in the waters of the **Mississippi River**, just below the **Coon Rapids Dam** or the **Ford Dam** near downtown St. Paul. On the hottest days of summer, big carp are attracted to the oxygen-rich shallows along the dams' concrete spillways; the deeper holes are home to more traditional game fish, including smallmouth bass and walleye.

For those who want to travel, **Lake Mille Lacs** (www.millelacs.com) and **Leech Lake** are home to big walleye and muskie. **Lake of the Woods** bills itself as the "**Walleye Capital of the World**." Call 800-382-FISH or visit www.lake-ofthewoodsmn.com for resort information. Plastic-coated maps that show the good fishing spots on each lake are sold at bait and sporting goods stores everywhere. Data on fish stocking and water quality, as well as consumption advice guidelines, are searchable by lake on the **Department of Natural Resources Lake Finder** web site, www.dnr.state.mn.us/lakefind/. Sadly, the increase in impervious surfaces and agricultural and industrial run-off has not only made consumption of fish an iffy proposition but has actually wiped out several area fisheries. Trout that once swam in suburban waters like Golden Valley Creek, Purgatory Creek, and Trout Brook no longer exist. Both **stocked and native trout**, however, can still be found in the **Rush River**, about an hour east of the

Twin Cities, in Wisconsin. A **Wisconsin fishing license** is required for anyone 16 or older. Licenses can be purchased online at http://dnr.wi.gov.

The **Minnesota Horse and Hunt Club** provides 600 acres of upland and wildfowl hunting, trap and skeet. Its grill features a wild game menu. They also sell started and finished German Shorthair Pointers, www.horseandhunt.com.

To learn about the best hunting grounds and fishing holes, tune in to **Ron Schara** and his black Labrador retriever Raven on **Minnesota Bound** on **KARE11** television weekends, or listen to Ron on **WCCO** radio (AM 830) at 5:30 on Saturday mornings. Schara has also written numerous books on hunting and fishing, and authors a monthly newsletter. Sign up for it on his web site, www.mnbound.com. For interesting articles, read **Minnesota Sportsman** magazine, www.minnesotasportsmanmag.com.

GARDENING

The **University of Minnesota Landscape Arboretum** (www.arboretum.umn.edu), otherwise known as "The Arb," is located on Highway 5 west of Chanhassen. It features over 1000 acres of public gardens, natural and native areas. Its **Gardening Information** page will connect you with a Master Gardener who will answer your gardening questions by e-mail. Need more info? Call the Arb at 952-443-1400 and leave a message. You can also contact the Hennepin County Master Gardener Helpline at 612-596-2118 and a Master Gardener will call you back. Other Helplines can be found at www.extension.umn.edu/gardeninfo/components/questions_yglines.html.

As long as you choose plants that are hardy in our zone (4a, minimum temperatures of minus 30 degrees Fahrenheit), you'll find Minnesota gardening quite enjoyable. And cultivate a taste for hostas—they're not only beautiful, but they're also reliably hardy. Check out the Master Gardeners' list of their top 25 plants for Minnesota at www.mg.umn.edu/top25/index.html. If you need to over-winter non-hardy roses, you'll want to use the **Minnesota Tip** method (see http://minnesotarosesociety.org/).

For nurseries and more gardening resources, see **Gardening** in the **Shopping** chapter. For a peek at what other people are growing, check with the **Arboretum Auxiliary** about its annual bus tour to private gardens. The information will be advertised in the papers and listed on the Arboretum's web site (see address and phone number above). In addition, many neighborhoods and members of plant societies open their garden gates for fundraising events. To accelerate your learning curve, get a subscription to the **Northern Gardener**, www.northerngardener.org. Other resources include:
- **Minnesota Native Plant Society**, www.mnnps.org
- **Northscaping**, an Internet community of northern gardeners and landscapers, www.northscaping.com

- **Minnesota Hosta Society**, www.mnhosta.org (You have to watch their 2010 National Convention promo video—it's Minnesota Priceless!)

GOLF

Having just moved, you may not be quite ready to join a country club, but don't worry, many public courses here are as good as the clubs—in fact, many are better! But for a unique Minnesota experience, try these: **Science Museum of Minnesota Big Back Yard**, **Baker National**, and **The Legends Club**. Okay, so the Science Museum is mini-golf—it's definitely fun and unique, and it will teach you about the effect of water on the landscape. For information, look on the museum's web site, www.smm.org.

Now for the real golf. Play **Baker National** in **Medina** if for no other reason than to see what the metro used to look like before it got so built up. Set amidst lakes and rolling fields, this challenging course is owned and operated by the **Three Rivers Park District**, www.threeriversparks.org. On the other side of the metro, **The Legends Club** in **Prior Lake** is #3 on *Golfweek*'s Top 10 Minnesota Public Courses, and #15 on *Golf Digest*'s Top Twenty Minnesota Courses, www.golfdigest.com.

A little farther afield, but well worth the trip, is **The Quarry** at Giant's Ridge, Biwabik, a fairly new modern-style course which debuted #16 on *Golf Digest*'s list of 100 Greatest Public Courses. Nearby are **The Legends**, also at Giant's Ridge, and **The Wilderness at Fortune Bay** on Lake Vermillion. All three were designed by the great modern course architect **Jeffrey Brauer**, who refers to this collection of northern Minnesota courses as his "Pinehurst." In the opposite direction, try **Willinger's** in Northfield, 952-652-2500, www.willingersgc.com.

For information about the courses above and to find a course that suits you, check out **MinnesotaGolf.com**, which has a clickable map and helpful course review section. To reserve tee times at most courses, call **Teemaster** at 952-525-1100, or make your reservations online at www.teemaster.com. Here are some locals' favorite public courses:

- **Baker National**, Medina, www.threeriversparks.org
- **Bunker Hills**, Coon Rapids, www.bunkerhillsgolf.com.
- **Chaska Town Course**, Chaska, www.chaskatowncourse.com; #5 on *Golfweek*'s list of Top Ten Minnesota Public Courses.
- **Edinburgh USA**, Brooklyn Park, www.edinburghusa.org.
- **Hidden Greens**, Hastings, costs half what the closer-in courses do, and is in the middle of a state game refuge, so it scores on beauty, too, www.hiddengreensgolf.com.
- **Keller Golf Club**, St. Paul, www.co.ramsey.mn.us/parks/golf/keller.htm
- **Meadowbrook**, Hopkins, www.minneapolisparks.org
- **Rush Creek**, Maple Grove, www.rushcreek.com; #7 on *Golfweek*'s Top Ten Minnesota Public Courses.

- **St. Croix National**, Somerset, Wisconsin, 715-247-4200, www.wpgolf.com/stcroix/index.html.
- **StoneRidge**, Stillwater, is a links-style course ranked #1 Public Access Golf Course in the Twin Cities by *Golfweek*, www.stoneridgegc.com.
- **Troy Burne**, Hudson, Wisconsin, www.troyburne.com.
- **The Wilds**, Prior Lake, www.golfthewilds.com; is #8 on *Golfweek*'s Top Ten Minnesota Public Courses.

For those interested in private clubs, both **Interlachen** in Edina (www.interlachencc.org) and **Hazeltine**, in Chaska (www.hngc.com), have made *Golf Digest*'s list of 100 Greatest Golf Courses, and are ranked 1 (Interlachen) and 2 (Hazeltine) on the magazine's list of Top 20 Minnesota Courses. Ranked 15th on this list is another interesting course, the **Tournament Players Club** of the Twin Cities (tpctwincities.com), a private course off 35W in Blaine/Circle Pines. Owned and built by the Professional Golfers Association, the TPC, which opened in the spring of 2000, is used once a year for a Champions Tour event; the rest of the time it is available to members. It is occasionally open to the public for charity events.

And don't forget—this *is* Minnesota; we don't give golf up for the winter here. For a quick getaway, work out your winter kinks on Breezy Point's links, near Brainerd. Their 9-hole course on the lake has tree-lined fairways and interesting hazards. Participants use regular golf clubs and tennis balls. Contact **Breezy Point Resort** online at www.breezypointresort.com or call 800-432-3777. Closer to home, **Wayzata** holds a Chilly Open fundraiser each year on **Lake Minnetonka**; and US Bank runs an 18-hole, all ages, mini-putt tournament in the Minneapolis Skyway system to raise money for the Boys and Girls Club, www.skywayopen.org.

HEALTH CLUBS AND GYMS

Many of the clubs listed below have locations throughout the Twin Cities.
- **Bally Total Fitness**; St. Louis Park, Fridley, Bloomington, Richfield, Eagan, St. Paul, Little Canada; 800-515-CLUB, www.ballyfitness.com.
- **Calhoun Beach Club Inc.**, 2925 Dean Pkwy, Minneapolis, 612-925-8300, www.calhounbc.com.
- **Life Time Fitness** health clubs and family recreation facilities; about two dozen locations throughout the Twin Cities; 952-380-0303, www.lifetimefitness.com.
- **Lonna Mosow's Center for Mind and Body Fitness**, 6409 City West Pkwy, Eden Prairie, 952-941-9448; www.lonnamosow.com.
- **The Marsh**, 15000 Minnetonka Blvd, Minnetonka; this peaceful, affirming exercise facility has a yoga tower and two pools along with the normal equipment rooms and aerobics classes. Physical therapy is available here as well.

The restaurant serves gourmet food and is open for lunch and dinner, 952-935-2202, www.themarsh.com.

- **SouthSide Athletic Club** includes a separate gym for serious powerlifters and bodybuilders, 12940 Harriet Ave S (35W and Burnsville Pkwy), Burnsville.
- The **University Club**, 420 Summit Ave, St. Paul, 651-222-1751, www.university clubofstpaul.com, is a formal old-school club, but does have fitness and health facilities, clay court tennis, an outdoor pool and children's swim team, and swimming and tennis privileges at Dellwood Hills Country Club.
- The Ys—**YWCA and YMCA**—have locations throughout the Twin Cities and western Wisconsin. A monthly membership may cost much less than for a private club, and volunteering at the Y can earn you a discount. Call 612-332-0501, 612-230-9622, or look online at www.ymcatwincities.org, ywcampls.org, www.ywcaofstpaul.org.

HIKING

The amount of green you see on the Minnesota State map speaks for itself—a good part of the northern third of the state is either state or national forest, and there are dozens of interconnected local, regional, and state parks and trails that wind throughout the metro. Four national parks are within a day's drive. For detailed information about trails, including ratings, look online at **www.trails.com**, or buy one of the numerous excellent hiking/biking guidebooks written about Minnesota, such as *60 Hikes within 60 Miles: Minneapolis and St. Paul* by Tom Watson. For more hiking opportunities see the **Quick Getaways** and **Lakes and Parks** chapters. Here are a few suggestions to get you started:

- **Afton State Park**, Hastings, www.dnr.state.mn.us/state_parks/afton; hike the rolling bluffs along the St. Croix River.
- **Carver Park Reserve**, west of Chanhassen off Highway 5, www.threeriver-sparks.org, has 14.5 miles of turf trails and another 9 miles of paved trails, and connects to the Lake Minnetonka Regional Trail.
- **Fort Snelling State Park**, Hwys 5 & 55, St. Paul, www.dnr.state.mn.us/state_parks/fort_snelling, is an historic site with trails that connect to the metro parkways.
- **Swede Hollow Park**, St. Paul, is an enchanted little nature area in the shadows of St. Paul's downtown skyscrapers. Site of an early immigrant shanty town, after the city condemned and burned the buildings in 1956, it reverted to nature. Part of the Bruce Vento Trail system, the stairs alone are a workout.

Local hiking clubs include:

- **St. Paul Hiking Club**, www.stpaulhike.org
- **Thursday Night Hikers** is a group of people who hike together every Thursday night throughout the year, except Thanksgiving. After the hike, they go

to a restaurant for dinner/ dessert and further conversation. Hikes are free and moderately paced, www.angelfire.com/mn/thursdaynighthikes/.

HORSEBACK RIDING

Hennepin County used to have the most horses per capita of any county in the U.S. Now, if you want to keep horses, you really need to move farther out. Washington County toward **Forest Lake**, **Medina/Maple Plain/ Independence** in western Hennepin County, **Jordan**, **Lakeville**, and **western Wisconsin** still have room—and zoning friendly to horses. **Baker Park Reserve** in Medina has just over nine miles of trails to ride; and **Murphy-Hanrehan Park Reserve** in Savage has 13.9 miles of horse trails plus a 20-horse camping spot, www.three-riversparks.org. The **Minnesota Valley National Wildlife Refuge** (www.fws.gov/midwest/minnesotavalley) allows riding on 13 miles of trails that cross the **Louisville Swamp** (off Highway 169 near **Jordan**). Be aware that trails can be flooded during spring and summer, and are used by hunters in the fall. Call the Visitor Center at 952-854-5900 for an update. Washington County allows horses in **Lake Elmo Park Reserve** and **Pine Point Park**. The **Minnesota Trail Riders Association** (www.mntrailriders.com) is a good resource for finding places—and even horses—to ride.

For a comprehensive list of Minnesota stables with some clickable links, look online at www.polocenter.com/stable/stableusmnm.htm. Here are some of the larger boarding, training, and trail riding facilities:

- **Alpine Farms**, Long Lake, 763-473-1361, www.alpine-farms.com; hunters, jumpers, dressage
- **Bob Jensen Stables**, Lakeville, 952-435-5774, bobjensenstables.com; Saddlebreds
- **Bunker Park Stables**, in Bunker Hills Regional Park in Andover, 763-757-9445, www.bunkerparkstable.com; guided trail rides, hay rides, sleigh rides, boarding and lessons
- **Hardwood Creek Farm**, Hugo, 651-429-4900, www.hardwoodcreek.net; Saddlebreds and Morgans
- **Minnesota Horse and Hunt Club**, Prior Lake, is a full-service boarding, training and lesson facility for hunters and jumpers, 952-226-1155, www.horseandhunt.com.
- **River Valley Ranch** boarding and guided trail rides, Carver, 952-361-3361, www.rivervalleyhorseranch.com
- **Triple S Ranch**, 108th St at Barnes Ave, Inver Grove Heights, 651-457-0559, triple-sranch.com; boarding, training, and lessons (hunt seat, Western, equitation, dressage, combined)
- **Twin City Polo Club**, West End Farm, Maple Plain (one mile south of Hwy 12 off County Rd 90), 763-479-4307, www.twincitypolo.com
- **Valiant Stables**, Stillwater, 651-430-1763, Saddlebreds, equitation

- **Westwind Stables**, Hastings, 651-480-1124, westwindstable.com; boarding, lessons, dressage and equitation, camps, hundreds of acres of trails
- **Woodloch Stable**, Hugo, 651-429-1303, woodlochstable.com; boarding, training, lessons, summer youth day camps

If watching the ponies is closer to what you have in mind, see **Horse Racing** under **Professional Sports**.

HORSE SHOWS AND EVENTS

- **Animal Humane Society Hunter and Jumper Show**, June, at Alpine Farms (see above)
- **Tanbark Cavalcade of Roses**, for Saddlebreds, is held at the Minnesota State Fairgrounds Coliseum, St. Paul, in June; www.statefair.gen.mn.us.

ICE SKATING/HOCKEY/BROOMBALL

If slip-sliding and gliding across a smooth lake surface under the stars is your idea of Heaven, you've come to the right place. Nearly every lake in the Twin Cities has a rink and warming house in winter. Some lake rinks are small and neighborhood-maintained, but **Centennial Lakes Park** in Edina (www.ci.edina. mn.us) is 10 full acres. They'll rent you skates, if you don't have your own, and the warming house has both indoor and outdoor fireplaces. **Lake of the Isles** and **Powderhorn Park** in Minneapolis are even more scenic, as is St. Paul's outdoor refrigerated rink in Landmark Plaza.

Most of the following ice arenas are inside and open year 'round, except for a week or two in summer when the ice has to be replaced. They're home to competitive skating clubs and hockey leagues, and also offer open skating for the general public. To find the rink nearest you, use **Rinkfinder** (www.rink-finder.com), a service of the Minnesota Ice Arena Manager's Association. Here are a few rinks to get you started:

- **Aldrich Arena**, Maplewood, 651-748-2510, www.co.ramsey.mn.us
- **Augsburg College Arena** is where they shot the movie *The Mighty Ducks*, Minneapolis, 612-330-1163, www.augsburg.edu/athletics/facilities.html.
- **Bloomington Ice Garden**, Bloomington, has Olympic-sized ice and seating for 2,500; 952-563-8842, www.ci.bloomington.mn.us
- **Burnsville Ice Center**, Burnsville, 952-895-4651, www.Burnsville.org
- The **Guidant John Rose MN Oval**, Roseville, www.skatetheoval.com, 651-792-7007, is the largest refrigerated outdoor skating facility in the world. Experts can hit 40 mph here, but it's also open to the public for regular **ice skating, speed skating, hockey**, and **bandy** in the winter and **in-line skating** in the spring, summer and fall. The adjacent indoor ice arena is open year-round for **hockey** and **figure skating**. Thinking about getting engaged? The rink has a scoreboard that can be used for personal messages!

- **The Depot**, Minneapolis, 612-339-2253, www.thedepotminneapolis.com/rink.htm
- **Eagan Civic Arena**, 651-675-5590, www.cityofeagan.com
- **Minnetonka Ice Arena**, Minnetonka, 952-939-8310, www.eminnetonka.com
- **Parade Ice Garden**, Minneapolis, 612-370-4846, www.minneapolisparks.org
- **Schwan's Super Rink**, Blaine, 763-717-3880, www.superrink.org
- **White Bear Lake Sports Center**, White Bear Lake, 651-429-8571, www.whitebearlake.org
- **YMCA Horse Camp**, 952-898-9622, www.ymcatwincities.org

HOCKEY

Minnesotans bleed hockey—it's in their genes. It used to be only boys, but now it's girls, too. It starts with kids so little they take breaks from skating to lick the ice and rises to the level of the NCAA champion men's and women's **University of Minnesota Hockey Gophers** (www.gophersports.com) and the legendary **1980 U.S. Olympic Team** with its "**Miracle on Ice.**" The sport is mythic here, and a lifestyle. There's lesson hockey, league hockey, pond hockey, school hockey, summer-camp hockey, traveling hockey, park hockey, and pick-up hockey. There's even **Power Hockey** for people in power wheelchairs. To sign up, call the **US Electric Wheelchair Hockey Association**, 763-535-4736 or look online at www.usewha.org.

If you have a child who wants to play hockey, it will take over your life—and most coaches and the other parents will expect you to accept that fact without complaint and schedule Christmas, weddings, and family vacations accordingly. Then make your first hockey-themed vacation a trip to Eveleth, on the Iron Range, to visit the **United States Hockey Hall of Fame** (www.ushockeyhall.com). Adults who'd like to learn to play hockey can sign up for **Adult Beginning Hockey**, which guarantees "no checking/no fighting," Augsburg Arena, 800-4-HOCKEY, www.hna.com. To learn more about adult hockey for both men and women, look online at **www.lifetimehockey.com**. For everything there is to know about every hockey program in the state, including camps and summer camps, go to **ArenaMaps.com**, which includes clickable links.

Pond Hockey (otherwise known as The Game As Nature Intended) is played on many lakes, including Lakes Calhoun and Nokomis in Minneapolis and on Lake Minnetonka. The season is five weeks long, during January and February. There are teams for men, women, and children. Contact your local Park Board to sign up for a league. The US Pond Hockey Championships are played here every January. Learn more at www.pondhockeynac.com and www.uspondhockey.com. In 2008, a documentary was made about pond hockey in Minnesota. Watch the trailer at www.pondhockeymovie.com. Since there are no zambonis, the players shovel the rinks between games!

We also play **broomball** here, which is like hockey, but played with a broom instead of a stick. Check it out or, if you're brave, go ahead and invite your new friends over for a broomball party or join one of the many coed, post-college teams. For information about either sport, check with your local park and recreation department or your local school district's Community Services—or simply ask at your favorite bar. **Lord Fletcher's** in Spring Park on Lake Minnetonka is where many of the broomball leagues play, 952-471-8513.

MARCH MADNESS

Kentucky has the Derby, but Minnesota has the **State High School Hockey Tournament.** Held every year in **March** in **St. Paul**, it's the state's biggest event after the state fair. For days, kids and parents wearing high school hockey jerseys clog the concourses at **Xcel Arena**, and every hotel room in St. Paul is transformed into a fire marshal's nightmare. Then there's usually a blizzard. Life can't get much more Minnesota than that! For everything you need to know to talk hockey tournament around the water cooler, visit the **Minnesota State High School League**'s web site, www.mshsl.org.

IN-LINE SKATING AND SKATEBOARDING

It is fitting that here in the home of **Rollerblade˚**, one of the most popular warm-weather activities is to strap on in-line skates and cruise the marvelous trail system. Heavily used lake routes, such as along **Lake Calhoun** and **Lake of the Isles**, have separate paths for people on and off wheels, so in-line skaters must mix it up with bikers. The **Summit Avenue bike lane** and **Mississippi River parkways** are popular in-line routes as well. In winter, the hallways of the Hubert H. Humphrey **Metrodome**, www.roller-dome.com, are regularly opened to in-line skaters. Or try the **Roller Garden**, 5622 West Lake Street, St. Louis Park, 952-929-5518, www.rollergarden.com, where lessons are available. The cost of each session includes roller skate rental, but in-line skates are extra. The **Minnesota Inline Skate Club**, www.skateminnesota.org, holds lots of fun events and reviews trails, giving them one to four wheels depending on how worthwhile they are to skate. Here are a few skate parks to try:

- **Roseville Aggressive Skate Park**, 2661 Civic Center Dr, Roseville, 651-792-7191, www.ci.roseville.mn.us
- **Southdale YMCA "Tri-City Skate Park,"** Southdale YMCA, Edina, 952-835-2567, www.ymcatwincities.org
- **3rd Lair Skate Park & Skate Shop**, 850 Florida Ave S, Golden Valley, 763-79 SKATE (75283), www.3rdlair.com
- **White Bear Lake YMCA "Wheel Park,"** in Polvin Park, 651-777-8103, www.ymcatwincities.org

JUST FOR KIDS

In addition to **Playgrounds and Amusement Parks**, below, you might be interested in:

- **Bounce On Air**, moonwalk and bouncers to rent for parties, 612-961-6580, www.bounceonair.com.
- **My Gym Children's Fitness Center**, 956 Prairie Center Dr, Eden Prairie; has classes for children ages 6 weeks to 13 years, and is available for birthday parties; 952-906-0028, www.my-gym.com.
- The **Minnesota Department of Natural Resources** has a number of programs for young naturalists as well as outdoor weekend workshops for families, www.dnr.state.mn.us/dnrkids/index.html.

KITEBOARDING

You'll see kiteboarders on Minnetonka and a number of other lakes. Look like fun? It is! On a big lake you can fly for miles!
- **Lakawa School of Kiteboarding**, 612-296-3201, www.lakawa.com

LACROSSE

Look on the **Minnesota Lacrosse Association** web site (www.mnlacrosse.com) for everything you need to know about how to get involved in this up-and-coming sport.

PAINTBALL

Paintball is all the rage for parties these days. You can go out to a farm or arena to play, or some companies will bring their paintball equipment to you. For links, check the **Minnesota Paintball Internet Guide** (www.mnpig.com).

PLAYGROUNDS AND AMUSEMENT PARKS

- **Carnival Thrillz**, 329 S Lake Ave, Canal Park, Duluth, 218-720-5868
- **Chutes and Ladders**, Hyland Park Reserve, Bloomington, has climbing options and slides suitable for almost any skill level, www.threeriversparks.org.
- **Lake Minnetonka Regional Park**, Minnetrista, www.threeriversparks.org
- **Valley Fair Amusement Park and Whitewater Country Waterpark**, Shakopee, www.valleyfair.com

RACQUET SPORTS

The courts listed here are either public courts or private institutions that offer daily rates or special deals for non-members. Keep in mind that most health clubs contain racquetball and indoor tennis courts; see listings below under **Health Clubs**. The following are indoor courts. Outdoor courts can be found at parks and schoolyards throughout the region. Don't overlook the school district community services catalogues as sources for lessons, leagues, and partners.

- **Commodore Squash Club**, 79 Western Avenue N, 651-228-0501, http://com modoresquashclub.com
- **Daytona Club**, 14740 N Lawndale Ln, Dayton, 763-427-6110, www.daytona golfclub.com
- **Fred Wells Ft. Snelling Tennis and Learning Center**, 100 Federal Dr, Minneapolis, near the junction of 62 and 55, 612-252-8367, www.tennisandlearning. org

ROCK AND ICE CLIMBING

The granite bluffs of the Upper Midwest offer worthy challenges to climbers. The best rock climbs nearby are the quartzite bluffs at **Devil's Lake State Park** near Baraboo, Wisconsin, about a four-hour drive southeast. It's a beautiful hiking area, too. Climbers also like the sheer basalt walls on the banks of the **St. Croix River at Interstate State Park** in Taylors Falls and the ice climbs along **Highway 61 out of Duluth**. For more information about Minnesota climbing, look online at www.mnclimbing.org. The **University of Minnesota–Duluth Recreational Sports Outdoor Program**, 1-218-726-7128, www.umdrsop.org, leads frozen river trips (skiing and frozen waterfall climbing), January through March. To practice on indoor walls and sign up for indoor and outdoor lessons, visit the following places:

- **Midwest Mountaineering**, 309 Cedar Ave S, Minneapolis, 612-339-3433, www.midwestmtn.com
- **P.J. Asch Outfitters**, 413 E Nelson St, Stillwater, 651-430-2286
- **REI Recreational Equipment**, 750 W 79th St, Bloomington, 952-884.4315, www.rei.com
- **University of Minnesota Center for Outdoor Adventure**, 1906 University Ave SE, Minneapolis, 612-625-6800, www.recsports.umn.edu/coa/rental. html, rents rock and ice climbing equipment to students, staff, and the public.
- **Vertical Endeavors**, 855 Phalen Blvd, St. Paul, 651-776-1430, www.vertical endeavors.com

RUNNING/WALKING

Even in the glacial cold of January you see hardy Minnesotans jogging along the streets and parkways. For those who are trying to rack up miles, the **Minneapolis Chain of Lakes** provides a flat and scenic way to achieve your goals. Here, according to the Minneapolis Park and Rec Board, are the walking distances around each lake: **Cedar**, 1.68 miles; **Lake of the Isles**, 2.6 miles; **Lake Calhoun**, 3.1; **Lake Harriet** 2.75; and **Lake Nokomis** 2.7. The trail around Cedar Lake is typically free of the crowds that populate the other running paths.

For route suggestions, race information, and running mates, contact the following clubs. (Also listed are a few events that [briefly] transform distance running here into a spectator sport.)

- **Active Life and Running Club (ALARC)** runs weekly in different locations around the Twin Cities. Started by the American Lung Association, it sponsors and promotes fitness events including a 14-week Marathon Training Program, www.alarc.com.
- **All-American Trail Running Association**, www.trailrunner.com, gives the run-down on trails all over the state.
- **Breast Cancer 3-Day Walk for the Cure** is a 60-mile trek that is, as they say, all about Saving Second Base. You do need to raise a significant amount of money to be able to participate—and to enjoy breast humor, www.the3day. org.
- **Frozen Half Marathon**, January, St. Paul, is one of the events of the St. Paul Winter Carnival, www.winter-carnival.com.
- **Get in Gear 10K**, April, Minneapolis, www.getingear10K.com
- **Grandma's Marathon**, June, Duluth, www.grandmasmarathon.com
- **James Page Blubber Run®, Walk or Whatever 5K**, September, Minneapolis, ends with BBQ and beer on Boom Island, www.blubberrun.net.
- **Lifetime Fitness Triathlon**, July, Minneapolis, is considered one of the world's best triathlon events, with cash awards to the pros, but thousands of local athletes also compete for the fun (and chance of being seen on national television), www.ltftriathlon.com.
- **Minnesota Distance Running Association** provides a variety of training programs led by certified coaches, publishes *RunMN Magazine*, and sponsors races around the metro that are free for MDRA members, 952-927-0983, www.runmdra.org.
- **Run N Fun** running stores are where the track teams shop; 868 Randolph Ave, St. Paul, 651-290-2747; Burnsville Crossing Center, 35E & County Road 42, Burnsville, 952-892-7386, www.run-n-fun.com
- **Medtronic Twin Cities Marathon**: this 26-mile road race winds around the lakes of Minneapolis and along the Mississippi River to the finish line at the state capitol. Held in crisp October, it is billed as the most beautiful marathon in America and attracts thousands of runners and cheering spectators who line every foot of the way. If you want to run in this race, enter early and train hard—the entries fill fast, and just so you know, there's a punishing uphill late in the race, www.mtcmarathon.org.
- **Twin Cities Race for the Cure**, Mother's Day, Mall of America, is a 1K–5K run/walk to raise money for breast cancer, www.racecure.org.

MARATHON TRAINING
- **Cool Running** covers the running news and has links to local clubs and events, www.coolrunning.com.
- **Dick Beardsley's Marathon Running Camp** and online coaching, http:// dickbeardsleyfoundation.org

- **Lake Superior College's** virtual campus offers 13-week credit and non-credit training courses for marathons and half-marathons. Running in Grandma's Marathon is the final exam, www.lssu.edu.

WALKING TO GET TO KNOW THE NEIGHBORHOOD

There are innumerable places in the Twin Cities where you can get your exercise and learn something at the same time. Here are just a few:

- **Eloise Butler Wildflower Garden and Bird Sanctuary**, off Theodore Wirth Pkwy, Minneapolis; all the naturalist-led walks are interesting, but twilight walks on the evenings just before the full moon are truly beautiful. Reservations are required, 612-370-4903, www.minneapolisparks.org.
- **F. Scott Fitzgerald Walking Tour of St. Paul**: The tour begins at 481 Laurel, where Fitzgerald was born, and continues down Summit Avenue to the Romanesque brownstone apartment building (593–599) Fitzgerald once described as, "A house below the average on a street above the average." This is where he was living when his first novel was accepted for publication, and it's reported that he ran down the street stopping traffic and telling drivers his news. For a printable map of the complete tour, click on http://caudle2.home.comcast.net/~caudle2/fscotwlk.htm.
- **Minnesota Historical Society** conducts walking tours year 'round. Check the Society's calendar of events for walks and dates, www.mnhs.org.
- **Minneapolis Riverfront** walking tours are offered most weekends. They begin and end at the Mill City Museum, 612-341-7555, www.millcitymuseum.org.
- The **Fish and Wildlife Service** offers numerous guided wildlife walks in the **Minnesota Valley National Wildlife Refuge**, including summer solstice, prairie-in-bloom, bird-watching, and full-moon hikes. Check the refuge's online calendar for times and dates: www.fws.gov/midwest/minnesotavalley/calendar.html or call 952-854-5900.
- **French Regional Park in Plymouth** is a particular favorite because its 10 miles of trails meet the needs of those who have difficulty walking as well as those of serious runners. One particularly gentle paved trail has rest stops every quarter of a mile. Similar "Trails at Your Pace" loops are found in many other Three Rivers parks, www.threeriversparks.org.
- **Minneapolis Architecture**: Architecture author and critic Larry Millett's *AIA Guide to Downtown Minneapolis* includes maps and pictures for do-it-yourself walking tours of Nicollet Mall, the Warehouse District, the central riverfront, and Elliot Park and Loring Park neighborhoods.

SAILING

See Sailing/Sailboat Rental under **Boating**, on page 377.

SCUBA DIVING

Diving is a year-round sport in Minnesota—no kidding. They just cut holes in the ice. Good dives are found at **Square Lake Park** in Washington County and in **Lake Superior**. There is also diving in the **Crosby-Ironton mines** "Up North." And you may have seen this on the national news—every winter thousands of "polar bear aspirants" take the Polar Bear Plunge to benefit Special Olympics at events across the state. Watch the video online at http://specialolympicsmin-nesota.org. The following places can get you certified and equipped, but also check with your school district's Community Services.

- **Martha Burns Swimming School**, 952-945-0346, www.marthaburns.com, offers scuba lessons for kids and adults.
- **Scuba Center Windsurfing**, 5015 Penn Ave S, Minneapolis, 612-925-4818, www.scubacenter.com
- **Scuba Daddy's Dive Shop**, 13761 Nicollet Ave S, Burnsville, 952-892-7181, www.scubadaddys.com

SKIING—CROSS-COUNTRY

Once it snows, cross-country ski tracks seem to magically appear on all the lakes, parks, and golf courses. You can follow them or, if you want to get out into the woods, try just about any of the Regional or State Parks listed in the **Lakes and Parks** chapter or the trails listed in **Biking** or **Hiking** above. To ski public land, anyone over age 16 will need a **Great Minnesota Ski** pass, available from the **Department of Natural Resources (DNR)**, 1-888-MNLICENSE (1-888-665-4236), www.dnr.state.mn.us/licenses/skipass. Day passes can be purchased at most parks. Money from ski passes is used to maintain the trails.

- Many county parks groom trails for skiing, and some of them offer other amenities as well.
  - ▷ Try **Baker Park Reserve**, Maple Plain, which also offers a sliding hill and cozy chalet.
  - ▷ The short (6.1K) trail at **French Regional Park** is lighted.
  - ▷ For more information about these parks and many others, visit the **www.threeriversparks.org** web site.
  - ▷ In town, **Wirth Park Winter Recreation Area**, Minneapolis, provides space for tubing and snowboarding, as well as cross-country skiing, www.theodorewirth.org
- To find more places to ski, order free maps and lodging information online from the **Minnesota Office of Tourism**, www.exploreminnesota.com, or check out **SkinnySki.com**, which features trail/snow/weather conditions all over the state— and rollerski information, too.
- The **City of Lakes Loppet** is an early-February cross-country ski festival held in Minneapolis. Events include skijoring (with your dog), ice bike racing, ski

games for young children, non-competitive nighttime skiing and snowshoe-ing, and real races for prize money, www.cityoflakesloppet.com. Get Loppet updates on Twitter at http://twitter.com/loppet.

- For an invigorating winter getaway, rent a cabin on the **North Shore** (the arrowhead-shaped part of the state, north of Duluth), and tour the area's granite bluffs and woods on cross-country skis.
- For a more isolated experience, the **Boundary Waters Canoe Area** is open to cross-country skiers in winter. You can even ski yurt-to-yurt if you want to! For full details call Boundary Country Trekking Adventure Vacations, Grand Marais, 800-322-8327, www.boundarycountry.com.
- Neighboring Wisconsin has skiing too! In fact, it is host to the country's most famous cross-country ski race, the **American Birkebeiner**, www.birkie.com. Starting at Hayward, Wisconsin, about a three hours' drive from the Twin Cities, this 51-kilometer race is held every February. The "Birkie," as it's affec-tionately known, is open to world-class competitors and well-conditioned amateurs. Call 800-872-2753 for information or pick up entry forms at local ski shops. You can also enter online.
- Even if you're not interested in racing, this region's 858,400-acre **Chequame-gon National Forest** is always a beautiful place to ski. For Wisconsin travel information look online at **www.travelwisconsin.com**.

LEARN TO SKI

Many parks offer free cross-country ski lessons, as do schools' community ser-vices programs, and ski shops. In the cities, call the following numbers for more information:

- **Minneapolis Parks and Recreation Board**, www.minneapolisparks.org
- **St. Paul Division of Parks and Recreation**, www.stpaul.gov

Cross-country ski equipment is available for rental at many parks and a few sports shops.

- **Hoigaard's**, Miracle Mile Shopping Center, 5425 Excelsior Blvd, St. Louis Park, 952-929-1351, http://hoigaards.com
- **REI**, 750 W American Blvd, Bloomington, 952-884-4315; 11581 Fountains Dr, Maple Grove, 763-493-7861; www.rei.com
- **Tonka Cycle and Ski**, 14731 Excelsior Blvd, Minnetonka, 952-938-8336, http://tonkacycleandski.com
- **University of Minnesota Center for Outdoor Adventure**, 1906 University Ave SE, Minneapolis, 612-625-6800, www.recsports.umn.edu/coa/rental. html, rents ski packages to students, staff, and the public

SKIING—DOWNHILL

While Minnesota is not mountainous, it is hilly, and its short runs have turned out some of the top U.S. Ski Team racers in the country—**Olympic Gold**

Medalist Lindsey Vonn learned to race at **Buck Hill** while teammate **Kaylin Richardson** trained at **Hyland Hills**. For the rest of us, the nearby slopes offer a fun day out, with more of our time spent skiing than riding lifts. Snowboarding is allowed everywhere, and all ski areas offer rentals. For additional sources of information, try the following:

- For snow conditions in Minnesota, Wisconsin, and the Upper Peninsula of Michigan, check out **www.mnsnow.com**.
- To find the perfect pair of skis, try **Joe's Ski Shop's Demo Center at Wild Mountain** ski area in **Taylors Falls**. By purchasing a Demo Pass, you can try several pairs of the latest skis. **Joe's Ski Shop** is located at 33 E County Rd B, St. Paul, 651-209-7800, www.joessportinggoods.com.
- The **Sitzmark Ski and Social Club** organizes ski (and other) trips for its membership. Check online for meetings and other events, www.sitzmarkmn.org.
- Look in **Minnesota Monthly** magazine (www.minnesotamonthly.com) for the latest on local downhill ski areas, cross-country trails, snowshoeing, dog-sledding, and winter getaways.

These are the region's most popular ski areas:

- **Afton Alps**, Afton, 651-436-5245, www.aftonalps.com
- **Buck Hill**, Burnsville, 952-435-7174, www.skibuck.com
- **Hyland Hills Ski Area and School**, Bloomington, 763-694-7800, www.three-riversparks.org
- **Indianhead Mountain** in the **Michigan Upper Peninsula** (UP) 225 miles northeast of St. Paul gets a LOT of snow. There are other ski areas and cross-country trails nearby. Wakefield, Michigan, 800-3-INDIAN, www.indian-headmtn.com.
- **Lutsen Mountain Ski Area** is the closest Minnesota comes to mountain skiing. Runs feature beautiful views of Lake Superior, and the area is criss-crossed with cross-country trails as well. Lutsen, 218-663-7281, www.lutsen.com.
- **Spirit Mountain**, Duluth, 218-628-2891, 800-642-6377, spiritmt.com
- **Welch Village**, North of Red Wing off Highway 61 on County Road 7, 651-258-4567, www.welchvillage.com
- **Wild Mountain Ski and Snowboard Area**, Taylors Falls, 651-465-6315, 800-447-4958, www.wildmountain.com

For certified ski and snowboard instruction or race coaching contact:

- **Team Afton Alpine Ski Team**, 651-436-7652, www.teamafton.com
- **Blizzard Ski and Snowboard School**, 763-559-3343, blizzardmn.com
- **Buck Hill Ski Racing**, 952-435-7174 or www.skibuck.com
- **Mt. Gilboa Alpine Racing Inc.**, 952-831-5025, www.teamgilboa.com
- **Otto Hollaus Ski School**, 952-406-8923, www.ottohollaus.com
- **Ski-Away**, www.skiaway.net, offers lessons for women taught by women.

- **SkiJammers Ski and Snowboard School**, 952-473-1288, www.skijammers. com

SNOWMOBILING

In winter, this is the state "sport" for Minnesotans who love their motorized vehicles. Minnesota has over 20,000 miles of snowmobile trails. More than 18,000 of those miles are managed and maintained by local snowmobile clubs. To plan your next snowmobile jaunt, there's no better resource than *Snowgoer* magazine, www.snowgoer.com. You can also look online at **dnr.state.mn.us** for locations of trails. Anyone planning to ride on a state or groomed trail in Minnesota must purchase a Minnesota Snowmobile State Trail Sticker. Those who ride only on private land or on lakes do not need the sticker. Purchase stickers when you register your vehicle, or from the DNR. Residents born after 1976 need a valid snowmobile safety certificate earned either in a traditional classroom course (dates and locations are available on the DNR web site at **www. mndnr.gov**) or from watching a Snowmobile Safety CD-ROM. Check the DNR web site for details.

SNOWSHOEING

Many state parks rent snowshoes for a very small fee, and offer guided snowshoe hikes, as well. **Three Rivers Park District** maintains snowshoe trails at 11 parks and reserves. It rents snowshoes by the hour at Hyland Hills in Bloomington, Elm Creek in Maple Grove, Baker in Maple Plain and Carver Park in Victoria. Snowshoes are provided for participants taking guided hikes, www.threeriversparks.org. In Minneapolis, the Park and Rec Board offers naturalist-led snowshoe hikes on the Chain of Lakes, Lake Nokomis, Loring Park, Minnehaha Park, Wirth Park and along the Mississippi River, with snowshoes provided. Moonlight hikes are held when there's a full moon. Register in advance, 612-313-7725, www.minneapolisparks. org.

SOCCER

Soccer is rapidly becoming Minnesota's most popular youth sport, with approximately 76,000 players ages 6 to 19. It's an exciting spectator sport as well.
- The 52 fields at the 172-acre **National Sports Center** in **Blaine** are home to the professional **Minnesota Stars** (www.nscminnesota.org) and also the site of the **USA Cup**, the premier youth soccer tournament in the country, www. usacup.com.
- Local soccer associations offer recreational, competitive, and Olympic development programs, and summer camps. For information about soccer programs in your community check your school Community Services guide

or contact the **Minnesota Youth Soccer Association**, 11577 Encore Cir, Minnetonka, 55343, 952-933-2384, 800-366-6972, www.mnyouthsoccer.org.

- In the South Metro, **Soccer Blast MN**, 3601 W 145th St, Burnsville, 952-895-1962, www.soccerblastmn.com, offers ISSE soccer training, year-round youth and adult recreational and competitive leagues—and you can rent a field and party room for your own private soccer party.

SWIMMING BEACHES

Rising mercury sends sweaty Minnesotans straight to the beaches—and there are hundreds from which to choose. Most are open from early June to mid-August. If you sign your children up for beach swimming lessons, be advised that June is often stormy. On the other hand, the beaches are sometimes closed on summer's hottest days because of parasites in the water that cause swimmers' itch. Consequently, pool lessons are often preferred.

- In the **Three Rivers** park system (www.threeriversparks.org), **Baker** (Maple Plain), **Bryant Lake** (Eden Prairie), **Cleary Lake** (Prior Lake), **Elm Creek** (Maple Grove), **Fish Lake** (Maple Grove), **French Regional** (Plymouth), **Lake Minnetonka Regional Park** (Minnetrista), and **Lake Rebecca** (Rockford) all have really nice swimming beaches with picnic facilities and playgrounds.
- **Lake Minnetonka Regional Park** and **Elm Creek Park Reserve** feature swimming ponds with filtered and chlorinated water. **"De-Bug" Beach Wheelchairs**, designed to allow access to areas that would normally be inaccessible for people who use wheelchairs, are available free of charge at both Elm Creek and Lake Minnetonka Regional Parks.
- Another chlorinated, sandy-bottomed swimming pond is at **Lake Elmo Park Reserve,** 1515 Keats Ave N, Lake Elmo, in **Washington County**.
- Nearby Stillwater is home to one of the area's best scuba diving lakes, **Square Lake**, www.co.ramsey.mn.us.
- There are a number of beaches in **Anoka County**, including **Bunker Beach Water Park** in Bunker Hills Regional Park, Coon Rapids, www.anokacountyparks.com.
- Back in the cities—**Minneapolis'** most popular beach is on **Lake Nokomis**, although the beaches on **Cedar**, **Calhoun**, and **Harriet** are also heavily used.
- In 2004, Minneapolis developed **LAURI**, the **Lake Aesthetic and User Recreation Index**, an online reference that rates Minneapolis lakes for water quality and aesthetics (that would be color and odor of the water, not the quality of the tattooed-topless at Cedar Lake's Hidden Beach). The online guide reports data for all the city's public swimming lakes: **Lake Calhoun, Cedar Lake, Lake Harriet, Lake Hiawatha, Lake of the Isles, Loring Pond, Lake Nokomis, Powderhorn Lake,** and **Wirth Lake**. Check out LAURI and the beaches' hours of operation, facilities, lessons, directions and parking,

etc., on the **Minneapolis Park and Recreation Board** web site, www.min-neapolisparks.org.

- **St. Paul** operates beaches on **Lake Phalen** and **Lake Como**. For directions, hours of operation, etc., look online at **St. Paul Parks and Recreation**, www.stpaul.gov/index.aspx?nid=243
- In the western suburbs, **Shady Oak Lake** on Shady Oak Road just outside of **Hopkins** is so heavily used, unless you get there early it's difficult to find a parking spot, www.hopkinsmn.com/boards/park/index.php.
- While many **Lake Minnetonka** cities maintain beaches for their residents, the primary public beach is at the **Excelsior Commons**. www.ci.excelsior.mn.us.

SWIMMING LESSONS

Given the amount of water we have in Minnesota, every child should learn to swim. Most schools and Community Services programs offer swimming lessons, but there are several private swimming schools as well. Among them:

- **Foss Swim School** has facilities in Blaine, Chanhassen, Maple Grove, Savage, St. Louis Park, and Woodbury, as well as seasonal locations in St. Louis Park and Edina and several country clubs, www.fossswimschool.com.
- **Martha Burns Swimming School** has several locations in Minneapolis and the western metro, and also offers scuba lessons for kids and adults, 952-945-0346, www.marthaburns.com.
- **YMCA** (ages 6 months to 16 years) 612-230-9622, www.ymcatwincities.com

SWIMMING POOLS AND WATER PARKS

You can hit the beach all winter long at the Twin Cities' indoor water parks. While many cities have municipal facilities, try these, too:

- **Eko Backen Waterslides**, New Scandia Township (near Forest Lake), offers snow-tubing in winter; 651-433-2422, http://ekobacken.com
- **Marriott Depot Waterpark**, 225 Third Ave S, Minneapolis; indoor water park, open to the public Thursday–Sunday; 612-375-1700, www.thedepotminne-apolis.com/courtyard
- **Tropics Indoor Water Park** is one of the nicest water parks around, 651-490-4700, shoreviewcommunitycenter.com.
- **Valleyfair Amusement Park & Whitewater Country Waterpark**, County Rd 101, Shakopee; included in Valleyfair's general admission: Ripple Rapids lazy river, Panic Falls slides, Raging Rapids flume ride; 952-445-6500, valleyfair.com
- **Water Park of America at the Grand Hotel Mall of America**, Bloomington, is billed as "America's Biggest Water Park and Resort;" 70,000-square-foot indoor water park features a 10-story water slide tower and arcade, www.waterparkofamerica.com.

- **Wild Mountain/Taylors Falls Recreation Area** is a water park at a ski resort. Attractions include an innertube ride, speed slide, a lazy river, and dedicated children's area; 7 miles north of Taylors Falls, 651-465-6315, www.wildmountain. com.
- **Wisconsin Dells** (www.wisdells.com), the self-proclaimed "Waterpark Capital of the World," is about 200 miles away, and is described on page 487.

WALKING

See **Running/Walking**, on page 394.

YOGA

Finding the right yoga class can be hard, but these studios should give you a place to start:

- **CorePower Yoga** has studios in Eden Prairie, Edina, Minneapolis, Minnetonka, St. Louis Park, and St. Paul. Get phone numbers and directions off the web site, www.corepoweryoga.com.
- **One Yoga**, 2100B Lyndale Ave S, Minneapolis, is a nonprofit that offers daily sliding fee classes and bi-monthly free introductory classes, 612-872-6347, www.one-yoga.org.
- **St. Paul Yoga Center**, 1162 Selby Ave, St. Paul, 651-644-7141; print out a coupon from the web site and try one class for free.
- **Yoga Center** also offers equestrian yoga, 212 3rd Ave N, Minneapolis, 612-436-4700; 4200 Minnetonka Blvd, St. Louis Park, 952-345-1953, www.yogacentermpls.com
- **Yoga House** emphasizes Ashtanga Yoga, 4402 France Ave S, Edina, 952-285-YOGA, www.yogahouse.net

SPORTING GOODS STORES

For those in need of gear, we offer the following list of places to start shopping. If you're not sure whether you want to buy an expensive item, inquire about testing or renting—some stores even offer season-long leases.

- **Cabela's**, 800-237-4444, www.cabelas.com, 3900 Cabela Dr, Owatonna, Minnesota, off I-35 south of the cities, 507-451-4545; Rogers, at the intersection of I-94 and Minnesota Hwy 101, 218-773-0282; Cabela's superdome-sized stores are a tourist attraction as well as the definitive sports equipment shopping experience.
- **Erik's Bikes and Boards** has stores throughout the metro, www.eriksbikeshop.com
- **Freewheel Bike** is one of the largest bike shops in the nation. It offers bike service, a public shop where you can do your own maintenance, maintenance classes, group rides, and bike rental. The Midtown location has bike

lockers and showers. Freewheel Mobile Service will come to you, 612-339-2235. Westbank Store, 1812 S 6th St, Minneapolis, 612-339-2235; Midtown Bike Center, on the Midtown Greenway at 2834 10th Ave S, Minneapolis, 612-238-4447, http://freewheelbike.com
- **The House Boardshop**, located at the junction of 35E and 694 at 300 S Owasso Blvd, St. Paul, 800-409-7669, 651-482-9995, www.the-house.com, has a great selection—and equally great prices—on windsurfing equipment and lessons, snowboards, and more.
- **Hoigaard's**, 5425 Excelsior Blvd., St. Louis Park, 952-929-1351, www.hoigaards.com, can outfit you for almost any sport. This is also a good place to look for a winter coat and patio furniture. Don't miss Hoigaard's annual ski tent sale.
- **Joe's Ski Shop**, 33 E County Rd B, St. Paul, 651-209-7800, 1-888-468-6563, joessportinggoods.com
- **Midwest Mountaineering**, 309 Cedar Ave S, Minneapolis (near the U of M), 612-339-3433, www.midwestmtn.com, carries outdoor equipment and clothing, and holds a spectacular fall sale.
- **Northstar Lacrosse**, 774 Main St, Hopkins, 952-938-0399, northstarlacrosse.com, is the place to go for lacrosse equipment.
- **Pierce Skate and Ski**, 208 W 98th St, Bloomington, 952-884-1990, www.pierceskateandski.com, has been *Ski Magazine*'s Gold Medal Shop for a decade.
- **REI**, www.rei.com, 750 W 98th St, Bloomington, 952-884-4315, and 1995 W County Rd B2, Roseville, 651-635-0211, Maple Grove, 763-493-7861, has bikes, skis, canoes, and camping gear—and a monster climbing wall.
- **Run N Fun**, run-n-fun.com, 14240 Plymouth Ave S, Burnsville, 952-892-7386, and 868 Randolph Ave, Saint Paul, 651-290-2747, is the racing headquarters for many high school and college track teams, and includes a Nike women's "concept shop."
- **Scuba Center Windsurfing**, 5015 Penn Ave S, Minneapolis, 612-925-4818, www.scubacenter.com
- **2nd Wind Exercise**, www.2ndwindexercise.com, has several locations throughout the metro. They sell new and used better-grade exercise equipment.
- **Seven Seas Chandlery**, Shorewood Marina and Yacht Club, Lake Minnetonka, 952-474-0600
- **Soccer Express USA**, www.soccerexpressusa.com, 653 S Snelling Ave, St. Paul, 651-698-8092, and 11016 Cedar Lake Rd, Minnetonka, 952-544-6662
- **Sportsman's Guide Outlet**, 490 Hardman Ave S, St. Paul, 651-552-5248, www.sportmansguide.com, sells overstocks, returns, discontinued items, and special purchases at 5 to 50% discounts.
- **Sports Hut**, 16875 County Rd 24, Plymouth, 952-473-8843.
- **Twin City Tennis Supply**, 4747 Chicago Ave S, Minneapolis, 612-823-9285, twincitytennis.com; this is where the champions shop.
- **West Marine** has stores in Minnetonka, Bloomington, and Stillwater, www.westmarine.com.

WITH 11,842 LAKES, AND 16.7 MILLION ACRES OF FORESTS, YOU could consider all of Minnesota one big park if you wanted to—and many people do! Approximately ten thousand years ago, when the most recent ice age ended, the receding glaciers left behind a landscape filled with lakes, marshes, bogs, and fens. When European settlers arrived they found this wet land difficult to develop, so thousands of acres were preserved, quite accidentally. Today, many of these wetlands are parks where thousands of people congregate for recreation and relaxation. Amazingly though, the wetlands almost didn't become parks.

By the 1880s, the Twin Cities' lakes had become popular locations for resorts and houses, and while state officials coveted the prime waterfront areas as regional parks, their plan was not well received. Citizens were afraid it was a speculation scheme by conspiratorial insiders. Park proponents prevailed, though, by citing the success of New York's Central Park. Soon, **Theodore Wirth**, in the persistent manner of New York City's Robert Moses, was tearing down houses on the east shore of Lake Calhoun and marshaling the park system into what it is today. Wirth Park is named after him.

Thanks to Theodore Wirth, **99%** of the residents of Minneapolis live within **six blocks** of a park.

Thanks to Wirth's template for development, parks are an integral part of all our other cities as well. Consequently, you can expect that anywhere you choose to live, there will be parks and trails nearby. The biggest plus, though, is the interconnectedness of the system. While there are gaps, and the linkages aren't perfect, every city, county, and regional planning agency within the metro area has as its goal the establishment of contiguous green space. Thanks to them we can easily bike from the far western suburbs to the Mississippi

Riverfront in Minneapolis and, with just a little more trouble, continue on to north of Stillwater. Thanks to the planners, too, there is public access to every lake and river—quite often, handicapped access, as well!

Download Twin Cities park, bike, and trail maps from the Metropolitan Council web site, **www.metrocouncil.org**. You will find clickable links to county, city, and regional parks there as well.

The following is a brief sampling of some of the metro's 136,900 acres of parks and open space. The highlighted parks were chosen because they offer very different experiences of this region. By visiting them, you will quickly be able to develop a broad perspective on your new home. For many more places to go and things to do, look under your specific interests in the **Sports and Recreation** chapter.

MISSISSIPPI RIVER

A place that never ceases to delight is the narrow corridor that the Mississippi River carves from Itasca through Minneapolis and St. Paul. This 72-mile route is one of the most diverse and complex ecosystems on earth. Shallow and narrow at its upper end, by the time the Mississippi reaches its confluence with the Minnesota River at Fort Snelling, it has become a wide and powerful feature of the largest inland navigation system on earth. At this point, it "becomes what the Mississippi IS," a symbol of our nation, a critical migration and transportation corridor at the heart of America's history, and one of the planet's most identifiable features when observed from outer space.

Within the 54,000-acre riverfront, dozens of state and local parks provide outstanding recreation opportunities. For those who feel the river is best experienced by watercraft, be sure to plan ahead and obtain navigational charts, particularly if you are boating on the section of the river that is part of the inland waterway system. (The U.S. Army Corps of Engineers posts downloadable **navigation charts** and revisions on its web site, www2.mvr.usace.army. mil/NIC2/mrcharts.cfm.) Not only are there locks, dams, and shoals to navigate, but you will also be sharing the channels with commercial barges that cannot maneuver out of your way. If that thought is enough to make you take back your captain's hat, try the **Padelford tour boats**, 651-227-1100 or 800-543-3908, www.riverrides.com. Their daily sightseeing cruises, running Memorial Day to Labor Day, also include lunch or dinner.

The pathways along either bank are lovely for walking and biking.

- The **St. Anthony Falls Heritage Trail** is a self-guided tour from the Stone Arch Bridge (built for trains 150 years ago and now the exclusive domain of pedestrians and bicyclists) to Nicollet Island and back to SE Main Street. Interpretive markers and kiosks along the way describe the birth of Minneapolis. If your mood is romantic, stroll here on a moonlit evening and enjoy the skyline reflected in the black river.

- If you're in a hurry, take a **Segway tour** of this area, www.humanonastick. com.
- For longer tours, you can follow **West River Parkway** and eventually reach **Minnehaha Park** on the city's far south side.
- Alternatively, follow **East River Parkway/East Mississippi River Boulevard** south, going through the University of Minnesota campus, to **Hidden Falls Park**, a picnic area on the riverbank.
- A little farther along the parkway is **Fort Snelling State Park**, the place where the Minnesota and Mississippi Rivers meet and the site of a stone fort built in the 1820s. The parkway ends at **Crosby Farm Nature Area**, off Gannon Road at Shepard Road, St. Paul. This secluded preserve of Mississippi River estuaries and marshes features a boardwalk through the marsh and is one of the few places in the metro area where nesting warblers can be found. The entrance to Fort Snelling State Park (www.dnr.state.mn.us/state_parks/fort_snelling/ index.html) is off Post Road, south of State Highway 5. A day-use park with no camping allowed, it boasts a swimming beach, handicapped-accessible fishing pier, and boat access.

CITY PARKS

Every city has a park system, but the biggest (and probably best) is that of **Minneapolis** (www.minneapolisparks.org), which encompasses 18 lakes and 6400 acres of parkland, including over 182 parks, gardens, playgrounds, and golf courses, and 49 year-round recreation centers. Because the city dedicates 15% of its land to parks, it has been named one of the top 10 green cities in the nation by *The Green Guide*. It has also been called the "closest thing to park nirvana" by the Trust for Public Land.

   St. Paul (www.stpaul.gov/depts/parks) has more miles of shoreline (17) along the Mississippi than any other municipality along the entire length of the river. Its series of 16 public parks provides over 3500 acres of floodplain and bluff-top wildlife habitat and opportunities for recreation. Though these incredible parks have, until recently, been viewed as individual sites, the city is in the process of consolidating and connecting them, and forming a new park that will be known as "**The National Great River Park**." You can access the river in many places along Mississippi River Boulevard. Unique to St. Paul are the city's elegant public squares, such as **Rice Park**, where the locals sit to relax and people-watch. In winter the squares twinkle with holiday lights—and, during St. Paul's Winter Carnival, with ice sculptures.

CITY PARK HIGHLIGHTS

- **Big Island Nature Park in Lake Minnetonka**, www.ci.orono.mn.us; has rustic hiking trails and great eagle-watching, and is accessible only by boat.

- **Minneapolis Chain of Lakes**, www.minneapolisparks.org; walk, bike, drive, or paddle around these lakes, which run north to south along the western edge of Minneapolis and are connected by water and a 12-mile system of walking and biking paths.
  - ▷ **Cedar Lake** has a quiet public swimming beach and fishing dock.
  - ▷ **Lake of the Isles** offers walking paths, canoe rentals, skating rinks (with a warming house) in the winter, and an off-leash dog park.
  - ▷ **Lake Calhoun** has swimming beaches and offers boat rentals and lessons.
  - ▷ **Lake Harriet** has swimming, boat rentals, a bandshell that hosts summer concerts, and the second oldest public rose garden in the United States.
- **Minnehaha Creek** connects with the above lakes. When the water is high enough, you can start at Gray's Bay in Minnetonka and canoe all the way through South Minneapolis to Minnehaha Park (on the Mississippi), via the creek.
- **Como Park Zoo, Conservatory, Amusement Park, and Golf Course**, 1431 N Lexington Pkwy, St. Paul, www.comozooconservatory.org, has something for everyone. In winter, the golf course becomes Como Ski Center. (See **Gardens** on page 415.)
- **Minnehaha Park and Falls**, 4801 Minnehaha Ave S, Minneapolis, www.minneapolisparks.org, is one park you can get to on the Hiawatha LRT. This 171-acre sports and nature area surrounds Minnehaha Falls, where Minnehaha Creek empties into the Mississippi River. On summer afternoons and weekends, the park is packed with family reunions and company picnics. There are well-marked paths for hiking and nature viewing. A particularly dramatic prospect is the frozen falls in mid-winter, as seen from the ski trails below. There's a great off-leash dog park at the park's south end.
- **Indian Mounds Regional Park** (www.stpaul.gov) is situated atop Dayton's Bluff east of downtown St. Paul. It was established in 1893, making it one of the oldest parks in the region. The six mounds here are thought to be burial sites for at least two American Indian cultures. At the north end of the park there is an overlook from which you can gaze down on Minnesota's capital city, and upon the transportation network that has given it life—the river, the railroad, the freeways, and the St. Paul Airport—all laid out before you like a map.
- **Springbrook Nature Center**, 100 85th Ave NE, Fridley, www.springbrooknaturecenter.org, has been voted the number one park/nature center for families in the greater metropolitan area by readers of *Parents* magazine. Check out their seasonal events such as Halloween Walk, Winterfest, and Spring Fling, which are appropriate even for very small children.
- **Woodlake Nature Center**, 6710 Lake Shore Dr, Richfield, www.woodlakenaturecenter.org, is a 150-acre natural area dedicated to environmental

education, wildlife observation, and outdoor recreation. Its three miles of trails are wheelchair accessible in summer, and one of the best places to go for a quick cross-country ski in winter.

COUNTY PARKS

While all counties have their own parks, the most extensive system is Hennepin and Scott counties' **Three Rivers Park District** (www.threeriversparks. org) in the western suburbs. The name "Three Rivers" derives from the fact that all park properties are located in watersheds that flow into one of three rivers: the Mississippi, Minnesota, or Crow. The district includes nearly 27,000 acres of park reserves, regional parks, regional trails and special-use facilities such as beaches, boat launches, interpretative centers, campsites, stables, and ski hills.

- **Elm Creek Park Reserve, Maple Grove**, www.threeriversparks.org, is the largest of all the Three Rivers Parks. With over 4900 acres, this park offers everything, including long hiking/biking loops through miles of mostly unspoiled Minnesota countryside. It also has a chlorinated upland swimming pond, massive children's play area, disc golf, and off-leash pet exercise area. In winter, the park offers cross-country skiing, snow-tubing, a beginner downhill and snowboarding hill, and provides lighted trails for evening skiing.
- **Hyland Lake Park Reserve, Bloomington**, www.threeriversparks.org, is a winter downhill ski and snowboard area, and a summer hiking/biking/golf practice center. Home to one of the metro's most popular creative play areas, the park also includes a six-mile grass loop dog-walking trail, and fishing pier on Hyland Lake.
- **Lake Elmo Park Reserve, Lake Elmo**, www.co.washington.mn.us, is 2165 acres in size (3 1/2 square miles) with 80% of its acreage set aside for preservation and protection. This 80% is being allowed to revert to native vegetation, so it will eventually resemble the land as it was prior to the arrival of the settlers in the mid-1800s. The park offers eight miles of turf trails for horses and mountain bikers, as well as an equestrian campground, swimming beach, and orienteering course. Trails are groomed for skiing in winter.

REGIONAL PARKS

The immediate metro includes 46 regional parks and park reserves, 22 regional trails, and 6 special recreation areas. Visit **www.metrocouncil.org/parks/ parks.htm** for an online, clickable map and parks directory.

- **Battle Creek Regional Park**, off Lower Afton Road, is an 1840-acre active recreation area with an off-leash dog park and tough mountain biking course. Check www.co.ramsey.mn.us/parks/trails for rules and trail maps.
- **Bunker Hills Regional Park**, Bunker Lake Blvd, www.anokacountyparks. com, is situated at the city borders of Ham Lake, Andover, Coon Rapids, and Blaine. Covering 1600 acres, this park has everything from stables where you

can rent a horse for a guided trail ride (www.bunkerparkstable.com) to a wavepool water park and top-rated golf course. In winter, take a sleigh ride or hitch up your dog and try skijoring (being pulled by your horse or dog) over the park's 12-kilometer skijoring course.

- **Lake Minnetonka Regional Park, Minnetrista**, www.threerivers parks.org, features a boat launch, fishing piers, creative play area and handicapped-accessible sandy-bottom chlorinated lake water swimming pond. Season passes are sold only on site.
- **Square Lake Regional Special Recreation Feature**, Stillwater, www. co.washington.mn.us, has some of the clearest water in Minnesota, and is a favorite of scuba divers from throughout the region.

REGIONAL TRAILS

One of the finest regional trail systems in the country is right here in the Twin Cities, where an extensive network of 22 regional trails connects local communities to park reserves and regional parks. Download trail maps from the **Metropolitan Council's web site**, www.metrocouncil.org/parks/map/parksmap.htm. Routes designated **"Trails… At Your Pace"** are generally a mile or less and have flat or gentle terrain, rest stops every ¼ mile, restrooms, and staffed facilities. Look for these trails at all **Three Rivers parks**, www.threeriversparks.org.

- **Big Rivers Regional Trail**, from Mendota Heights through Eagan to Lilydale, is a 4½-mile flat trail with spectacular views of Fort Snelling, the Minnesota River Valley, and the confluence of the Minnesota and Mississippi Rivers, www.co.dakota.mn.us/parks/index.htm. It links to the 72-mile Mississippi National River and Recreation Area, and through it to the rest of the metro trail system.
- The **Lake Minnetonka LRT Regional Trail** runs east-west along the shore of Lake Minnetonka from Victoria to Hopkins, where it connects with the **Cedar Lake LRT Trail** and continues into Minneapolis. There it connects with the **Luce Line State Trail** headed northwest, the **Midtown Greenway** headed east, and the **Minneapolis Grand Rounds**. The southern fork of this trail, called the **Minnesota River Bluffs LRT Trail**, begins in Chanhassen and runs through Hopkins and St. Louis Park, where it connects to the Minneapolis trails, www.threeriversparks.com.

STATE PARKS

Minnesota has 72 state park and recreation areas, a number of which are located within the metro area. Vehicle permits are required. They can be purchased at REI stores in the Twin Cities, at any state park, and from the DNR, 651-296-6157 or toll free 1-888-MINNDNR (646-6367), www.dnr.state.mn.us. Links to information about all Minnesota's state parks, including maps, fees, reservations, events and activities, and rules can be found at www.dnr.state.mn.us. This web site also includes the "**Lake Finder**," which contains data for more than 4500 lakes and rivers throughout Minnesota, including lake surveys, depth maps, water quality and clarity, stocking reports, and fish consumption advice (from the Department of Health). Check availability and make **campsite reservations** online at www.stayatmnparks.com or by phone, 1-866-85PARKS (1-866-857-2757).

- **Afton State Park**, on the banks of the St. Croix River near Hastings, offers over 20 miles of hiking, skiing, horseback riding trails across roller-coaster terrain of grassy ridges and deep wooded ravines. Though many of the paths are quite challenging, part of the trail system is handicapped accessible. You can camp here year-round in cabins or at very private campsites—one so secluded, it's only accessible by canoe. The Afton Alps downhill ski area is open to mountain bikers in summer. Fishing and swimming are also available within the park.
- **Blue Mounds State Park**, in the southwestern corner of the state near Luverne, has a 100-foot-tall quartzite cliff that looms over a herd of bison grazing the surrounding tall-grass prairie. The park is a favorite for rock climbing and bird watching. As long as you're in the vicinity, be sure to visit nearby Pipestone National Monument and the fascinating Jeffers Petroglyphs, near Windom.
- **Fort Snelling State Park**, 101 Snelling Lake Rd, St. Paul (by the airport): Located in the heart of the Twin Cities, where the Mississippi and Minnesota rivers converge, this park offers extensive hiking, bike and ski trails that link to Minnehaha Park and the Minnesota Valley National Wildlife Refuge. You can canoe here, swim, or play golf. Trails allow visitors to hike up to historic Fort Snelling for a view of military life in the 1820s. Ski alongside ice floes in the river in winter.
- **Hill Annex Mine State Park**, between Grand Rapids and Hibbing on U.S. Hwy 169, offers fossil and ADA-accessible mine tours of this historic open-pit iron-ore mine.
- **Interstate State Park**, on Hwy 8, just south of Taylors Falls, was formed by earthquakes and lava flows a billion years ago. Then, for another half a million years, the entire region was washed by advancing and retreating seas. Evidence of this fascinating geologic history can be seen in the rock formations found here as well as in the fossil remains of ancient animals. Both sides of the river offer rugged trails and spectacular views of the St. Croix River Valley. Taylors Falls Scenic Boat Tours (www.wildmountain.com/boat/boat_home.html) offers narrated cruises daily from May through mid-October. Taylors Falls Canoe and Kayak Rental (www.wildmountain.com/canoe/canoe_faqs.html) specializes in one-way canoe and kayak trips, which start in the park and continue downstream to either the Osceola Landing (7 miles) or William O'Brien State Park (17 miles). A shuttle takes you back to your car.
- **Itasca State Park**, 21 miles north of Park Rapids, is where the Mississippi River begins its 2,552-mile journey to the Gulf of Mexico. Wading across the

river at this point is a long-standing Minnesota tradition. Overnight lodging is available, as is a full-service restaurant.

- **Jay Cooke State Park**, about two and a half hours north of Minneapolis, east of Carlton on the St. Louis River, is the place to go for kayaking and white-water rafting. Linked to the Willard Munger State Trail, it is also perfect for backpackers, bikers, hikers, horseback riders, and cross-country skiers. There are a number of drive-in camping sites, some of which stay open in winter, and some of which are handicapped accessible.
  - ▹ For rafting information contact **Superior Whitewater Raft Tours,** 218-384-4637, www.minnesotawhitewater.com.
  - ▹ For kayaking lessons and opportunities to take group trips, contact the **University of Minnesota–Duluth Recreational Sports Outdoor Program**, 218-726-7128, www.umdrsop.org.

STATE TRAILS

Maps for these and other state trails are available online at www.dnr.state.mn.us/state_trails/index.html:

- The **Gateway State Trail** is part of the ambitious Willard Munger State Trail system, planned to connect St. Paul with Duluth. Eighteen miles long, the Gateway Trail begins in St. Paul at Cayuga/L'Orient Streets, travels northeast through the cities of Maplewood, North St. Paul, and Oakdale, through Washington County, and ends at Pine Point Regional Park, four miles northwest of the city of Stillwater. Along the way, the paved, multiple-use track cuts through a cross-section of urban areas, parks, lakes, and even some rural landscapes that are a surprise to most first-time trail users. East of Interstate 694, it includes a 9.7-mile unpaved, parallel treadway for horseback riding or carriage driving.
- Biking the **Luce Line**, from Plymouth west to Cosmos, is like taking a jaunt down a quiet country road. A 63-mile-long former railroad grade, it is paved for 30 miles, from Plymouth west to Winsted, with a parallel path for horseback riding.
- The **Minnesota River Valley State Trail** stretches for 47 miles along the south bank of the Minnesota River, from Fort Snelling to Belle Plaine. It is ideal for hiking, cross-country skiing, mountain biking, horseback riding, and snowmobiling, but be very careful if you use this trail during hunting season. Visit www.stayatmnparks.com to make reservations for the Quarry Campground and horsecamp sites.
- **Root River State Trail/Harmony–Preston State Trail** is a 42-mile-long multiple-use trail through the quaint and picturesque rural communities of southeastern Minnesota.
- The 63-mile paved **Willard Munger State Trail**, from Hinckley to Duluth, is a favorite of the in-line skating crowd.

SCENIC BYWAYS

Minnesota has 23 designated Scenic Byways, ranging from the **Waters of the Dancing Sky** in the northwestern corner of the state to the **Minneapolis Grand Rounds**. Here we list just two highlights. For complete information, look online at the state's tourism web site, **www.exploreminnesota.com**, or at the National Scenic Byways site, **www.byways.org**.

- The **Minneapolis Grand Rounds** (www.minneapolisparks.com/grandrounds/info_center.htm) is the nation's only urban scenic byway. As it makes its 50-mile circuit of the city, it offers impressive views of the downtown skyline, the Mississippi Riverfront, and Minneapolis Chain of Lakes. Human-made attractions along this route include the historic Stone Arch Bridge, the Walker Arts Center Sculpture Garden, and the city's historic mill district. Download a map of the route from the web site, or simply follow the signs.

- The **Great River Road Scenic Byway** begins at the headwaters of the Mississippi in Itasca State Park and follows the river all the way through the state down to Baton Rouge, Louisiana. The northern portion of the route runs through the magnificent forests of Minnesota's "Lake Country," an area which is also known for its unsurpassed fishing and hunting. Attractions along this leg include 18-foot-high statues of legendary Paul Bunyan and Babe his Blue Ox in Bemidji, and the Little Falls home of Charles Lindbergh. The Forest History Center in Grand Rapids shows visitors life as it was in a 1900-era logging camp. The southern portion runs from the Twin Cities to Winona. On this portion of the route, Highway 61 hugs the riverbluffs for some of the most stunning scenery and best bird watching in the state. (See **Quick Getaways**.)

REGIONAL LAKES

Fishing seasons for walleye, muskellunge, and large- and small-mouth bass are generally mid-May to mid-February. Fishing for lake trout runs mid-May through September. For more information on fishing, see **Fishing** in the **Sports and Recreation** chapter and check the DNR's web site, www.dnr.state.mn.us/fishing/index.html. For information about whether the ice is safe, or to find out about rules and regulations on various Hennepin County lakes and rivers, including Lake Minnetonka, the Mississippi River, and the Minnesota River, look online at the Hennepin County Water Patrol's web site, www.waterpatrol.org. Speaking of ice—the average ice-out date on Lake Minnetonka is April 15, although, in fact, the ice has never actually gone out on that date. The earliest the ice has ever gone out was March 11, 1878; the latest was May 8, 1856. The most common ice-out dates have been April 17 and 18th (9 times each). A list of all the ice-out dates since 1855 can be found on the Freshwater Society's web site, www.freshwater.org.

At over 14,000 acres, **Lake Minnetonka**, west of Minneapolis between highways 12 and 7, is the largest body of water in the Twin Cities area, and the ninth largest lake in the state. With over 120 miles of shoreline, it is accessible at numerous public boat ramps. The closest public launch site to Minneapolis is at Gray's Bay off Highway 101 in Minnetonka. Several national bass fishing contests are held here each year. Water skiers gravitate to St. Alban's Bay and the quieter waters at the west end of the lake. Those who wish to see and be seen head for the north side of Big Island, between Excelsior and Wayzata, or Lord Fletcher's at Spring Park. Families will enjoy Lake Minnetonka Regional Park, west of Excelsior, which features a swimming pond, boat ramp, and extraordinary playground. One of the best sailing grounds in the country, Minnetonka is home to several yacht clubs and sailing schools.

White Bear Lake, east of Hwy 61 at White Bear, is to the East Metro what Minnetonka is to the west. A shallow lake with a sandy bottom, it is a favorite for swimming, sailing, windsurfing, ice boating, and fishing for carp, bluegills, and bullheads.

FORESTS

Less than 1% of the oak, maple, and basswood Big Woods that spanned the middle of the state in the 1850s has survived into the 21st century.

However, a pristine, 43-acre Big Woods remnant does lie within **Eden Prairie's Riley Creek Conservation Area** off Dell Road, between Pioneer Trail and Flying Cloud Drive. The area is ideal for nature study and photography, but there are no trails. Unfortunately, it is severely pressured by surrounding development.

Another old growth forest, **Wolsfeld Woods** (http://wolsfeldwoods.org), Hwy 6 at Brown Rd, Long Lake, has fared better, and is home to 185 acres of trees so old and tall that sunlight pierces them like arrows.

Another tiny remnant of the Big Woods, 22-acre **Wayzata Cenacle Big Woods**, is located on Wayzata Boulevard, in the heart of downtown Wayzata, next door to Colonial Square Shopping Center.

The closest state forest to the TC metro is **Sand Dunes State Forest** in central Sherburne County. Open year 'round, it has something for everyone—hiking, canoeing, fishing, mountain biking, horseback riding, camping, hunting—all in a beautiful oak savanna forest and pine plantation.

Finally, a cautionary note to hikers and nature lovers: the woods and fields, even fairly close to houses, are not 100% safe during **deer hunting season**. Generally, bow season begins in mid-September and firearm season begins in early November. If you feel the need to take a late fall walk in the woods, be sure to wear hunter's "blaze" orange. And if you are taking Fido with you, put an orange vest on him as well. And make plenty of noise. For more information on hunting seasons and regulations check www.dnr.state.mn.us.

NORTH COUNTRY NATIONAL SCENIC TRAIL

The nation's longest hiking trail, the **North Country National Scenic Trail** is a work in progress. Viewed on a map, it looks like the path of an ant, beginning at Crown Point State Historic Site on the Vermont–New York border and meandering over 4000 miles through New York, Ohio, Pennsylvania, Michigan, Wisconsin, and Minnesota, and ending at Lake Sakakawea in North Dakota. Information, updates, and brochures can be obtained from the North Country National Trail Association, www.northcountrytrail.org; or access the National Park Service homepage, www.nps.gov.

GARDENS

Out-of-town visitors and locals alike delight in Minnesota's public gardens. Here are just a few:

- The **Eloise Butler Wildflower Garden and Bird Sanctuary** in Theodore Wirth Park in Minneapolis (www.friendsofeloisebutler.org) is a peaceful place to learn about and enjoy nature. The oldest public wildflower garden in the U.S., it was originally a botany lab for Minneapolis schoolteachers. Naturalist tours and programs are offered on weekends. Try the blindfolded sensory walks, "Pond Critters for Kids," and moonlight walks. MetroTransit buses stop at Glenwood Ave and Theodore Wirth Pkwy, just a short two-block walk to the garden's gate (follow the signs).

- **Lyndale Park Gardens**, also in Minneapolis, on the east side of Lake Harriet, www.minneapolisparks.org, is another peaceful urban oasis in the midst of the busy city. It has four distinctive gardens: the Rose Garden, the Perennial Garden, Peace (Rock) Garden, and the Perennial Trial/Hummingbird and Butterfly Garden. Immediately adjacent to the Peace Garden is the Thomas Sadler Roberts Bird Sanctuary. MetroTransit buses stop at the intersection of W 40th St and Bryant Ave S. The gardens are just a two-block walk west of the bus stop.

- Located in popular **Como Park** in St. Paul, the glass-domed Victorian-era **Marjorie McNeely Conservatory**, with its large collection of tropical palm trees and orchids, is a lovely escape on a minus 30° day. In summer, the park's outdoor Japanese garden is the perfect place to sit and enjoy a meditative cup of tea, 651-487-8200, www.comozooconservatory.org.

- **Noerenberg Memorial Gardens**, on County Rd 51 (North Shore Dr), overlooking Lake Minnetonka, www.threeriversparks.org, features a variety of unusual plantings, as well as an antique boathouse with a deck where you can sit and enjoy the peace and beauty of the lake. Combine a trip to this garden with lunch at the Minnetonka Art Center, practically across the road, www.minnetonkaarts.org.

- The **University of Minnesota Landscape Arboretum**, 3675 Arboretum Dr, Chaska, 952-443-1400, www.arboretum.umn.edu, is, at over a thousand acres, the largest and most diverse of Minnesota's horticultural sites. Special focus areas include a Japanese garden and restored prairie. The three-mile drive through the Arboretum takes visitors past many of the collections. A guided tour follows this route as well.

WISCONSIN PARKS

- The **Apostle Islands National Lakeshore**, off the south shore of Lake Superior near Bayfield, Wisconsin, www.nps.gov/apis, boasts attractions for everyone from amateur naturalists to serious sailors and lighthouse lovers. For sea kayakers, this 21-island freshwater archipelago is a paddler's paradise of sandstone caves, beaches, lighthouses, and big water. Others can visit the islands via public excursion boats. Camping and hiking are allowed on most. There are hotels, bars, and restaurants on Madeline Island, which is not part of the park. Madeline Island is served several times a day by a ferry from Bayfield harbor, three miles away. Read more about this area in **Quick Getaways**.
- The **Chequamegon-Nicolet National Forest**, www.fs.fed.us/r9/cnnf, covers over a million and a half acres in Wisconsin's Northwoods. It has five designated Wilderness Areas that are open for fishing, hunting, hiking, canoeing, and "no-trace" camping. A number of trails run through here, including the North Country National Scenic Trail. (For more information about the North Country Scenic Trail, see above.)
- The **National Freshwater Fishing Hall of Fame and Museum**, 10360 Hall of Fame Dr, Hayward, Wisconsin, http://freshwater-fishing.org, is partly housed inside a giant concrete, steel, and fiberglass Muskie "Shrine to Anglers."

Y OU'VE FOUND A PLACE TO LIVE, UNPACKED, AND GOTTEN SETTLED into your new home. Now it's time to get involved in the community. This chapter lists a variety of options for community involvement, from volunteering, to special interest activities, to places of worship.

VOLUNTEERING

Volunteering for an organization is a satisfying way to make a difference in your new community while at the same time meeting people who share similar interests. Incidentally, according to a 2009 report released by the federal Corporation for National and Community Service, the Twin Cities metropolitan area ranks first in the nation among large cities in the rate of volunteering, with 38.4% of residents participating. Area schools, sports teams, hospitals, and museums, of course, are always in need of additional volunteers.

VOLUNTEER PLACEMENT SERVICES

The following organizations coordinate many volunteer activities in the Twin Cities. Call them and they will help you find a place in need of your special talents:

- **Community Volunteer Service of the St. Croix Valley Area (CVS)**, 2300 Orleans St W, Stillwater, 651-439-7434, www.volunteercvs.org; connects people with volunteer opportunities in Washington and St. Croix counties.
- **Hands On Twin Cities Volunteer Resource Center** is the principal source for volunteer information in the region. Its web site allows you to browse volunteer projects by impact areas, county, and dates you're available, www.handsontwincities.org.
- **Junior League of Minneapolis**, 612-238-8460, www.jlminneapolis.org

- **Junior League of St. Paul**, 651-291-7377, www.jlsp.org
- **United Way First Call for Help**, 211, www.unitedwaytwincities.org
- **Volunteer Match**, www.volunteermatch.org; just put in your ZIP code and be matched with a local nonprofit that's looking for volunteers.

AREA CAUSES

The following are some of the Twin Cities service organizations that need volunteers:

AIDS

- **AIDS Project Minnesota**, 1400 Park Ave S, Minneapolis, 612-341-2060, www.mnaidsproject.org
- **The Aliveness Project**, 730 E 38th St, Minneapolis, 612-822-7946, www.aliveness.org

ANIMALS

- **Animal Humane Society**, *763-522-4325*, www.animalhumanesociety.org, needs both money and volunteers. Adoption centers are open until 8 p.m., and facilities are located throughout the metro:
  - ▷ **Buffalo,** 4375 Hwy 55 SE, 763-390-3647
  - ▷ **Coon Rapids,** 1411 Main St NW, 763-862-4030
  - ▷ **Golden Valley,** 845 Meadow Ln N, 763-522-4325
  - ▷ **St. Paul,** 1115 Beulah Ln, 651-645-7387
  - ▷ **Woodbury,** 9785 Hudson Rd, 651-730-6008
- **Como Park Zoo**, St. Paul, 651-487-8200, www.comozooconservatory.org
- **Minnesota Zoo**, Apple Valley, 952-431-9200, 24-hour Information Line 952-431-9500, www.mnzoo.com
- **Raptor Center at the University of Minnesota**, 1920 Fitch Ave, St. Paul, 612-624-4745, www.raptor.cvm.umn.edu. Established in 1974, The Raptor Center specializes in the medical care of eagles, hawks, owls, and falcons.
- **We Can Ride** (see under **Disability Assistance** on page 420.)
- **Helping Paws of Minnesota** (952-988-9359, www.helpingpaws.org); and **Can Do Canines** (formerly Hearing and Service Dogs of Minnesota), 763-331-3000, www.hsdm.org, http://can-do-canines.org/, always need people to raise and help train their assistance dogs.

THE ARTS

Many of our local theater companies depend upon volunteers. They are always in need of ushers for shows, as well as extra hands for many other purposes.
- **Minneapolis Institute of Art**, 2400 3rd Ave S, Minneapolis, 612-870-3013, www.artsmia.org

- **Minnesota Orchestra Volunteer Association**, 1111 Nicollet Mall, 612-371-5654, www.wamso.org
- **Walker Art Center**, 612-375-7600, www.walkerart.org

BUSINESS

- **SCORE**, http://score-mn.org; sponsored by the Small Business Administration, this organization of active and retired business people provides free business counseling. Local offices are in Minneapolis, St. Paul, and Burnsville.

CHILDREN/YOUTH

- **Big Brothers Big Sisters of the Greater Twin Cities**, 2550 University Ave, St. Paul, 651-789-2400, www.bbbs.org
- **Boys and Girls Clubs Twin Cities**, www.boysandgirls.org
- **Boy Scouts of America**, 5300 Glenwood Ave, Golden Valley, 763-231-7201, www.northernstarbsa.org
- **The Garage**, 75 Civic Center Pkwy, Burnsville, 952-895-4664, www.thegarage. net, is a teen hangout staffed by paid employees and volunteers. Its concerts showcase local teen performers.
- **Girl Scouts of Minnesota and Wisconsin River Valleys**, 5601 Brooklyn Blvd, Brooklyn Center, 763-535-4602, www.girlscoutsrv.org
- **Pillsbury United Communities**, www.puc-mn.org
- **Teens Alone** helps homeless teenagers in the West Metro and needs teen volunteers to get the word out to their schools and organize fund raisers, 952-988-TEEN, www.teensalone.org.
- **Two Wheel View/Trips for Kids–Twin Cities** provides out-of-school, outdoor learning experiences and coordinates local, regional, and international biking expeditions, 612-767-8586, 866-858-2453, www.twowheelview.org.

CROSS-CULTURAL UNDERSTANDING

- **Hallie Q. Brown Community Center** in the Summit-University neighborhood always has volunteer and internship openings, 270 N Kent St, St. Paul, 651-224-4601, www.hallieqbrown.org.

DISABILITY ASSISTANCE

- **Adaptive Recreation Office**, City of St. Paul, 651-266-6375, www.stpaul.gov/index.aspx?nid=1249
- **The ARC of Minnesota**, 651-523-0823, www.arcmn.org
- **Courage Center**, 3915 Golden Valley Rd, Golden Valley, 763-588-0811, www.couragecenter.org, is always looking for people with strong communications skills to volunteer with youth and adults who have physical disabilities.

The ski program is especially fun, but they also have need for martial arts instructors, archers, aquatic therapy—and that's just the A's. Download an application off the web site.

- **National Alliance for Mental Illness—Minnesota**, 800 Transfer Rd, St. Paul, 651-645-2948, www.namihelps.org
- **People Incorporated** helps people with mental illness and brain disorders, 317 York Ave, St. Paul, 651-774-0011, www.peopleincorporated.org
- **We Can Ride**, 952-934-0057, www.wecanride.org, offers therapeutic horseback riding and cart driving for children and adults at four locations: Hennepin County Home School in Eden Prairie; Woodpecker Woods in Delano; East Wind Farm, Marine on St. Croix; and the University of Minnesota Leatherdale Equine Center in St. Paul. Volunteer training begins each February.

DRINKING FOR CHARITY

- **Finnegans Irish Amber** beer's slogans include "Practice Random Pints of Kindness" and "Drink Like You Care." The nonprofit is possibly the only beer maker in the world that donates every penny of its profits to charity. Finnegans Beer is made and bottled at the Summit Brewery in St. Paul and sold in numerous bars and restaurants around the Twin Cities, www.finnegans.org.

ENVIRONMENT

- **Friends of the Mississippi**, www.fmr.org, work to protect the river and its watershed in the Twin Cities.
- **Land Stewardship Project**, www.landstewardshipproject.org
- **Minnesota Environmental Action Network** is made up of 16 conservation and environment nonprofits with a variety of volunteer needs, www.mnaction.org.
- **Nature Conservancy**, 1101 W River Pkwy, Ste 200, Minneapolis, 612-331-0750, www.nature.org/wherewework/northamerica/states/minnesota
- **Neighborhood Energy Connection** is a good place for those interested in energy-efficiency to volunteer. This home of **HourCar** can always use help in its office, 624 Selby Ave, St. Paul, 651-221-4462, www.spnec.org.
- **Sierra Club, North Star Chapter**, 2327 E Franklin, Minneapolis, 612-659-9124, www.northstar.sierraclub.org; this very active organization saved Pilot Knob (sacred to the Dakota and best vantage point from which to see the Twin Cities) in Mendota Heights from developers, and sponsors numerous fun outings and events such as the Tour de Sprawl.
- **University of Minnesota Landscape Arboretum**, Hwy 5 and Arboretum Dr, Chanhassen, 952-443-1400, www.arboretum.umn.edu

EVENTS

Every municipality has a summer festival run by volunteers. They're always fun—parades, concerts, contests, flea markets, art shows—something for everyone. And they're a GREAT way to get to know your neighbors.

- **Minneapolis Aquatennial**, www.aquatennial.org; this summer event is always looking for volunteers to work the numerous events, and it's a great way to feel like you're part of the community. Volunteers get a T-shirt, invitations to parties, and a chance to ride on the Volunteers' float in the Torchlight Parade. Volunteer online.
- **St. Paul Winter Carnival** is organized around winter games and sports, www.winter-carnival.com.

GAY, LESBIAN, BISEXUAL, TRANSGENDER

- **OutFront Minnesota**, 310 38th St E, Minneapolis, 612-822-0127, www.outfrontminnesota.org

HEALTH AND HOSPITALS

Most hospitals welcome volunteers—see the **Health Care** chapter in this book for a list of local institutions, and give the nearest one a call. For specific health issues, try one of the following:

- **American Cancer Society**, 2520 Pilot Knob Rd, Mendota Heights, 651-255-8100, www.cancer.org
- **American Heart Association**, 4701 W 77th St, Edina, 952-835-3300, www.americanheart.org
- **American Lung Association**, 490 Concordia Ave, St. Paul, 651-227-8014, www.alamn.org
- **Breast Cancer 3-Day Walk**, www.the3day.org
- **Cystic Fibrosis Foundation**, 651-631-3290, www.cff.org/Chapters/minnesota
- **NARAL Pro-Choice Minnesota**, 651-602-7655, www.prochoiceminnesota.org
- **Planned Parenthood of Minnesota**, www.plannedparenthood.org

HISTORY

- **Minnesota Historical Society**, www.mnhs.org

HOUSING AND HOMELESS SERVICES

- **CommonBond Communities**, www.commonbond.org, is a nonprofit developer and manager of affordable rental homes in Minnesota, Wisconsin, and Iowa. Volunteer opportunities include tutoring, leading exercise classes, and instructing in arts and crafts. Call 651-291-1750 to volunteer.

- **People Serving People** has need for both individuals and groups of volunteers, 614 S Third St, Minneapolis, 612-332-4500, www.peopleservingpeople.org.
- **St. Stephen's Shelter**, 2211 Clinton Ave, Minneapolis, 612-874-0311, www.ststephensmpls.org
- **Twin Cities Habitat for Humanity** is an organization of 20,000 volunteers, 10,000 donors, and a staff of 65 dedicated employees. Over the past years, Twin Cities Habitat has helped nearly 600 families become owners of quality, affordable housing. Volunteer online at www.tchabitat.org.

HUMAN SERVICES

- **American Red Cross**, www.redcrosstc.org
- **Amicus**, 100 N 6th St #347B, Minneapolis, 612-348-8570, www.amicususa.org, provides services for ex-inmates.
- **Emergency Food Shelf Network**, 8501 54th Ave N, New Hope, 763-450-3860, www.emergencyfoodshelf.org
- **House of Charity Soup Kitchen and Learning Center**, 510 S Eighth St, Minneapolis, 612-594-2000, www.houseofcharity.org
- **Metro Meals on Wheels**, 612-623-3363, www.meals-on-wheels.com; every community participates in this program. It's easy—volunteers deliver food to seniors and shut-ins, visit for a minute, and leave—but even this brief contact means the world to people who need this service.
- **Neighborhood Involvement Program (NIP)**; using a small staff and a lot of volunteers, NIP offers a variety of health care and social services to women, men, and children in need; 2431 Hennepin Ave S, Minneapolis, 612-374-3125, www.neighborhoodinvolve.org.
- **Phyllis Wheatley Community Center**, 1301 Tenth Ave N, Minneapolis, 612-374-4342, www.pwccenter.org
- **Sharing and Caring Hands**, 525 N 7th St, Minneapolis, 612-338-4640, www.sharingandcaringhands.org, has been in operation since 1985. Its founder, Sister Mary Jo Copeland, is often referred to as an "Urban Saint."
- **VEAP (Volunteers Enlisted to Assist People)**, 9728 Irving Ave S, Bloomington, 952-888-9616, www.veapvolunteers.org, is a grassroots agency founded in 1973 by thirteen churches in Richfield for the purpose of neighbors coming together to help other neighbors. VEAP volunteers help residents in Bloomington, Edina, Richfield, and a small portion of South Minneapolis.

HUNGER

- **Emergency Food Shelves**, www.emergencyfoodshelf.org
- **Feed My Starving Children**, 763-504-2919, www.fmsc.org, is a nonprofit Christian organization with sites in Chanhassen, Coon Rapids, and Eagan,

where children grades 3 and up and accompanying adults hand-pack meals that are shipped to more than 60 countries around the world.

- **Open Arms**, 1414 E Franklin Ave, 612-872-1152, www.openarmsmn.org, feeds people who are living with HIV/AIDS, ALS, breast cancer, and MS. They prepare and deliver about 250,000 meals a year.

LITERACY

- **English As A Second Language** classes, sponsored by school districts and Early Childhood and Family Education, always need volunteers to converse with the students.
- **Minnesota Literacy Council**, 756 Transfer Rd, St. Paul, 651-645-2277, www. themlc.org

POLITICS–PARTIES

- **Democratic Farmer Labor State Office**, www.dfl.org
- **Green Party**, www.mngreens.org
- **Independence Party**, www.independenceminnesota.org
- **Republican State Office**, www.mngop.com

POLITICS–PUBLIC INTEREST

- **Citizens for Election Integrity Minnesota** is a nonprofit, nonpartisan organization that organizes state-wide nonpartisan observations of audits or recounts in Minnesota, 612-724-1736, www.ceimn.org.
- **League of Women Voters of Minnesota**, 550 Rice St, St. Paul, 651-224-5445, www.lwvmn.org, is a nonpartisan political organization that encourages the informed and active participation of citizens in government.
- **Minnesota Common Cause,** nonpartisan citizens' lobby dedicated to improving the way state government operates, www.commoncause.org.
- **Minnesota Public Interest Research Group (MPIRG)**, is a grassroots, nonpartisan, nonprofit, student-directed organization that empowers and trains students and engages the community to take collective action in the public interest throughout the state of Minnesota, 2414 University Ave SE, Minneapolis, 612-627-4035, www.mpirg.org.
- **Minnesota Women's Political Caucus** works to increase the number of elected and appointed women in office, 550 Rice St, St. Paul, 651-228-0995, www.mnwpc.org

SENIOR SERVICES

- **Little Brothers—Friends of the Elderly**, 612-721-6215, www.littlebrothersmn.org

WOMEN'S SERVICES

- **Minnesota Coalition for Battered Women**, 651-646-6177 or 800-289-6177, www.mcbw.org
- **Minnesota Women's Consortium**, Minnesota Women's Building, 550 Rice St, St. Paul, 651-228-0338, www.mnwomen.org, is a unique statewide coalition of organizations that work to enhance equality and justice for women in Minnesota. There are many opportunities for volunteering here.
- **Sojourner Domestic Violence Project** provides safe shelter for women and children, Hopkins, 952-933-7433, 24-Hour Crisis Line 952-933-7422, www.sojournerproject.org.

MEETING PEOPLE

In addition to meeting people with like interests through your volunteer activities, you might also look at some of the following possibilities:

- **Cities Sports Connection**, 612-929-9009, www.cscsports.com, gives you the opportunity to sign up on their web site for social outings as well as adult recreation.
- **Localtweeps** (http://localtweeps.com/about) is an opt-in ZIP code level means of connecting local like-minded individuals—whether their interests are social or commercial. Members may use it to promote specific events and tweet-ups throughout a targeted ZIP code.
- **Minneapolis Institute of Arts' Circle** (for ages 21–44), offers opportunities to attend insider tours of local galleries, special museum events, and excursions to art crawls and other festivals, www.artsmia.org.
- The **Minnesota Orchestra's Crescendo Project** includes invitations to special events, Happy Hour get-togethers, pre- and post-concert receptions, seating with other Crescendo Project members, and opportunities to get to know the orchestra's musicians, www.minnesotaorchestra.org.
- **Minnesota Rovers Outdoors Club** emphasizes quiet sports such as hiking, canoeing, climbing, bicycling, and skiing. Trip costs (day/weekend/extended) are shared and coordinated by members. Hotline: 612-782-7139, www.MNRovers.org.
- The **Newcomers Clubs** directory includes a large number of organizations in the Twin Cities and surrounding areas that provide men and women the opportunity to meet and develop friendships with others who live in the area. Many organizations have general meetings as well as specific interest groups, www.newcomersclub.com/mn.html#Minneapolis
- **Ski Hawks Sport and Social Club**: This social club sponsors bike, ski, and snowboarding trips, rollerblading, and happy hours, www.mnskihawks.org.

- **UnCorked Twin Cities** is an un-stuffy wine events club that meets monthly at various TC restaurants. Membership is free, but you do pay for your food and drink, www.tc-uncorked.org.

Also, check out the **Sports and Recreation** chapter for more specific recreational activity–oriented groups, such as those for runners, bicyclists, etc.

PLACES OF WORSHIP

Another great way to meet people is at church. While the largest active Lutheran congregation in the USA can be found in south Minneapolis at the Mount Olivet Lutheran Church, www.mtolivet.org, not everybody in Minnesota is Lutheran. In fact, Lutherans may be outnumbered by Catholics—and those two religious traditions may well be outnumbered by everybody else!

Obviously there are too many active houses of worship in the metro area to list here but we offer the following as a place to start. For a complete listing look in the Yellow Pages under "Churches" and "Synagogues."

CHURCHES

AFRICAN METHODIST EPISCOPAL

- **St. Peter's AME Church**, 401 E 41st St, Minneapolis, 612-825-9750, stpeters amechurch.org/church_website.swf
- **St. James AME Church**, 624 Central Ave W, St. Paul, 651-227-4151, stjames stpaul.org

ANGLICAN

- **Anglican Church of St. Dunstan**, 4241 Brookside Ave S, St. Louis Park, 952-920-9122, stdunstananglican.org

APOSTOLIC

- **Rehoboth Church of Jesus Christ**, 916 31st Ave N, Minneapolis, 612-529-2234

ASSEMBLIES OF GOD

- **Bethel Assemblies of God**, Nicollet Ave & 57th St, Minneapolis, 612-866-3227
- **Summit Avenue Assembly of God**, 854 Summit Ave, St. Paul, 651-228-0811, summitag.org

BAPTIST

- **Bethesda Baptist Church**, 1118 S 8th St, Minneapolis, 612-332-5904
- **First Baptist Church**, 10936 Foley Blvd NW, Coon Rapids, 763-755-3748
- **Progressive Baptist Church**, 1505 Burns Ave, St. Paul, 651-774-5503

- **Wooddale Church**, 6630 Shady Oak Rd, Eden Prairie, 952-944-6300, www. wooddale.org

CHRISTIAN SCIENCE

- **First Church of Christ, Scientist**, 2315 Highland Pkwy, St. Paul, 651-291-7640
- **Second Church of Christ, Scientist**, 228 S 12th St, Minneapolis, 612-332-3368

CHURCH OF CHRIST

- **Minneapolis Central Church of Christ**, 1922 4th Ave N, Minneapolis, 612-374-5481, www.churches-of-christ.net
- **Church of Jesus Christ of Latter-Day Saints**
- **Latter-Day Saints Institute**, 1205 University Ave SE, Minneapolis, 612-331-1154
- **Church of Jesus Christ of Latter-Day Saints Family History Centers**, 2801 Douglas Dr N, Crystal, 763-544-2479; 4700 Edinbrook Pkwy, Brooklyn Park, 763-425-1865; and 9700 Nesbitt Ave S, Bloomington, 952 893-2393

CONGREGATIONAL

- **First Congregational Church of Minnesota**, 500 8th Ave SE, Minneapolis, 612-331-3816, www.firstchurchmn.org
- **Plymouth Congregational Church**, 1900 Nicollet Ave, Minneapolis, 612-871-7400, www.plymouth.org
- **Woodbury Community Church**, 2975 Pioneer Dr, Woodbury, 651-739-1427, wccmn.org

DISCIPLES OF CHRIST

- **First Christian Church**, 2201 First Ave S, Minneapolis, 612-870-1868, www. disciples.org

EASTERN ORTHODOX

- **Russian Orthodox Church**, 1201 Hathaway Ln NE, Fridley, 763-574-1001, www.stgeorgeroc.org
- **St. George Greek Orthodox Church**, 1111 Summit Ave, St. Paul, 651-222-6220, stgeorgegoc.org
- **St. Mary's Greek Orthodox Church**, 3450 Irving Ave S, Minneapolis, 612-825-9595, www.stmarysgoc.org
- **St. Michael's Ukrainian Orthodox**, 505 4th St NE, Minneapolis, 612-379-2695, www.uocofusa.org

EPISCOPAL

- **Cathedral Church of St. Mark**, 519 Oak Grove St, Minneapolis, 612-870-7800, ourcathedral.org

- **Christ Episcopal Church-Woodbury**, 7305 Afton Rd, Woodbury, 651-735-8790, www.christchurch-woodbury.org
- **Episcopal Diocese of Minnesota**, 1730 Clifton Pl, Minneapolis, 612-871-5311, www.episcopalmn.org
- **St. Alban's**, 6716 Gleason Rd, Edina, 952-941-3065, stalbansedina.org
- **St. David**, 13000 St. David's Rd, Minnetonka, 952-935-3336, stdavidsparish.org
- **St. Martin's by-the-Lake**, County Rd 15 and Westwood Rd, Minnetonka Beach, 952-471-8429, www.stmartinsbylake.org
- **St. Paul's, Franklin and Logan at Lake of the Isles**, 612-377-1273, www.stpaulsmpls.org
- **St. Paul's Church on the Hill**, 1524 Summit Ave, St. Paul, 651-698-0371, www.stpaulsonthehillmn.org
- **Trinity Episcopal Church**, 322 2nd St, Excelsior, 952-474-5263, www.trinityexcelsior.org
- **University Episcopal Center**, 310 Walnut St SE, Minneapolis, 612-331-3552, www.uec-mn.org

EVANGELICAL

- **Brookdale Covenant Church**, 5139 Brooklyn Blvd, Brooklyn Center, 763-535-6305, brookdalecovenant.org
- **Community Covenant Church**, 901 Humboldt Ave N, Minneapolis, 612-374-3935, www.cccminneapolis.org
- **Russian Evangelical Christian Church**, 1205 Tenth Ave, Shakopee, 952-496-0578

FRIENDS (QUAKERS)

- **Minneapolis Friends Meeting**, 4401 York Ave S, Minneapolis, 612-926-6159, minneapolisfriends.org
- **Twin Cities Friends Meeting**, 1725 Grand Ave, St. Paul, 651-699-6995, www.tcfm.org

INDEPENDENT/MULTIPLE AFFILIATIONS

- **Colonial Church of Edina**, 6200 Colonial Way, Edina, 952-925-2711, www.colonialchurch.org
- **Japanese Fellowship Church**, 4217 Bloomington Ave, Minneapolis, 612-722-8314, www.fellowshipdeaconry.org
- **Living Waters Christian Church**, 1002 2nd St NE, Hopkins, 952-938-4176,
- **Wayzata Evangelical Free Church**, 705 County Rd 101 N, Plymouth, 763-473-9463, www.wayzatafree.org

JEHOVAH'S WITNESSES

The national web site for Jehovah's Witnesses is www.watchtower.org.

- **Riverview Congregation (with Spanish)**, 1545 Christensen Ave, West St. Paul, 651-457-7139

LGBT CHURCHES

- **All God's Children Metropolitan Community Church**, 3100 Park Avenue S, Minneapolis, 612-824-2673, www.agcmcc.org
- **Dignity Twin Cities** meets at Prospect Park United Methodist Church (22 Orlin Ave SE) on the 2nd and 4th Sundays of the month, www.dignitytwincities. org.
- **Spirit of the Lakes United Church of Christ**, 4001 38th Ave S, Minneapolis, 612-729-7556, www.spiritucc.org
- **St. Joan of Arc**, 4537 3rd Ave. S, Minneapolis, 612-823-8205, www.stjoan.com
- **St. Paul-Reformation Lutheran Church**, 100 North Oxford Street, St. Paul, 651-224-3371, www.stpaulref.org

LUTHERAN

- **Beautiful Savior**, 5005 Northwest Blvd, Plymouth, 763-550-1000, www. beautifulsaviorlc.org
- **Bethlehem Lutheran Church**, 4100 Lyndale Ave S, Minneapolis, 612-312-3400, www.bethlehem-church.org
- **Calvary Lutheran Church**, 7520 Golden Valley Rd, Golden Valley, 763-545-5659, www.calvary.org
- **Como Park Lutheran Church**, 1376 W Hoyt Ave, St. Paul, 651-646-7127, www.comoparklutheran.org
- **Den Norske Lutherske Mindekirke (The Norwegian Lutheran Memorial Church, Mindekirke)**, 924 E 21st St, Minneapolis, 612-874-0716, mindekirken. org; just off Franklin Ave in Minneapolis, this old Norwegian-heritage church sponsors Norwegian classes and sometimes holds bilingual services.
- **Evangelical Lutheran Church Association**, 612-870-3610, www.elca.org
- **Hosanna Lutheran Church**, 9600 163rd St W, Lakeville, 952-435-3332, www. hosannalc.org
- **Holy Trinity Lutheran Church**, 2730 E 31st St, Minneapolis, 612-729-8358, www.htlcmpls.org
- **Luther Memorial Church LCA**, 3751 Sheridan Ave N, Minneapolis, 612-522-3639, www.hmonglutheranministry.org
- **Luther Seminary**, 2481 Como Ave, St. Paul, 651-641-3456, www.luthersem. edu
- **Mt. Calvary**, 301 County Rd 19, Excelsior, 952-474-8893, www.mountcalvary. org
- **Mt. Olivet Lutheran Church**, 5025 Knox Ave S, Minneapolis, 612-926-7651, www.mtolivet.org
- **Prince of Peace Lutheran Church**, 13901 Fairview Dr, Burnsville, 952-435-8102, www.princeofpeaceonline.org

MENNONITE

- **Faith Mennonite Church**, 2720 E 22nd St, Minneapolis, 612-375-9483
- **St. Paul Mennonite Fellowship**, 576 S Robert St, St. Paul, 612-388-5016, saintpaulmennonite.org

METHODIST

- **Hamline United Methodist Church**, 1514 Englewood Ave, St. Paul, 651-645-0667, hamlinechurch.org
- **Hennepin Avenue United Methodist Church**, 511 Groveland at Lyndale Ave, Minneapolis, 612-871-5303, www.haumc.org
- **North United Methodist Church**, 4350 Fremont Ave N, Minneapolis, 612-522-4497, gbgm-umc.org/northchurch
- **Walker Community United Methodist Church**, 3104 16th Ave S, Minneapolis, 612-722-6612, www.walkerchurch.org
- **Wesley United Methodist Church**, Marquette Ave & Grant St, Minneapolis, 612-871-3585, www.thewesleychurch.org
- **Woodbury United Methodist Church**, 7465 Steepleview Rd, Woodbury, 651-738-0305, www.woodburyumc.org
- **Metropolitan Community Churches**
- **All God's Children Metropolitan Community Church**, 3100 Park Ave S, Minneapolis, 612-824-2673, www.agcmcc.org; a consciously inclusive Christian faith community, reaching out to all with a primary focus to the LGBT community.

NON-DENOMINATIONAL

- **Cedarcrest Church**, 1630 E 90th St, Bloomington, 952-854-8390, www.cedarcrestchurch.net
- **The Rock** meets in Uptown Minneapolis on Friday nights; check their web site for details, 612-339-7625, www.rockthechurch.com

PRESBYTERIAN

- **Aldrich Avenue Presbyterian Church**, 3501 Aldrich Ave S, Minneapolis, 612-825-2479, www.aldrichchurch.org; sometimes holds services at the Lake Harriet Bandshell.
- **Arlington Hills Presbyterian**, 1275 Magnolia Ave E, St. Paul, 651-774-6028, arlingtonhillspresbyterian.org
- **Bryn Mawr Presbyterian Church**, 420 S Cedar Lake Rd, Minneapolis, 612-377-5222, www.brynmawrchurch.org
- **Macalester-Plymouth United Church**, 1658 Lincoln Ave, St. Paul, 651-698-8871, www.macalester-plymouth.org
- **Presbyterian Church Synod of Lakes & Prairies**, 2115 Cliff Dr, Eagan, 651-3574-1140, www.lakesandprairies.org
- **Presbytery of the Twin Cities**, 122 W Franklin Ave, Minneapolis, 612-871-7281, www.ptcaweb.org

- **Stadium Village Church**, 501 Oak St, SE, Minneapolis, 612-331-1632, www. stadiumvillagechurch.org
- **St. Luke**, 3121 Groveland School Rd, Minnetonka, 952-473-7378, www. stlukeweb.org
- **Westminster Presbyterian Church**, Nicollet Mall & 12th St, Minneapolis, 612-332-3421, ewestminster.org

ROMAN CATHOLIC

The web site for the Archdiocese of St. Paul and Minneapolis, www.archspm. org, provides information about St. Paul's majestic cathedral and offers links to other Catholic resources.

- **Archdiocese of St. Paul and Minneapolis**, 226 Summit Ave, St. Paul, 651-291-4400, www.archspm.org
- **Basilica of St. Mary**, 88 N 17th St, Minneapolis, 612-333-1381, www.mary. org
- **Cathedral of St. Paul**, 239 Selby Ave, St. Paul, 651-228-1766, www.cathedral-saintpaul.org
- **Dignity Twin Cities is a community of Catholic LGBT people**, their families and friends, 612-827-3103, www.dignitytwincities.org
- **Liberal Catholic Church of St. Francis**, 3201 Pleasant Ave, Minneapolis, 612-823-4276, www.liberalcatholic.org
- **NET (National Evangelization Teams) Ministries is an international Catholic youth ministry based in the Twin Cities. It holds monthly masses for teens**, 651-450-6833, www.netusa.org
- **Our Lady of Guadalupe**, 401 Concord St, St. Paul, 651-228-0506
- **Our Lady of Lourdes Church**, One Lourdes Place NE, Minneapolis, 612-379-2259, www.ourladyoflourdes.com, is the oldest continuously used church in the city. It was designated a U.S. historic landmark in 1934.
- **Pax Christi**, 12100 Pioneer Trail, Eden Prairie, 952-941-3150, www.paxchristi. com
- **Presentation of the Blessed Virgin Mary**, Larpenteur Ave at Kennard St, St. Paul, 651-777-8116, www.presentationofmary.org
- **St. Joan of Arc Church**, 4537 3rd Ave S, Minneapolis, 612-823-8205, www. stjoan.com
- **St. Olaf Catholic Church**, 215 S 8th St, Minneapolis, 612-332-7471, www. saintolaf.org
- **St. Patrick's**, 6820 Saint Patrick's Ln, Valley View and Gleason Rds, Edina, 952-941-3164, stpatrick-edina.org
- **St. Stephens Catholic Church and Shelter**, 2211 Clinton Ave S, Minneapolis, 612-874-0311, www.ststephensmpls.org
- **St. Victoria Catholic Church**, 8228 Victoria Dr, Victoria, 952-443-2661, www. stvictoria.net

UNITARIAN UNIVERSALIST

- **First Unitarian Society of Minneapolis**, 900 Mt. Curve Ave, Minneapolis, 612-377-6608, www.firstunitariansociety.org
- **Nora UU Church**, 12333 155th Ave, Hanska (about an hour and a half southwest of Minneapolis), 507-439-6240, norauuchurch.org; organized in 1881, this tiny country church is the only remaining Norwegian liberal congregation and the only existing rural church that was actually built to be a Unitarian church. The grounds, church, cemetery, log cabin museum filled with immigrant artifacts, and parsonage are well-kept and beautiful in their simplicity. The church's early October Smorgasbord fundraiser is an opportunity to enjoy a beautiful drive through Minnesota's farmlands at harvest time as well as an authentic Norwegian meal.
- **Unity Unitarian Church**, 732 Holly Ave, St. Paul, 651-228-1456, www.unityunitarian.org
- **Unitarian Universalist Association**, 122 W Franklin Ave, Minneapolis, 612-870-4823, www.psduua.org
- **White Bear Unitarian Universalist Church**, 328 Maple St, Mahtomedi, 651-426-2369, www.whitebearunitarian.org

UNITED CHURCH OF CHRIST

- **First Congregational Church of Minnesota**, 500 8th Ave SE, Minneapolis, 612-331-3816, www.firstchurchmn.org
- **Mayflower Congregational Church**, 106 E Diamond Lake Rd, Minneapolis, 612-824-0761, www.mayflowermpls.org
- **Macalester Plymouth United Church**, 1658 Lincoln Ave, St. Paul, 651-698-8871, www.macalester-plymouth.org
- **St. Anthony Park United Church of Christ**, 2129 Commonwealth Ave, St. Paul, 651-646-7173, www.sapucc.org
- **St. Paul's United Church of Christ**, 900 Summit Ave, St. Paul, 651-224-5809, www.SPUCConSummit.org
- **Wayzata Community Church**, 125 W Wayzata Blvd, Wayzata, is the largest UCC church in town, 952-473-8877, wayzatacommunitychurch.org

WESLEYAN

- **Oakdale Wesleyan Church**, 6477 N 10th St, Oakdale, 651-739-2940, www.oakdalechurch.org

SYNAGOGUES

The web site of the **Minneapolis Jewish Federation/St. Paul United Jewish Fund and Council** (www.jewishminnesota.org) contains links to local synagogues, arts and Jewish culture. Sign up on their web page and they will welcome you with a packet of information about the Jewish communities in the Minneapolis and St. Paul areas. This site also has links for singles. **TC Jew-**

folk, "The Twin Cities Hub for Hip Jewish Stuff," features content ranging from Hanukkah recipes to dating advice and politics, http://tcjewfolk.com/.

Newcomers should also check in at the **Jewish Community Center–Greater Minneapolis,** 4330 Cedar Lake Rd S, St. Louis Park, 952-381-3400, www.sabesjcc.org.

JEWISH—CONSERVATIVE

- **Adath Jeshurun Congregation**, 10500 Hillside Ln W, Minnetonka, 952-545-2424, www.adathjeshurun.org, is described as "a progressive, egalitarian" community. This synagogue is one of the most beautiful buildings and settings in the Twin Cities.
- **Beth El Synagogue**, 5224 W 26th St, St. Louis Park, 952-920-3512, www.beth elsynagogue.org
- **Temple of Aaron Congregation**, 616 S Mississippi River Blvd, St. Paul, 651-698-8874, www.templeofaaron.org

JEWISH—ORTHODOX

- **Adath Israel Synagogue**, 2337 Edgcumbe Rd, St. Paul, 651-698-8300, http://adath.blogspot.com
- **Bais Yisroel**, 4221 Sunset Blvd, St. Louis Park, 952-926-7867, www.baisyisroel.org
- **Kenesseth Israel Modern Orthodox**, 4330 W 28th St, St. Louis Park, 952-920-2183, www.kennessethisrael.org

JEWISH—RECONSTRUCTIONIST

- **Mayim Rabim**, 44th and York Ave S, Minneapolis, 612-922-5983, http://jrf.org/mayimrabim

JEWISH—REFORM

- **Mount Zion Temple**, 1300 Summit Ave, St. Paul, 651-698-3881, www.mzion.org
- **Temple Israel**, 2324 Emerson Ave S, Minneapolis, 612-377-8680, www.tem pleisrael.com

ISLAMIC CENTERS

The **University of Minnesota's Muslim Students Association** (300 Washington Avenue SE, Minneapolis) has developed an extensive list of resources including community centers, Islamic organizations, and Islamic businesses (tc.umn.edu/~muslimsa). Many Muslim restaurants, groceries, and fabric stores are concentrated along Central Avenue, north of downtown Minneapolis, and near the University.

- **Abuubakar As-Sadique Islamic Center**, 325 Cedar Ave S, Minneapolis, 612-333-2341, www.somalitalk.com/abubakar/

- **Islamic Center of Minnesota**, 1401 Gardena Ave NE, Minneapolis, 763-571-5604, www.islamiccentermn.org

EASTERN RELIGIONS

BAHA'I

- **Baha'i Faith**, 1680 Bellows St, West St. Paul, 651-455-7169
- **Baha'i Faith**, 4 Pine Tree Dr, Arden Hills, 651-482-9455
- **Baha'i Faith**, 426 Fairview Ave N, St. Paul, 651-641-0336
- **Baha'i Faith**, 3644 Chicago Ave, Minneapolis, 612-823-3494, bahai.org

BUDDHIST

- **Clouds in Water Zen Center**, 308 Prince St, St. Paul, 651-222-6968, www.cloudsinwater.org
- **Compassionate Ocean Dharma Center**, 3206 Holmes Ave, Minneapolis, 612-825-7658, www.oceandharma.org
- **Dharma Field Zen Center**, 3118 W 49th St, Minneapolis, 612-928-4868, www.dharmafield.org
- **Karma Kagyu Minneapolis**, 4301 Morningside Rd, Edina, 952-926-5048, www.ktcminneapolis.org
- **Minnesota Zen Meditation Center**, 3343 E Lake Calhoun Pkwy, Minneapolis, 612-822-5313, www.mnzenctr.com; posts information on the practice of Buddhism and activities of the Twin Cities Buddhist community on its web site.
- **Shambhala Center of Minneapolis**, 2931 Grand St NE, 612-331-7737; the Shambhala tradition has attracted interest because of its music and art. Visit www.shambhala-mn.org for more information.
- **Soka Gakkai International USA**, 1381 Eustis St, St. Paul, 651-645-3133, sgi-usamnnd.org

HINDU

- **Geeta Ashram Church**, 10537 Noble Ave N, Brooklyn Park, 763-493-4229, www.geetaashram.org
- **Hindu Mandir**, 10530 Troy Ln N (corner of 105th Ave and Troy Ln), Maple Grove 763-425-9449, www.hindumandirmn.org; the New Temple is a 42,000-square-foot building on a 40-acre property with landscaping designed to make it "a place of peace."
- **Meditation Center**, 631 University Ave NE, Minneapolis, 612-379-2386, the meditationcenter.org

For more information about Hinduism in the Twin Cities, check out www.hindumandirmn.org. This site is associated with the **Hindu Society of Minnesota**, where many events take place.

SIKH

- **Sikh Society of Minnesota**, 5831 University Ave NE, Fridley, 763-574-0886, mnsikhs.com

OTHERS

If you're an "eclectic practitioner," e.g., a Wiccan, Druid, tolerant Pantheist, etc., the multitraditional **Wiccan Church of Minnesota** (www.wiccanchurchmn.org) may be for you. In addition, the **Minnesota Atheists Online** (www.mnatheists.org) has a site that explains this oft-misunderstood belief system.

NEW AGE

- **Eckankar Spiritual Center**, Temple of Eck, 1200 W 78th St, Chanhassen, 952-380-2200, www.eckankar.org
- **Lake Harriet Community Church**, 4401 Upton Ave S, Minneapolis, 612-922-4272, www.www.lakeharrietspiritualcommunity.com, describes itself as "a spiritually diverse community that honors and explores all sacred beliefs and empowers the unique connection to the Divine Spirit within each of us."

WINTER

If you want to know what Minnesota is like in the winter, rent the movie *Grumpy Old Men*. You'll see that Minnesotans don't just endure the winter, we revel in it! As the mercury plunges, our spirits soar! When snow blankets the landscape and residents of states "Down Below" bundle in blankets and huddle in front of roaring fires, Minnesotans head outside. It's time for us to ski, skate, sled, snowboard, snowmobile, ice fish, or maybe even try our hands at clattering across "hard water" at 50 miles an hour in an iceboat. In fact, there's even more to do here in winter than in summer—and there are no mosquitoes!

With snow cover on the ground continuously for several months, it's no surprise that snowmobiles were invented right here. Originally developed as a serious way to get around in inclement weather, snowmobiles quickly became Minnesotans' preferred recreation vehicle. There are now over 20,000 miles of snowmobile trails in the state. Free snowmobile trail maps and license information are available from the Minnesota **DNR Information Center** (651-296-6157 or 1-888-646-6367, TTY: 651-296-5484 or 1-800-657-3929, 1-888-665-4236, www.info.dnr.state.mn.us). (See **Snowmobiling** in the **Sports and Recreation** chapter.)

The temperature usually takes a real tumble in November, with the record low for the month of −17; the all-time record low in Minneapolis is −41, in January.

Winter, which sets in here by November and lasts into April, is usually brought down by bitter cold weather systems that dip south from Canada. Be prepared for week-long periods of sub-zero (that's sub-zero, not sub-freezing) temperatures, and for the possibility of an April blizzard. Sign up with any local television station for email notification of snow emergencies, school closings, and late openings.

Take winter seriously: if you don't stay active in the cold weather months, cabin fever and shortness of daylight can result in malaise and even depression. That said, winters here can be a thrill, and the following information should help to smooth your way.

Download WCCO's storm-tracker app and never be caught unprepared.

APPAREL

Layering is the secret to staying comfortable. Make the layer closest to your skin something that wicks, or draws moisture away from your body. Patagonia long underwear is a favorite here, but there are other high-tech fibers and brands. And though turtlenecks are "out" in most parts of the country, they're always "in," in Minnesota. So are flannel-lined jeans. You'll need a heavy coat. Down-filled is usually considered warmest. Buy it here or from a catalogue company such as L.L. Bean, which rates its clothing for comfort at sub-zero temperatures. Bean's –50° Fahrenheit down hip-length or longer coats and parkas are popular here. For the proper clothing for more strenuous activities, consult the ski and sports stores. There are new fabric systems every year, many of which react with the body's temperature to store or release heat as needed to buffer the body against overheating as well as getting chilled.

Finally—feet. Warm feet are key. Snow boots will reduce your chances of suffering a major wipeout on the sidewalk, not to mention frozen toes. Insulated Sorel boots are rated for very cold temperatures and are especially good for those who have to stand around outside. Sorel also makes children's boots and winter booties for infants and toddlers. Other brands to look for include Columbia, Kamik, Merrell, and Baffin. You can compare many brands of cold-rated apparel at stores here or online at dealers such as Northland Marine (www.northlandmarine.com). Because falling on ice causes many injuries, stores also sell metal-studded detachable soles that fit on the bottoms of your boots. Stabil-icers and Yaktrax are two popular traction devices (sold by L.L. Bean, Northland Marine, www.32north.com, and local retailers).

Those who need winter wear and cannot afford it can receive help at Sharing And Caring Hands, Minneapolis, 612-338-4640; The Salvation Army, Metrowide, where coats are available from late October, 651-746-3412; CEAP, Brooklyn Park, 763-566-9600; Hope for the City, Minnetonka, 952-897-7799; Joseph's Coat, St. Paul, 651-291-2472; Neighbors, Inc, South St. Paul, 651-455-1508; CHAP Ministries, Burnsville, 952-890-8222; or Catholic Charities, Minneapolis, 612-664-8500. These organizations also welcome donations of coats and warm jackets, winter boots, hats, warm gloves, and other seasonally appropriate clothing.

Watch Out for Signs of Frostbite

If you're outside and feel tingling in your fingers or other exposed areas, notice a change in your skin tone, or lose feeling in your extremities, you probably have frostbite. What to do? For first-stage frostbite, slowly rewarm the affected tissue at room temperature, without rubbing, using body heat and blankets or applying warm cloths. If numbness remains after warming, seek immediate medical treatment.

One final category: dressing up. Minnesota couture usually includes long sleeves and boots—and people carry their good shoes. So if you're throwing a winter housewarming, be sure to save room by the front door for the pile of boots.

By the way, your teenager will not dress sensibly, so give it up. Generations of Minnesota teens have proven that you CAN stand at a bus stop dressed in jeans and a light jacket wearing neither hat nor gloves, with temperatures at 20 below, and survive.

DRIVING

If you have four-wheel drive you may think winter driving will be a cinch, but the truth is that, although four-wheel drive is better in snow, it is no better on ice. Front-wheel drive cars provide better control in icy conditions than rear-wheel drive, but none of it's any good if you're driving too fast, so slow down.

If the forecast includes bad road conditions, give yourself extra time to get to your destination, including a few minutes to warm up your car. If the weatherman happens to mention "black ice," be especially careful. Black ice is particularly prevalent at intersections, where car exhaust freezes, it also causes many accidents on bridges, freeway ramps, and at exposed locations where the wind whips across the pavement. Before winter really kicks in (sometime in October), take the following steps to winterize your vehicle. Change the radiator fluid and add anti-freeze. Some people switch to a lighter oil (more viscous at low temperatures) for winter. If you park outside overnight, 5W-30 or a synthetic oil will help your car start in the morning; if you park in a garage, 10W-30 is sufficient. Do consider buying snow tires and an engine block heater (the origin of the electrical cords you see hanging out of the grilles of some cars). These devices run a low electrical current through your engine to keep it warm overnight. They're particularly helpful if you don't have a garage, although you may find it impractical to run an extension cord out to your car. Finally, think about your battery. Be sure to clean the connections in the fall; and if it is four years old, replace the battery before winter. On those January mornings when it's −20° and you stick your key in the ignition and nothing happens, begging and swearing will not turn your engine over, but that new battery will.

Next, stash the following useful items somewhere inside your car:

- An ice scraper
- A cell phone
- A set of jumper cables, for yourself or for a coworker stranded in the parking lot;
- A bag of kitty litter (for traction) and a small snow shovel, to help dig your way out of a wipeout (car mats work for tire traction, too)
- A "stranded" emergency kit consisting of blankets, a bright-colored piece of cloth to use as a flag, Hot Hands heat packs, a candle in a coffee can (a makeshift heater), matches, a flashlight (with batteries that work), water and a couple of energy bars.

Once the Arctic weather has arrived, keep your gas tank from getting near empty—the water content of the fuel will actually freeze in the gas lines, preventing any fuel from getting to the engine. If you've never driven in snowy conditions before, a good place to practice is on a frozen lake, with your window rolled down in case your car goes through the ice. The trick to maintaining control when you start to "fishtail" (when the back wheels slide out to the left or right as you hit the brakes) is to steer, not too fast, into the direction that your back wheels are sliding. Try it; it works. Above all, drive as slowly as conditions demand.

As mentioned, you will have to leave a little extra time to drive anywhere. Many drivers make an extra key for their car, so they can go out, start up their vehicle, lock it, and return to get ready while the inside of the car gets nice and warm. The police however, counsel against doing this, because of the easy (and warm!) target you leave for a car thief. IN FACT, LEAVING YOUR CAR RUNNING UNATTENDED CAN GET YOU A TICKET IN SOME CITIES. An alternative: On particularly cold nights, start your car up for 10 minutes or so before going to bed; it gives your engine and battery an extra charge for the morning. One safety tip: don't run your car while it's parked inside a garage—people here die every year that way.

For specific rules on winter parking, see **Parking** in the **Getting Settled** chapter and check your city's web page. Did we remember to tell you to slow down?

HEATING

Heating costs take a big bite out of your monthly budget for at least half of the year, but Xcel Energy does have an online Home Energy Analyzer (www.energy-guide.com) which can help you find ways of reducing heating and other energy costs for your home.

TOP TEN WAYS TO SAVE ON YOUR HEATING BILL

Following are the top 10 recommendations from the state's Energy Information Center on how to reduce heating costs throughout the winter.

1. Turn your thermostat down 5 to 10 degrees while you are away or asleep. Every degree above 68° adds about 3% to your heating bill.

2. Turn your water heater temperature down to 120° or 125°.

3. Cover the interior of leaky or drafty windows with window film (sold at all hardware stores).

4. Have your furnace and water heater professionally cleaned and inspected annually to make sure they work efficiently and safely. Change your furnace filters monthly.

5. Replace your old furnace with a new, energy-efficient model. Look for the Energy Star label on all new home appliances.

6. Caulk and weatherstrip around doors and windows.

7. Vacuum your heat registers and return air vents regularly. If you have hot water heat, vacuum radiators or baseboard heaters. Make sure furniture and draperies do not block the heat flow.

8. Keep your curtains open when the sun is shining, in order to gain solar heat.

9. Bring your attic insulation up to an R-value of 38, but only after sealing all your attic bypasses. Bypasses leak warm, moist air into the attic, reducing the value of insulation.

10. Call your local utility and schedule a home energy audit, which will pinpoint other ways to weatherize your home to make it more energy-efficient.

HOME INSULATION

Insulation is taken seriously in this climate. The state building code requires a minimum of R-38 in ceilings with attics. To learn more about the state energy code, check with the **Minnesota Department of Commerce Energy Information Center** (651-296-5175, 800-657-3710, www.doli.state.mn.us/CCLD/PDF/sbc_1322.pdf). The **Center for Energy and Environment in Minneapolis** (612-335-5858, www.mncee.org) and the **St. Paul Neighborhood Energy Consortium** (651-221-4462, www.spnec.org) are even better resources for information about keeping your house cozy on those below-zero days.

You can actually save a considerable amount of money on heating and cooling by making some relatively modest improvements to your home. Caulking or weather-stripping doors and windows can save as much as 10% on your annual energy bill. Storm doors and windows prevent drafts and can save as much as 15% in cold months. Insulating your attic floor or top floor ceiling reduces energy costs by about 5%, and insulating exterior walls can save on both heating and cooling by 20%.

PETS

The two most important things you can do for your pet in the winter are to provide adequate shelter and plenty of water—animals cannot survive on the moisture in snow. You may also need to protect your pet's feet. Pet stores and catalogues sell dog booties, which protect tender paws from being cut or frozen while walking on the crusty snow. Look for booties that are tall enough to stay on. PetEdge.com sells waterproof tall booties with non-slip soles. You can also pick up booties from local pet stores and vendors at dog shows.

Many people appreciate the convenience of indoor-outdoor runs. It's an easy do-it-yourself project to install a dog door between the studs in a garage wall to create an out-of-the-elements place for your pet to sleep and be fed.

For those who dream of racing through the woods behind a team of huskies, you've come to the right state. See the **Dogsledding** section of the **Sports and Recreation** chapter. Locally, sled dog races are held during St. Paul's Winter Carnival and sometimes on Lake Minnetonka.

TORNADOES

The worst tornadoes in Twin Cities history occurred on May 6, 1965, when six tornadoes swept across the western and northern portions of the metro, killing 13 people and injuring 683.

This was the first night that the Twin Cities' civil defense sirens were ever used to warn about approaching tornadoes, and they are credited with saving many lives. We still depend on this warning system to let us know when to take cover. Take it seriously when you hear the sirens go off, because tornadoes are the deadliest weather we have. Cities test their civil defense sirens at 1 p.m. on the first Wednesday of the month.

Tornadoes have the power to lift cars and hurl them through the air. Their winds make deadly missiles of ordinary household objects, debris, and broken glass, and they sometimes stay on the ground for many miles. They are among the most violent natural forces on the planet—and by mid-April, we have a reasonable expectation of severe thunderstorms and tornadoes in the metro area.

So if you see strange clouds moving in, or hail, or if the sky starts to turn a sickly green, what should you do? Turn on the radio or television (preferably battery-powered) to any local station to get the weather forecast. They all have Doppler radar and can tell you minute-by-minute where the storm is and where it's going. An "NOAA weather radio" is a special comfort at night. New models can be set so that they are activated when a severe weather warning is issued—and you'll be awakened.

Severe weather warnings fall into two categories: watches and warnings. If a tornado "watch" is issued, it means that a tornado is "possible." If a tornado "warning" is issued and/or you hear a siren, it means that a tornado has actually been spotted, or is strongly indicated on radar, and it is time to go to a safe shelter immediately. What constitutes safe shelter? A basement is best, away from the west and south walls, preferably under a heavy piece of furniture. If you don't have a basement, go to an inside bathroom and get in the tub, or take shelter in a closet, hallway, or stairwell, and put something over you. Even if it's only a blanket, it might still protect you from flying glass. Outside, if you see a tornado and it isn't moving to your right or left relative to trees and power poles in the distance, it may be heading straight for you, so get down as low as you possibly can. If you're in a car, get out of the car and lie down on the ground or in a ditch, if it isn't raining. If it's raining, the ditch might flood. Do not—DO NOT—take shelter under a highway overpass; you might as well run into a wind tunnel. And do not stay in your car—most tornado deaths occur in mobile homes or cars. If you're out shopping, don't worry; just follow the manager's instructions—all public buildings here have shelters.

Finally, know where you are. Warnings and watches are normally given by county. If the weather service says a warning has been issued for Wright County, you need to know that that's west of Hennepin County and Minneapolis and, since storms here usually travel from west to east, if you are in western Hennepin County, you should be thinking about taking precautions. All the warnings in the world won't help if you don't know which city and county you are in. More than likely, you'll never really need to use this advice, but be prepared: Minneapolis does rank number eight on *USA Today*'s list of Top Twenty Tornado-Prone Cities.

WEATHER-RELATED RESOURCES

For current weather conditions as well as weather-related links, check any of the local radio or TV stations, or call 763-512-1111 for Time and Temperature. Lastly, Minnesota's popular Weatherguide Calendars are sold for $15.95 in most book and grocery stores, or order one from the Freshwater Society (952-471-9773, www.freshwater.org).

On weekdays you can get a forecast for the day on your phone. To sign up text the word WEATHER to 677677. Standard texting rates apply. To unsubscribe, text STOP WEATHER to 677677.

BY CAR

CONGESTION

For better or worse, most people in the Twin Cities get around by car. With increased growth and development, particularly in the outer suburbs, traffic congestion has intensified to the point that Minnesota now ranks tenth worst in the country with respect to congestion, according to results of a national traffic study released in 2009 by the Washington-based firm INRX.

- Our worst bottleneck is at **I-494 and Highway 169** in Eden Prairie.
- **Highway 100 at 84th St** (just south of 1-494) was identified by the report as the metro's second worst.
- Other spots that will have you pulling your hair out by the roots are:
  - ▹ **Westbound I-494 at Lyndale Ave** in Bloomington
  - ▹ **Eastbound 494 at France Ave**
  - ▹ **Southbound I-35W from 11th to 17th Ave** in downtown Minneapolis
  - ▹ **Westbound I-94 through Minneapolis** morning and evening
  - ▹ **The I-62 Crosstown/I-35 convergence** on the borders of Richfield and Minneapolis
  - ▹ **Highway 77 (Cedar Avenue) at 138th Street**
  - ▹ **I-35E and Highway 13**

The report also found that it takes metro area residents 13% longer to get where they're going during peak driving times. Another study identified our "rush hour" as 7.4 hours long.

Be sure to keep the above information in mind when choosing a place to live relative to where you work—unfortunately, it doesn't look like the situation is going to improve anytime soon. In fact, traffic congestion ranks as the No. 1

concern of Twin Cities area residents, according to a survey conducted by the Metropolitan Council.

> iOn Traffic Minnesota – Minneapolis St. Paul is an app that allows you to check traffic conditions on your intended route.

The state's attempts at addressing the metro's transportation problems start and stop as often as rush hour traffic. However, the publicly owned **Hiawatha Light Rail Transit** (LRT) line, which began operating between downtown Minneapolis and the Mall of America in 2004, has been carrying double its projected ridership, and is widely hailed as a success, as is its connecting arm, the **Northstar Commuter Rail**, which runs west/northwest from Target Field in downtown Minneapolis through Fridley, Coon Rapids, Anoka, and Elk River to Big Lake. The next piece of the network to come online will be the 11-mile Central Corridor light rail connecting St. Paul and Minneapolis downtowns via University and Washington Avenues. It is scheduled to begin operation in 2014.

For the present, most of the state's efforts are focused on roads. The **Minnesota Department of Transportation**, otherwise known as MnDOT (www.dot.state.mn.us) is busily adding lanes to every major road that passes through or around the Twin Cities, and addressed the problem of congestion on I-394 (the freeway between downtown Minneapolis and the western suburbs) and I-35W (from Burnsville to Minneapolis) by turning the **High Occupancy Vehicle** lanes into **toll lanes** during rush hours (see **MN-Pass** below).

At the same time, **MetroTransit**, the publicly owned transit company, has been caught in a budget squeeze (ironically caused in part by declining state automobile tax revenues), and has reacted by increasing fares and cutting routes, thus putting many former bus riders back into their cars.

Finally, the state's only other congestion-management tool, **freeway on-ramp metering**, has long been a bugaboo, even to drivers who are used to them. These on-ramp signal lights generally run during morning and evening peak periods, and are meant to keep cars flowing smoothly onto the highway. And yes, they are bona fide traffic lights, so you are required to stop until the light turns green; and yes, again—it is a moving violation to run a red meter. To find out how the traffic is actually moving each day, keep your radio tuned to **KBEM**, 88.5 FM, www.jazz88fm.com, for real-time accident and gridlock reports.

MN-PASS

For solo commuters caught in the **I-394 and I-35W** bottlenecks, there is a way to end-run some of the congestion, albeit an expensive one: their High Occupancy Vehicle (HOV) carpool lanes have been converted to rush hour toll lanes. While these express lanes are still free for motorcycles and cars carrying at least one passenger, solo drivers can use the lanes, too—for a price. Using the lanes can be as inexpensive as twenty-five cents one way if there isn't a lot of traffic, but—and this is a big but—as congestion starts to get worse, the tolls go up. Tolls are posted on overhead signs that change every few minutes, and can and do rise to a cost of as much as $8 for a one-way trip at the height of rush hour. Open a **toll-lane account** in person at 2055 Lilac Drive, Golden Valley; by phone at 866-397-4334; or on the Internet at www.mnpass.org. One last point of information, because the question keeps coming up: According to the people at MN-Pass, an infant does count as a passenger, so if you're driving with an infant in your car, you may use the toll lane without charge.

To see how Mn-PASS works, check out the I-394 MnPASS Express Lanes video on YouTube, www.youtube.com/watch?v=fPc2z0qPedQ.

MAJOR HIGHWAYS

As you get to know the area, you'll find alternatives to the big roads, but until then, here are some of the major arteries:

- **Interstate Hwys 35 and 94** are the main arteries through the cities. I-35 runs north and south and I-94 runs east and west. Both highways connect with the 494/694 ring around the metro area. I-35 splits in Burnsville into **35W**, which heads into Minneapolis, and **35E**, which goes through St. Paul. The two roads run through the northern suburbs before joining again in Lino Lakes and continuing as plain old I-35 up to Duluth.
- Lesser north-south routes serving St. Paul are **State Hwy 3** (South Robert St), which connects southeastern suburbs to downtown St. Paul; **State Hwy 61**, which winds along the Mississippi and cuts northwest into St. Paul (a beautiful drive near the river); and **State Hwy 5**, which goes directly east from the airport to West 7th St in St. Paul, or west along I-494 to Eden Prairie, where it becomes plain 5 again and continues through the southwest suburbs. **State Hwy 280** joins I-94 to **State Hwy 36**, an east-west route running north of St. Paul to Stillwater.
- Lesser north-south routes on the Minneapolis side are **State Hwy 77** (Cedar Ave), which is a link from Apple Valley to the Mall of America and the airport; **State Hwy 65**, which is a link from Blaine and the other northern suburbs; **State Hwy 100**, which runs from Bloomington through first-ring suburbs to Brooklyn Center; and **US 169**, which runs slightly to the west of Hwy 100, from Savage to Maple Grove, and then becomes a state highway heading north.
- **Interstate-94** is the main east-west thoroughfare. It does not split in two the way I-35 does, but instead comes into the Twin Cities area at Hudson, Wisconsin, passes directly through downtown St. Paul, then cuts past downtown Minneapolis, turning due north before heading out of town to the northwest.

If you are on 94 heading west from St. Paul, to continue westward, get onto I-394.

- Minor east-west arteries are **State Hwy 62** (the Crosstown), which runs from I-35W near the airport to Minnetonka, and **I-394**, which heads west out of downtown Minneapolis; I-394 ends at US 12, east of Long Lake. **US 12** continues due west out of the metro area. **Hwy 55** is a curious road that runs from near the airport, through North Minneapolis, and west to Wright County. The other major east-west route is **State Highway 36**, which runs through suburbs north of St. Paul to Stillwater.
- The main encircling arteries are **I-694** to the north and **I-494** to the south and west. Minneapolis–St. Paul International Airport is off I-494/State Highway 5 in Bloomington; see below for best routes by which to approach it. The Mall of America is also off I-494 in Bloomington.

COMMUTING OPTIONS

After you've sat on an on-ramp and read an entire newspaper a few afternoons in a row, you might start to consider carpooling or vanpooling. Not only will you save time, but you'll also save money and the environment. The Metropolitan Council estimates that the annual cost of driving a round trip of just 17 miles a day to work can be over $4000 a year. Calculate your own true cost of driving on the St. Paul Smart Trips web site, www.smart-trips.org/rideshare. Then, if you decide you'd like to travel as part of a group, MetroTransit/Rideshare which will link you with others who work/live in the same area. In case you're worried about getting trapped downtown in an emergency, with no way home, you can also register for the free **Guaranteed Ride Home Program**. Registered commuters receive two coupons every six months that are good for bus or cab rides in the event of an emergency or schedule conflict.

PARKING

Downtown Minneapolis has 17 parking ramps and 7 lots located in the warehouse, entertainment, and business districts. I-394 from the western suburbs empties directly into three parking ramps in the Warehouse District, immediately behind Target Center. A map of the facilities is available on the city's web site at www.ci.minneapolis.mn.us/parking/ramp-map.asp. Monthly parking varies from $25 a month at a boondocks lot to $205 a month at the Courthouse. Daily rates vary widely, but the first hour generally costs at least $3 in the heart of downtown.

Minneapolis also has 6800 parking meters. They accept only quarters and U.S. dollar coins, but you can purchase a parking card that works in meters the same as money. Cards are sold from dispenser machines located in parking ramps and at City Hall. For further information call 612-673-AUTO (2886) or look online at www.ci.minneapolis.mn.us/parking/parking-card.asp.

These parking cards (after St. Paul time has been loaded) also work in St. Paul, where much of the parking is on-street and metered, though popular St. Paul venues such as the Xcel Energy Center and the Science Museum do have their own attached ramp parking. For information about St. Paul's ramps, check out the clickable map posted on **St. Paul's Transportation Management Organization**'s (TMO's) web site, www.smart-trips.org. Click on any facility and see its monthly and hourly rates. The Smart Trips web site also offers commuters other services including information about park & ride lots. St. Paul's cards work in Minneapolis, after Minneapolis time is loaded.

CAR SHARING

Don't want the trouble and expense of keeping a car, but need one some of the time? Consider **HourCar** car sharing, www.hourcar.org. Managed by the non-profit **Neighborhood Energy Consortium** (**NEC**), www.thenec.org, HourCar has car hubs in Minneapolis and St. Paul, and at the University of Minnesota, Macalester College, and the University of St. Thomas. They offer pay-as-you-go and flat rate plans.

BY BIKE

"It's a cold, hard fact: The unforgiving and frigid city of Minneapolis is the country's top spot to be an urban cyclist."—*Bicycling Magazine*, May 2010

Surprisingly large numbers of Twin Citians bike to work, and Minneapolis and St. Paul do their best to make their cities bicycle friendly. There are designated bike lanes throughout downtown Minneapolis and 24 bike/pedestrian paths in St. Paul. Download a Minnepolis bike map off the city's web site, www. ci.minneapolis.mn.us/bicycles/where-to-ride.asp). Download a St. Paul Bike-Hike map at www.smart-trips.org/bikewalk. Find routes throughout the region at http://magic.cyclopath.org/.

For a small fee, the cities rent weather-sheltered, secure bicycle lockers at several locations. For rates and locations in Minneapolis, look online at www. ci.minneapolis.mn.us/bicycles/bikeparking-lockers.asp; for St. Paul, visit www. smart-trips.org/biking_walking.php. And don't forget the **Guaranteed Ride Home** (see above), so you don't have to worry about getting stuck after dark or in bad weather. Register online at www.metrotransit.org. For commuter seminars and the latest local developments, check the web site of **Transit for Livable Communities**, www.tlcminnesota.org.

PUBLIC TRANSPORTATION

Visit www.metrotransit.org with any mobile browser and it will redirect you to **NexTrip**, where you can get info on the next few buses/trains for any MetroTransit or suburban bus company bus/train, at any stop, including whether a bus is running late.

BY BUS

By going online to www.metrotransit.org, you can download bus schedules and a transit system map for the entire metro area, use the online "Trip Planner" tool, or order transit information and printed schedules to be sent to you by mail. If you prefer, you can visit one of the following **MetroTransit Stores** to pick up a map, talk to someone in person, or buy a pass:

- **Minneapolis Transit Store**, 719 Marquette Ave, open 7:30 a.m.–5:30 p.m., weekdays.
- **St. Paul Skyway Store**, 101 E Fifth St, US Bank Center, open 7:30 a.m.–5 p.m., weekdays.
- **SuperSaver Passes and Go-To Cards** can be purchased from many retailers including Cub Foods, Rainbow, banks, and check-cashing stores; city halls; and colleges.

The entire Twin Cities area is included in an integrated public transportation (bus/van/light rail) system known as **MetroTransit**. At the time of the writing of this book, however, with its budget shortfall bumping up against the current governor's vow not to raise taxes, MetroTransit has had to reduce or eliminate service on many of its bus routes.

It's interesting that the decline in bus service is coming at a time when there is a greater appetite for public transit than there has ever been before. Consequently, many of the suburbs have stepped up to the plate and are providing their own commuter and local neighborhood service. These include Apple Valley, Elk River, Plymouth, Maple Grove, Eden Prairie, and Woodbury. So if you wish to live in any of those suburbs, you may even be able to get around—or to work, at least—without a car. (See list of suburban bus lines below.) Simply park at a designated **Park & Ride** lot and take the bus into town. Park & Rides and bus stops are both marked with the "**T**" logo. Some Park & Rides and bus stops do not provide posted schedules, so it's a good idea to get a printed map and take it with you until you get comfortable using the system.

An adult non–rush hour base fare ($1.75) gets you 2½ hours of unlimited rides on buses and trains. Express routes, which travel between the downtowns and to the suburbs, cost 50 cents extra. Rush hour fares cost an additional

50–75 cents. Seniors and children age 6–12 can ride for 75 cents during non-rush hours, but this fare rises to $2 and $3 during rush hours. Children 5 and under ride free. People with disabilities always ride for 75 cents, but must show some form of proof of disability. (For information on disabled certification, call Customer Relations at 612-373-3333; also see the **Helpful Services** chapter.) The fare within either the Minneapolis or St. Paul **Downtown Zones** is 50 cents, anytime. You can pay as you go (drivers take cash, but don't make change), or buy special passes. If you're going to have to take more than one bus, pay the driver when you get on and ask for a transfer. **Transfers** are free and good for up to 2½ hours. You can buy a ticket with cash or a credit card from **vending machines** on the station platforms. A **monthly pass** gives you unlimited rides for a whole calendar month.

Even though all buses are equipped with wheelchair lifts, there is also a special transportation service available for people with disabilities. **Metro Mobility** is the **door-through-door** transportation system available to people in the Minneapolis/St. Paul area and certain adjoining suburbs. Customers who are certified can call transportation providers to schedule their trips. For more information, look online at www.metro-transit.org, or call 651-602-1111 (TTY 651-291-0904).

If MetroTransit routes aren't convenient for you, there are other options. Check the routes and schedules of the **University of Minnesota Transit Service** (www1.umn.edu/pts/index.htm), which runs buses from many locations throughout the city to the University, though usually only on weekdays. Anyone can ride them, and they cost the same as a city bus. **U-Pass** and **Metropass** deeply discounted transit passes are sold at many campus locations and the Fairview-University Medical Center Ticket Office, as well as at all MetroTransit stores and online at www.metrotransit.org. Campus shuttles are free and run continuously, http://www1.umn.edu/pts/busing/index.html. **Transit Link**, a shared **curb-to-curb** van and minibus service, is another option. Rides must be scheduled in advance, but they do accept standing orders. Your Transit Link driver can also give you a transfer ticket good for a bus ride. Fares are low, generally under $5 one way. Call **651-602-LINK (5465)** to reserve a ride. Of course, for any service within the metro area, you can always call MetroTransit's main number, 612-373-3333, 24-hour Automated Schedule Information Line 612-341-4BUS, or look online, www.metrotransit.org.

BUS SAFETY

While generally safe, problems can occur both on buses and at bus stops. Buses traveling through North Minneapolis have a history of having more problems than most. For your own safety, you may not want to ride these or certain other routes alone.

SUBURBAN BUS LINES

Call MetroTransit, 612-373-3333, www.metrotransit.com, for schedules and connection information for any of these suburban bus lines, although it's sometimes easier to find what you're looking for on their own web sites:

- **Maple Grove Transit**, Emergency Information Hotline 763-494-5994, www. ci.maple-grove.mn.us
- **Minnesota Valley Transit Authority**, www.mvta.com, serves Apple Valley, Burnsville, Eagan, Rosemount, and Savage.
- **Plymouth Metrolink** offers express bus service between Plymouth and downtown Minneapolis, 763-509-5535, www2.ci.plymouth.mn.us.
- **Ramsey Star Express** shuttles commuters to and from the 5th Street Transit Station in downtown Minneapolis during peak hours, 1-888-528-8880 or www.commutercoach.org.
- **Shakopee Transit BlueXpress** transports commuters to and from downtown Minneapolis, Info Line 952-496-8800, www.bluexpressbus.com.
- **SouthWest Transit**, 952-949-2BUS (2287), www.swtransit.org, provides service on very nice buses from the southwest suburbs to downtown Minneapolis, Uptown, Southdale Mall, Normandale Community College, and the University of Minnesota. It has Park & Ride lots in Victoria, Chaska, Chanhassen, and Eden Prairie.

TRAVELING TO SPORTS EVENTS

There really is such a thing as a **Free Ride**. Customers with game-day tickets can ride the train/bus for free to Minnesota Wild Hockey games at Xcel Energy Center. Free rides are valid from two hours before face-off until two hours after the game ends. Rides are also free to Minnesota Swarm lacrosse games at the Xcel.

Not free, but ever so convenient—Game Day Express buses, the LRT, and Northstar Rail will all drop you off at the front door to Target Field for Twins games. Buy an **Event 6-Hour Pass** for an easy roundtrip. Check MetroTransit's News page for other free rides.

TROLLEYS

Twin City Trolleys operates a fleet of vintage-styled trolleys and mini-coaches that are available for charter, www.twincitytrolleys.com. The free **Wayzata Towne Trolley** operates from May through October in the downtown Wayzata shopping district. Its Wednesday afternoon narrated **Gold Coast Tours** are a fun way to get to know the neighborhood. The trolley is also available for weekend and evening rental, www.wayzatachamber.com/town_trolley.html.

NATIONAL BUS SERVICE

- **Greyhound Bus Lines** (800-231-2222, www.greyhound.com) has terminals in the following Twin Cities locations:

- **Minneapolis**, 950 Hawthorne Ave, 612-371-3325
- **Minneapolis, University of Minnesota**, 300 Washington Ave SE (Coffman Union), 612-624-4636
- **St. Paul, Amtrak Station**, 730 Transfer Rd (Tickets are not sold at this location but may be purchased by mail 10 days in advance by calling Greyhound's Telephone Information Center at 1-800-231-2222.)
- **St. Paul**, 166 W University Ave, 651-222-0507
- **St. Paul, University of Minnesota**, 2017 Buford Ave (St. Paul Student Center), 612-625-9794

REGIONAL BUSES

There are also a number of **regional** and **specialty** bus lines you can use:

- **Go Rochester Direct**, 800-280-9270, www.gorochesterdirect.com; offers daily shuttles between Minneapolis–St. Paul Airport and Rochester.
- **Jefferson Bus Lines**, 2100 26th St, Minneapolis, 612-359-3400, Hotline 800-451-5333, www.jeffersonlines.com, primarily serves the southern part of the state. It also offers service to Brainerd, Duluth, Crookston, Grand Forks, and Winnipeg. Buses leave from the Greyhound depots in St. Paul and Hawthorne Ave in Minneapolis (see addresses above), from Coffman Union at the University, and from the Minneapolis–St. Paul Airport.
- **Northfield Lines**, 888-748-9634, www.northfieldlines.com; offers daily shuttles from the MSP-International Airport to Northfield.

BY LIGHT RAIL

The **Hiawatha Line** provides light-rail service every 5–15 minutes between 5 a.m. and 1 a.m., to 19 stations along Hiawatha Avenue between Target Field in the Minneapolis Downtown Warehouse District, the airport, and Mall of America in Bloomington. Bus routes are timed to connect with the LRT, as is **the Northstar Commuter Train.** The Northstar travels northwest between Target Field in downtown Minneapolis and Big Lake, with stops in Fridley, Coon Rapids, Anoka, and Elk River. Trains make five departures from Big Lake (with one return trip) in the morning and five departures from downtown Minneapolis (with one return trip) in the evening. On weekends the Northstar makes three roundtrips, with its schedule timed to coincide with Twins baseball games.

A rush-hour drive from Elk River to downtown Minneapolis normally takes at least 70 minutes; on the Northstar, it only takes 34.

Park & Ride lots for the LRT are located at Lake Street Midtown Station, Fort Snelling Station, and 28th Avenue Station (three blocks east of the Mall of America). Free Park & Ride lots for the Northstar are located at all its suburban stations. For connecting bus schedules, time between stations, and route maps, look online at www.metrotransit.org.

Because there are no fare boxes on trains, you must pay before boarding. Purchase tickets at kiosks on the station platforms using cash or credit card. LRT fares are the same as local bus fares ($2.25 during rush hours, $1.75 at all other times). Northstar fares range from $3.25 to $7 on weekdays and $2.50 to $5.25 on weekends. Seniors, children under age 5, and those who are disabled ride station-to-station for 75 cents, or the whole route for $1.75. If your trip begins on a bus, you must ask the bus driver for a rail-only transfer. Transfers from buses and light rail to the Northstar require an additional fare. Transfers from the Northstar to light rail and buses are free. Those going downtown for a game or movie can buy a **6-Hour Pass** at the rail station.

Train Brain (http://trainbrainapp.com) is an iPhone/iPod Touch app that uses the devices' GPS functionality to tell you when the next train is coming and how much the fare will cost—and count down to the train's scheduled arrival.

All station platforms are fully accessible, and trains are equipped with designated sections for customers using wheelchairs.

The popularity of the Hiawatha and Northstar lines has given momentum to the next project on the Twin Cities' rail wishlist, the **Central Corridor line,** which is scheduled to begin shuttling passengers back and forth between downtown Minneapolis and St. Paul in 2014. It would appear that the Twin Cities (which in the late 19th and early 20th centuries had 15 commuter rail lines) has caught the bug again. Now several more projects are under discussion, including the Southwest Corridor LRT, which would run from Eden Prairie into Minneapolis; Red Rock Commuter Rail, which would run from Hastings into St. Paul; and high-speed rail service between St. Paul and Chicago.

BY AIR

Airport police do not let you sit for a second when you're dropping off or picking up people. However, there is a free airport cell phone lot located approximately halfway between the two terminals on Post Road, off Highway 5. You can sit in your car there until your arriving party has collected their luggage and calls you to be picked up at the curb.

Minneapolis–St. Paul International Airport (www.mspairport.com) has changed a lot since the movie *Airport* was filmed here in 1970. Today it is one of the busiest airports in the world, serving 32 million passengers a year. Located on State Highway 5 between Bloomington and St. Paul, it is the commercial aviation center for the entire upper Midwest, and provides connecting service to regional airports including Rochester, Duluth, Fargo, Grand Rapids, and Hibbing.

The airport has two terminals: Terminal 1-Lindbergh (Main) and Terminal 2-Humphrey, Because the terminals are located on opposite sides of the runways, off separate roadways, you should find out which terminal your airline flies from before arriving at the airport. To determine which terminal your airline uses, check the airport's **Airlines** page. A single airline, Delta, dominates this market, and its flights use Terminal 1-Lindbergh.

To reach Terminal 1-Lindbergh by car, use the following routes:

- **From Minneapolis and points north**, take I-35W south to I-494 east. Travel east on I-494 to the Highway 5 exit. Terminal 1 is located directly off Highway 5. Follow the signs for Terminal 1. The exit is on the left beyond the Post Road exit.

- **From St. Paul and points northeast**, take I-35E south to the W 7th Street/MN-5 exit. Turn right onto W 7th Street/MN-5. Continue traveling west on MN-5. Terminal 1 is located directly off MN-5. Follow the signs to the Terminal 1 exit.

- **From western, southern, and southeastern suburbs**, take I-494 east to State Hwy 5 and follow the signs to Terminal 1. The terminal exit will be on the left beyond the Post Road exit.

Terminal 2-Humphrey can be reached using the same initial directions, but then go north from I-494 on 34th Avenue. It is well signed, as are its parking lots.

The airport can also be reached by taking the **Hiawatha LRT** from either downtown Minneapolis or the Mall of America. Trains stop at both terminals, and run between them every few minutes, 24 hours a day. There is no charge for travel between the two terminals. The **Terminal 1-Lindbergh** LRT station is located **below the Transit Center**, between the Blue and Red Parking ramps. From the Tram Level (one level below baggage claim), take the tram to the Transit Center. When you exit the tram, follow the signs to the light rail station, which is located underground. The **Terminal 2-Humphrey** light rail station is located on the north side of the Orange parking ramp. From the terminal, take the **skyway from Level 2** across to the parking facility. Follow the overhead signs through the parking facility. Take the escalators or elevators down one level to the station platform. Both stations are fully accessible. Maps to both are posted on the airport's web site.

If you have a layover and decide you want to go into Minneapolis or the Mall of America, allow about half an hour each way for the LRT to travel between the airport and warehouse district downtown, and 11 minutes to go to the Mall. Fares for travel to other locations are $2.25 during rush hours (Monday–Friday,

6–9 a.m. and 3–6:30 p.m.) and $1.75 at other times. Tickets are sold at vending kiosks at the rail stations. For more information, visit MetroTransit's web site, www.metrotransit.org.

AIRLINES

Service to Minneapolis is dominated by **Delta Airlines,** but a number of other airlines have a smaller presence here.

Airlines using **Terminal 1-Lindbergh**:
- **Air Canada Reservations**: 888-247-2262 or 1-316-686-3636, www.aircanada. com
- **Alaska Airlines Reservations**: 800-426-0333, www.alaskaair.com
- **American Airlines Reservations**: 800-433-7300, TTY 800-543-1586, www. aa.com
- **Continental Airlines Reservations**: 800-525-0280, www.continental.com
- **Delta Airlines Reservations**: 800-221-1212, TTY 800-831-4488, www.delta. com
- **Frontier Airlines Reservations**: 800-432-1359, www.frontierairlines.com
- **Midwest Airlines Reservations**: 800-452-2022, TTY 800-872-3608, www. midwestairlines.com; named Best Domestic Airline repeatedly over its 20-plus-year history. Its "Signature Service" includes chocolate chip cookies baked onboard.
- **United Airlines Reservations**: 800-241-6522, www.united.com
- **US Airways Reservations**: 800-428-4322, www.usairways.com

Airlines that use **Terminal 2-Humphrey**:
- **Air Tran Airways Reservations**: 800-247-8726, www.airtran.com
- **Icelandair Reservations**: 800-223-5500, www.icelandair.com (a local favorite!)
- **Southwest Airlines Reservations**: 800-435-9792, TTY 800-533-1305, www. southwest.com
- **Sun Country Airlines Reservations**: 800-359-6786, www.suncountry.com

PARKING

For jump-starts and towing: if you come back from a trip and your car won't start, the airport web page says to call Mark's Towing in Eagan at 651-454-1533. Some of the off-site lots provide free jump-starting.

New covered **parking ramps at both** terminals have done a lot to ease the on-site parking situation, but you might still want to check availability during busy travel times by checking online at www.mspairport.com/parking/surepark. aspx, or by calling the **Parking Information Hotline, 1-877-FLY-PARK** (1-877-359-7275). Long-term parking costs $16 a day at Terminal 2-Humphrey and

$20 a day at Terminal 1-Lindbergh; short-term parking costs $8 for the first two hours at both. Terminal 1 parking is usually crowded, especially during the winter holidays and Spring Break, so either park over at Terminal 2 adjacent to the LRT station and ride it over (easy! but allow 30 minutes), or park off-site.

Off-site parking—and taking a shuttle to the terminal—is cheapest and quite convenient. Shuttles run every few minutes around the clock. There are several **off-airport lots**:

- **Park 'N Fly**, 952-883-3606 , www.pnf.com, about 5 minutes away from the airport at 3700 American Blvd E (south of 494 off 34th St), offers outdoor parking for $11 a day ($57 per week), indoor ramp parking for $16 (discounts to seniors and AAA members).
- **Park 'N Go**, 7901 International Dr, Bloomington, off 34th St, 952-854-3386, www.parkngo.net/minneapolis.htm, charges $10.75 a day or $64.50 a week. AARP and government employee discounts are available.
- **Team Parking**, 651-690-1259, www.teamparking.com, is 3½ miles from the airport at 1465 Davern S, St. Paul (off Highway 5/West 7th). It offers outdoor parking for $11 a day, and indoor parking for $13 or $78 per week. Allow at least 15 minutes for the shuttle trip from lot to airport.
- **Heated valet parking** is available underneath Terminal 1 on Level T, but it's hard to find. To get to it, use the left inbound lane on the lower level roadway past the exit to Short Term and General Parking and past the rental car return ramp. Then follow the directional signs to the valet service entrance. It costs $10 for the first hour, $3 each additional hour; and $40 daily, May–October.

AIRPORT BUS, SHUTTLE, AND TAXI SERVICE

Taxis are available at both terminals. Follow the signs to the cab starter booth, where airport staff will call a taxi up from the queue for you. Downtown Minneapolis is approximately 16 miles (25 minutes) from the airport. Expect to pay around $34–$44. The distance to downtown St. Paul is approximately 12 miles and the fare is around $28–$34. All taxi fares are metered at a rate of up to $2.35 per mile and include a $3.00 trip fee that is added to the final metered fare.

City **bus** service is provided by MetroTransit. The airport's bus stop is located at the Lindbergh Terminal **Transit Center** on **Level 1** of the **Blue and Red parking ramps**. Passengers who arrive at the Humphrey Terminal 2 will need to take the LRT to the Lindbergh Terminal 1 and catch a city bus there.

Shared ride service between the airport and cities within a 25-mile radius is available from **SuperShuttle** (800-258-3826, www.supershuttle.com). Shuttles pick up and drop travelers off near the **Green** and **Gold parking ramps** across from Terminal 1-Lindbergh.

SCHEDULED TRANSPORTATION

Scheduled bus, van, and limousine service is provided by several companies that have **ticket counters** in the **Ground Transportation Center** in **Terminal 1-Lindbergh**. Advance reservations are highly recommended. Contact the individual companies directly for rates, routes, and other information:

- **Chippewa Airport Service** (service to Wisconsin), 877-811-4211 or 715-830-9400, www.chippewavalleyairportservice.com
- **Executive Express** (service to St. Cloud, Brainerd, Camp Ripley, and other cities in central Minnesota), 888-522- 9899, www.executiveexpress.biz
- **Go Rochester Direct** (service to Rochester/Mayo Clinic), 800-280-9270, www.gorochesterdirect.com
- **Jefferson/Greyhound Bus Lines** (service to Minnesota, Iowa, Wisconsin, North and South Dakota); buy tickets at the Rochester Direct counter, jeffersonlines.com, 800-451-5333
- **Land to Air Express** (service to Mankato and St. Peter), 888-736-9190, www.landtoairexpress.com
- **Premier Transportation** (hotel shuttle service to St. Paul suburbs), 612-331-7433 or 800-899-7433, www.premierTrans.com

CAR RENTAL

Airport rental car counters at Terminal 1-Lindbergh are located on the second and third levels between the Blue and Red parking ramps. Passengers can take the underground tram to the Blue and Red parking ramps. At Terminal 2-Humphrey, airport rental car counters are located in the Ground Transport Center on the ground level of the Purple parking ramp directly across from the terminal building.

AT-THE-AIRPORT CAR RENTAL
- **Alamo**, www.alamo.com, 877-222-9075
- **Avis Rent-A-Car**, www.avis.com, 800-831-2847
- **Budget**, www.budgetrentacar.com, 800-527-0700
- **Dollar**, www.dollar.com, 800-800-4000
- **Enterprise Rent-A-Car**, www.enterprise.com, 800-325-8007
- **Hertz**, www.hertz.com,
- **National Car Rental**, Minneapolis, www.nationalcar.com, 877-222-9058

OFF-AIRPORT CAR RENTAL
Shuttle buses to the off-airport car rental companies are accessible from the Terminal 1-Lindbergh Transit Center, between the Blue and Red Parking ramps.
- **Ace Rent A Car**, 1-800-243-3443, www.acerentacar.com

- **Thrifty Car Rental**, 952-854-8080, 800-847-4389, 800-367-2277, www.thrifty. com; Thrifty Car Rental has a branch office at the Millennium Hotel, 1313 Nicollet Ave.

LIMOS

If you want to arrive in style, all the limousine services make runs to the airport.
- **A Davis Limo Airport Express**, South Metro 952-882-1400, North Metro 612-290-2100, www.adavislimoairportexpress.com
- **All Day Limo**, 763-561-0407, www.alldaylimo.com
- **All Occasion Transportation**, serves Duluth, Minneapolis, St. Paul, Rochester, and Bloomington, 1-800-454-1380, www.alloccasionlimo.com
- **Archer Limo**, 763-503-9482, 877-503-9482, www.archerlimo.com
- **Kirk Limousine**, 612-221-6470, http://minnetonkalimo.com
- **Star Limousine**, 952-895-0095, 866-440-2907, www.limostar.com

TAXIS

Unless you are in one of the two downtowns or at the airport, you must telephone for a taxi rather than hailing one on the street. (See Taxis and Shuttles in **Useful Numbers and Web Sites**.)

TRAIN/AMTRAK

There are not a lot of passenger trains, but the **EmpireBuilder** stops in the Twin Cities on its route from **Chicago** (about 8 hours) to **Seattle** (48 hours plus).
- **Amtrak National Route Information**, 1-800-USA-RAIL (1-800-872-7245), www.amtrak.com
- **Amtrak Twin Cities Passenger Station** is open from 6 a.m. to midnight, 730 Transfer Rd, St. Paul, 651-644-1127. The number 16 bus route runs along University Ave, 0.27 miles south of the station. You can catch it at Transfer Rd and University and take it to downtown Minneapolis or St. Paul, but catching a taxi at the train station is probably the easiest and safest way to get to your destination.

WATER TAXI AND BOAT TOWING

- **H2O Towing & Taxi/Towboat U.S.** provides salvage, emergency pump-out, towing, jump-starts; 612-282-8616. Towing costs over $100 an hour, so become a member of BOATUS.com (800-395-2628) and save yourself a bundle.

HERE IN THE LAND OF SKY BLUE WATERS, PEOPLE TRY TO LIVE GREEN. We value our lakes, rivers, and forests, and care about protecting our Great Outdoors so we can pass it on to our children and grandchildren. While state policies leave a lot to be desired, individuals and cities have renewed their focus on environmental activism. Recycling is a way of life here, with 80 to 90% of households in Minneapolis and St. Paul engaged in recycling. So is bike commuting, with Minneapolis named *Bicycling Magazine*'s Top Spot To Be An Urban Cyclist in 2010. As for buildings, Target Field in Minneapolis is the greenest baseball stadium in the country, thanks to its use of recycled building materials, its reuse of water, and its auxiliary function as a public transportation hub.

The **Minnesota Energy Challenge** is a fun and easy web site where you can learn how to stay comfortable at home and still save money, www.mnenergychallenge.org.

If you think you're seeing the word Minneapolis a lot, well, you're right—the city has definitely taken a leadership role in the local environmental arena. In fact, Minneapolis, at number seven, is only a few blades less green than Portland, Oregon, which **SustainLane** says is the nation's most self-sustaining city. (They must have given Portland extra credit for recycling all those old VW vans!) In recognizing Minneapolis, SustainLane cited the city's innovations, such as giving Climate Change grants for projects that tackle global warming, tripling its number of farmers' markets since 2006, and creating a land use and development policy that encourages dense, green development along transit corridors.

And Minneapolis is not alone. The conglomerate Minneapolis/St. Paul metro area is number 11 on the Environmental Protection Agency's 2010 list of metropolitan areas with the most ENERGY STAR buildings. In addition, the U.S.

Department of Energy has named both Minneapolis and St. Paul Solar America Cities and charged them with developing ways to make solar energy more accessible for homes and businesses by the year 2015. Downtown St. Paul is using its grant to install solar thermal or hybrid solar thermal/photovoltaic systems, and will become a demonstration site for how diversified energy sources can power large-scale buildings and district systems. In downtown Minneapolis, over 130 square blocks are already heated and cooled using steam, so the city is using its grant to integrate solar into this system.

St. Paul has made its own strong commitment to environmentalism and energy efficiency with its **Neighborhood Energy Connection** (NEC), a nonprofit whose mission is to reduce pollution, conserve resources, and improve quality of life by offering tools for energy-efficient living. Among those tools are home energy audits and HourCar car-sharing (www.spnec.org, www.hourcar. org). Possibly even more impactful, however, is the city's **Eureka Recycling** (www.eurekarecycling.org). With a mission of demonstrating that waste is preventable, not inevitable, Eureka has sponsored a number of reuse and recycling projects including the **Twin Cities Free Market** (www.twincitiesfreemarket. org), an Internet-based exchange program that connects people who have reusable items to give away with people who want them. As of 2010, the Free Market exchange has kept over 11.4 million pounds of still-useful items out of the landfills.

Residents of most of the metro are required to put their lawn waste out for pickup in compostable bags, made of either paper or compostable plastic.

Out in the 'burbs, there's a lot more greenin' going on. Edina has created an Energy and Environment Commission, and even sent a delegate to the 2010 United Nations Climate Change Conference in Copenhagen. The city of Shoreview is rebuilding streets using pervious concrete paving that allows rainwater to pass through the pavement and soak into the soil underneath. And looking slightly into the future, Chisago City and Lindstrom are developing plans for the nation's first carbon-neutral industrial park, a complex that will be powered entirely by green bioenergy (that's prairie grass and wood waste to us laymen).

At the neighborhood level, groups such as Linden Hills Power & Light (www.lhpowerandlight.org) are working to shrink their neighborhoods' carbon footprints through education and community engagement.

Now for the bad news—sprawl. Minneapolis rivals LA for sprawl—and that's saying something. The TC used to be seven counties thick and now it's up to 11, with huge costs for the accompanying unplanned development. New schools, roads, police and fire, water, sewer, street lights, greater fuel consumption because of more people commuting for more hours each day, increased pollution—where are those ticked-off woodland creatures wreaking pain on would-be settlers a la *Furry Vengeance* when we need them? The one good thing that these hard times have accomplished is that, at least for now, growth in the exurbs has stopped cold; and the metro is actually strengthening at its center. The big question is, is it permanent, or merely a pause? It's really up to people like you, who are moving here, to decide.

The Twin Cities had the nation's third-largest exurban growth between 2000 and 2005, ahead, even, of sprawling Atlanta. In 2009, with people abandoning foreclosed and unsellable homes, for the first time ever, more people left the exurbs than moved in.

And more bad news— but this time with a happy ending. For the last several years there has been a downward spiral of state funding for the environment, so in November 2008, we Minnesotans took matters into our own hands and passed the Clean Water, Land and Legacy Amendment to the state constitution. Now a certain percentage of every state budget MUST be allocated to cleaning up our lakes and streams, protecting fish and wildlife habitat, and taking care of parks and trails.

If you're interested in how legislators are treating the environment, check out Conservation Minnesota's Legislative Scorecard at www.mnvotercenter.org/score/scorecard.

GREEN BUSINESSES

In October 2009, *Newsweek Magazine* released its first annual environmental rankings of America's 500 largest corporations (http://greenrankings.newsweek.com/top500/). The best rank was 1 and the worst, 500. So how did our local companies stack up? 3M, which manufactures high-efficiency lighting and low-toxicity building products, was in the top 50. Best Buy (recycles electronics), Medtronic (recycles nearly half its waste and has tried to eliminate the use of controversial substances such as PVC), Target (operates green buildings), and General Mills (reduced the amount of insecticides used on its crops) made into the top 100. Supervalu (our main food distributor), EcoLab, and CenterPoint Energy all ranked around 200 – making them greenies, as well. Xcel Energy, however, ranked 436th out of 500—not totally their fault since energy companies in general have adverse environmental impacts, but definitely not what we customers would hope.

Another member of our home team, locally based Caribou Coffee (www.cariboucoffee.com), supports sustainable coffee production by serving only Fair Trade and organic certified coffees. And it illuminates all its corporate-owned coffee shops with energy efficient compact fluorescent lightbulbs (CFLs).

GREENING YOUR HOME

Minnesota houses are tight—and closed up all winter. That means the air inside may be 100 times worse than the air outdoors. You'll need to take indoor air quality more seriously here than you might in some other areas, but you'll also find that a lot of things that make a huge difference here are easy and relatively inexpensive to do: Use paints that are "Low VOC"; change the filter on your furnace regularly; use plants to naturally filter the air; buy "Energy Star" appliances to conserve energy; use compact fluorescent light bulbs, which use 66% less energy and last up to 10 times longer. If you like your home to glow with candlelight, use soy candles.

Cleaning is critical to maintaining a healthy home, especially if family members suffer from allergies and asthma. Most allergists and green building organizations recommend central vacuum systems because they remove dirt and allergens without blowing air around during cleaning. Cleaning products are equally important. Look at labels to identify specific, eco-friendly ingredients such as grain alcohol, coconut or other plant oils, and plant-oil disinfectants such as eucalyptus, rosemary, or sage. Other non-polluting, simple ingredients such as plain soap and water, baking soda, and vinegar can clean most things—and save you money, too.

And if you're building a home, choose eco-friendly or recycled materials and create areas that have multiple uses, so you'll need to purchase fewer electronics.

Of course, the quickest and easiest way to have a green home is to buy one that is no bigger than you need—smaller homes consume fewer resources. Because of the climate, finding a tight, well-insulated home should not be difficult—the statewide building code requires that ceilings have an R-value of 38 or more. Look for windows with a U-factor of 0.35 or less. Then the trick is to make sure that the tight house has adequate ventilation; all new residential construction after 2000 must have mechanical ventilation in order to improve indoor air quality, but homes built before that may have "sick house" issues.

GREEN REMODELING

Savvy consumers know that the greenest building materials are those that someone else has already used. The nonprofit Green Institute (2801 21st Avenue South, Minneapolis, 612-724-2608; 1727 East Hwy 36, Maplewood, 651-379-1280; www.thereusecenter.com) has been a leader in the green building movement since the 1990s. It has developed a broad range of programs and initiatives including the ReUse Center and DeConstruction Services, which salvages and sells building materials. They also conduct residential energy efficiency workshops, sell conservation products, and are behind Minnesota GreenStar regionally appropriate green building guidelines. In 1998 The Green Institute built the first green commercial building in the Upper Midwest.

Designed as a "living experiment," the Phillips Eco-Enterprise Center, which is home to the Green Institute, is designed to be disassembled and reused, and even has showers for bike commuters and, of course, a "green" roof. Natural Built Home is another one-stop shop for eco-friendly cabinets, flooring, paints, plumbing and electrical supplies—and classes on how to use them (4020 Minnehaha Avenue in Minneapolis a few blocks from the 38th Street Light Rail Station, 612-605-7999, www.naturalbuilthome.com). You might also consider poking around the region's architectural salvage stores (see **Shopping for the Home** for listings).

If you're doing structural work, consider using green-certified wood products; the **Forest Stewardship Council** (www.fscus.org) is a widely known certification program. Use nontoxic or least-toxic glues and finishes whenever possible; local paint company **Valspar** (www.valspar.com) produces quality low-VOC (volatile organic compounds), low-odor paint.

ENERGY EFFICIENCY

Some Xcel Energy and CenterPoint Energy customers in the Twin Cities receive bills that allow them to see how their energy use compares with their neighbors'. The theory is that customers will be more likely to turn down the thermostat and turn off some lights if they can see where their energy consumption ranks against their neighbors.

Reducing your home's energy consumption, particularly its consumption of energy produced by fossil fuels or other non-renewables, is probably the single most effective way to create a greener home. In most homes, furnaces and air conditioners, appliances, and lighting are the biggest energy hogs, and you'll get the biggest bang for your buck by weatherizing your home and making these systems work more efficiently. The following steps are typically recommended for boosting your home's energy efficiency:

- **Insulate and weatherize your home.** Poorly insulated walls, ceilings, and floors allow heated or cooled air to escape from your house, needlessly raising your energy use (and energy bill). Also seal ductwork, insulate hot water pipes in non-conditioned spaces, and seal or caulk leaks around doors, windows, pipes, vents, attics, and crawlspaces. Replace or repair leaky old windows. These steps will also reduce drafts and increase comfort levels in your home.

- **Upgrade your heating and cooling systems.** Old furnaces and air conditioning units are usually much less efficient than new models. Once you've insulated and weatherized your home, consider replacing old units with new, efficient units, and make sure that they are properly sized for your home. A programmable thermostat can also help reduce energy consumption by adjusting the inside temperature automatically when you're at work or asleep. (Note: different rules apply for heat pumps.)

- **Upgrade inefficient appliances.** Replacing old, inefficient washing machines, dishwashers, water heaters, and especially refrigerators with more efficient models can have a major effect on your energy consumption (and, in the case of washing machines and dishwashers, on your water consumption, too).
- **Install efficient lighting.** Compact fluorescent light bulbs use 75% less energy and last up to 10 times longer than standard incandescent bulbs. They also generate less heat. For an assurance of quality, choose ENERGY STAR° bulbs.

Fortunately, you don't have to figure out how to accomplish these things on your own. An inexpensive **CenterPoint Energy** Home Energy Audit (www.centerpointenergy.com) will provide you with specific actions you can take to improve your home's energy efficiency. CenterPoint also offers rebates for upgrading heating and water heating equipment.

RENEWABLE ENERGY

Consider buying a home in an area that is served by a green utility. **Wind-powered turbines** that supply strictly local power needs have gone up in Maple Grove and Elk River (www.greatriverenergy.com) and have also been built—or are scheduled to be built—in Anoka, Buffalo, Chaska, Shakopee, and North St. Paul (www.mmpa.org). Even inner-ring suburbs such as St. Louis Park are toying with the idea. Look in the **Utilities** section of the **Getting Settled** chapter for details. And if it's inconvenient for you to live in any of those places, you at least have the consolation of knowing that Minnesota has passed a law requiring 25% of electricity to be renewable by 2030.

If you are interested in going further in your support of renewables, not only can you make your home more energy-efficient, but you can influence your city to become energy independent; you can even make energy in your home.

First, there's wind. According to a recent American Wind Energy Association report, Minnesota has the fourth-highest potential wind-generating capacity in the country. Wind farms, mostly in the western part of the state, already generate as much electricity as Xcel Energy's Monticello and Prairie Island nuclear power plants combined. New wind farms in southeastern Minnesota, which are just starting to come online in 2010, are expected to produce enough electricity to power nearly 300,000 homes. In fact, according to the University, wind power has the potential to provide 20% of our electricity. Even in the metro, which doesn't have the constant wind that lashes across outstate Minnesota's prairies, a 160-kilowatt metro windmill, when going full blast, can generate enough electricity to power about 100 homes. That's why some metro residents are starting to talk about building their own personal windmills—and why some cities (even as close to the central core as St. Louis Park) are considering allowing it.

Then there's solar. Minnesota has as much **solar capability** (sunlight intensity) as Houston, Texas. So as heating bills have gone up, more and more people have turned to solar to augment their other heating systems. Another option is a **heat pump**. Both air-source (ASHP) and ground-source (GSHP) heat pumps work in Minnesota, BUT the ability of the ASHP to efficiently provide heat falls dramatically as the outside air temperature drops, so it always requires a secondary heating system to provide adequate heat on cold days. GSHP systems are typically sized to meet cooling needs, and are too small to heat a house without the use of an additional heat source.

Finally, Minnesotan municipalities are starting to make use of another interesting renewable resource—**biomass** (in the form of methane from stock farms and landfills for electricity, and ethanol made from corn for fuel). In fact, one of the fastest growing business sectors in Minnesota is the ethanol industry, whose operations are already breathing renewed life into the Minnesota countryside (www.mda.state.mn.us/Home.aspx).

WATER CONSERVATION

Although everywhere you'll look you'll see a lake, water conservation is still important here: the metro has been flirting with long-term drought, and our groundwater supply is becoming depleted. It's a fact of life: water that is withdrawn can only be replaced through recharge, and recharge depends on precipitation and its ability to soak into the ground. One way to recharge the groundwater supply is by creating rain gardens—depressions that retain water and allow it to soak into the earth. Another way is by limiting the amount of impervious surface (roof, driveway, sidewalk) that covers your yard. Finally, reduce your demand. Did you know that producing one pound of beef requires 5,600 gallons of water, while producing one pound of chicken requires 815? That a typical person uses 70 gallons of water a day? Toilets account for about 27% of water use, clothes washers for 22%, showers for 18%, and LEAKS for 14%. So one of the easiest ways to reduce YOUR water use is to fix drips, take shorter showers, and install low-flow faucets. Yes, what you eat, how long you shower, how often you flush—it all makes a difference.

The **Minnesota League of Women Voters** is constantly studying water—has been for years. To learn more about the state's water issues, join the League, or look online at www.lwvmn.org for the League's reports. Another private nonprofit, the **Freshwater Society/Gray Freshwater Institute**, based on Lake Minnetonka, has been working since 1968 to promote the conservation, protection, and restoration of our freshwater resources and their surrounding watersheds. Check out their web site, http://freshwater.org, to learn about the state's water challenges, as well as the politics behind the issues. Proceeds from their Weatherguide calendars (available at the Society and nearly every grocery or book store around) support much of their work and will help you to learn about your new state.

LANDSCAPING

Don't forget to make your home green on the outside, too (and we're not talking about paint color). Reduce or eliminate pesticides and chemical fertilizers, and use as little supplemental water as possible. The University recommends—if your yard is sunny—taking out your bluegrass lawn and replacing it with one of the new ultra low maintenance grass mixes that not only nearly eliminate your need to water and fertilize, but cut way down on your mowing, too. You can see plots of various low-maintenance lawn mixes out at the U of M Arboretum in Chaska, www.arboretum.umn.edu, or read about them online at www.extension.umn.edu.

Landscaping with native plants is another great way to reduce your yard's environmental impact, and take back what has been taken away from us with respect to species diversity and beneficial organisms. Because native plants are adapted to the local climate and soils, they often practically take care of themselves; at the very least, they don't require constant watering and fertilization. To see what grows here, and what habitat they require, look online at **Minnesota Wildflowers, A Project for Environmental Justice**, www.minnesotawildflowers.info. **Prairie Restorations** in Princeton and other locations, www.prairieresto.com, has a large online catalogue, perfect for do-it-yourselfers, or will design, plant, and manage a native plant community for you. **Prairie Moon Nursery**, www.prairiemoon.com, is another good source for native plants and seeds. Short on ideas? The **Minnesota DNR** has designs for five native plant gardens on its web site, www.dnr.state.mn.us/gardens/nativeplants/index.html.

ENVIRONMENTALLY FRIENDLY PRODUCTS AND SERVICES

Minnesota 2020 compiles a "Buy Local" gift guide every year. Download the "Made in Minnesota" gift guide from their web site, www.mn2020.org.

Your pocketbook is one of your most powerful weapons in the environmental fight. Your decision to support environmentally friendly businesses not only helps those businesses, but indirectly creates additional consumer demand for environmentally benign choices (a demand that could ultimately change the behavior of less environmentally focused businesses). While it's hard to know what we're really getting when we attempt to buy "green" products, there are experts out there to guide us. Search for products by name and learn about their toxicity at **Environmental Working Group**, www.ewg,org. Another web site, **Goodguide.com**, rates the health, environmental, and social impacts of a wide range of products, including personal care, toys, and household cleaners. Below are a few resources for finding green products and services:

Hyperlocal, community-enhancing social commerce: "hyperlocal" in computer speak translates as "shopping your neighbors and the Mom-and-Pop stores down the street," and three guys from St. Anthony Park in St. Paul have set up a web site to help you do just this. **www.Buythechange.com** is based on the Craigslist model, but with a few twists. You not only find goods and services being sold by neighbors and local businesses, but one-third of all membership fees are contributed to nonprofits of the members' choosing. Check the webpage to see if your neighborhood participates—lots do, including Mac-Groveland in St. Paul and Powderhorn in Minneapolis. **Localtweeps** (http://localtweeps.com), from the same developers, is an opt-in ZIP code level means of connecting local like-minded individuals—whether their interests are social or commercial. Members use it to promote specific events and tweet-ups throughout a targeted ZIP code. Happy hour at the local, anyone?

GREEN FOOD

The "locavore" movement is alive and going strong in the Twin Cities, with everybody purchasing **CSAs** (Community Supported Ag, or crop shares) of locally grown produce, eggs, and meat. In addition, many farmers' markets accept only locally produced products. For more information, read the Minneapolis blog, **Simple, Good, and Tasty**, http://simplegoodandtasty.com, which promotes local, sustainable, and organic foods and the people who produce them. Order the **Minnesota Grown** directory of local food and plant sources at www3.mda. state.mn.us/mngrown/. A word about CSAs—nice as they are, this is Minnesota, and CSAs definitely reflect the eccentricities of our growing season. So plan to can a lot of tomatoes or—better yet—share with another family.

Restaurants have gotten into the act, as well, by featuring locally grown foods in season and composting their waste. A Minneapolis restaurant, the Red Stag (509 1st Avenue NE, 612-767-7766, www.redstagsupperclub.com), opened in 2007 as the first LEED-CI registered restaurant in Minnesota. By using new technologies, it cut its water use by approximately 70%, and energy use almost in half. By the way, Happy Hour starts at 3 p.m. and Tuesdays are Cheap Date Nights.

FURNITURE AND CLOTHING

You won't have any trouble finding clothing made of natural fibers here, but home furnishings may present a challenge.

- Uptown Minneapolis retailer **Moss Envy** stocks furniture and eco-friendly latex mattresses and other bedding, toys, personal accessories, cleaning products, hardware, and baby gear that are, as they say, "Recycled, Reclaimed,

Natural, Organic, or Sustainable," 3056 Excelsior Blvd, Minneapolis, 612-374-4581, www.mossenvy.com. Their Do It Green directory, www.doitgreen.org/greenpages, lists green businesses and organizations throughout Minnesota. Be sure to watch for the Do It Green/City Pages Holiday Gifts Fair that also features events like the low carbon cook-off and eco fashion show, and children's activities.

- **Room and Board**, 7010 France Ave S, Edina, 952-927-8835, www.roomandboard.com/rnb, sells natural latex mattresses that are covered in organic wool and cotton.
- Minneapolis-based organic children's brand **m.o.o.** (Making Organic Outstanding) is sold at Nordstrom and Von Maur in the Twin Cities and nationwide. Each garment comes with an ID number that makes it possible to trace its life from field to finished product, www.mookidsclothing.com.

GREENER TRANSPORTATION

In Minnesota, electricity costs about 6 cents per kilowatt hour, so a car can charge overnight for less than 50 cents.

Probably the single best transportation choice you can make is to live close to your place of work, or in a place where you can use public transit to get to around. MetroTransit has purchased a fleet of 170 hybrid electric buses, and uses next-generation fuels like biodiesel and ultra-low sulfur diesel for the rest (www.metrotransit.org/gogreener/index.asp); the Hiawatha LRT uses about a third less energy and emits about half the greenhouse gases of regular buses and trucks. The Central Corridor Light Rail will be cleaner yet, because it will run on electricity, and also, as seems likely, because many people will be able to walk to use it, instead of requiring bus transport. The Carbon Counter at www.metrotransit.org/gogreener/carboncounter.asp shows an estimate of how many pounds of CO_2 emissions public transit customers have saved so far this year by using buses and trains instead of driving alone. The **Transportation** chapter lists alternatives to travel by automobile, and the Neighborhoods sections include information about local public transit options.

The **Drive Less/Save More** web site (www.drivelesssavemore.com) offers many ideas for reducing the amount you drive, explains why driving less is good for your pocketbook, and offers a handy driving cost calculator to hammer the point home.

If you need or want to drive, consider driving a more fuel-efficient vehicle. The popular hybrids are good choices, but Minnesota is also becoming much more friendly to fully electric cars. St. Paul, in particular, is building infrastructure for electric vehicles by installing charging stations in parking ramps and even in street meters. Another plan is to build solar charging stations like the one at the 48th Street Light Rail stop in Minneapolis, which provides electricity for an HourCar that's parked there. Dealers are increasing, too. One spin-off from a local bike shop, the **Electric Vehicle Store** in St. Louis Park, http://theelectricvehiclestore.com, offers a variety of zero emission plug-in electric vehicles, including cars and trucks. For more info on living electric in "The Land of 10,000 Outlets," look online at the **Minnesota Electric Auto Association**'s web site, www.mneaa.com.

Whatever kind of car you drive, make sure the car gets routine maintenance to ensure that it runs as efficiently as possible. And if you're really serious about saving money, Edmunds.com says you can save up to 37% by driving less aggressively, and up to 14%—each—by lowering your speed and using cruise control. Finally, if you want to join an automobile club for roadside assistance and travel advice, consider **Better World Club** (503-546-1137, 866-238-1137, www.betterworldclub.com). Better World Club bills itself as the nation's only environmentally friendly auto club; they offer the usual menu of auto club services, along with discounts on hybrid rentals, bicycle roadside assistance, and a frequently hilarious electronic newsletter, Kicking Asphalt.

ALTERNATIVE FUELS

You can buy or modify cars to run on alternative fuels like grease from McDonald's or even natural gas, but by far the most popular alternative fuel is **biodiesel**. Biodiesel is essentially diesel fuel made from vegetable oil, and is usually sold blended with petroleum diesel fuel. Minnesota was the first in the country to mandate that 2% biodiesel be blended in all diesel fuel sold in the state. In recent years, it has increased the biodiesel requirement from 2% to 5%, making it the first state to move to such a high blend. There is a catch though— biodiesel performance does worsen in extremely cold temperatures. That fact, and a few schools that were forced to shut down because their diesel buses wouldn't run, has caused the Minnesota Department of Commerce to occasionally suspend the requirement during the winter.

Bear in mind, too, that the use of biodiesel—particularly biodiesel blended with petro-diesel—is not without potential particulate pollution problems. If you already own a diesel-powered vehicle, biodiesel is a great choice that reduces dependence on oil. However, you might think twice about buying a car just so you can fuel it with biodiesel. (New passenger car models with cleaner-burning diesel engines will become available in the next few years, which could change the calculus.)

Also remember that, although biodiesel is made from vegetable oil, it is *not* the same as straight vegetable oil (SVO) fuel (a.k.a. "French fry car fuel" like Willie Nelson uses). While most diesel engines can run on pure biodiesel or biodiesel blends—at most, you'll have to replace a hose or two—SVO fuel requires substantial modifications to your car (including in most cases a second fuel tank).

Ag state that we are, Minnesota also promotes the use of **ethanol**. Without trying to put the production of biofuels into context and making a true determination of their earth-friendliness, the statistics that are advertised claim that using 100% corn ethanol gets you approximately a 25% carbon reduction, and E85 gets a 15% carbon reduction if made with corn, but up to 120% if made using other feedstocks. Good news for flex-fuel car owners: Minnesota has a growing number of stations that have added E85 to their pump offerings, with station owners deciding to sell regular and E85, instead of regular and premium. At this time, there are over 40 stations that carry E85 throughout the metro; many of them are Holiday or Freedom gas stations. To find an E85 station near you, look online at http://e85prices.com.

To find E85 stations while on the road, use the link above or try this: The **Renewable Fuels Association** industry lobbying group (www.ethanolrfa.org) has developed a fuel locater application for Garmin and TomTom GPS systems that will map out fueling stations closest to the user's location and chosen destination.

SUSTAINABLE COMMUNITIES

Modern **Smart Growth** principles differ greatly from those that shaped the subdivisions and communities of the past. Years ago, planning and zoning regulations were intended to create single-use, strictly separated zones along a transportation network made up of arterial and feeder roads that cut through large swaths of undesigned landscape that developers were left to configure as they wished. The result was the single-family detached bedroom communities many of us grew up in. Today's Smart Growth principles aspire to create compact, walkable communities located in areas with existing infrastructure, ideally near transit, that include workforce housing, shopping, entertainment, and recreation. "Mixed use" is the new buzzword. Will you be able to live in a mixed use community in Minnesota? Maybe. We have done particularly well improving the mixed-use quality of the downtowns and some of our older suburbs. Are the far-out suburbs mixed use? Not so much. In fact, Minnesota has used sewer and the Northstar Commuter Rail to channel development the same way the roads did, and what we've gotten in return are a lot of high-density, aesthetically bereft, car-dependent bedroom communities; and the people who live far out where the sewer has been extended into Carver County, or in Elk River, near the end of the Northstar line, basically still have to come into the town to work and party.

GREEN ENTERTAINMENT

- Green-minded local experimental indie rock band **Cloud Cult** (www.cloud-cult.com) and its nonprofit recording label, **Earthology Records** (www.earthology.net), were formed by Craig Minowa when he was pursuing a degree in environmental science at the U of M. In keeping with Minowa's philosophy of life, Earthology uses organic and/or recycled materials to manufacture its albums, DVDs, prints, posters, and apparel. The company plants 10 trees for every 1000 albums sold. The band's 2008 album, *Feel Good Ghosts (Tea-Partying Through Tornadoes)*, addresses the group's environmental concerns in song. During their shows, band members Connie Minowa and Scott West each complete a painting onstage, which they auction off at the end of the concert, with the proceeds going to charity.

- **Brown Paper Tickets** is a Fair Trade ticketing company. A portion of their service fee goes back to the community. 24/7 Ticket Hotline: 1-800-838-3006, www.brownpapertickets.com
- Listen to **Everything Green** on Saturdays from noon until 1 p.m. on KTNF radio, AM950, or online at www.everythinggreenradio.com. The web site contains clickable links to the program's "green" sponsors, as well as tips and other useful information.

GREEN ORGANIZATIONS

- **1000 Friends of Minnesota** promotes conservation development or, as it says, it's trying to help Minnesota grow without wrecking the place. Its web site includes an animated map showing growth across the state from 1940 to 2030; www.1000fom.org.
- The **Alliance for Sustainability**, http://www.afors.org, is a Minnesota-based alliance of churches and others who support projects that are ecologically sound, economically viable, socially just, and humane.
- **Conservation Minnesota**, www.conservationminnesota.org, is a private nonprofit dedicated to turning conservation values into state priorities.
- **LandOf.org** is a web site that will help you access information about central cities, urban neighborhoods, developed suburbs, developing suburbs, small cities, and rural areas.
- The **Land Stewardship Project** is a grassroots membership organization made up of farmers as well as rural and urban residents, working together to secure a healthful food supply, preserve soil, water and wildlife, and support diversified, profitable family-sized farms, www.landstewardshipproject.org.
- The **Minnesota Public Interest Research Group** (MPIRG, www.mpirg.org) is another nonpartisan advocacy group for the public interest on issues of the environment, consumer protection, and social justice.

WHILE YOU SEARCH FOR A PERMANENT LIVING SITUATION, THE apartment search services listed in the **Finding a Place to Live** chapter can assist you with a short-term lease. Also consider the following options, which vary in expense and accommodation.

RESERVATION SERVICES

- **AAA**, www.aaa.com
- **Cheap Tickets**, www.cheaptickets.com
- **Expedia**, 800-EXPEDIA, www.expedia.com
- **Orbitz**, www.orbitz.com
- **Travelocity**, www.travelocity.com
- **Trip Advisor**, www.tripadvisor.com
- **Hotels.com**, www.hotels.com
- **Hotwire**, www.hotwire.com
- **Priceline**, www.priceline.com

LODGINGS

If you don't want to have to rent a car, stay in downtown Minneapolis or St. Paul, or along the Hiawatha LRT route.

MINNEAPOLIS DOWNTOWN

- **Crowne Plaza–Northstar** is located downtown on the skyway system; 618 Second Ave S, 612-338-2288, 1-800-556-STAR, www.msp-northstar.crowneplaza.com.

- The **Depot Renaissance Minneapolis Hotel** features an indoor ice rink and weekend water park; 225 Third Ave S (Washington Ave), 612-375-1700, www.thedepotminneapolis.com.
- The **Doubletree Guest Suites** feature spacious suites, including separate sitting areas complete with a sleeper sofa, 1101 La Salle Ave, 612-332-6800, www.minneapolisdoubletree.com.
- **Holiday Inn Metrodome** is located four blocks from the Hiawatha LRT line on the edge of the business district. It offers complimentary shuttle service within a three-mile radius, as well as oversized vehicle parking; 1500 Washington Ave, 612-333-4646, 800-448-DOME, www.metrodome.com.
- The **Marquette** is an older hotel in the IDS Center, an office complex situated on the Nicollet Mall in the middle of downtown Minneapolis; 710 Marquette Ave, 612-333-4545, www.marquettehotel.com.
- **Millennium Hotel Minneapolis**, 1313 Nicollet Mall, 612-332-6000, 866-866-8086, www.millenniumhotels.com, is connected to the Convention Center through the skyway system.
- **Minneapolis Hilton and Towers** is connected by skyway to the Convention Center; 1001 Marquette Ave S, 612-376-1000, 800-HILTONS, www1.hilton.com.
- **Radisson Plaza Hotel Minneapolis** is connected to the city's skyway system; 35 S 7th St, 612-339-4900, 800-333-3333, www.Radisson.com.
- **Sheraton Midtown**, two miles south of downtown on the Midtown Greenway bike path, is connected to Abbott Northwestern Hospital and Children's Hospital; 2901 Chicago Ave S, 612-821-7600, www.starwoodhotels.com.
- The landmark **Westin Minneapolis** was transformed from the historic Farmers & Mechanics Bank building, originally built in 1941; 88 S 6th St, Minneapolis, 612-333-4006, www.starwoodhotels.com.

ST. PAUL

- **Crowne Plaza–Riverfront** is a few blocks from the Ordway and Science Museum, 11 E Kellogg Blvd, 651-292-1900, www.cpstpaul.com.
- **Days Inn Midway Minneapolis/St. Paul** is located 3 blocks from the Twin Cities Amtrak Station. It provides complimentary shuttle service within a 2-mile radius; 1964 University Ave W, 651-645-8681, 800-329-7466, www.daysinn.com.
- **Embassy Suites Hotel Downtown St. Paul** features two-room suites, complimentary breakfast, and a complimentary manager's reception; 175 E 10th St, 651-224-5400, 800-329-7466, http://embassysuites1.hilton.com.
- **Holiday Inn RiverCentre** is across the street from Xcel Energy Center/RiverCentre and is home to an Irish pub, The Liffey; 175 W 7th St, 651-225-1515, 1-888-HOLIDAY, www.holiday-inn.com/stpaulmn.

SUBURBS

The Bloomington Strip (I-494 west of the MSP airport and Mall of America) is shoulder-to-shoulder with the greatest concentration of hotels in the metro, as well as numerous bars and restaurants. Tour groups and families focused on the Mall of America usually stay at the east end. You can find quieter accommodations at the west end of the strip in West Bloomington/ Edina.

- **AmericInn Motel and Suites**, off I-35W, has a water park and bowling center; 2200 Hwy 10, Mounds View, 763-786-2000, 800-634-3444, www.americinn. com/hotels/MN/MoundsView.
- **Baymont Inn and Suites** is near Medtronic and 3M; 6415 James Circle, Brooklyn Center, 763-561-8400, 877-229-6668, www.baymontinns.com.
- **Best Western Kelly Inn–Plymouth** is home to the Plymouth Playhouse comedy theater and a Green Mill restaurant; 2705 N Annapolis Ln, Plymouth, 763-553-1600, www.bestwesternplymouth.com.
- **Comfort Inn** has various metro area locations; 800-424-6423, www.comfortinn.com.
- **Country Inn & Suites**, 591 West 78th St, Chanhassen, 952-937-2424, 800-596-2375, www.countryinns.com
- **Crowne Plaza North** is located where I-694 merges with I-94, near Fridley; 7-mile jogging trail; 2200 Freeway Blvd, Brooklyn Center, 763-566-8000, 800-481-3556, www.minneapolisnorthhotel.com.
- **Embassy Suites Airport** is located one mile from the airport and from the Mall of America; other locations throughout the metro; 7901 34th Ave S, Bloomington, 952-854-1000, 800-329-746, http://embassysuites1.hilton.com.
- **Hampton Inn Minneapolis/St. Paul North**, 1000 Gramsie Rd, Shoreview, 651-482-0402, www.hamptoninn.hilton.com
- **Hilton Garden Inns**, 420 Inwood Avenue, Oakdale, 651-735-4100; 1975 Rahncliff Court, Eagan, 651-686-4605; 6350 Vinewood Lane, Maple Grove, 763-509-9500; 6330 Point Chase, Eden Prairie, 952-995-9000; www.hiltongardeninn.com
- **Holiday Inn–Burnsville** is located at I-35W/I-35E and County 42, by Burnsville Center and not far from Buck Hill Ski Area and the Minnesota Zoo; 14201 Nicollet Ave S, Burnsville, 888-463-7200 or 952-435-2100, www.hiburnsville. com.
- **Holiday Inn Select–Minneapolis–St. Paul International Airport**, is also close to the Mall of America, Three Appletree Sq, Bloomington, 952-854-9000, www.himspairport.com.
- **Marriott Southwest**, 5801 Opus Pkwy, Minnetonka, 952-935-5500, www. marriott.com
- **Oak Ridge Hotel and Conference Center** is across the road from Hazeltine National Golf Course; 1 Oak Ridge Dr, Chaska, 952-368-3100, www.dolceminneapolis-hotel.com.

- **Sheraton St. Paul Woodbury Hotel**, 676 Bielenberg Dr, Woodbury, 651-209-3280, www.starwoodhotels.com
- **Sofitel Minneapolis**, 5601 W 78th St, Edina, 952-835-1900, www.sofitel.com

UNIVERSITY AREA

- **Days Hotel University of Minnesota**, on the eastern edge of the campus, offers complimentary shuttle service to and from the University of Minnesota campus, Minneapolis area hospitals and clinics, and many other area locations; 2407 University Ave, Minneapolis, 612-623-3999, 800-329-7466, www.daysinn.com.
- **Radisson University Hotel** is across the street from the U of M Medical Center. It offers complimentary transportation within a 5-mile radius of the hotel. 615 Washington Ave Southeast, Minneapolis, 612-379-8888, 800-395-7046, www.radisson.com.

HOSTELS

The **City of Lakes International House** is located among the Victorian homes near the Minneapolis Institute of Arts. Convenient to downtown, it offers private rooms and dormitories, and a group kitchen. This hostel is only open to out-of-the-metropolitan-area and international visitors. It is on the bus line. Long-term housing may be available during the off-peak seasons. Reservations are recommended, but walk-ins are welcome; 2400 Stevens Ave S, Minneapolis, 612-874-0407, www.minneapolishostel.com.

SHORT-TERM RENTALS AND EXTENDED-STAY HOTELS

For a comfortable transition, the following hotels offer furnished rooms in convenient locations, such as downtown Minneapolis, near the airport, Eden Prairie, Plymouth, Maple Grove, Brooklyn Center, and Woodbury.

The **Extended Stay Hotel Network**, http://minneapolis.extendedstayhotelnetwork.com; lists extended stay and corporate housing accommodations throughout the metro.

- **Baymont Inns and Suites**, many locations, 877-229-6668, www.baymontinns.com
- **Bridgestreet Corporate Housing** manages buildings in downtown/Uptown Minneapolis, and has numerous other properties, including townhomes, throughout the metro; 800-278-7338, www.bridgestreet.com.
- **Country Inns and Suites**, many locations, 800-596-2375, www.countryinns.com

- **Embassy Suites Hotel St. Paul-Downtown**, 651-224-5400, and many other locations, 1-800-EMBASSY , http://embassysuites1.hilton.com
- **Holiday Inn Express Hotel & Suites**, 1-888-HOLIDAY, www.hiexpress.com
- **Northland Inn Luxury Suite Hotel**, 7025 Northland Dr, Brooklyn Park, 763-536-8300, 800-441-6422, www.northlandinn.com
- **Oakwood Corporate Housing**, locations throughout the Twin Cities, 952-888-8446, 877-902-0832; www.oakwood.com
- **Park Plaza**, 4460 W 78th St Cir, Bloomington, 952-831-3131, 1 800-791-9161, www.parkplaza.com
- **Residence Inn Minneapolis Downtown at the Depot**, 612-340-1300, ice skating; indoor water park open on weekends. Other locations throughout the metro, 800-331-3131, www.marriott.com.
- **Staybridge Suites by Holiday Inn**, many locations, including more in the eastern and northern metro than most other chains offer, 888-233-0369, www.ichotelsgroup.com.
- **TownePlace Suites**, 525 N 2nd St, Minneapolis (Downtown Warehouse District), 612-340-1000; 400 Zarthan Ave S, St. Louis Park, 952-847-6900, www.marriott.com; gets high marks from those who have stayed there; allows pets.

BED & BREAKFASTS

If you really want to learn about your new hometown, try a bed & breakfast for your initial stay. Innkeepers always know their way around.

- **Cathedral Hill Bed and Breakfast**, 488 Holly Ave, St. Paul, 651-998-9882, www.bbonthehill.com
- **Covington Inn** is one of America's few floating bed and breakfasts, with a permanent mooring on the Mississippi River on Harriet Island in downtown St. Paul, 651-292-1411, www.covingtoninn.com.
- **Elmwood House**, 1 East Elmwood Pl (corner of Nicollet & 51st St), Minneapolis, 612-822-4558, www.elmwoodhouse.us
- **Evelo's Bed and Breakfast** is located in the Lowry Hill East neighborhood, steps away from a bus stop and within walking distance of the Walker Art Center; 2301 Bryant Ave, Minneapolis, 612-374-9656.
- **Le Blanc House**, 302 University Ave NE, Minneapolis, 612-379-2570, www.leblanchouse.com, is located within walking distance of a variety of restaurants in downtown Minneapolis.
- **Wales House**, 1115 Fifth St SE, Minneapolis, is a five-minute walk from the University of Minnesota East Bank campus, 612-331-3931, www.waleshouse.com.

LUXURY LODGINGS

- **Le Meridien Chambers Luxury Art Hotel** is dead center in the Hennepin Theater District, 901 Hennepin Ave, Minneapolis, 612-767-6900, www.chambersminneapolis.com.
- The **Grand Hotel Minneapolis**, 615 Second Ave S, Minneapolis, 612-288-8888, 800-323-7500, www.preferredhotels.com, is clubby and quiet; a little out of the action, but only by a few blocks.
- **Graves 601**, 601 First Ave N, Minneapolis, opposite Target Center and First Ave, and connected by skyway to downtown shopping, 612-677-1100, 866-523-1100, www.graves601hotel.com.
- **Hotel Ivy**, 201 S Eleventh St, Minneapolis, 612-746-4600, www.starwoodhotels.com
- **Nicollet Island Inn** is located in a restored factory on an island in the middle of the Mississippi River; a local favorite; 95 Merriam St on Nicollet Island, Minneapolis, 612-331-1800, www.nicolletislandinn.com.
- The **Saint Paul Hotel** is one of *Condé Nast Traveler*'s "Top 75 Hotels in the U.S." Located across the square from the Ordway and Landmark Center, this historic hotel has always been the place to stay in St. Paul; 350 Market St, St. Paul, 651-292-9292, 800-292-9292, www.stpaulhotel.com.

ACCESSIBLE ACCOMMODATIONS

A word of warning: if you travel in a large van, the downtown parking ramps will probably not be able to accommodate your vehicle, even though the hotels and skyway system may be able to accommodate you. Some of the hotels do address this issue by offering valet parking, but you may have the best luck finding fully accessible accommodations outside the downtowns, where parking is usually on surface lots. Also note: federal law requires that if a hotel guarantees reservations for its regular rooms, it must also guarantee reservations for handicapped-accessible rooms. Here's a list of some hotels with accessible accommodations:

- **Crowne Plaza–Northstar** is located downtown on the skyway system; 618 Second Ave S, 612-338-2288, 1-800-556-STAR, www.msp-northstar.crowneplaza.com. Call the attached Northstar parking ramp to check on accessibility for your vehicle, 612-333-6127.
- **Minneapolis Hilton and Towers** is connected by skyway to the Convention Center. It offers valet parking and can accommodate large vans in an adjacent city-owned parking ramp; pets allowed; 1001 Marquette Ave S, 612-376-1000, 800-HILTONS, www1.hilton.com.
- **Holiday Inn Metrodome** is located four blocks from the Hiawatha LRT line on the edge of the business district. Located near the University of Minnesota campus and the HHH Metrodome, it offers complimentary shuttle service

within a three-mile radius, as well as oversized vehicle parking; 1500 Washington Ave, 612-333-4646, 800-448-DOME, www.metrodome.com.

- **Minneapolis Marriott City Center** is connected to the skyway. The hotel offers valet parking, and can accommodate oversize vans in an open lot a few blocks away; 30 S 7th St in the City Center shopping complex, 612-349-4000, 800-228-9290, www.Marriott.com.
- **Northland Inn and Executive Conference Center** is a suite hotel with fully accessible rooms; 7025 Northland Dr, Brooklyn Park, 763-536-8300, 800-441-6422, www.northlandinn.com.

Check Minnesota Beds and Breakfasts Online (www.bbonline.com/mn/) for places to stay on your getaways.

Once you've settled in, you'll eventually want to get away, if only for a day or two. Twin Citians tend to frequent the places described below. In addition to these, you may want to join the time-honored tradition of heading "**Up North**." It doesn't matter where you go—there are ten thousand lakes to choose from! Read about them on the Minnesota Tourism web site (www.exploreminnesota.com). One popular destination is **Brainerd**, about two hours' drive north—except on Friday afternoons, when it can take forever. With 465 lakes, 16 golf courses, five water parks, the 70-mile Paul Bunyan Trail, and International Speedway, Brainerd has plenty of things to do, even on rainy days. Call 800-450-2838 or check www.explorebrainerdlakes.com for specifics. And as long as you're headed that way, don't miss the 26-foot-tall statue of Paul Bunyan at Paul Bunyan Land's This Old Farm and Pioneer Village, seven miles east of Brainerd on Highway 18 (www.paulbunyanland.com). Don't ask why you should be interested in a giant statue, it's a Minnesota thing, as is breaking the short trip to Duluth at Tobies Restaurant in Hinckley—everybody does it, so you should, too!

HISTORIC VILLAGES AND THEIR VICINITIES

Stillwater, 20 miles east of St. Paul on the St. Croix River, and Excelsior and Wayzata, 20 miles west of Minneapolis on Lake Minnetonka, can best be reached by car. All three of these historic villages offer cute shopping, eating and drinking, and general poking around. Excelsior and Stillwater offer other recreation opportunities as well.

WAYZATA

Wayzata (www.wayzata.org), out I-394 from Minneapolis, has nothing to offer children, apart from Ben and Jerry's ice cream. Antiquing, however, is world class. Post-shopping, hang with the locals at Sunsets, under the clock tower on Lake Street (www.sunsetsrestaurant.com). For the best lunch around, drive a few minutes west on Highway 15 to the Minnetonka Center for the Arts (www. minnetonkaarts.org). The café there is open from 9 'til 2, Monday through Friday, as are the galleries, which are filled with local artists' work.

EXCELSIOR

Excelsior (www.ci.excelsior.mn.us), on Highway 7, has a much more family-friendly vibe. Founded in 1853, it has a distinct New England village feel, with a waterfront common area and a variety of colorful houses with cute gardens. Visit during Art on the Lake in June or Apple Days in September, and take a walking tour led by local author Bob Williams, who uses Excelsior as the setting for his books. Browse in the shops on Water Street, swim at the Commons, ride the old-fashioned trolley, or take a day or evening cruise. Excelsior is home port to several charter cruise lines, among them the *Queen of Excelsior* (www. qecruise.com). The *Minnehaha*, a 1906 streetcar boat that was raised and restored by community volunteers after being scuttled in Lake Minnetonka back in the 1920s, runs a scheduled route on weekends and holidays and will drop you off at the Wayzata dock so you can explore that village too (www. steamboatminnehaha.org).

Looking for more action? Rent a jet ski from Bay Rentals (952-474-0366) or a boat or kayak from Excel Boat Club (www.excelboatclub.com). You can even hire a guide to take you fishing. HookMasters (www.HookMasters.net) is based near Excelsior. Other guides can be found in the Yellow Pages under "Fishing Trips."

Don't miss:

- **Excelsior Bay Books**, 36 Water St, an independent bookstore well-known for its children's and fiction sections.
- **Leipold's Antiques and Gifts**, 239 Water St, 952-474-5880, which is known nationwide for its antique lighting fixtures.
- **Adele's Frozen Custard & Old Fashioned Ice Cream**, on Excelsior Blvd at the east end of town, is a good place to end your walking tour with a dish of the ultimate in ice cream.
- If you're looking for a meal, walk across the street and eat on the patio at the **Bayside Grill**.
- Be sure to catch a performance at the world-famous **Old Log Theater** (5175 Meadville St, 952-474-5951, www.oldlog.com). The Old Log serves excellent

dinners and is renowned for its British farces, as well as for the famous actors who have starred in them.

- If you decide to stay the night, the **Bird House Bed and Breakfast** is on Water Street, right in the heart of town (www.birdhouseinn.com).
- The next closest place to stay is Chanhassen, which has a **Country Suites by Carlson** (952-937-2424, 800-596-2375, www.countryinns.com/chanhassenmn).

STILLWATER

Stillwater (www.ilovestillwater.com) is another lively town with a history that pre-dates statehood. Nestled into the bluffs of the St. Croix River, this Birthplace of Minnesota was a thriving logging town into the late 1800s and is listed on the National Registry of Historic Places. Visitors can enjoy antiquing, canoeing and boating on the beautiful St. Croix, one of America's protected Wild and Scenic Waterways—or tour the river valley from a hot air balloon (**Aamodt's Hot Air Balloon Rides**, 651-351-0101, www.aamodtsballoons.com; **Stillwater Balloons**, Hot Air Balloon Flights, 651-439-1800, www.stillwaterballoons.com). This is one town that did not tear down its past in order to build its present; consequently many of its elegant old mansions survive and have been turned into bed and breakfasts. **Elephant Walk** (www.elephantwalkbb.com) and **Rivertown Inn Bed & Breakfast** (www.rivertowninn.com) are often recommended. The **Lowell Inn** (www.lowellinn.com) is the fanciest place in town and is well known for its Swiss fondue and beautifully restored rooms.

For dining, locals suggest **The Dock Café** (425 Nelson Street East, 651-430-3770, www.dockcafe.com), a great place to sit and watch the river traffic and eat burgers.

Visit Stillwater during **Lumberjack Days** (www.lumberjackdays.com) in July to watch professional and amateur loggers demonstrate logrolling, ax throwing, and other lumberjack skills.

If you love pottery, time your visit to coincide with the **St. Croix Valley Pottery Tour and Sale**. Similar to drive-around weekends in other artsy rural areas of the country, the St. Croix Valley Tour is held every spring—come snow or mosquitoes—on a 75-mile route along Highway 95, between Stillwater and Cambridge. For details and a map to the studios check the potters' web site (www.minnesotapotters.com).

The St. Croix National Scenic Riverway from Stillwater upstream to Taylors Falls is easy to navigate by canoe or powerboat and also attracts hikers, rock climbers, cross-country skiers, mountain bikers, and fishermen. There are three parks in this area: **St. Croix Islands Scenic Reserve**, **William O'Brien State Park**, and **Interstate Park at Taylors Falls**. Information is available online from the National Park Service (www.nps.gov/sacn) or from the Minnesota Department of Natural Resources (DNR) (www.dnr.state.mn.us). The **St. Croix Boat and Packet Company** offers St. Croix River charter cruises departing from the

Port of Stillwater, which is located downtown on the south end of Main Street (www.stillwaterriverboats.com).

POINTS NORTH

DULUTH

On the shores of Lake Superior, Duluth (www.visitduluth.com), about two hours' drive north of the Twin Cities up I-35, is an easy weekend destination. There are a lot of things to do, in every season: watch giant cargo ships from around the world enter Duluth's harbor under the Aerial Lift Bridge; downhill ski at city-owned Spirit Mountain (www.spiritmt.com); and bike, hike or in-line skate the Willard Munger Trail (www.dnr.state.mn.us/state_trails/willard_munger). At Canal Park, you can stroll the boardwalk and visit the police horse stable, or hop on a tour boat for a narrated harbor cruise. Kids love Canal Park's Adventure Zone, or watching the soaring raptors at Hawk Ridge, www.hawkridge.org.

> During the raptor migration people stand in line to make a contribution to "adopt" a bird for the privilege of holding it briefly and then releasing it. At the migration's peak in September thousands of birds a day fly by. The record number of raptors counted in ONE DAY: 102,321!!

Those looking for hardcore adventure can find it ice climbing on the lake's steep cliffs. The Casket Quarry within the city of Duluth has several "social" climbs. Information about Lake Superior ice climbs, guides, and gear can be found on the Climbing Central web site (www.climbingcentral.com) or contact the Ski Hut in Duluth (www.theskihut.com). An equally good source of information is Vertical Endeavors in St. Paul or Duluth (651-776-1430, www.verticalendeavors.com). If you're adventurous, and love the water, try kayaking in Lake Superior. The University of Minnesota–Duluth offers both sea kayaking and rock climbing tours (www.d.umn.edu).

For those who are looking for something a little less strenuous, walking the quiet residential streets of the historic East End is always a pleasure. The massive mansions and ornate Victorian houses here were built by wealthy turn-of-the-century businessmen who could afford to bring master craftsmen over from Europe to build their regal homes. Glensheen, at 3300 London Road, is a Jacobean mansion on the lake where two infamous murders took place. It's open to the public daily May–October, www.d.umn.edu/glen. (Check the **Literary Life** chapter for a book about Glensheen that will tell you the things they won't talk about on the tour.)

There are plenty of great places to stay in Duluth. If you're looking for a room with a lake view, try one of these:

- **Fitger's Inn**, a renovated brewery at 600 East Superior St, (888-FITGERS or www.fitgers.com).
- The **Cotton Mansion**, 3600 London Rd, (www.cottonmansion.com, 800-228-1997), an especially elegant bed and breakfast right next door to Glensheen.
- The interesting **Mountain Villas** on top of Spirit Mountain (866-688-4552, www.mtvillas.com).
- The **Canal Park** area is the perfect place to stay with children. Accommodations there range from a private "beach cottage" on **Park Point** (218-343-5030, www.parkpointbeachhouse.com) to **The Inn on Lake Superior**, 50 Canal Park Dr, 218-726-1111, 888-668-4352, www.theinnonlakesuperior.com, which welcomes pets and serves s'mores on the beach every night at 8.
- If you like to do your own cooking, **Beacon Pointe Condos**, www.beaconpointecondos.com, are located along the Lakewalk, just up from Canal Park.
- For many other options, check out **www.visitduluth.com/lodging**.

For those who prefer to camp, the Superior National Forest or one of the several state forests along the North Shore are favorite destinations. For Superior National Forest information call 218-626-4300 or 877-550-6777 (reservations), or check out www.fs.fed.us/r9/superior. You can make reservations online. For state forest information and reservations, contact the DNR (651-296-6157, www.dnr.state.mn.us).

Popular events in and near Duluth include **Grandma's Marathon**, from Two Harbors to Duluth in June, and the **North Shore Inline Marathon** over the same route in September; the **Two Harbors Folk Festival** is held in July, with the **Bayfront Blues Festival** in August. The 400-mile **John Beargrease sled dog marathon** (www.beargrease.com) starts and ends in Duluth. It is held in late January or early February.

NORTH SHORE OF LAKE SUPERIOR

If you have the time, continue up the **North Shore** of Lake Superior, the largest freshwater lake on earth. Its mild appearance on a calm day belies the fact that these are some of the most dangerous waters anywhere in the world. Highway 61 along the shore is lined with markers memorializing the ships that have wrecked on Superior's iron-red rocks.

The views as you drive along the lake through Superior National Forest are stunning and minimalist, often reduced to a slab of rock against sky and water. Park and hike to Gooseberry Falls and Split Rock Lighthouse—the routes are well-marked from the highway. **Split Rock Lighthouse State Park**, an hour's drive from Duluth, past Two Harbors, boasts a restored lighthouse that is probably Minnesota's most photographed historic attraction (www.mnhs.org/places/sites/srl). You can stay in a working lighthouse at the **Lighthouse Bed and Breakfast at Two Harbors**, www.lighthousebb.org. (This B&B is said to be haunted, which many visitors consider a plus.) For a North Shore visitors' guide, look online at www.northshoreinfo.com.

If you love good food, be sure to stop at one of the fabulous restaurants on the way up the coast—and that is not marketing hyperbole. **New Scenic Café**, www.newsceniccafe.com, is eight miles up Scenic Highway 65 from the east edge of Duluth. Beautiful garden, fabulous food! You'd never guess it began life as a 1950s drive-in, except that it's still unpretentious enough to wear your jeans. The kids' menu includes blackberry lemonade and "dirt and worms." A restaurant doesn't get any more family-friendly than that! **Nokomis Restaurant and Wine Shop**, www.nokomisonthelake.com, 17 miles up from Duluth, offers truly fine dining and, again, a great kids' menu. A four-year-old I know gives Five Stars to the Mac and Cheese!

A little farther up the coast, **Lutsen** is a famous resort area that offers downhill and cross-country skiing and snowmobiling in winter, and golf, hiking, sea kayaking, canoeing, fly fishing, and mountain biking in summer. There are numerous motels and resorts here, but the granddaddy of them all is **Lutsen Resort** (www.lutsenresort.com). Nearby **Bluefin Bay** at Tofte (800-BLUEFIN, www.bluefinbay.com) has received "Best Resort" honors multiple times.

Grand Marais, just up the road, is an artful little village, home to the **Grand Marais Art Colony** (www.grandmaraisartcolony.org), which offers workshops for visual artists and writers throughout the summer. Also here: the **North House Folk School** (www.northhouse.org), which offers courses in traditional northern crafts, from baking and boatbuilding to weaving and woodworking. **Naniboujou Lodge and Restaurant** (www.naniboujou.com), located 14 miles east of Grand Marais, is the kind of place where high tea is served in the solarium. It was built in the 1920s as an ultra-exclusive private club, with Babe Ruth as one of its charter members. When the stock market crashed in 1929, however, it took Naniboujou down with it. Since then it has been open to the public, and regular people have been able to eat in its colorful Native American–style painted dining room. This room, with its 20-foot-high domed ceiling, has been described as the "North Woods' answer to the Sistine Chapel." Lodging is available in rooms that are substantially more rustic, and don't have telephones or TVs. For other lodging, check online at http://grandmarais.com.

Seventeen miles north of Grand Marais, the **Gunflint Trail** (www.gunflint-trail.com) takes off into the **Boundary Waters Canoe Area Wilderness** (BWCAW). The BWCAW, which extends for 150 miles along the Canadian border, is a million-acre labyrinth of portage-linked lakes. Here you can canoe and camp just as primitively as the French-Canadian voyageur fur-traders did back in the 1700s. Cross-country skiing, snowshoeing, dog sled trips, and wolf-calling are popular activities in the wilderness in winter. Whatever the season, you are in close contact with nature including bears, moose, and mosquitoes—so be careful. Guides are available and permits are required for all visitors entering the BWCAW or neighboring **Quetico Provincial Park**, another million acres of wilderness on the Canadian side of the border. Visit in the middle of the week, or before Memorial Day or after Labor Day, and you will encounter fewer people. The main entry points to the BWCAW are through Crane Lake, Ely, Tofte, and Grand Marais, so that's where the outfitters are located. If you use an outfitter, as most people do, the outfitter will be able to arrange for your permit. For help finding outfitters, look online at the state's tourism web site (www.exploreminnesota.com) or contact the Grand Marais Chamber of Commerce www.grandmaraismn.com; the Ely Chamber of Commerce (800-777-7281, www.ely.org); or the Crane Lake Visitor and Tourism Bureau (800-362-7405, www.cranelake.org). For Gunflint Trail lodgings and outfitters call 800-338-6932, www.gunflint-trail.com. Do-it-yourselfers will find Boundary Waters permits available online at www.bwcaw.org.

Seven miles south of the Canadian border, **Grand Portage National Monument** was once a large fur-trading post. Tour the reconstructed fort and hike or cross-country ski the 8.5-mile portage footpath to the awe-inspiring 200-foot-high Pigeon River waterfall. For camping information look online at www.nps.gov/grpo.

Grand Portage is also the place to catch the ferry to **Isle Royale**, a wilderness park of rugged forests and unspoiled lakes located 22 miles out in Lake Superior. Home to wolves and moose, it is accessible only by boat or float-plane, April to October. Eighty percent of Isle Royale National Park is underwater and includes shallow warm-water ponds and fast streams as well as the cold, deep waters of Lake Superior. Sport fishing is popular here and trout, northern pike, walleye, and perch are abundant, especially in spring and fall. Travel in the park is by foot or boat—no pets, no bikes. Campers, including boaters, need a permit. Reservations for Rock Harbor Lodge or its housekeeping cabins may be made by calling the Lodge at 906-337-4993 (summer) or 866-644-2003 (winter). For complete information, look online at www.nps.gov/isro.

VOYAGEURS NATIONAL PARK

The quiet splash of the voyageurs' paddles dipping into sparkling water is long gone, replaced by crowds of house-boating wilderness-seekers and fishermen who throng to Voyageurs National Park, on the Canadian border, all summer long. Moose, bears, eagles, loons, and wolves seem to have gotten used to the crowds and are regularly spotted here, as well. Recreation is not limited to the water—the Park Service maintains a number of trails for hiking and cross-country skiing. Snowmobiling and ice fishing are allowed on the frozen lakes in winter. There are primitive boat-in campsites scattered throughout the park, but public and private campsites, accessible by car, are also available. Three park visitor centers offer information, guidebooks, maps, navigational charts, naturalist-guided trips and campfire talks: Rainy Lake Visitor Center is open year round; Kabetogama Lake Visitor Center and Ash River Visitor Center are open seasonally. There are also narrated boat tours that depart from the visitor centers and visit an old lumber camp, gold and mica mines, and the Ellsworth Rock Gardens. Reservations are suggested: 888-381-2873.

You can enter Voyageurs Park (www.nps.gov/voya) from four points along US 53 between Duluth and International Falls: Crane Lake, Ash River, Kabetogama, and Rainy Lake. Year-round food, fuel, lodging, and boat rentals are available outside the park at the four access points. Because this park spans the international border, you must report to customs before and after crossing the Canadian border. All passport and identification rules apply. For lodging and boat rental around Rainy Lake call 800-FALLS-MN or look online at www.rainylake.org; for Ash River, www.ashriver.com, for Crane Lake, www.visit-cranelake.com.

HEADING SOUTH

SOUTHEAST MINNESOTA BLUFF COUNTRY

In sharp contrast to the rocky wildness of Highway 61 along Lake Superior (the North Shore drive), Highway 61 heading south from the Twin Cities is a pastoral route across rolling farmland and the tall wooded bluffs of the Mississippi River. (See **Great River Road Scenic Byway** in the **Lakes and Parks** chapter.) About an hour out of the Twin Cities, **Red Wing** (www.redwing.org) is a popular day or weekend destination. A trip here can be anything you want it to be—a scenic drive, a day spent browsing the town's antique shops and pottery factory, or something more physical. Hike to the top of Barn Bluff and picnic with a view of Red Wing and the surrounding river valley that is breathtaking; or pedal the Cannon Valley Trail, which runs for 20 miles along the Cannon River. For golfers, there's scenic **Mississippi National Golf Links** (www.wpgolf.com/Mississippi). In spring, go to watch the eagles on Lake Pepin, and in winter go for the skiing at nearby Welch Village. Many go just to stay at the wonderful **St. James Hotel** (**800-252-1875**, www.st-james-hotel.com). If the St. James is full, there are several other delightful options, including a former dairy farm, **Round Barn Farm Bed and Breakfast and Bread** (www.roundbarnfarm.com).

Lake Pepin at **Lake City** (www.lakecity.org), 60 miles from Minneapolis, is another half-hour south of Red Wing. A natural wide spot in the Mississippi River, this is the place where water skiing was invented. The sailing is wonderful, as well, though it's shared with a lot of big boat recreational and commercial traffic. The lush broad flood plain and majestic river bluffs of Lake Pepin's shoreline make it prime territory for bird watching. The large **Lake City Marina** (651-345-4211, www.ci.lake-city.mn.us) has excellent shower and bathroom facilities as well as electric hook-ups, so you can sleep on board your boat if you choose to dock there.

A favorite fall color/apple-picking trip is to drive down the Minnesota side of the river on Highway 61, cross at Wabasha or Winona and come back up Wisconsin Route 35, stopping to eat at one of the fun restaurants in **Pepin, Wisconsin** (www.pepinwisconsin.com). The **Harbor View Café** (www.harbor viewpepin.com) is a perennial favorite, but it's first-come-first-served, and the line starts forming an hour before it opens—and they don't take credit cards. Laura Ingalls Wilder fans will enjoy seeing the Little House in the Big Woods, which is replicated just north of the town. **Laura Ingalls Wilder Days** are held annually in September. Along the way, visit **Frontenac**, on the Minnesota side, a village where little has changed since the 1880s. **Frontenac State Park** (www. dnr.state.mn.us/state_parks/frontenac) completely encircles the village and is a sanctuary for migratory warblers and bald and golden eagles. Hiking trails here overlook the valley and lead you to In-Yan-Teopa, a limestone arch that is thought to have been sacred to the Dakota and Fox Indians who lived in the region. Look for more bald eagles at Read's Landing near **Wabasha** (www.wabashamn.org). Wabasha is home to the **National Eagle Center** (www.nationaleaglecenter.org), as well as the place where they filmed *Grumpy Old Men.*

At **Winona** (www.visitwinona.com), two hours south of the cities, still on Highway 61, you hit serious apple country. Winona County Road 1 is known as Apple Blossom Drive, but it is **LaCrescent** (www.lacrescent.govoffice.com) that bills itself as the Apple Capital of Minnesota. Time your trip to catch the Apple Festival held here during the third week in September, or to catch the state's best display of fall color, a little later.

Lanesboro (www.lanesboro.com), a short distance away, was named one of the 50 Best Outdoor Sports Towns in America by *Sports Afield* magazine. Nestled in the Root River Valley, it lives up to its award-winning designation by offering a wide variety of invigorating outdoor activities, including biking, hiking, or cross-country skiing the picturesque 60-mile Root River Trail, paddling the river, hunting, fishing, and golf. Outfitter rentals and shuttle services are available through clickable links from the web site. For those looking for less strenuous activities, a drive along Highway 16, a National Scenic Byway, or a sidetrip down nearly any country road will provide you with a nostalgic glimpse into rural life in Amish country. Back in town, there is professional theater, homemade sauerkraut and root beer at **Das Wurst Haus German Village and Deli,** and that inimitable local greasy spoon, the **Chat 'n Chew**. Lodging choices range from camping to B&Bs and full-bore resorts.

GO EAST

WISCONSIN

Two hundred miles northeast of St. Paul, **Bayfield** (www.bayfield.org) and **The Apostle Islands National Lakeshore** (www.nps.gov/apis) are both romantic and sporty. There you can cruise one of the great sailing grounds of the world, fish one of the great fishing holes, bike, hike, golf, or learn about nature from rangers on the islands—or just stroll around and enjoy the ambience.

Start your vacation on the mainland in Bayfield, a gem of a town on the shore of Lake Superior that mixes art, antiques, and Victorian bed and breakfasts with hunting, fishing, camping, and sailing. Take a sailboat cruise on the three-masted schooner, the *Zeeto* (www.schoonerman.com/zeeto.htm), or charter a boat yourself. **Sailboats, Inc.** at Bayfield and Superior, operates a charter service/sailing school (800-826-7010, www.sailboats-inc.com). If you're adventurous, try sea kayaking. **Midwest Mountaineering** in Minneapolis (www. midwestmtn.com) presents kayaking clinics that cover trip planning details and route information for planning your own paddle through the Apostle Islands. **Living Adventure** (www.livingadventure.com), based in Ashland, Wisconsin, near Bayfield, offers kayak rental as well as guided tours—some strictly for women.

Bayfield is home to several active yacht clubs that conduct a full schedule of regattas. Try to catch the **Blessing of the Fleet** in June when fishing boats, sailboats, kayaks, rowboats, and even ferry boats decorated with flags weave their way through the Bayfield harbor in a colorful parade to welcome the summer season and receive an ecumenical blessing.

When you're ready to head to the islands, you'll find that getting there is half the fun. In the summer take the 25-minute ferry; in winter, when the lake is frozen, you can drive. In between, and most fun of all, is the wind sled, which is used when the ice road is deemed unsafe to travel. The wind sled runs on an uncertain schedule, but the ferry travels from Bayfield Dock to Madeline Island every half-hour (www.madferry.com). Sightseeing boats and island shuttles also depart from the Bayfield Dock. The Grand Tour half-day sightseeing trip will take you past all 22 of the Apostle Islands. For campers, there is a shuttle to Stockton Island from the mainland. Stockton is the largest island and has the most extensive trail system, as well as civilized camping facilities and an awesome swimming beach. Devil's Island is famous for its sea caves.

Madeline Island (www.madelineisland.com), the largest of the Apostle Islands, is not part of the park, but is developed with summer and year-round residences, hotels, and bed and breakfasts. Besides water sports, you can play golf and tennis, explore the island on a rented moped or bike, or bird watch in the Madeline Island Wilderness Preserve. Cold weather activities include the Run on Water five-mile race to Madeline Island over the Madeline Island Ice Road, and snowshoe racing.

Among the interesting lodging choices on Madeline Island are **The Inn** (800-822-6315, www.madisland.com), which offers townhouse accommodations and beach cottages, and **Brittany Bed & Breakfast** (www.brittanycabins. com), which is listed on the National Register of Historic Places. This peaceful waterfront complex was built in the style of an Adirondack camp, with a main house and several cottages. Its manicured croquet lawn begs for ladies in long white dresses and gentlemen in boaters. And after you peg out (finish the game, in croquet talk), be sure to stop for a glass of wine in the formal garden's tea house. **The Island Inn** (www.ontheisland.com) takes vacationing in an entirely different direction. It features rooms with a rustic décor and includes winter dogsledding among its entertainments.

Wisconsin Dells (www.wisdells.com) is where your kids will want to go—over and over and over. This self-proclaimed "Waterpark Capital of the World" is located off I-90 and I-94, about 200 miles from St. Paul. It has indoor and outdoor water parks, adrenaline-pumping roller coasters, jet boats, horses to ride, trains, mini-golf, cabarets, hypnosis shows…the list of attractions goes on forever. Be sure to take an amphibious vehicle tour (www.wisconsinducktours.com and www.dellsducks.com). Two tips from families who go there often: avoid the crowds by staying in a resort that has its own guests-only water park; and download all the coupons you can find from the various Dells web sites—it does get expensive.

For more Wisconsin travel information look online at www.travelwisconsin.com.

A LITTLE FARTHER AFIELD

CHICAGO

This just squeaks in as a "quick" getaway—it's an eight-hour drive, one way—but if you give yourself four days, you won't feel rushed. Or fly—there are often special fares between the Twin Cities and Chicago. Amtrak will get you there as well (800-USA-RAIL, www.amtrak.com). "The Windy City" needs no introduction, but as a reminder, you can visit the Art Institute, the Field Museum of Natural History, the Magnificent Mile of shopping on Michigan Avenue, the American Girl store, Millennium Park, the Cloud Gate sculpture, eclectic shops and pubs on Clark Street, Old Town, blues and jazz festivals, and more. Yes, the Cubs still play at Wrigley Field. For lots of trip planning help, look online at www.explorechicago.org.

BLACK HILLS, SOUTH DAKOTA

Minnesota was the jumping-off point for pioneers headed west in the late 1800s, and to get a taste of those good old days, plan a trip to **Deadwood, South Dakota**, in the heart of the Black Hills.

At 600 miles, this is not a "Quick Getaway" in the strict sense of the word, and the 9-10–hour drive out I-90 all the way across South Dakota to Mt. Rushmore is a whole lot more pleasant if your car has a DVD player. When you finally get there, though, you'll find there's plenty of action—real cowboys and Indians, gunslingers, rodeos and rock-and-roll. In early August, the region roars with motorcyclists who've come to the Black Hills for the **Sturgis Motorcycle Rally**, an event packed with concerts, racing, and general testosterone-testing. Should you miss that event, you can still match wits with one-armed-bandits (slot machines) in Deadwood gaming halls that date back to the Gold Rush days of the 1870s. Surprisingly, all of Deadwood is actually a national historic landmark, a fact to ponder while standing at the foot of Wild Bill Hickok's grave on the original Boot Hill, or while panning for gold at the Broken Boot Mine. Deadwood is also the gateway to over 300 miles of groomed snowmobile and bike trails. Lodging is available in cabins, condos, campgrounds, bed and breakfasts, and chain motels. Book reservations online at www.deadwood.net or by calling 866-601-5103. For more South Dakota travel information, look online at the state's tourism web site, www.travelsd.com.

FALL COLOR

Fall color in Minnesota tends to be yellow and short-lived, with leaves falling with the first hard rain. Check the U.S. Forest Service's hotline for weekly updates on peak fall color (800-354-4595, www.forestry.about.com/od/fallcolor/a/usfs_fall_hot.htm). Here are a few places the locals like to go to catch the Fall Color at its height:

- **Chippewa National Forest**, just west of Grand Rapids on Highway 38 (edge of the Wilderness Scenic Byway) or Highway 46 (the Avenue of the Pines), is located at the intersection of Minnesota's three major ecosystems: the aspen, birch, spruce, fir, and pines of the northern boreal forest; the maple-basswood hardwood forests typical in the southern part of the state; and the prairie west of the forest. The combination produces a range of fall colors not found anywhere else in the state.
- **North Shore** of Lake Superior, Highway 61 North (see above)
- **Southeastern Minnesota/Western Wisconsin Bluff Country**, Highway 61 South (see above)
- The **University of Minnesota Landscape Arboretum**, Highway 5 just west of Highway 41 in Chaska, www.arboretum.umn.edu

ADULTS ONLY GETAWAYS

Midwest resorts tend to run to families, fishermen, golfers, and, in winter, snowmobilers. That's fine, if you fit into that mold. But if what you're looking for is something more on the order of a romantic hideaway, there is a **Relais & Chateaux** hotel (www.relaischateaux.com) in Chetek, Wisconsin (www.chetek. com). Rustic and elegant at the same time, **Canoe Bay** (800-568-1995, www. canoebay.com) has been ranked the top hotel in the Midwest, and one of the Top 10 Most Romantic. Designed for couples, it's indulgent, quiet, and expensive—and only a two-hour drive east of the Twin Cities. Be sure to stop along the way in Chippewa Falls for a tour of the Leinenkugel Brewery (www.leinie. com). Reservations are suggested.

GOLF GETAWAYS

- A three-and-a-half hour drive from the Northern Metro, **Giants Ridge** (www. giantsridge.com) at Biwabik, on the Iron Range in Northern Minnesota, has been named one of *GolfWorld* magazine's "Top Six Golf Destinations in the World."
  - ▷ Its **Quarry** course, which opened in 2003, debuted at Number 16 on *Golf Digest*'s 2005–06 rankings of America's 100 Greatest Public Courses.
  - ▷ The resort's older course, **The Legend** (No. 88 on the 100 Greatest list), garnered a prestigious 4.5-star rating from *Golf Digest*, and has been named Minnesota's #1 Public Golf Course.
- Nearby **Fortune Bay Resort Casino** on Lake Vermillion (www.fortunebay. com) is home to **The Wilderness at Fortune Bay** (www.thewildernessgolf. com), *Golf Digest*'s choice for "America's Best New Upscale Public Golf Course for 2005."

For the newest, most comfortable lodgings, stay at the resorts.

ADDITIONAL RESOURCES

- For **general travel information** and an excellent comprehensive travel guide for the entire state, look online at the Minnesota Office of Tourism's web site, www.exploreminnesota.com.
- For **trip planning or park maps** check the Minnesota Department of Natural Resources web site, www.dnr.state.mn.us.
- To **reserve a campsite** at one of the many state parks, call the DNR's reservation line at 866-85PARKS, www.stayatmnparks.com.
- For a free **Wisconsin** vacation guide look online at www.travelwisconsin.com.
- **North Dakota** tourism information is available at www.ndtourism.com.
- **South Dakota** information is available at www.travelsd.com.
- **Travel Michigan** is online at www.michigan.org/travel.
- The **National Park Service** web site is www.nps.gov.
- For **road condition and detour information** call 511 or look online at www.511mn.org.

MOSQUITOES EAT YOU IN SUMMER AND THE COLD FLASH-FREEZES you in winter, but if you're a Minnesotan, you'll be out and about anyway, dismissing such life-threatening conditions as mild annoyances. All four seasons in the Twin Cities offer exciting annual celebrations, festivals, and shows. Here are just a few you may want to experience yourself.

JANUARY

- **Land O'Lakes Kennel Club Dog Show**, River Centre, St. Paul; all breeds. This is the largest indoor show in the region, www.infodog.com.
- **St. Paul Winter Carnival**; this spectacular annual event includes parades, dog sled races, ice carving, a treasure hunt, and fervent attempts by the Vulcans to warm up the winter. It runs into early February, www.winter-carnival.com.

FEBRUARY

- **Chilly Open**; play golf on frozen Lake Minnetonka in Wayzata! There are three courses and lots of hot food and drink, www.wayzatachamber.com.
- **City of Lakes Loppet**; this weekend festival of cross-country skiing includes participatory and spectator events for the whole family, www.cityoflakesloppet.com.
- **John Beargrease Dogsled Race**, Duluth; a 373-mile, four-day marathon, www.beargrease.com.

MARCH

- **Builders Association Spring Preview of Homes** offers tours of newly built homes to acquaint you with builders, and the latest trends and developments, www.paradeofhomes.org.
- **Minnesota State High School Basketball Tournaments**, www.mshsl.org.
- **Minnesota State High School Hockey Tournaments**, www.mshsl.org.
- **St. Patrick's Day Celebration**, March 17, St. Paul, www.stpatsassoc.org.

APRIL

- **Annual Smelt Run**, in rivers near Duluth.
- **Voltage Fashion Amplified** is Mnfashion Week's premier event, www.voltagefashionamplified.com.

MAY

- **Cinco de Mayo** is celebrated with a huge fiesta in the District del Sol in St. Paul's West Side, and in Minneapolis in restaurants and parks along E Lake St near the Mercado Central.
- **Festival of Nations**, RiverCentre, is Minnesota's largest multicultural extravaganza. It features ethnic cafés, folk dancing, and an international bazaar, www.festivalofnations.com.
- **Heart of the Beast May Day Parade**; giant puppets parade through the streets to Powderhorn Park on the first Sunday in May, www.hobt.org.
- **Minnesota Fishing Opener**, this huge event in the land of 10,000 lakes is the weekend we are all reminded that Minnesota has too many fishermen and too few roads heading "Up North."
- **Soundset Hip-Hop Festival**, Canterbury Park, Shakopee, www.soundsetfestival.com.

JUNE

- **Edina Art Fair**, W 50th St and France Ave; outdoor art and craft bazaar featuring artists, food, and entertainment, www.50thandfrance.com.
- **Gay-Lesbian-Bisexual-Transgender Pride Festival**, Loring Park, Grant and Willow sts, Minneapolis; includes music, dancing, and drag queens, www.tcpride.org.
- **Grand Old Day**, Grand Ave, St. Paul; this three-mile-long, family-friendly bash in the street includes a parade, food and drink, specials in Grand Ave stores, arts and crafts, and great music on stages in every block, www.GrandAve.com.

- **Grandma's Marathon**, Duluth; the route parallels the shore of Lake Superior from Two Harbors to Duluth and draws competitors from all over the world. Pick up information at local sports stores, www.grandmasmarathon.com.
- **Juneteenth**, held in mid-June in Theodore Wirth Park, Glenwood Ave N, Minneapolis, is a family festival celebrating black American culture with food, music, athletic events, and a film festival, www.juneteenth.com.
- **Rock the Garden Music Festival** in the Walker Art Center sculpture garden, www.walkerart.org.
- **Svenskarnasdag, Swedish Heritage Day**, on the last Sunday in June at Minnehaha Park, Minneapolis, is a traditional celebration featuring a Swedish/ English church service, ethnic food, and the crowning of Miss Svenskarnasdag, www.svenskarnasdag.com.

JULY

- **Basilica Block Party**, basilicablockparty.org, Basilica of St. Mary, Hennepin Ave and 17th St, Minneapolis; the church trades its choir for funky rock bands, two nights of music, food, drink, and a raffle. Buy tickets online at www.ticketmaster.com.
- **Lumberjack Days**, Stillwater's festival, commemorates its lumber mill days with ax throwing, logrolling, chainsaw carving, pole climbing, free concerts, and a Bunyanesque fireworks display, www.lumberjackdays.com.
- **Minneapolis Aquatennial** pays homage to all things water with 10 days of free events that appeal to all age groups and interests: Torchlight Parade, Milk Carton Boat Race, the world's highest-purse triathlon, water ski show, sailing regatta, logrolling competition, art fair, concerts, and Fireworks over the Mississippi. This is the biggest event of the summer, with many streets temporarily closed to traffic. This event is always looking for volunteers—it's a great way to feel like you're part of the community. To volunteer, check online at www.aquatennial.org.
- **Minnesota Orchestra's Viennese Sommerfest**, Orchestra Hall, Nicollet Mall; the setting for nearly a month of concerts with famous guest soloists inside Orchestra Hall, and free entertainment, food, and dancing outside in the Peavey Plaza Marketplace. For concert tickets call 612-371-5656 or 800-292-4141, or order online at www.minnesotaorchestra.org.
- **Rondo Days Festival and Parade**, Martin Luther King Recreation Center Park, St. Paul, is host to the biggest African-American celebration in Minnesota. It includes a parade, arts and crafts, and a drill team competition, http:// rondodays.org/history.htm.
- **Taste of Minnesota**, Harriet Island, St. Paul; Fourth of July weekend—three days of music, entertainment, food (some from local restaurants), and capital fireworks, www.tasteofmn.com.

AUGUST

- **Minnesota Renaissance Festival** is a loose recreation of a renaissance town fair. Located off Hwy 169, four miles south of Shakopee, it lasts seven weekends, mid-August to nearly the end of September. Make merry with jousting tournaments, finger food, entertainers, and unique arts and crafts. For directions and ticket information, call 800-966-8215, www.renaissancefest.com.
- **Minnesota State Fair**, State Fairgrounds, Snelling Ave, St. Paul, marks the end of summer with farm animals, art, fried food on a stick, and Princess Kay of the Milky Way carved in butter—what more could you want? Runs through Labor Day, 651-288-4400, TTY 651-642-2372, www.mnstatefair.org. For information about accessibility, wheelchair rental, and other services, contact guestservices@mnstatefair.org or call 651-288-4448. State Fair Express buses operate from the major malls. For automated express bus information, call 612-341-4287.
- **Uptown Art Fair**, Hennepin and Lake in Minneapolis; a street fair crowded with artists' booths, food, and entertainment. This is one of the largest outdoor art fairs in the Midwest, www.uptownminneapolis.com.
- **Wacipi (Pow Wow)**, west of Little Six Casino off County Rd 42 in the Shakopee/Prior Lake area, www.tpt.org/powwow; live three-day event featuring over 1000 dancers, performed by the Shakopee Mdewakanton (Dakota) Sioux Community.

SEPTEMBER

- **Fall Festival at the Minnesota Landscape Arboretum**, Hwy 5, Chanhassen, invites the public in for live music, children's activities, and apple and plant sales, www.arboretum.umn.edu/.
- **Jason DeRusha Day**, September 21, in Minneapolis; WCCO's "Good Question Man" is also an ace Tweeter (@DeRushaJ). On August 6, National Cheesecake Day, he tweeted, "How do you get a 'day' anyway? Good Question at 10. (Anyone have power to declare DeRusha Day?)" Then people around the TC swung into action. Somebody created a DeRusha Day web site and someone else started an online petition. Within hours, DeRusha was presenting the petition to the city, and a few weeks later he got back the happy news—September 21 is officially declared Jason DeRusha Day. Tweet him your congratulations and let him know how you're celebrating "His Day."
- **Laura Ingalls Wilder Days** in Pepin, Wisconsin, www.pepinwisconsin.com
- **North Shore In-Line Skating Marathon**, Two Harbors to Duluth, www.northshoreinline.com

- **Parade of Homes** is a tour of selected new homes in the Twin Cities, sponsored by the Builders Association of the Twin Cities, www.paradeofhomes.org.

OCTOBER

- **MEA Week**; the Minnesota Education Association holds its annual convention; area schools schedule parent conferences, and lots of families leave town.
- **Twin Cities Marathon**, www.twincitiesmarathon.org

NOVEMBER/DECEMBER

- This is a time for celebrating the Winter Solstice, Christmas, Hanukkah, Hmong New Year, Kwanzaa, and Ramadan, often with interfaith and cross-cultural events.
- Top of the list is a family trip to see **The Christmas Carol at the Guthrie**, www.guthrietheater.org, which has been presented annually for at least 20 years, or the **Holiday Pageant at the Open Eye Figure Theatre**, www.openeyetheatre.org.
- But there are plenty of other events and productions unique to Minnesota that are worth a try.
- The **American Swedish Institute**, 2600 Park Ave, Minneapolis, 612-871-4907, www.americanswedishinst.org, celebrates Christmas with a Scandinavian flair that includes decorations, music, and a full-blown Lucia festival.
- The **Black Nativity**, Penumbra Theater, St. Paul, www.penumbratheatre.org
- **A Capital New Year**, Rice Park and other downtown St. Paul locations, rings in the New Year with ice skating, live music, and midnight fireworks.
- **Hmong-Americans usher in the New Year** in December or January with several days of dancing, singing, and talent contests, at the St. Paul River Centre in downtown St. Paul, with sports tournaments are held at Como Park; www.mnhany.org.
- **Holiday Flower Show**, Como Park Conservatory, www.comozooconservatory.org
- **Holiday Lights at Phalen Park**, St. Paul, Thanksgiving through New Year's Eve, www.lightsinthepark.org
- **Holiday Traditions in the Period Rooms**; Minneapolis Institute of Arts, 3rd St, Minneapolis, is decorated for the holidays, www.artsmia.org.
- **Holidazzle** parades down Nicollet Mall in Minneapolis, www.holidazzle.com. Every Thursday, Friday, Saturday, and Sunday evening at 6:30 p.m., from Thanksgiving until just before Christmas, local volunteers dress up in light-

ed costumes and parade down the Nicollet Mall in Minneapolis. When the weather's good, the crowds are huge, so give yourself plenty of time to find a place to park, and try to get there early enough to sit in the "Hot Seats" in one of the skyways.

- **Kwanzaa** is celebrated with storytelling, music and crafts at the Minnesota History Center, 345 Kellogg Boulevard W, St. Paul, 651-259-3000, 800-657-3773, 651-282-6073 (TTY), www.mnhs.org
- The annual **Macy's Holiday Show**, which features animatronic puppets acting out a story children know, is a must-see holiday event for families, 700 Nicollet Mall, Minneapolis, www.macysinc.com, 612-375-2200
- Family-friendly **Reindeer Day** in early December in Linden Hills, www.reindeerrun.com/website, begins with the 5K Reindeer Run around Lake Harriet and continues with free sleigh rides, wagon rides, caroling, and a visit from Santa Claus!
- **Walk the Wild Side at the Minnesota Zoo** light display, Thanksgiving through December, www.mnzoo.com.
- **Winter Solstice Blessing, Drumming the Soul Awake**, is "Part theater. Part Shamanic ceremony. All cool," as they say. Minnesota Opera Center, 620 N First St, Minneapolis, www.drummingthesoulawake.com

FROM **SINCLAIR LEWIS** AND **F. SCOTT FITZGERALD** TO **CAROL BLY, Garrison Keillor**, Pete Hautman**,** and **Kao Kalia Yang**, many fine writers hail from or have written about Minnesota. Is it the weather? Below is a list of a few good reads with a Minnesota connection to get you started. For those who enjoy hearing authors talk about their work, the **Hennepin County Library Foundation** sponsors a series of authors' lectures every year called "**Pen Pals**." Order tickets online on the Hennepin County web site (www.hclib. org) or call 952-979-1111.

FICTION

- *A Superior Death* by Nevada Barr
- *A Finntown of the Heart* by Patricia Eilola
- *The Dog Says How* and *Holiday Inn* by Kevin Kling.
- *Excelsior* by Bob Williams
- *Haunted Ground* by Erin Hart
- *How To Steal A Car* and 2004 National Book Award Winner *Godless* are Young Adult books by Peter Hautman.
- *In the Lake of the Woods* by Tim O'Brien
- *Killing Time in St. Cloud* by Judith Guest
- *Main Street* by Sinclair Lewis is set in Sauk Center.
- *Nomad Diaries* by Yasmeen Maxamuud
- *Red Earth, White Earth* by Will Weaver
- *Silent Prey* by John Sandford
- *Staggerford* by Jon Hassler
- *Third Person Singular* by K J Erickson
- *Thunder Bay* by William Kent Kreuger
- *Until They Bring the Streetcars Back* by Stanley Gordon West

- *Welcome to the Great Mysterious* and *Angry Housewives Eating Bon Bons* by Lorna Landvik
- *The Wind Chill Factor* by Tom Gifford is a mystery set in Stillwater.

REGIONAL HISTORY

- *55000 Sunsets: 150 Years at Linwood Beach, Lake Minnetonka*, by Robert Gerlicher and Michael J. Peterson
- *All Hell Broke Loose,* by William H. Hull is the story of the November 11, 1940, Armistice Day storm—the worst blizzard that ever hit Minnesota.
- *Boundary Waters: The Grace of the Wild* by Paul Gruchow is a mixture of natural history and stories about pioneers on Isle Royale and the Gunflint Trail.
- *Bring Warm Clothes* by Peg Meier
- *Class Action* by Clara Bingham and Laura Leedy Gansler
- *The Conscience of a Liberal: Reclaiming the Compassionate Agenda* is by Paul Wellstone, U.S. Senator from Minnesota, 1990–2002.
- *The Days of Rondo* by Evelyn Fairbanks
- *Fitzgerald's Storm: The Wreck of the Edmund Fitzgerald* by Joseph MacInnis
- *Gunflint: Reflections on the Trail* and *Woman of the Boundary Waters* by Justine Kerfoot are by and about an elderly woman who lived alone in the Boundary Waters area.
- *The Latehomecomer* by Kao Kalia Yang
- *How To Talk Minnesotan* by Howard Mohr (get the audio version).
- *Kensington Rune Stone: New Light on an Old Riddle* by Theodore C. Blegen
- *Last Standing Woman* and *All Our Relations: Native Struggles for Land and Life* by Winona LaDuke
- *Me: a Memoir* by Brenda Ueland
- *Minnesota Treasures: Stories Behind the State's Historic Places* by Denis Gardner
- *Packinghouse Daughter: A Memoir* by Cheri Register
- *Prairie Days* by Bill Holm
- *Root Beer Lady* by Bob Cary is about Dorothy Molter, a woman who lived alone in her cabin in the Boundary Waters until her death in 1986.
- *Rudy! The People's Governor* by Betty Wilson is about Democratic governor Rudy Perpich, who served in the late 1970s.
- *Secrets of the Congdon Mansion* by Joe Kimball tells you everything they won't tell you on the tour of Glensheen in Duluth.
- *The Street Where You Live: A Guide to Street Names of St. Paul* by Don Emerson
- *Trial at Grand Marais* by Jean Andereck
- *Twin Cities Album: A Visual History* by Dave Kenney
- *Walking the Rez Road* by Jim Northrup

ARCHITECTURE

- *A Guide to the Architecture of Minnesota* by Tom Martinson and David Gebhard was published by the University of Minnesota Press in 1977, and is still considered the local architectural bible.
- *Cape Cods and Ramblers: A Remodeling Planbook for Post-WWII Houses* will help you time-tune houses from the 1940s, '50s and '60s. Residents of Blaine, Brooklyn Park, Columbia Heights, Coon Rapids, Crystal, Fridley, Golden Valley, Hopkins, Mounds View, New Brighton, New Hope, Robbinsdale, Richfield, Roseville and St. Louis Park can purchase the book from their city halls. Those who live outside those communities can get a copy from the City of Brooklyn Park, 763-424-8000.
- *Legendary Homes of Lake Minnetonka* by Bette Jones Hammel and Karen Melvin
- *Longfellow Planbook: Remodeling Plans for Bungalows and Other Small Urban Homes* can be purchased from the Longfellow Community Council, 4151 Minnehaha Ave S, Minneapolis 55406, 612-722-4529, www.longfellow.org.
- *Not So Big House* by Sarah Susanka

CHILDREN

- *Betsy-Tacy* books by Maud Hart Lovelace
- *Little House in the Big Woods* and *Little House on the Prairie* by Laura Ingalls Wilder are set in this region. The Wilder Pageant, presented every July in an outdoor amphitheater on the banks of Plum Creek, is complete with grasshoppers and the prairie fire. For information and to order tickets look online at www.walnutgrove.org.
- *One-Dog Canoe* by Mary Casanova
- *Red Sings from Treetops: A Year in Colors* by Joyce Sidman
- *Shadow Baby* and *Someday* by Alison McGhee
- *The Magician's Elephant* by Kate DiCamillo
- *Think Happy, I Like Me* and *Look Out Kindergarten Here I Come* by Nancy Carlson

GARDENING

- *Growing Perennials in Cold Climates* by Mike Heger and John Whitman
- *Landscaping with Native Plants of Minnesota* by Lynn Steiner
- *Northland Wildflowers: The Comprehensive Guide to the Minnesota Region* by John and Evelyn Moyle
- *Wetlands in Your Pocket, A Guide to Common Plants and Animals of Midwestern Wetlands* by Mark Muller

MINNESOTA IN PHOTOS

- *Barns of Minnesota* by Doug Olman and Will Weaver

- *Chased by the Light: A 90-day Journey* by Jim Brandenburg
- *Minnesota: A State of Beauty* by James LaVigne
- *Minnesota on My Mind* by Paul Gruchow
- *Minnesota Wild* by Les Blacklock

TRAVEL

- *Bicycle Vacation Guide, Minnesota and Wisconsin* by Doug Shidell, Brent Campbell, and Mike Wohnoutka
- *Biking with the Wind: Bicycling Day Trips in Minnesota and Wisconsin* by David Dixen
- *Prairie, Lake, Forest: Minnesota's State Parks* by Chris Niskanen and Doug Ohman
- *Paddling Minnesota* by Greg Breining

SPORTS

- *The Boys of Winter: The Untold Story of a Coach, a Dream, and the 1980 U.S. Olympic Hockey Team* by Wayne Coffey

THREE-DIGIT NUMBERS

- **211**, First Call for Help (social services information)
- **311**, City of Minneapolis
- **411**, Telephone Directory Assistance
- **511**, Road Conditions
- **711**, Minnesota Relay Assistance
- **911**, Police, Fire, or Medical Emergencies

EMERGENCIES

EMERGENCY

- **Fire, Police, Medical,** 911
- **Minnesota Poison Control Center,** 800-222-1222

EMERGENCY VETERINARIANS

- **Affiliated Emergency Veterinary Service** (Minneapolis side of the Twin Cities), www.aevs.com:
    - ▷ **Coon Rapids**, 1615 Coon Rapids Blvd, Coon Rapids, 763-754-9434
    - ▷ **Eden Prairie**, 7717 Flying Cloud Dr, Eden Prairie, 952-942-8272
    - ▷ **Golden Valley**, 4708 Hwy 55, Golden Valley, 763-529-6560
- **Animal Emergency Care (South Metro)**
    - ▷ **Apple Valley**, 14690 Pennock Ave, 952-953-3737
- **Animal Emergency Clinic (St. Paul side of the Twin Cities)**
    - ▷ **West St. Paul**, 301 University Ave, 651-293-1800
    - ▷ **Oakdale**, Interstate 694 & 10th St, 651-501-3766

- **Metropolitan Veterinary Referral Services**, 7562 Market Place Dr, Eden Prairie, maintains an emergency, trauma and critical care facility that accepts both walk-in and referral emergencies (952-943-2282, www.mvrs-mn.com).
- **Pet Poison Helpline**, 1-800-213-6680, www.petpoisonhelpline.com
- **University of Minnesota Emergency**; 24/7 call 612-625-9711; 8 a.m. to 4:30 p.m. call: Small Animal Hospital, 612-626-VETS (8387); Large Animal Hospital, 612-625-6700

CRISIS LINES

- **211**, United Way First Call for Help, is NOT an emergency line, but is a state-wide number that will direct you to the help you need
- **911**, Emergency
- **Drug Abuse Hotline**, 800-662-4357
- **Emergency Contraception**, 888-NOT-2-LATE
- **Jacob Wetterling Foundation** for missing and exploited children, 24hour helpline, 800-325-HOPE (toll-free), www.jwrc.org
- **Minneapolis Sexual Violence Center** (24-hour crisis line), 612-871-5111
- **Minnesota Coalition for Battered Women**, 651-646-6177 or 800-289-6177, www.mcbw.org/
- **Minnesota Domestic Abuse Hotline**, 866-223-1111, automatically connects you with resources nearest you.
- **National Domestic Abuse Hotline**, 1-800-799-SAFE (7233)
- **National Runaway Switchboard**, 800-621-4000
- **Sojourner Shelter** (from domestic abuse) 24-Hour Crisis Line 952-933-7422, www.sojournerproject.org
- **Suicide Prevention**, 612-347-2222
- **Teens Alone**, 952-988-TEEN, www.teensalone.org, helps homeless teenagers in the West Metro.

UTILITY EMERGENCIES

- **Electrical Outage**, 800-895-1999
- **Emergency Furnace Repair**, 612-333-6466 or 800-722-6821
- **Emergency/Gas Odor**, 800-895-2999
- **Gas Leak, Center Point Energy**, 612-372-5050, TTY/Voice 612-342-5471
- **Telephone Outage, Qwest**, 800-573-1311

NON-EMERGENCY NUMBERS

ALCOHOL AND DRUG DEPENDENCY

- **Alcoholics Anonymous**, Greater Minneapolis, 952-922-0880, www.aaminne-apolis.org; St. Paul, 651-227-5502, www.aastpaul.org

- **Crisis Connection** (24-hour), 612-379-6363

ANIMALS

See also **Veterinarians** on page 513 and **Emergency Veterinarians** on page 500.
- **Animal Humane Society of Hennepin County**, www.animalhumanesociety.org: 845 N Meadow Ln, Golden Valley, 763-522-4325; 1411 NW Main St, Coon Rapids, 763-862-4030; also boards dogs, cats, and other small animals, and provides pet grief support.
- **Animal Inn Boarding Kennel, Training School, and Pet Cemetery**, 651-777-0255, 888-777-0255, www.animalinntraining.com
- **Helping Paws of Minnesota**, 952-988-9359, www.helpingpaws.org
- **Minnesota Zoo**, 24-hour information line 952-431-9500 www.mnzoo.com
- **Wildlife Rehabilitation Center**, 2530 Dale St, Roseville, 651-486-WILD (9453), www.wrcmn.org

APPLIANCE AND ELECTRONICS RECYCLING

- **Carver County Environmental Center**, 116 Peavey Cir, Chaska, 952-361-1835 or 952-361-1800, www.co.carver.mn.us
- **Eureka Recycling**, 651-633-EASY, www.eurekarecycling.org
- **North Hennepin County Recycling Center and Transfer Station**, 8100, Jefferson Hwy, Brooklyn Park, 612-348-3777, www.hennepin.us
- **South Hennepin County Recycling and Problem Waste Drop-off Center**, 1400 W 96th St, Bloomington, 612-348-3777, www.hennepin.us
- **Twin Cities FreeNet**, www.tcfreenet.org

AUTOMOBILES

- **511**, road conditions
- **AAA**, 952-927-2600, 24-hour line 952-927-2727, ww2.aaa.com
- **Minneapolis Impound Lot**, 612-673-5777
- **Minnesota Department of Public Safety—Motor Vehicle Division**, 651-296-6911, www.dps.state.mn.us
- **St. Paul Impound Lot**, 651-266-5630
- **Automobile Service Centers—Vehicle Registration**, Driver's Licenses and Identification Cards

MINNESOTA

- **Minnesota Driver and Vehicle Services,** 445 Minnesota St, Suite 168, St. Paul, MN 55101, 651-296-6911, TTY 651-282-6555, www.dps.state.mn.us/dvs
- **Anoka County**, www.co.anoka.mn.us; State Exam Station, 530 W Main St, Anoka, 763-422-3401; North Metro Exam Station, Highway 35W & County Rd I, Arden Hills, 651-639-4057

- **Carver County**, www.co.carver.mn.us; Chaska Exam Station, 418 Pine St, Chaska, 952-448-3740
- **Dakota County**, www.co.dakota.mn.us; South Metro Driver's Exam Station, 2070 Cliff Road, Eagan, 651-688-1870; 217 Ramsey St, Hastings, 651-437-4884
- **Hennepin County**, www.co.hennepin.mn.us; 2455 Fernbrook Ln, Plymouth, 952-476-3042
- **Ramsey County**, www.co.ramsey.mn.us, 445 Minnesota St, St. Paul, 651-639-4057
- **Scott County**, www.co.scott.mn.us, Customer Service Center, Government Services Building, located at 200 W Fourth Ave, Shakopee, 952-496-8150
- **Sherburne County**, www.co.sherburne.mn.us, Department of Motor Vehicles, 600 Railroad Dr, Elk River, 763-422-3401 to schedule a road test appointment
- **Washington County**, www.co.washington.mn.us, Stillwater License Center, Valley Ridge, 1520 W Frontage Rd, Stillwater, 651-284-1000
- **Wright County**, www.co.wright.mn.us, 15 1st Ave S, Buffalo, 763-682-3963

WISCONSIN
- **Drivers' License Information**, 608-266-2353, www.dot.wisconsin.gov/drivers/drivers/apply/drivrlic.htm
- **Vehicle Registration**, www.dot.wisconsin.gov/drivers/vehicles/veh-forms.htm
- **Hudson, Wisconsin, DMV,** 2100 O'Neil Rd (near Carmichael Rd); open Wednesdays, 7:45 a.m. to 5:45 p.m.; Thursdays, 8:15 a.m. to 6:15 p.m.; and Fridays, 7:45 a.m. to 5:00 p.m. There is no direct phone number to that location, but the automated phone system number is 800-924-3570. Register vehicles at the St. Croix County Government Center, 1101 Carmichael Rd, Hudson, in the Clerk's Office, 715-386-4609, www.ci.Hudson.wi.us.

BIRTH/ DEATH CERTIFICATES

- **Minnesota Department of Health**, Attention: Office of the State Registrar, PO Box 64882, St. Paul, Minnesota 55164-0882, fax 651-291-0101, www.health.state.mn.us/divs/chs/osr/
- **Wisconsin Vital Records Office**:
  - **Birth,** www.dhfs.state.wi.us/VitalRecords/birth.htm
  - **Death,** www.dhfs.state.wi.us/VitalRecords/death.htm#D1

CHILD ABUSE/PROTECTION

- **United Way First Call for Help**, 211, 651-291-0211 or 800-543-7709, www.unitedwaytwincities.org

CITIZEN PARTICIPATION

- **Citizens' League**, 651-293-0575, www.citizensleague.net
- **League of Women Voters of Minnesota**, 651-224-5445, www.lwvmn.org

CONSUMER AGENCIES

- **Better Business Bureau of Minnesota**, 651-699-1111, 800-646-6222, http://minnesota.bbb.org
- **Consumer Checkbook**, 651-646-2057, www.checkbook.org; download reports
- **Minnesota Attorney General**, Hotline 651-296-3353, 800-657-3787, TTY 651-297-7206, TTY toll-free 800-366-4812, www.ag.state.mn.us
- **Minnesota Department of Commerce**, 651-296-2488, 651-296-5175, www.commerce.state.mn.us
- **Minnesota Public Utilities Commission**, 651-296-0406, 800-657-3782
- **University of Minnesota Extension Service**, www.extension.umn.edu

CRISIS LINES

See **Crisis Lines** under **Emergencies** on page 501.

EMERGENCIES

See **Emergencies** at the beginning of the chapter.

FOOD

- **Emergency Food Shelf Network**, 763-450-3860 or **First Call for Help**, 211, www.emergencyfoodshelf.org
- **University of Minnesota Extension Service** (cooking tips), www.extension.umn.edu

GAMBLING

- **Minnesota Compulsive Gambling Hotline**, 800-437-3641

GARDENING

- **University of Minnesota Extension Service and Landscape Arboretum Answer Line**, 1-800-854-1678 www.extension.umn.edu

DISABLED, SERVICES FOR

- **The ARC Minnesota** (advocacy and support for those who are developmentally disabled), 651-523-0823, www.arcmn.org

GOVERNMENT

MINNEAPOLIS
- **City Hall**, general information: 311, www.ci.minneapolis.mn.us

ST. PAUL
- **City Hall**, general information: 651-266-8500, www.stpaul.gov

COUNTY AND REGIONAL
MINNESOTA
- **Anoka County**, www.co.anoka.mn.us, 763-421-4760
- **Carver County**, www.co.carver.mn.us, 952-361-1500
- **Dakota County**, www.co.dakota.mn.us, 651-438-4418
- **Hennepin County**, www.co.hennepin.mn.us, 612-348-3000
- **Isanti County**, www.co.isanti.mn.us, 763-689-3859
- **Metropolitan Council**, www.metrocouncil.org
- **Ramsey County**, www.co.ramsey.mn.us, 651-266-2000
- **Scott County**, www.co.scott.mn.us, 952-445-7750
- **Sherburne County**, www.co.sherburne.mn.us, 763-241-2700
- **Washington County**, www.co.washington.mn.us, 651-439-3220
- **Wright County**, www.co.wright.mn.us, 763-682-3900

WISCONSIN
- **Pierce County**, Courthouse: 414 W Main St, Ellsworth, WI 54011, 715-273-3531, www.co.pierce.wi.us
- **Polk County**, Government Center: 100 Polk County Plaza, Suite 110, Balsam Lake, WI 54810, 715-485-9226, www.co.polk.wi.us
- **St. Croix County**, Government Center: 1101 Carmichael Rd, Hudson, WI 54016, 715-386-4600, www.co.saint-croix.wi.us

STATE
MINNESOTA
- **Attorney General**, www.ag.state.mn.us, 651-296-3353
- **Governor's Office**, 651-296-3391
- **Minnesota State Legislature**, information and bill tracking, www.leg.state.mn.us/leg/legis.asp
- **Secretary of State**, 651-296-2803; Elections: 651-215-1440; www.sos.state.mn.us

WISCONSIN
- **State of Wisconsin**, www.wisconsin.gov/state/index.html

HEALTH

- **Mayo Clinic Health Oasis**, www.mayoclinic.com
- **Minnesota State Council on Disability**, Voice/TTY, 651-361-7800, 800-945-8913, 711, www.state.mn.us/portal/mn/jsp/home.do?agency=MSCOD Minnesota Department of Health, www.health.state.mn.us
- **Neighborhood Health Care Network**, 651-489-CARE, www.nhcn.org; medical and dental referrals.

HOMEBUYING AND MAINTENANCE

- **National Association of Home Inspectors**, www.nahi.org; for a list of accredited home inspectors.
- **Twin Cities Bungalow Club**, www.bungalowclub.org, is a great source of advice about old houses of all styles.
- **Minnesota Real Estate Property Listings** (multiple listing service), www.mls.com

HOSPITALS

See **Health Care** chapter.

HOUSING

MINNEAPOLIS
- **311**, www.ci.minneapolis.mn.us

ST. PAUL
- **www.ci.stpaul.mn.us**
- **St. Paul Heritage Preservation Commission**, 651-266-9078
- **St. Paul Housing Information Office**, 651-266-6616

STATE/FEDERAL
- **Minnesota Department of Human Rights**, 651-296-5663, TDD, 651296-1283, 800-657-3704
- **Minnesota Department of Public Service Energy Information Center**, www.dpsv.state.mn.us
- **US Department of Housing and Urban Development**, 612-3703000, www.hud.gov; Discrimination Hotline, 800-669-9777

LIBRARIES

See **Getting Settled** chapter and listings at the end of neighborhood profiles.

MINNESOTA ONLINE

City/neighborhood specific web sites can be found at the end of each neighborhood profile, or check the **Surrounding Communities** section.

- **About.com**, http://minneapolis.about.com
- **Minnesota Grown**, www3.mda.state.mn.us/mngrown
- **Newcomers Club**, www.newcomersclub.com/mn.html#Minneapolis
- **Photo Tour of Twin Cities**, www.phototour.minneapolis.mn.us
- **Registered Offender List**, www.criminalcheck.com; type in your ZIP code and find registered offenders living in that neighborhood
- **Twin Cities Transplants**, www.imnotfromhere.com, is a support group for transplanted professionals.

MAPS

- **DNR Fishing Maps**, www.dnr.state.mn.us/lakefind/index.html
- **Metropolitan Council maps** of 46 regional parks and park reserves, 22 trails, and six special recreation areas, www.metrocouncil.org/parks/ r-pk-map.htm
- **Minnesota County maps**, www.metrocouncil.org/parks

NEWSPAPERS AND MAGAZINES

For clickable links to newspapers by county, look online at www.mnnews.com/ countylist.html. Also see **Newspapers and Magazines** in the **Getting Settled** chapter.

POLICE

See info sections at the end of individual **Neighborhoods and Communities** listings.

- **Emergency**, 911
- **Hennepin County Sheriff**, Non-Emergency, 763-525-6210
- **Minnesota State Patrol**, Non-Emergency, 651-582-1511

RADIO/TV STATIONS

See **Getting Settled** chapter.

RELOCATION

First Books Newcomer's Handbooks, www.firstbooks.com; relocation resources and information on moving to the USA as a whole, as well as Atlanta, Boston; Chicago; Los Angeles; Minneapolis–St. Paul; New York City; Portland, OR; San Francisco Bay Area; Seattle; Texas; and Washington, DC, and London, England, and China; also resources for moving pets and children.

- **HousingLink**, 612-522-2500, www.housinglink.org, is a free nonprofit service that provides information about affordable rental housing throughout the metro area.
- **LiveMSP** has pictures of neighborhoods in Minneapolis and St, Paul, www.livemsp.org
- **Mothers and More**, www.orgsites.com/mn/mothersandmore-stpaul, is a nonprofit dedicated to improving the lives of "sequencing women."
- **www.moving.org** is the web site of the 3200-member American Moving and Storage Association
- **Newcomers Clubs**, www.newcomersclub.com/mn.html#Minneapolis
- **www.move.com**, apartment rentals, movers, relocation advice, help finding pet-friendly rentals, and more.
- **www.usps.com**; relocation information from the U.S. Postal Service.
- **ZILLOW** lists most of the homes for sale in Minnesota, www.zillow.com

ROAD CONDITIONS

- **Road Condition Information**, 511
- **Snow Emergency Information**, Minneapolis, 311, 612-348-SNOW, www.ci.minneapolis.mn.us
- **Snow Emergency Information**, St. Paul, 651-266-PLOW, www.stpaul.gov
- **Wisconsin Traveler Information**, 511, 800-ROADWIS (800-762-3947), www.dot.wisconsin.gov/travel/road

SANITATION—GARBAGE & RECYCLING

See **Getting Settled** chapter.
- **Allied Waste**, 763-784-2104 (North Metro), 952-9415174 (Southwest Metro), 651-455-8634 (East Metro), www.alliedwastetwincities.com
- **Eureka Recycling**, 651-222-7678, www.eurekarecycling.org
- **Twin Cities Free Market (web-based**, reusable goods exchange), www.twincitiesfreemarket.org
- **Waste Management**, 952-890-1100, www.wm.com; serves most of metro

SENIORS

- **Senior Linkage Line**, 800-333-2433

SOCIAL AGENCIES

- **United Way First Call for Help**, 211, acts like directory assistance for those seeking help from social service organizations in Minnesota. This is NOT an emergency number, but it is answered 24 hours a day, and will refer you to the help you need.

SPORTS & RECREATION

PROFESSIONAL SPORTS

It's usually easiest to purchase tickets online.

- **Canterbury Park**, www.canterburypark.com; horse racing.
- **Minnesota Lynx**, www.wnba.com/lynx; women's professional basketball.
- **Minnesota Timberwolves**, Tickets 612-673-8373, www.nba.com/timberwolves; men's professional basketball.
- **Minnesota Twins**, 800-33-TWINS, http://minnesota.twins.mlb.com
- **Minnesota Vikings**, 612-33-VIKES, www.vikings.com; professional football.
- **Minnesota Wild**, 651-602-6000, http://wild.nhl.com; NHL hockey.
- **St. Paul Saints**, Tickets 651-644-6659, http://saintsbaseball.com; professional baseball

COLLEGE SPORTS

- **University of Minnesota** (all teams), www.gophersports.com

PARTICIPANT SPORTS & RECREATION

- **Minnesota Ski Areas**, www.twin-cities.com/ski
- **Boundary Waters**, www.canoecountry.com
- **Lake Finder**, www.dnr.state.mn.us/lakefind/index.html
- **Ski Conditions and Snow Depths**, www.onthesnow.com/minnesota/profile.html
- **Snow Conditions**, 651-296-6157, www.dnr.state.mn.us/current_conditions
- **Snow Sledding** (Bobsled, Skeleton, Luge, Tobogganing, Dogsled Tours and Racing), www.sledcity.com
- **Golf Tee Times**, www.teemaster.com

TAXES

FEDERAL

- **Internal Revenue Service**, 800-829-4477, www.irs.gov
- **Bloomington, Minneapolis, and St. Paul IRS Offices**, 651-312-8082
- **IRS Taxpayer Advocate Service**, 651-312-7999, 877-777-4778

PROPERTY TAXES

Call your city.

STATE

- **Minnesota Department of Revenue**, 600 N Robert St, St. Paul, MN 55101, www.taxes.state.mn.us
- **Income Tax Information and Forms**, 651-296-3781; budget cuts resulted in the shutting down of the state's toll-free number, but you can still access information and file electronically at www.taxes.state.mn.us. People with impairments should call 711 for Minnesota Relay Service.
- **Refund Status**, 651-296-4444

- **Taxpayers Rights Advocate**, 651-556-6013

TAXIS AND SHUTTLES

AIRPORT

- **Airport Taxi and Delivery**, www.airporttaxicabs.com; serves the entire Twin Cities metro area with vans and smoke-free cabs; accepts reservations up to 24 hours in advance; make reservations online.
- **West Metro**, 952-928-0000
- **East Metro**, 651-222-0000
- **Toll free**, 800-464-0555
- **Airport Southwest Taxi**, 952-937-0600; provides service to and from the airport; make reservations 24 hours in advance.
- **SuperShuttle**, 612-827-7777 (ext 1), www.supershuttle.com

MINNEAPOLIS

- **ABC Taxi**, 612-788-1111
- **Blue & White Taxi**, 612-333-3331
- **Red and White Taxi**, 612-871-1600
- **Suburban and Green & White Taxi**, 612-522-2222
- **Yellow Cab**, 612-824-4000

ST. PAUL

- **Citywide Cab**, 651-489-1111
- **St. Paul All City Cab**, 651-222-8294

SUBURBAN

- **Suburban Taxi**, 763-545-1234, 952-884-8888, www.suburbantaxi.com

TELEPHONE

- **Directory Assistance**, 411
- **Do Not Call List**, 888-382-1222
- **Online Directory**, www.dexonline.com
- **Qwest**, 800-244-1111, www.qwest.com

TOURISM

- **MetroConnections**, 612-333-8687, www.metroconnections.com, offers 3-hour tours to various sites in Minneapolis and St. Paul.
- **Minneapolis Heritage Preservation Commission free walking tour**, 350 5th St S, Minneapolis, 612-673-2615, www.ci.minneapolis.mn.us/hpc/walking-tours.asp

- **Minnesota Historical Society**, 345 Kellogg Blvd W, St. Paul, 651-259-3000, www.mnhs.org
- **Minnesota Office of Tourism**, www.exploreminnesota.com
- **Minnesota State Capitol**, 75 Reverend Dr. Martin Luther King Blvd, St. Paul, 651-296-2881, www.mnhs.org; free guided tours on the hour, also self-guided tours.
- **Mobile Entertainment's Magical History Tours**, 952-888-9200, www.magicalhistorytour.com; 3-hour tours by Segway of the Minneapolis Riverfront.
- **Padelford Packet Boat Co.**, Harriet Island, St. Paul; 651-227-1100, www.riverrides.com, offers narrated public excursions and private charters on the Mississippi River, May through October, from Boom island, Minneapolis, and Harriet Island, St. Paul.
- **Wabasha Street Caves Tours**, 215 S Wabasha St, St. Paul; 651-224-1191, www.wabashastreetcaves.com
- **Wisconsin Tourism**, www.wisconline.com

TRANSPORTATION

- **Department of Public Safety Driver and Vehicle Services** Office Locations, 651-297-2005, www.dps.state.mn.us/dvs
- **Minneapolis–St. Paul International Airport**, www.mspairport.com:
  - ▹ **Lindbergh (Main) Terminal #1**, 4300 Glumack Dr, St. Paul, 612-7265555
  - ▹ **Humphrey Terminal #2 (charter and other flights)**, 7150 Humphrey Dr, Minneapolis, 612-726-5800
- **Airport Police Department parking ramp escort service**, 612-7265577
- **Mn-PASS toll-lane** info and to open an account, 866-397-4334, www.mn-pass.org
- **State Department of Transportation**, 511, www.dot.state.mn.us

LOCAL PUBLIC TRANSIT AND COMMUTER SERVICES
- **MetroTransit**, 612-373-3333, TTY 612-349-7369, www.metrotransit.org; find out everything you need to know about local public transit options.

NATIONAL TRAIN & BUS SERVICE
- **Amtrak**, Reservations: please call a service representative at 800-USA-RAIL (800-872-7245), TDD/TTY 800-523-6590, www.amtrak.com
- **St. Paul/Minneapolis Midway Amtrak Passenger Station**, 730 Transfer Rd, St. Paul, 651-644-6012
- **Greyhound Bus Lines**, 950 Hawthorne Ave Station, Minneapolis, 612-371-3325, 612-371-3334 (baggage); University of Minnesota, Coffman Union, 300 Washington Ave SE, 612-624-4636; St. Paul Amtrak Station, 730 Transfer Rd; tickets are not sold at the Amtrak station but may be purchased by mail at least 10 days in advance through the Ticket Center on Greyhound.com or by

calling the Telephone Information Center at 800-231-2222, www.greyhound.com.

- **Rochester Direct**, Minneapolis International Airport, 612-726-5501, www.rochesterdirect.com
- **BadgerBus**, provides weekend transport for students between the University of Minnesota and University of Wisconsin campuses.

U.S. POSTAL SERVICE

- **U.S. Postal Service**, 800-275-8777, www.usps.com

UTILITIES

- **Diggers' Hotline** (buried cable locations in Wisconsin), 800-242-8511, www.diggershotline.com
- **Gopher State One Call** (buried cable locations in Minnesota) 651-454-0002, www.gopherstateonecall.org; call before you dig.

ELECTRICITY

- **Dakota Electric**, 651-463-6212, 800-874-3409, www.dakotaelectric.com
- **Minnesota Valley Electric Co-op**, 952-492-2313 www.mvec.net
- **Xcel Energy, Billing and New Accounts**: 800-895-4999; Street Lights Burned Out/Electrical Outage 800-895-1999; www.xcelenergy.com

NATURAL GAS

- **CenterPoint Energy**, 612-372-4727 or 800-245-2377 for Billing and New Accounts; Emergency Gas Leaks and Repairs, 612-372-5050, www.centerpointenergy.com

TELEPHONE

- **Do Not Call**, 888-382-1222, TTY 866-290-4236, www.ftc.gov/donotcall
- **Qwest**, 800-244-1111 Billing and New Accounts (serves almost all of the metro), www.qwest.com

SATELLITE AND CABLE

Call 1-866-49Cable to reach the cable company serving your area.

- **Charter Communications**, 1-888-GET-CHARTER, www.chartercom.com (Northwest Metro)
- **Comcast**, 800-COMCAST, www.comcast.com (most of the metro)
- **Direct TV satellite service**, 1-888-777-2454, www.directtv.com
- **Dish Network satellite service**, 888-236-2202, www.dishtv.com/
- **Mediacom**, 800-332-0245 for Billing and New Accounts; http://mediacomcable.com (west side of the cities)

UTILITY EMERGENCIES

- **Electrical Outage**, 800-895-1999
- **Emergency Furnace Repair**, 612-333-6466 or 800-722-6821
- **Emergency/Gas Odor**, 800-895-2999
- **Gas Leak, Center Point Energy**, 612-372-5050, TTY/Voice 612-342-5471
- **Telephone Outage**, Qwest, 800-573-1311

VETERINARIANS, EMERGENCY CLINICS

- **Affiliated Emergency Veterinary Service** (Minneapolis side of the Twin Cities), www.aevs.com:
  - ▷ **Coon Rapids**, 1615 Coon Rapids Blvd, Coon Rapids, 763-754-9434
  - ▷ **Eden Prairie**, 7717 Flying Cloud Dr, Eden Prairie, 952-942-8272
  - ▷ **Golden Valley**, 4708 Hwy 55, Golden Valley, 763-529-6560
- **Animal Emergency Care** (South Metro)
  - ▷ **Apple Valley,** 14690 Pennock Ave, 952-953-3737
- **Animal Emergency Clinic** (St. Paul side of the Twin Cities)
  - ▷ **West St. Paul**, 301 University Ave, 651-293-1800;
  - ▷ **Oakdale**, Interstate 694 & 10th St, 651-501-3766
- **University of Minnesota Veterinary Hospitals**, 1365 Gartner Ave, St. Paul, 612-625-9711 (24-hour emergency hotline)
- **Metropolitan Veterinary Referral Services**, 7562 Market Place Dr, Eden Prairie, maintains an emergency, trauma and critical care facility that accepts both walk-in and referral emergencies (952-943-2282, www.mvrs-mn.com).

VOTING

- **Minnesota Secretary of State's Office**, 651-296-2803, www.sos.state.mn.us

WATER TAXI AND BOAT TOWING

- **H2O Towing & Taxi/Towboat U.S.** provides salvage, emergency pump-out, towing, and jump-starts on Lake Minnetonka; 612-282-8616. Towing costs over $100 an hour, so become a member of BOATUS.com (800-395-2628) and save yourself a bundle.

WORSHIP

See **Places of Worship** in the **Getting Involved** chapter.
- **Minnesota Council of Churches**, 612-870-3600, www.mnchurches.org
- **Jewish Minnesota**, www.jewishminnesota.org

ZIP CODE INFORMATION

- **USPS**, 800-275-8777, www.usps.com

ELIZABETH CAPERTON-HALVORSON has lived in the Minneapolis area for over 30 years. Raised in Virginia, her experience as a newcomer began with her marriage to a Minnesotan—and nearly ended when she realized she had worn her winter coat through the entire summer the first year she lived in the Twin Cities. She and her family soon discovered the exhilaration of Minnesota skiing and the joy of sailing Lake Minnetonka by moonlight, and she now looks forward to the cycle of the seasons. She has worked as an elementary school teacher and newspaper reporter, and is currently a writer and editor of corporate communications. Her family's hobbies revolve around art, bridge, gardening, and sports.

READER RESPONSE

We would appreciate your comments regarding this fourth edition of the *Newcomer's Handbook® for Moving to and Living in Minneapolis–St.Paul.* If you've found any mistakes or omissions or if you would just like to express your opinion about the guide, please let us know. We will consider any suggestions for possible inclusion in our next edition, and if we use your comments, we'll send you a free copy of our next edition. Please e-mail us at readerresponse@firstbooks.com, or mail or fax this response form to:

Reader Response Department
First Books
6750 SW Franklin, Suite A
Portland, OR 97223-2542
Fax: 503.968.6779

Comments: _____

_____

_____

_____

_____

_____

_____

_____

_____

Name: _____

Address: _____

_____

_____

Telephone: (   ) _____

Email: _____

6750 SW Franklin, Suite A
Portland, OR 97223-2542
USA
P: 503.968.6777
www.firstbooks.com

Utilizing an innovative grid and "static" reusable adhesive sticker format, *Furniture Placement and Room Planning Guide…Moving Made Easy* provides a functional and practical solution to all your space planning and furniture placement needs.

MOVING WITH KIDS?

Look into *The Moving Book: A Kids' Survival Guide*.

Divided into three sections (before, during, and after the move), it's a handbook, a journal, and a scrapbook all in one. Includes address book, colorful change-of-address cards, and a useful section for parents.

Children's Book of the Month Club "Featured Selection"; American Bookseller's "Pick of the List"; Winner of the Family Channel's "Seal of Quality" Award

And for your younger children, ease their transition with our brand-new title just for them, *Max's Moving Adventure: A Coloring Book for Kids on the Move*. A complete story book featuring activities as well as pictures that children can color; designed to help children cope with the stresses of small or large moves.

NEWCOMERSWEB.COM

Based on the award-winning *Newcomer's Handbooks*, **NewcomersWeb.com** offers the highest quality neighborhood and community information in a one-of-a-kind searchable online database. The following areas are covered: Atlanta, Austin, Boston, Chicago, Dallas–Fort Worth, Houston, Los Angeles, Minneapolis–St. Paul, New York City, Portland (Oregon), San Francisco, Seattle, Washington DC, and the USA.

NEWCOMER'S HANDBOOKS`

Regularly revised and updated, these popular guides are now available for Atlanta, Boston, Chicago, China, London, Los Angeles, Minneapolis–St. Paul, New York City, Portland, San Francisco Bay Area, Seattle, Texas and Washington DC.

"Invaluable …highly recommended" – Library Journal

If you're coming from another country, don't miss the *Newcomer's Handbook® for Moving to and Living in the USA* by Mike Livingston, termed "a fascinating book for newcomers and residents alike" by the *Chicago Tribune*.

6750 SW Franklin Street
Portland, Oregon 97223-2542
Phone 503.968.6777 • Fax 503.968.6779
www.firstbooks.com

FIRST BOOKS

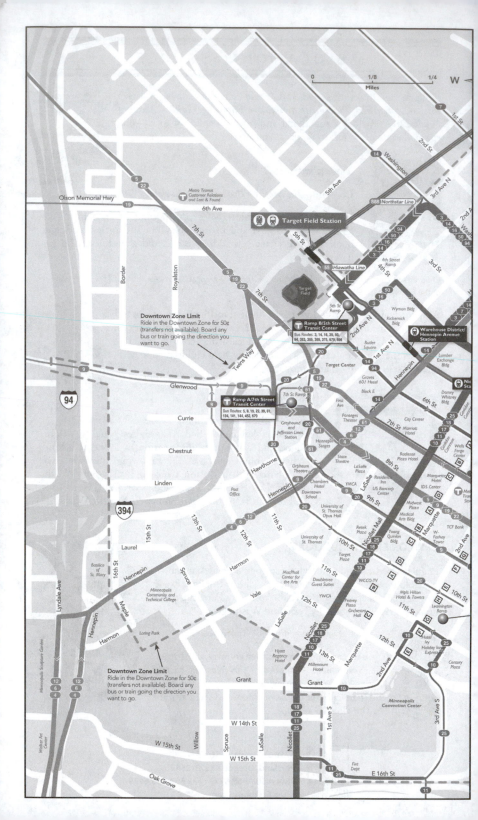

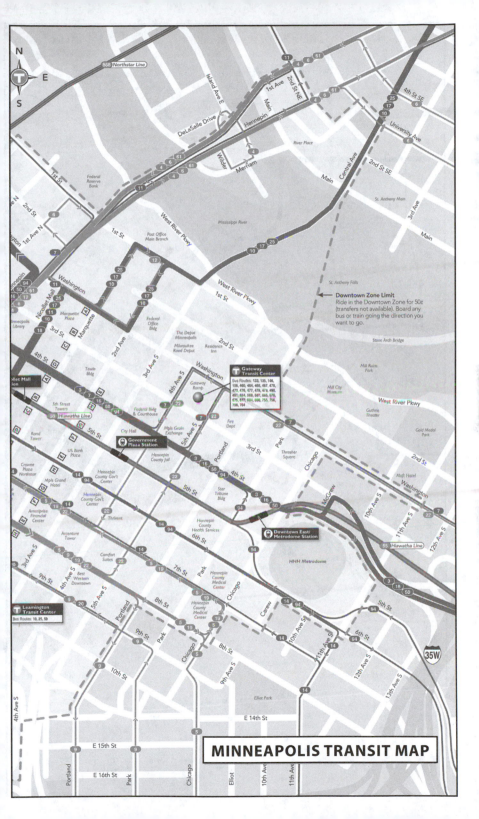

MINNEAPOLIS TRANSIT MAP

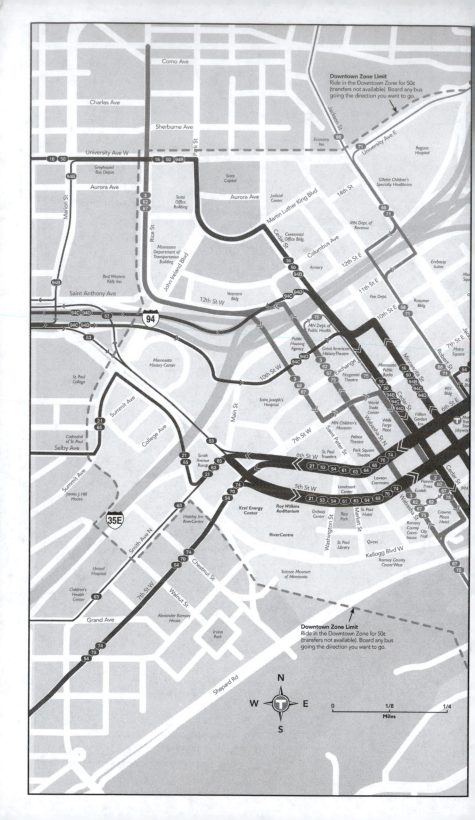

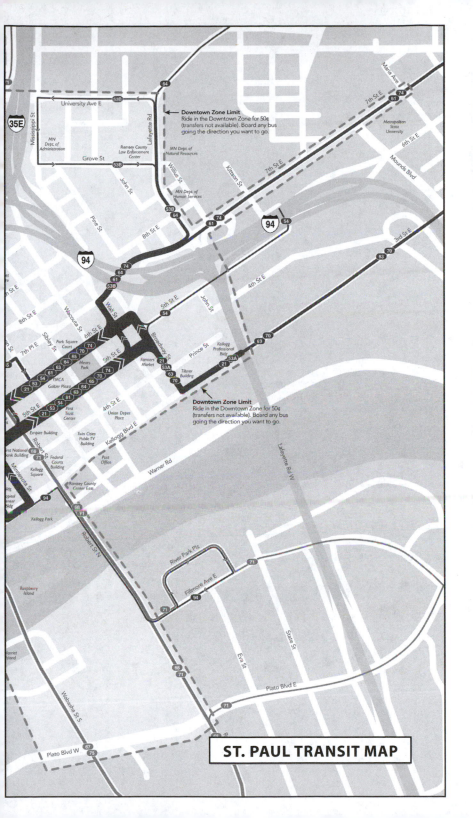

ST. PAUL TRANSIT MAP